Tolley's Data Pndbook

Third Edition
by

Susan Singleton
Singletons
www.singlelaw.com

Members of the LexisNexis Group worldwide

United Kingdom	LexisNexis UK, a Division of Reed Elsevier (UK) Ltd, 2 Addiscombe Road, CROYDON CR9 5AF
Argentina	LexisNexis Argentina, BUENOS AIRES
Australia	LexisNexis Butterworths, CHATSWOOD, New South Wales
Austria	LexisNexis Verlag ARD Orac GmbH & Co KG, VIENNA
Canada	LexisNexis Butterworths, MARKHAM, Ontario
Chile	LexisNexis Chile Ltda, SANTIAGO DE CHILE
Czech Republic	Nakladatelství Orac sro, PRAGUE
France	Editions du Juris-Classeur SA, PARIS
Germany	LexisNexis Deutschland GmbH, FRANKFURT and MUNSTER
Hong Kong	LexisNexis Butterworths, HONG KONG
Hungary	HVG-Orac, BUDAPEST
India	LexisNexis Butterworths, NEW DELHI
Ireland	LexisNexis, DUBLIN
Italy	Giuffrè Editore, MILAN
Malaysia	Malayan Law Journal Sdn Bhd, KUALA LUMPUR
New Zealand	LexisNexis Butterworths, WELLINGTON
Poland	Wydawnictwo Prawnicze LexisNexis, WARSAW
Singapore	LexisNexis Butterworths, SINGAPORE
South Africa	LexisNexis Butterworths, DURBAN
Switzerland	Stämpfli Verlag AG, BERNE
USA	LexisNexis, DAYTON, Ohio

© Reed Elsevier (UK) Ltd 2004
Published by LexisNexis UK

All rights reserved. No part of this publication may be reproduced in any material form (including photocopying or storing it in any medium by electronic means and whether or not transiently or incidentally to some other use of this publication) without the written permission of the copyright owner except in accordance with the provisions of the Copyright, Designs and Patents Act 1988 or under the terms of a licence issued by the Copyright Licensing Agency Ltd, 90 Tottenham Court Road, London, England W1T 4LP. Applications for the copyright owner's written permission to reproduce any part of this publication should be addressed to the publisher.

Warning: The doing of an unauthorised act in relation to a copyright work may result in both a civil claim for damages and criminal prosecution.

Crown copyright material is reproduced with the permission of the Controller of HMSO and the Queen's Printer for Scotland. Parliamentary copyright material is reproduced with the permission of the Controller of Her Majesty's Stationery Office on behalf of Parliament. Any European material in this work which has been reproduced from EUR-lex, the official European Communities legislation website, is European Communities copyright.

A CIP Catalogue record for this book is available from the British Library.
ISBN 0 754524957

Typeset by Columns Design Ltd, Reading, England
Printed and bound in Great Britain by Cromwell Press, Trowbridge, Wiltshire

Visit LexisNexis UK at www.lexisnexis.co.uk

To my children, Rachel, Rebecca, Ben, Sam and Jo,
whose use and abuse of the internet
has thrown up many an interesting data protection problem.

Introduction

2004 is an interesting time to be preparing the third edition of this Handbook. The Data Protection Act received more publicity than it had ever had before when it was 'blamed' in January 2004 for a failure properly to vet the killer in the Soham murder case. High profile cases, for example *Hello!* and Naomi Campbell, are going to the House of Lords and in December 2003 important new email marketing rules came into force. In addition, in late 2003 the court clarified very important issues in the *Durant case*, which will require rewriting of some of the data protection guidance. In addition, the Data Protection Office is committed to simplifying the documentation it has issued. This is a very welcome development. It is hard enough for data protection lawyers, such as myself, to read and remember the many pages of guidance the IC's office issues. It is even harder for those trying to carry on business, whilst grappling with data protection legislation in addition to the many other areas of legislation, such as employment law, which provide a huge regulatory burden on many.

This third edition of this Handbook is written with a new Information Commissioner, Mr Richard Thomas, in place. In his Annual Report (2003) he wrote:

> 'Protection. Information. Freedom. The heady vocabulary of my remit as the new Information Commissioner brings a weighty challenge of responsibility. It involves a direct influence on the kind of society we live in. How should the balance be drawn between respect for privacy and the fight against crime? How can people discover a great deal more about what public bodies are doing in their name and which may affect their lives – without creating a goldfish bowl where good government becomes impossible? Accountability is another key word. It is imperative – for both data protection and freedom of information – that no-one should be in any doubt about my independence. I have considerable autonomy. I have an extensive range of statutory duties and powers. My decisions and activities make a real difference to the behaviour of public and private organisations and their impact on individuals. I spend public money. All of this – and much else – means that I and my staff must be fully accountable. This Annual Report is one of the main instruments of that accountability.'

That introduction sums up the difficult issues addressed by data protection legislation. How to balance people's right to privacy with their right in some cases to life. It is rarely such a stark choice but getting the balance right is never easy. Many businesses struggle to achieve full compliance with data protection legislation. It is complicated and at times unclear. However, a criminal offence is committed if the Act is breached, so companies do need guidance such as this handbook seeks to provide. Do not hesitate to seek legal advice, however, if a real problem arises, even if it is just to confirm a view taken. Some companies spend thousands of pounds on achieving what they think is compliance and then find their competitors took a different, perhaps less cautious, but equally lawful view. Others proceed entirely ignoring the legislation and lose huge amounts of customer goodwill when a public data protection breach comes to light. Share prices have been known to drop in consequence. It is not an area of law which can be ignored and it brings with it positive benefits in any event. Employees and customers who think their personal data is safe, secure and respected are likely to remain good employees and customers. Those who think a company rides roughshod over their very personal information may take their employment or business elsewhere.

Virtually all businesses hold personnel records and many have substantial mailing lists. They need to use that personal data within the confines of the *Data Protection Act 1998*. Data protection legislation is thus relevant to most UK businesses and institutions. One of the greatest advantages of the PC and the Internet is the ease of access to, and ability to use, personal data in all its forms. However, many are concerned about the use of their data. This A–Z handbook aims to provide practical advice to UK businesses and institutions on compliance with UK data protection legislation, principally in the *Data Protection Act 1998*.

Individuals have widely different views on privacy issues. The legislation tries to achieve a fair compromise between freedom of expression and rights of privacy. An important practical consideration is ease of access to information. Often information has been available publicly for years, but has been difficult to access. Allowing access over the Internet means in practice availability is hugely eased. Data protection implications then arise.

In advising clients in my commercial law practice, the greatest wisdom one gains, after 20 years in the City and running one's own practice, is not knowledge of the law (which should be taken as read), but the ability to advise commercially and provide practical solutions – pragmatism and risk analysis. Applying this to the data protection area is particularly difficult. Those seeking to advise corporate directors of the seriousness with which data protection should be taken are not helped by the few prosecutions and low level of fines. However, there are certainly investigations each year (905 visits to premises and 91 cases were brought before the criminal courts, 80 resulted in conviction, and 11 cautions were administered in the year to March 2003), and a number of cases are settled without enforcement proceedings being launched. Consequently, for some businesses which handle large amounts of data, or in bigger companies with a high profile, complete compliance must be the aim.

Clearly it is necessary to notify (register) where personal data is held, and there are criminal penalties and fines for breach, but ensuring basic compliance should not be complicated or expensive for most companies. They need to understand that the legislation is in places overly complicated; no one knows with certainty what all its provisions mean and they should put such reasonable resources as they have into compliance without worrying unnecessarily over this legislative area. Breach of data protection legislation is not for most businesses a major concern or risk area. However a public breach, a security glitch, a difficult customer making public complaints, can result in appalling and very damaging publicity for bigger companies, so where possible procedures should be put in place to minimise the risk of such problems arising.

Increasingly in my practice jurisdictional issues are to the fore. For example the data may be in the US. It is used in the UK at a call centre, processed cheaply in India or the client runs an Internet betting operation in an offshore tax haven and ships personal data around. The EU/US Safe Harbor Agreement has not at the date of writing been adopted with much enthusiasm – only a handful of companies have taken part. As with many areas of e-commerce law, what is really needed is international harmonisation.

New data protection guidance and rules continues to be issued. On 11 December 2003 the UK implemented the EU privacy directive. The resulting *Privacy and Electronic Communications (EC Directive) Regulations 2003 (SI 2003/2426)* affect many companies, in particular in relation to their e-mail marketing. Important appeals in the *Naomi Campbell* and *Hello!* decisions, both to the House of Lords, are to be decided in 2004. The *Durant* decision came in time for inclusion in this third edition of the Handbook and provides useful guidance on what manual data is caught by the Act.

In 2004 the Information Commissioner, Richard Thomas, himself the author of a book *Plain English for Lawyers*, stated that he hoped to simplify data protection guidance. The legislation was unfairly blamed for failure to pass on crucial information in the Soham murder enquiry.

For those involved with personnel and human resources the *Employment Practices – Data Protection Code* provides detailed guidance. Parts 1 – 3 were finalised in 2003 and Part 4, on Medical Records, was issued as a draft in 2004. It is likely to come into force later in 2004 and is covered in draft form in this third edition of the Guide.

In preparing the third edition of this book in March 2004, I was struck by how many changes there had been since I produced the last edition only just over a year before.

Not content with leaving matters as they are, the EU is currently consulting on how the Directive has operated in practice as a result of which further changes may occur. As part of that process, consultation on employer surveillance of employees is being undertaken by the EU. In January 2004 the *Regulation of Investigatory Powers (Communications Data) Order 2003 (SI 2003/3172)* came into force, once dubbed the snoopers' charter, it entitles various Government bodies to share traffic data, but not content of e-mails and the like.

For human resources managers, data protection officers and similar staff, the day-to-day issues of data protection are more mundane. This book seeks to provide practical advice on the major topics in an accessible A–Z format. As it will be updated annually, readers are invited to e-mail suggestions for improvements to me at the address below.

Susan Singleton
Singletons
The Ridge
South View Road
Pinner
Middlesex
HA5 3YD
Tel: 020 8866 1934
Fax: 020 8866 6912
E-mail: susan@singlelaw.com
www.singlelaw.com

21 January 2004

Contents

Table of Cases

Table of Statutes

Table of Statutory Instruments

Table of European Material

Chapter 1 –
Automated Decision-taking

At A Glance

✓   Decisions made about individuals, particularly employees, by automated means can lead to injustices. The *Data Protection Act 1998 (DPA 1998)* includes protection where 'automated decision-taking' takes place.

✓   Individuals may, by written notice, require a data controller to ensure that no decision which significantly affects them is taken based solely on the processing by automatic means of their personal data (*DPA 1998, s 12*).

✓   Upon request, an individual has a right to be told the 'logic' behind a decision taken by these means (*DPA 1998, s 7*).

✓   Where a decision is taken about an individual based on automated means, and the individual has not served such a notice, then the data controller must notify the individual that such a decision has been taken as soon as is reasonably practicable.

Introduction   1.1

Section 12 of *DPA 1998* gives examples of personal data processing which may significantly affect the individual, where processing by automated means is the sole way of evaluating a data subject as to their:

- performance at work;
- creditworthiness;
- reliability; and
- conduct.

Normally, appraisal of an individual will be based on non-automated means. For example, checking the speed with which supermarket checkout employees scan goods is usually done by automated means, whereas assessing that person on whether they have a good manner with customers and wear appropriate clothes to work is not. Assessing workers simply by checking whether they have clocked into work on time is automated means, whereas using other factors alone or in

1

conjunction with this factor would be outside the scope of *section 12 of DPA 1998*. The provisions of *section 12* are based on *Article 15* of the *Data Protection Directive (95/46/EC)* which *DPA 1998* implements.

Example: Shortlisting for a Job   1.2

The shortlisting of those applying for a job based only on the evaluation of an applicant's attributes by automated means must safeguard applicants' interests. This will be the case if an applicant is rejected or treated in a way that is significantly different from other applicants solely as a result of an automated process. According to the Information Commissioner (previously known as the Data Protection Commissioner) (see **4 COMMISSIONER**) it will not be the case if the automated process merely provides information (for example, a score resulting from a psychometric test which is just one of a range of factors taken into account in a human decision). However, any automated system must process information about individuals fairly. In the Employment Practices Data Protection Code the Commissioner suggests the following standards:

Standards

- Ensure that shortlisting is carried out in a way which produces results that are objective, consistent and fair to applicants (implying the drawing-up and use of criteria for assessing applications) (Principle 1).

- Only use an automated system for shortlisting if the system can be demonstrated to produce results that are objective, consistent and fair to applicants (Principle 1).

- Where an automated system using some form of evaluation is used as the sole basis for a decision to reject an applicant, inform the applicant that an automated system has been used, give the applicant an opportunity to make representations, and consider these representations before a final decision is reached (Principle 6).

  This right will not apply if the automated process merely provides information, for example where the score resulting from a psychometric test is just one of a range of factors taken into account as part of a decision-making process that has an element of human intervention or scrutiny. Ensure that psychological and other complex tests are only used and interpreted by those who have received appropriate training.

In Part I: Recruitment and Selection of the Employment Practices Data Protection Code , the Commissioner suggests the following.

- Inform applicants if an automated shortlisting system will be used as the sole basis of making a decision, making provisions to consider representations from applicants against this and to take these into account before making the final decision.

> - Ensure all the applicants are informed that an automated system is used as the sole basis of shortlisting and how to make representations against any adverse decision. Test and keep the results produced by the system under review to ensure they properly and fairly apply the shortlisting criteria to all applicants.
>
> - Ensure that psychological and other complex tests are only used and interpreted by those who have received appropriate training.
>
> - Determine which such tests are operated within the organisation. Ensure all tests are properly assessed.

Data Subject Notice   1.3

Individuals are allowed, within 21 days of receipt of the data controller's notice, to serve a 'data subject notice' requiring the data controller to reconsider the decision taken or to take a new decision. Within 21 days of receipt of a data subject notice the data controller must give the individual a written notice specifying the steps they intend to take to comply with the data subject notice.

Exempt Decisions   1.4

Certain decisions are excluded from these provisions (*DPA 1998, ss 12(5)–(7)*). These can be set out in an order of the Secretary of State (none have been drafted at the time of writing).

An exempt decision can also occur where a decision is made during steps taken when considering whether to enter into a contract with the data subject, either:

- with a view to entering such a contract;
- in the course of performing such a contract; or
- where authorised or required to do so under an enactment.

However, the contracts and other exemptions above will not apply unless the effect of the decision is to grant a request of the data subject, or steps have been taken to safeguard the legitimate interests of the data subject, for example by letting them make representations.

Exemption Conditions   1.5

The conditions for exemption are:

- the decision must be taken in the course of steps taken:
    - for the purpose of considering whether to enter into a contract with the data subject,

   ○ with a view to entering into such a contract, or

   ○ in the course of performing such a contract; or

- the decision must be authorised or required by or under any enactment.

In addition, either:

- the effect of the decision must be to grant a request of the data subject; or

- steps must have been taken to safeguard the legitimate interests of the data subject (for example, by allowing them to make representations).

Examples of Exemptions   1.6

The relationship between employees and employers is contractual, and automated decision-taking in that area is likely to be an exempt decision as long as an unsuccessful employee or potential employee has a right of appeal or a right to make representations in some other effective way. The following examples are given by the Commissioner in the Employment Practices Data Protection Code (2000 Draft).

(a) An employer places the educational qualifications of job applicants into categories and then enters these into a computer system which produces a score for each applicant. Only those applicants with a score of 25 or over are shortlisted. This is an automated decision but, provided safeguards are in place for those not shortlisted, it is an exempt decision as it is taken for the purpose of considering whether to enter into a contract of employment with the applicant. Safeguards would be notifying applicants that an automated process is to be or has been used, giving them an opportunity to state why they should be considered separately and, if the case is valid, doing so.

(b) An employer produces a bulletin on its pension scheme with background information for those approaching retirement age. The system is programmed to send the bulletin to all those employees who are likely to receive a pension of more than £10,000 per year and are aged over 60. The decision on who receives the bulletin and who does not falls outside the specific requirements on automated decision-taking because although it is automated, it only affects the provision of background information and not benefits. It does not significantly affect employees.

(c) An employer has a system that scans application forms. The employer asks applicants to specify on the minimum starting salary that they would accept. The system automatically rejects those applicants that put more than £50,000 per year. The decision falls outside the specific provisions on automated decision-taking because it is not based on an evaluation of matters relating to the individual of the type referred to in *DPA 1998*.

Positive decisions in respect of an application for products or services are an example of one category of exempt decision. A lender operating a credit scoring system will fall within the exemption in many cases and be allowed to take a decision on that basis. The application has been made at the data subject's request.

In their documentation data controllers may want to add that they use automated processing to decide whether to enter into a contract with an individual.

Court Orders   1.7

A court, on application by the data subject, and where the person taking the decision ('the responsible person') has not complied with the requirements, can order the responsible person to reconsider their decision. No such order will affect the rights of any person other than the data subject and the responsible person.

An application for an order under *section 12* of *DPA 1998* may be made where the data controller has failed to notify the data subject that the decision was taken by automated means, or where the individual was not given 21 days to give notice to require the data controller to reconsider the decision or reach a different decision.

Generally, individuals are entitled to claim compensation from data controllers where *DPA 1998* has been contravened and the individual has suffered damage or damage and distress.

'Logic'   1.8

Section 7 of *DPA 1998* provides that where an individual's personal data will be processed by automatic means in order to evaluate matters relating to him or her (such as performance at work, creditworthiness, reliability or conduct), and this will constitute or be likely to constitute the sole basis for any decision which significantly affects that person, they are entitled to be informed by the data controller 'of the logic involved in that decision-taking'.

This means that when individuals make subject access requests they are entitled to be told of the logic involved in any automated decision-taking that comes within the scope of these provisions and affects or is likely to affect them. An employer need not provide the information in response to a broader subject access request unless it is referred to in the request. If it is the subject of a separate request, a separate fee can be charged. An employer is not required to provide information in response that constitutes a trade secret.

The use of the word 'logic' is unusual in a statute, as it is not defined. Presumably it can be interpreted as meaning 'reasons'. Under *section 7(2)* of *DPA 1998*, however, there is no need to provide this information unless the individual has made a request in writing and paid the relevant fee. Regulations may also deal with this area but have not yet been drafted.

Regulation 3 of the *Data Protection (Subject Access) (Fees and Miscellaneous Provisions) Regulations 2000 (SI 2000/191)* provides that the maximum fee for such a request is £10.

The Commissioner says:

> 'Neither the term "logic" nor the term "trade secret" is defined. The Commissioner takes the view that an employer is required to provide an explanation that enables the individual to understand the sorts of factors taken into account in the discussion and the way in which they are evaluated and translated into the decision. However, the employer is not required to give matters such as the precise weighting given to each factor which either the system supplier or the employer would reasonably want to keep secret from a competitor on the basis that it provides it with a significant competitive advantage.'

In respect of this right to information the Commissioner proposes the following standard.

Standard   1.9

- Ensure that on request, promptly, and in any event within 40 calendar days, workers are provided with a statement of how any automated decision-making process, to which they are subject, is used, and how it works.

  (Employment Practices Data Protection Code Part 2: Records Management.)

Action List   1.10

Businesses need to check the following in all areas of their business.

- Whether they do assess people by automated means alone. In many cases such means are just one of a number of factors, therefore *section 12 of DPA 1998* will not apply.

- Whether they notify individuals in accordance with *section 12 of DPA 1998* if they do assess by automated means.

- Keep a register of decisions made by automated means. This will allow individuals who have objected to these means to be noted.

- Ensure individuals are given the right to object as required by the legislation. A system should be set up to handle *section 12* notices which can operate across the whole business.

- Keep a register of individuals' applications for such decisions to be reconsidered.

- Change the terms and conditions of contracts with customers etc. so that sufficient protection is included to ensure, where possible, that the decision becomes an exempt decision.

- Check whether an exemption might apply, eg someone may be assessed by automated means in order to decide whether to hire them as an employee. This may be exempt under *section 12(4)* of *DPA 1998* due to the provisions of *section 12(6)* and *(7)* of *DPA 1998*.

FAQs   1.11

What is automated decision-taking under *DPA 1998*?

Automated decision-taking is the process by which decisions are made about individuals such as their work performance based on an automated means. This can lead to unfairness if other checks and balances are not used.

How does the Act regulate such decision taking?

Section 7 of *DPA 1998* states that individuals subject to automated decisions are entitled to be informed of the logic behind the taking of that decision. *Section 12* of *DPA 1998* gives individuals a right to serve a data subject notice asking a data controller to reconsider a decision taken by this method.

Are there any exemptions?

Yes, these are set out in *section 12(5)–(7)* of *DPA 1998*. The conditions for exemption include that the decision must be taken to consider whether to enter into a contract with the data subject.

Chapter 2 –
CCTV

At A Glance

✓   Closed circuit television often involves recordings of individuals and their movements. These are 'personal data' (*Data Protection Directive (95/46/EC), Art 14*).

✓   The Information Commissioner has issued a CCTV Code of Practice (July 2000) (see **APPENDIX 1**) which sets out what those operating CCTV systems must do to ensure compliance with the *Data Protection Act 1998 (DPA 1998)*, including in many cases putting up warning notices to tell people they are being recorded.

✓   In 2004 the Information Commissioner issued supplemental CCTV guidance following *Durant v FSA*, which states that most small businesses using CCTV are probably outside the *DPA 1998* entirely.

✓   Employers should also pay regard to the CCTV sections of the Employment Practices Data Protection Code (Part 3).

Recording and Use of Personal Data   2.1

Closed circuit television ('CCTV') involves the recording and use of personal data about individuals. CCTV pictures of individuals are defined as 'personal data' under *DPA 1998*. *Article 14* of the *Data Protection Directive (95/46/EC)* provides that the Directive applies to 'the techniques used to capture, transmit, record, store or communicate sound and image data relating to natural persons'.

Therefore, those using CCTV (such as employers and those with business premises who record customers and others inside and outside those premises) need to ensure they comply with *DPA 1998* in their use of such systems. It is important that individuals are told they are being recorded by displaying a notice in the shop, office or other premises as necessary.

In the 2004 Guidance on CCTV, the Information Commissioner concluded following *Durant v FSA* that those with a basic CCTV system, would probably no longer be covered by the *DPA 1998*.

This depends on what happens in practice. For example, small retailers would not be covered who:

- only have a couple of cameras;
- can't move the cameras remotely;
- just record on video tape whatever the cameras pick up; and
- only give the recorded images to the police to investigate an incident in their shop.

The shopkeepers would need to make sure that they do not use the images for their own purposes, eg checking whether a member of staff is doing their job properly, because if they did, then that person would be the focus of attention and they would be trying to learn things about them so the use would then be covered by the *DPA 1998*.

Those now outside the DPA for CCTV who were within it before are told:

> 'If you have already notified the Information Commissioner of your CCTV activities you will not have to renew this when it is due. Just let us know when you get your renewal reminder'.

Code of Practice   2.2

The Information Commissioner's Code of Practice on CCTV (July 2000), made under *section 51(3)(b)* of *DPA 1998*, gives guidance on how to ensure compliance with *DPA 1998* with respect to such systems. Ideally, those charged with ensuring legal compliance in this area should read and follow the detailed guidance. The Code of Practice is not intended to apply to 'targeted and intrusive surveillance activities' covered by the provisions of the *Regulation of Investigatory Powers Act 2000*, meaning the use of surveillance techniques by employers to monitor their employees' compliance with their contracts of employment. This will be covered by the Employment Practices Data Protection Code considered at **2.3** below. The CCTV Code of Practice does not cover security equipment installed in homes for security purposes or the use of cameras for journalism or media purposes.

Advice to Employers   2.3

The Employment Practices Data Protection Code, due to be finalised by the end of 2002, provides guidance on both video and audio monitoring of employees. The Information Commissioner believes that continuous monitoring by either video or audio equipment is 'particularly intrusive for employees'. Employers should not, therefore, routinely engage in this practice unless there are particular safety or security risks that cannot be properly addressed in less intrusive ways.

'Covert monitoring will only be justified in specific cases where openness would prejudice the prevention or detection of crime or the apprehension of offenders.'

The Information Commissioner has proposed standards (set out at **2.4** below) in this area in Part 3 of the Employment Practices Data Protection Code.

Standards – Video and Audio Monitoring   2.4

If video or audio monitoring are to be used covertly, take account of the following benchmarks.

Benchmarks

1. Carry out an impact assessment to determine what, if any, video and audio monitoring is justified by the benefits. Limit the scope of monitoring to what is strictly necessary to deliver these benefits.

2. Give workers a clear notification that video or audio monitoring is being carried out and where and why it is being carried out.

3. Ensure that people other than workers, such as visitors or customers, who may inadvertently be captured by monitoring, are made aware of its operation and why it is being carried out.

Notes and Examples

1. In making an impact assessment to determine whether video and audio monitoring is justified, and in determining its scope, the following should be considered.

    - Can video and audio monitoring be targeted at areas of particular risk, for example where there is a risk to safety or security?

    - Can monitoring be confined to areas where workers' expectations of privacy will in any case be low, for example areas to which the public have access?

    - Can video and audio capability be treated separately? Cases where both video and audio monitoring are justified are likely to be extremely rare.

    - Will the employer be in a position to meet its obligations to provide subject access to and, if necessary, remove information identifying third parties from audio and video recordings?

    See Part 2: Records Management of the Employment Practices Data Protection Code.

    Continuous video or audio monitoring is particularly intrusive for workers. The two combined are even more intrusive. The circumstances

    (cont'd)

in which continuous monitoring is justified are likely to be rare, for example work in particularly hazardous environments such as refineries or nuclear power stations, or where security is at risk.

2. Employers carrying out monitoring should make it clear to workers that monitoring is taking place and where and why it is being carried out. This could be done by ensuring that in areas subject to monitoring, a prominent sign is displayed that identifies the organisation responsible for the monitoring and why is it being done, and says who to contact regarding the monitoring. Simply telling workers that from time to time they may be subject to video or audio monitoring is not sufficient. Given the intrusive nature of such monitoring they should know exactly when it is taking place.

3. Not only workers, but also others who might be caught by monitoring should be informed that it is taking place and why it is taking place. Any notification given should identify the organisation responsible for the monitoring, its purposes, and should say who to contact regarding the monitoring.

Sample Form – CCTV Requests   2.5

Employers should ensure that whenever someone asks to view CCTV pictures they keep a record of the request and who has obtained the data. This record might be kept along the following lines.

Name of person requesting the footage:
Address:
Tel:
Fax:
Email:
Identification obtained from person named above to verify identity:
Legal basis on which information released:
Reason for request:
Manner in which footage was viewed and if tapes returned:

The Commissioner says that recorded images should not be made widely available, for example routinely making them available to the media or putting them on the Internet. There may be a case to disguise or blur some pictures.

Code of Practice   2.6

The draft advice to employers at **2.4** above is short. For more thorough guidance on CCTV under *DPA 1998*, the general guidance in this area in the CCTV

Code of Practice issued by the Information Commissioner should be considered. (The CCTV Code of Practice is reproduced in **APPENDIX 1**.)

Initial Assessment 2.7

The Commissioner advises that before CCTV or similar equipment is used it should be established who will be responsible for it, whether it is appropriate to use it at all and the reasons for doing so. Ideally the assessment process should be documented, including reasons behind any decisions made. The appointment of the data controller, indicating that they will be holding personal data, should be registered with the Information Commissioner. The purposes for which the equipment should be used should also be covered. Ideally security and disclosure policies should also be documented.

Siting Cameras 2.8

The way in which images are captured must comply with the First Data Protection Principle. The equipment should only monitor those areas intended to be monitored, although sometimes it is difficult not to record adjoining areas. In the CCTV Code of Practice the Information Commissioner refers to the recording of back gardens of neighbouring premises and states that neighbours should be consulted in advance.

In addition, operators of the equipment should not be able to alter the areas covered to examine other areas.

Examples 2.9

The following are examples of common situations that can occur due to the placement of CCTV cameras.

Sunbathing 2.10

The Commissioner states that 'individuals sunbathing in their back gardens may have a greater expectation of privacy than individuals mowing the lawn of their front garden'.

ATMs 2.11

In some cases it may be appropriate for the equipment 'to be used to protect the safety of individuals when using automated teller machines ('ATMs'), but images of PIN numbers, balance enquiries etc. should not be captured'.

Signs Used   2.12

Importantly, signs should be placed so that the public are aware that they are entering a CCTV zone, in order to comply with the First Principle. A sign at the entrance to a building society office may only need to be A4 size as it would be at eye level for all those entering the building. However, in car parks the size should be larger, such as A3, in order for them to be viewed by someone from their car.

Information on the Sign   2.13

The following information should be included on the sign:

- the identity of person responsible for the scheme;
- the purpose of the scheme; and
- details of whom to contact.

Recommended Wording   2.14

The Information Commissioner's recommended wording for the notice (where no image of a camera appears on the sign) is:

'Images are being monitored for the purposes of crime prevention and public safety. This scheme is controlled by the Greentown Safety Partnership. For further information contact 01234 567 890'.

Where there is an image of a camera on the sign the following wording is recommended:

'This scheme is controlled by the Greentown Safety Partnership. For further information contact 01234 567 890'.

Occasionally there may be exceptional and limited cases where the use of signs is not appropriate. For example, where specific criminal activity has been identified, surveillance is needed to obtain evidence and signs would prejudice the success of the operation. Even in such a case, the surveillance must not take place over a longer period than is necessary to obtain the evidence. The CCTV Code of Practice, Part II, section 3(e) sets out when the requirement for signs may be set aside. *Section 29(1) of DPA 1998* allows the processing of data to prevent crime to be excluded from the First Principle and this might be used in such cases where no sign appears.

Quality of Images   2.15

The Information Commissioner gives guidance in the CCTV Code of Practice on the need to ensure that the quality of the images is accurate, and that good quality tapes are used etc. If the system is to detect crime, obviously faces should be identifiable. If the system is in place to monitor traffic flow, for example, then cameras should not capture details of the drivers of vehicles. Sometimes an automatic facial recognition system is used to match images captured against a database of images. To ensure compliance with the Third and Fourth Data Protection Principles the sets of images must be clear enough to ensure an accurate match. In poorly lit areas infra red equipment may need to be installed.

Ideally a maintenance log of the system should be kept.

Processing the Images   2.16

The images must not be kept for longer than is necessary. In an example given by the Commissioner in the guidance, a publican may only need to keep recorded images for seven days (as they will generally be aware, should a brawl occur in their public house, as soon as the fight has started). Images of town centres and streets may not need to be kept for longer than 31 days, unless required as evidence in court proceedings. Images at ATMs may need to be kept for three months to resolve customer disputes about cash withdrawals. This period is based on the length of time it takes individuals to receive bank statements, the Commissioner states.

If images are kept for evidential purposes then they should be securely stored.

Access to and Disclosure of Images to Third Parties   2.17

The Commissioner proposes standards in the CCTV Code of Practice relating to third party access to, and disclosure of, images. Only those staff who need access to achieve the purpose for which the footage was obtained should have access, and access should be documented to ensure compliance with the Seventh Data Protection Principle.

Access by Data Subjects   2.18

Those filmed may wish to view themselves and can make a subject access request in that regard under *section 8* of *DPA 1998*. The Commissioner recommends the following.

'Data subjects should be provided with a standard subject access request form which:

(1)   indicates the information required in order to locate the images requested;

(For example: an individual may have to provide dates and times of when they visited the premises of the user of the equipment.)

(2)   indicates the information required in order to identify the person making the request;

(For example: if the individual making the request is unknown to the user of the equipment, a photograph of the individual may be requested in order to locate the correct image.)

(3)   indicates the fee that will be charged for carrying out the search for the images requested – a maximum of £10 may be charged for the search;

(4)   asks whether the individual would be satisfied with merely viewing the images recorded;

(5)   indicates that the response will be provided promptly and in any event within 40 days of receiving the required fee and information; and

(6)   explains the rights provided by *DPA 1998*.'

Individuals could be given a leaflet which describes the images being recorded. It may be necessary to hire an editing company to edit the tape to provide the relevant extract. If this is done then contract guarantees about confidentiality will need to be included as provided in the CCTV Code of Practice.

It is important to ensure that images of other people are not disclosed in responding to a subject access request. The CCTV Code of Practice, Part II, section 4 deals with this. If the individual will not be able to identify the other individual from the information given then it can be provided. It may also be provided where the other individual has consented, or it is reasonable in all the circumstances to comply with a request without the consent of the other person. Under *section 29* of *DPA 1998* (the 'criminal exemption') it may be reasonable to refuse a subject access request for footage where the information is held for the prevention or detection of crime or apprehension or prosecution of offenders.

Further Information   2.19

The British Standards Institute's BS 7958 'Closed Circuit Television (CCTV) – Management and Operation – Code of Practice' provides guidance on issues of security, tape management etc. and is referred to in the Information Commissioner's guidance on CCTV.

The Information Commissioner's CCTV Code of Practice under *DPA 1998* is under 'Codes of Practice' on the Data Protection website (www.informationcommissioner.gov.uk) and is reproduced in APPENDIX 1.

FAQs

Does CCTV fall within *DPA 1998*?

Yes, where individuals are recorded their images will be personal data under DPA 1998 and thus subject to its provisions.

What guidance is available from the Commissioner on this subject?

The Commissioner has issued a detailed code of practice on the use of CCTV under DPA 1998 which is on the website www.informationcommissioner.gov.uk under 'Codes of Practice' and in appendix 1 of this book.

What are the rules about telling people they are being recorded?

The Commissioner recommends that signs be placed so that the public know they are entering a CCTV zone otherwise breach of the first data protection principle may occur. The sign should identify the person running the scheme, state its purpose and give details of whom to contact.

What steps should businesses take before installing CCTV?

Before proceeding check the Commissioner's CCTV Code of Practice mentioned above and undertake an initial assessment to ensure it is clear who will be responsible for it.

Small User Checklist

This checklist is designed to help operators of small CCTV systems comply with the legal requirements of *DPA 1998* and it details the main issues that need to be addressed when operating a CCTV system. When used as part of a regular review process it should help to ensure that the CCTV system remains compliant with the requirements of the Act.

It is important that *DPA 1998* is complied with because failure to do so may result in action being taken under this Act. Failure to comply with data protection requirements will also affect the police's ability to use the CCTV images to investigate a crime and may hamper the prosecution of offenders.

If you use a CCTV system in connection with your business you should work through the checklist and address all the points listed. This will help to ensure that your CCTV system remains within the law and that images can be used by the police to investigate crime.

(cont'd)

Operation of the CCTV System

This CCTV equipment and the images recorded by it are controlled by .....
who is responsible for how the system is used and for notifying the
Information Commissioner about the CCTV system and its purpose (this is a
legal requirement of *DPA 1998*).

The above controller has considered the need for using a CCTV system and
has decided it is required for the prevention and protection of crime and for
protecting the safety of customers. It will not be used for other purposes.

	Checked (Date)	By	Date of next review
The controller is aware that notification to the Information Commissioner is necessary and must be renewed annually.			
Notification has been submitted to the Information Commissioner and the next renewal rate recorded.			
Cameras have been sited so that their images are clear enough to allow the police to use them to investigate a crime.			
Cameras have been positioned to avoid capturing the images of persons not visiting the premises.			
There are signs showing that a CCTV system is in operation visible to people visiting the premises and the controllers contact details are displayed on the sign where it is not obvious who is responsible for the system.			
The recorded images from this CCTV system are securely stored, where only a limited number of authorised persons may have access to them.			
The recorded images will only be retained long enough for any incident to come to light (eg for a theft to be noticed).			
Recordings will only be made available to law enforcement agencies involved in the prevention and detection of crime, and no other third parties.			
The operating equipment is regularly checked to ensure that it is working properly (eg the recording media used is of an appropriate standard and that features on the equipment such as the date and time stamp are correctly set).			
The controller knows how to respond to requests from individuals for access to images relating to that individual. If unsure the controller knows to seek advice from the Information Commissioner as soon as such a request is made.			

In 2004 the Information Commissioner issued supplementary guidance on CCTV following a decision in the case of *Durant v FSA*, which is at www.informationcommissioner.gov.uk. A copy of the guidance appears at the end of **APPENDIX 1**.

Chapter 3 –
Codes of Practice

At A Glance

✓ Under *section 51* of the *Data Protection Act 1998* (*DPA 1998*), the Commissioner is charged with issuing codes of good practice to be followed by data controllers.

✓ A CCTV Code of Practice has been issued and draft codes proposed in areas such as employer/employee relationships.

✓ In addition, the Commissioner comments on proposed general legislation which may have data protection implications.

✓ Three codes of practice were issued under the *Regulation of Investigatory Powers Act 2000* (*RIPA 2000*).

✓ The Commissioner, under *section 51(4)* of *DPA 1998* has a duty to encourage trade associations to bring out their own codes and to comment thereon.

✓ Codes have been issued in the financial services sector, on direct marketing, factors, fire officers, the Church of England, the Office of National Statistics and the General Medical Council.

Introduction   3.1

The Information Commissioner has a duty under *section 51* of *DPA 1998* to promote the following of good practice by data controllers. *Section 51(2)* of *DPA 1998* provides that she may arrange the dissemination of information as appears expedient to give information:

> '...to the public about the operation of [the Act], about good practice and about other matters within the scope of [his] functions under [the] Act, and may give advice to any person as to any of those matters'.

In her First Annual Report (June 2001) the Commissioner wrote:

> 'Codes of practice do not add to the regulatory burden, nor go beyond the requirements of the law already in place. Their aim is further to

explain the interpretation which this Office (as regulator) is taking of the requirements of *DPA 1998*'.

Good Practice   3.2

When new legislation is proposed the Commissioner will often comment on any adverse data protection implications. The Commissioner's general duty is to encourage good practice.

Definition of Good Practice   3.3

The codes of practice should set out good practice. *Section 51(9) of DPA 1998* defines good practice as:

> '...such practice in the processing of personal data as appears to the Commissioner to be desirable having regard to the interests of data subjects and others, and includes (but is not limited to) compliance with the requirements of this Act'.

Factors in Encouraging Good Practice   3.4

In considering the encouragement of good practice, the following factors are relevant.

- *Transparency*: that except in cases where it would be 'prejudicial to the prevention and detection of crime or the collection of taxes, data subjects should be fully informed of the uses to which their personal data may be put'.

- *Fairness*: that personal data should be processed in a way which is fair to data subjects. The Commissioner states that 'although fairness may be difficult to define in precise terms, clearly it is a concept which embraces the notion of equity and is opposed to action which is discriminatory'.

- *Purpose limitation*: having collected information for specified purposes, that information should not be used or disclosed for other purposes (once again except in cases where there is prejudice to the prevention and detection of crime or the collection of taxes).

- *Security*: ensuring that data are stored in a manner appropriate to the sensitivity of those data and are not disclosed to others.

Commenting on Proposed Legislation   3.5

Set out below are four recent examples of the Commissioner commenting on or criticising proposed legislation. This is likely to be more common than the issuing of formal codes of practice.

(*a*)   The draft *Nursing and Midwifery Order 2001* envisaged a public register of nurses and midwives including their home addresses, which the Commissioner said would not be compliant with *DPA 1998*.

(*b*)   *Social Security Fraud Act 2001* (*SSFA 2001*) – here the Commissioner considered that the objectives of the Department of Social Security could be achieved by less intrusive means than were set out in the Social Security Fraud Bill. The Act provides that where benefit fraud is suspected, investigating officers can ask organisations to provide them with any information for the purpose of the prevention and detection of crime (under the exemption to data protection legislation set out in *DPA 1998, s 29*). However, they cannot compel organisations to provide information under the exemption.

In the explanatory notes to *SSFA 2001* the Department of Trade and Industry states that 'Many organisations are bound by a duty of confidentiality to their customers and are therefore uncertain whether they should provide information on this basis. Consequently, investigating officers obtain very little information in this way.' The Commissioner reports in her First Annual Report (June 2001) that she was pleased to see the Government take account of these comments by way of amendment before the Bill was enacted.

(*c*)   *Criminal Justice and Police Act 2001* (*CJPA 2001*) – here, as with *SSFA 2001*, the Commissioner commented on the proposed legislation. *Section 51* of *CJPA 2001* gives powers to seize equipment such as personal computers which might contain personal data and *section 82* of *CJPA 2001* provides restrictions on the use and destruction of fingerprints and samples which may have data protection implications.

(*d*)   Before the enactment of the *Health and Social Care Act 2001* (*HSCA 2001*), it was subject to criticism and comment by the Commissioner. *Section 60* of *HSCA 2001* concerns the control of patient information. It enables the Secretary of State to require or permit patient information to be shared for medical purposes where he considers that this is in the interests of improving patient care or in the public interest.

In May 2002 the Commissioner issued Guidance on the Use and Disclosure of Health Data.

The Issuing of Codes of Practice   3.6

Where the Commissioner thinks it appropriate or the Secretary of State directs by order, the Commissioner shall prepare codes of practice for guidance as to good practice and disseminate them to those people she considers appropriate.

It is such codes, enacted under *section 51(3)* of *DPA 1998*, which are considered in this chapter. The codes should be produced 'after such consultation with trade associations, data subjects or persons representing data subjects' as the Commissioner deems appropriate. There are also duties on the Commissioner in *section 51(6)* of *DPA 1998* to disseminate information about EU decisions.

If the Secretary of State has ordered the production of the code, which is unlikely to occur often, then the code of practice resulting from that exercise must under *section 52(3)* of *DPA 1998* be laid before each House of Parliament.

Codes have long been issued in the data protection field, including under the *Data Protection Act 1984* (*DPA 1984*).

The Usefulness of Codes of Practice   3.7

In her invitation to tender document (August 2001) the Commissioner implicitly recognises the fact that codes of practice can entrench 'one time interpretation', by suggesting that Part 2: Records Management of the Employment Practices Data Protection Code should perhaps exist as a web-based reference document only and be updated regularly as and when the Commissioner's interpretation of the law develops. This would accommodate the problem of changes in interpretation.

Invitation to Tender   3.8

A lot of work goes into producing a code of practice so it is not surprising that not many have been issued. On the second proposed code (the first was the CCTV Code of Practice) the Commissioner, having produced a draft which was much criticised, put out an invitation to tender for help in finalising the code (the Employment Practices Data Protection Code).

Trade Associations   3.9

Trade associations are defined in *section 51(9)* of *DPA 1998* as 'includes any body representing data controllers'.

Practical Advice   3.10

Codes of practice should be contrasted with the guidance which the Commissioner issues in a number of areas which is not subject to the provisions of *section 51* of *DPA 1998*. However, for practical purposes the effect is the same – businesses and others are provided with advice on how the Commissioner views particular areas or practices under *DPA 1998* and can act accordingly.

In either case the Commissioner may be wrong in her interpretation of the law and the codes could be legally challenged in appropriate cases. However, the cautious data controller will seek to operate in accordance with all relevant codes and guidance.

Issued Codes of Practice   3.11

The Commissioner has issued the following codes of practice (list current at January 2004):

- CCTV Data Protection Code of Practice;

- The Employment Practices Data Protection Code Part 1 Recruitment and Selection;

- The Employment Practices Data Protection Code Part 1 Recruitment and Selection Notes;

- The Employment Practices Data Protection Code Part 2 Employment Records;

- The Employment Practices Data Protection Code Part 3 Monitoring at Work;

- The Employment Practices Data Protection Code Part 3 Monitoring at Work Supplementary Guidance

- The Employment Practices Code Part 3 Small Business Code

- The Employment Practices Code Part 4 Information about Workers' Health;

- Small Business Information; and

- Code of Practice on Telecommunications Directory Information and Fair Processing.

CCTV Code of Practice   3.12

The CCTV Code of Practice was the first code of practice to be issued by the Commissioner under *DPA 1998*. It was issued in July 2000 after a consultation related to CCTV (see **2 CCTV**).

Employment Practices Data Protection Code   3.13

In late 2000 the Commissioner issued a Draft Code on the Use of Personal Data in Employer/Employee Relationships. This was heavily criticised by employers in many areas and, illustrating how important the consultation process is, the Commissioner agreed to make major revisions before finally releasing the Code in 2002. In 2002 Parts 1 and 2 of the Employment Practices Data Protection Code were issued, Part 3 was issued for further consultation and Part 4 was issued as a draft for comments in 2003.

The Code is divided into sections:

- recruitment and selection (Part 1);

- management of employment records (Part 2);

- monitoring at work (Part 3); and

- medical testing (including drug testing, genetic testing etc.) (Part 4).

Its main target is human resources practitioners in larger businesses and will be supplemented with additional material to support the Code, for example guidance leaflets for small businesses, employees etc. Interestingly, the Commissioner also suggested that research might be commissioned into how other codes of practice in areas other than data protection operate in practice.

Structure of Codes 3.14

Codes of practice under *DPA 1998* have so far always included recommended standards (some of which are quoted from in this book). Of those standards parts are obligatory, with compliance being necessary to comply with *DPA 1998*, and other parts are voluntary, but it would be good or best practice to follow them.

Regulation of Investigatory Powers Act 2000 3.15

Under *RIPA 2000* codes of practice are also issued. These are also considered under the topic 'Confidentiality and Security'. The following codes came into force in August 2002.

- The Interception Code of Practice.
- Covert Human Intelligence Sources Code of Practice.
- Covert Surveillance Code of Practice.

Industry Guides 3.16

Various guides and codes of practice are produced by industry, and details of some of these are given at **3.17–3.20** below.

A Duty to Consider Codes of Trade Associations 3.17

Section 51(4) of *DPA 1998* provides that the Commissioner shall encourage trade associations to prepare and disseminate codes of practice to their members. If a trade association submits a code to the Commissioner for consideration, then the Commissioner has a duty to consider that and consult with data subjects and those who represent them, and then to notify the trade association of whether, in the opinion of the Commissioner, the code does promote the following of good practice.

Under *section 51(8)* of *DPA 1998* the Commissioner is allowed to charge for services such as approving trade associations' codes, although it is thought she has not done so to date.

Financial Services 3.18

In September 2000 the main trade associations in the financial services sector published guidance on the Act entitled 'The New Data Protection Act 2000: A

Practitioner's Handbook'. Each chapter includes practical examples for banks and other financial institutions. Appended to the book are many examples and practical advice (see **22 FINANCIAL SERVICES**). Copies can be ordered from the British Bankers' Association website at www.bba.org.uk under Services/Publications.

Direct Marketing 3.19

In August 2000 the Direct Marketing Association's Colin Fricker, produced 'A Guide to the Data Protection Act 1998 For Direct Marketing'.

Other Industry Guides 3.20

In her First Annual Report (June 2001) the Commissioner mentions the financial services and direct marketing guidelines mentioned at **3.18** and **3.19** above, as well as commenting on guidance produced by:

- the Factors and Discounters Association;
- the Chief and Chief Fire Officers Association;
- the Church of England;
- the Office of National Statistics; and
- the General Medical Council.

The Commissioner has welcomed the fact that the NHS Executive is to convene a working group of interested parties to develop a code of practice for the NHS (referred to in her 2nd Annual Report).

EU Codes of Practice and Standards 3.21

The Information Commissioner supports the European Union Codes of Practice. The Federation of European Direct Marketing Associations ('FEDMA') have produced a code of practice relating to direct marketing under the *Data Protection Directive (95/46/EC)*, and the International Commerce Exchange ('ICX') has prepared a comprehensive code for EU-based multi-nationals who wish to follow one system of good practice throughout their international operations, the Commissioner reports in her First Annual Report.

OECD Privacy Statement Generator for Websites 3.22

In 2000 the Organisation for Economic Co-operation and Development ('OECD') Privacy Statement Generator for websites was adopted, and can be found at http://cs3-hq.oecd.org/scripts/pwv3/pwhome.htm.

Summary 3.23

Codes of practice are rarely likely to be issued. The CCTV Code of Practice is useful and detailed (see **2 CCTV**). The Employment Practices Data Protection Code will be finalised in 2004. Parts 1 to 3 were finalised in 2003.

All codes of practice are under 'Codes of Practice' on the Commissioner's website at www.informationcommissioner.gov.uk.

FAQs 3.24

What is the purpose of codes of practice under *DPA 1998*?

The Information Commissioner has a duty to issue codes of practice under *DPA 1998* whose purpose is to aid businesses and other institutions to achieve compliance with the Act.

What codes of practice have been issued to date?

At the date of writing only one code has been finalised, dealing with CCTV. A four part code on employment practices has partly been released and should be finalised by the end of 2002.

How are the codes of practice accessed?

The codes are all on the Commissioner's website under 'Codes of Practice' at www.informationcommissioner.gov.uk

How do industry codes fit in?

The Information Commissioner is keen to encourage trade associations to produce their own sector-specific codes of practice, such as one proposed for the NHS. This relieves the Commissioner of the burden of researching particular areas and enables the Commissioner to check and then approve the relevant industry code.

Chapter 4 –
Commissioner

At A Glance

✓ The Information Commissioner is an independent public official who reports to Parliament.

✓ The role of Information Commissioner involves duties under both the *Data Protection Act 1998* (*DPA 1998*) and the *Freedom of Information Act 2000* (*FIA 2000*).

✓ Under *section 59* of *DPA 1998* the Commissioner is restricted from disclosing certain information.

Introduction   4.1

The current Information Commissioner (as of 2002) is Richard Thomas, a solicitor and formerly the Director of Public Policy at city law firm Clifford Chance. Mr Thomas succeeded Mrs Elizabeth France, who departed at the end of her eight year term to take up the position of the UK's first Telecoms Ombudsman. Under the *Data Protection Act 1984* (*DPA 1984*) the Commissioner was called the 'Registrar' and then renamed 'Data Protection Commissioner'. *FIA 2000* led to a new title and responsibilities for the Commissioner as of 30 January 2001, when the post was renamed the 'Information Commissioner', and was given a dual role under both that legislation and *DPA 1998*.

Role of the Commissioner   4.2

The role of the Commissioner is self-described thus:

> 'The Commissioner is an independent supervisory authority and has an international role as well as a national one. In the UK the Commissioner has a range of duties including the promotion of good information handling and the encouragement of codes of practice for data controllers, that is, anyone who decides how and why personal data, (information about identifiable, living individuals) are processed.'

Under *section 6(2)* of *DPA 1998* the Commissioner is an independent person appointed by the Queen. She reports to Parliament directly. The duties of the Commissioner include:

- the promotion of the following of good practice by data controllers and, in particular, compliance with *DPA 1998*;

- the dissemination of information on *DPA 1998*; and

- encouraging the development of codes of practice to show good practice under *DPA 1998*.

Section 6 of *DPA 1998* sets out these provisions. There are more detailed provisions in *Schedule 5* to *DPA 1998*. In legal terms, the Information Commissioner is a 'corporation sole'. The Commissioner and her officers and staff are not servants or agents of the Crown. This chapter examines the Commissioner's main duties, responsibilities and powers, first under *DPA 1998* and then under *FIA 2000*.

The 2003 Annual Report of the Commissioner summed up the mission of the office as follows:

> 'We shall develop respect for the private lives of individuals and encourage the openness and accountability of public authorities by promoting good information handling practice and enforcing data protection and freedom of information legislation; and by seeking to influence national and international thinking on privacy and on information access issues'.

Requests for Assessment and Workload   4.3

The Commissioner deals with requests for assessment made under *section 42* of *DPA 1998*, which can be made by someone affected by the processing of personal data. A request for assessment is not strictly called a 'complaint' under *DPA 1998*.

The Commissioner has a duty to make an assessment where such a request is made, except where she has not been given sufficient information to be satisfied as to:

- the identity of the person making the request; or

- the ability to identify the processing concerned.

Most of the requests for assessment are made by individuals who believe their data has not been properly processed under *DPA 1998*. The Commissioner has powers to make assessments in relation to businesses and their compliance with the Act.

Dealing with a Request   **4.4**

In deciding how to deal with a request, the Commissioner takes account of a variety of factors, such as whether the issue raised is a 'matter of substance'; whether the complainant has shown undue delay in making the request; and whether there is a right of subject access in respect of the personal data concerned. The Commissioner's threshold criteria for determining when to handle a request for assessment are whether:

- the request is made by or on behalf of a person who is, or who believes himself to be, directly affected by the processing in question;

- the Commissioner is satisfied as to the identify of the person making the request;

- the Commissioner can identify the processing in question; and

- the processing is of personal data.

The person who made the request should be told by the Commissioner whether an assessment has been made as a result, and of any views formed or action taken by the Commissioner in consequence.

In a 'considerable number of cases', insufficient information is given to make an assessment (see the Commissioner's First Annual Report (June 2001)). In those cases written advice is given and the Commissioner treats them as 'enquiries'. In the period to 31 March 2001 the Commissioner's office dealt with 8,875 requests for assessment and enquiries, which included 1,721 complaints about breaches of telecommunications regulations (unsolicited faxes etc.). In 27.4 per cent of cases in that period advice was given; in 3.9 per cent a request for assessment was declined; and in 4 per cent the requirements for assessment were not met. 55,500 telephone enquiries were received by the Information Line (working out to be 9.12 enquiries per line per hour). These represent 35 per cent of calls received by the office overall.

Factors to Consider   **4.5**

In making assessments, the Commissioner can make either a verified or unverified assessment. In deciding which of the following factors are taken into account, as described in the Commissioner's First Annual Report, the Commissioner decides:

'whether:

- the request raises, on the basis of the impact on the person making the request or on whose behalf the request is made and the wider impact, what we consider to be a matter of substance;

- the request is made without undue delay;

- the request is from a person who is entitled to make a subject access request in respect of the personal data in question;

- an assessment has previously been carried out in respect of the processing in question;

- the matters to which the request relates are being or could better be dealt with by another body or alternative mechanism;

- the matters to which the request relates have already been resolved;

- the issues raised by the request are fundamentally about data protection (rather than data protection being merely incidental to the main issues); and

- an investigation by the Commissioner is likely to require resources disproportionate to the value of the assessment.'

Education   4.6

A principal duty of the Commissioner is to educate people about the legislation concerning data protection. To that end, an important part of her role and that of her staff is the issuing of Codes of Practice (see **3 CODES OF PRACTICE**), guidance, telephone advice, and attending workshops and issuing leaflets to ensure as many people as possible are aware of *DPA 1998* and its provisions. For example, in August 2000 the Commissioner implemented a national television advertising campaign. Education packs for schools are also prepared. Further details on the Commissioner's role in this area are included in Chapter 4 of the First Annual Report.

Inspection Visits and Search Warrants   4.7

As well as handling complaints and assessments, the Commissioner organises inspection visits. There were about 900 such visits to premises in the year to 31 March 2003 in the course of investigations into criminal breaches of *DPA 1998*.

Departments   4.8

The Commissioner's office is divided into different departments although this is not laid down by statute and may change from time to time. The Commissioner has an investigations department and also a legal department. The legal department considers, amongst other matters, whether prosecutions should be brought, and in the year to 31 March 2003, 91 cases were brought before the criminal courts, 80 resulted in conviction, and 11 cautions were administered (3rd Annual Report, to 31 March 2003).

Cautions   4.9

The Commissioner's current policy is to administer 'cautions' rather than prosecuting offenders, although in September 2002 a toughening up was announced so this may change. In the year to 31 March 2002 cautions were administered in 13 cases. 5 cautions were administered in relation to the offence of failure to notify (pursuant to *section 17(1)* of *DPA 1998*). In 2003 11 cautions were administered.

Enforcement and Information Notices 4.10

When the Commissioner decides to prosecute, an enforcement notice is served, often preceded by a preliminary enforcement notice. Where the Commissioner simply wants information, an information notice is served. In 2000/01 four enforcement notices and five preliminary enforcement notices were served. No information notices were served.

17 ENFORCEMENT, REMEDIES AND POWERS provides further information regarding the Commissioner's powers. In brief, the Commissioner can serve enforcement notices on those who are contravening the legislation.

Holding of Office 4.11

The Commissioner holds office for up to five years at a time, with a maximum of 15 years' service. Should the Commissioner reach 65 years of age while in office, he or she must leave office on completion of the year of service during which the birthday occurs. A reappointment for a third term is not allowed unless by reason of special circumstances. The role is a paid role with a salary and pension, the details of which are set out in *paragraph 3* of *Schedule 5* to *DPA 1998*. *DPA 1998* provides for the appointment of a Deputy Commissioner and another member of staff.

Freedom of Information Role 4.12

The Information Commissioner's role was created with effect from 30 January 2001 when the then Data Protection Commissioner took on responsibility for *FIA 2000*. *FIA 2000* must be implemented in full by 30 November 2005.

The Commissioner issues guidance on *FIA 2000*. Both roles cover aspects of information policy and the Government has said that 'joint responsibility will allow the Information Commissioner to provide an integrated and coherent approach to information handling and will provide a single point of contact for public authorities and the public.' (*FIA 2000 Overview, June 2001*).

In relation to freedom of information the Commissioner has the following duties.

- Approve/revoke publication schemes.
- Promote the following of good practice.
- Promote public authorities' compliance with *FIA 2000*.
- Disseminate information and give advice about *FIA 2000*.

- With consent, assess whether a public authority is following good practice.

- Report annually to Parliament.

FIA 2000 allows the Commissioner to charge for certain services.

Where a breach of *FIA 2000* occurs, for example where an individual has requested information of a public body and the information has been refused or the individual has received no reply, then they can apply to the Information Commissioner for a decision as to whether the request has been addressed in accordance with *FIA 2000*. The Information Commissioner may then serve a decision notice on the public authority and the applicant stating what must be done to comply.

The duties of the Commissioner also include the service of information or enforcement notices on public authorities. Notices can be issued requiring information to be disclosed in the public interest. However, a Cabinet Minister can override such notice (an executive override), and there is no appeal procedure following such a ministerial certificate. This illustrates a limitation on the powers of the Commissioner in the *FIA 2000* field. At the date of writing it is not yet known how often the executive override will be exercised.

Where the Commissioner serves a notice, the other party may appeal to the Information Tribunal.

The Role 4.13

The Information Commissioner position created from 30 January 2001 was not just a renaming of the Data Protection Commissioner. The Commissioner describes it as a 'new organisation' which expects to double in size by 2005 when *FIA 2000* is fully in force. The Commissioner's role is therefore likely to broaden and change as *FIA 2000* comes fully into force. New premises and staff will be sought and internal procedures will be formalised. Legislative change may also occur.

The Commissioner and Disclosure 4.14

Section 59 of *DPA 1998* provides that the Commissioner, members of her staff and agents of the Commissioner must not disclose information which has been obtained by the Commissioner under *DPA 1998*, relates to an identified or identifiable individual or business, and is not available to or has never been available to the public from other sources, unless the disclosure is made with lawful authority.

'Lawful authority' is defined in *section 59(2)* of *DPA 1998* as being applicable in cases where:

- a disclosure is made with the consent of the individual or business;

- information was provided for the purpose of its being made available to the public;

- the disclosure is made to discharge functions under *DPA 1998* or *FIA 2000* or an EU obligation;

- the disclosure is made for the purposes of proceedings (whether criminal or civil); or

- having regard to the rights and freedoms or legitimate interests of any person, the disclosure is necessary in the public interest.

The Commissioner said in the First Annual Report that *section 59* of *DPA 1998* 'imposes inappropriate restrictions on [her] ability to disclose information about [her office's] activities'. Such a restriction may not be compatible with the Data Protection Office's own duties to disclose information under *FIA 2000*.

If a member of the Commissioner's staff or the Commissioner breaches *section 59* of *DPA 1998* they commit an offence.

Transparency Consultation Paper   4.15

The Commissioner wishes to establish a policy on the extent and manner in which information coming into her office in connection with her data protection functions should be published. A consultation paper was published setting out the legislative background and some policy considerations in 2001. As seen at 4.14 above, *section 59* of *DPA 1998* imposed a criminal sanction on the Commissioner, her staff or agents if they disclose information obtained in the course of their duties otherwise than in accordance with the rules laid out in that section of *DPA 1998*.

To date, the Commissioner has been open about her office's activities, while protecting the privacy of complainants. The office issues guidance, annual reports, codes of practice, press releases and other publications. *Section 1* of *FIA 2000* provides that:

> 'Any person making a request for information to a public authority is entitled:
>
> (*a*)   to be informed ... whether it holds information ... ; and
>
> (*b*)   ... to have that information communicated to him.'

There are certain types of information which the Commissioner believes should be kept confidential, such as information about complainants, details of informants, details of those who complain under 'whistleblowing' legislation (the *Public Interest Disclosure Act 1998*), evidence obtained from third parties in the course of investigation, and information such as trade secrets entrusted in confidence. The Commissioner feels a certain balance must be achieved. Restrictions under *section 59* of *DPA 1998* only apply to information:

- obtained for statutory functions;

- relating to an identifiable individual or business; and

- not previously available to the public from other sources.

Where the restrictions in *section 59* of *DPA 1998* apply, there is a list of circumstances in which information can be disclosed. The Commissioner states that three useful rules permitting disclosure might apply in particular cases, as set out below.

- Where the individual or business has consented.

- Where the information was provided with the object of being disclosed under *DPA 1998*.

- Where the disclosure is for the purposes of any civil or criminal legal proceedings.

It should be clear from the circumstances where one of these three rules applies. A typical case of information being provided for disclosure under *DPA 1998* would be notification particulars which are to be included on the Register of Companies. The two other rules permitting disclosure of restricted information are more general. They can provide further bases for the data protection office giving out information. They are:

- where the disclosure is for the purposes of and is necessary for the discharge of statutory functions or a community obligation; or

- where the disclosure is, having regard to the rights and freedoms or legitimate interests of any person, necessary in the public interest.

The consultation paper stated that the Commissioner has come to the conclusion that the best way of reconciling the tension between the various legislative provisions and policy issues would be to 'adopt formally a policy about the information which she considers expedient to disseminate to the public thereby crystallising her duty to disseminate that information under *section 51(2)* of *DPA 1998*. Information published under that duty would seem to be disclosed with lawful authority by virtue of *section 59(2)(c)(i)* of *DPA 1998*.'

Contacting the Commissioner 4.16

The contact details of the Commissioner and her office are as follows:

Information Line	
Tel: 01625 545 745	Email: mail@informationcommissioner.gov.uk
To notify	
Tel: 01625 545 740	Email: mail@notification.demon.co.uk
Switchboard: 01625 545 700	
Fax: 01625 524 510	
DX 20819 Wilmslow	

FAQs   **4.17**

Who is the Information Commissioner?

The Information Commissioner is Mr Richard Thomas who succeeded Mrs Elizabeth France, who held the post for eight years, in 2002.

What are the main duties of the Information Commissioner?

The Commissioner's principal duty is to enforce *DPA 1998* and to educate businesses and individuals about the legislation.

How long does the Commissioner remain in post?

The Act provides that the Commissioner holds office for up to five years at a time but with a maximum of 15 years' service (ie three five year terms).

What other roles does the Commissioner have?

The Commissioner liases with data protection commissioners abroad and also is in charge of the *Freedom of Information Act 2000* enforcement.

Chapter 5 –
Compensation, Damages
and Prevention of Processing

At A Glance

✓ Those suffering damage through a breach of the *Data Protection Act 1998* (*DPA 1998*) can recover damages (*DPA 1998, s 13*).

✓ In limited cases compensation for distress, where no damage is also suffered, may be available.

✓ Under *section 10* of *DPA 1998* there is also a right to prevent processing which causes damage or distress.

✓ Under the *Privacy and Electronic Communications (EC Directive) Regulations 2003, s 30* damages can be recovered where a person has suffered loss through a breach of the regulations, eg where they have received unsolicited emails in breach of those regulations.

Introduction 5.1

DPA 1998 provides redress for those who have suffered through a breach of the legislation.

The provisions do not seem to have been widely used, although a threat to seek such redress may in practice lead to a payment which would of course not then be recorded in any court decision.

This section looks at the right to recover compensation under *section 13* of *DPA 1998* and also the right for data subjects to sue to prevent processing which causes them damage or distress under *section 10* of *DPA 1998*.

Compensation 5.2

Under *section 13* of *DPA 1998*, individuals have the right to sue for the damage they have suffered if the requirements of *DPA 1998* have not been met by a data controller. The individual must have suffered 'damage' by reason of any contravention by a data controller of any *DPA 1998* requirement. The compensation is paid by the data controller for that damage. Under *section 13* compensation is also available for 'distress'.

Where distress rather than damage is caused, then compensation is only paid where:

- the individual also suffers damage by reason of the contravention (in other words the claim is for both damages and distress and both claims are valid); or

- the contravention relates to the processing of personal data for the special purposes.

Section 3 of *DPA 1998* defines 'the special purposes' as being journalism and artistic and literary purposes. Therefore if a tabloid newspaper publishes details of the confidential extra-marital affair of a individual, and the individual suffers distress but no provable economic damage, then the individual can sue for damages. However, if the same facts were published, but by the disgruntled wife pasting notices on trees and lamp posts on the road where the man lives (which is not journalism or literary or artistic publication) then the husband can sue the wife for the distress, even if no damage is shown.

Case Examples   5.3

Naomi Campbell v MGN Limited [2003] 1 All ER 224, Court of Appeal (14 October 2002) – subject to appeal to the House of Lords (case pending, 2004)

Naomi Campbell, the internationally renowned fashion model, sought damages for breach of confidentiality and compensation under *section 13* of *DPA 1998* in relation to newspaper articles with photographs which had been published by the defendants in The Mirror in February 2001. At first instance (*Campbell v Mirror Group Newspapers plc, QBD, 27 March 2002*) she won. She claimed that as a result of the articles she had suffered distress, embarrassment and anxiety, which were aggravated by later publications in The Mirror and the defendant's conduct of the trial. The articles revealed that contrary to her previous false assertions she was a drug addict and that she was attending meetings of Narcotics Anonymous to beat her addiction. Some details of those meetings were published in The Mirror together with photographs of her leaving a meeting in Chelsea. Her barrister accepted that The Mirror was entitled to publish that she was a drug addict and the fact that she was having therapy. He contended that the information that the therapy was being obtained through Narcotics Anonymous and the details of her attendance at meetings were private and confidential matters and that there was no overriding public interest to justify their publication. No damages were pursued for infringement of privacy.

The Mirror denied that it had acted in breach of confidence, that the information published was sensitive personal data and that the defendants were in breach of any duty under *DPA 1998*. They did not dispute that she was entitled to damages and/or compensation, including aggravated damages or compensation, assuming that she established breach of confidence and/or breach of duty under the Act against the defendants. The Mirror argued that if information published was confidential, its publication 'was legitimate in that the public interest in favour of publication outweighed any public interest in the protection' of Miss Naomi Campbell's rights of confidentiality. The Mirror said that she was an internationally famous supermodel 'so well-known as to be recognised immediately by appearance and name by a high proportion of the general public' and well-known for her commercial ventures and as a figurehead for charitable causes. She had not only been 'for many years the subject of extensive media attention and coverage relating to her private and personal life, activities and conduct', but also she had courted such attention and coverage including voluntarily disclosing otherwise inaccessible details about her private and personal life and feelings. Although she had discussed with the media that she had undergone therapy for behavioural problems and anger management, she had falsely and publicly asserted that she had not fallen prey to drug abuse thereby misleading the public. The High Court referred to the case of *Douglas v Hello! Ltd [2001] QB 967* (see below) and examined five questions under the DPA 1998 section of the judgment.

1. Was the personal data 'sensitive personal data' within *section 2 of DPA 1998*? Yes.

2. Was the defendant exempted from liability under *section 32 of DPA 1998*? No. the Court of Appeal did not agree with this and said *section 32* did apply.

3. If the defendant is not exempt under *section 32*, did the defendant contravene the First Data Protection Principle under *section 4(4) of DPA 1998*? Yes.

4. If the defendant contravened the First Data Protection Principle, has the defendant established a *section 13(3) of DPA 1998* defence? No ('utterly failed' the court said).

5. Compensation.

The High Court decided as follows (but was later overruled by the Court of Appeal). In relation to compensation, the court said 'In my judgment "damage" in *section 13(1)* and *section 13(2)(a)* [of *DPA 1998*] means special or financial damages in contra-distinction to distress in the shape of injury to feelings.'

In awarding her £2,500 damages the High Court said:

'Although I am satisfied that Miss Naomi Campbell has established that she has suffered a significant amount of distress and injury to feelings caused specifically by the unjustified revelation of the details

(cont'd)

41

of her therapy with Narcotics Anonymous, apart from that distress and injury to feelings she also suffered a significant degree of distress and injury to feelings caused by the entirely legitimate publication by the defendants of her drug addiction and the fact of therapy about which she cannot complain. In determining the extent of distress and injury to feelings for which she is entitled to compensation, I must consider her evidence with caution. She has shown herself to be over the years lacking in frankness and veracity with the media and manipulative and selective in what she has chosen to reveal about herself. I am satisfied that she lied on oath about the reasons for her rushed admission to hospital in Gran Canaria and I have doubts about the accuracy of her accounts of the assaults on her assistants and her dealings with Mr Matthew Freud, the publicist. Nevertheless I am satisfied that she genuinely suffered distress and injury to feelings caused by the unjustified publication and disclosure of details of her therapy in the two articles of the 1st and 5th February 2002 complained of. I assess damages or compensation in the sum of £2,500.'

The court then turned to the matter of aggravated damages. It is for the claimant to establish that she has suffered increased distress and injury to feelings caused by the conduct of the defendants after the publication of the articles. Any damages awarded by way of aggravation can only be compensatory and must not reflect any punitive element. The court said:

'I am satisfied that Miss Carroll's article [an article in the Mirror about the matter] sounds in aggravated damages. That article did not only criticise the merits of her claim in strong and colourful language but also ..."Trashed her as a person" in a highly offensive and hurtful manner. That trashing entitles her to aggravated damages. I assess aggravated damages in the sum of £1000.'

In total Miss Campbell was awarded £3,500. An article on the High Court decision, 'Naomi Campbell: Drugs, Distress and the Data Protection Act', is in the June/July 2002 issue of the Computers and Law (www.scl.org) by Nigel Wildish and Marcus Turle of Field Fisher Waterhouse.

Court of Appeal

However, in October 2002 the Court of Appeal overturned these findings. It said:

'The primary information that had been conveyed to the appellants [The Mirror Group Newspapers Plc] was that Miss Campbell was regularly attending Narcotics Anonymous. The fact she was a drug addict was a secondary inference from this primary fact, albeit an inescapable inference. We find the suggestion that The Mirror should have published the secondary inference without publishing the primary fact to be lacking in realism. What is it suggested The Mirror should have published? Naomi Campbell is a drug addict. The Mirror has discovered she is receiving treatment for her addiction? Such a story, without any background detail to support it, would have bordered on the absurd. We consider that the detail given, and indeed the photographs, were a legitimate, if not an essential, part of the journalistic package designed to demonstrate that Miss Campbell had been deceiving the public when she said she did not take drugs.

Given that it was legitimate for the appellants to publish the fact she was a drug addict and receiving treatment, it does not seem it was particularly significant to add the fact the treatment consisted of attendance at meetings of Narcotics Anonymous. We consider that the detail given, and indeed the photographs, were a legitimate, if not an essential, part of the journalistic package designed to demonstrate that Miss Campbell had been deceiving the public when she said she did not take drugs. Given that is was legitimate for the [newspaper] to publish the fact she was a drug addict and receiving treatment, it does not seem it was particularly significant to add the fact the treatment consisted of attendance at meetings of Narcotics Anonymous.'

The Court of Appeal said that Miss Campbell is an internationally famous model. She has courted, rather than shunned, publicity. In part, this has been to promote other ventures in which she is involved. In interviews she volunteered information about aspects of her private life and behaviour, including limited details about her relationships with male friends. She acknowledged she had behavioural problems, including difficulty in keeping her temper. When talking to the media, Miss Campbell went out of her way to aver that, in contrast to many models, she did not take drugs, stimulants or tranquillisers. This was untrue. She had, in fact, become addicted to drugs. On one occasion it became known Miss Campbell had entered a clinic, the Cottonwood de Tucson Centre in Arizona.

The explanation she gave was [that] she was having therapy aimed at dealing with behaviour and anger problems. The reality is she was also being treated for drug abuse. The judges agreed the initial Mirror story had been sympathetic to the model but a follow-up article was not, following her complaint her privacy had been invaded. She also complained that clinical details of her treatment had been published. The court held:

'We do not consider the information that she was receiving therapy from NA was to be equated with disclosure of details of medical treatment.'

They said it was also inevitable Miss Campbell's identity would be known to others attending meetings of NA with her. They continued:

(cont'd)

'We do not consider a reasonable person on reading Miss Campbell was a drug addict would find it offensive that the Mirror also disclosed she was at NA.'

Disclosure of her NA sessions was not 'of sufficient significance to shock the conscience and justify the intervention of the court'. The judges insisted The Mirror was entitled to tell of Miss Campbell's addiction and treatment under *Article 10* of the *Human Rights Act 1998*. The information published was justified in order to provide a factual account of her drug addiction that had the detail necessary to carry credibility. Provided publication of confidential information is justifiable in the public interest, the journalist must be given reasonable latitude as to the manner in which that information is conveyed to the public or his right to freedom of expression will be unnecessarily inhibited. The court applied *A v B plc [2002] 3 WLR 542* (a confidentiality case).

The court said that on the data protection legislation the court said that the exemption in *section 32* of *DPA 1998* did apply. Where a data controller was responsible for the publication of hard copies which reproduced data previously processed by means of equipment operating automatically, the publication formed part of the processing and fell within *DPA 1998*. *Section 32(1) to (3)* of *DPA 1998* provided widespread exemption from the Act, provided that the data controller reasonably believed that publication would be in the public interest and that compliance was incompatible with the special purpose of journalist. The subsections must be given their natural meaning, and must apply both before and after publication. Miss Campbell had sought to argue that the exemption in *section 32(1)* depended on the processing being undertaken with a view to publication, therefore the processing could not include the publication. However the Court of Appeal said that it was the data which was exempt. Where under *section 32* the data became exempt as a result of a reasonable belief of the journalist that the publication would be in the public interest, the data remained subject to the exemption after that. Here the *section 32* exemption applied.

The Information Commissioner's March 2003 report summarised the case as follows:

Case commentary

'In this case the Court of Appeal has confirmed and clarified various "routine" matters of interpretation relating to both *Directive 95/46/EC* and the *DPA 1998*, making various helpful passing comments on the general ambit of these provisions. The Court confirmed that the definition of "processing" in the *DPA 1998* is "very wide" and that "publication must be treated as part of the operations covered by the requirements of the Act." Some legal commentators have characterised the Court of Appeal's judgment in this case as a denial of any right to privacy. In the Commissioner's view this is quite wrong; rather, the Court are still feeling their way in that direction.

On the central question of where the law stands on the "Article 8 v Article 10 issue", the courts are, in the Commissioner's view, still slowly and carefully moving towards establishing a common law concept of privacy within, alongside or, possibly, outside the realms of the law of confidence. In an appropriate case, on the particular facts, the courts will almost inevitably find there to be a "breach of privacy" as opposed to a "breach of confidence". But what will be an appropriate case? What will be the particular facts? How will the case by case approach work? What will be an "unjustifiable publication"? At this stage the Commissioner's prediction is that the courts will move further down this road in a case involving a genuine private person, not a celebrity or other public figure. The Court of Appeal clearly adopted a wide approach to the "special purposes" exemption at *section 32* of the *DPA 1998*, making it clear that it can apply after, as well as before, publication. The Commissioner would though want to make it clear that the exemption does not provide unlimited exemption from the whole Act for the media. This is very clearly not the case. The *section 32* exemption only applies in relation to particular provisions of the Act, and only to the extent that there is a reasonable belief that compliance with any such provision would prejudice any of the "special purposes", including journalistic purposes. It does not provide carte blanche for the media. The Commissioner notes that the Court of Appeal's judgment is currently the subject of an appeal to the House of Lords which is not expected to be heard before the publication of this Report. The Commissioner awaits with interest their Lordships' judgment in this important case.' (Information Commissioner, 3rd Annual Report to 31 March 2003.)

House of Lords

In January 2004 the appeal to the House of Lords began. The result was not known at the date of writing.

Douglas v Hello Ltd and Privacy

Another relevant case in relation to privacy is *Douglas and Others v Hello! Ltd [2001] 2 All ER 289* where the court said:

'…we have reached a point at which it can be said with confidence that the law recognises and will appropriately protect a right of personal privacy. The reasons are twofold. First, equity and the common law are today in a position to respond to an increasingly invasive social environment by affirming that everybody has a right to some private space. Secondly, and in any event, the *Human Rights Act 1998* requires the courts of this country to give appropriate effect to the right to respect for private and family life set out in *art 8* of the

(cont'd)

[*ECHR*]...the two sources of law now run in a single channel because, by virtue of *ss 2* and *6* of the *Human Rights Act*, the courts of this country must not only take into account jurisprudence of both the European Commission of Human Rights and the European Court of Human Rights which points to a positive institutional obligation to respect privacy; they must themselves act compatibly with that and the other convention rights. This...arguably gives the final impetus to the recognition of a right of privacy in English law...the right, grounded as it is in the equitable doctrine of breach of confidence, is not unqualified.'

In *Douglas* the court went on to provide that what a 'concept of privacy does ... is accord recognition to the fact that the law has to protect not only those people whose trust has been abused but those who simply find themselves subjected to an unwanted intrusion into their personal lives. The law no longer needs to construct an artificial relationship of confidentiality between intruder and victim: it can recognise privacy itself as a legal principle drawn from the fundamental value of personal autonomy.'

Many cases on privacy are summarised in the Appendix to the Information Commissioner's 3rd Annual Report.

Lord Ashcroft v A-G

In Lord Ashcroft v A-G [2002] EWHC 1122 (QB) the court said:

'29. The position under the [*Data Protection Act*] 1998... is entirely different: [*from the earlier Act*] there is a free-standing duty on data [controllers] under *section 4(4)* to comply with the principles which are set out in *Schedule 1, Part I*. By *section 13* breach of those principles does sound in damages, as does breach of any of the requirements of the 1998 Act. *Section 14* confers a right to rectification, blocking, erasure or destruction of personal data. Although enforcing compliance with the principles is for the Commissioner, it is clear that [his] jurisdiction is non-exclusive so far as claims for damages by data subjects are concerned.

'35. As I have already held, a right to damages does arise under the 1998 DPA for breach of the principles contained therein. The Claimant alleges that the disclosure of the documents amounted to a breach of the seventh principle [of the DPA 98], which requires data [controllers] to take appropriate technical and organisational measures against disclosure. I disallow this part of the pleading for the same reason I disallowed the [DPA 84 eighth principle] allegation [see above]..., namely that disclosure may be evidence of breach of the obligation to take such measures but cannot in itself amount to such a breach.'

Lord Ashcroft won his case and £500,000 of legal costs from the Government.

Right to Prevent Processing 5.4

Section 10 of *DPA 1998* contains a right for data subjects to prevent the processing of any data which will cause them damage or distress. Individuals can exercise this right at any time by notice in writing to the data controller.

The Data Subject Notice 5.5

A data subject notice is given to stop someone processing data or to prevent them beginning to do so. The notice is for them to stop or cease for a specific purpose, or in a certain manner. It must relate to data being used or processed in relation to which the complainant is the data subject. The right set out by *section 10* of *DPA 1998* cannot be used by someone where the processing of data relates to someone else. The period of notice to be given in such a case should be that which is 'reasonable in the circumstances'.

Section 10 of *DPA 1998* applies where, with reference to the data subject:

- the processing of those data or their processing for that purpose or in that manner is causing or is likely to cause substantial damage or substantial distress to him or to another; and

- that damage or distress is or would be unwarranted.

As can be seen above, if the processing of data about a person causes distress to someone else then *section 10* of *DPA 1998* can be invoked. Thus, processing data about someone's husband may distress the wife and in such a case the husband could complain, even if he were not personally distressed or damaged.

When Section 10 Does Not Apply 5.6

Section 10 of *DPA 1998* does not apply where the conditions in *paragraphs 1–4* of *Schedule 2* to *DPA 1998*, are met. These are the conditions relevant to the First Data Protection Principle (data processing). *Section 10* of *DPA 1998* does not apply:

- where the data subject consents;

- where the processing is necessary to perform a contract to which the data subject is a party or to take steps at the request of the data subject with a view to entering into a contract;

- if the processing is necessary for compliance with a legal obligation, other than an obligation imposed by contract; and

- if the processing is necessary to protect the vital interests of the data subject.

In addition, *section 10* of *DPA 1998* will not be applicable where the Secretary of State so orders.

Once a notice is received from a data subject under *section 10* of *DPA 1998* the data controller has 21 days from receipt of the data subject notice to return a notice to the data subject stating that the controller has complied with the notice or intends to do so. Otherwise, a statement must be issued detailing reasons for regarding the notice of the data subject as unjustified and how, if at all, the data controller intends to comply with part of it.

If the controller so refuses to comply, a court – upon application of the data subject – may order the data controller to take such steps to comply with the notice or part of it as the court thinks fit (*DPA 1998, s 10(4)*). No data subject can be obliged to serve a data subject notice nor will they lose rights if they do so. A failure by a data subject to exercise its rights above does not affect any other right under *DPA 1998* by virtue of *section 10(5)*. Indeed, in many cases the data subject will choose to make an application for assessment (complaint) to the Information Commissioner rather than suing for damages. Suing for damages, given the small loss the data subject has probably suffered (at least in financial terms), is rarely likely to be worthwhile because of the costs of litigation.

Unsolicited Communications and Damages   5.7

There are also rights to claim damages for breach of the *Privacy and Electronic Communications (EC Directive) Regulations* 2003, eg for sending unsolicited emails without consent. The regulations provide:

(1)   'A person who suffers damage by reason of any contravention of any of the requirements of these Regulations by any other person shall be entitled to bring proceedings for compensation from that other person for that damage.

(2)   In proceedings brought against a person by virtue of this regulation it shall be a defence to prove that he had taken such care as in all the circumstances was reasonably required to comply with the relevant requirement'.

Summary   5.8

There have been few publicised cases where individuals have sued to recover damages. However, in practice many individuals write to those who have caused them damage or distress themselves, and through their solicitors, both to require that such processing be stopped and to recover damages. Frequently a small sum is offered in settlement and that is the end of the matter. No litigation results.

FAQs

Can damages be recovered for breach of *DPA 1998*?

Yes, under *section 13* of *DPA 1998* compensation can be claimed where an individual has suffered damage by contravention of a provision by a data controller.

Has anyone ever recovered damages to date?

There may well have been settlements, and the *Campbell v Mirror Group Newspapers Plc* case in 2002 resulted in the model Naomi Campbell recovering both £2,500 standard damages, and £1,000 aggravated damages according to the High Court judgment, although the Court of Appeal set this aside.

What rights do individuals have to prevent the processing of their data?

Section 10 of *DPA 1998* gives a broad right to a data subject to prevent processing of any data which causes them damage or distress. A notice must be served and the procedure in *section 10* followed.

How much can be recovered in damages?

DPA 1998 does not specify the sum. In the *Campbell* case the ordinary damages were £2,500, but were overturned by the Court of Appeal (October 2002). It is likely that damages of this kind set by a judge, not a jury, will be low.

Chapter 6 –
Confidentiality and Data
Security: Seventh Principle

At a glance

✓ The Seventh Data Protection Principle requires that personal data be kept safe and secure.

✓ Security should also extend to e-mails, and companies must set up appropriate security procedures. In some cases encryption will be necessary.

✓ Codes of practice under the *Regulation of Investigatory Powers Act 2000 (RIPA 2000)* on the interception of communications, on the use of covert human intelligence sources and on covert surveillance have been issued and should be considered in this field.

✓ Security and data protection issues arising from the use of CCTV are addressed in the CCTV Code of Practice (see **2 CCTV**).

Appropriate Measures   6.1

The Seventh Data Protection Principle states that appropriate technical and organisational measures must be taken against unauthorised or unlawful processing of personal data and against accidental loss or destruction of, or damage to, personal data (*Data Protection Act 1998 (DPA 1998), Sch 1, Part I, para 7*).

Data controllers handling personal data need to ensure they take appropriate security measures to protect that data. The Seventh Principle, like all the principles, applies whether or not the data controller has notified their holding of data. The nature of the data determines to some extent the precautions which must be taken in relation to it. Sensitive data, as defined in *DPA 1998* (such as data about race), needs to be treated even more carefully than other data.

Levels of Security   6.2

Relevant factors to the levels of security provided include:

- the state of technological development; and

- the cost of implementing a measure.

These factors are mentioned in the Seventh Data Protection Principle. One example might be a newsagent whose computer screen can be seen by customers. Customers therefore have access to the personal data of those who have paid for their newspapers and their addresses. The Commissioner has held in one instance that this breached *DPA 1998*. Criminals could in such a case see whose newspapers had been cancelled for holidays. If the screen is turned to the counter the breach of the Act is removed.

The level of security must be appropriate to:

- the harm that might result from such unauthorised or unlawful processing or accidental loss, destruction or damage; and

- the nature of the data to be protected.

British Standard BS 7799 is helpful for companies assessing whether their security precautions are adequate. The Information Commissioner recommends compliance with BS 7799 in the Employment Practices Data Protection Code.

Practical Guidance   6.3

The Seventh Data Protection Principle refers to appropriate measures being taken to protect data. The following practical guidance is given by the Commissioner in the Employment Practices Data Protection Code.

'The holding of inaccurate data will be unlawful processing in that it contravenes the requirements of the *Data Protection Act 1998*. An employer should have in place technical and organisational measures to protect against inaccuracy. Technical measures might include a system that has accuracy and consistency checks built into the software. Organisational measures might include requiring employees to confirm the accuracy of the information held about them from time to time.'

Employees   6.4

The data controller must take reasonable steps to ensure the reliability of any employees who have access to the personal data (*DPA 1998, Sch 1, Part II, para 10*). *DPA 1998* does not specify what those steps should be. Under the *Data Protection Act 1984* (*DPA 1984*) there was an identical provision, and the Registrar recommended asking the following questions.

- Is proper weight given to the discretion and integrity of staff when they are considered for employment in or promotion/a move to an area where they have access to personal data?

- Are staff aware of their responsibilities? (A compliance or education programme on the Act will help with this.)

- Do disciplinary rules and procedures take account of the Act's requirements and are they enforced?

- If the employee is found to be unreliable, is his access to personal data immediately withdrawn?

Example **6.5**

A case study given in the Commissioner's First Annual Report (June 2001) describes an example of a breach of the Seventh Data Protection Principle. A council employee sent to the Data Protection Office a large amount of employee personnel information found in a black bin liner in a skip at the council depot where he was employed. He said the manager of the depot disposed of the personnel files of employees working at the depot by placing them in black bin liners and from there into skips to be transported to a public refuse tip, and that he had found two additional bags which contained similar information.

The documents which had been retrieved contained a large amount of personal data about the employees and their relatives, including details of:

- their pay;

- their relatives;

- applications for leave; and

- medical information about sick leave.

Most of the documents retrieved were copies of manual documents which did not then fall within the scope of *DPA 1998*. The Commissioner said:

'However, there was one document, a sickness record relating to the complainant, which appeared to have been computer-generated. On this basis we notified the council concerned that we had formed the view that there had been a contravention of the Seventh Data Protection Principle in this case.'

The council's response was to explain that although systems and procedures were in place at the depot these had not been strictly followed. The result of the case was that all depots were issued with shredders and the management was reminded of the procedures. All employees then received data protection awareness training, and data protection liaison officers throughout the council were told of the incident and asked to apply the lessons learned in their own areas.

E-mails 6.6

The use of e-mail can cause security problems. In the Employment Practices Data Protection Code the Information Commissioner says that an employer who allows the transmission of confidential employee information by e-mail without taking proper security measures will breach the Seventh Principle. Some companies use encryption to protect e-mail in transit, but it can still then be vulnerable at either end. Employers need to be aware that even deleting a confidential e-mail does not mean it is irretrievable. Indeed, the Commissioner's guidance on subject access rights under *section 7* of *DPA 1998* and e-mails includes a section on possible obligations upon employers to retrieve deleted e-mails in response to a subject access request.

Encryption 6.7

Encryption is one method of security which can be used to protect e-mails, although it can cause problems when it concentrates too much power in the hands of the employee who has the encryption key. *RIPA 2000* was heavily criticised during its passage through Parliament because it permits the police to require an employee to hand over an encryption key without telling the employer they have done so, and indeed makes it an offence for the employee to inform their employer of this. *Section 49(2)* of *RIPA 2000* sets out the principal provision requiring an individual to hand over a key.

Under *section 53* of *RIPA 2000*, a person to whom a *section 49* notice has been given is guilty of an offence if he 'knowingly fails, in accordance with the notice, to make the disclosure required by virtue of the giving of the notice'. A jail sentence of up to two years and/or a fine can be imposed on an individual who does not comply.

Section 54 of *RIPA 2000* is called 'tipping off', and states that where the notice served said 'to keep secret the giving of the notice, its contents and the things done in pursuance of it', and the individual does not do this, they can be jailed for up to five years and/or fined.

There are defences under *section 54* where:

- the disclosure was effected entirely by the operation of software designed to indicate when a key to protected information has ceased to be secure; and

- that person could not reasonably have been expected to take steps, after being given the notice or (as the case may be) becoming aware of it or of its contents, to prevent the disclosure.

Under *section 54(6)* of *DPA 1998* there are also certain defences involving disclosures to legal advisers, or where the disclosure was to the Interception of Communications Commissioner, the Intelligence Services Commissioner or any Surveillance Commissioner or Assistant Surveillance Commissioner.

Codes of Practice 6.8

Several codes of practice have been made under *RIPA 2000*. They all contain sections relevant to data protection and security, and in essence require the authorities to comply with *DPA 1998* in carrying out their duties.

Code of Practice on Interception of Communications 6.9

This code of practice, published on 7 August 2002, sets out the powers and duties conferred or imposed under *Chapter 1* of *Part 1* of the *Regulation of Investigatory Powers Act 2000* regarding the regulation of the interception of communications. It gives guidance to intelligence agencies and others on warrants and the disclosure, copying, retention and other safeguards necessary for materials obtained through warranted interception. It is primarily intended for used by those public authorities listed in *section 6(2)* of the Act, but will also prove useful to postal and telecommunication operators and other interested bodies.

Code of Practice on the Use of Covert Human Intelligence Sources 6.10

RIPA 2000 deals with other aspects of interception too, and a Draft Code of Practice on the Use of Covert Human Intelligence Sources has been issued (1 August 2002), in part covering security issues (see **6.11** below).

Retention and Destruction of the Product and Records of the Use of a Source 6.11

> '2.16 Where the product obtained from a source could be relevant to pending or future criminal or civil proceedings, it should be retained in accordance with established disclosure requirements for a suitable further period, commensurate to any subsequent review.
>
> 2.17 In the cases of the law enforcement agencies (not including the Royal Navy Regulating Branch, the Royal Military Police and the Royal Air Force Police), particular attention is drawn to the requirements of the code of practice issued under the *Criminal Procedure and Investigations Act 1996*. This requires that material which is obtained in the course of a criminal investigation and which may be relevant to the investigation must be recorded and retained.
>
> *(cont'd)*

> 2.18 There is nothing in the 2000 Act which prevents material obtained from properly authorised use of a source being used in other investigations. Each public authority must ensure that arrangements are in place for the handling, storage and destruction of material obtained through the use of a source. Authorising officers must ensure compliance with the appropriate data protection requirements and any relevant codes of practice produced by individual authorities in the handling and storage of material.'
>
> *Draft Code of Practice on the Use of Covert Human Intelligence Sources*
> *(in force 1 August 2002)*

Regulation of Investigatory Powers (Communications Data) Order 2003   6.12

The *Regulation of Investigatory Powers (Communications Data) Order 2003 (SI 2003/3174)*, which came into force on 5 January 2004, has security implications.

The *Anti-terrorism, Crime and Security Act 2001* required the retention of communications data by ISPs as these were needed to fight terrorism. Once obtained, the *RIPA 2000* provisions allow access to many other agencies for purposes unconnected with terrorism. The data concerned includes information from telephone companies, ISPs and interactive television providers. The data also describes the caller and the means of communication (eg, subscriber details, billing data, email logs, personal details of customers and records showing the location where mobile phone calls were made). It does not include content.

In addition to the police, Inland Revenue, Customs and Excise, MI5, MI6 and Government Communications Headquarters, the new Order gives certain other agencies rights to access communications data. These are fewer in number than in the original proposal, which critics had called the 'Snoopers' Charter', but do include:

- the Financial Services Authority;
- the Office of Fair Trading;
- the Maritime and Coastguard Agency;
- the UK Atomic Energy Constabulary;
- the Scottish Drugs Enforcement Agency;
- the Radio Communications Agency;
- NHS bodies, in connection with health and fraud;
- local authorities (but not parish councils); and
- the Office of the Police Ombudsman for Northern Ireland.

The Order can be viewed at http://www.hmso.gov.uk/si/si2003/20033172.htm

Code of Practice on Covert Surveillance   6.13

Under *RIPA 2000* there is also a Code of Practice on Covert Surveillance (see www.homeoffice.gov.uk/ripa/code_of_practice/covert_surveillance.htm). As regards the Police (including Service Police), the National Criminal Intelligence Service, the National Crime Squad and HM Customs & Excise it says:

> '**2.16** Where the product of surveillance could be relevant to pending or future criminal or civil proceedings, it should be retained in accordance with established disclosure requirements for a suitable further period, commensurate to any subsequent review.

> **2.17** In the cases of the law enforcement agencies (not including the Royal Navy Regulating Branch, the Royal Military Police and the Royal Air Force Police), particular attention is drawn to the requirements of the code of practice issued under the *Criminal Procedure and Investigations Act 1996*. This requires that material which is obtained in the course of a criminal investigation and which may be relevant to the investigation must be recorded and retained.

> **2.18** There is nothing in the 2000 Act which prevents material obtained from properly authorised surveillance from being used in other investigations. Each public authority must ensure that arrangements are in place for the handling, storage and destruction of material obtained through the use of covert surveillance. Authorising officers must ensure compliance with the appropriate data protection requirements and any relevant codes of practice produced by individual authorities relating to the handling and storage of material.'

Faxes   6.14

Security issues relating to fax machines should also be considered by readers. Sometimes a confidential fax is sent to a machine where many people can pick it up and read the contents, and sometimes faxes are misdirected by using the wrong number. All these activities could amount to breach of the Seventh Data Protection Principle.

Standards   6.15

- Apply proper security standards, such as those identified in BS 7799, that take account of the risks of unauthorised access to or accidental loss or destruction of or damage to employment records (Principle 7).

- Institute a system of access controls and passwords that ensure staff access to employment records is strictly on a 'need to know' basis (Principle 7).

- Keep a log of non-routine access to employment records and, as far as possible, use systems that record an audit trail of all access to computerised records whether routine or not (Principle 7).

- Take steps to ensure the reliability of staff who have access to employee records (Principle 7).

- Treat accessing, disclosing or otherwise using employee records without authority as a serious disciplinary offence. Make staff aware of this and also that such conduct may constitute a criminal offence (Principle 7; *DPA 1998, s 55*).

- Pay particular attention to the risks of transmitting confidential employee information by e-mail or fax by:

  o only transmitting information between locations if a secure network or comparable arrangements are in place or if, in the case of e-mail, encryption is used;

  o ensure that all copies of e-mails and fax messages received by managers are held securely;

  o provide a means by which managers can effectively expunge e-mails they receive or send from the system and make them responsible for doing so;

  o draw the attention of all employees to the risks of sending confidential, personal information by e-mail or fax; and

  o ensure that the information systems security policy properly addresses the risk of transmitting employee information by e-mail (Principle 7).

Data Processors and Security   6.16

Where a data processor is given the job of processing data on behalf of a data subject, then the data controller must do the following (*DPA 1998, Sch 1, Part II, para 11*):

- choose a data processor providing sufficient guarantees in respect of the technical and organisational security measures governing the processing to be carried out; and

- take reasonable steps to ensure compliance with those measures.

Where processing is carried out by a data processor the Seventh Data Protection Principle will not be complied with unless:

- the processing is carried out under a contract in writing and under which the data processor is to act only on instructions from the data controller; and

- the contract requires the data processor to comply with obligations equivalent to those imposed on a data controller by the Seventh Data Protection Principle.

These obligations on data processors require the data controller to be very careful when choosing a data processor.

CCTV   6.17

The Commissioner's CCTV Code of Practice (see **2 CCTV**) (www.informationcommissioner.gov.uk/cctvcop.htm) gives guidance on how to ensure compliance, *inter alia*, with the Seventh Data Protection Principle with respect to such systems. It includes ensuring that all requests for access to CCTV pictures are recorded and details kept of who has obtained the data. Consideration should be given to the harm which might result from the disclosure of the data. The nature of the data should also be considered. The more sensitive the data the more security measures are required.

Sensitive Personal Data   6.18

Some data is classed as 'sensitive personal data' under *section 2* of *DPA 1998* (see **42 SENSITIVE PERSONAL DATA**). The conditions for processing such data are contained in *Schedule 3* to *DPA 1998*. There is a requirement that such data is only processed with the explicit consent of the data subject or other conditions are met. Data controllers have to be particularly careful to preserve confidentiality of sensitive personal data.

Confidentiality and the Commissioner   6.19

Section 59 of *DPA 1998* imposes strict duties on the Commissioner and her staff to keep information confidential. In 2001 she issued a consultation document on transparency suggesting important changes in this area. *Section 59* can hamper her work. Details of this can be found in **4 COMMISSIONER**.

Further Information   6.20

The *RIPA 2000* Codes of Practice are on the Home Office website (www.homeoffice.gov.uk).

FAQs

What duties do data controllers have to keep personal data secure and safe?

The Seventh Data Protection Principle requires that personal data be kept safe and secure. Appropriate technical and organisational measures must be taken to prevent unauthorised access to data.

What assistance is there available from the Information Commissioner for this purpose?

The Information Commissioner issued in 2002 an Audit Manual (extracts of which appear in **APPENDIX 4**) which provides valuable assistance to companies seeking to ensure compliance with the legislation.

Does the nature of the data have an effect on the protective steps to be taken?

Yes, if the data is not secret or important the measures taken would not need to be as stringent, whereas if it were sensitive personal data such as about someone's health then a greater duty would arise.

What measures must data controllers take to check on staff?

DPA 1998 requires data controllers take reasonable steps to ensure the reliability of any employees who have access to personal data.

Chapter 7 –
Credit References and
Access to Credit Files

At A Glance

✓ Legal liability can attach to the giving of references.

✓ The *Consumer Credit Act 1974* (*CCA 1974*) was amended by the *Data Protection Act 1998* (*DPA 1998*) such that individuals could make credit access requests only under the 1998 Act and not under *section 159* of *CCA 1974*. There is a seven day response period for credit requests under *section 7* of *DPA 1998*.

✓ The use of third party data in the consumer lending process needs particular care. The Commissioner has issued guidance in this area including Model Letters for credit reference agencies and others.

Introduction   7.1

Few businesses will offer credit to new customers without a credit reference. As most customers want to operate on credit terms, credit references are a very important area both in the UK and abroad. Where an adequate reference cannot be obtained, businesses have to deal on a 'cash up front basis', which is not conducive to good cash flow and unacceptable for many businesses. The data protection implications of credit references are important because often the information contained in the reference is 'personal data' under *DPA 1998*, and compliance with the Act is therefore necessary. This section examines credit references under *DPA 1998* and also access to credit files generally. Reference in that respect should be made also to **43 SUBJECT ACCESS REQUESTS**.

Reluctance to Give References   7.2

Clearly, simply stating that 'XYZ plc' is good for £10,000 credit is not a statement containing any personal data at all, so the starting point for businesses is to ascertain the extent to which the references they may give or need will contain any personal data, and thus whether *DPA 1998* is relevant or not. However, even if the Act is not applicable, companies are increasingly showing reluctance to give references for other legal reasons. Normally there is no fee for the giving of such a reference, and if the consequence is to expose the person giving the reference to possible legal liability then it may be simpler to refuse to give references at all.

Legal Liability   7.3

Some companies already have such a policy in relation to employee references. Rarely is there a contractual or other legal obligation to give a reference, although these issues should always be considered. When an employee is dismissed it may well be the term of a settlement agreement that a reference will or will not be given. In such a case the provisions of the contract should be followed. The other areas of legal liability might include liability in tort for negligent misstatement or liability for defamation if the statement is defamatory.

Disclosure   7.4

Under the *Data Protection Act 1984* (*DPA 1984*) credit references could not be disclosed to data subjects under subject access rights. *DPA 1998* reversed that, leading to many companies ceasing to provide such references (they are not happy that those about whom they write will see what they have written). Under consumer credit legislation, credit reference agencies do not have to disclose the names of referees.

Overlap with the Consumer Credit Act 1974   7.5

Section 62 of *DPA 1998* made some substantial changes to *CCA 1974*. In particular, individuals (but not those trading in partnership) lost their right of subject access under *section 158* of *CCA 1974*, and instead have subject access rights under *section 7* of *DPA 1998* (but with an enhanced seven day response period). Individuals in partnerships, however, have rights to see data held about them under both *DPA 1998* and *CCA 1974*.

However, the right of individuals/data subjects under *section 159* of *CCA 1974* was not modified or removed by *DPA 1998* and remains. This section grants the right to give notice to a credit reference agency for the removal or amendment of an entry where the individual considers the entry to be both incorrect, and to cause prejudice if it is not corrected.

When an individual makes a request under *section 7* of *DPA 1998*, and is also entitled to information under *section 159* of *CCA 1974*, then under *section 9(3)* of *DPA 1998* the individual should be provided with the information. The data controller cannot simply say that the *section 7* request is requested and that *section 159* of *CCA 1974* must be used. Each year around one million references are made for access to information credit reference files.

Proposed Changes to Consumer Credit Law   7.6

In July 2001 the Government proposed major changes to *CCA 1974*, although not specifically in any area which affects data protection. The Department of Trade and Industry consultation document, 'Tackling loan sharks and more: Consultation document on modernising the Consumer Credit Act 1974', arose from its Task Force on over-indebtedness which was set up in October 2000 (see www.dti.gov.uk/consultations). The changes are likely to result in:

- greater information being given to those seeking credit;

- a rise in the £25,000 limit above which certain protection does not arise; and

- the enabling of online credit agreements, which should save costs.

Use of Third Party Data in the Consumer Lending Process   7.7

Historically, it was in accordance with the Data Protection Tribunals and Enforcement Notices agreed between the Credit Reference Agencies and the Data Protection Registrar in April 1992 that information on individuals other than a credit applicant could be included under two conditions:

- where the third party has resided concurrently with the credit applicant; and

- where it was reasonably believed that the third party has been living as a member of the same family as the applicant in a single household.

The Credit Industry Application for Change   7.8

In November 2000 the credit industry submitted an application to the Information Commissioner to allow the use of 'third party data' in the consumer lending process. The proposals were in response to concerns that the industry's current use of 'third party data' was becoming increasingly contentious. The result of a detailed review, the proposals would give the individual reassurance that their own information will not be seen or used inappropriately in connection with credit applications. The Commissioner in her press release at the time said:

'For example, no longer will a parent's credit information be seen by their children when a copy of a credit file is requested. But, at the same time, the individual will be protected from over-commitment and fraud by enabling the credit industry to continue to use aspects of "third party data".'

Changes   7.9

The changes included the following.

- There will no longer be an assumption made that there is a financial connection simply on the basis of a shared surname and address – parents and children are no longer automatically assumed to be formally connected.

- When customers request a copy of their credit file, the process will be amended so that an individual will only see their own credit data and not that of any financially connected 'third party'.

- Individuals will be able to opt-out of the automatic use of their financial partner's data enabling them, on occasion, to be assessed in their own right.

- An 'alert process' using household data will be created, providing lenders with the ability to detect fraud. Consideration is also being given to the use of this system as a means of assessing over-commitment within a financial unit.

At the time of writing these changes have not yet been put into force.

Credit Reference Agencies as Data Controllers   7.10

In January 2001 the Information Commissioner issued guidance on the definition of 'data controller' under *DPA 1998*. She said that the credit reference agency and agency customers/subscribers are data controllers as they both decide why and how they process personal data.

The credit reference agency's tasks, amongst other things, include obtaining, recording, holding, organising, adapting, altering and disclosing personal data. The agency customer/subscriber consults, obtains or retrieves personal data disclosed to it by the agency before using such data; for example, to inform a decision on whether to supply a customer. It is the ability to decide these things that makes them data controllers.

Information for Data Subjects   7.11

The Commissioner produces a leaflet 'No Credit?' (August 2001) (available by calling 0870 442 1211 or online at www.informationcommissioner.gov.uk) which explains how data subjects can ascertain what information is held about them on their credit file. It is the lender rather than the credit reference agency who informs the data subject about why they might have been refused credit on a particular occasion.

Common Complaints   7.12

The most common complaints to the Commissioner about credit reference files relate to:

- the amount of data which appears in the file, and in particular the fact that there may be information about a person other than the applicant for credit;

- the accuracy of one or more of the entries which appear on the file; and

- the length of time for which a record continues to appear on a file.

Others of Less Creditworthiness   7.13

There have been a number of well-publicised cases where individuals have been unable to obtain credit because others of less creditworthiness live with them or have lived at the same address. The Commissioner says the following in her guidance.

'The circumstances in which information about another person may appear on your credit reference file are set out in an Enforcement Notice which resulted from a decision of the Data Protection Tribunal. The rules are complex, and the following is a summary of them:

- the agencies must not supply information about anyone who has not lived at the same address at the same time as you;

- the agencies can provide information where the name is the same or similar and the address is the same as yours;

- the agencies can provide information about someone of a different name where the agency knows beforehand that it applies to you;

- the agencies can provide information about other people as long as those others have the same surname as you and they have been liv-ing, at either your present or last address, at the same time as you (it is this provision which enables the agencies to include informa-tion about family members at the same address on your credit file);

- the agencies can provide information about people with different surnames from you where they already have information from which it is reasonable for them to believe that these other people are or have been living as a member of your family in a single household (at either your present or last address); and

- the agencies must not supply information about any other person (even those indicated above) if the agency has information from which it is reasonable to believe that either that person is not you or that there is no financial connection between you and that person.'

Allowable Information 7.14

Agencies are only allowed to give information about:

- the data subject;
- people with the same name, or a very similar name, living at the address;
- other family members living in the household;
- people with the same name, or a very similar name, who have, in the past, lived with the data subject at his or her current or last address; and
- other people who have, in the past, lived with the data subject as part of the family at the current or last address.

Agencies must not report financial information about other people if:

- they have not lived at the data subject's current or last address as a member of the family at the same time as the data subject; and
- the agencies have information which makes it reasonable to believe that the data subject has no financial connection with them.

However, agencies can supply the names of other people, whether or not they are members of the family, who are or have been listed on the electoral roll at the data subject's addresses.

When individuals make access requests relating to their financial standing they are assumed to be limited to that area unless the request says otherwise.

Disassociation 7.15

Individuals can apply to be 'disassociated' from someone who lives at their address, but not from information on the electoral role. This information can continue to be associated with the complainant even if they object.

Model Letters 7.16

Credit Reference Agencies 7.17

The Commissioner suggests the following wording for data subjects wanting to find out which credit reference agencies have been used.

---

123 Any Street
Anytown, A45 6EC
21 March 200–

Dear Loan Company

Data Protection Act 1998

Please tell me the name and address of any credit reference agency which you have asked to give information about me. I expect a reply within seven working days of your getting this letter.

Yours faithfully

Adam Neil Other

Disassociation 7.18

For disassociation the Commissioner suggests the following text.

---

123 Any Street
Anytown, A45 6EC
10 June 200–

Dear Credit Reference Agency

Your reference 123456–7890

Thank you for sending me my file. The information on it about John James Other relates to my adult son. He has now left home and I no longer have any financial connection with him. Please 'disassociate' us, so that financial information about him no longer appears on my file, and information about me does not appear on his.

Yours faithfully

Adam Neil Other

Inaccurate Data 7.19

One of the major credit complaints is about the lack of accuracy of the data. There is a right to have inaccurate data 'rectified'. The agencies obtain data from the electoral role and from bodies such as the Registry Trust Limited (who keep the Registry of County Court Judgments) and financial institutions. The agencies will often offer to add a 'Notice of Correction' to the data subject's file. This is a statement of up to 200 words written by the individual saying why the information is not correct or is misleading. An example of such a notice is given at **7.21** below.

Sample Wording for Data Correction 7.20

The Commissioner suggests the following sample wording for having the data corrected.

---

123 Any Street
Anytown, A45 6EC
18 June 200–

Dear Credit Reference Agency

Your Reference 123456–7890

Thank you for sending me my credit reference file.

I no longer owe any money to Anytown Lending Company Limited. The file shows that I did get into arrears on my loan and they recorded a default. I have now paid this off. I enclose a letter from the company which confirms this. I expect a reply within 28 days of your getting this letter. Please make it clear that the debt has been cleared.

Yours faithfully

Adam Neil Other

Sample Wording for Notices of Correction 7.21

Under *CCA 1974* the agency has to notify the data subject within 28 days as to whether the data has been corrected as specified in **7.20** above. Further model wording from the Commissioner is given below for notices of correction.

---

123 Any Street
Anytown, A45 6EC
10 August 200–

Dear Credit Reference Agency

Your Reference 123456–7890

Thank you for your letter of 15 July 200–.

I note that you will not remove the entry from my file. Please add the following notice of correction to my file.

NOTICE OF CORRECTION

I, Mr Adam Neil Other, of 123 Any Street, Anytown, A45 6EC would like it to be known that the judgment recorded against me for £200 relates to a bill which I could not pay because I was made redundant in 1996. I paid the bill in full after I got a job in 1997. I would ask anyone searching this file to take these facts into account.

> I look forward to receiving confirmation from you within 28 days of receiving this letter that you have added this notice of correction to my file.
>
> Yours faithfully
>
> Adam Neil Other

Writing to the Commissioner 7.22

If correspondence such as that at **7.20** and **7.21** above does not result in a correction or notice, the Commissioner recommends that data subjects write to her along the following lines. In addition, there are rights under *DPA 1998* to have an assessment made as to whether or not the companies are complying with *DPA 1998*.

> 123 Any Street
> Anytown, A45 6EC
> 23 September 200–
>
> Dear Information Commissioner
>
> I am writing under *section 159(5)* of the *Consumer Credit Act 1974.*
>
> I got my file (reference number 123456–7890) from (the name of the credit reference agency) and asked them to change an entry about (details of the entry: county court judgment/ sheriff court decree/bankruptcy etc). Because they would not remove this from my file, I sent the agency a notice of correction to add to my file explaining the situation. It is now more than 28 days since I wrote and they have not told me whether they have put the notice on the file.
>
> I believe that if the notice of correction is not added to my file, it will not be clear why this situation happened and as a result I may be refused credit. Please can you contact the agency and resolve the matter. I enclose copies of all my letters to the agency and copies of the letters to and from the court.
>
> Yours faithfully
>
> Adam Neil Other

Breaches by Credit Grantors 7.23

The Commissioner says:

> 'We cannot accept that a failure of a credit grantor to produce a copy of the signed credit agreement is, on its own, evidence that your debt does not exist and therefore should not appear on your credit file. If the credit grantor can supply some other evidence of the agreement and you have no evidence to contradict this then it is likely to be proper for the debt to continue to appear.'

Nor is she likely to accept that the failure of a credit grantor to produce evidence of notification to the data subject of the purposes for which the data will be collected is a reason for requiring the deletion of the data.

Duration   7.24

The Fifth Data Protection Principle requires that personal data are held no longer than is necessary. The Commissioner says that:

> 'In general, credit reference agencies retain records for six years for the use of credit grantors in deciding whether or not to grant you credit. Records of bankruptcies are held for six years after the date of bankruptcy, records of County Court Judgments are held for six years from the date of the judgment, whether or not they are subsequently satisfied. Account records are held for six years from the date of the last entry on that record. In the Commissioner's view, it is not inappropriate for both a default and a subsequent judgment or bankruptcy to appear on a credit file.'

Finally, those suffering through inaccurate credit data as in any other area, may be able to claim compensation (see **5 COMPENSATION, DAMAGES AND PREVENTION OF PROCESSING**).

Transitional Provisions   7.25

Complicated transitional provisions apply in this area – see *Schedule 8* to *DPA 1998*.

Access to Credit Files for Data Subjects   7.26

Individual data subjects' access rights under *section 7* of *DPA 1998* differ for credit files – the period for production is seven days.

FAQs 7.27

The Commissioner's Questions and Answers contain the following guidance on access to credit files.

'Q. How can I obtain a copy of my credit file?

A. Credit grantors exchange information with each other about their customers. They also have access to the electoral roll and to publicly available financial information, which will have a bearing on an individual's credit worthiness, including County Court Judgments and Scottish decrees. This information is held by credit reference agencies. In order to get a copy of the information which relates to your financial standing (i.e.(ie your credit file), you should write to the two main credit reference agencies. These are:

- Equifax plc, Credit File Advice Service, PO Box 3001, Glasgow, G81 2DT; and

- Experian Ltd, Consumer Help Service, PO Box 8000, Nottingham, NG1 5GX.

You should send a fee of £2.00 and provide your full name and address, including postcode, and any other addresses you have lived at during the last 6 years and details of any other names you have used or been known by in that time. Unless the agencies require any further information to locate your file, they have 7 working days from the receipt of your letter in which to provide you with a copy of your file. For further information look at the paper 'No Credit' @ www.informationcommissioner.gov.uk under Guidance & other publications/sub heading your rights.'

Chapter 8 – Crime

At A Glance

✓ Breach of the *Data Protection Act 1998* (*DPA 1998*) may involve the commission of a criminal offence under the Act.

✓ Proceedings are initiated by the Information Commissioner's Office which also operates a Police Working Party.

✓ Under *section 61* of *DPA 1998*, offences committed under the Act with the consent or connivance of a director or similar officer will result in liability on that individual.

✓ Examples of breaches are listed in the Commissioner's First Annual Report (June 2001) and include the offences of unlawful disclosure, unlawful use and unlawful procurement.

✓ A new Criminal Records Bureau has been established to which employers will have access to check what general criminal offences their staff or proposed staff may have committed.

✓ The Council of Europe has developed a Cybercrime Convention.

✓ The *Computer Misuse Act 1990* (*CMA 1990*) makes computer hacking a criminal offence. Hacking can be used to access personal data.

✓ Criminal offences can also be committed in relation to computer software, and organisations such as BSA and FAST will investigate and/or civil or criminal proceedings may follow.

Introduction 8.1

Data protection can often become a criminal issue. The methods used to obtain the data may be criminal. Investigators may have broken into an office or hacked into a computer in breach of *CMA 1990*. **32 OFFENCES** looks in detail at the criminal offences created by *DPA 1998*.

Statistics   8.2

In 2001/2002 there were 33 criminal convictions for breach of *DPA 1998* (21 in 2000/2001):

- 2 were for being an unregistered data user;

- 18 were for unlawfully procuring information;

- 12 were people using data for an unregistered purpose; and

- 1 was an employee disclosing data.

13 cautions were administered up to 31 March 2002 (according to the Information Commissioner's 2nd Annual Report).

New Media and Telecoms   8.3

The fast development of communications such as mobile phones and the Internet has been used by criminals. There is a conflict between privacy and law enforcement. Law enforcement agencies want access to communications which may contain personal data. The *Regulation of Investigatory Powers Act 2000* contains important provisions about when the police and others can access e-mails and monitor telephone calls and Internet use etc. (See **3 CODES OF PRACTICE** for details about codes issued in this area relating to surveillance; also **38 RECORDING TELEPHONE CALLS AND E-MAILS**.)

The Commissioner, in her First Annual Report (June 2001), writes that in some cases new media provides new opportunities for surveillance: 'one example is the use of the increasingly precise location data generated by mobile phones to track individuals' movements'. She writes that the use of such data where it is a key element in addressing specific criminal activity will be justified, provided that proper controls are in place. The Commissioner recommends a proportionate response.

Personal Data as a Business   8.4

Some individuals make a business of obtaining personal data and pass it on to clients for a fee. In August 2000 the Commissioner set up a joint initiative with the then Department of Social Security, the Inland Revenue and the Commissioner's Office to stop such people. A number of organisations were reported to be subject to 'close scrutiny' when the Commissioner published her Annual Report in June 2001.

Commencement of Criminal Proceedings   8.5

In England and Wales, proceedings for a criminal offence under *DPA 1998* are commenced only by the Commissioner or by or with the consent of the Director of Public Prosecutions. Scotland has a different legal regime and there the

Procurator Fiscal brings the proceedings. In Northern Ireland, proceedings are started by the Commissioner or by or with the consent of the Director of Public Prosecutions for Northern Ireland. *Section 60* of *DPA 1998* contains these provisions. It also sets out the penalties of fines or prison sentences.

The Commissioner operates an EU Data Protection Commissioners' Police Working Party amongst other working groups. Criminal activities in relation to data are closely followed by both the Commissioner and police forces.

Liability of Directors etc   8.6

Body Corporate   8.7

If an offence is committed under *DPA 1998* by a body corporate and it is proved to have been committed

> '...with the consent or connivance of or to be attributable to any neglect on the part of any director, manager, secretary or similar officer of the body corporate or any person who was purporting to act in any such capacity, he as well as the body corporate shall be guilty of that offence and be liable to be proceeded against and punished accordingly.'
>
> (DPA 1998, s 61(1))

Shareholders   8.8

If the shareholders of a company manage its affairs, then *section 61(1)* of *DPA 1998* (see **8.7** above) also applies to any acts or defaults of a member of the company or shareholder. This is unusual as normally shareholders do not carry the same type of legal liability as directors. In 2001 the Government announced a sweeping review of company law which will lead to the duties of directors being codified for the first time in a statute, as well as other changes. The Company Law Review report was published in July 2001 (see www.dti.gov.uk/cld/review.htm) and draft legislation is currently awaited. This will include obligations in relation to data protection as well as other areas. *Section 61(3)* of *DPA 1998* also contains provisions about Scottish partnerships.

Examples   8.9

The Commissioner's First Annual Report (June 2001) gives examples of convictions for offences under *DPA 1998* including the following.

Unlawful Disclosure   8.10

A telecoms employee passed information on to a friend about a female customer's telephone account in order to assist that friend with a domestic situation. He was convicted of the unlawful disclosure of data.

Unlawful Use 8.11

An employee left his employer to set up on his own, taking data on his computer with him. He was convicted of having unlawfully used the data for his own purposes. His new company was also prosecuted for failing to notify.

Unlawful Procurement – Bank 8.12

A bank employee used the bank's online credit checking facilities to do a credit search which had nothing to do with her work and which related to her domestic situation. She was convicted of unlawfully procuring information from the credit reference agency.

Unlawful Procurement – DVLA 8.13

In two cases, convictions were secured for obtaining information from the Driving and Vehicle Licensing Agency (DVLA) by deception about registered keepers of cars. The prosecutions were for unlawfully procuring information from the DVLA.

Victim Support 8.14

An individual was the victim of a crime. Acting under good motives, the police passed his details to a third party which provides counselling services to victims, but did so without the consent of the individual. The police force accepted this was an error after the individual complained and agreed to ensure that they would review procedures to ensure victims' wishes were respected.

Prosecutions 8.15

Below is a list from the Commissioner's First Annual Report (June 2001) of prosecutions from 1 April 2000 to 31 March 2001 which resulted in convictions. The Report also gives the hearing date, court and result (all guilty), and the costs ordered to be paid in addition to the sentences below. These costs are up to £1,000 in addition to the fines below. No one was sent to prison.

Offence (section of DPA 1998)	Sentence (£)
5(1)	100
5(1)	200
5(1)	250
5(1)	450
5(1)	750
5(1)	800
5(1)	1,000
5(1)	1,000
5(1)	2,000
5(1)	3,000
5(1)	Absolute Discharge
5(1)	Conditional Discharge 12 months
5(2)(b)	250
5(2)(d)(3) × 3	1,400
5(6)	200
5(6)	250
5(6)	Conditional Discharge 12 months
5(6)	Conditional Discharge 2 years

In 2001/2002 similar penalties were imposed as summarised in the Commissioner's second Annual Report.

Criminal Records Bureau   8.16

In 2002 the new Criminal Records Bureau began issuing 'disclosures' – criminal conviction certificates based on information on the Police National Computer. Many employers will take these disclosures into account when recruiting new staff.

Cybercrime   8.17

The Council of Europe has developed a Cybercrime Convention. This would to some extent harmonise the laws in this area internationally. The UK Information Commissioner has concerns that the retention of traffic data beyond that needed for technical and commercial reasons, as provided in the current draft, would be a breach of the right to private life in *Article 8* of the *European Convention on Human Rights*, and indeed now the *Human Rights Act 1998* in the UK.

Computer Misuse Act 1990   8.18

CMA 1990 makes it a criminal offence to gain unauthorised access to computer systems, and separately makes it a further offence to modify material having gained such access. There are few prosecutions, although a special department of police forces around the country handles this area – the Computer Crimes Unit. Many employers do not want to draw public attention to problems with their own security, so offences are covered up or not much reported. Even when prosecutions are brought before local courts the penalties are often weak. A UK man was arrested in August 2001 on charges that he created and released the W32-Leave worm, a virus-like program that was designed to let hackers take control of home computers. The man was charged under *CMA 1990*, and if he is convicted could be jailed for up to five years.

Such hacking will usually involve access to personal data, for example someone may obtain details of the credit card and spending habits of a famous person through hacking. The data which is then accessed will be personal data under *DPA 1998*. Other countries have similar hacking legislation, so a hacker who has been hacking in many nations may find him or herself prosecuted in a number of different locations. The US Department of Justice is active in the computer crime area and has a cybercrime website at www.cybercrime.gov.

Copyright, Designs and Patents Act 1988   8.19

Crimes in this field can also be committed under the *Copyright, Designs and Patents Act 1988*, although sentences can be light. Some computer software owners will seek to have a criminal prosecution brought against a computer software pirate or counterfeiter as a threat of a jail sentence can be more of a deterrent to some individuals than a large damages claim or the seizure of the infringing programs.

FAST and BSA   8.20

Bodies such as the Federation Against Software Theft ('FAST') (www.fast.org.uk) and the Business Software Alliance ('BSA') (www.bsa.org/uk) will obtain court orders on behalf of their members to seize infringing products. However, this is in relation to copyright infringement, not a breach of data protection legislation. They also help companies ensure that all software used within the business is properly licensed, and run a telephone line for infringements to be reported, with rewards of thousands of pounds paid to those tipping off the organisation about infringement of copyright where this leads to a successful prosecution.

Pirated Software   8.21

Businesses buying software online need to ensure it is not pirated. The BSA estimates that more than 90 per cent of the software sold on auction sites is pirated. The BSA runs an Online Investigative Unit which recently looked at counterfeit software on Internet auction sites in the US and Europe. Its investigation,

'Operation Bidder Beware', found sales of pirated or counterfeit software from vendors in the UK, Germany and the US. Each of the 13 defendants caught in the US faces damages of up to $150,000 per work infringed.

Further Information   8.22

In addition to this chapter, see **3 CODES OF PRACTICE**, **32 OFFENCES** and **38 RECORDING TELEPHONE CALLS AND E-MAILS**.

Federation Against Software Theft (FAST)
Clivemont House
54 Clivemont Road
Maidenhead
Berkshire
SL6 7BZ
Tel: 01628 622 121
Fax: 01628 760 355
E-mail: fast@fast.org.uk
Website: www.fast.org.uk

Business Software Alliance (BSA)
79 Knightsbridge
London
SW1X 7RB
Tel: 0800 510 510
Website: www.bsa.org/uk

US Department of Justice Computer Crime
Website: www.cybercrime.gov/

FAQs   8.23

Is breach of *DPA 1998* a criminal offence?
Yes, the Information Commissioner obtains criminal convictions for breach of the Act in magistrates' courts with fines of up to £5,000 being imposed.

How many prosecutions are there each year?
Numbers vary but about 20–40 appears to be the norm.

Can individuals be personally liable under *DPA 1998*?
If an offence by a body corporate is committed under the Act, then under *section 61(1)* of *DPA 1998* a director, manager, secretary or other similar office can be guilty of an offence where they consented to it, connived in it or it was attributable to neglect on their part.

How do other bodies get involved, such as FAST?
FAST will obtain court orders on behalf of their members but these are civil procedures and obtained with leave of the court.

Chapter 9 –
Data Controller

At A Glance

✓ The data controller is the principal entity charged with compliance with the *Data Protection Act 1998* (*DPA 1998*) as regards the personal data which it processes.

✓ There will often be more than one data controller for particular data.

✓ The Commissioner has issued useful guidance on this definition.

✓ Anonymisation of data can be a sensible procedure, however it will not necessarily render such data outside the scope of *DPA 1998*.

Introduction   9.1

'Who is the data controller?' is one of the most common questions asked of IT lawyers by their clients. This chapter seeks to provide some guidance on this topic. In 2001 the Information Commissioner issued some useful guidance on definitions under the *Data Protection Act 1998* (*DPA 1998*) including the definition of a data controller, set out at **9.2** below and examined in this chapter. Data controllers may be companies, partnerships or individuals who control the use of personal data. Under the *Data Protection Act 1984* (*DPA 1984*) they were called 'data users'. Data controller is the equivalent term under *DPA 1998*.

Definition of a Data Controller   9.2

A data controller is a person who either alone, jointly or in common with other persons 'determines' the purposes for which and the manner in which any personal data are processed or are to be processed (*DPA 1998, s 1(1)*). Where personal data is processed because of an enactment which requires such processing, then the data controller is the person on whom the obligation to process the data is imposed by the enactment (*DPA 1998, s 1(4)*).

Alone or Jointly

A data controller will be covered by *DPA 1998* whether they act alone or jointly with others. There may therefore be two or more data controllers in relation to any piece of personal data. All data controllers would have to notify their holding of data and follow *DPA 1998*. Where data is controlled in 'common', those so holding it will all be data controllers. This may be the case where data controllers share a pool of personal data and each process it independently of each other.

Commissioner's Advice on the Interpretation of the Expression 'Data Controller'

In January 2001 the Information Commissioner issued guidance on the interpretation of the definition 'data controller' and 'personal data' (see **9.13** below). The former is considered below.

The Commissioner draws attention to *section 4(4)* of *DPA 1998* which provides that:

> ' ... it shall be the duty of a data controller to comply with the Data Protection Principles in relation to all personal data with respect to which he is the data controller.'

Jurisdictional Issues

DPA 1998 only applies where the data controller is established in the UK and the data are processed in the context of that establishment, or the controller uses equipment in the UK for processing the data 'otherwise than for the purposes of transit through the UK' (*DPA 1998, s 5(1)(b)*). 'Transit' means transient passing of the data such as where data is sent by e-mail and passes, often unnoticed, across servers in several states before ending up at the recipient.

Who is Established in the UK?

If a data controller based abroad sends data to the UK and uses equipment in the UK to process the data then *DPA 1998* applies. *Section 5(3)* of *DPA 1998* deals with who is established in the UK. The following are so classified:

(*a*)   individuals ordinarily resident in the UK;

(*b*)   companies registered in the UK;

(*c*)   partnerships or other unincorporated associations formed under the law of any part of the UK;

(*d*)   anyone else not within (*a*)–(*c*) who maintains in the UK an office, branch or agency through which they carry on any activity or who maintains in the UK a regular practice.

Nominated Representatives 9.7

Where a data controller is not established in the UK or any other state of the European Economic Area, but they use equipment to process data in the UK, then they must nominate a representative established in the UK (*DPA 1998, s 5(2)*). Few other sections of *DPA 1998* refer to such a representative. *DPA 1998, Sch 1, Part II, para 3*, which sets out the information which should be given to data subjects to ensure their data is fairly processed, includes a requirement that if there is a nominated representative under the Act then the identity of the representative must be given, along with the other information which has to be provided such as the identity of the data controller and the purpose for which the data is processed.

Consequences of Being a Data Controller 9.8

Data controllers are the bodies or individuals who have the principal duties to comply with *DPA 1998*. They must accede to requests for subject access and must follow the Eight Data Protection Principles.

Group Companies and Data Controllers 9.9

The controller is the person who determines the purposes for which and the manner in which the data is processed. A data controller must be a legal person, so it could be one subsidiary company, rather than the parent company. It is likely that for many corporate groups, most if not all of the group companies will have to notify ('register').

Delegation 9.10

The data controller(s) must decide the purposes for which personal data are, or will be, processed, and the way in which personal data are, or will be, processed. The Commissioner recognises, however, that a person may decide the purposes for which personal data are to be processed, but may delegate responsibility for the way in which those data are to be processed to another person. She advised:

> 'In such a situation, the person determining the purposes will be the data controller because the Commissioner takes the view that when a person determines the purposes for which personal data are to be processed, a decision as to the manner in which those data are to be processed is inherent in that decision. The Commissioner's view is that the determination of the purpose for which personal data are to be processed is paramount in deciding whether or not a person is a data controller.'

Joint Controllers 9.11

In deciding the purposes for which data are processed, it does not have to be exclusively processed by one data controller. There may be joint control of the data. 'Jointly' covers where the determination is exercised by acting together equally. 'Determination in common' is where data controllers share a pool of personal data, each processing independently of the other.

The Commissioner's advice is as follows.

> 'It is likely to be the case that data users under the previous data protection regime are data controllers under the new regime. However, it is important to appreciate the difference between the two definitions as it is quite possible that persons who were not data users under the 1984 Act will be data controllers under the Act. It is also possible that persons who carried on a computer bureau, as defined in the 1984 Act, and who were not also data users may find that they fall within the definition of data controller in the Act rather than the definition of "data processor".'

Example 9.12

A good illustration of the difference between the concepts of data user and data controller is in the context of credit reference agency data. Credit reference agencies were data users under *DPA 1984* and are data controllers under *DPA 1998*. The agency customers or subscribers who had access to credit reference agency data by way of a remote terminal, on a read-only basis, were not considered to be data users under *DPA 1984*. This was because they had no control of the content of the agency data and therefore fell outside the definition of data user.

Under *DPA 1998*, the Commissioner's view is that the credit reference agency and agency customers/subscribers are data controllers. This is because they each decide why and how they process personal data. Remember that the concept of 'processing' is very wide. The word can be used to encompass all manner of activities and operations that a particular data controller may want to perform on the personal data in question.

In respect of the credit reference agency, it, amongst other things, obtains, records, holds, organises, adapts, alters and discloses personal data. The agency customer or subscriber consults, obtains or retrieves personal data disclosed to it by the agency before using such data, for example, to inform a decision on whether to supply a customer. It is the ability to decide these things that makes them data controllers.

There will be many other examples of people, businesses and organisations who were not subject to *DPA 1984* but who are subject to *DPA 1998* because of the fact that they are now data controllers.

Personal Data   9.13

The question of what constitutes personal data is also addressed in detail by the Commissioner. She suggests certain questions in assessing any particular case, and these are set out at **9.14–9.21** below.

What Determines Whether Data Relate to an Individual?   9.14

Whether data relates to an individual is a question of fact. One issue is whether a data controller can form a connection between the data and the individual. Data do not have to relate solely to one individual and the same data may relate to two or more people and still be personal data about each of them; for example, joint tenants of a property, holders of a joint bank account or even individuals who use the same telephone or e-mail address. Information may relate to an individual in a business capacity and not just to their private life. Information about the business of a sole trader will amount to personal data as information about the business will be about the sole trader. Information about an individual in a partnership will be personal data if it relates to a specific partner. This will be more likely in a small partnership.

Although *DPA 1998* refers to individuals and not other legal entities such as limited companies, there will be situations where information about a limited company or other legal entity amounts to personal data because it relates to a specific individual, for example, the performance of a department. According to the Commissioner information relating solely to the legal entity will not be personal data.

Does the Act Only Relate to Living Individuals?   9.15

Yes. *DPA 1998* is only concerned with living individuals and so if the subject of the information is dead, then the information cannot be personal data.

The Individual Must be Capable of Being Identified. How Does the Commissioner Approach this Issue?   9.16

The individual must be capable of being identified from data in the possession of the data controller, or from those data and other information in the possession of, or likely to come into the possession of, the data controller. The issue of information likely to come into the data controller's possession has always puzzled the writer. A data controller could always promise to itself never to let certain information come into its possession and thus could avoid the information being personal data. The writer has had at least one client in this class.

The Commissioner recognises that an individual may be 'identified' without necessarily knowing the name and address of that particular individual. The Commissioner's view is that it is sufficient if the data are capable of being processed by the data controller to enable the data controller to distinguish the data subject from any other individual. This would be the case if a data subject could be treated differently from other individuals.

Examples of this are as follows.

- The capture of an image of an individual by a CCTV camera may be done in such a way that distinguishable features of that individual are processed and identified from the captured images. This will amount to personal data.

- In the context of the Internet, many email addresses are personal data where the e-mail address clearly identifies a particular individual, for example the address elizabethfrance@dataprotection.gov.uk.

In the majority of cases the ability to 'identify' an individual will be achieved by knowing the name and address of an individual, or by the data controller being in possession of some other information. The definition also allows for an individual to be identified from data together with information 'likely to come into the possession of' the data controller. It will be for a data controller to satisfy himself whether it is likely that such information will come into his possession to render data personal data. This will depend largely on the nature of the processing undertaken by a data controller, the Commissioner says.

This issue is clearly relevant in the context of personal data which a data controller wishes to keep anonymous (see **9.20** below).

Example 9.17

The following example is given by the Commissioner.

If information about a particular web user is built up over a period of time, perhaps through the use of tracking technology, with the intention that it may later be linked to a name and address, then that information is personal data. Information may be compiled about a particular web user, but there might not be any intention of linking it to a name and address or e-mail address. There might merely be an intention to target that particular user with advertising, or to offer discounts when they re-visit a particular website, on the basis of the profile built up, without any ability to locate that user in the physical world. The Commissioner takes the view that such information is, nevertheless, personal data. In the context of the online world the information that identifies an individual is that which uniquely locates him in that world, by distinguishing him from others.

CCTV Images   9.18

Another way in which information may come into the possession of a data controller is in relation to an image captured on CCTV. This might produce an
image which is not of a distinguishable individual, but the actual identity of that
individual may become apparent from other information likely to come into the
possession of the data controller.

What is Meant by the Expression 'Possession' in this Context?   9.19

The concept of possession is very wide. In the Commissioner's view possession
does not necessarily mean that the identifying data are in the physical control of
the data controller, or likely to come under his physical control. A data controller
enters into a contract with a data processor for the processing of personal data.
The arrangement is that the data processor may receive some of the identifying
data from a third party and some from the data controller. The data are processed
in accordance with the terms of the contract. The data controller determines the
purposes for which and the manner in which the personal data are to be processed
by the data processor but may not have sight of all or any of the information
which identifies a living individual. The data controller would, however, be
deemed to be in possession of those data. The data controller could not argue in
such a situation that the identifying data are not in his 'possession' and absolve
himself of his responsibilities as data controller.

Can Personal Data be Made Anonymous?   9.20

The issue of information in the possession of, or likely to come into the possession of, a data controller has an impact on a data controller who seeks to make
anonymous the personal data he is processing by stripping those data of all personal identifiers.

The Commissioner says:

> 'The fact that personal data may be anonymised is referred to in *Directive
> 95/46/EC* (the "Directive"), at Recital 26, and in the matter of *R v The
> Department of Health ex parte Source Informatics Limited [2000] 1 All ER
> 786*. In that case it was acknowledged by the Court of Appeal that the
> Directive does not apply to anonymised data. In anonymising personal
> data the data controller will be processing such data and, in respect of
> such processing, will still need to comply with the provisions of the Act.'

The Commissioner recognises that the aim of anonymisation is to provide better
data protection. However, some people use it to avoid the onerous obligations of
DPA 1998. The Commissioner thinks it is a good thing but very hard to achieve.
The fact that the data controller is in possession of this data set which, if linked to
the data which have been stripped of all personal identifiers, will enable a living

individual to be identified, means that all the data, including the data stripped of personal identifiers, remain personal data in the hands of that data controller and cannot be said to have been anonymised. The fact that the data controller may have no intention of linking these two data sets is immaterial.

A data controller who destroys the original data set retaining only the information which has been stripped of all personal identifiers and who assesses that it is not likely that information will come into his possession to enable him to reconstitute the data, ceases to be a data controller in respect of the retained data.

Whether or not data which have been stripped of all personal identifiers are personal data in the hands of a person to whom they are disclosed, will depend upon that person being in possession of, or likely to come into the possession of, other information which would enable that person to identify a living individual.

It should be noted that the *disclosure* of personal data by a data controller amounts to processing under *DPA 1998*.

For example, the obtaining of clinical information linked to a National Health Service number by a person having access to the National Health Service Central Register will amount to processing of personal data by that person, because that person will have access to information enabling him to identify the individuals concerned.

It will be a duty upon someone processing data to take measures to ensure that the data cannot be reconstituted to become personal data and to be prepared to justify any decision made on processing of the data.

In the case of data collected by the Office of National Statistics, where there is a disclosure of samples of anonymised data, it is conceivable that a combination of information in a particular geographic area may be unique to an individual or family who could therefore be identifiable from that information. In recognition of this fact, disclosures of information are done in such a way that any obvious identifiers are removed and the data presented so as to avoid particular individuals being distinguished.

If data have been stripped of all personal identifiers such that the data controller is no longer able to single out an individual and treat that individual differently, the data cease to be personal data. Whether this has been achieved may be open to challenge. Data controllers may therefore be required to justify the grounds for their view that the data are no longer personal data. When a subject access request is received, a data controller must be able to identify the data relating to the data subject making the request, to enable him to provide information specific to that data subject. In making a subject access request, a data subject might provide the data controller with sufficient information to enable his data to be distinguished from data relating to other individuals, in a situation where the data controller would not otherwise be able to do so from the information in his possession, which he may have stripped of all personal identifiers. In this case the data relating to the individual making the request become personal data, but the information provided by the data subject does not render the other data being held personal data unless the data controller believes that it is likely that information will come into his possession to render the other data personal data.

If there are any doubts as to whether data are personal data, the Commissioner's advice would be to treat the data as personal data, having particular regard to whether those data are sensitive personal data. In respect of such data, if a subject access request is received and the data controller cannot satisfy himself as to the identity of the person making the subject access request, or as to his ability to locate the information to which the subject access request relates because the data have been stripped of identifiers, then the data controller would not be obliged to comply with that subject access request, advising the data subject accordingly.

What About Expressions of Opinion or Intention? 9.21

The definition of personal data contained in *DPA 1998* now expressly includes any indication of the intentions of the data controller or any other person in respect of an individual. This aspect of the definition was not included in the definition of 'personal data' in *DPA 1984*. The consequence of this may mean, for example, that an employer who processes appraisals of employees would have to disclose not only his opinions of the employees, but also any intention to offer or decline promotion on the basis of those opinions subject to any exemption available at any particular time.

General 9.22

To date, there have been no cases reported addressing the question of these definitions in order to provide judicial guidance as to their meaning.

FAQs 9.23

9.14–9.21 above contain frequently asked questions in relation to 'data controllers'.

Chapter 10 –
Data Processor and
Processing

At A Glance

✓   Data processors process personal data on behalf of data controllers.

✓   Data processing definitions were examined by the European Court of Justice in 2003 in *Bodil Lindqvist* (Case C-101/01).

✓   The data controller is responsible for ensuring that the data processor acts properly in relation to the data (*Data Protection Act 1998 (DPA 1998), Sch 1, Part II, paras 11, 12*).

✓   The data processor does not need to notify their holding of personal data, although many data processors are also data controllers.

✓   Example letter from data controller to data processor.

Introduction   10.1

DPA 1998 contains special provisions in relation to those who process data. Processing includes most uses of data. Anyone who processes personal data on behalf of a data controller is called a 'data processor'. A data controller will have a higher duty of care where they have someone else process data on their behalf than would otherwise be the case.

A major change from the *Data Protection Act 1984 (DPA 1984)* is that now a data processor does not have to notify their holding of personal data nor comply with the Data Protection Principles. *DPA 1998* requires that the data controller must impose a control on the data processor by contract terms to ensure *DPA 1998* is followed. However, many data processors are also data controllers so the relaxation in the rules for data processors contained in *DPA 1998* has not had a major impact. *DPA 1998, Sch 1, Part II, paras 11* and *12* contain provisions relating to data processors.

What is Processing?   10.2

Processing means obtaining, recording or holding the information or data, or carrying out any operation or set of operations on the information or data.

This might include things such as:

'(*a*)   organisation, adaptation or alteration of the information or data,

(*b*)   retrieval, consultation or use of the information or data,

(*c*)   disclosure of the information or data by transmission, dissemination or otherwise making it available,

(*d*)   alignment, combination, blocking, erasure or destruction of the information or data.'

(DPA 1998, s 1(1))

In most instances of data use, processing is involved because of the width of the definition above. The definition of processing is much broader than under *DPA 1984*.

The Commissioner, in the Introduction to *DPA 1998*, writes:

'It is a compendious definition and it is difficult to envisage any action involving data which does not amount to processing within this definition. It is important for data controllers to bear in mind the extension of the concept of processing in the Act and not assume any similarity with the term as used in the 1984 Act'.

Processing by Reference to Data Subject   10.3

Processing otherwise than in relation to the data subject is now also covered by *DPA 1998*, although transitional provisions apply. *DPA 1984* did not include this. As of 24 October 2001 (the end of the first transitional period under *DPA 1998*), eligible automated data which are processed by reference to the data subject are exempt from the requirement in the First Data Protection Principle for one or more of the conditions for processing to be complied with, and such data *not* processed by reference to the data subject are exempt from:

- the First Data Protection Principle, except paragraphs 2 and 3 of the Fair Processing Code (which requires data controllers to tell data subjects about certain matters);

- the Second, Third, Fourth and Fifth Principles; and

- the rectification, blocking, erasure and destruction provisions.

The 'Guide to the Data Protection Act 1998 for Direct Marketing' by Colin Fricker (2000) describes the position under *DPA 1984* which meant that those processing a direct marketing database of businesses with 'names of key office holders such as sales directors would not normally fall within the scope of "processing" – and would therefore normally fall outside the scope of the Act – if the names of the sales directors were added to enhance the likelihood of targeting an offer of a business product or service to a personal who had the relevant internal responsibilities but where the actual name or personal characteristics of the sales director were of no consequence per se.'

Some may think removing contact names from a database will remove the application of *DPA 1998*. If living individuals are able to be identified from the data when added to other information in the possession of or likely to come into the possession of the data controller then *DPA 1998* will apply.

> 'So, processing leading to mail addressed to "The Prime Minister" or "The Chairman, XYZ Bank" is likely to fall within the Act as the identity of such persons should be known, or become known, as a matter of course. However a list of job titles such as sales directors, marketing managers of businesses etc. is unlikely to be regarded as falling within the definition of personal data in the normal course of events.'
>
> *Colin Fricker, Guide to the Data Protection Act 1998 for Direct Marketing (2000, DMA)*

European Data Protection Case   10.4

In Bodil Lindqvist (Case C-101/01), in November 2003, the European Court of Justice looked at the Data Protection Directive (Directive 95/46) and held that referring to various persons on an Internet page and identifying them, either by name or by other means, constitutes processing of personal data by automatic means within the meaning of community law. Mrs Lindqvist was involved in preparing people for confirmation in the parish of Alseda (Sweden). At the end of 1998 she set up Internet pages on her personal computer, at home, to enable parishioners preparing for confirmation to obtain easily the information they were likely to need. Those pages contained information on Mrs Lindqvist and 18 of her colleagues in the parish, including their first names and sometimes their full names.

Mrs Lindqvist also described the work done by her colleagues and their hobbies in mildly humorous terms. In several cases their family circumstances, their telephone number and other information was given. She also mentioned that one of her colleagues had injured her foot and was working part-time on medical grounds.

Mrs Lindqvist was fined SEK 4,000 (approximately EUR 450) for processing personal data by automatic means without notifying the Datainspektion (the Swedish supervisory authority for the protection of electronically transmitted data) in writing, for transferring data to third countries without authorisation and for processing sensitive personal data (ie details about a foot injury and part-time work on medical grounds).

She appealed against the decision to the Göta hovrätt, which asked the Court of Justice of the EC whether the activities with which Mrs Lindqvist was charged were contrary to the provisions of the Data Protection Directive, which is intended to ensure the same level of protection in all the Member States for the rights and freedoms of individuals in that regard.

The court held that the act of referring, on an Internet page, to various persons and identifying them by name or by other means (giving their telephone number or information about their working conditions and hobbies) constitutes 'the processing of personal data wholly or partly by automatic means'. Moreover, reference to the state of health of an individual amounts to processing of data concerning health within the meaning of the Data Protection Directive.

Such processing of personal data does not fall within the category of activities for the purposes of public security nor within the category of purely personal or domestic activities, which are outside the scope of the Directive.

The court states that the directive also lays down specific rules intended to allow the Member States to monitor the transfer of personal data to third countries. However, given the state of development of the Internet at the time the directive was drawn up and the absence of criteria applicable to use of the Internet, it takes the view that the community legislature did not intend the expression 'transfer of data to a third country' to cover the loading of data onto an Internet page even if such data is thereby made accessible to persons in third countries.

The provisions of the Directive do not in themselves entail a restriction contrary to the principle of freedom of expression or other fundamental rights. It is for the national authorities and courts responsible for applying the national legislation implementing the Directive to ensure a fair balance between the rights and interests in question, including those fundamental rights.

Processor   10.5

DPA 1998 defines a data processor as, in relation to personal data:

> 'any person (other than an employee of the data controller) who processes the data on behalf of the data controller'
>
> (DPA 1998, s 1(1))

Companies have to act through their employees and their use of the data on behalf of the employer does not make the employee a data processor, as some business people erroneously believe. However, a third party company or independent contractor processing data for their customer will be a data processor.

A data processor is the equivalent of a computer bureau under *DPA 1984*. In her January 2001 guidance on certain definitions under *DPA 1998* (see **9 DATA CONTROLLER**) the Commissioner wrote:

> 'It is also possible that persons who carried on a computer bureau, as defined in the 1984 Act, and who were not also data users may find that

they fall within the definition of data controller in the Act rather than the definition of "data processor".'

Whether that is the case in a particular instance will depend on the particular circumstances as seen above. The term 'data processor' catches more businesses than the old computer bureau definition. It will apply, for example, to market researchers who collect data for a data controller and also disposal contractors.

Schedule 1, Part II – the Seventh Principle and Data Processors   10.6

DPA 1998, Sch 1, Part II, paras 11 and *12* state that where processing is carried out by a data processor on behalf of a data controller then the data controller must, in order to comply with the Seventh Principle (security – see **6 CONFIDEN-TIALITY AND DATA SECURITY: SEVENTH PRINCIPLE**),

'(*a*)   choose a data processor providing sufficient guarantees in respect of the technical and organisational security measures governing the processing to be carried out, and

(*b*)   take reasonable steps to ensure compliance with those measures.'

Such processing by a data processor will not, on the part of the data controller, comply with the Seventh Principle unless the processing is carried out under a contract which is made or evidenced in writing (which presumably even since the advent of the *Electronic Communications Act 2000* would not include being made by e-mail, although in practice a prosecution on that basis would be unlikely to be brought if clear e-mailed terms had been agreed), and under which the data processor is to act only on instructions from the data controller. The contract must require the data processor to comply with obligations equivalent to those imposed on a data controller by the Seventh Principle.

In practice this means that those using data processors need to ensure written contracts are in place, otherwise the data controller may breach the Seventh Principle.

Heather Rowe of Lovells, in her book 'Data Protection Act 1998: A Practical Guide' (Tolley), suggests the following practical steps which data controllers should take.

● Users should check their standard forms for appointment of third parties to process their data and ensure that appropriate references to the Seventh Principle are incorporated as well as including references to the appropriate level of control of the data by the data controller.

● Users should ask themselves who is a data processor. Is it the person who processes a company's payroll (almost certainly yes), but what about the person who shreds confidential paperwork. Could that be personal data?

● Users should also consider, when appointing a new processor, incorporating detailed questionnaires in tender documents, say, requiring the prospective processor to describe its security measures so that they can be carefully assessed.

95

- The Commissioner has suggested that data controllers should review that their existing security measures are appropriate for the types of data they are processing. She has suggested that reference to the British Standards Institute Standard BS 7799 may help data controllers assess the adequacy of their current data protection regime.

- New contracts must contain an ongoing right of audit/inspection of the processor's security procedures

(Heather Rowe, Lovells, Data Protection Act 1998: A Practical Guide (Tolley))

The following sample letter from a data controller to a data processor is also suggested by the same source.

An Example of a Draft Letter from a Data Controller to a Data Processor

[appropriate officer to Data Processor]

[address of Data Processor]

[For the attention of: [appropriate representative of Data Processor]]

Dear [Sir] [ ]

Processing contract between [Data Processor] and [Data Controller]

We refer to the processing contract between us dated [ ] ('the Contract') under which you have undertaken to provide certain processing services ('Services') on our behalf.

On 1 March 2000 the Data Protection Act 1998 ('the Act') became law. Under that Act, by virtue of the Seventh Data Protection Principle contained in Schedule 1 of the Act, "data controllers" (in the case of our relationship with you, that will be [full name],) are obliged to impose certain obligations of security in relation to personal data upon their 'data processors' which, in the context of the Contract, is you.

Since it is our legal requirement to include such a provision in our Contract, we would be grateful if you would undertake to us as set out below. [In consideration of that undertaking, we would be prepared to contemplate continuing future relationships with you.] If you are unable to give such an undertaking, then we may [be forced to seek services elsewhere in the future] [will not renew the Contract] [on expiry of the Contract] since, if we are unable to obtain appropriate assurances from you, we will be in breach of our legal obligations under the Act.

The assurance that we seek from you is that you undertake to us to comply with the obligations of a 'data controller' under the provisions of the Seventh Data Protection Principle, as set out in Schedule I, Part II of the Act as regards any personal data you process in providing the Services. In addition, you:

(*a*) Warrant and undertake that you have and will have at all times during the term of the Contract appropriate technical and organisational measures in place acceptable to us to protect any personal data accessed or processed by you against unauthorised or unlawful processing of personal data and against accidental loss or destruction of, or damage to, personal data held or processed by you [(such measures as at the date of this letter being described in the attached Annex)] and that you have taken all reasonable steps to ensure the reliability of any of your staff which will have access to personal data processed as part of the Services;

(*b*) Undertake that you will act only on our instructions in relation to the processing of any personal data provided to you by us, [or] on our behalf, [or] by our employees [or former employees];

(c) Undertake [to provide the Services at least to the level of security set out in the Annex to this Letter and] to allow us (or our representative) access to any relevant premises owned or controlled by you on reasonable notice to inspect your procedures described at (a) above and will, on our request from time to time, prepare a report for us as to your then current technical and organisational measures used to protect any such personal data.

[(d) Undertake to consider all [reasonable] suggestions which we may put to you to ensure that the level of protection you provide for personal data is in accordance with this Letter and to make changes suggested unless you can prove to our reasonable satisfaction that they are not necessary to ensure ongoing compliance with your warranty and undertaking at (a) above.]

Breach of any of the above warranties or undertakings will entitle us to terminate the Contract forthwith.

Any terms defined in the Act will have the same meaning in this letter.

Please indicate your agreement to the provisions set out above by signing and returning the attached copy of this letter.

Yours faithfully,

....

For and on behalf of [Data Controller]

....

Accepted and Agreed

[Data Processor]

....

Annex

The Current Security Procedures

(Heather Rowe, Lovells, Data Protection Act 1998: A Practical Guide (Tolley).)

Processing Sensitive Personal Data   10.7

The processing of sensitive personal data (see **42 SENSITIVE PERSONAL DATA**) is addressed in the *Data Protection (Processing of Sensitive Personal Data) Order 2000 (SI 2000/417)*.

Summary   10.8

Most uses of data amount to processing under the definitions in *DPA 1998*. The important practical point to note from this section is that if a data processor is used to process the data, the data controller must impose contractual provisions as stipulated in *DPA 1998* on the data processor as described above.

FAQs   10.9

Who is a data processor under *DPA 1998*?

A data processor is defined in *section 1(1)* of *DPA 1998* as any person other than an employee of the data controller who processes the data on behalf of the data controller. This is the equivalent of the old 'computer bureau' term under *DPA 1984*.

What contract terms are needed before a data controller can hand personal data over to a data controller?

Schedule 1, Part II, paragraphs 11 and *12* of *DPA 1998* provide that data processors must provide security guarantees and data controllers must enforce them. In practice this means ensuring there is a contract in place and model wording is given in this chapter at **10.6** which could be used.

What is 'processing' under DPA 1998?

Processing is defined in *section 1(1)* of *DPA 1998* as obtaining, recording or holding the information or data or carrying out any operation or set of operations on the information or data. This covers most activities which can be done with personal data.

Does the Act apply when the data is processed otherwise than by reference to a data subject?

Yes, this was one of the changes *DPA 1998* brought about – see **10.3** above.

Chapter 11 –
Data Subject

At A Glance

✓ A data subject is an individual under the *Data Protection Act 1998* (*DPA 1998*) whose personal data is controlled by a data controller (*DPA 1998, s 1(1)*).

✓ Data subjects must be living individuals. Limited companies cannot be data subjects.

✓ *DPA 1998* applies to data controllers established in the UK even if they process data relating to those living abroad.

✓ Consideration should be given to when data can be made anonymous, such that it then comes outside the scope of protection under *DPA 1998*. Guidance from the Information Commissioner is available in this area.

Introduction   11.1

Those about whom data is held are known as data subjects under the *Data Protection Act 1984* (*DPA 1984*). *Section 1(1)* of *DPA 1998* defines this as 'an individual who is the subject of personal data'. There is no definition of data subject in the *Data Protection Directive* (*95/46/EC*).

• The data subject is required to be a living individual.

• A limited company cannot be classified as a data subject.

• A partnership is a group of living individuals. Individual partners would be data subjects, as would members of a limited liability partnership under the *Limited Liability Partnerships Act 2000*.

• Animals cannot be data subjects. The position on unborn children is not clear.

The definition of data subject is identical to that under *DPA 1984*.

Living Individuals 11.2

The use of the word 'living' in the legislation has led to some concern about whether the law could apply to those who had been living but have then died. However that appears not to be the case.

'In fact, a literal interpretation of the Directive might arguably have applied the definition to individuals who had died, but the Home Office have interpreted this sensibly.'

(Heather Rowe, Data Protection Act 1998 – A Practical Guide (Tolley 2000))

'Does the Act only relate to living individuals?

Yes. The Act is only concerned with living individuals and so if the subject of the information is dead, then the information cannot be personal data.'

(Guidance on Personal Data, Information Commissioner)

Given the Commissioner's view above, it seems reasonable for data controllers to assume that *DPA 1998* will not apply to personal data they hold about people who have died.

Personal Data 11.3

Data controllers assessing what constitutes personal data should consider the guidance which the Commissioner has issued on the subject. For that purpose, the individual must be capable of being identified from data in the possession of the data controller, or from those data and other information in the possession of, or likely to come into the possession of, the data controller.

'The Commissioner recognises that an individual may be "identified" without necessarily knowing the name and address of that particular individual. The Commissioner's view is that it is sufficient if the data are capable of being processed by the data controller to enable the data controller to distinguish the data subject from any other individual. This would be the case if a data subject could be treated differently from other individuals.'

This guidance may be revised in 2004 following the decision in *Durant v Financial Services Authority [2003] EWCA Civ 1746*.

In this case the court looked at what is personal data and asked if information relating to the investigation by the Financial Services Authority of Mr Durant's complaints against Barclays was 'personal data'?

The judges found that in conformity with the 1981 Council of Europe Convention (Convention 108) and the Council Directive (EC) 95/46, the purpose of *section* 7 of the *DPA 1998* is to enable an individual to check whether a data controller's processing of his personal data unlawfully infringes his privacy and, if so, to take steps, for example under *section 14* or *section 10*, to protect it. It is not an automatic key to any information, readily accessible or not, of matters in which he may be named or involved. Nor is it to assist him, for example, to obtain discovery of documents that may assist him in litigation or complaints against third parties. It is likely, in most cases, that only information that names and directly refers to him will qualify:

> 'Mere mention of the data subject in a document held by a data controller does not necessarily amount to his personal data. Whether it does so in any particular instance depends on where it falls in a continuum of relevance or proximity to the data subject as distinct, say, from transactions or matters in which he may have been involved to a greater or lesser degree'.

The judgment highlighted these issues:

> 'The first is whether the information is biographical in a significant sense, that is, going beyond the recording of the putative data subject's involvement in the matter or an event that has no personal connotations…The second is one of focus. The information should have the putative data subject as its focus rather than some other person with whom he may have been involved or some transaction or event in which he may have figured or have had an interest'.

These notions were summarised as information affecting a person's privacy, whether in his personal or family life, business or professional capacity.

The mere fact that a document is retrievable by reference to his name does not entitle him to a copy of it under the *DPA 1998*.

The court found that none of the personal data sought by Mr Durant amounted to personal data and, therefore, his claim fell at the first hurdle.

In December 2003, the Data Protection Commissioner commented as follows on this decision:

> 'The Commissioner welcomes the extent to which this judgment provides firm guidance and greater clarity as to the meaning of "personal data" and "relevant filing system". These have always been complex issues and any jurisprudence in this area is helpful. The Commissioner particularly welcomes the fact that the Court has reiterated the fundamental link between data protection and privacy rights'.

The Commissioner recognised that the interpretation suggested by Lord Justice Auld is more restrictive than the approach adopted by the Commissioner to date. In 2004 the guidance issued by the Commissioner's Office will be reviewed and amended to reflect this difference of approach. All the Commissioner's responsibilities, including existing and future casework, will be carried out in accordance with this judgment.

In February 2004 further guidance was given on this decision – see **CHAPTER 30** and **CHAPTER 35**.

The Data Subject   11.4

In most cases there is not much doubt about who a data subject is. Sometimes personal data will contain information about several data subjects, and then the issue arises of ensuring that where a subject access request is received, information about one data subject is not disclosed to the other without consent, but the identity of the data subject themselves is largely clear.

By way of example, Susan Singleton is a data subject. Her sole legal practice, Singletons, operates as a sole trader. Singletons is the trading name and is not a data subject. The publisher of this book, Reed Elsevier (UK) Limited, is a limited company registered at Companies House. The company cannot be a data subject as it is not a living individual.

Age and Data Subjects   11.5

Individuals of any age can make a subject access request and this includes children. In her guidance 'Subject Access to Social Services Records' (November 2000) (accessible under Guidance on the Commissioner's website), the Commissioner says that:

> 'Subject access requests may be made by the individuals to whom the data relate irrespective of age or any other criteria. A data subject can make a request through agents such as a solicitor or advice worker, although they may be asked for evidence that they are acting on behalf of the data subject. In cases where data subjects are incapable of understanding or exercising their rights, for instance because they are too young or suffer from a severe mental handicap, then subject access requests may be made by parents or other persons who are legally able to act on behalf of the data subjects. In many cases a social services department may choose to disclose information about a client who is incapable of exercising his or her rights to a parent or other third party. However, it cannot be compelled to make the disclosure if the third party does not act on behalf of the data subject in law.'

In the February 2001 Advice Sheet 'The Disclosure of Examination Results by Schools to the Media', the Commissioner comments on the issue of children giving consent. The rights which *DPA 1998* gives data subjects are not affected by their ages, she says. The Commissioner generally advises that providing people are able to understand their rights then it is they and not their parents or guardians who should be informed of the uses and disclosures of data, and who have the right to object to processing. In most cases, therefore, it is sufficient to provide information in advance notifying pupils that their examination results will be published. In a small number of cases, it may be that pupils are not capable of understanding their rights or of understanding the consequences of publication. In these cases, schools should provide the relevant information to parents or guardians.

For example, a premature baby born at 21 weeks gestation, and arguably damaged during its delivery by the doctors, where litigation may result, could therefore make a subject access request. Presumably despite its birth below the normal lawful age for abortion in the UK, the fact it has 'lived' will make it a living individual entitled to exercise a request under *DPA 1998* through the agency of its parents or solicitors, whereas had the child died before birth, it may not be a 'living individual' and thus could not make a request whether through an agent or not. However, the Act does not state at what point life begins so the issue is not free of doubt.

The Direct Marketing Association's 2003 *Code of Practice for all Direct Marketing Mediums and Sectors* includes a section on on-line marketing to children. The European Commission is also looking at this area. The USA has legislation (the *Children's Online Privacy Protection Act of 1998*) which requires websites directed at children aged 13 and under to obtain parental consent before obtaining data from the children.

Territorial Application 11.6

DPA 1998 protects personal data relating to British citizens and foreigners, protecting those living abroad as much as those living in the UK. *Section 5 of DPA 1998* provides that the Act applies to data controllers who are established in the UK and the data is processed in the context of their establishment, or they are established elsewhere but they use equipment in the UK to process data in the UK.

A UK business processing data about customers in Japan, for example, deals with 'data subjects' even if all those people are Japanese residents who have never been to the UK.

International Co-operation 11.7

The *Data Protection (International Co-operation) Order 2000 (SI 2000/190)* gives the Commissioner powers to enforce *DPA 1998* over data controllers who are processing their data in the UK, but to whom the Act does not apply because of *section 5* of *DPA 1998*, and where they are processing data within the scope of the functions of a supervisory authority in another member state. Upon the request of that authority the Commissioner can then act. The Commissioner sends the authority details of the action taken as he/she thinks fit.

Similarly the Commissioner may request a supervisory authority in another EEA state to exercise its functions under *Article 28(3)* of the *Data Protection Directive (95/46/EC)* in relation to that processing.

Anonymising Data   11.8

Data will not fall within *DPA 1998* if it does not relate to a data subject. Some data controllers will seek to strip data of all personal identifiers.

The *Data Protection Directive (95/46/EC)* refers to the anonymising of data, as did the case *R v The Department of Health ex parte Source Informatics Limited [2000] 1 All ER 786*. Here the court held that the Directive does not apply to anonymised data. The Commissioner's view in guidance on the definition of 'personal data' is that it is hard to anonymise data but that it is laudable, where possible, to strip data of information 'relating to a data subject, which is not necessary for the particular processing being undertaken … This does not amount to anonymisation but is in line with the requirements of the Data Protection Principles.'

Normally where anonymisation is sought the data controller still keeps the original data out of which the personal identifiers have been stripped. The Commissioner says in her guidance:

'The fact that the data controller is in possession of this data set which, if linked to the data which have been stripped of all personal identifiers, will enable a living individual to be identified, means that all the data, including the data stripped of personal identifiers, remain personal data in the hands of that data controller and cannot be said to have been anonymised. The fact that the data controller may have no intention of linking these two data sets is immaterial.'

However, if a data controller destroys the original data set and only keeps the information which has been stripped of all personal identifiers, and assesses that it is not likely that information will come into his possession to enable him to reconstitute the data will then cease to be a data controller for that data which is kept.

Commissioner's Examples   11.9

The obtaining of clinical information linked to a National Health Service number by a person having access to the National Health Service Central Register will amount to processing of personal data by that person, because that person will have access to information enabling him to identify the individuals concerned.

The person processing the data should take the steps needed to ensure that the data cannot be reconstituted so as to become personal data. They must also be prepared to 'justify any decision they make with regard to the processing of the data'.

In the case of data collected by the Office of National Statistics, where there is a disclosure of samples of anonymised data, it is conceivable that a combination of information in a particular geographic area may be unique to an individual or family who could therefore be identifiable from that information. In recognition of this fact, disclosures of information are done in such a way that any obvious identifiers are removed and the data presented so as to avoid particular individuals being distinguished.

'If data have been stripped of all personal identifiers such that the data controller is no longer able to single out an individual and treat that individual differently, the data cease to be personal data. Whether this has been achieved may be open to challenge. Data controllers may therefore be required to justify the grounds for their view that the data are no longer personal data.'

Identifying the Data Subject   11.10

Normally there is little doubt, in relation to data which is not anonymised, as to whether or not it is data about a 'data subject' or not. Another issue, however, is ensuring that the individual data subject is whom they say they are. Reference should be made here to **6 CONFIDENTIALITY AND DATA SECURITY: THE SEVENTH PRINCIPLE** in this respect.

Those making subject access requests must provide the data controller with enough information to enable the data to be distinguished from data relating to other individuals. If the data controller, as seen above, has stripped the data of personal identifiers he may then find it hard to determine whose data is whose. If this stripping exercise, undertaken with laudable objectives, has not so fully anonymised the data that it is not 'personal data' at all (which the Commissioner believes will rarely be achieved) then the subject access request must still be complied with. The data relating to the individual making the request may become personal data but the information provided by the data subject does not, the Commissioner believes, 'render the other data being held personal data unless the data controller believes that it is likely that information will come into his possession to render the other data personal data'.

'If there are any doubts as to whether data are personal data the Commissioner's advice would be to treat the data as personal data, having particular regard to whether those data are sensitive personal data. In respect of such data, if a subject access request is received and the data controller cannot satisfy himself as to the identity of the person making the subject access request, or as to his ability to locate the information to which the subject access request relates because the data have been stripped of identifiers, then the data controller would not be obliged to comply with that subject access request, advising the data subject accordingly.'

(Information Commissioner – Guidance on Definition of Personal Data)

FAQs 11.11

Who is a data subject under *DPA 1998*?

The Act only applies to data relating to data subjects. These must be living individuals and it does not include companies.

Can data be anonymised so data subjects cannot be identified?

Yes, but usually *DPA 1998* still applies because other information the data controller has in its possession enables it still to identify the individuals – see **11.8**.

What is the jurisdictional ambit? Does *DPA 1998* protect foreigners?

The Act protects personal data relating to those living in the UK whether they are British or not (*DPA 1998, s 5*).

Chapter 12 – Direct Mail

At A Glance

✓ The direct mail industry makes much use of personal data and thus is subject to the *Data Protection Act 1998* (*DPA 1998*).

✓ Under *section 11* of *DPA 1998* individuals have a right to object to their personal data being used for the purposes of direct marketing.

✓ The Mailing Preference Service is a voluntary service in which companies can participate. Participants will check whether individuals have opted out of direct mail before marketing to them by post.

✓ Email, telephone and fax marketing is dealt with in the *Privacy and Electronic Communications (EC Directive) Regulations 2003 (SI 2003/2426)*.

Introduction   12.1

The direct mail industry makes major use of personal data and must fully comply with *DPA 1998*. **13 DIRECT MARKETING** looks at general direct marketing issues under the Act and the various preference services available where individuals can register so as not to receive certain unsolicited communications in various areas. This topic examines specifically 'direct mail' sent by post.

Most direct mail is addressed to individuals and thus uses personal data under *DPA 1998*. (See **35 PERSONAL DATA**.) However, the legislation will not apply in most cases. In particular, the Mail Preference Service described at **12.7** below will not apply where:

- mailings are anonymously addressed, such as to 'the householder';

- without a name but simply stating the postal address; or

- leaflets are delivered by hand to the door without any recipient's name appearing on them,

because those mailings do not include personal data in most cases.

Rights to Object to Direct Mail   12.2

Under *section 11* of *DPA 1998* individuals have a right to object to their personal data being used for the purposes of direct marketing. *Section 11* is closely allied to *section 10* of *DPA 1998* which gives the right to prevent processing which is likely to cause damage or distress.

Section 11 provides:

'(1)   An individual is entitled at any time by notice in writing to a data controller to require the data controller at the end of such period as is reasonable in the circumstances to cease, or not to begin, processing for the purposes of direct marketing personal data in respect of which he is the data subject.

(2)   If the court is satisfied, on the application of any person who has given a notice under subsection (1), that the data controller has failed to comply with the notice, the court may order him to take such steps for complying with the notice as the court thinks fit.'

Under this section direct marketing means 'the communication (by whatever means) of any advertising or marketing material which is directed to particular individuals' (*DPA 1998, s 11(3)*).

The application of this is wider than simply in relation to direct mail and is concerned with other forms of direct marketing as well.

Section 11 of *DPA 1998* implements *Article 14* of the *Data Protection Directive (95/46/EC)* which requires every state in the EU to allow data subjects rights to object on request and free of charge to the processing of their personal data for direct marketing purposes. The Direct Marketing Association's ('DMA') 'Guide to the Data Protection Act for Direct Marketing' points out that *DPA 1998* does not include a provision in the Directive that Member States must make individuals aware of their rights in this area and that under EU law, in the event of a conflict between national and EU law, EU law will prevail. Anyone who suffers loss because the UK has not implemented an EU directive properly can sue the Government for damages, but may only act as if the directive were in force against a state entity.

It is probably the role of the Information Commissioner to make individuals aware of this right rather than the data controller. Does the data controller have to put on all its marketing material when it gathers personal data that individuals have a right of opt-out in this way?

Example: Wording of Opt-out Provision and Response 12.3

The DMA suggests some wording in its guide (see **12.6** below). One suggestion made is to add a phrase such as:

'We may wish to send you promotional material about our other products/services.'

This might be appropriate in an off the page advertisement where the data would not be passed on or shared with anyone else. Then additional words could be added:

'If you don't want us to do this please let us know by writing to the above address.'

or:

'If you would prefer us not to do this please tick this box when sending in your order'.

Dealing with Suppression Requests 12.4

When a business receives a written notification under *section 11* of *DPA 1998*, the Information Commissioner recommends as follows.

'Dealing with direct marketing suppression requests

The *Data Protection Act 1998* gives individuals the right not to have their personal data processed for direct marketing purposes. When collecting data, for example from customers, you should give them the opportunity to let you know whether or not they wish to receive marketing material from you. If they do not, you must ensure that you can suppress their details on any mailing lists you use. If you intend to pass personal data to other companies for direct marketing purposes, again you must first check with the individuals concerned if they are happy for you to do this. This should be done when you first collect the data, perhaps on an application form. You must not pass on the details of anyone who says that they object to their details being used in this way. If you have not previously sent out marketing material or passed on details to third parties for marketing, you should obtain the consent of existing customers before beginning to process their data for either of those purposes.'

Direct Mail Issues   12.5

There are no special rules in relation to the dispatch of mail by post rather than by other means (see **13 DIRECT MARKETING**). However, the preference service described at **12.7** below is specific to the use of postal services.

DPA 1998 and Direct Mail – A Guide   12.6

The 'Guide to the Data Protection Act 1998 for Direct Marketing' is published by the DMA and written by Colin Fricker, former DMA Director of Legal and Regulatory Affairs.

Specific explanation, interpretation and guidance is given in the Guide in relation to:

- increased controls over data processing;

- the new express provision that gives individuals a right to opt-out of receiving a company's own future direct marketing approaches;

- the type of information that must be provided to the data subject;

- what opt-outs are necessary and the wording to be used in different circumstances;

- the restrictions on the transfer of data to countries outside the European Economic Area; and

- the increased rights of data subjects and the notification process.

The Mailing Preference Service   12.7

The Mailing Preference Service ('MPS') was set up as and remains a non-profit organisation. It is a member of the Committee of Advertising Practice and enables individuals to register so as not to receive unsolicited post/mail from companies which participate in the voluntary scheme. The scheme does not remove the rights under *section 10* of *DPA 1998* which state that every data subject has to notify the data controller individually that they do not want to receive unsolicited mail.

The direct mail industry funds the Mailing Preference Service. It pays a levy whenever a particular volume mailing service of Consignia (the Post Office) is used.

What the Mailing Preference Service Does   12.8

The MPS will remove a name from mailing lists or have it added to many lists; it works both ways around. Individual data subjects can register on the following link www.mpsonline.org.uk/MpsR/html/Register.asp and use forms which appears there for completion.

Points to Note 12.9

The MPS says:

- '● Your name will remain on file for five years. If you want to continue receiving the service beyond this date, you will need to apply again.

- ● If you are currently receiving mailings with an incorrect version of your name and address, you will need to contact the mailer directly to correct this information.

- ● You will still receive mailings from companies with whom you have done business in the past, as well as from some small local companies. If you wish to stop these mailings you should contact the companies directly.

- ● Allow at least three months for mail to start to decrease.

- ● Unaddressed material is not covered by MPS.

- ● Please remember to let us know of any change of address.'

The Information Commissioner describes the scheme thus:

'When you provide your surname and address to the MPS they will place the information on their consumer file which is then made available to those members of the direct marketing industry who subscribe to the MPS scheme. They undertake to ensure that the mailing lists they use and supply are "cleaned" of any names and addresses which appear on the MPS file, the result being that you should not, in future, receive their mailings.

Membership of the MPS by direct marketers is not a specific requirement of the Data Protection Act 1998. However the Data Protection Commissioner strongly supports the scheme. In some circumstances she can insist that direct marketers who do not currently subscribe to the scheme, do so in future. Furthermore, several direct marketing industry codes of practice specify that direct marketers should clean their lists against the MPS file. This means there is substantial voluntary adherence to the scheme.

You can register your details with the MPS free of charge and your registration will be effective for five years. However, the MPS can only assist in respect of mailings, which are personally addressed. It is unable to assist with mailings, which are unaddressed, or those, which are addressed to "the occupier". It is also unlikely to prevent the mail you may receive from organisations you have done business with – you should write to those organisations directly and request that they exclude you from their marketing lists.'

Fax, Email and Telephone Marketing 12.10

Fax, email and telephone marketing are covered by separate legislation not discussed in this chapter – the *Privacy and Electronic Communications (EC Directive) Regulations 2003* which have applied since 11 December 2003.

Further Information 12.11

The Direct Marketing Association's 'Guide to the Data Protection Act for Direct Marketing' The Guide costs £75 (members) and £150 (non-members).	www.dma.org.uk

Mailing Preference Service FREEPOST 22 London W1E 7EZ Tel: 020 7766 4410.

See also **13 DIRECT MARKETING**, **31 MARKETING** and **33 OPT-IN AND OPT-OUT**.

FAQs 12.12

Is the Mailing Preference Service compulsory?

No, only those businesses who have chosen to subscribe to the service will check whether data subjects have registered so as not to receive unsolicited direct mail. Other businesses must simply comply with *DPA 1998* in general terms.

Does the position with faxes differ?

Yes, the legislation requires that those sending unsolicited faxes must check the Fax Preference Service register and must not send any unsolicited faxes to partnership or individuals without their consent.

Are there any industry guides to direct mail and *DPA 1998*?

Yes, the DMA has published a 'Guide to the Data Protection Act 1998 for Direct Marketing'. For further information see www.dma.org.uk.

Chapter 13 – Direct Marketing

At A Glance

✓ Direct marketing normally involves processing of personal data.

✓ Under *section 11* of the Data Protection Act 1998 *(DPA 1998)* individuals can object to their personal data being processed for such purposes.

✓ Mailing preference schemes of various types exist to enable individuals to object to direct marketing.

✓ Special rules apply to direct marketing by fax, telephone and email in the *Privacy and Electronic Communications (EC Directive) Regulations 2003 (SI 2003/2426)*. Detailed FAQs for the Information Commissioner on the Regulations appear at the end of this Chapter.

Introduction   13.1

Direct marketing takes many forms, from unsolicited e-mails ('spam') to telephone calls. This section examines direct marketing in general. For further information on direct mail, see **12 DIRECT MAIL**.

Various preference schemes are available under which individuals can register to object to direct marketing. *Section 11* of the *DPA 1998* enables individuals to notify individual data controllers that they do not want their personal data processed for direct marketing purposes.

purposes. The principal legislation is the *DPA 1998* and the *Privacy and Electronic Communications (EC Directive) Regulations 2003 (SI 2003/2426)*. Part 1 of the Information Commissioner's guidelines on the Regulations tries to define direct marketing as follows:

> '*Section 11* of the *DPA 1998* refers to direct marketing as "the communication (by whatever means) of any advertising or marketing material

which is directed to particular individuals". The Commissioner regards the term "direct marketing" as covering a wide range of activities which will apply not just to the offer for sale of goods or services, but also to the promotion of an organisation's aims and ideals. This would include a charity or a political party making an appeal for funds or support and, for example, an organisation whose campaign is designed to encourage individuals to write to their MP on a particular matter or to attend a public meeting or rally'.

Notice to Data Controllers   13.2

Under *section 11* of *DPA 1998*, notice must be given in writing to a data controller to cease – or not to begin – processing personal data relating to the individual for direct marketing purposes. Individuals can apply to the court for an order to that effect if the data controller does not comply with the notice.

Privacy and Electronic Communications (EC Directive) Regulations 2003   13.3

The *Privacy and Electronic Communications (EC Directive) Regulations 2003* implemented the EU Privacy Directive in the UK on 11 December 2003. They are the principal UK legislation on email, telephone and fax marketing in the data protection field. The Information Commissioner has issued guidance on the Regulations and FAQs. The FAQs on the email marketing part of the Regulations is included at the end of this Chapter. Part 1 of the guidance is included in **APPENDIX 8** and the regulations themselves are included in **APPENDIX 7**. The Regulations deal with direct marketing and some other data protection issues, for example the use of location data/tracking devices, cookies and telecoms issues, eg calling line identification and the right to withhold numbers.

Safety   13.4

Regulation 5 provides that a provider of a public electronic communications service must take measures, if necessary, in conjunction with the provider of the electronic communications network by means of which the service is provided, to safeguard the security of the service. It also requires the provider of the electronic communications network to comply with the service provider's reasonable requests made for the purposes of taking the measures. 'Public electronic communications service' has the meaning given by *section 151* of the *Communications Act 2003* and 'electronic communications network' has the meaning given by *section 32* of the same act. There are also obligations under *regulation 5* to require service providers to provide subscribers to that service with certain information set out in the regulations. A 'subscriber' is defined as 'a person who is party to a contract with a provider of public electronic communications services for the supply of such services'.

Rights to Refuse Access to Information 13.5

Regulation 6 says that an electronic communications network may not be used to store or gain access to information in the terminal equipment of a subscriber or user. A 'user' is defined as 'any individual using a public electronic communications service', unless the subscriber or user is provided with certain information and is given the opportunity to refuse the storage of, or access to, the information in his or her terminal equipment.

Traffic Data 13.6

Regulations 7 and *8* set out restrictions on the processing of traffic data relating to a subscriber or user by a public communications provider. 'Traffic data' is defined as: 'any data processed for the purpose of the conveyance of a communication on an electronic communications network or for the billing in respect of that communication'. 'Public communications provider' is defined as: 'a provider of a public electronic communications network or a public electronic communications service'. Traffic data concerns who has sent a message to who, rather than the content of the message, so this is a provision of more interest to telecoms companies than users of the Internet.

Regulation 9 says people can have non-itemised bills on request. *Regulation 10* says that users must be able to prevent calling line identification on a call-by-call basis and to provide subscribers to the service with a means of preventing the presentation of such identification on a per-line basis.

Location Data 13.7

Regulation 14 imposes certain restrictions on the processing of location data, which is defined as:

> 'any data processed in an electronic communications network indicating the geographical position of the terminal equipment of a user of a public electronic communications service, including data relating to the latitude, longitude or altitude of the user; the direction of travel of the user; or the time the location information was recorded'.

Some companies make staff carry a pass which contains a chip that can track them. Milk floats, lorries and some cars contain tracking devices. *Regulation 14* says:

> 'Location data relating to a user or subscriber of a public electronic communications network or a public electronic communications service may only be processed:
>
> •   where that user or subscriber cannot be identified from such data; or

- where necessary for the provision of a value added service, with the consent of that user or subscriber'.

Nuisance Calls   13.8

Regulation 15 deals with tracing malicious or nuisance calls. *Regulation 16* makes provision in relation to emergency calls, which are defined in *regulation 16(1)* as calls to the national emergency number 999 or the European emergency number 112.

Automatic forwarding   13.9

Regulation 17 requires the provider of an electronic communications service to a subscriber to stop, on request, the automatic forwarding of calls to that subscriber's line and also requires other communications providers to comply with reasonable requests made by the subscriber's provider to assist in the prevention of that forwarding.

Directories   13.10

Regulation 18 applies to directories of subscribers and sets out requirements that must be satisfied where data relating to subscribers is included in such directories. It also gives subscribers the right to verify, correct or withdraw their data in directories.

Automated Calling Machines   13.11

Regulation 19 prohibits transmission of communications of recorded material for direct marketing purposes by an automated calling system, unless the line called is that of a subscriber who has notified the caller that he or she consents to such communications being made.

Direct Marketing   13.12

More attention has been focussed on the unsolicited email provisions of the regulations than any other. *Regulations 20, 21* and *22* set out the circumstances in which persons may transmit, or instigate the transmission of, unsolicited communications for the purposes of direct marketing by means of facsimile machine, make unsolicited calls for those purposes or transmit unsolicited communications by means of electronic mail for those purposes. The extracts from the Information Commissioner's (IC's) FAQs on direct marketing are given at the end of this chapter. Part 1 of the IC's guidance on this aspect of the regulations is contained in **APPENDIX 8**.

Regulation 22 (electronic mail) applies only to transmissions to individual subscribers (the term 'individual' means 'a living individual' and includes 'an incorporated body of such individuals'). It may be hard for list-holders to know if subscribers are individual subscribers or not. Sole traders and partnerships appear to be individual subscribers. In practice, it is likely to be easier to obtain express consent from everyone rather than distinguish between corporate and other subscribers in obtaining such consent. An email address may well not reveal whether the individual or a company subscribes.

As it is perhaps, for some, the most important provision in the Regulations it is worth looking at *regulation 22* in detail:

'22(1) This regulation applies to the transmission of unsolicited communications by means of electronic mail to individual subscribers.

Except in the circumstances referred to in paragraph (3), a person shall neither transmit, nor instigate the transmission of, unsolicited communications for the purposes of direct marketing by means of electronic mail unless the recipient of the electronic mail has previously notified the sender that he consents for the time being to such communications being sent by, or at the instigation of, the sender.

A person may send or instigate the sending of electronic mail for the purposes of direct marketing where:

- that person has obtained the contact details of the recipient of that electronic mail in the course of the sale or negotiations for the sale of a product or service to that recipient; [This means an unsolicited email to an individual subscriber can only be sent if that person was a previous customer in addition to the requirements below].

- the direct marketing is in respect of that person's similar products and services only; and

- the recipient has been given a simple means of refusing (free of charge except for the costs of the transmission of the refusal) the use of his contact details for the purposes of such direct marketing, at the time that the details were initially collected, and, where he did not initially refuse the use of the details, at the time of each subsequent communication.

A subscriber shall not permit his line to be used in contravention of paragraph (2).

Regulation 23 prohibits the sending of communications by means of electronic mail for the purposes of direct marketing where the identity of the person on whose behalf the communication is made has been disguised or concealed, or an address to which requests for such communications to cease may be sent has not been provided.

Regulation 24 sets out certain information that must be provided for the purposes of *regulations 19, 20* and *21*.

Unsolicited Faxes   13.13

Regulation 25 puts a duty on the Office of Communications, for the purposes of *regulation 20*, to maintain and keep up-to-date a register of numbers allocated to subscribers who do not wish to receive unsolicited communications by means of fax for the purposes of direct marketing. This replaces the existing fax regulations.

Sales Calls   13.14

Regulation 26 imposes a similar obligation for the purposes of *regulation 21* in respect of individual subscribers who do not wish to receive calls for the purposes of direct marketing.

Consequences of Infringement   13.15

Regulation 27 provides that terms in certain contracts which are inconsistent with these Regulations shall be void.

Exemptions   13.16

Regulation 28 exempts communications providers from the requirements of these Regulations where exemption is required for the purpose of safeguarding national security and further provides that a certificate signed by a Minister of the Crown to the effect that exemption from a requirement is necessary for the purpose of safeguarding national security shall be conclusive evidence of that fact. It also provides for certain questions relating to such certificates to be determined by the Information Tribunal referred to in *section 6* of the *DPA 1998*.

Regulation 29 provides that a communications provider shall not be required by these Regulations to do, or refrain from doing, anything if complying with the requirement in question would be inconsistent with a requirement imposed by or under an enactment or by a court order, or if exemption from the requirement is necessary in connection with legal proceedings, for the purposes of obtaining legal advice or is otherwise necessary to establish, exercise or defend legal rights.

Damages   13.17

Regulation 30 allows a claim for damages to be brought in respect of contraventions of the Regulations. It will be interesting to see what damages claims follow.

Data Protection Enforcement 13.18

Regulations 31 and *32* make provision in connection with the enforcement of the Regulations by the Information Commissioner under the *DPA 1998*.

Regulation 34 amends the *Telecommunications (Lawful Business Practice) (Interception of Communications) Regulations 2000 (SI 2000/2699)* and *regulation 35* amends the *Electronic Communications (Universal Service) Order 2003 (SI 2003/1904)*.

Timing and Enforcement 13.19

The Office of the Information Commissioner will enforce the regulations.

Any breaches of enforcement orders issued by the Information Commissioner will be a criminal offence liable to a fine of up to £5,000 in a magistrates court or an unlimited fine if the trial is before a jury. In addition, anyone who has suffered damages because the Regulations have been breached has the right to sue the person responsible for compensation. These are the normal remedies for breach of the *DPA 1998*, with which many readers will be familiar.

EU Basis 13.20

The *Privacy and Electronic Communications (EC Directive) Regulations 2003* are necessary for the implementation of the EC Directive on Privacy and Electronic Communications (2002/58/EC). The Directive updates the current Telecoms Data Protection Directive (Directive 97/66/EC) in the light of new technologies and, in particular, ensures that the privacy rules currently applicable to phone and fax services also apply to email and to the use of the Internet. Those regulations deal with fax marketing.

Further Information 13.21

The Regulations are available at
www.dti.gov.uk/industry_files/pdf/regulations_20030918.pdf.

The DTI page on the regulations is www.dti.gov.uk/industries/ecommunications/directive_on_privacy_electronic_communications_200258ec.html.

Guidance notes on the law are available at www.informationcommissioner.gov.uk.

The Interactive Advertising Bureau (IAB) provides independent guidance for Internet users and online operators on the use of cookies and how to notify users of them under the new rules at www.allaboutcookies.org.

Direct Marketing Authority 13.22

In May 1997, the board of the Direct Marketing Association ('DMA') approved proposals to reform the governance of the direct marketing industry by bringing the then disparate direct marketing self-regulatory services together under one administration by creating a new body, the Direct Marketing Authority, to act as the final arbiter on complaints referred to it by the DMA governance secretariat. It is the Authority, not the Association, which runs the various preference schemes.

The Direct Marketing Authority operates preference schemes such as the Mailing Preference Service ('MPS') (see **13.6** below), the Telephone Preference Service ('TPS') (see **13.7** below), and the Fax Preference Service ('FPS') (see **13.8** below). It also runs the Direct Mail Accreditation and Recognition Centre ('DMARC'), List and Data Suppliers Group ('LADS') and the List Warranty Register ('LWR').

It complements the work of the Advertising Standards Authority, which administers the general advertising code ('BSCAP'). The Direct Marketing Authority has a quasi-judicial function and considers complaints arising from the other self-regulatory bodies. It ensures all DMA members stick to the DMA Code of Practice, doing this, in particular, by considering complaints made against member organisations by consumers. It can issue a private or public admonition to the member concerned, and it may also suspend or expel a company from membership of the Association. Its powers extend to cover breaches of the TPS, FPS and MPS licences and of DMARC accredited suppliers' terms and conditions whether committed by DMA members or by non-DMA members.

The Direct Marketing Association 13.23

The DMA (www.dma.org.uk) requires its members to adhere to codes of practice in this field. It is a trade organisation for those involved in direct marketing in the UK. It is also a member of the International Federation of Direct Marketing Associations ('IFDMA') and the Federation of European Direct Marketing ('FEDMA').

Preference Services 13.24

Various preference services are operated, in most cases on a self-regulated basis, by the Direct Marketing Authority. They enable individuals to register so that they do not receive certain forms of direct marketing materials.

Mailing Preference Service 13.25

Individuals and businesses can register so as not to receive unsolicited mail under the MPS. It is not compulsory for companies to join. For further information on the service see **12 DIRECT MAIL**.

Telephone Preference Service 13.26

Similarly, the TPS only applies to those companies which have voluntarily chosen to be a member of the scheme. The TPS can be contacted by telephoning 020 7766 4420. Further details are available on the DMA website at www.dma.org.uk. This is likely to become compulsory during 2004.

Fax Preference Service 13.27

The FPS is slightly different from those mentioned above. It was set up under the *Directive on the Processing of Personal Data and the Protection of Privacy in the Telecommunications Sector (97/66/EC)* ('*Telecommunications Directive*') and is of universal application. It allows those businesses who object to unsolicited faxes to register, and those sending unsolicited faxes must check first before sending the fax.

For individuals, the *Telecommunications (Data Protection and Privacy) Regulations 1999 (SI 1999/2093)* implemented the Directive in the UK and give all individuals including sole traders and partners (no matter how large the partnership) the right not to receive unsolicited faxes unless they have consented, whether they have registered or not. It is unlawful under those Regulations to send an unsolicited fax to an individual without his or her consent. However, they were supplanted by the *Privacy and Electronic Communications (EC Directive) Regulations 2003* on 11 December 2003.

The FPS can be contacted by telephoning 020 7766 4422. Information relating to regulations in the area of direct marketing by fax is given later in this section.

E-mail Preference Service 13.28

Junk e-mail or 'spam' is a major data protection problem for many individuals and businesses. The DMA has set up an e-mail preference service ('e-MPS') which currently operates on a voluntary basis. e-MPS is described as 'a suppression file only and it is not released to marketers or any other third parties who may wish to send commercial messages.'

According to the organisers, those using the e-MPS send their e-mail address lists electronically to e-MPS at a nominal charge per annum. All e-mail addresses registered with e-MPS are removed from the service users' lists, thus being 'cleaned' and then returned electronically to the marketer.

Under *DPA 1998*, those who wish to send data to be cleaned against the e-MPS file can do so only if they have a processing contract with the US DMA. (See **20 EXPORT OF DATA**.)

The *Directive on Privacy and Electronic Communications (2002/58/EC)* ('*E-privacy Directive*'), when in force, will require that individuals consent to unsolicited e-mails. The Directive must be implemented by regulations in the UK and elsewhere in the EU by 31 October 2003 (for the *E-privacy Directive* – see www.dti.gov.uk/cii/regulatory/telecomms/telecommsregulations/comms_dpd.s html).

Advertising Standards Authority Cases 13.29

As well as complying with the Regulations, many businesses must also comply with the Advertising Standards Authority (ASA) Code . On 17 December 2003, the ASA issued rulings against two companies that had sent unsolicited commercial email without the explicit consent of recipients. This broke the ASA code of practice, which came into force in March.

One case concerned a company called 'Business in a Box'. Its email contained only the word 'Hi' in its subject line and then told people about an opportunity to make millions of pounds. The marketers were accused of sending unsolicited commercial email without consent and of sending an email that did not make clear prior to opening that it was an advert.

The ASA upheld the complaint on both grounds and highlighted other concerns:

> 'The Authority pointed out that the advertisers had not suppressed the complainants' details on the Authority's request. It noted the advertisers had offered a business opportunity but considered that, because the advertisers' website included their full name and geographical address, the email did not mislead on that point. The Authority considered that the email had not made clear, before opening, that it offered a business opportunity because it stated "Hi" in the subject field. The Authority understood that the complainant was not a customer of the advertisers and the advertisers had not sought the complainant's consent before they sent the email. The Authority considered that the advertisers had not substantiated the claim ... By joining us you up your chances by 1 in 26,000! [sic] much better odds than the Lottery! ... and had not made clear throughout the email that the nature of the work they were advertising was a business opportunity'.

The second case related to five emails sent by one of the UK's leading PC sellers, Evesham Technology, trading as lowestonweb.com (the website of which makes no reference to the more popular Evesham.com). The recipients had not consented to receiving the emails.

The ASA upheld the complaints on the grounds that while the marketers had used data purchased from another company, it had not checked whether the data supplier – and consequently the email addresses supplied – were bona fide.

Further Information 13.30

The DMA has four offices. These are in London, Edinburgh, Leeds and Bristol.

DMA (UK)
Haymarket House
1 Oxendon Street
London
SW1Y 4EE
Tel: 020 77321 2525
Fax: 020 7321 0191
E-mail: dma@dma.org.uk

DMA North
8th Floor
29 Wellington Street
Leeds
Yorkshire
LS1 1O
Tel: 0113 244 7103
Fax: 0113 244 7224
E-mail: sharon@dma.org.uk

DMA West
University of the West of England
Dupont Bristol Centre
Cold Harbour Lane
Bristol
BS16 1OD
Tel: 0117 976 2599
Fax: 0117 976 3839
E-mail: anna@uwe.ac.uk

DMA Scotland
41 Comely Bank
Edinburgh
EH4 1AF
Tel: 0131 315 4422
Fax: 0131 315 4433
E-mail: joscobie@dma.org.uk

The DMA has available a range of publications on its website (www.dma.org.uk) including the following.

- An Introduction to Direct Marketing.

- Best Practice Guidelines for Fax Marketing.

- 10 Best Practice Guidelines for List Suppliers.

- DMA Guide to the List Industry.

- DMA Guide to Renting Business Lists.

- DMA Guide to Renting Consumer Lists.

- DMA Broadcast Guidelines.

- DMA Best Practice Guidelines for Responsible Sampling.

- DMA Best Practice Guidelines for Catalogue and Home Shopping.

- Labour and Direct Marketing Guidelines.

- NVQs and SVQs in Direct Marketing and Telesales.

- Suggested Terms and Conditions for Contract of Agreement between Client and Agency.

- The Advertisers' Perspective on Address Management.

The publications are free of charge. For copies contact Patricia Burrows at the DMA. E-mail: patricia@dma.org.uk. Tel: 020 7766 4445.

FAQs   13.31

What is direct marketing?

Direct marketing is the use of any method of communicating with a potential customer to seek business from them such as direct mail, telephone, fax or e-mails.

What guidance is available for small and medium sizedmedium-sized businesses grappling with preference registers?

In 2001 the DMA launched two new enhancements to the Telephone and Fax Preference Services to help small and medium-sized enterprises ('SMEs') to comply with the *Telecommunications (Data Protection and Privacy) Regulations 1999 (SI 1999/2093)*. The TPS and FPS Online Interrogation Services now allow smaller businesses the opportunity to check instantly whether a telephone or fax number is registered with the relevant Preference Service and determine if contact can legally be made or not.

The new services are aimed at those companies that may be having difficulty complying with the Regulations because they:

- use manual records to source prospect numbers;

- only want to check low volumes of numbers;

- work off site; or

- can not afford the extensive list screening services to which larger companies subscribe.

By registering and accessing the TPS or FPS websites and paying a minimum monthly charge of just £50, companies can search up to 500 numbers.

Who is the data controller when a marketing list if bought in?

The company buying the list will be processing the data on its own behalf and will become a data controller or it. The supplier of the list presumably retains it for other clients too and is also a data controller of it.

FAQs and the Privacy and Electronic Communications (EC Directive) Regulations 2003
13.32

Direct marketing by email under the Regulations – Practical FAQs

These FAQs are based on some of the FAQs in the Information Commissioner's guidance on the Regulations, which will be updated regularly so the latest position should always be checked. 'We' below means the Information Commissioner's Office.

One difficult issue is over opting in and out. The IC's office says:

'By itself, the failure to register an objection will be unlikely to constitute valid consent. However, in context, a failure to indicate objection may be part of the mechanism whereby a person indicates consent. For example, if you receive a clear and prominent message along the following lines, the fact that a suitably prominent opt-out box has not been ticked may help establish that consent has been given: eg "By submitting this registration form, you will be indicating your consent to receiving email marketing messages from us unless you have indicated an objection to receiving such messages by ticking the above box".

'In summary, the precise mechanisms by which valid informed consent is obtained may vary. The crucial consideration is that individuals must fully appreciate that they are consenting and must fully appreciate what they are consenting to'.

How do the Regulations apply to marketing by electronic mail?

The Regulations define electronic mail as 'any text, voice, sound, or image message sent over a public electronic communications network which can be stored in the network or in the recipient's terminal equipment until it is collected by the recipient and includes messages sent using a short message service' (Regulation 2 'Interpretation' refers).

In other words, both email and text/picture/video marketing messages are considered to be 'electronic mail'.

(cont'd)

We consider that this rule also applies to voicemail/answerphone messages left by marketers making marketing calls that would otherwise be 'live'. Therefore, there are stricter obligations placed upon those marketers who make live calls but who wish to leave messages on a person's voicemail or answerphone.

For the avoidance of doubt, faxes are not considered to be 'electronic mail'. Fax_marketing is covered elsewhere in the Regulations . Also, so-called 'silent calls' or calls where a fax or other electronic signal is transmitted are not covered by these Regulations. This is because no marketing material is transmitted during such calls.

The law requires the following:

1. You cannot transmit, or instigate the transmission of, unsolicited marketing material by electronic mail to an individual subscriber unless the recipient of the electronic mail has previously notified *you*, the sender, that he or she consents, for the time being, to receiving such communications. There is an exception to this rule which has been widely referred to as the 'soft opt-in' (Regulation 22(2).)

2. A subscriber shall not permit their line to be used to contravene Regulation 22(2). (Regulation 22(4).)

3. You cannot transmit, nor instigate the transmission of any marketing by electronic mail (whether solicited or unsolicited) to *any subscriber* (whether corporate or individual) where:

    (a) the identity of the sender has been disguised or concealed; or

    (b) a valid address to which the recipient can send an opt-out request has not been provided. (Regulation 23 refers.)

What is the difference between a 'solicited marketing message' and an 'unsolicited marketing message that you consent to receiving'?

Put simply, a 'solicited message' is one that you have actively invited. We accept that this invitation can be given via a third party. An 'unsolicited marketing message that you have opted into receiving' is one that you have not invited but you have indicated that you do not, for the time being, object to receiving it. If challenged, marketers would need to demonstrate that you have positively opted into receiving further information from them.

What would constitute a 'valid address' for the purpose of Regulation 23?

In an online environment, this could be a valid email address. We do not consider that the provision of a premium rate, national rate or freephone number would satisfy this obligation.

Is there any difference between an individual subscriber_and the recipient of marketing material by electronic mail (Regulation 22(2))?

Yes, there is a difference. The Directive which these Regulations give effect to states that unsolicited marketing should not be sent by electronic mail to an individual subscriber unless the subscriber has given consent. However, this Regulation refers to the consent of the recipient. We consider that the practical interpretation of the meaning of 'the recipient' is the intended recipient. Where a household member has an individual email address then the consent of that individual is required unless the soft opt-in criteria are satisfied. Where a household has a household email address (eg familyname@domainname.com) then the consent of someone who there is no reason to believe does not speak on behalf of the family is sufficient unless the soft opt-in criteria are satisfied.

What is 'soft opt-in' (Regulation 22(3))?

This is what the law goes on to state:

You may send or instigate the sending of electronic mail for marketing purposes to an individual subscriber where:

(a) you have obtained the contact details of the recipient in the course of a sale or negotiations for the sale of a product or service to that recipient;

(b) the direct marketing material you are sending is in respect of your similar products and services only; **and**

(c) the recipient has been given a simple means of refusing (free of charge except for the cost of transmission) the use of his contact details for marketing purposes at the time those details were initially collected and, where he did not refuse the use of those details, at the time of each subsequent communication.

In other words, if you satisfy these criteria, you do not need prior consent to send marketing by electronic mail to individual subscribers. If you cannot satisfy these criteria you cannot send marketing by electronic mail to individual subscribers without their prior consent.

How does the Information Commissioner interpret 'in the course of a sale or negotiations for the sale of a product or service'?

A sale does not have to be completed for this criterion to apply. It may be difficult to establish where negotiations may begin. However, where a person has actively expressed an interest in purchasing a company's products and services and not opted out of further marketing of that product or service or similar

(cont'd)

products and services at the time their details were collected, the company can continue to market them by electronic mail unless and until that person opts out of receiving such messages at a later date.

For the avoidance of doubt, the Commissioner does not consider that 'negotiations for the sale of a product or service' includes the use of cookie technology to identify a person's area of interest when they are browsing your website. Unless that person has expressly communicated their interest to you by, for example, asking for a quote, no 'negotiations' can be said to have taken place for the purpose of these Regulations.

As another example, if you send an email to a national retailer asking them if they are going to open a branch in your town, you would expect a response of 'yes' with details or 'no' perhaps with details of their other stores in your area. This query does not, however, constitute part of a negotiation for the sale of a product or service. It does not constitute an invitation to the retailer to send you further information about their products or services. Nor does it indicate consent to receive further promotional emails from that retailer. The retailer could send you emails promoting their products and services if you:

- expressly invited them to;

- consented to their suggestion that they send you promotional emails; or

- did not object to the receipt of emails in the course of a sale or negotiations for a sale.

How does the ICO interpret 'similar products and services'?

We are taking a purposive approach here. In our view, the intention of this section is to ensure that an individual does not receive promotional material about products and services that they would not reasonably expect to receive. For example, someone who has shopped online at a supermarket's website (and has not objected to receiving further email marketing from that supermarket) would expect at some point in the future to receive further emails promoting the diverse range of goods available at that supermarket.

Ultimately, if an individual feels that the company has gone beyond the boundaries of their reasonable expectation that individual can opt-out, something which most responsible marketers will be keen to avoid. For the time being, therefore, we will be focussing particular attention on failures to comply with opt-out requests. We will continue to monitor the extent to which marketers take the reasonable expectations of individual subscribers into consideration.

This Regulation does not spell out our obligation to respect an opt-out request from individual subscribers? Does this mean we don't have to comply with such requests?

In our view, if you can only send marketing by electronic mail to individual subscribers where they have provided prior consent, implicit in this is the option to withdraw that consent at a later stage. We would cite the inclusion of the phrase 'for the time being' in support of our view. We will take enforcement action against those companies within UK jurisdiction who persistently fail to comply with opt-out requests from individual subscribers.

Text/picture/video messaging

Surely SMS marketing can't be subject to the same rules as conventional email – after all, the standard mobile phone screen can only hold 160 characters!

The practical limitations of standard mobile screens do not mean that marketers can ignore the rules. Information about the marketing you intend to do can be given before you send a marketing message or even before you collect the mobile number in question. For example, in an advert or on a website where the recipient signs up for the service.

Assuming the recipient has clearly consented to the receipt of messages, each message will have to identify the sender and provide a valid suppression address. This may take as few as 18 characters (eg PJLtdPOBox97SK95AF).

If, however, the sender is relying on the relaxation of the prior consent rule (ie soft opt-in), there is an additional obligation to provide a simple means of refusing further marketing with every message. This may well take 40 characters or more (eg PJLtdPOBox97SK95AF.2STOPMSGSTXT'STOP'TO (then add 5 digit short code)).

Do we have to screen against TPS if we are sending unsolicited marketing by text/picture/video messages?

TPS registration indicates a general objection to receiving live marketing calls. Text/picture/video messages are defined as 'electronic mail' under the Regulations and, as such, they should not be sent without the prior consent of the individual subscribers unless the 'soft opt-in' criteria are satisfied. You are, therefore, not obliged to screen against TPS before so doing because you should already have established prior consent or satisfied the 'soft opt-in' criteria.

However, you must ensure that you identify yourself in any text/picture/video messages that you send and provide a valid address to which opt-out requests can be sent. If you are sending the message on a soft opt-in basis, you are obliged to provide simple means of refusing further messages, which is free of charge except for the cost of transmitting the refusal. For the avoidance of doubt, if you only supply a premium rate or national rate number in these circumstances you would not satisfy this obligation.

(cont'd)

We carried out a marketing exercise by sending unsolicited text/picture/video messages before these Regulations came into force and only received a few opt-outs. Does this mean that we have consent to contact those other numbers because the subscribers didn't opt-out the first time round?

No, it does not mean you have consent to send further messages in this way. Provided you obtained the details in accordance with existing privacy law and used them recently, you can use them again. However, you must provide an opportunity for an opt-out with each subsequent message that is free of charge to exercise, except for the cost of transmission. For the avoidance of doubt, the use of premium or national rate lines for opt-out requests will not satisfy this requirement.

We will collect email addresses/mobile phone numbers as part of a competition, could this be considered as being 'in the course of negotiations for the sale of a product and service'?

A great deal will depend on the context and on what you tell the person when you collect their details. Arguably, where a competition is part of an inducement to raise interest in a product or service, this constitutes part of the negotiations for a sale. However, where you are unclear about what you will do with a person's email address or mobile phone number when you collect those details or where this information is not readily accessible, you are less likely to be able to rely on the 'soft opt-in'. If you have collected a person's name with their email address and/or mobile phone number and you have not been clear about what you are going to do with that information, you may also be in breach of the First Data Principle.

Mailing lists compiled before 11 December 2003

Can we still use our own electronic mail mailing list that we compiled before 11 December 2003?

We recognise that this new legislation imposes upon marketers a higher standard for data collection than they were obliged to follow before 11 December 2003. For the time being, we take the view that where your own mailing lists were compiled in accordance with privacy legislation in force before 11 December 2003 and have been used recently, you can continue to use them unless the intended recipient has already opted out. You are reminded that it is our view that privacy legislation in force before 11 December 2003 did not permit the sending of unsolicited text/picture/video messages without prior consent.

When using our existing lists after 11 December 2003, do we need to provide an opt-out opportunity or do we just have to provide a valid address for opt outs?

If your existing lists were compiled on a clear prior consent basis, you only need to provide a valid address with every message. In either case, you must always ensure that you do not conceal your identity.

However, if your existing lists were compiled in accordance with privacy legislation in force before 11 December but were not compiled on a clear prior consent basis, you must provide an opt-out opportunity with every message. This accords with the requirements of the 'soft opt-in' criteria.

As best practice, companies may wish to provide an opportunity to opt-out in every message, even if they are not obliged to. This may alleviate any practical difficulties that may arise in using lists compiled both before and after 11 December 2003 for the same mailing exercise.

While we are prepared to take a pragmatic view on pre-existing lists for the time being, we will expect marketers to ensure that any opt-out requests received either before or after 11 December 2003 are acted upon promptly. Responding promptly to an opt-out request is not a new requirement and organisations should already have efficient systems in place to deal with such requests.

For the avoidance of doubt, contact details should be 'suppressed' rather than deleted when an opt-out request is received. This should ensure that a person's opt-out request is recorded, retained and respected until such time as that person provides consent which over-rides their previous opt-out request. It is our view that over-riding consent would only be valid where it is provided to the sender directly from the person concerned.

Third party electronic mailing lists

Must any consent or invitation to market by electronic mail always be provided directly to the sender? If so, does this mean that we can never use bought-in/rented lists after 11 December 2003?

Notwithstanding our view about over-riding consent (see previous point), there is nothing in the Regulations which expressly rules out the provision of consent via a third party. However, if you are buying or renting a list from a broker, you will need to seek assurances about the basis upon which the information was collected.

We are prepared to exercise some latitude in the use of mailing lists that were compiled before 11 December 2003 in accordance with existing privacy legislation.

(*cont'd*)

However, it is difficult to see how third party lists can be compiled and used legitimately after 11 December 2003 on any other basis than one where the individual subscriber expressly invites, ie solicits marketing by electronic mail. This is because unsolicited marketing can only be sent to an individual subscriber where he or she has 'previously notified the sender that he or she consents for the time being to such communications being sent by, or at the instigation of, the sender'. (Regulation 22(2).)

The following is a list of scenarios that may apply to your list. It is by no means exhaustive.

1. List of individual subscribers who have INVITED contact from third parties on a particular subject

    You can send marketing material by electronic mail to contacts on this list provided that:

    - this person has not already sent an opt-out request to you;

    - you do not conceal your identity when you contact them; and

    - you ensure that you have provided a valid contact address for subsequent opt-out requests.

    Given individuals' increased caution over disclosure of their contact details to third parties for marketing purposes, you should seek assurances on the veracity of such a list, ie are these genuine invitations for contact from anyone on a particular subject as opposed to 2. or 3. below.

2. List of individual subscribers who have INVITED contact from third parties on unspecified subjects

    You can send marketing material by electronic mail to contacts on this list provided that:

    - this person has not already sent an opt-out request to you;

    - you do not conceal your identity when you contact them; and

    - you ensure that you have provided a valid contact address for subsequent opt-out requests.

    Given individuals' increased caution over disclosure of their contact details to third parties for marketing purposes, you should seek assurances on the veracity of such a list, ie are these genuine invitations for contact from anyone on any subject as opposed to 3. below.

3. List of individual subscribers who have CONSENTED TO receiving unsolicited marketing material by electronic mail from third parties on a particular subject (ie list compiled on an opt-in basis)

    You can send marketing material by electronic mail to contacts on this list provided that:

- this person has not already sent an opt-out request to you;

- you do not conceal your identity; **and**

- you ensure that you have provided a valid contact address for subsequent opt-out requests.

Given individuals' increased caution over disclosure of their contact details to third parties for marketing purposes, you should seek assurances on the veracity of such a list.

Where this consent was given after 11 December 2003, it is more likely that this person has genuinely consented to receiving unsolicited marketing messages from third parties about a particular subject (ie products and services similar to those in which they have already expressed an interest). It may, however, be difficult to demonstrate that the intended recipients have 'notified the sender' and a great deal will depend on the wording of any statement made when the information was collected.

Where this consent was given before 11 December 2003, you may wish to check with the broker how recently it was compiled and whether it has already been used by their other clients. A list compiled in 2003 should have been compiled in the knowledge of the general requirements of these Regulations. Although we would be prepared to take a pragmatic view on the use of lists compiled in accordance with privacy legislation before 11 December 2003, you may wish to consider whether using a list compiled before 1 January 2003 is going to yield a sufficiently positive response because it may well be out of date.

To summarise, if there is no express invitation to receive marketing messages, you will need to consider whether any list you use constitutes a list of notifications of consent to you, the sender. Another point to consider is that the older the list that you buy or rent, the less likely it is that those contacts on the list are going to respond positively to marketing messages. It may even damage the reputation of your business to send poorly targeted unwanted marketing messages. You have a general obligation to ensure that the recipient is provided with a valid address for opt-out requests in every message. Should you receive such an opt-out request, you must ensure that you suppress that individual's details immediately. We will pay particular attention to those companies that fail to respect opt-out requests.

Can we advertise the products and services of third parties via electronic mail?

If you are offering a 'host mailing' service, you are not disclosing your mailing list to a third party but you are willing, for a fee, to promote their goods and

(cont'd)

services alongside yours. It is unlikely you could send such messages on a 'soft opt-in' basis because they are not your 'similar products and services'. You could, however, send such material on a clear 'opt-in' basis provided you identify that you, and not the third party, are the sender.

Can we pass our list of email addresses/mobile numbers on to a third party for them to use for marketing purposes?

If the email addresses/mobile numbers in question are those of individual subscribers, the third party will not be able to use them to send unsolicited marketing material unless the subscriber has consented to receiving it from that third party (ie 'the sender'). You must make it clear who you are proposing to pass the details on to and what sort of products and services they will be offering.

For example, a positive response to a phrase such as: 'We would like to pass your details on to specially selected third parties so that they can send you more information about holidays in America. Do you agree to this?' is likely to be sufficient to allow third parties to use those contact details for promoting holidays in America by electronic mail.

A phrase such as 'We will pass your details on to third parties unless you write to us and tell us that you don't agree' will not be sufficient. You should not use contact lists which have been obtained in these circumstances.

The decision about what happens to an individual's electronic contact details must rest with the individual. No disclosure can be made to third parties for their marketing purposes unless that individual actively consents to such a disclosure taking place.

Group companies/trading names

How do the rules on marketing by electronic mail apply to marketing by different companies within a group of companies?

If you disclosed individual subscribers' contact information within your group in compliance with existing data protection rules prior to 11 December 2003 and those other group companies have already used that information and not received an opt-out request, that contact information can still be used by those other group companies, as long as further opt-out opportunities are provided with every subsequent message for more information about whether a valid address or an opt-out opportunity is required for subsequent communications.

Moving forward, you will, as a minimum requirement, have to ask individuals whether they consent to receiving unsolicited marketing by electronic mail from other group companies when you collect their contact details. In an online environment, you could provide a link listing those group companies.

You may even wish to consider providing separate opt-in opportunities for each company on that list in order to give the individual greater choice and to target your group's marketing more efficiently.

Another option you may wish to consider is providing an opportunity for the individual to invite (ie solicit) contact from other companies within the group.

Our company has a number of different trading names, surely an opt-in for one of the trading names is an opt-in for all the trading names because there is only one legal entity?

If you trade under several different names, particularly where those names are strong brands, you cannot assume that a customer who agrees to receive mailing from one trading entity is agreeing to receive marketing from your other trading entities. They may not even be aware of any connection between different trading names. You would need to ensure that the individual is made aware that they will receive unsolicited marketing from all of your trading names when they opt-in to receiving marketing from you. Similarly, when an individual opts-out of receiving unsolicited marketing from one of your trading names, this opt-out applies to all of your trading names unless they make it clear otherwise.

If you are collecting information on a 'soft opt-in' basis, you may have considerable difficulty in satisfying the 'similar products and services' criteria, if you want to send further unsolicited marketing relating to your full range of trading names. You could avoid this difficulty by providing an opportunity for the individual to invite contact from the wide range of trading names within the company.

Loyalty Schemes

We operate a loyalty scheme for our own products and services. How do the Regulations apply here?

If someone participates in a loyalty scheme, the minimum that they can expect to receive from you is an update about how many points/vouchers they have earned. In our view, under the 'soft opt-in' rule, you can send them further information about other incentives that are available under the scheme unless and until they opt-out of receiving such further information. Once they have opted-out of receiving further information about other offers that are available under the scheme, you should not send such further information unless and until they opt back into receiving it again.

(cont'd)

135

We operate a loyalty scheme in partnership with other companies. A great deal of information is transferred across the scheme and the partners do not necessarily offer similar products and services, how do the Regulations apply here?

Dealing first of all with the information you have already collected, we will assume that you have collected that contact information in accordance with your obligations under the *DPA 1998*. Each partner can continue to use contact information which was collected before 11 December 2003 for marketing by electronic mail, provided the information has been recently used by that partner and provided no opt-outs have been received for more information about whether a valid address or an opt-out opportunity is also required for subsequent communications. Moving forward, you may need to revisit the data protection and privacy wording of your application form where you are collecting information in order to conduct marketing exercises by electronic means. You must ensure that individuals are fully aware of the nature of the promotions you propose to send. The minimum that an individual can expect to receive from you is an update about how many points/vouchers they have earned. In our view, under the 'soft opt-in' rule, you can send them further information about other incentives offered by all the participating companies in the scheme unless and until they opt-out of receiving such further information. Where there are a number of partners in a loyalty scheme, you may find it easier to provide an opportunity for the individual to invite (ie solicit) further marketing contact from each partner where those partners propose to contact the individual independently of this scheme.

Business to business

How do the Regulations apply to business to business marketing by electronic mail?

Your obligations are as follows:

1.   You must not conceal your identity when you send, or instigate the sending of, a marketing message by electronic mail to anyone (including corporate subscribers); and

2. You must provide a valid address to which the recipient (including corporate subscribers) can send an opt-out request. (Regulation 23.)

Only individual subscribers have an enforceable right of opt-out under these Regulations. This is where that individual withdraws the consent that they previously gave to receiving marketing by electronic mail (that consent only being valid 'for the time being'. (Regulation 22(2).)) This right is not extended to corporate subscribers.

Although recipients who are corporate subscribers do not have an enforceable opt-out right under the Regulations, where the sending of marketing material to the employee of a company includes the processing of personal data (ie the marketer knows the name of the person they are contacting), that individual has a fundamental and enforceable right under the *DPA 1998*, *s 11* to request that a company cease sending them marketing material.

In our view, it makes no business sense to continue to send marketing material to a business contact who no longer wishes to hear from you. Arguably, by failing to respect a business to business opt-out request you may give the impression that you are unconcerned about your commercial reputation. You should note that persistent failure to comply with a *Section 11* request, whether or not it relates to a business to business communication, may result in our taking enforcement action against you.

How do these Regulations apply to unsolicited marketing material sent by electronic mail to individual employees of a corporate subscriber where that material promotes goods and services which are clearly intended for their personal/domestic use?

The Commissioner has no authority to take enforcement action based on the content of emails sent to corporate subscribers, even though that content may be entirely inappropriate for business to business communications.

In the 'Spam' report of an Inquiry by the All-Party Parliamentary Internet Group (APPIG) there was a recommendation that the Information Commissioner set out clear guidance as to how business-to-business communications are to be distinguished from messages intended for individual subscribers. This recommendation was prompted by the observation of one of the witnesses to the inquiry that an invitation to buy Viagra sent to the sales address of a shipping company could only be construed as being sent to an individual since it would not be of any business relevance. The problem is that the 'opt-in' and 'soft opt-in' rules do not extend to the sending of marketing emails to corporate subscribers. In the example quoted, the subscriber will be the shipping company because that is the person which is party to a contract with a provider of public electronic communications systems. This means, therefore, that even an email addressed to an individual within the company will not be covered by the Regulations, although it may be subject to the *DPA 1998* and a *Section 11* notice could be issued. In other words, the fact that an email sent to a corporate subscriber's address is obviously aimed at an individual (because it promotes a product that is for personal/domestic use) is not, for the purposes of the Regulations, relevant. Email communications sent to a corporate subscriber are simply not covered by the Regulations except in so far as there is a requirement to identify the sender and to provide contact details.

(cont'd)

How do the Regulations apply to the sending of text/picture/video messaging to mobile phones which are supplied to individual employees by corporate subscribers?

The law applies in exactly the same way as it does to the sending of emails to corporate subscribers.

Electronic mail marketing to partnerships

How do the Regulations apply to the sending of marketing messages by electronic mail to partnerships?

A non-limited liability partnership in England, Wales or Northern Ireland is an individual subscriber under these Regulations. This means that such a partnership (which may consist of several individuals and which may have a large number of employees) is afforded the same protection under these Regulations as a residential subscriber or a sole trader. This protection is not available to limited liability partnerships, to Scottish partnerships or to corporate subscribers, which include small and medium sized limited companies.

Strictly speaking, marketers must get prior consent to send emails to any email address used by an unincorporated partnership unless the 'soft opt-in' criteria apply. This may be the generic contact email address of the partnership, eg mail@partnershipname.com, or it may be the separate email addresses used by individuals (partners, associates and other employees) working at that partnership.

This issue was the matter of some debate during the Department of Trade and Industry's consultation exercise prior to the implementation of these Regulations.

What does this mean in practice?

Although, strictly speaking, the partnership could be viewed as the commercial equivalent of a large household, we recognise that there may be circumstances when the wishes of the subscriber, ie the unincorporated partnership (which is legally responsible for charges incurred on its lines) might over-ride the wishes of the employee. For example, an employer may insist that an employee keeps in regular contact with conference organisers. The employer's wishes in respect of unsolicited emails from conference organisers would over-ride the wishes of the employee.

However, if one individual working at the partnership consents to receiving unsolicited marketing material from the organiser, this does not mean that every individual working at the partnership has consented to receiving such material from the organiser.

Marketers must also remember that where they know the name of the person they are seeking to contact, that person's contact details must be processed in accordance with the Eight Data Protection Principles of the *DPA 1998*. For example, where the *DPA 1998* applies, all individuals have a fundamental opt-out right under *Section 11*.

Who is able to give consent on behalf of individuals working at a partnership?

If you are targeting an individual working at a partnership, you must ensure you obtain the consent of the individual (or a person who can be reasonably assumed to be entitled to give consent on that individual's behalf, eg a secretary or assistant) before sending unsolicited electronic mail to that individual unless the 'soft opt-in' criteria apply.

Partnerships may wish to ensure that their key frontline staff, eg switchboard operators, receptionists, administrators and secretaries are advised of any office policy regarding the disclosure of employee contact details.

Individuals employed by partnerships must remember that in respect of their work email address and mobile phone, it is ultimately their employer's consent choices which take precedence over their individual choices.

Who is able to give consent on behalf of the partnership?

Marketers must ensure that they have obtained consent from a person working for that partnership who, it is reasonable to assume, has the authority to give such consent. Partnerships may wish to ensure that their key frontline staff, eg switchboard operators, receptionists, administrators and secretaries, are advised of any office policy regarding the disclosure of office contact details.

Electronic mail marketing to sole traders

How do the Regulations apply to the sending of marketing messages by electronic mail to sole traders?

Sole traders are also individual subscribers under the Regulations. That said, we have recognised in earlier enforcement that marketers may have difficulty in distinguishing sole traders from small limited companies, particularly where a sole trader's contact details are available in business directories. However, marketers should use their best efforts to ensure that they do not send marketing messages by electronic mail to sole traders in contravention of the Regulations. For example, it is possible to check free of charge on the Companies House website (www.companieshouse.gov.uk) whether or not a trading entity is a limited company.

(cont'd)

Pan-European marketing

We plan to conduct a pan-European marketing campaign. Which jurisdiction's rules do we need to comply with?

It is our understanding that you must comply with the laws of the jurisdiction in which you are based. However, you should bear in mind that when implementing the EU Directive, each Member State was given the option to decide whether the rights given to individual subscribers should extend to corporate subscribers. Some jurisdictions have chosen to do so to a greater extent than the UK has done. You may create a negative impression about your business if you don't respect the laws of the country to which you are sending your messages. We cannot offer guidance on how to comply with the legislation of other jurisdictions and you should seek your own legal advice if you wish to conduct pan-European marketing campaigns.

Marketing by more than one medium

We collect individuals' addresses, telephone numbers, mobile numbers and email addresses for marketing purposes on a paper form. We have limited room on the form and we have to provide other information in order to comply with other legislation. What is the minimum amount of information we have to provide in order to comply with data protection rules?

You do not need to provide reams of legalese in order to comply with your data protection obligations. If you are collecting information in order to market a person by a variety of media, the simplest method is to adopt the highest standard and apply it even where you do not need to.

Under the *DPA 1998*, the bare minimum that you are obliged to tell people is who you are and what you plan to do with their information, including any unexpected uses, such as processing for marketing purposes and/or disclosures to third parties. Because you plan to market by electronic means, you also need to provide consent options. The very highest standard would be to provide the individual with the opportunity to solicit information from you, eg:

> 'Please contact me by post, by telephone, by text/picture/video message, by email with further information about your products and services (tick as applicable).'

However, if you use this wording, you cannot send marketing material to them by post, telephone, text message or email unless the individual ticks the box to invite further contact from you.

Charities/political parties/not for profit organisations

We are a charity/political party/not-for profit organisation, can we take advantage of 'soft opt-in'?

No, not unless you are promoting commercial goods and services, for example those offered by your trading arm. We recognise that this puts such organisations at a disadvantage and raised this point in our response to the consultation exercise, conducted by the Department of Trade and Industry, in advance of these Regulations. However, the EU Directive from which these Regulations are derived specify that the rules on marketing by electronic means apply to commercial relationships.

You may wish to revisit the wording of your data protection and privacy statements so that a person would actively 'invite' promotional information from you via electronic mail. As outlined above, there is a difference between a person actively soliciting promotional material by electronic mail and that same person consenting to the receipt of any promotional material you choose to send them by electronic mail (ie unsolicited marketing material). Alternatively, you could ask them whether they consent to the receipt of unsolicited marketing material.

You remain obliged to identify yourself and to provide a valid address for opt-outs in each electronic mailing.

Chapter 14 –
Distance Selling Regulations

At A Glance

✓ The Distance Selling Directive (97/7/EC) was implemented in the UK by the Consumer Protection (Distance Selling) Regulations 2000 (SI 2000/2334). In 2004 the DTI proposed changes to the Regulations, which are not yet in force. In 2003 draft guidance on the existing Regulations, as they apply to IT, was issued.

✓ These Regulations set out certain information which must be given to consumers purchasing most goods or services at a 'distance', such as in response to unsolicited mail or telephone calls, or via a website. This has a major impact on wording to be used in connection with direct marketing. Sample wording is provided.

✓ The Regulations give individuals the right to cancel contracts made by these means within a statutory withdrawal period.

✓ Major changes are made in the area of inertia selling, which concerns unsolicited goods and services.

✓ A separate *Directive on the Distance Marketing of Financial Services (2002/65/EC)* must be implemented by 9 October 2004.

Introduction   14.1

Directive 97/7/EC on distance selling contracts contains provisions relating to unsolicited e-mails which are very relevant in the data protection area. The UK implemented the Directive with the *Consumer Protection (Distance Selling) Regulations 2000 (SI 2000/2334)*. The Regulations have been in force since 31 October 2000.

The Regulations apply to contracts made at a distance via the following mediums:

● unaddressed printed matter;

● addressed printed matter;

● letters;

- press advertising with order form;

- catalogue;

- telephone with human intervention;

- telephone without human intervention (eg automatic calling machine, audiotext);

- radio;

- videophone (telephone with screen);

- videotext (microcomputer and television screen) with keyboard or touch screen;

- e-mail;

- facsimile machine (fax); and

- television (teleshopping).

The Regulations are not principally a data protection measure, although they are very relevant for those involved with direct marketing.

In 2004 the DTI proposed changes to the Regulations, which are not yet in force. In 2003 draft guidance on the existing Regulations, as they apply to IT, was issued.

Example: Application of the Regulations 14.2

Questions to determine whether the *Consumer Protection (Distance Selling) Regulations 2000 (SI 2000/2334)* apply.

(a) Does our business supply goods or services to consumers directly rather than just to other businesses?

If no, then the Regulations do not apply.

If yes then:

(b) Does our business supply to consumers by distance methods?

If yes, the Regulations apply.

Distance methods are defined below, but are essentially most selling methods which are not face to face. E-commerce, telesales and mail order come within the Regulations.

Timing 14.3

A distance contract is one where the consumer and supplier do not have face-to-face contact up to and including the moment when the contract is concluded.

The *Distance Selling Directive (97/7/EC)* covers the sale of goods or services concluded via e-commerce as well as other means of distance selling such as mail order and telephone sales, and fax.

The *Consumer Protection (Distance Selling) Regulations 2000 (SI 2000/2334)* include certain key features set out below.

- The consumer must be given clear information about the goods or services offered.

- After making a purchase, the consumer must be sent confirmation.

- The consumer has a cooling-off period of seven working days.

- Local Trading Standards Departments and the Office of Fair Trading receive new powers.

The Regulations do not apply to all distance contracts, the most important exception being for financial services. A separate *Directive on the Distance Marketing of Financial Services (2002/65/EC)* must be implemented by 9 October 2004.

Distance Contract   14.4

The list of means of distance communications covered by the *Distance Selling Directive (97/7/EC)* (see **14.1** above) includes direct mail and e-mail. The *Consumer Protection (Distance Selling) Regulations 2000 (SI 2000/2334)* only apply to organised distance selling contracts. If the business does not normally sell to consumers in response to telephone calls then the Regulations do not apply. The Department of Trade and Industry ('DTI') state the following on this point in their guide to the *Distance Selling Regulations* (see **14.1** above).

'If, for example, you do not usually sell goods or services by distance, but you agree to do so in response to a one-off request from a consumer over the phone, you do not need to comply with the Regulations. However if your business regularly handles 'one-off' requests from consumers and is organised so that it can deal with such requests (i.e. there is for example a mail order facility) you do need to ensure that you fulfil the Regulations.'

(Para 3.9, The Consumer Protection (Distance Selling) Regulations 2000: A Guide for Business).

The definition in the Regulations states:

'"Distance contract" means any contract concerning goods or services concluded between a supplier and a consumer under an organised distance sales or service provision scheme run by the supplier who, for the purpose of the contract, makes exclusive use of one or more means of distance communication up to and including the moment at which the contract is concluded'.

The Regulations apply where there is exclusive use of distance communications. The DTI states that this means the consumer has no face-to-face meeting with an employee, representative of the business, or someone acting on the business' behalf up to and including the time the consumer confirms the order.

Exclusions   14.5

Exclusions include any contract:

- for the sale or other disposition of an interest in land except for a rental agreement;

- for the construction of a building where the contract also provides for a sale or other disposition of an interest in land on which the building is constructed, except for a rental agreement;

- relating to financial services, a non-exhaustive list of which is contained in *Schedule 2* of the Regulations and includes:

  o   investment services,

  o   insurance and reinsurance operations,

  o   banking services, and

  o   services relating to dealings in futures or options;

- concluded by means of an automated vending machine or automated commercial premises;

- concluded with a telecommunications operator through the use of a public pay-phone; and

- concluded at an auction (including Internet auctions).

The major provisions of the *Distance Selling Directive (97/7/EC)* (relating to compulsory information to be given to consumers and the right to cancel a contract) do not apply to contracts for the provision of accommodation, transport, catering or leisure services, where the supplier undertakes – when the contract is concluded – to provide these services on a specific date or within a specific period.

Application to Home Supermarket Shopping   14.6

The DTI, in its guide for business, suggests the following in relation to supermarket deliveries.

'This exception (from information and cancellation provisions) will not generally apply to the growing market for home deliveries by supermarkets. Such deliveries are normally ordered specifically on each occasion by telephone, on the Internet or by fax. The consumer must be informed of the price and delivery arrangements etc. in accordance with *Regulation 7* at the time he places the order and receive a written confirmation of the order, at the latest at the time of delivery. There is, however, a specific exception to the right to cancel in respect of the supply of perishable goods'.

Premium-rate Telephone Services 14.7

With regard to premium-rate telephone services, consumers must be given prior information such as the cost of using the service before they are charged. In paragraph 5.6 of their guide for business, the DTI indicates that the business may provide the information required before the contract is made. The business does not need to provide written confirmation of the service but must ensure the consumer is able to obtain the postal address of the supplier's place of business in order to know where to send consumer complaints if necessary. Premium-rate websites must provide the information clearly before the charge is applied, for example at a point prior to the consumer switching to the premium rate service.

Prior Information Right 14.8

Those involved with direct marketing should note in particular the compulsory information which must be given to consumers. The Regulations give the consumer the right to receive clear information about the goods or services before deciding to purchase. This is called the prior information right.

Regulation 7 of the *Consumer Protection (Distance Selling) Regulations 2000 (SI 2000/2334)* states that this must be provided in good time prior to the conclusion of the contract. The supplier must:

- provide to the consumer the following information:
  - the identity of the supplier and – where the contract requires payment in advance – the supplier's address,
  - a description of the main characteristics of the goods or services,
  - the price of the goods or services including all taxes,
  - delivery costs where appropriate,
  - the arrangements for payment, delivery or performance (if no specified delivery date is given then this must be within 30 days of the order),
  - the existence of a right of cancellation except in the cases referred to in *Regulation 13*,
  - the cost of using the means of distance communication where it is calculated other than at the basic rate, for example premium rate telephone charges,

- o   the period for which the offer or the price remains valid, and

- o   where appropriate, in the case of contracts for the supply of goods or services to be performed permanently or recurrently, the minimum duration of the contract;

- inform the consumer if he proposes, in the event of the goods or services ordered by the consumer being unavailable, to provide substitute goods or services (as the case may be) of equivalent quality and price; and

- inform the consumer that the cost of returning any such substitute goods to the supplier in the event of cancellation by the consumer would be met by the supplier.

The supplier must ensure that the information required above is provided in a clear and comprehensible manner appropriate to the means of distance communication used, with 'due regard in particular to the principles of good faith in commercial transactions and the principles governing the protection of those who are unable to give their consent such as minors'.

The supplier must ensure that 'his commercial purpose is made clear when providing the information'. In the case of a telephone communication, the identity of the supplier and the commercial purpose of the call shall be made clear at the beginning of the conversation with the consumer.

Confirmation of the Prior Information in Writing or By E-mail   14.9

Confirmation of the prior information in writing or in another appropriate durable medium, eg fax or e-mail must be given. The *Distance Selling Directive (97/7/EC)* on which the *Consumer Protection (Distance Selling) Regulations 2000 (SI 2000/2334)* are based requires that the consumer be given information in writing or another 'durable medium that is available and accessible to him'. It does not say what this means so the DTI take the view that e-mail is a durable medium in the sense that it is open to the consumer to retain the information. Giving the details verbally is not, however, enough.

The written confirmation must give details of:

- the prior information (see **14.8** above);

- how to exercise the right to cancel and if the consumer is responsible for return of the goods;

- any guarantees and after sales services; and

- how to end any open-ended service contract, such as gas, telephone, cable or satellite TV, etc.

The information must be provided at the latest by the time the goods are delivered, or in the case of services, before or at any early state during performance of the contract. However, for Internet selling it makes more sense to give the information both on the website before purchase and in the confirmation e-mail on receipt and acceptance of order.

Cooling Off   14.10

A 'cooling off' period is given of seven working days from the day after delivery of the goods, in which the consumer can withdraw from the contract, unless extended by an additional three months because notice of the period was not given to the consumer at the relevant time (see **14.12** below). The DTI states:

> 'If the contract is made on Monday, Tuesday will be the first working day of the cooling off period and the seventh working day will be Wednesday of the following week (unless there are any public holidays during this period). If the sale is agreed on Thursday the seventh working day will fall on Monday in the second week following the sale to allow for the two intervening weekends'.

The statutory right of withdrawal below does not apply for:

(a)   the supply of services if the supplier has complied with *Regulation 8(3)* and performance of the contract has begun with the consumer's agreement before the end of the cancellation period applicable under *Regulation 12*;

(b)   the supply of goods or services, the price of which is dependent on fluctuations in the financial market which cannot be controlled by the supplier;

(c)   the supply of goods made to the consumer's specifications or clearly personalised, or which by reason of their nature cannot be returned or are liable to deteriorate or expire rapidly;

(d)   the supply of audio or video recordings or computer software if they are unsealed by the consumer;

(e)   the supply of newspapers, periodicals or magazines; or

(f)   for gaming, betting or lottery services.

Cooling Off Extension   14.11

The cooling off period extends for an extra three calendar months where the supplier has not given notice of the seven day period to the customer. This point illustrates the importance for businesses in amending their terms and conditions to cover these rights, so that the legal position can to some extent be ameliorated. *Regulation 11(3)* of the *Consumer Protection (Distance Selling) Regulations 2000* (*SI 2000/2334*) state:

> 'Where a supplier who has not complied with *regulation 8* (information requirements) provides to the consumer the information referred to in *regulation 8(2)*, and does so in writing or in another durable medium

available and accessible to the consumer, within the period of three months beginning with the day after the day on which the consumer receives the goods, the cancellation period ends on the expiry of the period of seven working days beginning with the day after the day on which the consumer receives the information'.

Where the supplier never supplied the information requirement then 'the cancellation period ends on the expiry of the period of three months and seven working days beginning with the day after the day on which the consumer receives the goods' (ie three months and seven working days).

Often delivery is contracted to be to a third party. In such a case this is treated as if the consumer had received the goods on the day on which they were received by the third party (*SI 2000/2334, Reg 11(5)*).

The DTI point out that the cooling off period is to give the consumer the chance he or she would have had in a conventional shop to 'examine the goods or to reflect on the nature of the service before deciding to buy'.

The effect of a notice of cancellation is that the contract shall be treated as if it had not been made. For contracts for the supply of goods the cancellation period ends on the expiry of the period of seven working days beginning with the day after the day on which the consumer receives the goods.

Paragraph (d) in 14.10 above is causing problems for some lawyers. It is obviously logical that goods of which the consumer could avail themselves, use/read etc. and then conveniently return cancelling the contract should be excluded from the cancellation right. It is a shame that not all computer software is excluded – only that which is 'unsealed'. Unsealed is not defined. This can create problems if, for example, a company supplies software to consumers online who have first given a credit card number. In such cases, the services are provided within the cancellation period, and there is nothing to 'unseal' except on a very broad and purposive interpretation of the provision which perhaps in practice is the best one to take, unless and until it is challenged. It would be advisable to include the relevant wording to ensure the cancellation period is seven (not 30) days. It may also be possible to argue that software is the provision of services, rather than supply of goods (assuming it falls into either category at all which, following the decision in *St Albans v ICL (CA) [1996] 4 All ER 481* it does not) including the provisions set out in *Regulation 8(3)* of SI 2000/2334 (see below).

In the DTI's consultation document *IT Consumer Contracts Made at a Distance – Guidance on Compliance with the Distance Selling and Unfair Terms in Consumer Contracts Regulations October 2003 OFT672* para 4.92, the DTI says:

> 'Consumers have the right to cancel software that conforms with the contract where the software is sealed and has not been unsealed by them. You should tell consumers that they have cancellation rights if they do not unseal the goods. The "seal" on the software may be the security seal on the inner packaging, or software may be "sealed" electronically'.

This is helpful draft guidance, but it does show the DTI's position is that consumers somehow need to be told they have a right to cancel software contracts before breaking open the cellophane seal, or where downloaded before they unseal electronically. How they can download electronically and not unseal and then cancel is unclear. The DTI does not elaborate. Some software suppliers, where consumers download online, have simply taken a pragmatic view that this exclusion of the right to cancel is designed to prevent illegal copying and thus does not give consumers cancellation rights. That is an acceptable commercial view of the spirit of the exclusion in this part of the regulations.

Regulation 8(3) states:

> 'Subject to *regulation 9*, prior to the conclusion of a contract for the supply of services, the supplier shall inform the consumer in writing or in another durable medium which is available and accessible to the consumer that, unless the parties agree otherwise, he will not be able to cancel the contract under *regulation 10* once the performance of the services has begun with his agreement.

Suppliers of services such as solicitors and accountants who provide chargeable advice to clients by telephone, e-mail or fax (and thus form a contract at a distance) may be caught by the Regulations (but only as regards 'consumer' clients such as those wanting wills to be written or personal tax advice or a divorce, etc.) It seems that even in such cases the right to cancel may apply. Could this be the case if the services are provided within the seven day cancellation period? Unless the service provider gives notice under *Regulation 8(3)*, the customer could theoretically cancel after receipt of the advice, possibly even after having signed a valid will, for example, provided under such advice within the seven days, the will, presumably, remaining valid. In most cases, therefore, providers are advised to include a new condition in their contracts.

Unless agreed otherwise with the supplier, there is a right to receive goods or services within 30 days. This accords with the period which is usual in the mail order industry in any event.

Example: Wording of Condition   14.12

> A sample of suitable wording is provided below.
>
> > 'For consumer customers where we carry out work for you, you have a right to withdraw your instructions, without any charge, by giving us a notice in writing or by e-mail at any time within seven working days from instructing us. This does not apply if we start work within this period and you do hereby consent to our starting work right away.'

Books   14.13

Another problem that could arise with the *Consumer Protection (Distance Selling) Regulations 2000 (SI 2000/2334)* is that although there is an exclusion from cancellation for magazines (which obviously is necessary to stop people buying the magazine, reading it and then sending it back) there is, illogically, no such exclusion for books. Internet booksellers who often despatch books the day after ordering must be encountering significant problems with the Regulations.

Examples: Online Supplier's Right to Cancel   14.14

Example 1

'You may normally cancel your purchase (where we have accepted your order and delivered the product) if you notify us within the 14 days following the day the product was delivered. You can do this by:

- returning the product to one of our shops (take the card you used to buy it with you and the receipt); or

- notifying us by telephone on _____; or

- notifying us by letter or e-mail at _____.

You may only return your product if it is complete, unused and in good condition with the box, packaging and accessories with which it came. Recorded tapes, compact discs, DVDs, software and minidiscs must be sealed. Free gifts sent with the product must be returned too.

We cannot refund your money when:

- you cannot provide proof of purchase, or

- when there is a service contract with the product (such as on a mobile telephone) which has already started.

If you do not return the goods in person, you will receive the refund in 30 days of notifying us of your cancellation.'

The terms should also deal with the consumer's rights if there are defects and/or manufacturers' warranties.

Example 2

'You have the right to cancel your contract with us at any time during the period which commences on the day the contract comes into existence and ends on the expiry of seven working days after the date of delivery of the products.

If the goods are to be rejected in the time limit set out above, you must comply with the returns procedure set out below. In that case we will accept any returned goods if the return is complete and with a valid proof of purchase and, in the case of an order which you wish to cancel, if the return is in unused and re-saleable condition.

You can contact us at the address or telephone number set out at the end of these terms with details of your original order number and receipt and we will arrange to collect the return. Subject to the terms provided below, your credit or debit card will then be debited with the cost of return delivery charge being £___ per return.

You will then receive e-mail notice that your return is registered with our carrier who will collect the goods within _____ working days of your contacting us as provided above.

If you prefer, you can return the goods to one of our stores with details of your order number, receipt and card details.

You will receive a full refund of the purchase price and the delivery charge to be credited to your card. Faulty products have to be returned before the refund will be made.

If there is a defect or discrepancy in the order then you will not have to pay the return delivery charge mentioned above. When the return arrives at our office it will be considered by us and if the goods are found to be defective or there was a discrepancy the return delivery charge will be credited to your card.'

Example: Companies With More Than One Type of Product   14.15

This example would be appropriate for a company which supplies some products that include contracts which can be cancelled and others which cannot (see final clause).

'If you do not wish to buy the goods you have received then you can return them as new within 14 days either for a refund or replacement. We can arrange   to   collect   the   goods   from   you   by   telephoning _____ or take them to the post office obtaining a certificate of posting as your proof of the return. The return is free of charge by either means.

If you do not return the goods in the same condition in which you received them, and not within 14 days, then we reserve the right to charge you for the goods.

Your right of return does not apply to food hampers, wines, spirits, personalised merchandise and certain electrical goods and other items where indicated in the product description.'

Cold Calling   14.16

When a supplier 'cold calls' someone at home, confusion can often arise over what is on offer and who is behind the call. The DTI hope the *Consumer Protection (Distance Selling) Regulations 2000 (SI 2000/2334)* will prevent this. Under these Regulations suppliers who cold call consumers at home must identify clearly the company they represent and the commercial purpose of their call at the beginning of the conversation.

How to Send the Cancellation Notice   14.17

The consumer must send the cancellation notice in writing only (including by fax or e-mail). The notice is given to the supplier or the person whom the supplier has nominated for this purpose.

Goods Returned Damaged   14.18

Consumers who use or damage the goods are not entitled to exercise the cancellation right. This is a very important point in practice. However if the goods are defective, then under sale of goods law the consumer may be allowed to reject them or sue for breach of contract. When, in 2002, the UK implements the *Consumer Guarantees Directive (1999/44/EC)*, there will be additional rights to reject goods which do not conform to the contract with stipulated six and 18 month periods. The Directive should have been implemented by 1 January 2002, but is expected to be implemented in late 2002 or 2003.

Goods and Services – Mobile Phones   14.19

The cancellation period differs between goods and services as seen above. The DTI in 'The Consumer Protection (Distance Selling) Regulations 2000: A Guide for Business' refers to mobile contracts where a phone is sold, but a service contract is undertaken with the customer. The DTI believes that the *Distance Selling Directive (97/7/EC)* does not deal with this kind of circumstance, stating that 'if the hardware is given away or sold at a significantly discounted price the contract could be treated as one for service provision, and cancellation would mean the phone must be returned too. So the cooling off period would run for seven working days from the date of the contract. If the phone is sold at full price with limited additional elements then probably the cancellation period for goods would apply, so that it ends seven working days after delivery of the phone'.

Refunds   14.20

Whilst in some industries, such as the clothing industry, it is common (provided the goods are undamaged) to let the consumer return them for various reasons, there has until now been no right for the consumer to return even undamaged goods. If the goods are defective that is a different matter. Rights of rejection exist under the *Sale of Goods Act 1979* as amended by the *Sale and Supply of Goods Act 1994* and are included in many consumer contracts. Leaving that aside, the law now allows returns.

In the past, many clothing suppliers have allowed exchanges or credit notes but have not given monetary refunds unless the law requires it, for example if the goods are defective. This practice has worked well, but has been altered by the *Consumer Protection (Distance Selling) Regulations 2000 (SI 2000/2334)*. If the consumer cancels the contract all money paid has to be returned within 30 days of the date the notice of cancellation is given. Usually this means crediting the payment or credit card. Goods purchased by distance methods are rarely paid for in cash, although sometimes they are paid by cheque.

One of the DTI's frequently asked questions in its Guide to the Regulations is whether a refund must be paid for a gift wrapping service for goods ordered. The answer is no because the service has already been carried out so cannot be cancelled, but normal delivery costs must be refunded where a consumer has paid for those separately.

Recovering the Goods   14.21

Ownership in the goods reverts to the seller when the consumer exercises the right to cancel. The consumer has to take reasonable care of the goods even after giving the cancellation notice. The goods should be returned as new.

Nevertheless, the supplier is obliged to collect the goods unless the contract says otherwise. The consumer simply has to make them available for collection. The supplier cannot force the consumer to return the goods unless the contract terms say so. Suppliers, therefore, would be well advised to include such a term in their contracts stating that the consumer must return the goods, making it much less likely that the cancellation right will be exercised.

The supplier has to notify the consumer within 21 days when the supplier will collect the goods, and if this is not done then the consumer does not have to look after them with reasonable care anymore, although the consumer must still be given a refund by the supplier in such a case.

If the consumer has been told in the contract – and written confirmation is provided – that they have to return the goods, then the consumer has to take care of them for up to six months and indefinitely if the supplier serves a notice requiring them to be handed over. If a consumer does not undertake due care in looking after the goods the supplier can claim any resulting loss in value. In practice, if the goods are destroyed this might be the whole value of the goods. It is unlikely that a supplier in such a case offset the refund of the price against this, due to the length of time involved. The refund will have to have been made before the consumer has returned the goods.

Delivery Dates   14.22

Most mail order companies are already subject to specific legislation which requires them to deliver in 30 days or else tell consumers this will not be the case. The *Consumer Protection (Distance Selling) Regulations 2000 (SI 2000/2334)* do the same thing across all distance selling sectors. Goods must be delivered or services provided within 30 days from the date when the order was placed and if the deadline cannot be met then the consumer must be told before the period expires and must refund money paid in a further 30 days, unless the consumer agrees to accept substitute goods or services or to propose a revised delivery date. If the consumer does not agree the later delivery date, which he or she may well not do, eg if the goods were for a birthday etc., then the contract is cancelled and the consumer is paid his or her money back.

Changes to Unsolicited Goods Law   14.23

The *Consumer Protection (Distance Selling) Regulations 2000 (SI 2000/2334)* also make changes to the *Unsolicited Goods and Services Act 1971 (UGSA 1971)*. The Act is amended slightly by the Regulations, but only in relation to goods sent from 31 October 2000 (see *SI 2000/2334, reg 22(4)*).

The Act makes it an offence to demand payment for goods known to be unsolicited. The person receiving the goods does not have to pay for or return goods if they do not want them. Until October 2000 the law contained particular periods after which the goods could be kept by the recipient. *Article 9* of the *Distance Selling Directive (97/7/EC)* bans the supply of unsolicited goods and services where supply involves a demand for payment (free samples etc. are unaffected).

The Regulations provide that in the case of unsolicited goods, (ie those where the recipient has no reasonable cause to believe that they were sent with a view to being acquired for the purposes of a business and where the recipient has not agreed to acquire or return them) the recipient may, as between himself and the sender, 'use, deal with or dispose of the goods as if they were an unconditional gift to him ... The rights of the sender to the goods are extinguished.'

The *Distance Selling Directive (97/7/EC)* also exempts the consumer from the 'provision of any consideration' in cases of unsolicited supply. In this context, the DTI said in a 1999 consultation that it considered that this means the consumer is under no obligation to enable the supplier to retrieve the goods and services but can treat them as his or her own property from the time of receipt. The Regulations now provide for this.

The reference for the consultation paper is URN 99/1257 and it is on the Internet at www.dti.gov.uk/cacp/ca/goodserv.htm.

The DTI advises that anyone who receives a demand for payment for unsolicited goods should report the matter to their local Trading Standards department.

What are Unsolicited Goods? 14.24

Inertia selling is defined in the *Consumer Protection (Distance Selling) Regulations 2000 (SI 2000/2334)* as to be where:

- unsolicited goods are sent to a person ('the recipient') with a view to his/her acquiring them;

- the recipient has no reasonable cause to believe that they were sent with a view to their being acquired for the purposes of a business; and

- the recipient has neither agreed to acquire nor agreed to return them.

Regulation 24 states:

'A person who, not having reasonable cause to believe there is a right to payment, in the course of any business makes a demand for payment, or asserts a present or prospective right to payment, for what he knows are:

- unsolicited goods sent to another person with a view to his acquiring them for purposes other than those of his business; or

- unsolicited services supplied to another person for purposes other than those of his business;

is guilty of an offence and liable, on summary conviction, to a fine not exceeding level 4 on the standard scale.'

The Regulations also prohibit in such cases the demanding of payment, the threatening of legal proceedings, the placing of an individual on a list of defaulters, or the invoking debt collection procedures.

Action for Companies 14.25

- Check if the *Consumer Protection (Distance Selling) Regulations 2000 (SI 2000/2334)* apply to the particular business.

- Are the goods or services excluded?

- Are the sales to consumers rather than businesses?

- Assuming the Regulations apply, check that the correct information is given to consumers.

- Check compliance with other requirements such as 30 day delivery dates.

- Ensure the right to cancel is implemented.

- Take legal advice in cases of doubt.

Future Legislation 14.26

In its guide to the Regulations the DTI list future legislation relevant in this field, the status of which is included at the time of publication.

- *E-commerce Directive* – implemented by the *Electronic Commerce (EC Directive) Regulations 2002 (SI 2002/2013)* on 21 August 2002.

- *Directive on Distance Marketing of Financial Services (2002/65/EC)* – to be implemented by 9 October 2004.

- Draft Directive on General Product Safety – currently being negotiated to amend existing such directives.

- Directive on Consumer Credit – currently under review.

- Brussels *Regulation 44/2001/EC* on jurisdiction – in force from 1 March 2002.

- Worldwide agreement on jurisdiction – currently under discussion in the Hague Conference on private international law.

Distance Selling and Financial Services 14.27

In June 2002 EU Ministers agreed the *Directive on the Distance Marketing of Financial Services* in the EU Council. Described as 'common rules for selling contracts for credit cards, investment funds, pension plans, etc. to consumers by phone, fax or Internet', the Commission described its main features as:

- the prohibition of abusive marketing practices seeking to oblige consumers to buy a service they have not solicited ('inertia selling');

- rules to restrict other practices such as unsolicited phone calls and e-mails ('cold calling' and 'spamming');

- an obligation to provide consumers with comprehensive information before a contract is concluded; and

- a consumer right to withdraw from the contract during a cooling off period, except in cases where there is a risk of speculation.

'Distance marketing' means selling by telephone, fax, proprietary computer networks and the Internet. A Directive regulating the distance selling of (all other) goods and services was adopted in 1997 and entered into force in 2000 (as discussed earlier in this chapter). Financial services were excluded from the scope of the 1997 Directive. The *Directive on the Distance Marketing of Financial Services (2002/65/EC)* prohibits 'inertia selling', which involves sending unsolicited financial products or services to a consumer and charging the consumer for their use.

'Cold faxing', or unsolicited communication about such products and services by fax is also prohibited.

The legislation gives EU Member States two optional ways of treating 'spamming' (unsolicited communication by e-mail) and 'cold calling' (the same practice by telephone). The Commission says 'Under the first option ('opt-in') cold calling and spamming are prohibited unless the consumer has expressly consented; under the second option ('opt-out') this is prohibited only if the consumer has signalled his/her objection, eg by entering his/her name in a registry set up for this purpose.' (See **33** OPT-IN AND OPT-OUT.)

Sellers of financial services and products are also obliged to provide consumers with a comprehensive package of information before an eventual contract is concluded. This package should include the identity, and contact details of the supplier, the price and payment arrangements, contractual rights and obligations, as well as information about the performance of the service offered. Information on the technical quality and nature of the financial service must also be provided in accordance with the rules of the Directives on credit, insurance and investment services or with relevant national rules for services not currently subject to Community legislation.

Cancellation of Financial Services Distance Contracts
14.28

The *Directive on the Distance Marketing of Financial Services (2002/65/EC)* also gives consumers the right to cancel a contract within 14 days after signing, extended in the case of life insurance and pension plans to 30 days. This right does not, however, apply to financial services which may be subject to price speculation, such as sales of foreign currency and securities. The Commission says that Member States may also exclude mortgage or property credit from this right of withdrawal from a contract. In addition, in the event of the fraudulent use of payment cards or other non-cash means of payment consumers will be able to cancel transactions and be entitled to reimbursement of any sums charged.

The *Directive on the Distance Marketing of Financial Services (2002/65/EC)* must be implemented by 9 October 2004.

Further Information
14.29

A DTI introductory guide for business is available on the DTI website (www.dti.gov.uk/ccp/topics1/guide/distsell.htm).

As stated above, the *Consumer Protection (Distance Selling) Regulations 2000 (SI 2000/2334)* are available on the Stationery Office website at www.hmso.gov.uk.

Copies of the introductory leaflet for business entitled 'Home Shopping: New Rights for Consumers' can be obtained by telephoning the DTI Order Line on 020 7215 6024. It can also be found on the DTI website at www.dti.gov.uk/cacp/ca/dsdbulletin.htm.

A 1999 consultation document on unsolicited goods laws is available from the DTI's website at www.dti.gov.uk/cacp/ca/goodserv.htm.

The DTI has also published a detailed booklet, entitled 'The Consumer Protection (Distance Selling) Regulations 2000 : A Guide for Business' (October 2000). This is also available from the DTI's Publications department by telephoning the Order Line above, or on the DTI website at www.dti.gov.uk/ccp/topics1/pdf1/bus_guide.pdf.

In October 2003 the DTI published a useful draft consultation paper *IT Consumer Contracts Made at a Distance – Guidance on Compliance with the Distance Selling and Unfair Terms in Consumer Contracts Regulations – A Consultation Paper OFT672*. The paper can be viewed at www.dti.gov.uk"

FAQs   14.30

Q1 Won't the unconditional right to cancel damage new dot.com home shopping businesses?

A Many home shopping websites already offer a no-quibble money back guarantee – and they are still in business. If you are selling a good, product or service at a competitive price, very few consumers are going to cancel.

Q2 I provide a gift-wrapping service and the option of express delivery – do I have to refund the cost of these services if the consumer cancels after delivery?

A Where delivery or gift-wrapping constitutes a separate and additional service, it cannot be cancelled once it has been carried out, but in our view normal delivery costs do have to be refunded following cancellation.

Q3 What about rogue consumers who use the goods and then cancel at the end of the cooling off period, and send the goods back in poor condition?

A The Regulations [*Consumer Protection (Distance Selling) Regulations 2000 (SI 2000/2334)*] are quite clear that the consumer is responsible for taking care of the goods if they decide to cancel. If the goods are damaged and not saleable as new, the supplier is entitled to seek recompense.

Q4 What if the consumer does not return the goods?

A The consumer has a duty to restore the goods to the supplier ie return them or make them available for collection. If he does not he is in breach of the law and the supplier can seek recompense. The Regulations do not require the consumer to return the goods but if the contract says he must and he does not, the supplier can charge the consumer for the direct costs of recovery.

Q5 I sell mobile phone contracts by mail order, these include a service and the phone – the cooling off periods are different for goods and services so how will this work?

A The Directive does not provide expressly for this situation. Our guidance is that if the hardware is given away or sold at a significantly discounted price the contract could be treated as one for service provision and cancellation would mean the phone must be returned too. So, the cooling off period would run for seven working days from the date of the contract.

If a phone is sold at full price with limited additional elements then probably the cancellation period for goods would apply, so that it ends seven working days after delivery of the phone.

Q6 Would the electronic purse type of card be covered under the 'payment card' definition?

A We understand that this type of card is like carrying cash in your pocket – if you lose it you have no more security than if you lose cash. The same applies to transactions made on the Internet using these cards.

Q7 What other laws apply to distance selling?

A All existing consumer legislation applies to distance selling, whether online or offline, just as it does to conventional shopping.

Some of the main consumer laws in force in the UK are:

- *Consumer Credit Act 1974* (as amended by the *Distance Selling Regulations*);
- *Consumer Protection Act 1987*;
- *Consumer Protection (Distance Selling) Regulations 2000 [SI 2000/2334]*;
- *Fair Trading Act 1973*;
- *General Product Safety Regulations 1994 [SI 1992/2328]*;
- *Package Travel, Package Holidays and Package Tours Regulations 1992 [SI 1992/3288]*;
- *Sale of Goods Act 1979*;
- *Supply of Goods and Services Act 1982*;
- *Timeshare Act 1992*;
- *Trade Descriptions Act 1968*;
- *Unfair Contract Terms Act 1977*;
- *Unfair Terms in Consumer Contracts Regulations 1999 [SI 1999/2083]*; and
- *Unsolicited Goods and Services Act 1971* (as amended by the *Distance Selling Regulations*).

Crown Copyright, Department of Trade and Industry

Chapter 15 – E-mails

At A Glance

✓ Marketing by e-mail is covered by the *Data Protection Act 1998* (*DPA 1998*).

✓ The *E-commerce Directive* and implementing legislation set out important rules in this area.

✓ The law on unsolicited emails and direct marketing is contained in the *Privacy and Electronic Communications (EC Directive) Regulations 2003 (SI 2003/2426)* and the E-privacy Directive (2002/58/EC).

✓ Information in e-mails may be 'personal data' and may need to be considered in dealing with a subject access request. Detailed guidance is available from the Commissioner.

Introduction   15.1

DPA 1998 applies to personal data in most forms, including that contained in e-mails. This section considers two different subjects:

• sending unsolicited e-mails; and

• subject access rights and information in e-mails.

Data controllers therefore need to ensure that their data protection policies and processes allow for this and that staff are told how to handle e-mails in this context. This chapter examines the law on the use of e-mail for marketing purposes and the sending of unsolicited e-mails. The *Privacy and Electronic Communications (EC Directive) Regulations 2003 (SI 2003/2426)* and the E-privacy Directive (2002/58/EC), on which the regulations were based, sets out the law in this area in the UK. This chapter also looks at the guidance given by the Information Commissioner on e-mails and subject access rights under *DPA 1998*.

Distance Selling Directive   15.2

Article 10.2 of the *Distance Selling Directive (97/7/EC)* provides that methods of distance selling other than faxes and automated calling machines may only be used where there is no clear objection from the consumer. However, the UK regulations implementing the Directive did not contain that provision (*Electronic Commerce (EC Directive) Regulations 2002 (SI 2002/2013)*. The UK, however, then implemented Directive 2002/58/EC by the *Privacy and Electronic Communications (EC Directive) Regulations 2003*, which set out the rules in this area. Consideration of an opt-in or an opt-out system (is given in **33 OPT-IN AND OPT-OUT**). In addition, there is the *Directive on the Distance Marketing of Financial Services (2002/65/EC)*, which must be implemented by 9 October 2004. (See **14 DISTANCE SELLING REGULATIONS.**)

The *Distance Selling Directive* covers unsolicited e-mails sent by businesses to consumers for the purposes of distance selling contracts under the Directive. Business to business e-mails are not covered, nor does the Directive cover all contracts. Financial service contracts are excluded and are covered under a separate directive.

The Directive defines a consumer as 'any natural person who, in contracts covered by this Directive, is acting for purposes which are outside his trade, business or profession'. The type of e-mail will determine whether the recipient has been sent it in the capacity of a consumer. An e-mail sent to someone at work about a business conference is clearly a business e-mail. One sent to them about family holidays at a resort would not be.

Codes for E-commerce   15.3

The Government is working with the Alliance for Electronic Business ('AEB') and the Consumers' Association, in consultation with the Office of Fair Trading, to develop:

● additional core principles to meet consumer concerns about e-commerce which will be developed further by the AEB and other bodies that issue e-commerce codes, including how consumers can avoid unsolicited e-mail;

● a new body, with the title of TrustUK, to accredit e-commerce codes that also accord with the core principles for codes described above;

● a 'hallmark' that accredited codes may use on their websites or incorporate into their logos;

● the use of existing links to establish international complaints handling networks;

● a way to market the e-commerce hallmark internationally;

● work with the European Commission to encourage the development of an EU-wide code; and

- work with the Organisation for Economic Co-operation and Development on its guidelines for consumer protection in e-commerce.

This aims to ensure the Government's intent that the UK provides the best environment in the world for electronic trading, as well as reducing the problems for consumers of unsolicited bulk e-mails.

Electronic Commerce Directive and Electronic Commerce (EC Directive) Regulations 2002   15.4

The *Electronic Commerce Directive (2000/31/EC)* ('*E-commerce Directive*') on certain legal aspects of information society services, in particular electronic commerce, in the Internal Market (OJ L178/1 17.7.2000) introduced some changes in this area considered in detail below. It is neutral on opt-in or opt-out as regards unsolicited e-mails. Where Member States permit unsolicited e-mails, *Article 6* of the *E-commerce Directive* requires them to ensure that service providers established on their territory make unsolicited e-mail clearly identifiable as such as soon as it shows up in the recipient's in-tray, in recognition of the additional communication costs of the recipient and the need to promote responsible filtering initiatives by industry.

The *Electronic Commerce (EC Directive) Regulations 2002 (SI 2002/2013)* brought the Directive into force on 21 August 2002. The DTI has issued a comprehensive set of guidance notes and a short guide for SMEs on the Regulations (see www.dti.gov.uk/cii/ecommerce/europeanpolicy/ecommerce_directive.shtml).

Other States' Rules   15.5

The Department of Trade and Industry ('DTI') say that a number of Member States (for example Austria, Italy, Germany and Sweden) either have or are likely to implement the e-mail provision of the *Distance Selling Directive* by opt-in, although others, such as Belgium, have gone for opt-out.

Article 2(f) of the *E-commerce Directive* defines 'commercial communications', such as advertising and direct marketing. *Article 6* makes these communications subject to certain transparency requirements to ensure consumer confidence and fair trading.

The DTI, in their August 2001 consultation document on the Directive, state that 'In order to allow individuals to deal more easily with unwanted intrusion, *Article 7* requires commercial communications by e-mail to be clearly identifiable and senders to consult and respect opt-out registers'. *Article 8* of the *E-commerce Directive* deals with regulated professions and requires them to respect certain rules of professional ethics in their use of commercial communications; these should be reflected in codes of conduct to be drawn up by professional associations.

In most EU Member States there is no obligation to indicate on a website that commercial communication is involved or to indicate on whose behalf it appears. The Directive requires the provider of the commercial communication to give contact details to assist the consumer in lodging and resolving complaints or securing enforcement by the authorities.

These rules were examined when the EU was seeking agreement, now reached, on the E-privacy Directive.

Unsolicited Commercial Communications Under the E-commerce Directive   15.6

The DTI says that

> 'Some commercial communication practices can be seen as intrusive and undermine the confident use of the Internet by consumers. The undisciplined sending of bulk e-mails can also impair the functioning of networks. Responsible and disciplined unsolicited advertising, respecting rules on the processing of the personal data of the target, is legitimate and well-established in most forms of communication (eg mail or telephone), subject to safeguards in law and self-regulatory practice. In the case of online advertising, the Directive depends on empowering the recipient and on industry codes of conduct as the first lines of defence against these risks'.

The Four Rules under the E-Commerce Directive 15.7

The *E-commerce Directive*, which has applied since 21 August 2002, brought four new rules which complement the *Data Protection Directive (95/46/EC)*, the *Distance Selling Directive (97/7/EC)* and the *Telecoms Data Protection Directive (97/66/EC)*, which is now largely superseded.

- *Article 5* requires all providers of information society services (including advertisers) to give at least their name, geographic address, e-mail contact details and the particulars of any supervisory authority to which they belong so that recipients of unwanted e-mails can readily take action to avoid receiving such communications in future.

- *Article 6* requires all commercial communications, solicited or unsolicited, to be identifiable as such, and also requires the senders to identify clearly the natural or legal person on whose behalf the e-mail was sent.

- *Article 7* provides that unsolicited commercial communications must be clearly identifiable as such as soon as they are received so that individuals or their Internet access service providers can delete them (or use filtering software to block or delete) without the need to read them.

- *Article* 7 also requires Member States to ensure that senders of unsolicited commercial communications consult regularly and respect opt-out registers through which individuals can indicate that they do not want to receive such communications.

The Information Commissioner will enforce these powers with regard to the fair processing of data and industry codes of conduct (as envisaged in *Article 16* of the *E-commerce Directive*). The powers are designed to provide a high level of legislative and self-regulatory safeguards against unwanted e-mail.

Opt-out Registers – Legal Obligation to Consult   15.8

The *E-commerce Directive* requires Member States to provide for senders of unsolicited commercial communications to 'consult regularly and respect the opt-out registers in which natural persons not wishing to receive such commercial communications can register themselves'.

Member States need to provide for this whether or not they effectively ban such communications by:

- having national opt-in arrangements;

- maintaining national opt-out systems; or

- having no national systems at all.

The Directive is careful to avoid specifying that opt-out should necessarily be operated on a national basis since this may not be the most effective way of dealing with cross-border communications in a global market.

Application of National Rules to Cross-border Unsolicited E-mail   15.9

The exclusion of the 'permissibility of unsolicited e-mail' from country of origin supervision in the Annex to the *E-commerce Directive* indicates that Member States may continue to choose to apply their own national controls, for example by enforcing an opt-in system. *Article 21(2)* of the *E-commerce Directive* provides for possible proposals in 2003 on 'the possibility of applying the internal market principles to unsolicited commercial communications by electronic mail' in the light of legal, technical and economic developments.

Unsolicited Commercial Communications in the UK under the Communications Directive and Privacy and Electronic Communications (EC Directive) Regulations 2003   15.10

The European Commission has adopted the *Directive on Privacy and Electronic Communications* ('*E-privacy Directive*') (*2002/58/EC*) which was implemented on 11 December 2003 (see **15.13** below). This provides for an opt-in with e-mails only being sent to those who have expressly chosen to receive them, a reversal of the currently perceived position under English law.

The DTI states:

> 'The UK's position has been that harmonised opt-in is a disproportion-ate response to the perceived problems of unsolicited commercial com-munications and that Member States should continue to be able to choose their approach at least until the outcome of that review. In the meantime, mail and e-mail addresses would, in many cases, be covered by data-protection legislation, enabling the Information Commissioner to take action on behalf of the individual.'

Main Bodies Involved   15.11

The DTI usefully lists the bodies involved in the UK with unsolicited e-mails in the 'Consultation Document on the Implementation of the E-Commerce Directive' (10 August 2001) (see www.dti.gov.uk/cii/ecommerce/europeanpol-icy/ecommerce_directive.shtml).

- **The Information Commissioner**

  Where a data controller processes personal data in the form of e-mail addresses subject to *DPA 1998* and continues to send unsolicited commer-cial communications to those individuals who have expressly advised the company concerned that they do not wish to receive such communications or have registered free with the e-mail Preference Service ('e-MPS') or another opt-out scheme, the Commissioner would take the view that this would involve unfair processing. The Commissioner has not received a sig-nificant number of complaints about this but could issue an Enforcement Notice (the breach of which would render the company liable for criminal prosecution and a fine of up to £5,000 in a Magistrates court for each breach) where it seemed the only way to ensure compliance in the face of persistent transgression. Sending unsolicited commercial communications has a low marginal cost, and there is an absence of public directories from which e-mail addresses could, in the absence of any indication to the con-trary, be collected fairly in the first place (unlike, for example, telephone or fax). Given that e-mail addresses often constitute personal data because they contain an individual's name, those capturing individuals' addresses should ensure that those individuals have an appreciation of any further use that might be made of the data.

The Information Commissioner also takes the view that direct marketing includes the promotion of an organisation's aims and ideals and that, therefore, e-mails canvassing for political or charitable purposes are direct marketing communications.

- **Direct Marketing Association ('DMA')**

Until now, promotion of the e-MPS has largely been online, but the DMA is considering ways to make the service more widely known, including the supply of information to citizens' advice bureaux, trading standards offices and direct-marketing companies for use by their customer services departments.

The DMA's online code for e-commerce stipulates that members must use the e-MPS and not send e-mail communications to individuals who have registered an objection to receiving such communications. In respect of this code, the DMA has obtained approval from TrustUK, a non-profit organisation run by the Alliance for Electronic Business (which includes the Confederation of British Industry, the Computing Software and Services Association, the DMA, e centre^{UK} and the Federation of the Electronics Industry) and the Consumers' Association.

- **Advertising Standards Authority ('ASA')**

Advertising and sales promotion in the non-broadcasting media in the UK is subject to a self-regulatory system of control overseen by the ASA. The ASA is an independent body, and the High Court has rejected an application for judicial review of its adjudication on the British Code of Advertising and Sales Promotion (the code of conduct drawn up by the advertising industry's Committee of Advertising Practice by which all advertisers agree to abide). The Code effectively requires companies involved in direct sales promotion to use their own, the e-MPS or another more appropriate preference service in respect of unsolicited e-mail.

- **Internet Service Providers Association ('ISPA')**

ISPA represents some 90% of the UK dial-up market for Internet access. It is currently preparing information for its website on how individuals can deal with unwanted e-mails and is also encouraging ISPA members to provide information to their users if they do not already do so. Many Internet service providers ('ISPs') already provide this information on their websites and in customer 'starter' packs. ISPs' customer services assist any individual reporting unsolicited commercial communications so far as they are able. ISPs' contract terms and conditions require all customers to comply with UK legislation. In addition, ISPs' Acceptable Use Policies form the basis for ISPs to manage between themselves the optimum functioning of their networks by setting out clear prohibitions against potentially disruptive unsolicited e-mails sent in bulk. Therefore, ISPA and its members have a number of avenues to reduce the incidence of unwanted unsolicited commercial communications through contractual relations, codes of conduct and peer pressure on ISPs that allow their subscribers to send such communications.

●   **The e-MPS**

The e-MPS is a global service hosted in the United States and supported by the DMA worldwide. It allows individuals to enter their details free on a register if they do not wish to receive unsolicited commercial communications and direct marketers to clean their names or e-mail addresses from lists of targets for a nominal charge, currently $100 per year (see www.e-mps.org).

Commercial and Spam E-mails and the Electronic Commerce (EC Directive) Regulations 2002   15.12

The *Electronic Commerce (EC Directive) Regulations 2002* (*SI 2002/2013*), which implemented the *E-commerce Directive* in the UK from 21 August 2002, deal with commercial communications and unsolicited e-mails in *Articles* 7 and 8. Reference should also be made to the DTI's guidance notes on the Regulations of which it has issued two sets – a short summary for SMEs and a set of detailed guidance notes.

'Commercial communications

7. A service provider shall ensure that any commercial communication provided by him and which constitutes or forms part of an information society service shall–

(*a*)   be clearly identifiable as a commercial communication;

(*b*)   clearly identify the person on whose behalf the commercial communication is made;

(*c*)   clearly identify as such any promotional offer (including any discount, premium or gift) and ensure that any conditions which must be met to qualify for it are easily accessible, and presented clearly and unambiguously; and

(*d*)   clearly identify as such any promotional competition or game and ensure that any conditions for participation are easily accessible and presented clearly and unambiguously.

Unsolicited commercial communications

8. A service provider shall ensure that any unsolicited commercial communication sent by him by electronic mail is clearly and unambiguously identifiable as such as soon as it is received.'

Reference should be made here to the general rules on opt-in and opt-out under *DPA 1998* (see **33 OPT-IN AND OPT-OUT**).

Privacy and Electronic Communications (EC Directive) Regulations 2003 and E-privacy Directive   15.13

The *E-privacy Directive* was implemented on 11 December 2003 by the *Privacy and Electronic Communications (EC Directive) Regulations 2003*. The *E-privacy Directive* sets out new legislative provisions in *Article 13* as follows.

'Article 13

Unsolicited communications

...

2. Notwithstanding paragraph 1 [which deals with automated calling systems], where a natural or legal person obtains from its customers their electronic contact details for electronic mail, in the context of the sale of a product or a service, in accordance with Directive 95/46/EC, the same natural or legal person may use these electronic contact details for direct marketing of its own similar products or services provided that customers clearly and distinctly are given the opportunity to object, free of charge and in an easy manner, to such use of electronic contact details when they are collected and on the occasion of each message in case the customer has not initially refused such use.

3. Member States shall take appropriate measures to ensure that, free of charge, unsolicited communications for purposes of direct marketing, in cases other than those referred to in paragraphs 1 and 2, are not allowed either without the consent of the subscribers concerned or in respect of subscribers who do not wish to receive these communications, the choice between these options to be determined by national legislation.'

The effect of paragraphs 2 and 3 is that where a business has sold goods or services to a customer it can market to them if the customer has been allowed to object when the data is collect (*E-privacy Directive, Art 2*). However, where the data is bought in from a third party no such emails can be sent without consent.

Article 13 of the Directive goes on to deal with other direct marketing issues:

'4. In any event, the practice of sending electronic mail for purposes of direct marketing disguising or concealing the identity of the sender on whose behalf the communication is made, or without a valid address to which the recipient may send a request that such communications cease, shall be prohibited.

5. Paragraphs 1 and 3 shall apply to subscribers who are natural persons. Member States shall also ensure, in the framework of Community law and applicable national legislation, that the legitimate interests of sub-

scribers other than natural persons with regard to unsolicited communications are sufficiently protected.'

This was then implemented in the UK implementing regulations as follows (see also **Chapter 13** and **Appendix 8**, which includes the IC's guidance on the regulations as regards unsolicited emails):

'22—(1) This regulation applies to the transmission of unsolicited communications by means of electronic mail to individual subscribers. [From here it is clear unsolicited emails to corporate subscribers are completely excluded. This means spam email to people at work will largely continue unabated and this has drawn much criticism. Nor is there any definition of an individual subscriber]

'3.6 Except in the circumstances referred to in paragraph (3), a person shall neither transmit, nor instigate the transmission of, unsolicited communications for the purposes of direct marketing by means of electronic mail unless the recipient of the electronic mail has previously notified the sender that he consents for the time being to such communications being sent by, or at the instigation of, the sender.

'3.7 A person may send or instigate the sending of electronic mail for the purposes of direct marketing where—

'3.7.1 that person has obtained the contact details of the recipient of that electronic mail in the course of the sale or negotiations for the sale of a product or service to that recipient; [This means an unsolicited email to an individual subscriber can only be sent if that person was a previous customer in addition to the requirements below].

'3.7.2 the direct marketing is in respect of that person's similar products and services only; and

'3.7.3 the recipient has been given a simple means of refusing (free of charge except for the costs of the transmission of the refusal) the use of his contact details for the purposes of such direct marketing, at the time that the details were initially collected, and, where he did not initially refuse the use of the details, at the time of each subsequent communication'.

A subscriber shall not permit his line to be used in contravention of *paragraph (2)*.

Regulation 23 prohibits the sending of communications by means of electronic mail for the purposes of direct marketing where the identity of the person on whose behalf the communication is made has been disguised or concealed or an address to which requests for such communications to cease may be sent has not been provided.

Regulation 24 sets out certain information that must be provided for the purposes of *regulations 19, 20* and *21*.

Data Protection and Access to Information in E-mails 15.14

Under *section 7* of *DPA 1998* data subjects have a right of access to much of the data held about them. (On this topic generally see **43 SUBJECT ACCESS REQUESTS**.) The Information Commissioner under *section 42* of *DPA 1998* has a duty to examine forms of processing and offer guidance. She has now issued such guidance in relation to access to personal data held in e-mails, and this guidance is summarised below. Importantly, data controllers do need to consider *section 7* in relation to information in e-mails; they can require data subjects who are exercising their rights to help identify the information required, and in extreme cases the controller may have to retrieve information in a deleted e-mail (this is technically possible).

An organisation which operates an e-mail system falls within the definition of a data controller if the e-mails processed or stored within its system identify living individuals and either:

● are held in automated form in live, archive or back-up systems, or have been 'deleted' from the live system but are still capable of recovery; or

● are stored, as print outs, in relevant filing systems (that is non-automated or 'manual' systems, organised according to criteria relating to individuals and allowing ready access to specific pieces of information).

In some cases data controllers may be able to take advantage of the transitional provisions contained in *DPA 1998*. In brief, transitional relief may be claimed if the processing of personal data was already underway immediately before 24 October 1998.

Some protection by the transitional relief provisions expired on 23 October 2001. The decision in *Durant v Financial Services Authority [2003] EWCA Civ 1746* may require some of the guidance of the IC in this area to be revised, but that had not yet occurred at the time of writing.

Making Assessments 15.15

In making an assessment of an alleged failure by a data controller to give access to personal data held in e-mails, the Commissioner will consider a number of questions including the following.

'(*a*) Has the data subject provided sufficient information to the data controller to enable him to locate the data in question?

(*b*) Do the e-mails exist?

(c)   Do they contain personal data covered by the Act?

(d)   Do they contain personal data relating to third parties and, if so, should this information be withheld or disclosed?

(e)   What information (other than a copy of the personal data) should be provided in response to a subject access request?

(f)   If access has not been granted, should enforcement action be taken?'

Each of these questions is considered in turn in the guidance from the Commissioner as set out at **15.16** below.

Information Needed to Find the Data   15.16

Sometimes data subjects are trying to be difficult and they ask for all data held about them. *Section 7(3) of DPA 1998* states that:

'Where a data controller–

(a)   reasonably requires further information in order to satisfy himself as to the identity of the person making a request under this section and to locate the information which that person seeks ...

the data controller is not obliged to comply with the request unless he is supplied with that further information.'

In most cases an open-ended request will not satisfy this provision.

Information which may assist the data controller might include:

- the fact that the data may be held in the form of e-mails;

- the names of the authors and recipients of the messages;

- the subjects of the e-mails;

- the dates or range of dates upon which the messages have been sent;

- whether it is believed that e-mails are held as 'live' data or in archived or back-up form; and

- any other information which may assist the data controller in locating the data.

In making an assessment, the Commissioner has to take a view on whether the data subject has failed to provide information that the data controller reasonably needs to narrow down the search. If so, then it is likely to be concluded that there has been no breach of *DPA 1998*. By contrast, where a data controller appears to be making demands for information which the data subject cannot reasonably be expected to give and where it appears that a copy of at least some of the personal data requested could be provided, then it is likely to be judged that there has been a breach, the Commissioner says.

Does the E-mail Exist?   15.17

Sometimes the individual data subject states that there is information they have not been given but they know it is there. Where the evidence submitted by the data subject showing that the e-mails in question exist or existed in the past is inconclusive, the Commissioner must form a judgement based not only on the information supplied but also upon other similar cases, particularly ones involving the same data controller.

If the Commissioner is satisfied that the e-mails are likely to exist, 'then the alleged failure to respond to the access request will generally be put to the data controller for comment. E-mails may be held locally, for instance on a stand-alone PC, and not be immediately accessible by data protection officers/systems administrators. In putting the concerns of data subjects to data controllers, therefore, the Commissioner will seek to ascertain that a proper search has been carried out for the e-mails in question.'

Do the E-mails Contain Personal Data Covered by the Act?   15.18

This is an interesting question, and the Commission says there are a number of different aspects to it. In particular, it will be important to determine whether the transitional provisions are relevant and whether the e-mails are held in the form of 'live' data or otherwise, for instance as back-up or archive data.

E-mails are caught if they contain information about identifiable living individuals unless they have been printed off, deleted and stored in manual filing systems falling outside the scope of *DPA 1998* (for instance references to an individual in the e-mailed minutes of a meeting which have been printed off and stored on the 'Meetings File').

In all other cases with the implementation of *DPA 1998*, the e-mails will be caught because of the ending of provisions contained in the *Data Protection Act 1984 (DPA 1984)*, in particular:

- the text preparation exception which took outside the scope of *DPA 1984* the processing of personal data for the sole purpose of the preparation of the text of a document;

- the exemption relating to back-up data; and

- the part of the definition of 'processing' which specified that in order to process personal data, processing must take place 'by reference to the data subject'.

Even though data may have been 'deleted' from the live system, the e-mails will be caught if they can be recovered by, say, the systems administrator before their final destruction.

'A "deleted" e-mail may still constitute personal data if it can be retrieved, albeit with some difficulty, by the data controller', the Commissioner says. Some e-mails contain personal data but fall outside the scope of *DPA 1998* since those data are not processed by reference to the data subject. An example may be a reference to an individual in the minutes of a meeting which are kept as a record of the meeting. This is an example given by the Commissioner. Others will clearly fall within the scope of the Act, for instance where the name of the data subject appears in the title of the e-mail or she/he is the sender or recipient. Other cases will be less clear cut.

However, the Data Protection Tribunal decision in the Equifax enforcement case *Equifax Europe Ltd v Data Protection Registrar (June 1991)* helps, the Commissioner says. This suggests that if an e-mail is stored because it contains information about an individual and may be accessed to discover information about an individual then processing takes place by reference to the data subject regardless of how the search is carried out.

Third Party Data and Human Rights 15.19

E-mails often contain personal data about third parties. In responding to subject access requests, therefore, controllers will need to have regard to the tests set out in *section 7(4)–(6)* of *DPA 1998*. In making assessments, the Commissioner will seek to assure herself that the tests have been properly applied as they would whenever a record contains information relating to a third party.

In addition, the Commissioner will consider the effect of *Article 8* of the *European Convention on Human Rights*. This specifies that:

'Everyone has the right to respect for his private and family life, his home and his correspondence'

and:

'There shall be no interference by a public authority with the exercise of this right except such as in accordance with the law and is necessary in a democratic society in the interests of national security ... or for the protection of the rights and freedoms of others.'

On an area where there has been a lot of recent publicity, the Commissioner writes:

'If an e-mail was written in a private rather than an official capacity, then it is likely that only exceptional circumstances will justify disclosure of third party information without the consent of the individual concerned.

Cases which involve possible breaches of Article 8 provisions will be considered on their individual merits.'

Other Section 7 Rights 15.20

Section 7 of *DPA 1998* is the section which gives individuals the right of access to their data. It also contains a number of rights in addition to the right to be given a copy of personal data. In particular, individuals have the right to be informed whether they are the subject of personal data being processed by the controller and, if so, to be given a description of:

- the personal data in question;

- the purposes of the processing;

- the recipients or classes of recipients; and

- the sources of the personal data (if known to the controller).

It can be hard for the controller to reconstitute data which has been deleted from a live system in order to provide a copy. However, it may still be able to provide some of this information. In particular, it may be helpful to explain that the purposes of the processing are to erase the data and that only in exceptional circumstances would those data be reconstituted and used for other purposes (for instance as evidence in serious criminal cases or as evidence in industrial tribunals).

Good Practice Tip 15.21

'As a matter of good practice controllers should develop clear policies as to the circumstances under which they would reconstitute "deleted" data before they are faced with subject access requests.'

Information Commissioner Guidance on Data Protection Act and E-mails

The Commissioner's Enforcement Policy 15.22

The following is the Information Commissioner's policy on enforcement.

Unless the personal data contained in e-mails are covered by the transitional provisions in *DPA 1998*, in principle data subjects have a right of access and the Commissioner has the power to take enforcement action in the event of non-compliance. Notices are not served automatically, however, and in deciding whether it is proper in particular cases to serve a notice, the Commissioner will take a number of factors into account.

She will consider first whether the data controller has been given sufficient evidence to locate the data. If transitional relief is available to the data controller, exempting back-up data and processing which does not take place by reference to the data subject, this question may be relatively simple. If the Commissioner considers that the controller can locate the data but has not provided a copy to the data subject then she will be more inclined to recommend enforcement.

If transitional relief is not available and *DPA 1998* extends to data not held on 'live systems', then the data subject may have had to provide more information to enable the data controller to locate the data. Data held other than on 'live systems' may include back-up data and data which have been 'deleted' but not yet finally erased.

In practice, however, the Commissioner might exercise her discretion and not seek to enforce a data subject's rights if she is satisfied that to give access would involve disproportionate effort on the part of the controller. In forming a judgement as to whether the effort involved would be disproportionate, she will consider the following.

- What is the nature of the data and the likely effect on the individual if the data are or are not retrieved? The more serious the possible effect, the more likely it will be that the Commissioner will take action.

- What is the controller's policy in relation to archive or other 'non-live' data? If it is to retrieve data only in exceptional circumstances (for example serious criminal allegations) then it may be disproportionate to have to retrieve data in response to a request from a data subject who only wants a copy out of interest. In attempting to determine what a data controller's policy is, the Commissioner may request sight of policy documents and/or an account of the practices followed by the controller in the past.

- How hard would it be for the controller to retrieve the data? Is it possible to retrieve small amounts of data or is it necessary to reconstitute large computer archives? How much will it cost?

- In the case of back-up data is there any evidence to suppose that this version differs materially from that held on the live system?

Summary   15.23

The Commissioner's approach is that where e-mails are held on live systems and can be located, she will seek to enforce subject access if this has been denied. Where data are held elsewhere, the Commissioner will weigh the interests of the data subject against the effort that the controller would have to take to recover the data and in many instances may be likely to decide not to take action.

The decision not to take action does not imply that a complaint will not be assessed nor does it deny the individual the right to seek access through the courts.

Further Information   **15.24**

See also **29 INTERNET, 34 OPT-IN AND OPT-OUT** and **44 SUBJECT ACCESS REQUESTS**, and the Commissioner's guidance on the Internet on her website. See **38 RECORDING TELEPHONE CALLS AND E-MAILS** for Part 4 of the Employment Code relating to rules on surveillance of employee communications.

The Information Commissioner

The Office of the Information Commissioner Wycliffe House Water Lane Wilmslow Cheshire SK9 5AF Tel: 01625 545 700 Fax: 01625 524510 E-mail: data@dataprotection.gov.uk Website: www.informationcommissioner.gov.uk

Useful Internet Addresses

DTI Guidance Notes on the Electronic Commerce (EC Directive) Regulations 2002	www.dti.gov.uk/cii/ecommerce/euro-peanpolicy/ecommerce_directive.shtml

Directives

Directive 95/46/EC of the European Parliament and of the Council of 24 October 1995 on the protection of individuals with regard to the processing of personal data and on the free movement of such data (OJ L 281, 23.11.1995, p 31)
Directive 97/7/EC of the European Parliament and of the Council of 24 May 1997 on the protection of consumers in respect of distance contracts (OJ L 1444, 4.6.1997 p 19)
Directive 97/66/EC of the European Parliament and of the Council of 15 December 1997 concerning the processing of personal data and the protection of privacy in the telecommunications sector (OJ L 24, 30.1.98, p 1) largely superseded by Directive 2002/58/EC
Directive 2000/31/EC of the European Parliament and of the Council of 8 June 2000 on certain legal aspects of information society services, in particular electronic commerce, in the Internal Market (Directive on electronic commerce – 'E-commerce Directive') (OJ L 178/1, 17.7.2000, p 1)

Directive 2002/58/EC of the European Parliament and of the Council of 12 July 2002 concerning the processing of personal data and the protection of privacy in the electronic communications sector (Directive on privacy and electronic communications – 'E-privacy Directive') (OJ 31.7.02 L201/37)Implemented by the Privacy and Electronic Communications (EC Directive) Regulations 2003

Directive 2002/65/EC of the European Parliament and Council of 13 September 2002 concerning the distance marketing of consumer financial services (OJ 9.10.02 L271.16)

FAQS

Can we send unsolicited e-mails to potential customers legally?

Yes, under current law, provided they have not objected. The *E-privacy Directive (2002/58/EC)* when in force will prevent your doing this without express consent, except to your own customers, but this has not yet been implemented in the UK.

Are e-mails subject to *section 7* subject access rights under *DPA 1998*?

Yes, the Information Commissioner has issued guidance on this subject which is considered in this chapter.

Do we need to put anything about privacy on the footer of our e-mails?

Probably not, unlike on your website where a privacy policy is a good idea. You may want to add that the information is confidential and add a disclaimer. It is possible you might want to warn the other party that the e-mail may be read not just by the recipient but also by other members of staff.

Chapter 16 –
Employment

At A Glance

✓ Employers handle lots of personal data and the Information Commissioner has issued an Employment Practices Data Protection Code.

✓ In 2002 the European Commission began consulting on employer surveillance and e-mails.

✓ There is a staff administration exemption from the *Data Protection Act 1998 (DPA 1998)* under the *Data Protection (Notification and Notification Fees) Regulations 2000 (SI 2000/188)* which may keep some employers outside of the obligation to notify under *DPA 1998*.

✓ An exemption under *Schedule 7* to *DPA 1998* exists for certain confidential employment references, providing exemption from the subject access provisions in *section 7* of *DPA 1998*.

✓ Those exporting personal data of employees from the European Economic Area ('EEA') should obtain their consent and comply with the Eighth Data Protection Principle.

✓ Under *section 61* of *DPA 1998* directors can be personally liable for certain offences under the Act.

✓ Under *paragraph 10* of *Schedule 1* to *DPA 1998* employers must take proper steps to ensure that their employees who will have access to personal data are suitable.

Introduction   16.1

Employers handle large amounts of personal data. Most need to have notified their holding of data with the Information Commissioner. This chapter examines the principal ways in which *DPA 1998* will apply to employers and their employees. Credit reference issues in this context are dealt with in **7 CREDIT REFERENCES AND ACCESS TO CREDIT FILES** and are therefore not included here. On 13 September 2001 the European Commission issued Opinion 8/2001 'on the processing of personal data in the employment context' (5062/01/EN/Final WP

48). In order to contribute to the uniform application of the national measures adopted under the *Data Protection Directive (95/46/EC)*, the Working Party has set up a subgroup to examine this question and has adopted an extensive document. In 2002 it began consulting on employer surveillance of employee e-mails (see www.europa.eu.int/yourvoice).

In late 2000 the Information Commissioner began issuing an Employment Practices Data Protection Code. Parts 1, 2 and 23 have been finalised and Part 4 (Medical Records) was issued for consultation to be agreed in 2004. The guidance provides some useful pointers, some of which are examined in this chapter.

Manual Records   16.2

DPA 1998 covers some manual records as well as computer records. The Commissioner says in the Employment Practices Data Protection Code that it is likely that many employment records, because of their structured nature, will come within the scope of the Act even if they are paper-based, but some will not.

Durant v Financial Services Authority [2003] EWCA Civ 1746 is likely to lead to changes to the guidance discussed in this chapter, in due course, about what manual data is caught. In February 2004 further guidance on manual data and its interpretation since the case was issued by the IC, which is considered in CHAPTER 30. It found that most employment records held in manual form are likely to be outside the *DPA 1998*. This is extremely important for those involved with human resources and most of the guidance described in this chapter will need to be reassessed by the IC in 2004 in the light of the *Durant* case. It is best to take legal advice before implementing expensive data protection policies, particularly if they relate to manual data which may not fall within the Act at all.

The Act applies to manual data which is part of a relevant fling system. The questions asked about employment and other data are:

1.   Whether the material was a set of information relating to an individual?

2.   Whether the material was structured either by reference to individuals or by reference to criteria relating to individuals? and

3.   Whether it was structured in such a way that specific information relating to a particular individual was readily accessible?

The judgment summarised the meaning of 'a relevant filing system' as a 'system':

'1)   in which the files forming part of it are structured or referenced in such a way as to clearly indicate at the outset of the search whether specific information capable of amounting to personal data of an individual requesting it under *section* 7 is held within the system and, if so, in which file or files it is held; and

2)   which has, as part of its own structure or referencing mechanism, a
        sufficiently sophisticated and detailed means of readily indicating
        whether and where in an individual file or files specific criteria or
        information about the applicant can be readily located'.

Importance of the Code   16.3

The Commissioner will take into account the extent to which an employer has
complied with the Employment Practices Data Protection Code when determining whether there has been a breach of the Principles and, if there has, whether
formal action is appropriate.

General Issues Under DPA 1998   16.4

There are some types of personal data where it does not matter too much if the
data is incorrect. In an employment record, for example, the name of the
employee's wife is not particularly material, although even that may become
important if death benefits have to be paid. Those who have bought a car from a
supplier may move house. It is not important if their new address is not changed
and the personal data record is not up-to-date. However, with disciplinary matters in employment accuracy is very important indeed, and it is likely that
employees will increasingly use failure to comply with data protection obligations
against employers in unfair dismissal cases.

Within many companies it is most frequently the human resources department
which has to address data protection legal issues, and often the data protection
manager within an organisation is involved in the personnel side of the company.

Staff Administration Exemption   16.5

The *Schedule* to the *Data Protection (Notification and Notification Fees) Regulations
2000 (SI 2000/188)* includes an exemption for staff administration. This is an
exemption from the requirement of the employer to notify (register) under *DPA
1998*. However, most employers will find they have to register because of some
other use of data within their business as a whole.

The exemption is from the requirement to notify, not from compliance with all
the principles of *DPA 1998* in relation to that data. So, for example, it will still be
necessary to comply with the Eight Data Protection Principles, such as keeping
data safe and secure and up-to-date.

The staff administration exemption is for processing:

- for the purposes of appointments or removals, pay, discipline, superannuation, work management or other personnel matters in relation to the staff of
  the data controller;

- of personal data in respect of which the data subject is:

  ○   a past, existing or prospective member of staff, or

  ○   any person, the processing of whose personal data is necessary for the exempt purposes;

- personal data which is the name, address and other identifiers of the data subject or information about qualifications, work experience or pay or other matters, the processing of which is necessary for exempt purposes;

- which does not involve disclosure of the personal data to any third party other than with the data subject's consent or where necessary to make the disclosure for the exempt purposes; and

- does not involve keeping the personal data after the relationship between the data controller and the staff member ends, unless and for as long as is necessary for the exempt purposes.

Note that these requirements must all be met before this provision applies.

Staff   16.6

The *Data Protection (Notification and Notification Fees) Regulations 2000 (SI 2000/188)* define staff as including employees or office holders, workers under *section 296* of the *Trade Union and Labour Relations (Consolidation) Act 1992*, people working under any contract for services and volunteers.

Third Party   16.7

The exemption only applies where there is no disclosure to a third party except with the data subject's consent or where this is necessary for the exempt purposes.

However, in the Notification Handbook the Commissioner states the limitations of this exemption.

> '**Your data subjects are restricted to** any person the processing of whose personal data is necessary for staff administration.
>
> **Your data classes are restricted to** data which are necessary for staff administration.
>
> **Your disclosures other than those made with the consent of the data subject are restricted to** those third parties which are necessary for staff administration.
>
> **Retention of the data:** The personal data are not kept after the relationship between you and the data subjects ends, unless and for so long as it is necessary to do so for staff administration.'

Notwithstanding these limitations, some companies will be able to rely on this exemption and may not even have to be registered under *DPA 1998*. However, if a business should have registered or notified and has not, it is still legally obliged to comply with the principles of the Act, including the right of subject access in *section* 7 of *DPA 1998*.

Confidential Employment References   16.8

Paragraph 1 of *Schedule 7* to *DPA 1998* provides that references given in confidence by the data controller are exempt, but only from the subject access provisions in *section 7* of *DPA 1998*. They are not exempt from all the other provisions of the Act. The reference must relate to education, training or employment, or prospective such matters of the data subject, the appointment or prospective appointment of the data subject to any office, or the provision or prospective provision by the data subject of any service. The last category is not an employment one.

Note that this provision only applies to confidential references. In addition, it only applies to references given by the data controller. If the data controller has on its file, after checking an employee's past employment history, references written by a former employer, the employee can obtain those from the new employer under *section* 7 of *DPA 1998*. The Commissioner's 'Introduction to *DPA 1998*' (accessible at www.informationcommissioner.gov.uk), page 25 says that 'the exemption is not available for such references when they are received by the data controller'.

Credit references are considered in **7 CREDIT REFERENCES AND ACCESS TO CREDIT FILES.**

There are special exemptions from *DPA 1998* for Crown Employment, judicial appointments and the armed forces which are not addressed here.

In Part 1: Recruitment and Selection of the Employment Practices Data Protection Code the Information Commissioner says the following on references.

> **'Isn't there an exemption in the Act for confidential references?**
>
> There is no such general exemption from the right of subject access. There is, however, a special exemption from the right of access to a confidential reference from the organisation which gave it. This exemption does not apply once the reference is in the hands of person or organisation to whom the reference has been given. The recipient is, though, entitled to take steps to withhold information that reveals the identity of third parties such as the author of the reference.'

Part 2: Records Management of the Code, section 10 on references states that 'Employers give a variety of references about workers (both current and former); for example, character references may be given in connection with legal proceedings, and financial references may be given in connection with a mortgage application. References are also given to prospective new employers.'

Employers should be aware of the difference between a reference given in a personal capacity and one given in a corporate capacity. A corporate reference is one given on behalf of the employer by one of its staff. Many employers have rules about who can give such a reference and what it can include. The employer is still legally responsible for making sure data protection standards are met. A personal reference is one given by a member of staff in an individual capacity. It may refer to work done but it is not given on behalf of the employer. References that are given in a personal capacity do not, at least in data protection terms, incur a liability for the employer.

Under a special exemption in *DPA 1998*, a worker does not have the right to request access to a confidential job reference from the organisation which has given it. However, once the reference is with the recipient then no such special exemption from the right of access exists, although the recipient is entitled to take steps to protect the identity of third parties such as the author of the reference.

Standards: Confidential Employee References   16.9

The following standards are proposed by the Information Commissioner.

1. Set out a clear company policy stating who can give corporate references, in what circumstances, and the standards that apply to the granting of access to them. Make anyone who is likely to become a referee aware of this policy.

2. Avoid providing confidential references about a worker unless you are sure that this is the worker's wish. Corporate referees must be confident that the individual has named them as referee.

3. As far as possible, establish at the time a worker's employment ends whether or not the worker wishes references to be provided to future employers or to others.

4. Be prepared to give access to corporate references you have provided even though in some cases *DPA 1998* allows for their exemption from subject access.

5. When responding to a request from an individual to see his or her own reference, make a judgement as to what information it is reasonable to release concerning the identities of third parties, using the guidelines given later in this Code [Employment Practices Data Protection Code].

Notes and examples

1. It is in the employer's interest to make clear to staff and even former staff the limits it places on their authority to give corporate references. A good indicator of whether a reference has been given in a corporate

capacity is if it is written on corporate headed notepaper with the referee providing his or her job title.

2. The provision of references on workers is common practice but they do contain personal information, often of a private nature. Employers should therefore be sure that the worker is content for a reference to be provided. Requests that are clearly from reputable businesses and which request that the reference is returned to a recognised address can generally be taken at face value, but if there are any doubts the employer should check with the worker.

3. This should help to clarify the expectations of workers who leave. If a worker wishes for references to be provided in future caution should still be exercised as to whom references should be provided.

4. Good data protection practice is to be as open as possible with workers about information which relates to them. Workers should be able to challenge information that they consider to be inaccurate or misleading, particularly when, as in the case of a reference, this may have an adverse impact on them.

5. When considering the release of such information, bear in mind that the release of information that identifies the author of a reference in his or her business capacity rather than in a private capacity is less likely to intrude on his or her private life.

Export of Data and Employees   16.10

One area which employers have to watch carefully is sending personal data about employees abroad. The Eighth Data Protection Principle prohibits export to countries outside the EEA except where there is adequate protection. If the employee consents to the export then it is allowed. A clause should therefore be considered in employment contracts, in contracts with employment agencies and on application forms for jobs.

Data export by employers is addressed in the Employment Practices Data Protection Code. Often employers will send employee details abroad.

Liability of Directors   16.11

An officer of a company proven to have committed a breach of *DPA 1998* through his or her neglect or with their consent is guilty of an offence under *section 61* of *DPA 1998*. This applies to directors, managers, secretaries or similar officers or anyone acting in their capacity.

Checking Up on Employees 16.12

The data controller must take reasonable steps to ensure the reliability of any employees of his who have access to the personal data (*DPA 1998, Sch 1, Part II, para 10*). *DPA 1998* does not say what those steps should be. Under the *Data Protection Act 1984* (*DPA 1984*), which included an identical such provision, the following questions were recommended to be asked, in guidance of the Registrar.

- Is proper weight given to the discretion and integrity of staff when they are considered for employment or promotion or a move to an area where they have access to personal data?

- Are staff aware of their responsibilities? (A compliance or education programme on the Act will help with this.)

- Do disciplinary rules and procedures take account of the Act's requirements and are they enforced?

- If the employee is found to be unreliable, is his access to personal data immediately withdrawn?

Part 4 of the Employment Practices Data Protection Code deals with surveillance of employees – see **38 RECORDING TELEPHONE CALLS AND E-MAILS.**

Advertisement 16.13

Individuals send confidential data, sometimes comprising sensitive personal data, to prospective employers after seeing job advertisements. In the Employment Practices Data Protection Code the Information Commissioner suggests the following standards to be used in the advertisement.

Standards: Advertisement 16.14

Advertising includes any method used to notify potential applicants of a specific job vacancy or range of vacancies, using such media as notices, newspapers, radio, television and the internet.

The benchmarks

1. Inform individuals responding to job advertisements of the name of the organisation to which they will be providing their information and how it will be used unless this is self-evident.

2. Recruitment agencies, used on behalf of an employer, must identify themselves and explain how personal data they receive will be used and disclosed unless this is self-evident.

3. On receiving identifiable particulars of applicants from an agency ensure, as soon as you can, that the applicants are aware of the name of the organisation now holding their information.

Notes and examples

1. Individuals providing personal data in response to a job advertisement, even if only giving their name and address, should be aware of who they are giving their details to. They should be made aware of this before they supply their details. Individuals should not be asked simply to provide their details to a PO Box Number or to an inadequately identified answering machine or website. Provide this explanation:

   a. in the advertisement if postal, fax or e-mail responses are sought;

   b. in the advertisement or at the start of the telephone call if telephone responses are sought;

   c. on the website before personal data are collected via an online application form.

   Advertisements for specific jobs need not state how the information supplied will be used, provided that this is self-evident. Only where the link between the information being asked for and its potential use is unclear need an explanation be given. For example, if an advertisement for a specific job simply asks those interested to send in personal details and these might also be passed on to a sister company to see if it has any suitable vacancies, this should be explained in the advertisement.

2. Where a recruitment agency places an advertisement on behalf of an employer, the identity of the agency must be given. The agency must also be identified as such if this is not apparent from its name.

   The agency should also inform the applicant if it intends to use the information supplied by the applicant for some purpose of which the applicant is unlikely to be aware, for example where the information will be used to market goods or services to the applicant. If the information supplied in response to a recruitment advertisement is to be retained for use in connection with future vacancies, the advertisement should make this clear.

3. An advertisement placed by a recruitment agency need not show the identity of the employer on whose behalf it is recruiting. The agency may pass information to the employer provided that the applicant understands that his or her details will be passed on. Once the employer receives identifiable particulars it must, as soon as it can, inform the applicant of its identity and of any uses it might make of the information received that are not self-evident. It can arrange for the agency to provide this explanation on its behalf.

   If for whatever reason the employer does not want to be identified to the applicant at an early stage in the recruitment process, it is acceptable for the agency to only send anonymised information about a candidate to the employer, and for the agency or employer to provide information as to the employer's identity once the employer has expressed interest in receiving personally identifiable information about the applicant.

Collecting and Keeping Employment Records
16.15

The Information Commissioner, in Part 2 of the Employment Practices Data Protection Code, looks at general obligations for employers as regards the keeping of records, as well as records in particular categories. This section is concerned with the collection of information, particularly about new workers, and with ensuring that records are and remain accurate. The following standards are proposed for workers, with explanatory notes below.

Standards: Collecting and Keeping Employment Records
16.16

The benchmarks

1. Ensure that newly appointed workers are aware of the nature and source of any information kept about them, how it will be used and who it will be disclosed to.

2. Inform new workers and remind existing workers about their rights under *DPA 1998*, including their right of access to the information kept about them.

3. Ensure that there is a clear and foreseeable need for any information collected about workers and that the information collected actually meets that need.

4. Provide each worker with a copy of information that may be subject to change, eg personal details such as home address, annually or allow workers to view this online. Ask workers to check their records for accuracy and ensure any necessary amendments are made to bring records up-to-date.

5. Incorporate accuracy, consistency and validity checks into systems.

Notes and examples

1. It is not generally necessary to seek a worker's consent to keep employment records. It will usually be sufficient to ensure that the worker is aware that records are being kept and is given an explanation of the purposes they are kept for and the nature of any intended disclosures unless these details are self-evident. However, if sensitive data are collected, then consent may be necessary.

2. One way of doing this is to prepare a fact sheet for workers telling them how information about them will be used, and of their right of access to it.

3. For example, employers often require an emergency contact to be used should a worker be taken ill at work. If they ask for 'next of kin' they will not necessarily obtain the information needed.

---

4. Some employers may decide that it is not practicable to provide each worker with a copy of their personal details annually. If so they must ensure they have an effective alternative for ensuring records are kept accurate and up to date. In some cases employers may be able to take advantage of the capabilities of automated systems. For example, workers' PCs could prompt them to check their personal details from time to time and require them to acknowledge that they have done so. Employers must be prepared to give access to records when a worker makes a subject access request, but employers should not rely on this alone as a means of ensuring accuracy.

5. For example, a computerised personnel system could have a built-in facility to automatically query the input date of birth of workers, high-lighting ages above or below the normal working age. Similar 'flagging' can be used to automatically alert the organisation to information that may be out of date. This could be used as part of a deletion policy. Systems which incorporate audit trails showing who has created or altered a record and when also assist in ensuring accuracy. They enable the employer to trace the sources of inaccurate records and to take action to prevent recurrence.

    Many businesses buy computerised personnel systems 'off the shelf'. The business should make sure the system facilitates data protection compliance. The legal responsibility for compliance rests clearly with users rather than suppliers of systems. Users cannot simply blame the system. The Information Commissioner does though recognise that it may take businesses some time to bring existing systems up to the desired standards. This will be taken into account should the possibility of enforcement action arise as a result of a breach of *DPA 1998*.

Discipline, Grievance and Dismissal   16.17

The activity of disciplining or dismissing workers, or the handling of their grievances, will generally involve the processing of personal data, such as the consultation of records or the compilation of dossiers of information about those involved, the Information Commissioner says in Part 2 of the Employment Practices Data Protection Code.

Workers have the same rights of access to files containing information about disciplinary matters or grievances about themselves as they do to other personal data held, unless this information is associated with a criminal investigation in which case an exemption might apply.

It is not the purpose of the Code to provide general guidance as to how disciplinary, grievance or dismissal proceedings should be conducted. Advice about this is available in guidance issued by the Advisory, Conciliation and Arbitration Service ('ACAS') and other bodies.

Standards: Discipline, Grievance and Dismissal   16.18

1.	Remember that *DPA 1998* applies to personal data processed in relation to discipline, grievance and dismissal proceedings.
2.	Do not access or use information you keep about workers merely because it might have some relevance to a disciplinary or grievance investigation if access or use would be either:

- incompatible with the purpose(s) you obtained the information for, or

- disproportionate to the seriousness of the matter under investigation.

3. Ensure that there are clear procedures on how 'spent' disciplinary warnings are handled.

4. Ensure that when employment is terminated the reason for this is accurately recorded, and that the record reflects properly what the worker has been told about the termination.

Notes and examples

1. *DPA 1998* applies to personal data including those held in connection with disciplinary or grievance investigations and proceedings. This means that:

- subject access rights apply, even when responding to a request might impact on a disciplinary investigation or on forthcoming proceedings. Access rights also apply to opinions expressed about workers and to information indicating the employer's intentions in respect of them. Access need not be provided if doing so would prejudice the investigation of criminal matters.

- personal data to be used as evidence to support disciplinary proceedings must not be obtained by deception or by misleading those from whom they are obtained as to why they are required or how they will be used.

- records used in the course of disciplinary and grievance proceedings must be accurate and sufficiently detailed to support any conclusions that are drawn from them.

- records relating to disciplinary and grievance investigations, proceedings and action must be kept secure. Be particularly careful that such records are only made available to those staff whose duties require that they should have access to them. Where information is to be provided to a worker's representative or legal adviser, check that this person has been authorised by the worker to act on his or her behalf.

- records of allegations about workers that have been investigated and found to be without substance should not normally be retained once an investigation has been completed. There are some exceptions to this where for its own protection the employer has to keep a limited record that an allegation was received and investigated, for example where the allegation relates to abuse and the worker is employed to work with children or other vulnerable individuals. There may also be a case for keeping records of unsubstantiated allegations of bullying or abuse of workers by a colleague, provided that it is made clear in the record what is an unsubstantiated allegation and what has been established as fact.

2.   Information about workers must not be used in a way that is incompatible with the purpose(s) for which the information was obtained. For example, a worker in a business that issues credit cards might also be a holder of one of the business' cards. The business should not access information it obtains about the worker because he or she is a cardholder, for use in connection with disciplinary or grievance investigations arising from his or her employment. Similarly, an employer might store e-mail messages for a limited period to ensure the security of its communications system. It must not access stored, personal messages sent by or to workers for incompatible purposes such as checking whether workers have been making adverse comments about their managers. A purpose will not be incompatible if workers have been told in advance that information obtained from them will be used for that purpose. Where the use of information about workers in disciplinary or grievance investigations is not incompatible, it must still be fair. Personal information about workers should not be accessed if the intrusion into workers' privacy would be out of proportion to the seriousness of the matter under investigation. For example, an employer storing e-mail messages might suspect that within a group of workers there is someone who has been spending too long conducting personal business in the employer's time. Accessing the content of all messages, including private and personal ones, sent by all members of the group is unlikely to be justified simply on the basis of tracking down the culprit even if workers have been told their messages might be accessed in the course of disciplinary investigations. This is because the nature of the offence would not justify the degree and extent of the intrusion, particularly given the availability of other less intrusive means of enforcing any rules the employer might have. On the other hand, accessing the personal e-mails of one particular worker where there is evidence that the worker has been using e-mail messages to racially or sexually harass another worker might well be justified.

2.   Disciplinary procedures generally provide for warnings to 'expire' after a set period of time. Ensure the procedure clarifies what is meant by 'expire'. For example, is the warning removed from the record or is it simply disregarded in determining a future disciplinary penalty? Put in place arrangements, such as a diary system, to ensure that the procedure is put into practice and that where the procedure provides for warnings to be removed or deleted, that this is actually done.

3.   A breach of the Act's requirement of accuracy could arise, for example, where a worker has been allowed to resign but, because he or she has been left with little choice, the employer has recorded 'dismissed'. Particular care should be taken in distinguishing resignation from dismissal.

Comments   16.19

None of these proposals are unduly onerous, unlike some other provisions of the Employment Practices Data Protection Code.

Inaccurate CVs   16.20

Not all candidates go to the lengths of the lady who, applying for a job as a reporter on The Sun newspaper, wrote 'SEX' across the top of her application to draw attention to herself. (She got the job: see The Times, 31 May 2000). However, many resort to leaving gaps on their CV, distorting facts or just telling lies. Many businesses now have procedures in place to try to identify inaccurate CVs and lying interviewees but this is not easy, particularly when the obligation also to comply with data protection legislation also arises.

In one case a well-known chef received a written apology from another chef after he was given a day to apologise or be sued for lying on his CV. A recruitment agency telephoned the chef to check that the candidate had worked for him as claimed on the CV. In fact they had apparently never met. The candidate wrote on his CV that he had worked for the chef as a senior sous-chef at a prestigious London restaurant. He had stated that the best food he had ever produced had been at that restaurant between 1994 and 1997, and that it has been hard, exacting work with very long hours. Moving from kitchen to office the situation is not much better. Many employees claim degree qualifications they do not have. They cover up gaps in their CV by saying they stayed longer at their previous employer than they did.

Libel and Slander   16.21

There is no general law prohibiting telling lies. However some laws can be breached depending on what is said. If a libellous statement has been made about a third party they can bring an action for libel or, if it is not written down, for slander, under the laws of defamation. This is unlikely to occur in an interview as most interviewees know it does not reflect very well on them if they start criticising their ex-employer.

Misrepresentation   16.22

Other relevant areas of law are the laws of negligent mis-statement and misrepresentation. A negligent mis-statement is a statement made to people who would be expected to rely on it and on which they do rely and suffer provable loss. Misrepresentation is also a tort or legal wrong which could be relevant where people lie on a CV or indeed any other document. The employer may be offering the job because the individual has a first from Oxford in law, when in fact they scraped a third in theatre studies at an ex-polytechnic and would not have even made the short list if this were the case. If when the lie comes to light the employer has to start the recruitment process over again and the employer has suffered loss, such as through having to spend money all over again on advertising and recruitment agencies' fees, then a recoverable loss against the employee can be shown and damages recovered. However in practice there is not sufficient money at stake to make an action worthwhile and the only issue is whether the lie is sufficiently bad to justify dismissing the employee. For example, the woman with children who is known as Mrs Smith but has never married her partner may describe herself as married on the CV even though in law she is not. This may be completely irrelevant to her job on the till of the local supermarket, but in a strict religious school it may be a justifiable policy not to recruit people 'living in sin' and the consequences might be different.

Some statements are of course open to opinion. A lot of prospective employees write about themselves in glowing terms such as 'team player', 'excellent all-rounder' etc. Often this is very far from the truth. Such broad statements are unlikely to cause legal problems. In assessing whether a statement on a CV which is untrue is a misrepresentation or not, note that a statement of opinion is not a misrepresentation nor a statement of intention. In one case a man said someone would make a very desirable tenant (knowing full well they were in arrears with their rent). A misrepresentation was found. A statement of intention may be actionable as a misrepresentation when at the time it was made the person making the statement had no intention to put it into effect.

Section 8 of the *Unfair Contract Terms Act 1977* provides that where a term in a contract excludes or restricts liability for misrepresentations made before the contract was made or any remedy available to any part to the contract by reason of misrepresentation, then that term is not valid unless it satisfies the requirement of reasonableness in the Act.

Case Law   16.23

In *Esso Petroleum Co v Mardon [1976] QB 801* the company had told a prospective tenant of a lease for a filling station a forecast of probable sales. Damages for negligent misrepresentation succeeded. When statements are made about the future, the courts look at whether it was reasonable for the person to have relied on that representation. Is the person just passing on information for what it is worth but clearly may not really know whether those facts are true or not? Damages can be recovered for fraudulent misrepresentation and often for negligent misrepresentation under *section 2(1)* of the *Misrepresentation Act 1967*. Where the misrepresentation was innocent, in most cases no damages can be recovered unless the representation is or becomes a contract term. Most lies on CVs risk being held to be fraudulent misrepresentations rather than innocent mistakes.

(cont'd)

In *Box v Midland Bank [1981] 1 Lloyd's Rep 434* someone sought a large loan from Midland Bank. His manager gave the impression it would be a formality, but would need head office approval. The bank manager allowed him overdraft facilities in the meantime. The loan application was refused by the head office and the man claimed damages for misrepresentation as he had suffered loss through thinking the loan would be forthcoming. The court found that the bank manager owed a duty to the man not to mislead him with careless advice.

Seeking Legal Advice   16.24

In any case, it is essential to speak to an employment lawyer before dismissing someone if a lie on their CV comes to light. Now that the maximum damages for unfair dismissal have been raised from £12,000 to £60,000 and there are unlimited rights to damages in certain areas, such as where there is sex discrimination, it is important to take advice before dismissing someone. It may be that a warning is more appropriate.

Practical Tips   16.25

In practice, it is best to try to put employees off lying on their application by using an application form rather than their own CV. This makes it much harder for them to lie as the information they have to supply is given on the form. Also, the employer has the opportunity to add to the form statements such as that all qualifications will be checked, and telling people to add all examinations which they passed, but not those they failed, and asking for the full name of the institution they attended (eg 'Oxford' is not the same as 'Oxford University'). A statement such as as:

> 'We require details on this form to be entirely accurate and up-to-date. If we subsequently find you have not completed this form accurately we reserve the right to treat this as serious misconduct and ultimately to dismiss you.'

Commissioner's Advice   16.26

In Part 1 of the Information Commissioner's Employment Practices Data Protection Code of Practice verification and data protection issues are addressed.

The term 'verification', as used in the Code, is the process of checking that details supplied by applicants are accurate and complete. Verification, therefore, should not go beyond the checking of information that is sought in the application or supplied later in the recruitment process, although in this Code it also includes the taking up of references provided by the applicant. The process can include confirmation of qualifications and financial information if this is justified in order to meet the requirements of the position. Some specialised agencies now offer a verification service.

The benchmarks

1.　Explain to applicants as early as is reasonably practicable in the recruitment process the nature of the verification process and the methods used to carry it out.

2.　If it is necessary to secure the release of documents or information from a third party, obtain a signed consent form from the applicant unless consent to their release has been indicate in some other way.

3.　Give the applicant an opportunity to make representations should any of the checks produce discrepancies.

Notes and examples

1.　Applicants may not always give complete and accurate answers to the questions they are asked.

　　Employers are justified in making reasonable efforts to check the truthfulness of the information they are given. The verification process should be open; applicants should be informed of what information will be verified and how this will be done. Where external sources are to be used to check the responses to questions, this should be explained to the applicant.

　　Access to certain records needed for the verification process may only be available to the individual concerned. You should not force applicants to use their subject access right to obtain records from a third party by making it a condition of their appointment. This is known as 'enforced subject access'.

　　Requiring the supply of certain records in this way, including certain criminal and social security records, will become a criminal offence under the Act when the Criminal Records Bureau starts to issue 'disclosures'.

2.　For example, some organisations will require a signed approval form from an individual before they confirm his or her qualifications to a third party.

3.　Where information obtained from a third party differs from that provided by the applicant, it should not simply be assumed that it is the information provided by the applicant that is incorrect or misleading. If necessary, further information should be sought and a reasoned decision taken as to where the truth lies.

　　As part of this process the applicant should be asked to provide an explanation where information he or she has provided is suspected of being incorrect or misleading. This is necessary to ensure that the data held are accurate and processed fairly.

No Enforced Subject Access   16.27

The Commissioner has always been of the view that forcing potential employees to exercise their right of access in order to provide the employer with a copy of a record held by a third party is a breach of the law. Requiring the supply of certain records will become a criminal offence when *sections 112, 113* and *115* of the *Police Act 1997* come into force.

Standards: Pre-employment Vetting   16.28

The term 'pre-employment vetting' as used in the Employment Practices Data Protection Code means actively making enquiries from third parties about an applicant's background and circumstances. It goes beyond the verification of details addressed earlier. As such it is particularly intrusive and should be confined to areas of special risk, the Information Commissioner says. It is for example used for some government workers who have access to classified information.

In some sectors vetting may be a necessary and accepted practice. Limited vetting may be a legal requirement for some jobs, for example under the *Protection of Children Act 1999*. The Department of Health is developing a Protection of Vulnerable Adults list which employers intending to recruit individuals to work with certain vulnerable adults may be required to consult. *DPA 1998* does not necessarily prohibit the use of such vetting, but regulates whether and how it may be carried out.

The benchmarks

1. Only use vetting where there are particular and significant risks to the employer, clients, customers or others, and where there is no less intrusive and reasonably practicable alternative.

2. Only carry out pre-employment vetting on an applicant at an appropriate point in the recruitment process. Comprehensive vetting should only be conducted on a successful applicant.

3. Make it clear early in the recruitment process that vetting will take place and how it will be conducted.

4. Only use vetting as a means of obtaining specific information, not as a means of general intelligence gathering. Ensure that the extent and nature of information sought is justified

5. Only seek information from sources where it is likely that relevant information will be revealed. Only approach the applicant's family or close associates in exceptional cases.

6. Do not place reliance on information collected from possibly unreliable sources. Allow the applicant to make representations regarding information that will affect the decision to finally appoint.

---

7. Where information is collected about a third party, eg the applicant's partner, ensure so far as practicable that the third party is made aware of this.

8. If it is necessary to secure the release of documents or information from a third party, obtain a signed consent form from the applicant.

Notes and examples

1. Checks should be proportionate to the risks faced by an employer and be likely to reveal information that would have a significant bearing on the employment decision. The risks are likely to involve aspects of the security of the employer or of others. They could range from the risk of breaches of national security, or the risk of employing unsuitable individuals to work with children through to the risk of theft or the disclosure of trade secrets or other commercially confidential information.

2. As a general rule

    • do not routinely vet all applicants;

    • do not subject all short-listed applicants to more than basic written checks and the taking up of references, eg against the list of persons considered unsuitable to work with children compiled under the *Protection of Children Act 1999*. Do not require all short-listed applicants to obtain a 'disclosure' from the Criminal Records Bureau.

3. This information could be provided on the initial application form or other recruitment material. Explain to the applicant the nature, extent and range of sources of the information that will be sought. Make clear the extent to which information will be released to third parties.

4. An employer intending to use pre-employment vetting must determine carefully the level of vetting that is proportionate to the risks posed to his or her business. Employers must be very clear as to what the objectives of the vetting process are and must only pursue avenues that are likely to further these objectives. Vetting should be designed in such a way that only information that would have a significant bearing on the employment decision is likely to be obtained.

5. In exceptional cases an employer might be justified in collecting information about members of the family or close associates of the applicant. This is most likely to arise in connection with the recruitment of police or prison officers.

    If sensitive data are collected one of the conditions listed on page 30 of the Code must be satisfied.

6. Employers should use all reasonable means to ensure that any external sources used as part of the vetting process are reliable. Where the vetting

(cont'd)

results in the recording of adverse information about an applicant, the applicant should be made aware of this and should be given the opportunity to make representations, either in writing or face to face.

7. Where information about a third party, eg the applicant's partner, is to be recorded, the collection must be fair and lawful in respect of the third party. This will mean informing third parties that information about them has been obtained and informing them as to the purposes for which it will be processed, unless this would not be practicable or would involve disproportionate effort, for example where the employer does not have contact details for the third party or the information will be kept in an identifiable form for only a very short period. In such cases there is no obligation to act.

8. During the vetting process information might be sought from a third party, eg a previous employer that the applicant has not given as a referee. If the information is subject to a duty of confidentiality, the third party will need some basis on which to justify its release. The employer might obtain consent for this from the applicant in order to avoid the need for the third party to contact the applicant to seek consent.

The Employment Practices Data Protection Code also contains useful standards on the areas of selection testing and interviews. The Commissioner suggests keeping records for those who were not successful when applying for jobs for no longer than four months. However, this is just a recommendation rather than a requirement of *DPA 1998*.

Advice to Employers   16.29

1. Require that original examination certificates be brought to the interview or sent on beforehand. Make copies. It is worth checking at the institutions concerned. It is not particularly difficult to forge a certificate these days.

2. Ask the employees about their qualifications, particularly if they sound unusual or dubious, and study their reaction.

3. Ask the obvious questions about gaps on the CV and take the employee through their career history. It is much better they are honest and say they spent six months between work unemployed than extend their departure date from the previous job.

4. Take up references and try to do this relatively early on. If only two out of three ex-employers are named, see if contact can be made with the missing one. It might have the most relevant information.

5. Look out for signs of lying in the interview such as individuals shifting in their seat, becoming less forthcoming, blushing or avoiding eye contact.

6. If it is found someone has lied do not recruit them. They may be dishonest in other ways and not prove a worthwhile employee.

Employment Records 16.30

Section 3 of Part 2: Records Management of the Information Commissioner's Code provides a huge amount of suggested advice and guidance for employers in the area of employment records which is too lengthy to consider here. The Commissioner considers the following areas set out at **16.31–16.37** below.

Standards: Sickness Records 16.31

Sickness records are likely to include sensitive data. The Information Commissioner sees a problem with requiring explicit consent requirements for sensitive data and the need for employers to keep sickness records. *DPA 1998* cannot have been intended to prohibit employers from keeping such data.

The term 'sickness record', as used in Part 2 of the Code, means a record which contains details of the illness or condition responsible for a worker's absence. Similarly the term 'accident record' means a record which contains details of the injury suffered. The term 'absence record' is used to describe a record that may give the reason for absence as 'sickness' or 'accident' but does not include any reference to specific medical conditions.

Sickness and accident records will include information about workers' physical or mental health. The holding of sickness or accident records will therefore involve the processing of sensitive personal data. This means one of the conditions for processing sensitive personal data must be satisfied.

Part 4 of the Code, which deals with medical information about workers, provides further information about occupational health schemes, and is expected to be issued by the end of 2002.

The Information Commissioner proposes the following standards.

The benchmarks

1. Keep sickness and accident records separately from absence records. Do not use sickness or accident records for a particular purpose when records of absence could be used instead.

2. Ensure that the holding and use of sickness and accident records satisfies a sensitive data condition.

3. Only disclose information from sickness or accident records about a worker's illness, medical condition or injury where there is a legal obligation to do so, where it is necessary for legal proceedings or where the worker has given explicit consent to the disclosure.

(cont'd)

---

4.   Do not make the sickness, accident or absence records of individual workers available to other workers, other than to provide managers with information about those who work for them in so far as this is necessary for them to carry out their managerial roles.

Notes and examples

1.   Do not access information about sickness or injury when only information about the length of absence is needed. For example, when calculating a benefit, it may only be necessary to see the length of absence rather than the nature of the sickness responsible for the absence.

2.   The Act does not prevent employers from keeping sickness and accident records about their workers. Such records are clearly necessary for an employer to review the ability of workers to undertake the work for which they are employed, and for other purposes such as the detection of health and safety hazards at work and the payment of health-related benefits to workers. Where an employer is obliged by law to process sensitive personal data, for example under health and safety or social security legislation, it is easy to satisfy a sensitive data condition. In other cases, particularly involving sickness records, it may be less clear cut that a sensitive data condition is satisfied. Because of this some employers have sought to rely on obtaining the worker's explicit consent for the processing. The Commissioner recognises that employers need to keep some sickness records but doubts the validity of consent as a basis for the processing of the health data involved. [The Commissioner] takes the view that an employer keeping and using sickness records in a reasonable manner is likely to satisfy one of the other sensitive data conditions. Whilst the Act, as it currently stands, does not place this question beyond doubt, [the Commissioner] understands the Government is considering changes to the law that will do so.

3.   This benchmark does not apply to the disclosure of the number of days of absence such as might be involved, for example, in giving a reference.

4.   For example, 'league tables' of sickness absences of individual workers should not be published because the intrusion of privacy in doing so would be disproportionate to any managerial benefit. It is permissible for a manager to access the record of an individual's sickness in order to investigate repeated or long term absence. It is also permissible to publish totals of sickness absence by department or section provided that individual workers are not identifiable.

Standards: Security   16.32

The Commissioner says 'Care should be taken with the use of e-mail. An employer that allows the transmission of confidential employee information by e-mail without taking appropriate security measures will be in breach of the Seventh Data Protection Principle'. Reference should be made here to **15**

E-MAILS. Encryption may protect e-mail in transit but it is still vulnerable at either end. If a confidential e-mail is 'deleted' a copy may nevertheless be retained on the system. There are also risks with the use of fax. A confidential fax message may be received on a machine to which many people have access. It can also easily be misdirected, for example, by mis-keying the fax number of the intended recipient.

Security, in this context, is concerned with the safe storage of both manual and electronic files, preventing unauthorised access to such files and preventing their unintended destruction.

The benchmarks

1. Apply security standards that take account of the risks of unauthorised access to, accidental loss or destruction of, or damage to, employment records.

2. Institute a system of secure cabinets, access controls and passwords to ensure that staff can only gain access to employment records where they have a legitimate business need to do so.

3. Use the audit trail capabilities of automated systems to track who accesses and amends personal data.

4. Take steps to ensure the reliability of staff that have access to workers' records. Remember this is not just a matter of carrying out background checks. It also involves training and ensuring that workers understand their responsibilities for confidential or sensitive information. Place confidentiality clauses in their contracts of employment.

5. Ensure that if employment records are taken off-site, eg on laptop computers, this is controlled. Make sure only the necessary information is taken and there are security rules for staff to follow.

6. Take account of the risks of transmitting confidential worker information by fax or e-mail. Only transmit such information between locations if a secure network or comparable arrangements are in place. In the case of e-mail deploy some technical means of ensuring security, such as encryption.

Notes and examples

1. It is beyond the scope of this Code to set general security standards that may have no special relevance to employment records. BS7799: 1995 (Code of Practice for Information Security Management, British Standards Institution, ISBN: 580236420) provides guidance and recommendations which, if followed, should address the main risks. Not all the controls described in BS 7799 will necessarily be relevant to all organisations but many are as applicable to small as well as to large organisations.

(cont'd)

---

2.   For example, confidential worker information should not be stored on laptop computers that do not have adequate access controls, ie controls that would prevent access to the information stored on the computer should it be stolen or misplaced. Give access to such information sparingly; for example, access to confidential worker information should not normally be given to technical staff for use in testing computer hardware or software. The basic principle should be that information about workers is only available to those who need it to do their job. Access rights should be based on genuine need not seniority.

3.   Computer systems increasingly incorporate audit trails. These can record automatically when and how records have been altered and by whom. In some cases they also record when a record has been accessed and by whom. Where systems detect unusual patterns of access to personal information, for example where one worker accesses information noticeably more frequently than other workers in a similar position, this should be investigated and if necessary preventative action taken.

4.   It is important to check the reliability of workers who have access to personal information. They should be made aware of the security regime that surrounds it. Where appropriate a confidentiality clause should be incorporated into their contracts. Do not overlook workers in management positions as they may pose as great a risk as other workers, or even a greater one, as they may enjoy wider access to information than other workers.

5.   There should be a procedure for taking employment records, whether computerised or in paper files, off-site – if this is allowed at all. This should make clear who, if anyone, is allowed to take information and what information they can take. It should address security risks, eg laptops not to be left unattended in vehicles. Do not overlook senior managers who may think procedures like this do not apply to them.

6.   There are risks with the use of faxes. A confidential fax message may be received on a machine to which many people have access. It can also easily be misdirected, for example, by miskeying the fax number of the intended recipient. Do not use general company e-mail addresses or fax numbers for the transmission of confidential information.

An employer must not allow the transmission of confidential worker information by e-mail without taking appropriate security measures. Encryption may protect e-mail in transit but it may still be vulnerable at either end. If a confidential e-mail is 'deleted' bear in mind that a copy may nevertheless be retained on the system.

To secure fax and e-mail systems:

- ensure that copies of e-mails and fax messages containing sensitive information received by managers are held securely and that access to them is restricted.

- provide a means by which managers can permanently delete e-mails from their personal work-stations that they receive or send and make them responsible for doing so.

- check whether 'deleted' information is still stored on a server. If so, ensure that this too is permanently deleted unless there is an overriding business need to retain it. In any event, restrict access to information about workers held on servers. Don't forget that those providing IT support have access to servers. They may be outside contractors.

- draw the attention of all workers to the risks of sending confidential or sensitive personal information by e-mail or fax.

- ensure that your information systems security policy properly addresses the risk of transmitting worker information by e-mail.

Standards: Pension/insurance Schemes 16.33

It will not always be the case that information made available by an employee to the pension provider or medical insurer of the employer needs to be seen by the employer 'unless this is a necessary consequence of the funding or other arrangements of the scheme. For example, there is no obvious reason why an employer requires access to medical information in connection with private medical insurance', the Commissioner says. For permanent health insurance, however, the employer may need to know the information.

The proposed standards are set out below.

Pension or insurance-based schemes such as those offering private medical care are often used to provide benefits for workers. These schemes are usually controlled by a third party but can be administered in-house. Some employers also insure their business against sickness by key workers. It is beyond the scope of the Code to address comprehensively the operation of insurance or pension schemes or the data protection obligations that arise from them. These benchmarks relate only to the obligations on an employer that is party to such an arrangement.

The benchmarks

General

1. Do not access personal data required by a third party to administer a scheme, in order to use it for general employment purposes.

(cont'd)

2.   Limit your exchange of information with a scheme provider to the minimum necessary for operation of the scheme bearing in mind the scheme's funding obligations. Make sure that if sensitive data are involved a sensitive data condition is satisfied.

Pension schemes

1.   Do not use information gained from the internal trustees or administrators of pension schemes for general employment purposes.

Insurance schemes

1.   If your business takes on the role of broker or your staff act as group secretary for a private medical insurance scheme, ensure that personal data gathered are kept to a minimum, limit access to the information and do not use it for general employment purposes.

2.   Ensure that when a worker joins a health or insurance scheme it is made clear what, if any, information is to be passed between the scheme controller and the employer and how it will be used.

Notes and examples

1.   Care must be taken to ensure that information legitimately required in connection with the administration of the scheme is not made available to the employer unless this is a necessary consequence of the funding or other arrangements of the scheme. Mechanisms can be put in place to ensure this. For example, information, perhaps about medical or pensions history, passed from workers to a scheme administrator via the employer could be provided in a sealed envelope so that it remains confidential.

2.   An employer's funding of a pension or insurance scheme does not give the employer the right to receive information about individual workers who are members of the scheme unless this is necessary for the operation of the scheme, eg to enable the employer to deduct contributions from pay or to decide whether to continue funding. This does not prevent the provision of anonymised, statistical information which should be used wherever possible. Some employers insure their businesses against sickness by key workers. If, as is likely, the insurer requires information about the worker's sickness in the event of a claim and the employer supplies this, one of the sensitive data conditions must be satisfied.

3.   Although the trustees or administrators may in some cases be workers or directors, information that they receive in their capacity as trustees or administrators of the pension scheme should not be used in relation to general employment issues. For example, a medical report on a new worker that is needed because he or she has applied to join the employer's pension scheme may not be used in connection with decisions about the worker's eligibility for sick pay.

4. Whilst there is no obvious reason why an employer should require access to medical information in connection with private medical insurance, the same is not necessarily true of permanent health insurance. If a worker becomes unfit for work and makes a claim, the insurer might justifiably approach the employer to determine whether suitable alternative work is available. This could involve the disclosure of some health information. In such cases notify the worker concerned about the disclosure and make the information available to the worker on request.

5. This may require an explanation of how the funding obligations for the scheme fall on the parties involved.

Standards: Equal Opportunities   16.34

This is concerned with the monitoring of the ethnic origins, religious beliefs, sex or disability of workers or other personal characteristics to promote equality of opportunity in the workplace. *DPA 1998* does not prevent this but requires that the use of information that identifies individual workers should be kept to a minimum.

The benchmarks

1. Information about a worker's ethnic origin, disability or religion is sensitive personal data. Ensure that equal opportunities monitoring of these characteristics satisfies a sensitive data condition.

2. Only use information that identifies individual workers where this is necessary to carry out meaningful equal opportunities monitoring. Where practicable, keep the information collected in an anonymised form.

3. Ensure questions are designed so that so that the personal information collected through them is accurate and not excessive.

Notes and examples

1. The sensitive data conditions should mean that most equal opportunities monitoring can take place without the need to obtain a worker's consent.

2. Effective equal opportunities monitoring may mean employers have to keep records about workers' backgrounds and their work history in a form that identifies them. For example, if your organisation wants to track how many people with disabilities are being promoted and to what grades, it is difficult to see how this can be done without keeping records in a form that identifies them. Where tracking of individuals is involved it will not always be possible to use only anonymised

(cont'd)

information. However, where the employer only wants to monitor the proportion of external candidates with particular characteristics that apply for jobs, this alone will not justify the keeping of information about unsuccessful candidates in a form that identifies them. Although the removal of identifying details, eg name, may assist the protection of privacy, records will not be truly anonymous if they can still be linked back to individual workers, for example by putting serial numbers on 'anonymous' questionnaires but keeping a list of which worker was given a particular questionnaire. Do not give workers the impression that information about them is anonymised unless this is truly the case.

3. Employers should take account of the advice of relevant bodies before designing, distributing, collating and evaluating an Equal Opportunities monitoring initiative and incorporating it into procedures. Public sector employers will also need to take into account the requirements of the *Race Relations Act 1976 (Statutory Duties) Order 2001 (SI 2001/3458)* and the *Race Relations (Amendment) Act 2000*. Advice about the forms, procedures and ethnic grouping categories to be used in equal opportunities monitoring are available from bodies such as the Commission for Racial Equality, the Equal Opportunities Commission and the Disability Rights Commission.

4. For example, do not limit the range of choices of ethnic origin to such an extent that individuals are forced to make a choice that does not properly describe their ethnic origin. Employers should consider carefully precisely what they are trying to monitor and should not collect unnecessarily detailed information about workers' nationality or linguistic group. Again, they should seek advice from bodies such as the Commission for Racial Equality about this. If monitoring involves the employer assigning workers to categories, perhaps in the case of those who decline to assign themselves, the record must make clear, whenever information is extracted, that the categorisation is merely the employer's assumption and is not a matter of fact.

Standards: Marketing   16.35

It may seem unlikely that an employer would market to employees, but many will market their own products, particularly in bigger companies, perhaps offering a staff discount at the same time. There may also be marketing of aims or ideals, the Information Commissioner says. Employees have a right not to have their data used for this purpose.

Standards: Fraud Prevention/detection   16.36

Some employers, particularly in the public sector, use workers' records in the prevention and detection of fraud, for example, in order to check that they are not paying State benefits to those who by virtue of their employment are not entitled to receive them. Such exercises frequently involve data matching – the electronic comparison of data sets held for different purposes in order to identify inconsistencies or discrepancies which may indicate fraud.

The benchmarks

1. Consult Trade Unions or other worker representatives, if any, or workers themselves before starting a data matching exercise. Act on any legitimate concerns raised in consultation before starting the exercise.

2. Inform new workers of the use of payroll or other data in fraud prevention exercises and remind them of this periodically.

3. Do not disclose worker data to other organisations for the prevention or detection of fraud unless:

    - you are required by law to make the disclosure, or

    - you believe that failure to disclose, in a particular instance, is likely prejudice the prevention or detection of crime, or

    - the disclosure is provided for in workers' contracts of employment.

Notes and examples

1. There is no obligation to set up representative bodies where they do not already exist, nor is consultation currently mandatory under employment law. However, consultation provides an opportunity to identify and address data protection risks and concerns, helping to ensure that the data matching is fair to the workers concerned.

2. This information could for example be included in a fact sheet for workers or other arrangements adopted to meet the benchmarks earlier in this Code.

3. The fact that disclosure of information may be required by law does not remove the obligation to inform workers. This is only removed if informing workers would be likely to prejudice the prevention or detection of crime, for example by amounting to a 'tip off' to the worker that he or she is under investigation for suspected fraud.

Outsourcing Data Processing 16.37

Frequently, organisations do not process all the data they hold on workers themselves but outsource this to other organisations. Organisations which process the data on behalf of other organisations include specialist businesses which run payroll systems, sister companies which manage the centralised computer system on which group worker records are kept, and organisations which provide a secure facility for the storage of archived manual records. Such organisations are termed 'data processors' in *DPA 1998*. Part 2 of the Employment Practices Data Protection Code deals with this issue.

The benchmarks

1. Satisfy yourself that any data processor you choose adopts appropriate security measures both in terms of the technology it uses and how it is managed.

2. Have in place a written contract with any data processor you choose that requires it to process personal information only on your instructions, and to maintain appropriate security.

3. Where the use of a data processor would involve a transfer of information about a worker to a country outside the European Economic Area, ensure that there is a proper basis for making the transfer.

Notes and examples

1. Where an employer outsources a service to a data processor, it falls to the employer to ensure that the data processor puts in place appropriate technical and organisational security measures. The employer must also take reasonable steps to ensure the processor complies with these measures. In deciding what are appropriate security measures account must be taken of the nature of the data being processed and the harm that might result from a security breach.

    In terms of practical steps the obligations on the employer might involve checking whether a potential data processor is certified to BS7799, and/or putting clauses in a contract to give the employer access to the data processor's audit or security reports. It may also mean visiting the data processor periodically to check that the service that has been outsourced is being provided securely. The aim is to ensure that once personal information has been handed over to a data processor, it is no less well protected than it would have had to have been were it to have remained with the employer.

    BS7799: 1995– Code of Practice for Information Security Management can be obtained from the British Standards Institution, ISBN: 580236420.

2. There must be a written contract in place between the employer and the data processor, or at least evidence in writing that there is such a contract.

3. The Act imposes restrictions on the transfer of personal data to countries outside the EEA. Countries in the EEA are the Member States of the European Union together with Iceland, Norway and Liechtenstein. The Information Commissioner provides separate detailed guidance on international transfers The European Commission provides both a model contract that can be used to legitimise a transfer outside the EEA and a list of countries outside the EEA that are deemed to provide adequate protection by virtue of their data protection law. The European Commission has also entered into a special arrangement with the USA known as 'the safe harbor'.

Workers' Access to Information about Themselves
16.38

As explained above, workers, like any other individuals, have a right to gain access to information that is kept about them. This right is known as subject access. The right applies, for example, to sickness records, disciplinary or training records, appraisal or performance review notes, e-mails, word processed documents, e-mail logs, audit trails, information held in general personnel files and even interview notes. The right of access is not confined to information in computerised files, as *DPA 1998* also covers structured paper records. A fee of up to £10 can be charged by the employer for giving access.

Responding to a subject access request involves:

- telling the worker if the organisation keeps any personal information about him or her,

- giving the worker a description of the type of information the organisation keeps, the purposes it is used for and the types of organisations which it may be passed on to, if any;

- showing the worker all the information the organisation keeps about him or her, explaining any codes or other unintelligible terms used;

- providing this information in a hard copy or in readily readable, permanent electronic form unless providing it in that way would involve disproportionate effort or the worker agrees to receive it in some other way; and

- providing the worker with any additional information the organisation has as to the source of the information kept about him or her.

There are a number of exemptions from the right of subject access which can be relevant in an employment context.

Standards: Workers' Access to Information about Themselves
16.39

The benchmarks

1. Establish a system that enables your organisation to recognise a subject access request and to locate all the information about a worker in order to be able to respond promptly and in any case within 40 calendar days of receiving a subject access request.

2. Check the identity of anyone making a subject access request to ensure information is only given to the person entitled to it.

3. Provide the worker with a hard copy of the information kept, making clear any codes used and the sources of the information.

(cont'd)

4. Make a judgement as to what information it is reasonable to withhold concerning the identities of third parties using the guidelines given later in this Code.

5. Inform managers and other relevant people in the organisation of the nature of information relating to them that will be released to individuals who make subject access requests.

6. Ensure that on request, promptly and in any event within 40 calendar days, workers are provided with a statement of how any automated decision-making process, to which they are subject, is used, and how it works.

7. When purchasing a computerised system ensure that the system enables you to retrieve all the information relating to an individual worker without difficulty. Ensure that the supplier of a system that you will use to take automated decisions about workers provides the information needed to enable you to respond fully to requests for information about how the system works.

Notes and examples

1. This is linked closely to the benchmarks in the section on Managing Data Protection. A subject access request need not mention the Act. When a worker makes a written request to an employer for access to information about him or her, this should be recognised as a subject access request and handled accordingly. Unless the employer knows what personal data are held about workers and who is responsible for the data, it will be difficult to fully respond to subject access requests. It may be necessary to carry out some form of audit to find out what information about workers is held. There should then be a system for ensuring all relevant information is located and provided in the event of a request being made. An employer can, however, ask a worker making an access request for information to help it locate the information about the worker, for example by asking 'when were you employed by us and in which department?'

2. In smaller organisations where workers make access requests in person identity checks may not be necessary, but in large organisations it should not simply be assumed all requests are genuine. Making a false subject access request is one method that can be used by those trying to get access to information about workers to which they are not entitled. See Disclosure Requests, Benchmark 5 (see **16.41** below) at for more information about this.

3. The employer must provide a copy of the subject access information in a permanent form unless providing it in that form would involve disproportionate effort. Even if disproportionate effort would be involved in providing a copy, the employer must still give access to the record, perhaps by allowing the worker to inspect it. The Act does not define 'disproportionate effort'. Matters to be taken into account include the

cost, the length of time it would take, the difficulty of providing the information, and also the size of the organisation to which the request has been made. These factors have to be balanced against the impact on the data subject of not providing a copy. Given the significance of employment records, an employer should only rely on the disproportionate effort exemption from providing a copy in exceptional circumstances.

One area that can cause employers difficulties is access to e-mail. Workers are entitled, under subject access, to copies of e-mails about them. Employers are not though required to search through all e-mail records merely on the off-chance that somewhere there might be a message that relates to the worker who has made the request. For information to fall within the Act's subject access provisions, the worker must be the subject of the information. This means, for example, that an e-mail about a worker must be provided. However, an e-mail that merely mentions a worker, perhaps because his or her name appears on the e-mail's address list, need not be provided. Employers should check wherever there is some likelihood that messages might exist, for example in the mail box of the worker's manager. In doing so they should take into account any details the worker has provided to assist them in locating the information about him or her.

It is sometimes asked whether an employer will be a data controller for personal e-mail messages held on its system. If it is not a data controller for such messages it does not have to provide access to them. Employers will though usually be data controllers for all e-mail messages held on their systems. This is because they will keep at least some control over how and why messages are processed, for example by restricting the purposes for which workers can send personal e-mails or by retaining or monitoring personal e-mails to ensure the security of their systems.

Employers are free to agree alternatives to formal subject access with workers, but no pressure should be put on workers not to make or to withdraw subject access requests. For example, a worker might agree to withdraw a formal request if the employer provides particular information, about which the worker is concerned, free of charge. However if the worker proceeds with a formal request the employer must provide a full response.

4. Information released to a worker could include information that identifies another person, for example a fellow worker. This other person is referred to as a 'third party'. Responding fully to a subject access request could lead to the third party's rights under the Act being violated. One example is when a complaint is received about a worker and releasing information on the complaint, in its entirety, would identify the complainant to the worker. In many cases simply removing the third party's name from the information before it is released to the worker will solve

(cont'd)

the problem. However this will not always be the case. Sometimes the worker might be able to work out the third party's identity from the information itself, for example 'only X could possibly have written that about me'. The employer has to strike a balance between the right of the worker to access and the right of the third party to privacy. Before releasing information to the worker the organisation should follow a clear decision-making process to ensure it gets the balance right.

5.   Managers and others need to be aware of the extent and nature of the information that an individual could gain access to. This should encourage them to record only what is truly relevant and useful.

6.   Such automated systems are most common in recruitment exercises. An example of a decision that is covered is where an individual is short-listed purely on the basis of answers provided through a touch-tone telephone in response to psychometric questions posed by a computer. Workers have a right, under the Act, to know the logic behind any such automated decision. Either a separate request can be made for which a fee of £10 can be charged, or, if specifically stated, the request can be included in a more general subject access request. Specific benchmarks relating to automated tests can be found under Section 5, Short-Listing, in the Recruitment and Selection part of the Code.

7.   Responsibility for responding fully to a subject access request rests with the employer rather than the systems supplier. An employer cannot blame the shortcomings of the system it uses, or a lack of information provided by the systems supplier, as a defence for its failure to respond properly to a subject access request.

Disclosure Requests   16.40

The topic of disclosure requests is concerned with requests for information about individual workers that come from outside the employer's organisation. An employer has a responsibility to its workers to be cautious in responding to such requests. It risks a breach of the Act if it does not take sufficient care to ensure the interests of its workers are safeguarded. In some cases though the employer has no choice but to respond positively to a request for disclosure. This is where there is a legal obligation to disclose. It is not *DPA 1998* but other laws that create such obligations. Where they do so the Act does not stand in the way of disclosure.

In some other cases the employer has a choice whether or not to disclose, but provided sensitive data are not involved it is clear that *DPA 1998* will not stand in the way of disclosure. This is where the circumstances of the disclosure are covered by one of the exemptions from the 'non-disclosure provisions' of the Act.

Standards: Disclosure Requests 16.41

Benchmarks

1. Establish a disclosure policy to tell staff who are likely to receive requests for information about workers how to respond, and to where they should refer requests that fall outside the policy rules.

2. Ensure that disclosure decisions that are not covered by clear policy rules are only taken by staff who are familiar with the Act and this Code, and who are able to give the decision proper consideration.

3. Unless you are under a legal obligation to do so, only disclose information about a worker where you conclude that in all the circumstances it is fair to do so. Bear in mind that the duty of fairness is owed primarily to the worker. Where possible take account of the worker's views. Only disclose confidential information if the worker has clearly agreed.

4. Where a disclosure is requested in an emergency, make a careful decision as to whether to disclose, taking into account the nature of the information being requested and the likely impact on the worker of not providing it.

5. Make staff aware that those seeking information sometimes use deception to gain access to it. Ensure that they check the legitimacy of any request and the identity and authority of the person making it.

6. Ensure that if you intend to disclose sensitive personal data, a sensitive data condition is satisfied.

7. Where the disclosure would involve a transfer of information about a worker to a country outside the European Economic Area, ensure that there is a proper basis for making the transfer.

8. Inform the worker before or as soon as is practicable after a request has been received that a non-regular disclosure is to be made, unless prevented by law from doing so, or unless this would constitute a 'tip off' prejudicing a criminal or tax investigation.

9. Keep a record of non-regular disclosures. Regularly check and review this record to ensure that the requirements of the Act are being satisfied.

Notes and examples

1. Junior or inexperienced staff should not be left to make difficult decisions about disclosure without guidance. A policy should be established. This does not need to be lengthy or complex but should set out some basic rules for staff who are likely to receive requests.

2. Ensure that unusual requests not covered by the disclosure policy are forwarded to those who have a proper grasp of the legal issues involved.

(cont'd)

3. In some cases you will be under a legal obligation to disclose. Where this is the case you have no choice but to do so. The Act does not stand in your way provided you only disclose no more than you are obliged to.

   In some cases you will not be under a legal obligation to disclose but you will be able to rely on an exemption in the Act if you choose to do so. This is most likely to arise in the case of criminal or tax investigations or where it is necessary for you to disclose to obtain legal advice or in the course of legal proceedings such as an employment tribunal. In such cases provided sensitive data are not involved, it is clear the Act will not stand in the way of disclosure. You should still take a balanced decision whether to disclose taking into account the interests of the worker. If the information requested is confidential, for example information about sickness or earnings, only disclose if you have obtained the worker's consent or you are satisfied the public interest served by disclosure is sufficiently strong to justify the breach of confidence.

   In other cases you risk a breach of the Act if you disclose. Where it is reasonable to do so inform the worker about the request for disclosure and take account of any objection. If confidential information is involved you should not disclose if there is an objection. If the information is not confidential, for example dates of employment, position employed in, still only disclose if in all the circumstances you are satisfied that it is fair to do so. This can be a difficult decision but you should remember that you must mainly consider what is fair to the worker. If it is not reasonable or not possible to contact the worker and they have not indicated their consent to disclosure in any way, you should not disclose confidential information unless it is clearly in the worker's interest that you do so. With non-confidential information still only disclose if in all the circumstances, including in particular what the worker's view would be likely to be, you are satisfied that it is fair to do so.

4. Even in emergencies care should be taken to protect the interests of workers whose information might be disclosed. How urgent is the situation? Is it a matter of life and death? In many cases there is, for example, no reason why requests cannot be submitted in writing given the wide availability of fax and e-mail facilities.

5. Always establish the identity and authority of the person making a request for disclosure before providing any information about workers. Those seeking disclosure, particularly on the telephone, are often persuasive. Approaches to an employer are a favourite route for those trying to get access to information to which they are not entitled eg debt collectors, private investigators, recruitment agencies or journalists. Employers should be aware that people requesting information might use deceit, for example by pretending to be from the Inland Revenue, and should guard against this. They should also be aware that sometimes officials, perhaps from a Government department, may not fully understand their own powers to demand information. They may mistakenly

tell an employer it is required by law to disclose information about workers when this is not the case. Where practicable, obtain the request in writing. Take particular care with telephone requests, for example by calling back to a known number. In particular:

- establish the authority, if any, of the person making a request. If this is not clear, seek further information from the person concerned.

- inform the Commissioner where requests based on deception are detected and there appears to be a reasonable prospect of obtaining evidence as to who is behind the deception.

- where those requesting information maintain that the employer is under a legal obligation to respond, ensure that the request is received in writing and spells out the basis on which the legal obligation is asserted. Check that any assertion they make is valid and that the law is not being misrepresented.

6. The processing of sensitive data involved in a disclosure must satisfy a sensitive data condition.

7. The Act imposes restrictions on the transfer of personal data to countries outside the EEA. Countries in the EEA are the Member States of the European Union together with Iceland, Norway and Liechtenstein. The Information Commissioner provides separate detailed guidance on international transfers. The European Commission provides both a model contract that can be used to legitimise a transfer outside the EEA and a list of countries outside the EEA that are deemed to provide adequate protection by virtue of their data protection law. The European Commission has also entered into a special arrangement with the USA known as 'the safe harbor'.

8. A non-regular disclosure would be one where a one-off enquiry is received about an individual worker, perhaps from the Inland Revenue or a local authority housing benefits department. It would not include, for example, information on tax deductions supplied regularly to the Inland Revenue on all workers or the regular passing of information to a trade union on subscriptions deducted from pay for its members.

Where there is a non-regular disclosure, even one required by law, and the information that is to be or has been disclosed might be challenged by the worker, make a copy available to the worker and give the worker an opportunity to check its accuracy. Even if the accuracy of the information is not in doubt it may well be helpful to the worker to know that a disclosure of information about him or her has been made, for example to the Child Support Agency. There will though be cases, for example an enquiry from the Inland Revenue seeking confirmation of tax deducted, where the employer might reasonably conclude that to specifically inform the worker would involve disproportionate effort.

Mergers and Acquisitions   16.42

Business mergers and acquisitions will generally involve the disclosure of worker data. This is addressed in Part 2 of the Employment Practices Data Protection Code. This may take place during the evaluation of assets and liabilities prior to the final merger or acquisition decision. Once a decision has been made it is also likely to take place either in the run-up to or at the time of the actual merger or acquisition. It should be remembered that a new employer's use of workers' information acquired as the result of a merger or acquisition is constrained by the expectations the workers will have from their former employer's use of the information.

Standards: Mergers and Acquisitions   16.43

The benchmarks

1. Ensure, wherever practicable, that information handed over to another organisation in connection with a prospective acquisition or merger is anonymised.

2. Only hand over personal information prior to the final merger or acquisition decision after securing assurances that it will be used solely for the evaluation of assets and liabilities, it will be treated in confidence and will not be disclosed to other parties, and it will be destroyed or returned after use.

3. Advise workers wherever practicable if their employment records are to be disclosed to another organisation before an acquisition or merger takes place. If the acquisition or merger proceeds make sure workers are aware of the extent to which their records are to be transferred to the new employer.

4. Ensure that if you intend to disclose sensitive personal data a sensitive personal data condition is satisfied.

5. Where a merger or acquisition involves a transfer of information about a worker to a country outside the European Economic Area ('EEA') ensure that there is a proper basis for making the transfer.

6. New employers should ensure that the records they hold as a result of a merger or acquisition do not include excessive information, and are accurate and relevant.

Notes and examples

1. Wherever practicable, information from which individual workers cannot be identified should be used, so details such as names and individual job titles should be omitted. This might be possible where, for example, a company merely wants to know how many workers of a particular type are employed and their average rates of pay. In other cases a

company might require detailed information about particular workers in order to appraise a company's human resources assets properly. This might be the case where the expertise or reputation of individual workers has a significant bearing on the value of the company. Similarly where a company has a significant liability, perhaps as the result of a worker's outstanding legal claim, it may have to disclose information identifying the worker with details of the company's liability.

In some cases even the removal of names from the information will not prevent identification, for example where without a name it is still obvious that the information relates to a particular senior manager. Removal of names may nevertheless help protect privacy, even if identification is still possible.

Remember that handing over sickness records will entail the processing of sensitive personal data (see 4 below).

2. It is important to gain formal assurances about how the information will be used. Information should be returned or destroyed by the shredding of paper or the expunging of electronic files, should the merger or acquisition not go ahead. The provision of information is sometimes achieved by the use of a 'data room' in which information about the business is made available to prospective purchasers. Strict conditions must be accepted by those granted access to the 'data room'.

3. Businesses may not always expect to be involved in mergers or acquisitions and may not therefore have told their workers, at the time they were recruited, what would happen to their personal information in such an event. Reasons of commercial confidentiality and legal duties relating to matters such as 'insider trading' may make it difficult to be explicit at the time the merger or acquisition is being considered. In some circumstances the corporate finance exemption in the Act may be relevant and may relieve companies of the obligation to inform workers of the disclosure of their information. This could occur, for example, where providing an explanation to workers could affect the price of a company's shares or other financial instruments.

One business may also be under a legal obligation to disclose to another . This is likely to be the case where the *Transfer of Undertakings (Protection of Employment) Regulations 1981 (TUPE 1981)* come into play. Where there is a legal obligation to disclose, there is an exemption from some of the provisions of the Act. The employer is relieved of the obligation to inform workers of the disclosure if this would be inconsistent with the disclosure, perhaps because it would breach commercial confidentiality.

4. The processing of sensitive personal data involved in a disclosure related to an acquisition or merger must satisfy a sensitive data condition. This will not be an obstacle where there is a legal obligation on one business

(cont'd)

to disclose to another, but may well prevent the disclosure of sensitive personal data in the run up to a merger or acquisition where there is no such obligation and the worker has not been asked for and given explicit consent.

5. The Act imposes restrictions on the transfer of personal data to countries outside the EEA. Countries in the EEA are the member states of the European Union together with Iceland, Norway and Liechtenstein. The Information Commissioner provides separate detailed guidance on international transfers. The European Commission provides both a model contract that can be used to legitimise a transfer outside the EEA and a list of countries outside the EEA that are deemed to provide adequate protection by virtue of their data protection law. The European Commission has also entered into a special arrangement with the USA known as 'the safe harbor'.

It is the new employer who now has a responsibility for the type and extent of personal data retained and who will have liability for them under the Act. The new employer must not assume that the personal data it receives from the original employer are accurate or relevant and not excessive in relation to its purposes. Within a few months of the merger or takeover it should review the records it has acquired, for example by checking the accuracy of a sample of records with the workers concerned and should make any necessary amendments.

Other Issues   16.44

The Information Commissioner's Employment Practices Data Protection Code also provides guidance on agency or contract staff and also a large section on employee monitoring in Part 3 (see **15 E-MAILS**). Medical data is also addressed in Part 4 of the Code (issued in draft for comment by early 2004).

Advice   16.45

Personnel managers and all those involved in the recruitment process, some of whom may know little about employment or data protection law if they are simply general managers interviewing a potential member of staff, do need guidance from their employer. They should therefore err on the side of caution. Such advice might include the following.

- *DPA 1998* gives individuals such as prospective employees important rights in relation to their personal information. Employees should consult their legal department before doing anything with such personal data about which they are unsure or to which the potential employee may not have consented, even if the recruitment agency tells them this is acceptable. Areas to watch include sending a CV to offices outside the EU and passing on the details to anyone else, even if they believe the employee might be glad they have passed their CV to a manager in another company who is also looking for such members of staff.

• When interviewing be careful about the notes taken. *Section 7* of *DPA 1998* gives individuals rights to see copies of the personal data held about them. This would include information written in e-mails and information you write down whether in handwriting, in a personal organiser or on the company's computer systems.

• If this information is inaccurate or biased it may be used against the company later if legal proceedings follow.

• There is nothing to stop notes being taken in interviews, and indeed it is a crucial part of the recruitment process that they are. For example, interviewers should note information that the employee mentions which had been left off the CV. However company policy on discrimination should always be followed.

• If in doubt take advice from the legal department.

Further Information 16.46

| Employment Practices Data Protection Code | www.informationcommissioner. gov.uk under Codes of Practice |
| European Commission Opinion 8/2001 (13 September 2001) 'on the processing of personal data in the employment context' (5062/01/EN/ Final WP 48) | http://europa.eu.int/comm/ internal_market/en/datprot/ wpdocs/index.htm |

In relation to inaccurate CVs see the following.

| Lies We Live By: The Art of Self-Deception, Eduardo Gianetti and John Gledson, Bloomsbury, £12.79 |
| Detecting Lies and Deceit, Aldert Vrij, Wiley, £24.99
Freedom, Fame, Lying and Betrayal, Lesek Kolakowski, Penguin, £6.99 |

See **38 RECORDING TELEPHONE CALLS AND E-MAILS** for recommended standards for employee surveillance (Part 4 of the Employment Practices Data Protection Code).

FAQs

FREQUENTLY ASKED QUESTIONS of Information Commissioner (taken from Part 2 of the Employment Practices Data Protection Code)

Aren't paper files exempt from DPA 1998 – are we OK if we don't computerise our records?

No. Manual data held within a 'relevant filing system' are now covered by the Act. This is defined as any set of information which is structured either by reference to individuals or by reference to criteria relating to individuals in such a way that specific information relating to a particular individual is readily accessible. An example of a relevant filing system would be a personnel file with a worker's name or individual reference number on it, in which it is possible to find information about the worker such as starting date, performance mark at last appraisal, or previous employer.

Do I have to get a worker's consent to keep records about him or her?

Consent to hold personal data relating to workers is not usually required. An employer can usually rely on the last of the conditions laid down in *Schedule 2* of the Act which states that personal data may be processed for the purposes of legitimate interests pursued by the data controller. Indeed the Commissioner considers it misleading to seek consent from workers if they have no realistic choice.

Employers are more likely to need the consent of workers if they are processing sensitive personal data rather than non-sensitive personal data. In this case, the consent must be 'explicit'. However, even then, sensitive personal data can be processed without explicit consent in a number of circumstances, for example where the processing is necessary in order to enable the employer to comply with any legal obligation associated with employment. Data about the racial or ethnic origin of workers may be held in order to comply with the law relating to racial discrimination.

What about sickness records?

Sickness records will almost certainly contain information about workers' physical or mental health. They will therefore include sensitive data. Where they are kept in order to enable employers to meet the requirements imposed on them by the law in relation to statutory sick pay it is clear that a sensitive data condition can be satisfied and consent will not be needed. With more general sickness records the position is less clear cut. The Commissioner recognises that employers need to keep some sickness records and it is unsatisfactory should they have to rely on the consent of workers to do so. She takes the view that an employer keeping and using sickness records in a reasonable manner can rely on the condition that the processing is necessary in order to enable the employer to comply with any legal obligation associated with employment. *DPA 1998*, as it currently stands, does not place the question beyond doubt but the Commissioner understands that Government is considering changes to the law that will do so. Even though consent is not needed, employers should of course ensure that workers are aware of what information about them is kept in sickness records and how it is used.

Is a worker entitled to access to all our confidential records, including references?

There is no general exemption from the worker's right of access to information about him/her simply because the information is 'confidential'. There is, however, a special exemption from the right of access to a confidential reference when in the hands of the organisation which gave it. This exemption does not apply once the reference is in the hands of the person or organisation to whom the reference has been given. The recipient may though be entitled to take steps to withhold information that reveals the identity of other individuals such as the author of the reference. This would not usually justify withholding the reference in its entirety.

How do I deal with requests by workers for access to information where the information identifies someone else? We get this problem a lot when workers want access to disciplinary files and similar documents.

Such requests require careful handling and there is no simple solution to your problem. Employers should be prepared to disclose information to a worker that identifies work colleagues, provided that the information is about colleagues acting in a business capacity and is not of a particularly private or sensitive nature. However, there are cases where information should be withheld. This might be the case where, for example, giving access would allow a worker accused of bullying to find out the identity of his or her accuser.

How can the company be expected to keep accurate records if workers give us wrong information?

Provided that the employer has taken reasonable steps to ensure the accuracy of the information, the data protection principle that requires personal information to be accurate will not be breached.

If the Act forces us to delete information, how are we supposed to protect ourselves against allegations that we have discriminated against someone?

The Act doesn't require that all information is deleted straight away. However, information that is retained for a particular purpose should not be

(cont'd)

kept for longer than is necessary for that purpose. This does not rule out keeping information to protect against legal action. Employers should however consider carefully what information they hold and why they hold it. A 'risk analysis' approach to data retention is therefore recommended.

We are looking at centralising our group's employment records at our headquarters in the USA. Can we do this?

Personal data must not be transferred outside the European Economic Area ('EEA') unless adequate protection is provided in the destination country. Some countries provide adequate protection by virtue of their data protection law. The USA is not one of these. In the USA a special arrangement known as the 'safe harbor' has been created. If your company is a member of the safe harbour transfer is allowed. There are also other alternatives such as providing adequate protection through the terms of a contract between your company in the UK and its parent in the USA. Detailed guidance on international transfers of personal data is provided on the Legal Guidance section of the Commissioner's website.

Can we disclose personal data to prospective purchasers of our business?

The Act doesn't necessarily prevent this. However, if it is not unduly difficult to do so and the prospective purchasers' needs can still be met the information should be anonymised, for example by providing the numbers of workers in each grade rather than their names. If personal information needs to be made available the employer should ensure that the prospective purchaser signs up to conditions on how it will be used. Employers should also ensure that information is returned or destroyed if the sale of the business does not proceed.

Checklist

16.48

Completing this checklist is not a requirement of either *DPA 1998* or the Employment Practices Data Protection Code but is meant to assist you in implementing the Code. The checklist is aimed at the person in the organisation who is responsible for implementation. Who has responsibility for the various actions will depend on the make-up of your organisation.

I Managing Data Protection

Possible action points

1.1   Establish a person within the organisation responsible for ensuring that employment practices and procedures comply with the Act and for ensuring that they continue to do so. Put in place a mechanism for checking that procedures are followed in practice.

Action ✓

Ensure that someone is responsible for delivering compliance.
Ensure the person responsible reads all relevant parts of the Code.

Obtain all written employment procedures and note unwritten procedures and practices and check them against the relevant parts of the Code.

Eliminate areas of non-compliance.

Inform those who need to know why certain procedures have changed.

Introduce a mechanism for checking that procedures are followed in practice, for example, occasional audits and spot checks and/or a requirement for managers to sign a compliance statement.

1.2   Ensure that business areas and individual line managers that process information about workers understand their own responsibility for data protection compliance and if necessary amend their working practices in the light of this.

Action ✓

Prepare a briefing to departmental heads and line managers about their responsibilities.

Distribute or deliver the briefing and be available to answer questions.

1.3   Assess what personal data about workers are in existence and who is responsible for them.

Action ✓

Consider using the checklists produced in conjunction with other parts of the Code to assess all personal data.

Check with personnel functions as to the types of data that are held.

Check with departments as to the types of data that are held.

1.4   Eliminate the collection of personal data that are irrelevant or excessive to the employment relationship. If sensitive data are collected ensure that a sensitive data condition is satisfied.

(cont'd)

Action ✓

Consider each type of personal data that are held and determine whether any information could be deleted or not collected in the first place.

Check that the collection and use of any sensitive personal data satisfies at least one of the sensitive data conditions.

1.5 Ensure that workers are aware of the extent to which they can be criminally liable if they knowingly or recklessly disclose personal data outside their employer's policies and procedures. Make serious breaches of a data protection rules a disciplinary offence.

Action ✓

Prepare a guide explaining to workers the consequences of their actions in this area.

Make sure that an infringement of data protection procedures is clearly indicated as a disciplinary offence.

Ensure that the guide is brought to the attention of new staff.

Ensure that staff can ask questions about the guide.

1.6 Allocate responsibility for checking that your organisation has a valid notification in the register of data controllers that relates to the processing of personal data about workers, unless it is exempt from notification.

Action ✓

Consult the Data Protection Register website (www.dpr.gov.uk) to check the status of your organisation regarding notification.

Check whether your organisation is exempt from notification using the website.

Check whether all information about workers is described there, if your organisation is not exempt.

Allocate responsibility for checking and updating this information on a regular basis, for example every 6 months.

1.7 Consult trade unions or other workers' representatives, if any, or workers themselves over the development and implementation of employment practices and procedures that involve the processing of workers' data.

Action ✓

On formulating new practices and procedures, assess the impact on processing personal data.

Consult with workers or workers representatives about the processing.

Take account of their suggestions and concerns.

2 Collecting and keeping general records

Possible action points

2.1 Ensure that newly appointed workers are aware of the nature and source of any information stored about them, how it will be used and who it will be disclosed to.

Action ✓

Decide on how best to inform new workers about how information about them will be held, used and disclosed. Possible different ways include distribution of a fact sheet, information given on an intranet or inclusion of relevant material in an induction course.

Inform HR professionals, department and line managers about this information and how it is to be made available to new workers.

In large organisations, randomly check with a sample of new workers, that they did in fact receive this information. Rectify any communication gaps.

2.2 Inform new workers and remind existing workers about their rights under the Act, including their right of access to the information kept upon them.

Action ✓

Ensure that information given to new workers includes information about their rights under the Act.

If your organisation has not done so previously, distribute this information to existing workers.

Set up a system to remind existing workers of this information.

2.3 Ensure that there is a clear and foreseeable need for any information collected from workers and that the information collected actually meets that need.

Action ✓

Review all forms where information is requested from workers.

Remove or amend any questions which require the worker to provide information extraneous to your needs.

Ensure that questions are constructed in such a way that their answers consist only of the information that is actually required.

2.4 Provide each worker with a copy of information that may be subject to change, eg personal details such as home address, annually or allow workers to view this on-line. Ask workers to check their records for accuracy and ensure any necessary amendments are made to bring records up-to-date.

(cont'd)

Action ✓

Determine the different types of personal data kept about workers and whether they are likely to be subject to change.

Decide whether data that change could easily be viewed electronically.

Make any changes to systems necessary to enable this.

Ensure that the system restricts access to individuals' records so that each worker can only get access to his or her own record.

If it is only possible for workers to view data manually, consider how this can be best be done.

Inform HR, departments and line managers of any new arrangements.

Make provision to amend any details that are incorrect on individual workers' files.

2.5   Incorporate accuracy, consistency and validity checks into systems.

Action ✓

Review computerised systems to see if accuracy checks can be easily built in.

Put in place arrangements to ensure that when systems are updated or new systems purchased they facilitate data protection compliance.

3 Security

Possible action points

3.1   Apply security standards that take account of the risks of unauthorised access to, accidental loss of, destruction of, or damage to employment records.

Action ✓

Obtain a copy of BS7799 if you do not have one already.

Compare its recommendations to your own existing procedures.

Put in place measures to rectify any shortfalls.

3.2   Institute a system of secure cabinets, access controls and passwords to ensure that staff can only gain access to employment records where they have a legitimate business need to do so..

Action ✓

Review who in your organisation has access to personal data.

Determine whether it is necessary to give access to everyone who currently has it.

Deny access to those who have unnecessary access to personal information about others.

Make sure manual files that hold personal data are securely held with locks and only those who should have access retain the key.

In the case of computerised records, ensure that passwords are set up to limit unauthorised access.

3.3   Use the audit trail capabilities of automated systems to track who accesses and amends personal data.

Action

Check whether computerised systems that retain personal data currently have audit trail capabilities.

If they do, check that the audit train is enabled.

If they do not, see if it would be possible to create audit trails of who accesses and amends personal data.

If you have a system with audit trails, ensure that regular checks occur to detect unauthorised or suspicious use.

Set up a procedure to investigate patterns of unusual or unauthorised access of personal data.

3.4   Take steps to ensure the reliability of staff that have access to workers' records. Remember this is not just a matter of carrying out background checks. It also involves training and ensuring that workers understand their responsibilities for confidential or sensitive information. Place confidentiality clauses in their contracts of employment.

Action ✓

Carry out background checks on staff that will have access to workers' records, for example by taking up references.

Review the contracts of workers who deal with personal data.

Write confidentiality clauses into contracts concerning the disclosure and unauthorised use of personal data.

Set up induction training for these staff that contains explanation about their responsibilities.

Organise refresher training as and when necessary.

Ensure that all senior staff are aware of their responsibilities in this area.

3.5   Ensure that if employment records are taken off-site, eg on laptop computers, this is controlled. Make sure only the necessary information is taken and there are security rules for staff to follow.

Action

Formulate a procedure for taking laptop computers off-site (or review the existing procedure). Include points regarding the information that may be taken off-site, security of passwords and keeping the laptop in view or secured at all times.

Inform all workers, including senior staff, of the procedure.

(cont'd)

3.6   Take account of the risks of transmitting confidential worker information by fax or e-mail. Only transmit information between locations if a secure network or comparable arrangements are in place. In the case of e-mail deploy some technical means of ensuring security, such as encryption.

Action   ✓

Review procedures for sending and receiving personal data via faxes.

Ensure that all managers use a secure system if personal data are to be transmitted by fax.

Advise all managers about permanently deleting e-mails that contain personal data from their work-stations.

Check whether deleted e-mails will still be kept on a server. Wherever possible ensure these too can be permanently deleted. In any case, restrict access to them. Check that your information systems security policy properly addresses the risk of transmitting worker information by e-mail.

4 Sickness and Accident Records

Possible action points

4.1   Keep sickness and accident records separately from absence records. Do not use sickness records for a particular purpose when records of absence could be used instead.

Action   ✓

Review how sickness and accident records are currently kept.

If necessary, change the way information on sickness and accidents is kept so that information on workers' health is not accessed when only information on absence is needed.

Inform those accessing both sickness / accident and absence records of when it is and is not necessary to access the full sickness or accident records.

4.2   Ensure that the holding and use of sickness and accident records satisfies a sensitive data condition.

Action   ✓

Check current practices on the use of sickness records against the sensitive data conditions in the Code.

Take any remedial action necessary.

Inform those handling sickness records of any changes in procedures or practices.

4.3   Only disclose information from sickness or accident records about a worker's illness, medical condition or injury where there is a legal obligation to do so, where it is necessary for legal proceedings or where the worker has given explicit consent to the disclosure.

Action ✓
Ensure that all those who deal with workers sickness records are aware
in which circumstances there may be a legal obligation to disclose.

Ensure when appropriate, written consent is obtained from the worker.

4.4   Do not make the sickness, accident or absence records of individual
      workers available to other workers, other than to provide managers with
      information about those who work for them in so far as this is necessary
      for them to carry out their managerial roles.

Action ✓
Review current procedures for use of sickness records.

Ensure no 'league tables' of individual records are published.

Ensure that managers are aware of the sensitive nature of sickness
records.

5 Pension and insurance schemes

Possible action points

5.1   Do not access personal data required by a third party to administer a
      scheme, in order to use it for general employment purposes.

Action ✓
Identify and review schemes currently in operation in your business.

Identify where information could possibly 'leak' from a scheme to an
employment context.

Identify ways of stopping this occurring, for example by passing
information in sealed envelopes.

5.2   Limit your exchange of information with a scheme provider to the min-
      imum necessary for operation of the scheme bearing in mind the
      scheme's funding obligations. Make sure that if sensitive data are
      involved a sensitive data condition is satisfied.

Action ✓
Review the exchange of information with any scheme providers.

Identify and eliminate any personal information passed to you by the
scheme provider that is not essential to the operation of the scheme.

5.3   Do not use information gained from the internal trustees or administra-
      tors of pension schemes for general employment purposes.

Action ✓
Inform trustees and administrators of their general data protection
responsibilities. In particular make sure they know they must not use
personal information acquired in their capacity as trustee or
administrator in their capacity as employer.

(*cont'd*)

5.4   If your business takes on the role of broker or your staff act as group secretary for a private medical insurance scheme, ensure that personal data
gathered is kept to minimum, limit access to the information and do not
use it for general employment purposes.

Action   ✓
Consider carefully what information is needed to administer the
scheme.

Limit access to personal data arising from the administration of the scheme.

Ensure that information gathered in this context is not used for any
other purposes.

5.5   Ensure that when a worker joins a health or insurance scheme it is made
clear what, if any, information is passed between the scheme controller
and the employer and how it will be used.

Action   ✓
Assess the information given to workers when they join a health or
insurance scheme.

If no specific mention is made about the transfer of information, amend
the documentation about the scheme accordingly.

6 Equal opportunities monitoring

Possible action points

6.1   Information about a worker's ethnic origin, disability or religion is sensitive personal data. Ensure that equal opportunities monitoring of these
characteristics satisfies a sensitive data condition.

Action   ✓
Check your organisation's current equal opportunities monitoring
against the sensitive data conditions in the Code.

Make any necessary changes to the monitoring procedure in the light of
these.

6.2   Only use information that identifies individual workers where this is
necessary to carry out meaningful equal opportunities monitoring.
Where practicable, keep the information collected in an anonymised
form.

Action   ✓
Review current practices. Check whether any monitoring form gives
the impression that information is anonymous, when in fact, it can be
traced back to individuals.
If identifiable information is held but it can be anonymised, do this.
When there is no reasonable alternative but to be able to identify
individuals, check whether the monitoring form states this and explains
how the data are to be used.

Make any necessary changes to procedures and ensure that HR staff involved in monitoring understand why these changes have been made.

6.3   Ensure questions are designed so that so that the personal information collected through them is accurate and not excessive.

Action ✓
Check that questions allow people to identify themselves accurately. For example, in ethnic origin monitoring, do not limit the range of choices given so that workers are forced to make a choice that does not properly describe them.

If you assign workers to categories ensure the record is clear that it is your assumption and not a matter of fact.

7 Marketing

Possible action points

7.1   Inform new workers if your organisation intends to use their personal information to deliver advertising or marketing messages to them. Give workers a clear opportunity to object (an 'opt-out') and respect any objections whenever received.

Action ✓
Review whether your business markets its, or anyone else's, products or services to current or former workers.

Ensure that any new worker who will receive marketing information from your company has been informed that this will happen.

Ensure that a clear procedure for 'opting-out' is made known to all workers.

7.2   Do not disclose workers' details to other organisations for their marketing unless individual workers have positively and freely indicated their agreement (an 'opt-in').

Action ✓
Review whether your business discloses workers' details. If so, put in place a procedure to ensure that a worker's details are not passed on until you have received a positive indication of agreement from him or her.

7.3   If you intend to use details of existing workers for marketing for the first time either in ways that were not explained when they first joined or that they would not expect, do not proceed until individual workers have positively and freely indicated their agreement (an 'opt-in').

Action ✓
When considering this type of campaign, construct an approval form to send to workers.

(cont'd)

Distribute the form to every worker to be targeted.

Only conduct the campaign to those workers who have given a positive indication of agreement.

8 Fraud detection

Possible action points

8.1 Consult trade unions or other worker representatives, if any, or workers themselves before starting a data matching exercise. Act on any legitimate concerns raised in consultation before starting the exercise.

Action ✓

Inform trade unions and other workers' representatives of any proposed data matching exercise.

Discuss with workers how the plan will work in detail.

Listen and take account of legitimate concerns raised.

8.2 Inform new workers of the use of payroll or other data in fraud prevention exercises and remind them of this periodically.

Action ✓

Explain how fraud prevention exercises operate to new workers as part of information given about data protection. (See **2.2**)

Set up regular reminders to workers on how the data matching exercise works – e.g. every 6 months.

Set up regular reminders to workers on how the data matching exercise works – eg every 6 months.

8.3 Do not disclose worker data to other organisations for the prevention or detection of fraud unless:

- you are required by law to make the disclosure, or

- you believe that failure to disclose, in a particular instance, is likely to prejudice the prevention or detection of crime, or

- the disclosure is provided for in workers' contracts of employment.

Action ✓

Ensure staff who would be approached by outside agencies for this type of information, understand the rules of disclosure.

9 Workers' Access to Information About Themselves

Possible action points

9.1   Establish a system that enables your organisation to recognise a subject access request and to locate all the information about a worker in order to be able to respond promptly and in any case within 40 calendar days of receiving a request.

Action   ✓

Assess all personal data held on workers (See **1.3**).

Ensure that the information is accessible.

Establish who in the organisation is responsible for responding to subject access requests.

Ensure that all workers who are likely to receive subject access requests can recognise them and know who to pass them to.

Have a checklist in place listing all places where personal data might be held that should be checked.

Use the checklist to gather all personal data in time to enable a response within 40 days.

If your organisation plans to charge a £10 fee, set up an administration system for handling this.

9.2   Check the identity of anyone making a subject access request to ensure information is only given to the person entitled to it.

Action   ✓

Brief anyone responsible for responding to a subject access request to check the identity of the person making it.

9.3   Provide the worker with a hard copy of the information kept, making clear any codes used and the sources of the information.

Action   ✓

In the checklist used to gather all personal data include a check to ensure that the information supplied is intelligible, that it includes sources and that if at all possible it is in hard copy form.

Ensure that everyone involved in responding to subject access requests is aware of these requirements.

9.4   Make a judgement as to what information it is reasonable to withhold concerning the identities of third parties using the guidelines given later in this Code.

Action   ✓

Brief those handling subject access requests on how to make decisions concerning third party information.

Include the guidelines on this as part of the checklist.

(cont'd)

9.5   Inform managers and other relevant people in the organisation of the nature of information that will be released to individuals who make subject access requests.

Action   ✓

Brief managers as to what type of information about them may be released.

Make sure this information is re-circulated from time to time.

9.6   Ensure that on request, promptly and in any event within 40 calendar days, workers are provided with a statement of how any automated decision-making process, to which they are subject, is used, and how it works.

Action   ✓

Determine whether your organisation has any automated systems which are used as the sole basis for decision-making, for example during short-listing.

If so, document how the system works and the basis of its decisions.

Distribute this information to those who are responsible for responding to requests about the process.

Make sure those responding to such requests are aware of the requirement to respond to do so within 40 calendar days.

If your organisation plans to charge a £10 fee, make sure that those responding to requests are aware of this and that there is a suitable administration system in place.

9.7   When purchasing a computerised system ensure that the system enables you to retrieve all the information relating to an individual worker without difficulty. Ensure that the supplier of a system that you will use to take automated decisions about workers provides the information needed to enable you to respond fully to requests for information about how the system works.

Action   ✓

If you are unsure of how the system works, obtain the relevant information from the system supplier.

Put in place arrangements to ensure that when systems are updated or new systems purchased they facilitate responses to subject access requests.

10 References

Possible action points

References Given:

10.1 Set out a clear company policy stating who can give corporate references, in what circumstances, and the policy that applies to the granting of access to them. Make anyone who is likely to become a referee aware of this policy.

Action ✓

Determine who is allowed to give corporate references, this may, for example, be done by grade. Check whether your organisation distinguishes between corporate and personal references. If not, consider doing so.

Draw up a policy explaining how reference requests should be handled, outlining the types of information that can be provided and the extent to which workers are given access. Ensure the policy is brought to the attention of anyone who is likely to receive a reference request.

10.2 Do not provide confidential references about a worker unless you are sure that this is the worker's wish.

Action ✓

As part of the policy, issue a requirement that all referees must be satisfied that the subject wishes the reference to be provided.

10.3 Establish at the time a worker's employment ends, whether or not the worker wishes references to be provided to future employers or to others.

Action ✓

As part of an Exit Policy, include on file a record of whether the worker wishes references to be provided.

References received:

10.4 When responding to a request from a worker to see his or her own reference and the reference enables a third party to be identified, make a judgement as to what information it is reasonable to withhold, using the guidelines given later in this Code.

Action ✓

Brief those responsible for responding to requests for access to references received on how to make decisions concerning third party information.

Provide them with the guidelines on this.

(cont'd)

11 Disclosure requests

Possible action points

11.1 Establish a disclosure policy to tell staff who are likely to receive requests for information about workers how to respond, and to where they should refer requests that fall outside the policy rules

Action ✓

Distribute information, based on this Code, on how to handle disclosure requests.

Ensure that all those likely to handle disclosure requests receive the information.

Give examples of situations where a member of staff might need to refer a request to a higher authority within the organisation.

Provide contact details of whom staff should contact, should they be unsure of how to deal with a disclosure request.

11.2 Ensure that disclosure decisions that are not covered by clear policy rules are only taken by staff who are familiar with the Act and this Code, and who are able to give the decision proper consideration.

Action ✓

Determine who will be responsible for dealing with disclosure requests not covered by the policy.

Organise any necessary training for those who will take on this role.

11.3 Unless you are under a legal obligation to do so, only disclose information about a worker where you conclude that in all the circumstances it is fair to do so. Bear in mind that the duty of fairness is owed primarily to the worker. Where possible take account of the worker's views. Only disclose confidential information if the worker has clearly agreed.

Action ✓

Ensure that those responsible for dealing with disclosure requests not covered by clear policy rules or where there is no legal obligation to disclose give them proper consideration.

Make sure that they take full account of what is fair to workers.

11.4 Where a disclosure is requested in an emergency, make a careful decision as to whether to disclose, considering the nature of the information being requested and the likely impact on the individual of not providing it.

Action

Make sure staff who are likely to receive such requests know whether they can handle them themselves or if not, who to refer them to. If they handle them themselves make them aware of their responsibility to assess the nature of the emergency and determine whether the request could be submitted in writing.

11.5 Make staff aware that those seeking information sometimes use deception to gain access to it. Ensure that they check the legitimacy of any request and the identity and authority of the person making it.

Action ✓
As part of the disclosure policy, make it a requirement that staff check the identity of any person making a request, the authority of the individual concerned and the basis for the request.

Ensure that when a request is made on the basis of a stated legal obligation, that it is received in writing, spelling out the legal obligation on which it is based. If the legal basis is relied upon, have in place an arrangement to check it against the law.

11.6 Ensure that if you intend to disclose sensitive personal data, a sensitive data condition is satisfied.

Action ✓
Ensure that those who respond to disclosure requests are familiar with the sensitive data conditions as set out in this Code.

11.7 Where the disclosure would involve a transfer of information about a worker to a country outside the European Economic Area, ensure that there is a proper basis for making the transfer.

Action ✓
Review the Information Commissioner's guidance at www.informationcommissioner.gov.uk Guidance & Other Publications: Legal Guidance: International transfers if you intend to pass workers' information outside the EEA.

Determine the basis for making the transfer.

11.8 Inform the worker before or as soon as is practicable after a request has been received that a non-regular disclosure is to be made, unless prevented by law from doing so, or unless this would constitute a "tip off" prejudicing a criminal or tax investigation.

Action ✓
For each non-regular disclosure, make a judgment as to whether the worker can be informed and whether a copy of the information can be provided to the him or her. (A reminder of this could be placed in any system for handling non-regular disclosures.)

In cases where it can be provided, do this as soon as possible.

11.9 Keep a record of non-regular disclosures. Regularly check and review this record to ensure that the requirements of the Act are being satisfied.

Action ✓
Set up a system for non-regular disclosures recording the details of the person who made the disclosure, the person who authorised it, the

---

(cont'd)

person requesting the disclosure, the reasons for the disclosure, the information disclosed and the date and time.

Also set up a system to regularly check and review this record.

12 Publication and other disclosures

Possible action points

12.1   Only publish information about workers where:

- there is a legal obligation to do so, or
- the information is clearly not intrusive, or
- the worker has consented to disclosure, or
- the information is in a form that does not identify individual workers.

Action   ✓

Assess the current information published about named workers i.e. in annual reports or on the website or in other publications.

Assess the current information published about named workers ie in annual reports or on the website or in other publications.

Assess whether there is a legal obligation to name the worker.

Assess whether workers would expect to be named in the context of the publication.

Determine whether it is necessary to obtain consent from workers who are named.

If so, set up an arrangement for obtaining consent from workers who are named in publications in the future.

12.2   Where information about workers is published on the basis of consent, ensure that when the worker gives consent he or she is made aware of the extent of information that will be published, how it will be published and the implications of this.

Action   ✓

In any arrangement for obtaining consent for the publication of information on named workers, ensure that the worker is made aware of the full extent of any information to be published and where it is to be published. This is particularly important if information is to be published on the internet.

12.3   Only supply personal information about workers to a trade union for its recruitment purposes if:

- the trade union is recognised by the employer,

- the information is limited to that necessary to enable a recruitment approach, and

- each worker has been previously told that this will happen and has been given a clear opportunity to object.

Action ✓

your organisation has a recognised trade union that is requesting personal information about workers for a recruitment drive, inform all workers and give them an opportunity to object if they so wish.

12.4 Where staffing information is supplied to trade unions in the course of collective bargaining, ensure the information is such that individual workers cannot be identified.

Action ✓

Review your arrangements for the supply of information in connection with collective bargaining.

Ensure in future all information on workers is supplied in an anonymised way.

13 Mergers and acquisitions

Possible action points

13.1 Ensure, wherever practicable, that information handed over to another organisation in connection with a prospective acquisition or merger is anonymised.

Action ✓

Ensure that in any merger situation, that those responsible for negotiation are aware of the Code.

Assess any request from the other organisation. If at all possible, limit the information given to anonymised details.

Ensure that those entrusted with negotiations are aware of and comply with the sensitive data conditions in the Code.

13.2 Only hand over personal information prior to the final merger or acqui-sition decision after securing assurances that it will be used solely for the evaluation of assets and liabilities, it will be treated in confidence and will not be disclosed to other parties, and it will be destroyed or returned after use.

Action ✓

Remind those negotiating that they must receive strict assurances about how personal data will be used and what will happen to them should discussions end.

Consider setting up a 'data room' with accompanying rules of access.

13.3 Advise workers wherever practicable if their employment records are to be disclosed to another organisation before an acquisition or merger

(cont'd)

takes place. If the acquisition or merger proceeds make sure workers are aware of the extent to which their records are to be transferred to the new employer.

Action ✓
Inform workers if their employment records are to be disclosed unless it is not practicable to do so or an exemption in the Act applies.

13.4 Ensure that if you intend to disclose sensitive personal data a sensitive personal data condition is satisfied.

Action ✓
Ensure that those who are responsible for disclosing information about workers are familiar with the sensitive data conditions as set out in this Code.

13.5 Where a merger or acquisition involves a transfer of information about a worker to a country outside the European Economic Area (EEA) ensure that there is a proper basis for making the transfer.

Action ✓
Review the Information Commissioner guidance at www.informationcommissioner.gov.uk Guidance & Other Publications: Legal Guidance: International transfers if you intend to pass workers' information outside the EEA.

Determine the basis for making the transfer.

13.6 New employers should ensure that the records they hold as a result of a merger or acquisition do not include excessive information, and are accurate and relevant.

Action ✓
When taking over an organisation assess personal data you now hold as outlined in 1.3 and 1.4.

14 Discipline, grievance and dismissal

Possible action points

14.1 Remember that the Data Protection Act applies to personal data processed in relation to discipline, grievance and dismissal proceedings.

Action ✓
Assess your organisation's disciplinary procedures and grievance procedures. Consider whether they need to be amended in the light of the Code.

Ensure that managers are aware that subject access rights apply even if responding to a request might impact on a disciplinary or grievance investigation or on forthcoming proceedings, unless responding would be likely to prejudice a criminal investigation.

Ensure that those involved in investigating disciplinary matters or grievances are aware that they must not gather information by deception.

Ensure that records used in the course of proceedings are of good enough quality to support any conclusion drawn from them.

Ensure that all records are kept securely.

Check that unsubstantiated allegations have been removed unless there are exceptional reasons for retaining some record.

14.2 Do not access or use information you keep about workers merely because it might have some relevance to a disciplinary or grievance investigation if access or use would be either:

- incompatible with the purpose(s) you obtained the information for, or

- disproportionate to the seriousness of the matter under investigation.

Action ✓

Make those in the organisation who are likely to carry out investigations aware that they do not have an unrestricted right of access to all information held about workers under investigation.

Put in place a system to ensure that decisions on whether access is justified take into account the provisions of this Code and the Act.

14.3 Ensure that there are clear procedures on how "spent" disciplinary warnings are handled.

Action ✓

Determine what is meant by a "spent" warning in your organisation. Assess the disciplinary procedure and decide whether it needs to be amended to clarify what happens once a warning period has expired.

Set up a diary system, either manual or computerised, to remove spent warnings from individual's records, if this is a requirement of your procedure.

14.4 Ensure that when employment is terminated the reason for this is accurately recorded, and that the record reflects properly what the worker has been told about the termination.

Action ✓

Ensure that if a worker has resigned, even if asked to do so, that this is recorded on his or her record, as "resigned" rather than "dismissed".

(cont'd)

15 Outsourcing data processing

Possible action points

15.1 Satisfy yourself that any data processor you choose adopts appropriate security measures both in terms of the technology it uses and how it is managed.

Action   ✓

Check whether the data processor has in place appropriate security measures. Is it, for example, certified to BS7799?

Check that the processor actually puts their security measures into practice.

15.2   Have in place a written contract with any data processor you choose that requires it to process personal information only on your instructions, and to maintain appropriate security

Action   ✓

Check that any contract you have with a data processor includes clauses ensuring proper data security measures.

If there is no contract, put one in place.

15.3   Where the use of a data processor would involve a transfer of information about a worker to a country outside the European Economic Area, ensure that there is a proper basis for making the transfer.

Action   ✓

Review the Information Commissioner guidelines at www.informationcommissioner.gov.uk Guidance & Other Publications: Legal Guidance: International transfers if you intend to pass workers' information outside the EEA.

Determine the basis for making the transfer.

16 Retention of records

Possible action points

16.1   Establish and adhere to standard retention times for the various categories of information to be held on the records of workers and former workers. Base the retention times on business need taking into account relevant professional guidelines.

Action   ✓

Decide on standard retention times for categories of information held in employment records. Consider basing these on a risk analysis approach.

Only retain information on records that is still needed; eliminate personal data that is no longer of any relevance, once the employment relationship has ended.

Assess who in your organisation retains employment records (see 1.3). Make sure no one retains information beyond the standard retention times unless there is a sound business reason for doing so.

If possible, set up a computerised system which flags data retained for more than a certain time as due for deletion.

16.2 Anonymise any data about workers and former workers where practicable.

Action   ✓

Where statistical information only is required, anonymise details.

16.3 If the holding of any information on criminal convictions of workers is justified, ensure that the information is deleted once the conviction is 'spent' under the Rehabilitation of Offenders Act.

Action   ✓

Use a computerised or manual system to ensure spent convictions are deleted from the system.

Identify when your organisation may need to make exceptions to this, for example convictions in connection with workers who work with children.

16.4 Ensure that records which are to be disposed of are securely and effectively destroyed.

Action   ✓

Review arrangements for dealing with old records to ensure they are securely disposed of.

Advise anyone holding employment records of these arrangements for disposal.

Check that computer records that are to be deleted are in practice removed completely from the system.

Make sure that computer equipment that has held employment records is never sold on unless you are sure the records have been fully removed.

These FAQs and the Checklists which follow them are copyright of the Information Commissioner 2002 and are contained in Part 2 of the Employment Practices Data Protection Code.

Chapter 17 – Enforcement, Remedies and Powers

At A Glance

✓ Requests for assessment of compliance with the *Data Protection Act 1998* (*DPA 1998*) can be made to the Information Commissioner's office under *section 42* of *DPA 1998*.

✓ The Information Commissioner's Enforcement Strategy (October 2002) highlights more rigorous proposals for taking active enforcement action against those breaching *DPA 1998*.

✓ *Section 40* of *DPA 1998* entitles the Commissioner to issue an enforcement notice requiring compliance with the legislation.

✓ Information notices may be served by the Commissioner requiring information to be provided.

✓ Examples of undertakings given are provided in this chapter.

✓ Compensation can be awarded by the courts but not by the Commissioner.

Introduction   17.1

The Information Commissioner has substantial powers under *DPA 1998* to enforce the provisions of the Act. The dual role also gives the Commissioner powers under the *Freedom of Information Act 2000*. **4 COMMISSIONER** looks at the assessment procedure, whereby a complainant or data controller can request the Commissioner to undertake an assessment. Section 7.2 of the Commissioner's Legal Guidance on the Act (October 2001) describes the assessment procedure in detail. **5 COMPENSATION, DAMAGES AND PREVENTION OF PROCESSING** of this book examines the compensation which can be recovered under the legislation. This chapter looks at other enforcement issues under the legislation, including in particular remedies and powers under *DPA 1998* (see **17.9** below).

There are huge demands on the IC's office's time. In the Annual Report to 31 March 2003 he stated:

'The considerable, and increasing, demands that have been placed on the Office during the period under review have caused us to look closely at our existing resources and how we can best use them. The challenges have been great. For example, we currently handle some 12,000 requests yearly from members of the public to assess whether the Data Protection Act is being complied with. We deal with many thousands of written requests from businesses and other record holders for advice about how best to comply with the law. In the period under review our enquiry line dealt with nearly 60,000 telephone enquiries, often difficult or complex ones. Although we are satisfied that we generally provide a good service, we intend to improve our service standards across the board.

'In response to the pressures described above, we are in the process of reviewing all aspects of the way our Office is run. This involves looking, for example, at staffing issues and at the way we handle information within our organisation. Most importantly, we are reviewing how we deliver our services to the considerable numbers of individuals and businesses who, quite rightly, expect prompt, clear, responses to their enquiries about how to comply with the potentially complex pieces of law we are responsible for promoting compliance with.

'Our corporate strategy for the future will focus on the external and internal challenges we face over the next three years and beyond. It sets out our direction and defines what we need or want to do and what sort of organisation we want to be. Dominating all our plans is the need to ensure that our priorities address the major challenges we face'.

Assessment   17.2

Briefly, requests for assessment can be made by anyone who is directly affected by any processing of personal data under *section 42* of *DPA 1998*. The Commissioner has a wide discretion; see **4 COMMISSIONER** in relation to how such assessments are handled.

Enforcement   17.3

Section 40 of *DPA 1998* empowers the Information Commissioner to serve enforcement notices on the data controller where there has been a contravention of one of the Data Protection Principles. The notice will specify what the controller must do, such as stop processing data in breach of *DPA 1998*. The Commissioner generally pursues a 'softly softly' approach to enforcement, and may well simply gently bring a breach to the attention of the controller rather than serving the notice in heavy-handed fashion (see **4 COMMISSIONER** and the Commissioner's Annual Reports (June 2001 and June 2002) , from which it can be seen that few enforcement notices are actually served). However, in assessing whether to serve such a notice, the Information Commissioner will consider if the contravention has caused or is likely to cause any person damage or distress.

> 'An enforcement notice must not require any of the provisions of the notice to be complied with before the end of the period within which an appeal can be brought against the notice unless the enforcement notice contains a statement of urgency. If an appeal is lodged the notice need not be complied with pending the determination or withdrawal of the appeal.'
>
> *Paragraph 7.3, Data Protection Act 1998: Guidance of Information Commissioner (October 2001)*

There is power to enclose a requirement that the notice be dealt with urgently by way of a 'statement of urgency', but even then there is still a period of seven days, beginning with the day on which the notice is served, before the requirement applies.

An enforcement notice may be cancelled or changed in particular circumstances, for example when the Commissioner considers that the notice (or part of it) need not be complied with in order to ensure compliance with the Data Protection Principle or Principles in question.

The Information Commissioner's Enforcement Strategy (October 2002)

The Commissioner has reviewed the approach to enforcement in response to the changes brought about by the Data Protection Act 1998 (the '1998 Act') in terms of assessments casework. The Commissioner has been aware for some time that compliance casework has not resulted in a significant amount of enforcement activity. In the vast majority of cases compliance has been achieved without the need for such action to be taken against data controllers. Relying upon such casework as the only means of identifying compliance issues is necessarily reactive and does not actually reflect the various different ways in which compliance issues are brought to the attention of the Commissioner.

In fact such issues have increasingly come to the Commissioner's attention through reports in various media, through enquiries made by members of the public which do not amount to requests for assessment as well as, more generally, through 'monitoring' of external activity such as public consultation exercises, the passage through Parliament of proposed legislation and the consequences of technological developments.

The Commissioner's primary aim in reviewing the enforcement strategy is to take a more pro-active stance in terms of investigating compliance issues leading to more enforcement action being taken. To do this effectively in the context of the significant changes that the role and Office have undergone the review sought to identify the internal structure and system that might best enable the Commissioner to decide upon and manage a programme of investigation that will result in the exercise of the formal enforcement powers under both the 1998 Act and the Freedom Of Information Act 2000 (the 'FOI Act').

(At the end of this chapter the full Enforcement Policy is given.)

The enforcement strategy aims to be more 'pro-active' and result in more actions. The change involved the following.

1. Formation of an Enforcement Board to identify compliance issues that merit pro-active investigation, and to create and manage a strategic investigations programme. The board is made up of seven representatives including the Information Commissioner, both Deputy Commissioners, two Assistant Commissioners, the Head of Investigations, and the Legal Adviser (in an advisory capacity).

2. The creation of an Enforcement Team which will include implementing the Enforcement Board's investigations programme, pursuing any necessary enforcement action, and identifying additional areas of non-compliance identified by the IC's compliance teams. The team will be made up of staff from the IC's compliance, investigations and legal departments.

The Enforcement Board first met in July 2002 and decided to focus on two areas for the rest of that year to 31 March 2003.

1. The compliance issues identified by the Commissioner's Website Compliance Survey (published earlier in 2002).

2. Subject access requests for manual records held by Central Government Departments.

Information Notices   17.4

DPA 1998 gives the Commissioner powers to serve an 'information notice' on a data controller once she has received a request for assessment or of IC's own volition. The notice will tell the data controller to provide information to the Information Commissioner and give a period in which to do so.

Special Information Notices   17.5

Special information notices can also be served where the Information Commissioner suspects that personal data is not being processed only for 'special purposes' or with a view to publication for journalistic purposes.

'Special purposes' under *section 32* of *DPA 1998* mean purposes of journalism, artistic purposes or literary purposes. There is only an exemption for processing data for special purposes where the following conditions are met:

● the data is processed only for those purposes;

● it is undertaken to publish journalistic, literary or artistic material and the controller reasonably believes that it is in the public interest; and

● the data controller reasonably believes that compliance with the provision in respect of which the exemption is claimed is incompatible with the special purposes.

Fines 17.6

8 CRIME gives a chart of the fines which were imposed for breach of *DPA 1998* in the Commissioner's First Annual Report (June 2001). Fines may be imposed for breach of obligations under the legislation such as failure to notify the holding of data or breach of the Data Protection Principles under the legislation. Fines are a maximum of £5,000.

Example Undertakings: Thames Water 17.7

Undertakings under *DPA 1998* are relatively few and far between.

The Commissioner published undertakings given by Thames Water Utilities Limited following proceedings started in 1999.

In January 1999 the Commissioner served a notice to take enforcement action on Thames Water Utilities Limited over the contravention of the First Data Protection Principle. The enforcement notice said that Thames had unfairly processed personal data in breach of the First Principle. Thames had unfairly processed personal data held by individual customers for the supply of water for the purpose of marketing non-water-related goods and services both from Thames and others. However, Thames appealed on 11 February 1999, so the Commissioner reconsidered and decided that an undertaking about the future processing of personal data would suffice.

The undertaking was as follows:

1. Subject to paragraphs 2 to 5 below, in connection with marketing or trade promotion, the data controller shall only process personal data which is or has been obtained by the data controller or its predecessors (*a*) from its individual customers for the provision of water supply, sewerage, drainage and sewage disposal services (hereinafter called 'the Services') to premises for the purpose of the Services or (*b*) as a result of the Services to such customers, for the following purposes:

   (i) the provision of the Services to premises and informing customers of the existence and nature of loyalty schemes in connection with the Services; for the avoidance of doubt, the data controller shall be entitled to describe the nature and benefits available under any such loyalty scheme and any relevant conditions, but without identifying the third party provider of those benefits except as otherwise permitted under this undertaking;

   (ii) the marketing or promoting by the data controller, on its own behalf or on behalf of third parties, of the supply, installation, servicing or repair of appliances and goods relating to the Services, including water efficiency and conservation;

   (cont'd)

(iii)   the marketing or promoting by the data controller, or by the data controller on behalf of an associated retail arm, of such goods or materials as are at the time of the marketing or promotion available for customers to purchase or hire at one or more retail premises of such retail company; and

(iv)   informing customers as to where further information may be obtained from the data controller on the loyalty schemes,

provided that the processing does not lead to the disclosure of personal data by the data controller to a third party.

2.   Consent. No restriction as aforesaid shall apply to the processing of personal data of customers in the categories set out below:

(i)   where individual customers have expressly consented to the type or types of marketing and promotions and disclosure (if any) for which their personal data is intended to be processed; or

(ii)   where individual customers supplied by the data controller with the Services to their premises either:

(*a*)   at or before the time when arrangements for the Services were made:

(i)   have been informed of the type or types of marketing or promotions and disclosure (if any) for which their personal data is intended to be processed; and

(ii)   have been given the choice to agree or not to such processing and either:

(*aa*)   have responded then and there, and in their response have consented or not objected to such processing; or alternatively

(*bb*)   thereafter and before such processing took place have returned a document to the data controller, or by other means of communication received by the data controller have indicated that they consent to, or by not filling in an 'opt-out' box, or by other means, have indicated that they did not object to such processing; or

(*b*)   at any time when currently supplied by the data controller with Services to their premises:

(i)   have been informed of the type or types of marketing or promotions and disclosure (if any) for which their personal data is intended to be processed; and

(ii)   have been given the choice to agree or not to such processing, and either:

(*aa*)   have responded then and there, and in their response have consented or not objected to such processing; or alternatively (*bb*)   thereafter and before such processing took place have returned a document to the data controller, or by other means of communication received by the data controller have indicated that they consented to, or by not filling in an 'opt-out' box or by other means, have indicated that they did not object to such processing.

3.   Where an individual customer supplied by the data controller with the Services at a premises is subsequently supplied by the data controller with the Services at other premises then, upon notice to the customer, any previous consent, non-objection or objection previously notified to the data controller in the manner set out in paragraph 2 above shall remain valid unless and until revoked by the customer.

4.   Indirect disclosure. No processing under paragraphs 1 or 2 above shall be undertaken by reference to selected criteria whereby individual customers, to whom the data controller supplies the Services to premises, who respond to a third party marketing or promotion, would disclose to the third party personal information concerning themselves, other than name and address and the fact that they are a customer of the data controller, unless prior to, or at the time of receiving the marketing or promotional communication, the customers are informed of the type of personal information that might be disclosed by such response.

5.   For the avoidance of doubt:

    (1)   the prohibition above does not apply to personal data obtained and held for functions other than the regulated function/s of the supply of the Services;

    (2)   marketing or promotions permitted under paragraph 1 may be independent of or accompanying a communication from the data controller (including the data controller's bills and circulars);

    (3)   consent shall not be inferred from the failure of any person to return any leaflet or other document containing an opportunity to opt-out;

    (4)   the prohibition above does not apply to the circulation of the annual charitable leaflet for Water Aid.

Comment: The undertakings show how important it is to ensure compliance with the First Data Protection Principle. The points at paragraph 5 'for the avoidance of doubt' are illuminating. Consent is not implied where someone fails to return a document which contains a chance to opt out. Readers in similar utility companies should not necessarily assume that the same undertakings would precisely be permitted to avoid enforcement action in their own business, but they do provide useful guidance as to what the Commissioner finds acceptable.

Remedies and Compensation 17.8

Compensation was addressed in **5 COMPENSATION, DAMAGES AND PREVENTION OF PROCESSING** to which reference should be made, but the following is worthy of note in the context of remedies in this chapter. *DPA 1998* gives rights to those who suffer damage or damage and distress through a breach of the Act, allowing them to recover compensation where the data controller cannot prove it took reasonable care to comply. Normally compensation is only payable for damage, but will also be available for distress if the processing was for 'special purposes' (see **17.5** above). If the processing occurs there may also in certain cases be a breach of the law of confidence.

Enforcement Action by ICSTIS under E-commerce Legislation – Greenock and Premium Call 17.9

Enforcement for data protection breaches can also occur under other related legislation in the data protection field, such as the legislation implementing the *E-commerce Directive*. The UK premium rate services regulator ICSTIS fined and barred two adult websites based in other EU Member States – Spanish company Greenock and German-based Premium Call GmbH. Those sites' promotional material repeatedly referred to sexual acts involving children, while the dialler software used to access the sites at premium rate charges of £1.50 per minute downloaded automatically without users' knowledge. ICSTIS said it appeared to be deliberately designed to mislead users into running up huge phone bills. It fined Greenock £75,000 and Premium Call £50,000 and banned access to both services for two years. Both companies were told to compensate those who had complained to ICSTIS. The action of ICSTIS was notified to the European Commission and the UK Department of Trade and Industry, as required by the *E-commerce Directive*. Both cases were also reported to the National Hi-Tech Crime Unit.

The Office of Fair Trading also have powers to impose 'Stop Now' orders in enforcing that and other distance selling legislation which is very relevant to those involved with direct marketing.

Applying for Compensation 17.10

Compensation can be applied for either to the court or initially may simply be negotiated with the infringer of the data subject's rights. Unless a payment of compensation is agreed between the data controller and the data subject as a result of negotiations between them, the application may be made by the data subject to the court for compensation alone, or it may be combined with an application in respect of any breach of *DPA 1998*. The Commissioner has no power to award compensation.

In her Legal Guidance (October 2001) on *DPA 1998* the Commissioner poses the question 'How much will the court award if a claim for compensation is successful?' and replies as follows:

'There are no guidelines as to appropriate levels of compensation for a claim under the Act and the Commissioner is not routinely advised of the outcome of cases where individuals have made a successful claim for compensation under the Act. The judge hearing the case has discretion in these matters and would have to take into consideration many factors including the seriousness of the breach and the effect upon the claimant, particularly when considering damages for distress.'

In the case of *Campbell v Mirror Group Newspapers Plc (QBD, 27 March 2002)* the High Court awarded £3,500 but the decision was overturned on appeal in October 2002.

Further Information   17.11

See also **5 COMPENSATION, DAMAGES AND PREVENTION OF PROCESSING**, and **4 COMMISSIONER** where the assessment procedure is addressed.

FAQs   17.12

How is *DPA 1998* enforced?

The Information Commissioner under *section 40* of *DPA 1998* can issue enforcement notices to require that data controllers comply with the Act. However in general the IC favours a software approach of encouragement except in the worst cases of infringement.

Can the Information Commissioner award compensation?

Lots of data subjects complain to the Information Commissioner expecting to get a compensation award and are disappointed. Only the courts can award compensation.

What is an information notice?

An information notice is issued under *DPA 1998* by the Information Commissioner who will by the notice ask a data controller to provide information.

The Information Commissioner's Enforcement Strategy

The Commissioner has reviewed her approach to enforcement in response to the changes brought about by the Data Protection Act 1998 (the '1998 Act') in terms of assessments casework. The Commissioner has been aware for some time that compliance casework has not resulted in a significant amount of enforcement activity. In the vast majority of cases compliance has been achieved without the need for such action to be taken against data controllers. Relying upon such casework as the only means of identifying compliance issues is necessarily reactive and does not actually reflect the various different ways in which compliance issues are brought to the attention of the Commissioner.

In fact such issues have increasingly come to the Commissioner's attention through reports in various media, through enquiries made by members of the public which do not amount to requests for assessment as well as, more generally, through 'monitoring' of external activity such as public consultation exercises, the passage through Parliament of proposed legislation and the consequences of technological developments.

The Commissioner's primary aim in reviewing her enforcement strategy is to take a more pro-active stance in terms of investigating compliance issues leading to more enforcement action being taken. To do this effectively in the context of the significant changes that her role and Office have undergone the review sought to identify the internal structure and system that might best enable the Commissioner to decide upon and manage a programme of investigation that will result in the exercise of her formal enforcement powers under both the 1998 Act and the Freedom Of Information Act 2000 (the 'FOI Act').

The review has resulted in the Commissioner agreeing to the following.

1. The establishment of a panel drawn from Senior Management and to be called the Enforcement Board. The members of the Enforcement Board are as follows:

    - The Information Commissioner.

    - Both Deputy Commissioners.

    - Two Assistant Commissioners.

    - The Head of Investigations.

    In addition, the Legal Adviser (or Deputy Legal Adviser) will attend all meetings of the Enforcement Board in an advisory capacity.

    One of the primary functions of the Enforcement Board will be to identify compliance issues warranting pro-active investigation and to formulate and manage a strategic programme of investigation (for the year) with a view to consideration of formal enforcement action.

The Enforcement Board will also consider prospective enforcement activity and make recommendations to the Commissioner (or in her absence, a Deputy Commissioner) who will decide at the meetings whether or not to proceed to enforcement activity and, if so, in what way.

The Commissioner's decision to proceed is to be taken on the basis of reasonable and consistent criteria (to be developed by the Enforcement Board) as well as taking account of issues such as resources and competing priorities across the Office.

Unless the decision-making function is formally delegated by the Commissioner, her attendance (or in her absence at least one of her Deputies) at any meeting of the Enforcement Board is necessary where decisions are to be taken at such meeting.

2.   The establishment of a dedicated Enforcement Team which will serve three primary functions, namely:

   ● To carry out the programme of investigation devised by the Enforcement Board and to pursue any resulting enforcement action;

   ● To identify additional areas of non-compliance that may be investigated through working closely with compliance teams. These would then be brought to the attention of the Enforcement Board for their consideration; and

   ● To provide administrative support to the Enforcement Board.

The Enforcement Team will be made up of staff drawn from the Commissioner's Compliance, Investigations and Legal departments. In this way it is hoped that team members will acquire and develop new skills and practical expertise from one another.

The Enforcement Team will assist the Commissioner by enabling more thorough investigation of major compliance issues than is currently feasible. The work of the Enforcement Team will, it is hoped, better inform the efforts of the Commissioner and her staff in achieving compliance with the legislation she promotes and enforces.

The first meeting of the Enforcement Board was held on 12 July 2002. It considered, and the Commissioner decided upon, an initial programme of investigation for the remainder of the financial year. At the same meeting the Enforcement Board discussed the appropriate resource initially required for the Enforcement Team to deal with the agreed programme.

The Commissioner has decided on two areas of investigation into non-compliance during the current financial year (ie up to 31 March 2003). They are as follows:

(cont'd)

- Compliance issues arising out of the Website Compliance Study funded by the Commissioner and conducted by UMIST;

- Issues surrounding the exercise of the right of subject access (under section 7 of the 1998 Act) since 24 October 2001 to manual records held by Central Government Departments.

The Commissioner, with the Management Board, will review and decide upon the continued feasibility of the Enforcement Board and Enforcement Team structures each year after the end of the financial year and in advance of publication of the Commissioner's Annual Report. She will review progress against the Team's enforcement programme and also the annual programme itself. Further information about the respective functions of the Enforcement Board and Enforcement Team are set out in the respective appendices attached to this paper.

The Functions of the Enforcement Board

Background

The Commissioner's existing structures and systems do not easily accommodate any initiative the Commissioner may wish to take in terms of investigating and enforcing compliance with the Data Protection Principles (and in time the requirements of the Freedom of Information Act 2000) other than those the subject of complaints/casework. The formation of an Enforcement Board is intended to provide the Commissioner with a means of addressing compliance issues that come to her attention through any of the various sources identified. The Enforcement Board is intended to enable the Commissioner to prioritise and plan Data Protection and Freedom of Information compliance investigations and take effective enforcement action in relation to both on her own initiative. The Enforcement Board, it is hoped, will provide the Commissioner with the means to meet the objective of more enforcement activity.

The Enforcement Board's remit does not extend to consideration of the investigation and prosecution of criminal offences under either the Data Protection or Freedom of Information Acts. The Commissioner's existing policies and procedures remain unchanged in these respects. The successful discharge of the Enforcement Board's strategic function will, however, depend on it being aware of all investigative and enforcement action being conducted (including criminal matters) – see 8 below.

Functions

The Enforcement Board will exercise the following functions.

1. Identify Data Protection and Freedom of Information compliance issues that warrant proactive investigation/monitoring with a view to consideration of enforcement action;

2. Formulate and manage a programme of investigative/enforcement activity addressing such issues;

3. Consider whether or not the Commissioner should decide to proceed to enforcement action, and if so in what way, in respect of any particular case or issue presented to it (orally or in writing);

4. In those cases where the Board recommend enforcement action, and such recommendation is accepted by the Commissioner (or in her absence, one of the Deputy Commissioners) this will be recorded as a decision of the Commissioner (or Deputy);

5. Ensure that sufficient resource is available to carry out such investigation instituted by the Commissioner and/or such enforcement action as the Commissioner decides should be taken, and by whom;

6. Apply, keep under review and develop reasonable and consistent criteria both for and against enforcement action;

7. Advise Compliance Managers on likely stance on enforcement;

8. Ensure that all enforcement activity (including in this respect investigations and prosecutions) is recorded and monitored and, where necessary, prioritised;

9. Direct the Enforcement Team on the publicising of its decisions and action taken as a result.

The Enforcement Board

The Enforcement Board comprises the following:

- The Information Commissioner.

- Both Deputy Commissioners.

- Two Assistant Commissioners (preferably one from each of private and public sector compliance).

- The Head of Investigations.

Unless the decision-making function is formally delegated by the Commissioner, the attendance of the Commissioner, or in her absence one of the Deputy Commissioners, is necessary in any Enforcement Board meeting at which a decision on enforcement action is to be taken.

As with the Management Board, other than the Commissioner (or in her absence one of the Deputy Commissioners), in the absence of formal delegated authority from the Commissioner, the remaining members of the Enforcement Board can only act in an advisory capacity.

(cont'd)

259

The role of the Legal Adviser

The role of the Legal Adviser at Enforcement Board meetings is limited to the provision of legal advice to the Commissioner and the Enforcement Board. The role may be likened to that of a Magistrates' Clerk. As such the Legal Adviser is not a member of the Enforcement Board.

The Legal Adviser (or Deputy Legal Adviser in his absence) should attend all Enforcement Board meetings so as to advise the Commissioner and the Board on any legal issues that may arise in the course of Board meetings and which are not otherwise addressed in written or oral reports or representations made to the Board.

Meetings

It is proposed that the Enforcement Board meet formally once a month, preferably on a fixed day each month. Such scheduled meetings are expected to last no more than two hours. Ad hoc meetings may be arranged on the basis that all decisions made in such meetings are recorded and reported to the next formal meeting.

Decisions arising out of the deliberations of the Board must be recorded and the record approved by the Board prior to circulation/publication. Minutes of formal meetings should be approved at the following formal meeting. Minutes of any ad hoc meetings must be recorded and approved by those attending the meeting in question.

Crucial to the efficient and effective operation of the Enforcement Board will be its dedicated secretariat, to be called the Enforcement Team (see Appendix 2).

The Functions of the Enforcement Team

Background

The Enforcement Team will provide a focal point for the combined and coordinated efforts of the Commissioner's Compliance, Investigation and Legal Departments to carry out the programme devised and set by the Enforcement Board to achieve compliance with the Data Protection Principles (and in time the requirements of the Freedom of Information Act 2000). It will do this by providing a continuous dedicated support team to the Enforcement Board and by conducting investigative and enforcement activity arising from the Enforcement Board's annual programme.

One of the primary objectives behind the setting up of the Enforcement Team is to broaden the Office's existing skills base in terms of investigatory practice and techniques in the area of non-compliance with the Data Protection

Principles and the requirements of the Freedom of Information Act, as well as to refine and improve such skills.

Functions

The functions of the Enforcement Team are as follows.

1.   To investigate those compliance issues identified by the Enforcement Board in their programme and, where directed to do so by the Board, pursue any enforcement action resulting;

2.   To identify additional areas of non-compliance that may be investigated through working closely with compliance teams. These could then be brought to the attention of the Enforcement Board for consideration.

3.   As well as dealing with the more pro-active workload referred to above, the Team will have an important procedural role to play in the organisation and administration of other, more reactive cases and issues referred to the Board for consideration by the Compliance, Investigations and Legal Departments. This will allow the Commissioner's existing procedures for enforcement work to be accommodated subject to them being reviewed and revised to take account of the new structures for dealing with enforcement work.

4.   To provide administrative support to the Enforcement Board. This will include the organisation and administration of Board meetings themselves. The Team will be expected to collate management information on current investigative and enforcement activity and provide this to the Board to inform their deliberations. The Team will also be responsible for the keeping of records of decisions taken by the Commissioner at Board meetings, and of action taken as a result of those decisions.

Copyright the Information Commissioner

Chapter 18 – European Aspects

At A Glance

✓ The *Data Protection Act 1998* (*DPA 1998*) implements the *Data Protection Directive* (*95/46/EC*) in the UK.

✓ All EU states should have implemented the Directive by now.

✓ Where a Government fails to implement a directive correctly, those suffering loss may be able to sue for damages under EU law.

✓ There are some areas where the UK may not have properly implemented the Directive.

Introduction   18.1

DPA 1998 implements the *Data Protection Directive* (*95/46/EC*) in the UK with effect from 1 March 2000. The Directive gives all Member States some choices and options in how they will implement the Directive so that laws will not be identical throughout the EU. However, they will be very similar indeed.

Effect of Late Implementation   18.2

All Member States should have implemented the *Data Protection Directive* by 24 October 1998. The UK implemented it on 1 March 2000. The effect of this under European law is that from that date (24 October 1998) all State bodies or emanations of the State should already have been acting as if the Directive were in place.

Secondly, anyone who has suffered loss or damage through the failure to implement the Directive on time may be entitled to claim damages from the Government for the late implementation. However, this is unlikely as such cases are expensive and difficult to bring about.

Status of Implementation of the Data Protection Directive   18.3

The European Commission publishes a chart of implementation around the EU, and this is summarised below. However the position regularly changes so always check the latest position. It can be found at:
www.europa.eu.int/comm/internal_market/en/dataprot/law/impl.htm

Member State	State of legislative procedure	Next steps
Belgium	1) Consolidated text of the Belgian law of December 8, 1992 on Privacy Protection in relation to the Processing of Personal Data 2) Modified by the implementation law of December 11, 1998 (O.J. 3.2.1999). English version: www.law. kuleuven.ac.be/icri/papers/ legislation/privacy/engels/ 3) Secondary legislation adopted on 13 February 2001 and published in the Official Journal 13 March 2001. 4) Entry into force 1 September 2001 (exception for information when the data were not collected from the data subject then 3 years more).	
Denmark★	1) The Act on Processing of Personal Data (Act No. 429) of 31 May 2000 English version: www.datatilsynet.dk/include/show. article.asp?art_id=443&sub_url=/ lovgivning/indhold.asp&nodate=1 2) Entry into force: 01.07.2000.	
Germany★	1) The Federal Data Protection Act (Bundesdatenschutzgesetz) was adopted 18 May 2001, published in the Bundesgesetzblatt I Nr. 23/2001, page 904 on 22 May German version: www.bfd.bund.de/ information/bdsg_hinweis.html English version:The Federal Data Protection Act will covers Federal public authorities as well as private sector. 2) Entry into force: 23 May 2001. Six Länder (Brandenburg, Baden–Württemberg, Bayern, Hessen. Nordrhein-Westfalen, Schleswig-Holstein) adopted new DPLs	

Member State	State of legislative procedure	Next steps
	persuant to the Directive. These acts apply to the public sector of the respective 'Länder'. Brandenburg: Gesetz zum Schutz personenbezogener Daten im Land Brandenburg (Brandenburgisches Datenschutzgesetz – bgDSG) in der Fassung der Bekanntmachung vom 9. März 1999: www.brandenburg.de/land/lfdbbg/ gesetze/bbgdsg.htm Baden-Württemberg: Gesetz zum Schutz personenbezogener Daten (Landesdatenschutzgesetz – LDSG) vom 27. Mai 1991, zuletzt geändert durch Artikel 1 des Gesetzes zur Änderung des Landesdatenschutz- gesetzes und anderer Gesetze vom 23. Mai 2000: www.baden-wuerttemberg. datenschutz.de/ldsg/ldsg-inh.html Bayern: Bayerisches Datenschutz- gesetz (BayDSG) vom 23. Juli 1993, zuletzt geandert durch Gesetz zur Anderung des Bayerischen Datenschutzgesetzes vom 25.10.2000 (Inkrafttreten zum 01.01.2001): www.datenschutz-bayern.de/recht/ baydsg_n.pdf Nordrhein-Westfalen: Gesetz zum schutz personenbezogener Daten (Datenschutzgesetz Nordrhein- Westfalen-DSG NRW-) in der Fassung der Bekanntmachung vom 9. Juni 2000: www.lfd.nrw.de/ fachbereich/fach_3_1.html Hessen: Hessisches Datenschutz- gesetz (HDSG) in der Fassung vom 7 Januar 1999 www.datenschutz.hessen.de/f02set. htm Precise page (one of the frames): www.datenschutz.hessen.de/ hdsg99/Inhalt.htm Schleswig-Holstein : Schleswig- Holsteinisches Gesetz zum Schutz personenbezogener Informationen vom 9. Februar 2000 www.datenschutzzentrum.de/ material/recht/ldsg-neu/ldsg-neu. htm	

Member State	State of legislative procedure	Next steps
	Sachsen-Anhalt : Gesetz zum Schutz personenbezogener Daten der Bürger (DSG-LSA) www.datenschutz.sachsen-anhalt.de/dsg-lsa/inhalt.htm	
Spain	1) Ley Orgánica 15/1999, de 13 de diciembre de Protección de Datos de Carácter Personal. ('B.O.E.' núm. 298, de 14 de diciembre de 1999). Original version: www.agenciaprotecciondatos.org/datd1.htm English version: 23750 ORGANIC LAW 15/1999 of 13 December on the Protection of Personal Data. 2) Entry into force: 14.01.2000.	
France	1) Law 78–17 of 6 January 1978 2) Draft implementation law of July 2001 www.justice.gouv.fr/actua/loicnild.htm	Discussed in Parliament
Greece	1) Implementation Law 2472 on the Protection of individuals with regard to the processing of personal data 2) Entry into force: 10 4.1997	
Italy	1) Protection of individuals and other subjects with regard to the processing of personal data Act no. 675 of 31.12.1996. English version: http://www.dataprotection.org/garante/prewiew/1,1724,448,00.html?sezione=120&LANG=2 2) Entry into force: 8.5.1997 3) Additional legal acts previewed by Act no. 676 of 31.12.1996 (in particular, the Legislative Decrees no. 123 of 09.05.97, no. 255 of 28.07.97, no. 135 of 08.05.98, no. 171 of 13.05.98, no. 389 of 06.11.98, no. 51 of 26.02.99, no. 135 of 11.05.99, no. 281 and no. 282 of 30.07.99 ; the Presidentials decrees No. 501 of 31.03.98, No. 318 of 28.07.99)	'Renew of the delegation to the Government to complete Law 675. • Act n. 127 of 24.03.2001 • Provisions concerning the adoption of the numerous security mea sures for the processing of personal data referred to in art. 15 of act n. 676 of 31.12.1996 • Adoption of the Code of conduct and professional practice applying to the processing of personal data for historic purposes.' • Act n. 325 of 3.11.1999
Ireland*	Draft bill to be approved by the Government and submitted to Parliament	

Member State	State of legislative procedure	Next steps
Luxembourg*	A new DPL was submitted to Parliament beginning October 2000.	
The Netherlands	1) DPL approved by the Senate on 06.07.2000 (O.J. 302/2000). Original and English version: Personal Data Protection Act (Wet bescherming persoonsgegevens), Act of 6 July 2000 2) Entry into force on 1 September 2001. 3) Secondary legislation adopted.	
Austria	1) Bundesgesetz über den Schutz personenbezogener Daten (Datenschutzgesetz 2000 . DSG-2000) vom 17.08.1999 Original version: www.bka.gv.at/datenschutz/dsg2000d.pdf English version: HTML version: http://www.bka.gv.at/datenschutz/dsg2000e.htm PDF version: www.bka.gv.at/datenschutz/dsg2000e.pdf 2) Entry into force: 1.01.2000. 3) Adopted ordinances: Verordnung des Bundeskanzlers über den angemessenen Datenschutz in Drittstaaten (Datenschutzan-gemessenheits- Verordnung – DSAV), Federal Law Gazette II Nr. 521/1999, about countries with adequate DP legislation (Switzerland and Hungary); Verordnung des Bundeskanzlers über das bei der Datens-chutzkommission eingerichtete Datenverarbeitungsregister (Datenverarbeitungsregister-Verordnung 2000 – DVRV), Federal Law Gazette II Nr. 520/1999, about the registration procedure; Verordnung des Bundeskanzlers über Standard- und Musteranwendungen nach dem Datenschutzgesetz 2000 (Standard- und Muster-Verordnung 2000 – StMV), Federal Law Gazette II Nr. 201/2000, about exceptions from notification.	

Member State	State of legislative procedure	Next steps
Portugal	1) Directive implemented by Law 67/98 of 26.10.1998. 'Lei da protecçao de dados pessoais' English version: www.cnpd.pt/Leis/ lei_6798en.htm 2) Entry into force: 27.10.1998	
Sweden	1) Directive implemented by SFS 1998:204 of 29.4.98 and regulation SFS 1998:1191 of 03.09.98 English version: www.datainspektionen.se/in_ english/default.asp?content=/in_ english/legislation/data.shtml 2) Entry into force: 24.10.1998.	
Finland	1) The Finnish Personal Data Act (523/1999) was given on 22.4.1999 English version: www.tietosuoja.fi/ uploads/hopxtvf.HTM 2) Entry into force: 01.06.1999.	
United Kingdom	1) Data Protection Act 1998 www.hmso.gov.uk/acts/acts1998/ 19980029.htm 2) Passed: 16.07.1998 3) Subordinate legislation passed on 17.02.2000 www.lcd.gov.uk/foi/ foidpunit.htm 4) Entry into force: 01.03. 2000.	

* *Indicates that measures implementing Commission Decision 95/46/EC have not been notified.*

(Taken from the Europa website (address as above); Chart up to date 12 February 2002).

EU Data Protection Commissioners   **18.4**

National Data Protection Commissioners   **18.5**

Austria Büro der Datenschutzkommission Ballhausplatz 1 1014 Vienna Tel: 00 43 1 531 15 25 25 Website: www.bka.gv.at/datenschutz
Belgium Commission de la protection de la vie privée Boulevard de Waterloo 115 B-1000 Brussels Tel: 00 32 25 42 72 00 Website: www.privacy.fgov.be
Denmark Registertilsynet Christians Brygge, 28, 4 sal DK–1559 Copenhagen V Tel: 00 45 33 14 38 44 Website: www.datatilsynet.dk
Finland Office of the Data Protection Ombudsman Albertinkatu 25, 3.kerros PL 315 PO Box 315 Tel: 00 35 89 18 251 Website: www.tietosuoja.fi
France Commission Nationale de l'Informatique et des Libertés 21 Rue Saint Guillaume 75340 Paris Tel: 00 33 15 37 32 222 Website: www.cnil.fr
Germany Der Bundesbeauftragte für den Datenschutz Friedrich-Ebert-Str. 1 53173 Bonn Tel 00 49 1888 7799 0 Website: www.bfd.bund.de

Greece
Hellenic Data Protection Authority
Omirou 8
PC 10564 Athens
Tel: 00 30 10 33 52 604
Website: www.dpa.gr

Iceland
Data Protection Commission
RauðPararstig 10
IS-105 Reykjavik
Tel: 00 354 510 9600

Ireland
Data Protection Commissioner
Irish Life Centre, Block 4
Talbot Street
Dublin 1
Tel: 00 353 1874 8544
Website: www.dataprivacy.ie

Italy
Garante per la protezione dei dati personali
00186 Rome
Piazza di Monte Citorio n 121
Tel: 00 39 06 696 77 1
Website: http://astra.garanteprivacy.it

Luxembourg
Commission en matière d'utilisation des données nominatives dans les
traitements informatiques
Ministère de la Justice
Boulevard Royal 16
L–2934 Luxembourg
Tel: 00 35 24 78 45 46

Netherlands
College Beschmering Persoonsgegevens
Postbus 93374
2509 AJ Den Haag
Tel: 00 31 70 381 13 00
Website: www.cbpweb.nl

Norway
The Data Inspectorate
PO Box 8177
N-0034 Oslo
Tel: 00 47 22 39 69 00
Website: www.datatilsynet.no

Portugal Commissão Nacional de Protecção de Dados Rue de São Bento, 148, 3 1200 Lisbon Tel: 00 35 213 928 400 Website: www.cnpd.pt
Spain Agencia de Protección de Datos C/Sagasta 22 28004 Madrid Tel: 00 34 91 399 62 00 Website: www.agenciaprotecciondatos.org
Sweden The Data Inspection Board Box 8114 S–104 20 Stockholm Tel: 00 46 86 57 61 00 Website: www.datainspektionen.se
United Kingdom The Office of the Information Commissioner Wycliffe House Water Lane Wilmslow Cheshire SK9 5AF Tel: 00 44 16 25 54 57 00 Website: www.informationcommissioner.gov.uk

Implementation Issues   18.6

Areas where the UK may not have implemented the *Data Protection Directive* properly include the fact that the Directive has a definition of 'consent'. The provisions in the Directive but not in *DPA 1998* require data subjects to consent 'unambiguously'.

Other EU Work   18.7

The Information Commissioner's Office participates in the Working Party of Data Protection Commissioners set up under *Article 29* of the *Data Protection Directive*. In 2001 the Working Party principally worked on transborder data flow issues and the US Safe Harbor Agreement.

In 2001 the Working Party adopted a report from its Internet task force on data protection and the Internet (mentioned in the UK Information Commissioner's First Annual Report (June 2001)).

Retaining Traffic Data – E-security   18.8

The *Directive on Privacy and Electronic Communications (2002/58/EC) (E-privacy Directive)* deals with certain privacy issues relating to 'traffic data'. *Article 6* provides that traffic data relating to subscribers and users processed and stored by the provider of a public communications network or publicly available electronic communications service must be erased or made anonymous when it is no longer needed for the purpose of the transmission of a communication. Traffic data necessary for the purposes of subscriber billing and interconnection payments may be processed. Such processing is permissible only up to the end of the period during which the bill may lawfully be challenged or payment pursued.

For the purpose of marketing electronic communications, *article 6(3)* provides that for services or for the provision of value added services, the provider of a publicly available electronic communications service may process the data referred to in *article 6(1)* to the extent and for the duration necessary for such services or marketing, if the subscriber or user to whom the data relate has given his/her consent. Users or subscribers must be given the possibility to withdraw their consent for the processing of traffic data at any time.

The service provider must inform the subscriber or user of the types of traffic data which are processed and of the duration of such processing for the purposes mentioned in *article 6(2)* and, prior to obtaining consent, for the purposes mentioned in *article 6(3)*.

Such processing of traffic data must be restricted to persons acting under the authority of providers of the public communications networks and publicly available electronic communications services handling billing or traffic management, customer enquiries, fraud detection, marketing of electronic communications services or providing a value added service, and must be restricted to what is necessary for the purposes of such activities.

The Directive was implemented by the *Privacy and Electronic Communications (EC Directive) Regulations 2003 (SI 2003/2426)*.

Regulation of Investigatory Powers (Communications Data) Order 2003 and Traffic Data   18.9

In January 2004 the *Regulation of Investigatory Powers (Communications Data) Order 2003 (SI 2003/3172)* came into force allowing some public authorities access to customer data held by telecoms companies and Internet service providers. The regulations are made under the *Regulation of Investigatory Powers Act 2000 (RIPA 2000)*. Earlier 2001 terrorism legislation required the retention of communications data by ISPs, as these were needed to fight terrorism. Once obtained, the *RIPA 2000* provisions allow access to many other agencies for purposes unconnected with terrorism. The data concerned is information, which includes information from telephone companies, ISPs and interactive TV providers and it describes the caller and the means of communication (eg subscriber details, billing data, email logs, personal details of customers and records showing the location where mobile phone calls were made). It does not include content.

In addition to the police, Inland Revenue, Customs and Excise, MI5, MI6 and GCHQ, the *Regulation of Investigatory Powers (Communications Data) Order 2003* gives some other agencies rights to access communications data. These are fewer in number than in the original proposal which critics called the 'Snoopers' Charter', but do include:

- the Financial Services Authority;

- the Office of Fair Trading;

- the Maritime and Coastguard Agency;

- the UK Atomic Energy Constabulary;

- the Scottish Drugs Enforcement Agency;

- the Radiocommunications Agency;

- NHS bodies, in connection with health and fraud;

- local authorities (but not parish councils); and

- the Office of the Police Ombudsman for Northern Ireland.

The *Regulation of Investigatory Powers (Communications Data) Order 2003* can be viewed at http://www.hmso.gov.uk/si/si2003/20033172

Recent Developments 18.10

New Legislation 18.11

The *Anti-terrorism, Crime and Security Act 2001* led to the Information Commissioner commenting that:

> 'The provisions could have a significant impact on the privacy of individuals whose data are retained. If there is a demonstrable and pressing need for these provisions, an appropriate balance must be struck between personal privacy and the legitimate needs of the law enforcement community. There are particular concerns that leaving matters to a voluntary code of practice, or to agreements, may pose difficulties for data protection and human rights compliance. Although recent events have prompted these measures to be brought forward, law enforcement agencies will make use of them on a day-to-day basis for a variety of matters. Careful consideration must be given to ensure that the provisions are appropriate to addressing these more routine needs.'

Case Law 18.12

In November 2001, in the case of *Brian Robertson v Wakefield City Council (High Court, 16 November 2001)*, the High Court held that the UK, in permitting the use of the electoral roll for commercial purposes had not, in *DPA 1998*, properly implemented the *Data Protection Directive (95/46/EC)*. Voters should not have their data used for such purposes when it was gathered to enable them to vote.

Further Information 18.13

Information on the implementation of the *Data Protection Directive* is on the European Commission's website at www.europa.eu.int/comm/internal_market/en/dataprot/law/impl.htm

The EU European Policy Approach to E-security is on the Internet at www.europa.eu.int/information_society/eeurope/news_library/pdf_files/netsec_en.pdf

FAQs 18.14

What is the European basis for *DPA 1998*?

DPA 1998 implemented the *Data Protection Directive* in the UK. The Act must therefore follow the provisions of the Directive.

Have there been any cases where *DPA 1998* has been held to conflict with the Directive?

Yes, in *Robertson v Wakefield* the court found that by not amending electoral legislation properly the Government had not in the Act properly implemented the directive.

Does the Information Commissioner have an EU role?

Yes, the Information Commissioner's office liaises with other information commissioners around the EU.

Chapter 19 – Exemptions

At A Glance

✓   There are many exemptions from the *Data Protection Act 1998* (*DPA 1998*) including those for staff administration and some forms of marketing.

✓   Comprehensive coverage of the exemptions to *DPA 1998* appears in the Commissioner's Legal Guidance (Chapter 5, October 2001).

✓   The decision in *Baker v Home Department (October 2001)* held that the security services could not just apply a blanket ban on subject access in major areas.

✓   In a Swedish case the exemption under the *Data Protection Directive* (*95/46/EC*) for the processing of data for journalistic purposes in the public interest was held to apply.

Introduction   19.1

DPA 1998 contains many complex exemptions in a wide range of areas. Few are blanket exemptions. Most give exemption from one aspect only, such as the right of subject access under *section 7* of *DPA 1998*. They therefore have to be considered very carefully indeed. This section simply provides a broad overview of the exemptions available. The staff administration exemption was also considered under **16 EMPLOYMENT**.

Exemptions in Notification Regulations   19.2

The *Data Protection (Notification and Notification Fees) Regulations 2000* ('*Notification Regulations*') (*SI 2000/188*) appear wide-ranging, but in practice most companies will find the processing they do with their data takes them outside the exemptions. Few businesses will be able to avoid notification (registration) under *DPA 1998* simply because of these provisions. This was the same under the *Data Protection Act 1984* (*DPA 1984*) which contains some fairly similar exemptions.

Section 17 of *DPA 1998* provides that no one must process personal data without registration or notification. The exemption below provides an exemption from this provision. In effect the data controller does not have to register. However, all the other obligations under *DPA 1998* apply, such as the Eight Data Protection Principles and the requirement to give individuals access to their personal data under *section 7* of *DPA 1998*.

Staff Administration Exemption   19.3

The staff administration exemption covers data processing for the purposes of appointments or removals, pay, discipline, superannuation, work management or other personnel matters in relation to the staff of the data controller where the personal data is in respect of a part, existing or prospective member of staff or any one the processing of whose personal data is necessary for the exempt purposes.

The exemption is limited to cases where the personal data is just the name, address and other identifiers of the data subject, information as to qualifications, work experience or pay, or other matters, the processing of which is necessary for the exempt purposes. In addition, the data must not be disclosed to a third party other than with the data subject's consent or where necessary for the exempt purposes. It must not involve keeping the personal data after the relationship has ceased.

Most employers will be outside this requirement.

Advertising, Marketing and Public Relations Exemption   19.4

A very limited exemption applies where data processing is for the purposes of advertising or marketing the data controller's business or activity, and it:

- solely relates to data of past, existing or prospective customers or suppliers;

- is only the name, address or other identifier; and

- does not involve disclosure without data subject consent, as in relation to the staff administration exemption (see **19.3** above).

The information must not be kept after the relationship ends, except where necessary for the exempt purposes.

Accounts and Records Exemption   19.5

Where data processing is:

- to keep accounts;

- to decide whom to accept as a customer or supplier;

- to keep records of purchases, sales or other transaction to ensure payments and deliveries are made; or

- for financial or management forecasts,

then it may be possible to be exempt from registration but not the other requirements of *DPA 1998*. This is limited as set out in *paragraph 4* of the *Schedule* to the *Notification Regulations (SI 2000/188)*, by requirements such as the data must only consist of data about customers and suppliers, which consists just of their name, address and other identifiers, and which relates only to their financial standing. It must not involve disclosure to third parties nor any retention of the information after the relationship is over.

Non-profit Making Organisations   19.6

There is an exemption from the *Notification Regulations (SI 2000/188)* where the processing is carried out by a body or association which is not established or conducted for profit. It applies where the data is just about past, existing or prospective members or any person in regular contact with the body or organisation, and must only be a name, address or other identifier and concern eligibility for membership. No disclosure may take place without the data subject's consent and after the relationship is over the data should be destroyed.

Manual Records   19.7

There is no general exemption for manual records under the *DPA* 1998, but the *Michael John Durant v Financial Services Authority [2003] EWCA Civ 1746* decision led the IC to issue guidance in February 2004, which concludes that most manual records fall outside the Act – see **CHAPTER 30**. Also new 2004 guidance on CCTV, included in **APPENDIX 1**, concludes many small businesses using CCTV also fall outside the *DPA 1998* following that case.

Other Exemptions   19.8

Other exemptions are contained in *DPA 1998*. However, it is essential to read *DPA 1998* in relation to these exemptions, as they provide exemptions from particular sections of *DPA 1998* rather than from the whole Act. A summary of the exemptions is contained in Chapter 5 of the Commissioner's Introduction which is on the website at www.informationcommissioner.gov.uk.

- National security (see the *Baker* decision at 19.13 below).

- Crime and taxation.

- Health and social work (in this respect note the *Data Protection (Subject Access Modification) (Social Work) Order 2000 (SI 2000/415)*, *Data Protection (Subject Access Modification) (Education) Order 2000 (SI 2000/414)* the *Data Protection (Subject Access Modification) (Health) Order 2000 (SI 2000/413)* (see **19.10** below).

- Regulatory activity.

- Journalism, literature and art – 'special purposes' (see the Swedish case at **19.15** below) under *DPA 1998* (this is an exemption from all the Data

Protection Principles except the Seventh Principle (security) and also an exemption from *sections 7, 10, 12,* and *14(1)–(3)* of *DPA 1998* where:

- the processing is with a view to the publication of journalistic, literary or artistic material;

- the data controller reasonably believes it is in the public interest (not a very onerous requirement); and

- the data controller believes that compliance with the provision in *DPA 1998* is incompatible with the special purpose.

- Research, history and statistics.

- Information available to the public under the law.

- Legal disclosures and legal proceedings (see *Totalise v Motley Fool* case at **19.14** below).

- Domestic purposes (family and householder affairs).

- *Schedule 7* to *DPA 1998* exemptions:

  - confidential references;

  - armed forces;

  - judicial appointments and honours;

  - Crown employment;

  - management forecasts;

  - corporate finance (and note the provisions of the *Data Protection (Corporate Finance Exemption) Order 2000 (SI 2000/184)*);

  - negotiations;

  - examination marks;

  - examination scripts;

  - legal professional privilege; and

  - self incrimination.

Also relevant are exemptions under *DPA 1984* such as for manual data, processing otherwise than by reference to the data subject, back-up data etc., in cases where there are lengthy periods before *DPA 1998* will apply.

Information Commissioner's Guidance on the Exemptions   19.9

In October 2001 the Commissioner issued her Legal Guidance on *DPA 1998* which includes, in Chapter 5, comprehensive consideration of the exemptions under the Act briefly mentioned above. Her guidance, along with secondary legislation relevant to the exemptions, is considered in more detail at **19.10–19.11** below.

Orders Made in Relation to Health, Education and Social Work 19.10

The orders made in relation to health, education and social work are made under *section 30* of *DPA 1998*. They include the *Data Protection (Subject Access Modification) (Health) Order 2000 (SI 2000/413)* ('*Health Order*'). This provides an exemption from subject access for data relating to the physical or mental health or condition of the data subject, to the extent to which the application of *section 7* of *DPA 1998* would be likely to cause serious harm to the physical or mental health or condition of the data subject or any other person.

The Commissioner states in her Legal Guidance:

> 'Before deciding whether this exemption applies, a data controller who is not a health professional (as defined in *DPA 1998*) is obliged to consult the health professional responsible for the clinical care of the data subject, or if there is more than one, the most suitable one.'

The Commissioner recognises that in many cases there will be more than one health professional responsible for the patient's clinical care at the time a subject access request is made. Data controllers should ensure that they have systems in place to enable the most suitable health professional to be identified and consulted to enable the data controller to comply with a subject access request within the statutory time limit of 40 days.

Where a request for subject access is made by someone other than the data subject (ie by someone with parental responsibility for a child or, in relation to Scotland, by such a person on behalf of someone under the age of 16, or by a person appointed by a court to manage the affairs of the data subject), the data controller should consider the following:

- any expectation of confidentiality the data subject may have had at the time the information was provided or obtained; and

- any wishes expressed by the data subject with regard to the disclosure of personal data relating to his physical or mental health or condition.

In specific circumstances, which are set out in the *Health Order 2000 (SI 2000/413)* where certain personal data are processed by the Court, there is also an exemption from the subject information provisions.

The *Data Protection (Subject Access Modifications) (Education) Order 2000 (SI 2000/414)* ('*Education Order*') provides for modifications and exemptions:

- where the personal data consist of information constituting an education record;

- where disclosure of the information pursuant to a subject access request would be likely to cause serious harm to the physical or mental health or condition of the data subject, or to some other person; or

- in some circumstances, where disclosure would reveal that the data subject is, or may be at risk of child abuse (as defined in the Order).

The *Data Protection (Subject Access Modifications) (Social Work) Order 2000 (SI 2000/415)* ('*Social Work Order*') provides for modifications and exemptions where the personal data relate to social work falling within any of the descriptions set out in the Order.

Processing for the Special Purposes   19.11

Data processing for special purposes is governed by *section 32* of *DPA 1998*.

'Special purposes' means any one or more of the following:

- the purposes of journalism;
- artistic purposes; and
- literary purposes.

Section 32 of *DPA 1998* provides four conditions which must all be present before the processing of personal data for the special purposes can qualify for any exemption from *DPA 1998* under this section. The conditions are that:

- the personal data are processed only for the special purposes;
- the processing is undertaken with a view to the publication by any person of any journalistic, literary or artistic material;
- the data controller reasonably believes that, taking account in particular of the special importance of the public interest in freedom of expression, publication would be in the public interest; and
- the data controller reasonably believes that, in all the circumstances, compliance with the provision in respect of which the exemption is claimed is incompatible with the special purposes.

In her Legal Guidance under *DPA 1998* the Commissioner says:

'If all the conditions are satisfied, the exemption available is from the following provisions of the Act:

- the *Data Protection Principles* except the *Seventh Data Protection Principle* (concerning security and other measures);
- *section 7* of *DPA 1998* – subject access;
- *section 10* of *DPA 1998* – right to prevent processing likely to cause damage or distress;
- *section 12* of *DPA 1998* – rights in relation to automated decision-taking;

- *section 12A* of *DPA 1998* – the rectification, blocking, erasure or destruction of certain inaccurate manual data during the transitional periods (see Chapters 4 and 6 [of the Commissioner's Legal Guidance]); and

- *section 14(1)–(3)* of *DPA 1998* – provisions relating to rectification, blocking, erasure and destruction of inaccurate data.'

Confidential References   19.12

Personal data which consist of a confidential reference given, or to be given, by the data controller for specified purposes (education, training or employment, appointment to office or provision of any service) are exempt from subject access. The Commissioner says:

'This exemption is not available to the data controller who receives such references. In other words, where Company A provides an employment reference concerning one of its employees to Company B, if the employee makes a subject access request to Company A, the reference will be exempt from the disclosure. If the employee makes the request to Company B, the reference is not automatically exempt from disclosure and the usual subject access rules apply.'

Section 28 Exemption (National Security): The Baker Case   19.13

In the recent case of *Norman Baker MP v Secretary of State for the Home Department (1 October 2001)*, under *DPA 1998* it was decided that the security service/Secretary of State was wrong to say that a blanket exemption (under national security exemption provisions) applied when a *section 7* of *DPA 1998* subject access request was refused. The security service had said subject access requests would only be permitted *in* the categories of staff administration, building security CCTV and commercial agreements, in which three categories in any event the security service held no data relating to the data subject, Mr Baker. This was held to be wrong in law by the Data Protection Tribunal. It asked:

'When does national security take precedence over human rights?

Where the context is national security, judges and tribunals should supervise with the lightest touch appropriate; there is no area (foreign affairs apart) where judges have traditionally deferred more to the executive view than that of national security; and for good and sufficient reason'.

They found however, that there were no reasonable grounds for the Secretary of State to issue the certificate which led to the failure to disclose whether any information (except in the three categories mentioned at **19.11** above) was held.

Section 28 of DPA 1998 provides an exemption from a number of provisions of the Act if exemption from any such provision is required for the purpose of safeguarding national security. In effect, such an exemption is, the Commissioner says, 'asserted by means of certificates, signed by a Minister of the Crown, certifying that exemption from all or any of the provisions is or was required for the requisite purpose. Such a certificate is conclusive evidence of that fact'. Any person directly affected by the issuing of such a certificate may appeal to the Data Protection Tribunal against the certificate.

The Tribunal is specially constituted to hear such appeals and is subject to different rules than in the case of appeals against enforcement and information notices under the *Data Protection Tribunal (National Security Appeals) Rules 2000 (SI 2000/206)*. The first appeal to be heard by this Tribunal was the one which considered the *Baker* case. As this was the first appeal, the parties consented to the proceedings taking place in public (subject to certain restrictions to protect the identity of some witnesses).

Section 35 Exemption: Totalise v Motley Fool
19.14

Section 35 of DPA 1998 provides that personal data are exempt from the non-disclosure provisions where the disclosure is required by or under any enactment, by any rule of law or by order of a court. Under *section 35(2)* of DPA 1998 there is a similar exemption where the disclosure is necessary for the purpose of legal proceedings or for obtaining legal advice, or is otherwise necessary for the purposes of establishing, exercising or defending legal rights.

In the case *Totalise plc v Motley Fool Ltd and Another (2001, upheld by CA 2002)*, where the websites Motley Fool and Interactive Investor were reluctant to hand over confidential personal data of who was behind an alias, where the man operating the alias was posting defamatory material about Totalise on the bulletin boards concerned, the companies said *section 35* of DPA 1998 would allow them to *resist* disclosure, not force them to disclose. They said it should be construed narrowly – that it should apply only for the data controller to obtain legal advice or to establish, exercise or defend legal rights. The court did not agree.

An interesting issue in relation to this area is raised. Totalise could not use *section 7* of *DPA 1998* to obtain the data they wanted because it is a company not an individual. Had a defamation of a director of Totalise occurred instead, the director exercising a right under *section 7* against the websites might have obtained the identity of the anonymous poster, who went by the name of Z Dust, unless this allows another individual to be identified (the director would have made his request in order to have the third party individual, the person defaming him, identified. However, disclosure under *section 7* is allowed which identifies third parties such as this where it is reasonable or where the individual consents. If the Internet Service Provider ('ISP') website conditions did not offer people posting messages anonymity, then the ISP may be entitled to give the director in such a case the information required. In addition, a *section 7* request is much cheaper than a High Court application (£10 as opposed to presumably at least £10,000–£20,000).

Example of Exemptions – Sweden   19.15

On 12 June 2001, the Swedish Supreme Court ruled in the first criminal case concerning the use and processing of personal data. The *Swedish Personal Data Act*, based on the *Data Protection Directive (95/46/EC)*, came into force in 1998. Since then the Act has been heavily criticised, *inter alia*, for limiting the freedom of expression. The case involved a public Internet website on which a Swedish person (X) listed and named a number of individuals, several of them politicians and bank directors at Swedish banks. On the site X criticised several of the named individuals and accused them, among other things, of plundering. X also argued that some of them were responsible for the bankruptcy of X's company. The prosecutor claimed that the publishing of personal data constituted an unlawful distribution of personal data to a third country.

The website was held by the defence to be a 'forum' that threw light on the damage caused by Swedish banks, financial institutions and private capitalists during the Swedish bank crisis in the late 1980s and early 1990s. X further claimed that the personal data had been published solely with a journalistic purpose and was therefore exempt from the requirements of the legislation. An exemption exists for the processing and publication of personal data undertaken solely with a journalistic purpose (see **19.11** above). It is not clear if this provision relates to everyone or just mass media companies.

The lower court in Sweden found that part of the purpose behind the publishing of the personal data was to spread knowledge of the disparaging remarks on the site. Therefore the purpose behind X's listing of the personal data had not been solely journalistic. The court held the exemption applies however not just to professional journalists, but to others too.

The Supreme Court clarified the law concerning the exemption granted to journalistic publication stating that it applies not only to professional journalists and media enterprises, but to the ordinary people too. The court also identified a journalistic purpose underlying X's website and furthermore made it clear that the presence of disparaging or offensive remarks must be considered a normal part of the pubic debate. Therefore it was found that the publishing of the personal data did form part of a solely journalistic activity and thus was not a criminal offence under the Personal Data Act.

To read the case go to: www.notisum.se. For more information contact: Erik.Bergenstrahle@lindahl.se.

Section 32 Exemption   19.16

In *Campbell v Mirror Group Newspapers [2003] 1 All ER 224* the Court of Appeal, overturning the High Court, held that Express Newspapers were free to publish details about the supermodel Ms Campbell's attendance at Narcotics Anonymous meetings because of the exemption in *section 32* of *DPA 1998*.

Section 32 reads:

'(1) Personal data which are processed only for the special purposes are exempt from any provision to which this subsection relates if-

(a) the processing is undertaken with a view to the publication by any person of any journalistic literary or artistic material,

(b) the data controller reasonably believes that having regard in particular to the special importance of the public interest in freedom of expression, publication would be in the public interest, and

(c) the data controller reasonably believes that, in all the circumstances, compliance with that provision is incompatible with the special purposes ...

(3) In considering for the purposes of subsection (1)(b) whether the belief of a data controller that publication would be in the public interest was or is a reasonable one, regard may be had to his compliance with any code of practice which-

(a) is relevant to the publication in question, and

(b) is designated by the Secretary of State by order for the purposes of this subsection.

(4) Where at any time ("the relevant time") in any proceedings against a data controller under section 7(9), 10(4), 12(8) or 14 or by virtue of section 13 the data controller claims, or it appears to the court, that any personal data to which the proceedings relate are being processed-

(a) only for the special purposes and

(b) with a view to the publication by any person of any journalistic, literary or artistic material which, at the time twenty-four hours immediately before the relevant time, had not previously been published by the data controller, the court shall stay the proceedings until either of the conditions in subsection (5) is met.

(5) Those conditions are-

(a) that a determination of the Commissioner under section 45 with respect to the data in question takes effect or

(b) in a case where the proceedings were stayed on the making of a claim, that the claim is withdrawn.

(6) For the purposes of this Act "publish", in relation to journalistic, literary or artistic material, means make available to the public or any section of the public.'

In this decision the Court of Appeal said that *section 32(1)* to *(3)* of *DPA 1998* provides widespread exemption from the Act provided that the data controller reasonably believed that publication would be in the public interest and that compliance was incompatible with the special purpose of journalism. The subsections must be given their natural meaning, and must apply both before and after publication. Miss Campbell had sought to argue that the exemption in *section 32(1)* depended on the processing being undertaken with a view to publication, therefore the processing could not include the publication. However, the Court of Appeal said that it was the data which was exempt. Where under *section 32* the data became exempt as a result of a reasonable belief of the journalist that the publication would be in the public interest, the data remained subject to the exemption after that. Here the *section 32* exemption applied.

Case commentary

The IC's Commentary on the case, in the March 2003 Annual Report, said:

'In this case the Court of Appeal has confirmed and clarified various "routine" matters of interpretation relating to both Directive 95/46/EC and the *DPA 98*, making various helpful passing comments on the general ambit of these provisions. The Court confirmed that the definition of "processing" in the *DPA 98* is "very wide" and that "publication must be treated as part of the operations covered by the requirements of the Act". Some legal commentators have characterised the Court of Appeal's judgment in this case as a denial of any right to privacy. In the Commissioner's view this is quite wrong; rather, the Court are still feeling their way in that direction. On the central question of where the law stands on the "*article 8* v *article 10* issue', the courts are, in the Commissioner's view, still slowly and carefully moving towards establishing a common law concept of privacy within, alongside or, possibly, outside the realms of the law of confidence. In an appropriate case, on the particular facts, the courts will almost inevitably find there to be a "breach of privacy" as opposed to a "breach of confidence". But what will be an appropriate case? What will be the particular facts? How will the case by case approach work? What will be an 'unjustifiable publication'? At this stage the Commissioner's prediction is that the courts will move further down this road in a case involving a genuine private person, not a celebrity or other public figure. The Court of Appeal clearly adopted a wide approach to the "special purposes" exemption at *section 32* of the *DPA 98*, making it clear that it can apply after, as well as before, publication. The Commissioner would though want to make it clear that the exemption does not provide unlimited exemption from the whole Act for the media. This is very clearly not the case. The *section 32* exemption only applies in relation to particular provisions of the Act, and only to the extent that there is a reasonable belief that compliance with any such provision would prejudice any of the "special purposes", including journalistic purposes. It does not provide carte blanche for the media. The Commissioner notes that the Court of Appeal's judgment is currently the subject of an appeal to the House of Lords which is not expected to be heard before the publication of this Report. The Commissioner awaits with interest their Lordships' judgment in this important case.' (IC's Annual Report for year to March 2003.)

This decision is being appealed to the House of Lords, so the latest position should always be checked.

The Privacy Code   19.17

The *Data Protection (Designated Codes of Practice) (No. 2) Order 2000 (SI 2000/1864*, which revoked *SI 2000/418)* designates for the purposes of *section 32(3) of DPA 1998* the codes of practice listed in the Schedule to this Order. These are:

- the code published by the Broadcasting Standards Commission under *section 107* of the *Broadcasting Act 1996;*

- the code published by the Independent Television Commission under *section 7* of the *Broadcasting Act 1990;*

- the Code of Practice published by the Press Complaints Commission;

- the Producers' Guidelines published by the British Broadcasting Corporation; and

- the code published by the Radio Authority under *section 91* of the *Broadcasting Act 1990.*

Compliance with any of the designated codes may be taken into account when considering for the purposes of *section 32(1)(b)* of *DPA 1998* whether the belief of a data controller that the publication of any journalistic, literary or artistic material would be in the public interest was reasonable.

Part 3 of the Press Complaints Commission Code says:

'Privacy

(i)   Everyone is entitled to respect for his or her private and family life, home, health and correspondence, A publication will be expected to justify intrusions into any individual's private life without consent.

(ii) The use of long lens photography to take pictures of people in private places without their consent is unacceptable.

Note: Private places are public or private property where there is a reasonable expectation of privacy.'

Further Information   19.18

Information on the exemptions is contained in the Information Commissioner's Legal Guidance (October 2001).

FAQs   19.19

Are all sectors covered by *DPA 1998*?

DPA 1998 contains exemptions not for sectors but for categories of data which vary considerably and many are not exemptions from the entirety of *DPA 1998*, but parts.

Are references exempted?

Not entirely. Confidential employment references are excluded in certain cases – in the hands of the employer who wrote the reference but not subsequent employers.

Have there been any cases on exemptions?

Yes, the case of *Baker* where the court held the Government had used the national security exemption much too broadly.

Chapter 20 –
Export of Data

At A Glance

✓ Data can be freely exported within the European Economic Area ('EEA').

✓ Data can be exported freely to approved countries designated by the European Commission.

✓ Data can be exported under the US/EU Safe Harbor Agreement to those US companies who have registered under that agreement

✓ Data can be exported elsewhere as long as the Eighth Data Protection Principle is followed, eg by using the European Commission's model clauses for data export (reproduced in **APPENDIX 3**). The Information Commissioner has issued guidance on adequacy and transborder data flows.

✓ The European Commission has issued useful Frequently Asked Questions guidance about the model clauses for data export (reproduced in **APPENDIX 2**).

Introduction   20.1

On 18 June 2001 the European Commission approved important new standard clauses for those exporting data from the EEA. There are many misconceptions at large about export of personal data under the *Data Protection Act 1998* (*DPA 1998*). These appear in Appendix 3. Many believe there is simply a ban on the export of data outside the EEA. In fact *DPA 1998* permits export in many situations. The Eighth Data Protection Principle in *Schedule 1* of *DPA 1998* simply provides that export from the EEA is not permitted unless that country ensures an adequate level of protection in relation to the processing of personal data.

> 'Personal data shall not be transferred to a country or territory outside the European Economic Area, unless that country or territory ensures an adequate level of protection of the rights and freedoms of data subjects in relation to the processing of personal data.'
>
> *(DPA 1998, Sch 1, Part I, Para 8.)*

An adequate level of protection is one which is adequate in all the circumstances of the case, having regard in particular to:

- the nature of the personal data;

- the country or territory of origin of the information contained in the data;

- the country or territory of final destination of that information;

- the purposes for which and period during which the data are intended to be processed;

- the law in force in the country or territory in question;

- the international obligations of that country or territory;

- any relevant codes of conduct or other rules which are enforceable in that country or territory (whether generally or by arrangement in particular cases); and

- any security measures taken in respect of the data in that country or territory.

This is not an exhaustive list.

Schedule 4 of *DPA 1998* provides for circumstances in which the Eighth Data Protection Principle does not apply to a transfer of data. These are where:

(*a*) the data subject has given their consent to the transfer;

(*b*) the transfer is necessary:

    (i) for the performance of a contract between the data subject and the data controller; or

    (ii) for the taking of steps at the request of the data subject with a view to the data subject entering into a contract with the data controller;

(*c*) the transfer is necessary:

    (i) for the conclusion of a contract between the data controller and a person other than the data subject which:

        (A) is entered into at the request of the data subject, or

        (B) is in the interests of the data subject, or

    (ii) for the performance of such a contract;

(*d*) the transfer is necessary for reasons of substantial public interest.

    The Secretary of State may specify by order the circumstances in which a transfer is to be taken to be necessary for reasons of substantial public interest. No order to this effect has been made to date;

(*e*) the transfer:

    (i) is necessary for the purpose of, or in connection with, any legal proceedings (including prospective legal proceedings);

(ii)   is necessary for the purpose of obtaining legal advice; or

(iii)   is otherwise necessary for the purposes of establishing, exercising or defending legal rights;

(*f*)   the transfer is necessary in order to protect the vital interests of the data subject;

(*g*)   the transfer is part of the personal data on a public register and any conditions subject to which the register is open to inspection are complied with by any person to whom the data are or may be disclosed after the transfer;

(*h*)   the transfer is made on terms which are of a kind approved by the Information Commissioner as ensuring adequate safeguards for the rights and freedoms of data subjects. It is not the practice of the Information Commissioner to consider or approve individual draft contracts submitted to her; and

(*j*)   the transfer has been authorised by the Information Commissioner as being made in such a manner as to ensure adequate safeguards for the rights and freedoms of data subjects.

The Information Commissioner has issued guidance on transborder data flows which looks at how such requirements might be met.

Approved Countries 20.2

The European Commission, as at January 2004, had approved the following countries as having adequate national data protection safeguards to permit export without restriction, subject always, of course, to the general provisons of the *DPA 1998* as they would apply in the UK:

Guernsey

- Commission Decision of 21 November 2003 on the adequate protection of personal data in Guernsey – OJ L 308, 25 November 2003.

Argentine

- Commission Decision C(2003) 1731 of 30 June 2003 – OJ L 168, 5 July 2003.

Canada

- Commission Decision 2002/2/EC of 20.12.2001 on the adequate protection of personal data provided by the Canadian Personal Information Protection and Electronic Documents Act – O.J. L 2/13 of 4 January 2002.

- See also Frequently Asked Questions on the Commission's adequacy finding on the *Canadian Personal Information Protection and Electronic Documents Act* (March 2002).

Switzerland

- Commission Decision 2000/518/EC of 26.7.2000 – O. J. L 215/1 of 25 August 2000.

Hungary

- Commission Decision 2000/519/EC of 26.7.2000 – O.J. L 215/4 of 25 August 2000.

The adequacy list is at
http://europa.eu.int/comm/internal_market/privacy/adequacy_en.htm

In 2003 and 2004 the EU and US were debating transfer of air passengers' personal data for security purposes – see Brussels, 16.12.2003 COM(2003) 826 final *Communication from the Commission to the Council and the Parliament Transfer of Air Passenger Name Record (Pnr) Data: A Global Eu Approach* Safe Harbor Agreement.

20.3

The US/EU Safe Harbor Agreement (Commission decision 2000/520/EC (OJ L 215 of 25.08.2000, p. 7–47)) permits data exports to the US to those companies within the scheme.

In July 2000 after months of negotiation the United States and European Union reached an accord on data protection, which covers e-commerce but not financial services. It has been designed to aid businesses shipping personal data between the EEA and US. The *Data Protection Directive (95/46/EC)*, which was implemented in the UK by *DPA 1998*, contains restrictions on export of data to countries such as the US which do not have the same type of data protection laws in place. Failure to comply with such laws will be considered a deceptive business practice and a prosecutable offence. The US Department of Commerce keeps a register of industry self-regulators and monitors those companies to ensure they comply with privacy rules. The Federal Trade Commission and the US judicial system can impose sanctions on companies that violate the rules. (See also **41** 'SAFE HARBOR' AGREEMENT.)

The Seven Safe Harbor Principles   20.4

Organisations must comply with the seven safe harbor principles if exporting data to the US. The requirements of the principles are set out in **20.5–20.11** below.

Notice   20.5

Organisations must notify individuals about the purposes for which they collect and use information about them. They must provide information about how individuals can contact the organisation with any inquiries or complaints, the types of third parties to which it discloses the information and the choices and means the organisation offers for limiting its use and disclosure.

Choice   20.6

Organisations must give individuals the opportunity to choose ('opt-out') whether their personal information will be disclosed to a third party, or used for a purpose incompatible with the purpose for which it was originally collected or subsequently authorised by the individual. For sensitive information, affirmative or explicit ('opt-in') choice must be given if the information is to be disclosed to a third party or used for a purpose other than its original purpose or the purpose authorised subsequently by the individual.

Onward Transfer (Transfers to Third Parties)   20.7

To disclose information to a third party, organisations must apply the notice and choice principles. Where an organisation wishes to transfer information to a third party that is acting as an agent, it may do so if it makes sure that the third party subscribes to the safe harbor principles or is subject to the *Data Protection Directive (95/46/EC)*. As an alternative, the organisation can enter into a written agreement with such a third party requiring that the third party provide at least the same level of privacy protection as is required by the relevant principles.

Access   20.8

Individuals must have access to personal information held about them by an organisation and be able to correct, amend, or delete that information where it is inaccurate, except where the burden or expense of providing access would be disproportionate to the risks to the individual's privacy in the case in question, or where the rights of persons other than the individual would be violated.

Security   20.9

Organisations must take reasonable precautions to protect personal information from loss, misuse and unauthorised access, disclosure, alteration and destruction.

Data Integrity   20.10

Personal information must be relevant for the purposes for which it is to be used. An organisation should take reasonable steps to ensure that data is reliable for its intended use, accurate, complete, and current.

Enforcement 20.11

In order to ensure compliance with the safe harbor principles, there must be:

- readily available and affordable independent recourse mechanisms so that each individual's complaints and disputes can be investigated and resolved and damages awarded where the applicable law or private sector initiatives so provide;

- procedures for verifying that the commitments companies make to adhere to the safe harbor principles have been implemented; and

- obligations to remedy problems arising out of a failure to comply with the principles. Sanctions must be sufficiently rigorous to ensure compliance by the organisation. Organisations that fail to provide annual self-certification letters will no longer appear in the list of participants and safe harbor benefits will no longer be assured.

To provide further guidance, the US Department of Commerce has issued a set of FAQs that clarify and supplement the safe harbor principles.

The Agreement began to operate in November 2000. After a slow start, with only Dun and Bradstreet registering (apart from some non-commercial bodies) Microsoft has announced it is joining the scheme, and in May 2001 the Direct Marketing Association also announced its support for the safe harbor agreement. It believes it will be the first trade association to offer its members free seals of approval through the arrangement.

The US authorities have a safe harbor website which is at www.export.gov/safeharbor/.

Commissioner's Guidance 20.12

The Information Commissioner has issued detailed guidance on the export of personal data (see **20.16** below).

European Commission Model Clauses 20.13

The European Commission has issued model clauses which would ensure the adequacy required by the Eighth Data Protection Principle in any export of data to data controllers and therefore it is likely that many companies will be agreeing with the imposition of such clauses on the recipients of their data outside the EU.

The model clauses can be accessed at http://europa.eu.int/comm/internal_market/privacy/modelcontracts_en.htm.

At the same time, the Commission issued some very useful FAQs which complement those already issued in relation to the EU Safe Harbor agreement. The clauses are annexed to a Commission Decision (OJ L181/19, 4.7.2001). Article 1 of the Decision provides that the annexed standard clauses will ensure adequate protection on the export of data. Under Article 3 a member state is given power to withdraw the protection of the clauses, for example where a data importer has not complied with the clauses.

Export can be made even to countries without adequate levels of protection under *Schedule 4* of *DPA 1998* which concerns cases where the Eighth Principle does not apply. These are also contained in *Article 26* of the *Data Protection Directive (95/46/EC)* and include cases where:

- the data subject has given his or her consent unambiguously to the proposed transfer;

- the transfer is necessary for the performance of a contract between the data subject and the controller or the implementation of pre-contractual measures taken in response to the data subject's request;

- the transfer is necessary for the conclusion or performance of a contract concluded in the interest of the data subject between the controller and a third party;

- the transfer is necessary or legally required on important public interest grounds, or for the establishment, exercise or defence of legal claims;

- the transfer is necessary in order to protect the vital interests of the data subject; or

- the transfer is made from a register which according to laws or regulations is intended to provide information to the public and which is open to consultation either by the public in general or by any person who can demonstrate legitimate interest, to the extent that the conditions laid down in law for consultation are fulfilled in the particular case.

Finally, national authorities may authorise on a case-by-case basis specific transfers to a country not offering an adequate protection where the exporter in the EU adduces adequate safeguards with respect to the protection of privacy by fundamental rights and freedoms of individuals, and as regards the exercise of the corresponding rights. This could be undertaken, for example, by contractual arrangements between the exporter and the importer of data, subject to the prior approval of national authorities.

In 2002 the Commission issued data export clauses where the export is to 'data processors'. They are reproduced in **APPENDIX 3**. The European Commission, in its FAQs on the clauses, explains that it intends to start work on other standard contractual clauses 'in particular to deal with low risk transfers that may allow for a lighter approach to be followed. A first decision is likely to concern the transfer of data to a subcontractor for the mere processing, a category of transfers excluded from the scope of the Decision).' The Commission is hoping to receive drafts of clauses from industry associations for it to consider.

The way the model clauses work is that each EU Member State will recognise the standard clauses as complying with the provisions of the legislation on data export.

Member States will be free to impose a licensing system for such exports, although it is believed to be unlikely that the UK would do so. The European Commission also believes that some Member States may require the contract containing the model clauses to be 'deposited' at a central registry. Again it is unlikely to be required in the UK. The Commission has said that some Member States have already announced that they will request the deposit of the contract, which may cause confidentiality problems. Apparently it will be possible to ensure that only those clauses dealing with an individual's personal data will be in the public domain. There will also be cases where Member States will be able to block export of data. The European Commission says these include cases where:

- it is established that the law to which the data importer is subject imposes upon him the need to derogate from the relevant data protection rules beyond the restrictions necessary in a democratic society as provided for in *Article 13* of *Directive 95/46/EC* where those derogations are likely to have a substantial adverse effect on the guarantees provided by the standard contractual clauses;

- a competent authority has established that the data importer has not respected the contractual clauses; or

- there is a substantial likelihood that the standard contractual clauses in the annex are not being or will not be complied with and the continuing transfer would create an imminent risk of grave harm to the data subjects.

It is expected that this safeguard clause will be very rarely used.

The Commission says it is permissible to add additional clauses to the standard contractual clauses such as additional guarantees for the individuals (eg online procedures or relevant provisions contained in a privacy policy etc.).

The clauses refer to joint and several liability. However, if one party is not responsible for an event relating to data loss which causes damage then it would not then be liable. Data exporters may choose to sue the data importer, the data exporter or both. The European Commission states:

> 'Although an action against the data exporter before a European court seems the preferable way for an individual to obtain compensation, he or she may decide to take action against the data importer, if, for example the data exporter has disappeared or filed for bankruptcy. In these cases, the data importer may be sued before the data exporter's courts [clause 10] or before the courts of his own country if so permitted under private international law.'

Using the Clauses   20.14

The clauses have now been adopted and some lawyers are having to struggle to provide practical advice on their use. Firstly they are very long, although companies familiar with lengthy agreements should not encounter any difficulties.

Others may find the provisions unacceptable. The Commission decision and clauses are 18 pages long and the clauses have three appendices of additional terms attached. Also attached are:

- a definitions section;

- a schedule which needs to be completed setting out the purposes for which the data will be exported;

- warranties from the data exporter and importer; and

- provisions about mediation and jurisdiction.

A data exporter might simply include a clause in a contract stating that the export would be governed by the Commission's Model Clauses (www.europa. eu.int/comm/internal_market/en/media/datprot/news/clausesdecision.pdf) rather than rewriting the clauses. Then, in the said contract, he should specify the variables required for the contract, such as the names of the data exporter and importer, purpose of export, the length of time the data will be held etc. This is probably not what is intended by the Commission. However, it seems legally permissible and may be more palatable to foreign data recipients who might otherwise be put off by the standard clauses' wording.

CBI Clauses 20.15

Some bodies are still lobbying the EU about the model clauses. The CBI had earlier drawn up its own model clauses and these may still be submitted to the Information Commissioner and/or the EU for approval. As an alternative the CBI may redraft them in the light of the EU clauses. Other bodies have their own clauses as well which again may need to be redrafted.

44 TRANSBORDER DATA FLOWS also makes mention of proposals in this area, including the International Chamber of Commerce's proposals.

Further Information 20.16

The Information Commissioner's guidance 'The Eighth Data Protection Principle and Transborder Dataflows' is accessible under 'International Transfers' at http://wood.ccta.gov.uk/dpr/dpdoc.nsf.

The European Commission's model clauses can be found online at http://europa.eu.int/comm/internal_market/privacy/modelcontracts_en.htm.

The European Commission's FAQs on its new model clauses for data export are at www.europa.eu.int/comm/internal_market/en/media/dataprot/news/clauses-faq.htm.

The EU data protection principal information page is at http://europa.eu.int/comm/internal_market/privacy/index_en.htm.

The EU third countries adequacy list for data export is at http://europa.eu.int/comm/internal_market/privacy/adequacy_en.htm.

The US authorities have a Safe Harbor Agreement website which is at www.export.gov/safeharbor/. See also **41 'SAFE HARBOR' AGREEMENT**.

See also **44 TRANSBORDER DATA FLOWS**.

The FAQs for data export appear in **APPENDIX 2**.

Chapter 21 –
Fair Processing

At A Glance

✓   The First Data Protection Principle requires that personal data be processed fairly and lawfully.

✓   Data subjects should be told the purposes for which their data will be used.

✓   *Schedule 2* to the *Data Protection Act 1998* (*DPA 1998*) sets out the conditions required for processing and is known as the 'Fair Processing Code'.

✓   The Commissioner's Legal Guidance on *DPA 1998* (October 2001) contains further information on fair processing.

Introduction   21.1

Those who use personal data must comply with the Data Protection Principles set out in *DPA 1998*. In practice, the First Principle has the most impact. It requires that data must be processed fairly and lawfully. Specific information must be supplied to data subjects when the data is obtained, including details of the purposes for which the data will be processed. Sensitive personal data is subject to even more stringent requirements (see **42 SENSITIVE PERSONAL DATA**).

First Principle   21.2

Paragraph 1 of *Schedule 1* to *DPA 1998* provides that personal data shall be processed fairly and lawfully and shall not be processed unless the conditions in *Schedule 2* to *DPA 1998* are met. For sensitive personal data, such as data about sex, race, religion, the conditions in *Schedule 3* to *DPA 1998* should be met, such as obtaining explicit consent.

The *Schedule 2* conditions are therefore crucial, and they comprise of what the Data Protection Commissioner calls the Fair Processing Code.

The 'Information Requirements'   21.3

Data subjects must be notified of:

- the identity of the data controller;

- the identity of any representative appointed for the purposes of *DPA 1998*, if any, by that data controller (this will usually not apply);

- the purpose or purposes for which the data are intended to be processed; and

- any further information which is necessary, having regard to the specific circumstances in which the data are to be processed to enable the processing in respect of the data subject to be fair.

Businesses need to ensure individuals are given the information listed above.

One of the new Orders under *DPA 1998*, the *Data Protection (Conditions under Paragraph 3 of Part II of Schedule 1) Order 2000 (SI 2000/185)*, addresses 'fair processing', and is examined in more detail at **21.4** below.

Disproportionate Effort   21.4

The *Data Protection (Conditions under Paragraph 3 of Part II of Schedule 1) Order 2000 (SI 2000/185)* (as amended by the *Data Protection (Miscellaneous Subject Access Exemptions) (Amendment) Order 2000 (SI 2000/1865)* in relation to the adoption of children) deals with a number of areas under *DPA 1998* where data is not treated as fairly processed unless certain requirements have been met concerning the giving of information to data subjects. However, these information provisions vary, and sometimes the requirements can be ignored where disproportionate effort might be involved. Of course, it is not always easy to know exactly what 'disproportionate effort' is and the risk is that businesses will use this as an excuse to avoid the provisions of *DPA 1998*.

The Order therefore states that where a data controller seeks to rely on this provision, they must still provide the relevant information to any individual who requests it. If they cannot readily decide whether they are processing information about the individual because of a lack of identifying information, the data controller must write to the individual explaining the position. The controller must keep a record of the reasons why he believes the disapplication of the information provisions is necessary.

> 'Para. 3.1.7.6 of the Legal Guidance (October 2001) of the Commissioner provides that what does or does not amount to disproportionate effort is a question of fact to be determined in each and every case.
>
> In deciding this the Commissioner will take into account a number of factors, including the nature of the data, the length of time and the cost

involved to the data controller in providing the information. The fact that the data controller has had to expend a substantial amount of effort and/or cost in providing the information does not necessarily mean that the Commissioner will reach the decision that the data controller can legitimately rely upon the disproportionate effort ground. In certain circumstances, the Commissioner would consider that a quite considerable effort could reasonably be expected. The above factors will always be balanced against the prejudicial or effectively prejudicial effect to the data subject and in this respect a relevant consideration would be the extent to which the data subject already knows about the processing of his personal data by the data controller.'

Conditions for Processing under the Act   21.5

Part II of *Schedule 1* to *DPA 1998* provides that in assessing whether the First Principle is complied with, regard must be had to the method by which the data is obtained, including whether anyone was deceived or misled about the purposes for which the data was processed. It goes on to provide that the information described above must be given at the 'relevant time' (when the data is first processed in most cases).

The Schedule 2 Conditions   21.6

Schedule 2 sets out the Fair Processing Code. It comprises the conditions necessary for data to be fairly processed. The following six requirements can be met.

1.   The data subject has consented to the processing.

2.   The processing is necessary to perform a contract (necessary is a strong obligation and it means more than simply desirable).

3.   The processing is necessary to comply with a legal obligation.

4.   The processing is necessary to protect the data subject's 'vital interests' (this means a matter of life or death).

5.   The processing is necessary for reasons such as the administration of justice.

6.   The processing is necessary for the purposes of legitimate interests of the data controller or third parties.

The Commissioner takes the view that in assessing fairness, the first and paramount consideration must be given to the consequences of the processing to the interests of the data subject. Her Legal Guidance says:

'This view was supported by the Data Protection Tribunal in the context of the *Data Protection Act 1984* (*DPA 1984*) in the cases of *CCN Systems Limited and CCN Credit Systems Limited v The Data Protection Registrar [Case DA/90 25/49/9]* and *Infolink v The Data Protection Registrar [Case DA/90 25/49/9]*. The Commissioner will also look at the purposes and nature of the processing in assessing fairness. Even though a data controller may be able to show that information was obtained and personal data processed fairly and lawfully in general and on most occasions, if it has been obtained unfairly in relation to one individual there will have been a contravention of the First Principle.'

The *Schedule 3* conditions which apply to sensitive personal data are dealt with in **42 SENSITIVE PERSONAL DATA.**

Consent   21.7

The Commissioner's Legal Guidance (which can be found at www.informationcommissioner.gov.uk) addresses the meaning of the provisions set out by *Article 2(h)* of *Directive 95/26/EC* in some detail, and in particular examines what is needed to establish consent. One of the conditions for process-ing is that the data subject must have consented to the processing.

The Commissioner's view is that consent is not particularly easy to achieve, and that data controllers should consider other conditions in *Schedule 2* to *DPA 1998* (and *Schedule 3* to *DPA 1998* if processing sensitive personal data) before looking at consent. No condition carries greater weight than any other. All the conditions provide an equally valid basis for processing. Consent is not defined in *DPA 1998*. The existence or validity of consent will need to be assessed in the light of the facts. To assist in understanding what may or may not amount to consent in any particular case, it is helpful to refer back to the *Data Protection Directive (95/46/EC)*. This defines the data subject's consent as:

'...any freely given specific and informed indication of his wishes by which the data subject signifies his agreement to personal data relating to him being processed'.

The Commissioner's View on Giving Consent   21.8

'The fact that the data subject must "signify" his agreement means that there must be some active communication between the parties. A data subject may "signify" agreement other than in writing. Data controllers cannot infer consent from non-response to a communication, for exam-ple from a customer's failure to return or respond to a leaflet.

The adequacy of any consent or purported consent must be evaluated. For example, consent obtained under duress or on the basis of mislead-ing information will not be a valid basis for processing.

Where a data subject does not signify his agreement to personal data relating to him being processed, but is given an opportunity to object to such processing, although this does not amount to consent for the pur-poses of the Act, it *may* provide the data controller with the basis to rely upon another Schedule 2 condition, for example, the legitimate interests condition, provided that the data subject is given the right to object before the data are obtained.'

Appropriate Consent   21.9

Consent must be appropriate to the particular circumstances. For example, if the processing is intended to continue after the end of a trading relationship, then the consent should cover those circumstances. The Commissioner adds:

> 'However, it must be recognised that even when consent has been given it will not necessarily endure forever. While in most cases consent will endure for as long as the processing to which it relates continues, data controllers should recognise that, depending upon the nature of the consent given and the circumstances of the processing, the individual may be able to withdraw consent.'

In her FAQs on data protection and the internet the Commissioner states that in many cases a right to object is sufficient for non-sensitive personal data.

Explicit and Non-explicit Consent   21.10

There is a distinction in *DPA 1998* between the nature of the consent required to satisfy the condition for processing and that which is required in the case of the condition for processing sensitive data. The consent must be explicit in the case of sensitive data. The use of the word 'explicit', and the fact that the condition requires explicit consent to the processing of the personal data, suggests that the consent of the data subject should be absolutely clear. In appropriate cases it should cover the specific detail of the processing, the particular type of data to be processed (or even the specific information), the purposes of the processing and any special aspects of the processing which may affect the individual, for example, disclosures which may be made of the data.

Foreseeability of Future Data Use   21.11

The Commissioner does say that the level of detail appropriate to a consent will vary and in some cases implied consent may be sufficient.

> 'A blanket consent to the processing of personal data is unlikely to be sufficient as a basis on which to process personal data, particularly sensitive personal data...As guidance...the Commissioner would advise that data controllers consider the extent to which the use of personal data by them is or is not reasonably foreseeable by data subjects. To the extent to which their use of personal data is not reasonably foreseeable, data controllers should ensure that they provide such further information as may be necessary.'

Timing 21.12

It does not say in *DPA 1998* when the data subject should be given the fair processing information where the data is obtained from data subjects. The Commissioner believes that this should be at the time when the data is obtained (Introduction, page 13, para 1.12.3).

Further Information 21.13

See the Commissioner's Legal Guidance (October 2001), at www.informationcommissioner.gov.uk.

FAQs 21.14

Which Data Protection Principle requires that data be processed fairly?

The First Data Protection Principle.

Where is the obligation explained in the legislation?

Schedule 2 to *DPA 1998* sets out the Fair Processing Code and the Information Commissioner has issued general guidance under *DPA 1998 inter alia* on these principles.

What does the Code say about disproportionate effort?

The Schedules to *DPA 1998* provide that disproportionate effort need not be expended and the Information Commissioner says that what this is, is a question of fact in each case.

Chapter 22 –
Financial Services

At A Glance

✓   The *Data Protection Act 1998* (*DPA 1998*) applies to financial services companies, many of whom hold considerable amounts of personal data about individuals.

✓   Importance guidance on the financial services sector can be purchased from the British Bankers' Association ('BBA') and others.

✓   The consequences of personal data being incorrect in the hands of a financial services company are likely to be worse than with mere marketing data, thus particular caution should be exercised.

✓   Often financial services companies will process data by automated means (*DPA 1998, s 12*), such as when credit scoring.

✓   Monitoring of financial services companies' calls and emails may have data protection implications.

✓   An exemption from the subject access provisions exists in the category of corporate finance.

✓   *Regulation of Investigatory Powers (Communications Data) Order 2003* gives the FSA access to certain data.

General   22.1

Financial services companies need to comply with *DPA 1998* in general. In particular, consideration should be given to fair processing of data (see **21 FAIR PRO-CESSING**) and to automated decision-taking (see **22.2** below and **1 AUTOMATED DECISION–TAKING**).

Automated Decision-taking   22.2

Section 12 of *DPA 1998* provides that an individual is entitled, by written notice, to require a data controller to ensure that no decision which significantly affects that individual is based solely on the processing by automatic means of personal data of which that individual is the data subject. The Commissioner's Legal Guidance (October 2001) on *DPA 1998* says:

> 'The Act includes specific examples of the purposes for which such automated decision-taking might be employed, ie. evaluating matters relating to the data subject such as his performance at work, his credit-worthiness, his reliability or his conduct. This is not an exhaustive list.'

Many financial services companies make use of automated decision-taking and need to be conscious of their obligations in this respect. **1 AUTOMATED DECISION-TAKING** also deals with this subject in general. If no notice has been given by an individual as mentioned above and a decision is based solely on automatic processing, the data controller must notify the individual that the decision was taken on that basis as soon as reasonably practicable. Within 21 days of receiving such notification, an individual is entitled by written notice (the 'data subject notice') to require the data controller to reconsider the decision, or to take a new decision on a different basis. Within 21 days of receiving the data subject notice, the data controller must give the data subject a written notice specifying the steps the data controller intends to take to comply with the data subject notice.

Exempt Decisions   22.3

There is an exemption under *DPA 1998* for some decisions made this way, known as 'exempt decisions'. The Commissioner summarises this as follows.

To qualify as an exempt decision certain conditions must be met as follows.

Firstly:

- the decision must be taken in the course of steps taken:
    - for the purpose of considering whether to enter into a contract with the data subject,
    - with a view to entering into such a contract, or
    - in the course of performing such a contract; or
- the decision must be authorised or required by or under any enactment.

Secondly:

- the effect of the decision must be to grant a request of the data subject; or
- steps have been taken to safeguard the legitimate interests of the data subject (for example, by allowing, the data subject to make representations).

In addition, the Secretary of State may prescribe other circumstances in which an automated decision may qualify as an exempt decision. No order to this effect has been made to date.

Credit scoring is one obvious way in which a financial services company may become involved in automated decision-taking of this kind.

Monitoring 22.4

Financial services companies in particular engage in the monitoring of employees' telephone calls and emails. The *Telecommunications (Lawful Business Practice) (Interception of Communications) Regulations 2000 (SI 2000/2699)* permit monitoring for most purposes under the *Regulations of Investigatory Powers Act 2000*. Those monitored should be informed that it is taking place. (See also **15 EMAILS** and **16 EMPLOYMENT**. **28 INTERNET** covers the *Telecommunications Regulations.*)

Corporate Finance 22.5

DPA 1998 contains a corporate finance exclusion from the subject access provisions where the data are processed for 'a corporate finance service' (as defined in *DPA 1998, Sch 7, para 6*) provided by 'a relevant person' (*DPA 1998, Sch 7*). The exemption is only available to the extent to which the application of the subject information provisions could, or in the reasonable belief of the data controller could, affect the price or value of particular instruments of a price-sensitive nature. 'Instrument' is defined in *paragraph 6(3)* of *Schedule 7* to *DPA 1998* and includes, for example, company shares.

The Information Commissioner in her Legal Guidance (October 2001) says 'this exemption may be material in due diligence enquiries arising from company takeovers or mergers'.

Economic or Financial Interests 22.6

If required, the exemption is also available for the purpose of safeguarding an important economic or financial interest of the United Kingdom. *DPA 1998* provides that the Secretary of State may, by order, specify matters to be taken into account when determining whether exemption from the subject information provisions is required for the purpose of safeguarding an important economic or financial interest of the United Kingdom as specified in the *Data Protection (Corporate Finance Exemption) Order 2000 (SI 2000/184)*. The Order provides that one such matter is the inevitable prejudicial effect on the orderly functioning of financial markets or the efficient allocation of capital with the economy resulting from the occasional or regular application of the subject information provisions to data specified in the order.

The Information Commissioner says

'The court may make an order requiring a person taking a decision in respect of the data subject (referred to in the Act as "the responsible person") to reconsider the decision or to take a new decision which is not based solely on processing by automatic means. The court will only make such orders if it is satisfied that the responsible person has failed to comply with the data subject notice.'

Industry Guidance 22.7

In September 2000 the main trade associations in the financial services sector published guidance on *DPA 1998* called 'The New Data Protection Act 2000: A Practitioner's Handbook'. Each chapter includes practical examples for banks and other financial institutions. Appended to the book are the following useful documents.

Appendix 1: Definitions within the Act.

Appendix 2: An explanation of transitional periods.

Appendix 3: Industry-wide examples of model notification. Wordings and the Office of the Data Protection Commissioner's (ODPC's) guidance leaflet on using her office's 'information padlock'.

Appendix 4: Putting it into practice: Who needs to do what to comply.

Appendix 5: Industry-wide examples of model subject access forms.

Appendix 6: BBA guidance: 'What banks need to tell customers about the personal information they collect: BBA Guidance on standard data protection notifications for customer application forms and data collection systems'.

Appendix 7: Finance and Leasing Associaton (FLA) model data protection notice (for implementation by FLA members 24 October 2000).

Appendix 8: FLA guidance for motor and caravan dealers (for implementation by FLA members 24 October 2000).

Appendix 9: Confederation of British Industry (CBI) and International Chamber of Commerce (ICC) model contract clauses.

Regulation of Investigatory Powers (Communications Data) Order 2003 And FSA Access to Information 22.8

The *Regulation of Investigatory Powers (Communications Data) Order 2003 (SI 2003/3172)* gave the Financial Services Authority (FSA), and some other public authorities, access to information known as 'communications data' from providers of communications services regulated under the *Regulation of Investigatory Powers*

Act (RIPA 2000). Communications data is information about the use people make of services such as the post, telephone or email. The FSA already had powers to obtain communications data under existing legislation, so this Order did not materially increase or reduce the FSA's powers. It did, however, bring them within a common statutory regime that applies to other authorities.

The FSA is not allowed to intercept telephone calls, letters or emails – these powers remain reserved for authorities such as the police and intelligence services. The FSA is, however, able to use *RIPA 2000* powers to obtain details of a subscriber behind a telephone number or when and to whom calls or emails were sent by particular subscribers.

The effect of including the FSA in the Order was to bring it and other public authorities within the *RIPA 2000* regime, which includes a process for the authorisation of the use of such powers, access to a tribunal for anyone affected by them and administrative arrangements for an independent oversight by an external body. The FSA already had rigorous procedures to ensure that individual privacy rights are respected and that it only obtains communications data where it is necessary and proportionate to do so – these procedures will now be supervised within the same statutory framework that applies to other authorities.

Andrew Procter, Director of Enforcement at the FSA, said in 2003 when the proposals were announced:

> 'Communications data, such as telephone billing information and Internet protocol addresses, are often a vital element of our investigations into serious offences like insider dealing, making misleading statements or conducting unauthorised business. Those offences are increasingly being committed by telephone or through the Internet. Although the FSA has been able to obtain communications data using its investigative powers under the *Financial Services and Markets Act 2000*, we welcome our inclusion as an authority under *Chapter II of RIPA 2000*. This means that the FSA's access to communications data will be subject to the same framework of regulation and statutory oversight as other public authorities obtaining this sensitive kind of information. In our view, this is an important means of ensuring that an appropriate balance is struck between the protection of privacy and our statutory objective to reduce crime in the financial services sector'.

The FSA's explanation on the background to this is as follows:

'1.   The *RIPA 2000* is intended to ensure that the surveillance and certain other investigative activities of government departments and public authorities are compliant with the privacy requirements of the European Convention on Human Rights.

'2.   *RIPA 2000* is divided into four main parts:

- Part I: Interception of Communications (Chapter I covers Interception of the Content of Communications; Chapter II covers Acquisition and Disclosure of 'Communications Data');

- Part II: Surveillance and Covert Human Intelligence Sources;

- Part III: Encryption; and

- Part IV: Oversight and Complaints.

'3.   Part I of Chapter II will come into force at the same time as the Order giving the FSA and other authorities powers under *RIPA 2000*.

'4.   The addition of further authorities to the list of 'relevant public authorities' in Chapter II attracted some criticism.

'5.   Chapter II provides a permissive authorisation regime for obtaining 'communications data'. Communications data does not contain any content, but is information about the circumstances in which a communication has been sent. The provisions of Chapter II apply equally to postal, telephone and Internet services.

'6.   *RIPA 2000* defines three types of communications data: subscriber information (eg names and addresses of people to whom services are provided), service use information (eg itemised telephone billing records) and traffic data (eg information identifying the precise location from which a communication has been made).

'7.   Subscriber data is the type of communications data obtained most frequently by the FSA and has been particularly important when the FSA has been seeking to establish whether investment business has been conducted without the FSA's authorisation. For example, the FSA often comes across websites promoting regulated activities or bogus high yield investment schemes masquerading as regulated activities. The FSA says it will need to identify the person posting the site and this can often only be done by obtaining subscriber data, such as registration details, from the web host. Alternatively, there may be a telephone number listed on the site and the FSA will contact the relevant telephone service provider to identify the person who holds that number. The FSA makes over 100 such requests for subscriber data each year.

'8.   Service use data is the type of communications data most commonly sought by the FSA in support of insider dealing investigations. For example, on occasion the FSA has noticed that large quantities of a particular stock have been traded shortly before a public announcement affecting the price of the stock (eg an impending take-over). Itemised telephone billing records have helped show whether the people who traded had contact with possible sources of information at critical times and might prove to be crucial evidence in a prosecution. In the course of the last year access to this type of data has been authorised on 12 occasions.

'9.   Traffic data is obtained by the FSA least frequently but can be highly valuable, it says, for its investigations into insider dealing or the making of misleading statements. For example, on a number of occasions the FSA has become aware of entries posted on Internet-based investment bulletin boards suggesting that a particular stock is likely to rise in value and encouraging readers to invest. 'In instances where the information in the posting is not true, this may be a misleading statement made in an attempt to manipulate the price of the stock. In order to help identify who made the statement, the FSA will need to obtain from the bulletin board operator the Internet Protocol address for the email posting the entry. We anticipate obtaining traffic no more than 10 times a year', the FSA said at the time this was announced.

'10.   The FSA regulates the financial services industry and has four objectives under the *Financial Services and Markets Act 2000*:

- maintaining market confidence;

- promoting public understanding of the financial system;

- securing the appropriate degree of protection of consumers; and

- fighting financial crime.'

The FSA aims to maintain efficient, orderly and clean financial markets and help retail consumers achieve a fair deal.

Further information 22.9

Copies of 'The New Data Protection Act 2000: A Practitioner's Handbook' can be ordered from the BBA website at www.bba.org.uk under Publications.

For monitoring see **29 LAWFUL BUSINESS PRACTICE REGULATIONS**.

FAQs 22.10

Are financial services excluded from *DPA 1998*?

Certainly not. Financial services companies handle huge amounts of personal data and must comply with the legislation.

Are there corporate finance exceptions?

There is a very limited exemption in the corporate finance field in *paragraph 6* of *Schedule 7* to *DPA 1998* but only from the subject access provisions but only in relation to a corporate finance service provided by a relevant person.

Chapter 23 –
Forms

At A Glance

✓ Companies seeking compliance with the *Data Protection Act 1998* (*DPA 1998*) will want to draw up various forms to be used by staff and those making subject access requests.

✓ In addition, there are forms which a data controller may use in notifying their holding of personal data under *DPA 1998* and an online question-naire included in the Information Commissioner's Notification Handbook.

✓ In the employment and credit sector, companies often devise their own standards or use forms recommended by their relevant trade association.

✓ Two examples of the Information Commissioner's forms for aspects of notification are included for information.

✓ Solicitors can advise clients in drawing up forms in this field.

Introduction   23.1

DPA 1998 does not set down defined forms for use by data controllers so many companies have drawn up their own. Appendix 5 of 'The New Data Protection Act 2000: A Practitioner's Handbook' contains model forms for subject access in the financial services industry which may be used but are not mandatory (see **22 FINANCIAL SERVICES**).

Notification Form   23.2

A fee of £35 is payable for notification of the holding of data. This covers one year. Guidance on how to notify is found in the Notification Handbook (available from the Commissioner's Office or via the website at www.informationcommissioner.gov.uk).

Registrable Particulars   23.3

Information to be provided on the notification form includes the following regis-trable particulars relating to the data controller:

- their name and address;

- if they have nominated a representative, the name and address of the representative;

- a description of the personal data being or to be processed and of the category(ies) of data subject to which they relate;

- a description of the purpose(s) for which the data are being or are to be processed;

- a description of any recipient(s) to whom the data controller intends or may wish to disclose the data;

- the name or a description of any countries or territories outside the European Economic Area to which the data controller transfers, intends to transfer or may wish to transfer the data; and

- where the personal data are of a type which is exempt from the prohibition against processing personal data without notification and where the notification does not extend to such data, a statement of that fact.

Security Measures   23.4

When a notification is made by a data controller he must also provide, in addition to the registrable particulars, a general description of the security measures taken to protect the personal data. However, this information will not appear on the register.

Padlock Symbol   23.5

Some companies have chosen to use the Commissioner's padlock sign to inform data subjects that their data is being gathered. Use of the symbol is not compulsory.

34 PADLOCK (USE OF THE SIGN CALLED 'PADLOCK') examines the signpost. It is often used on forms.

Employment and Credit   23.6

For details concerning forms in the credit field see **7 CREDIT REFERENCES AND ACCESS TO CREDIT FILES**. In relation to employment see **16 EMPLOYMENT**.

Changing a Register Entry   23.7

**THE DATA
PROTECTION
REGISTRAR**

Form DPR2
Application for Alteration or
Removal of a Register Entry
Data Protection Act 1984

Form DPR2 3/93

87908 **H**

Name & address of applicant (Currently held on the Register)

Company Reg.No.

User Number (issued
on the confirmation of
your Register entry).

Post Code

	Registration Numbers of Register entries to be altered		Registration Numbers of Register entries to be removed
Alteration of a Register entry (See Note 1)		**Removal of a Register entry** (See Note 2)	

Describe Alterations overleaf

Declaration (See Note 3)   **To be completed by all applicants**

To the best of my knowledge and belief, the particulars given in this form and on any
continuation sheets are correct and complete. I confirm that I am the Data User or Computer
Bureau named above or that I am authorised to act on behalf of that Data User or Computer
Bureau.

Signature _____   Date _____

Name _____

Position _____   Tel.No._____

Send your application to:
Changes Section, Office of the Data Protection Registrar,
Wycliffe House, Water Lane, Wilmslow, Cheshire SK9 5AF
See Notes 4-6 about confirmation of changes, and changes of name and address.

Notes

1. Write here the registration numbers of entries to be altered. Note that any alterations requested on this form will be applied to all of the
Register entries listed here. Give details of alterations overleaf.

2. Write here the registration numbers of entries to be removed from the Register. Please note that once an entry has been removed it cannot
be reinstated.

3. It is an offence knowingly or recklessly to furnish the Registrar with information which is false or misleading in any material respect.

4. Confirmation of the removal or alteration requested on this form will be sent by the Registrar to the contact name given in the Register entry.

5. Please remember there are 3 address sections which may be affected – data user, subject access and contact. Changes of contact name
and address have no effect on the Register itself, but will be recorded for use by the Registrar and confirmed to the new address.

6. If a new name is that of a different legal person a new application should be made using forms DPR1 or DPR4.

NB There is no fee for an application for alteration or removal of a Register entry.

Details of Alterations to Register Entries

Please explain in your own words, and us clearly as possible, the nature of the alteration you wish to make. You should clearly indicate to which section of the Register entry the alteration applies.

If the alteration is particularly complex, or is to add a purpose to your Register entry, you may find it easier to complete a new Part B form. If you do this you must clearly mark the Part B form "For addition to Register entry" or "To replace previously submitted Part B on Register entry". The Register reserves the right to ask applicants who request an alteration to use this method if the proposed alteration described is unclear.

Now sign the Declaration overleaf

You are advised to keep a copy of your application

In making any requests for alterations to a Register entry, you should refer to the booklet *Notes—to help you apply for Registration,* and where appropriate, to the *Registrar's Guidelines.* These, and copies fo Forms DPR1, DPR2 and DPR4 can be obtained from Information Services, Office of the Data Protection Registrar, Wycliffe House, Water Lane, Witmslow, Cheshire, SK9 5AF, Telephone Wilmslow (0625) 535777.

A4 398/0962 Dd 03498 100M TP

Purpose Form – To Add a Purpose to a Register Entry   23.8

DP Data Protection	***PURPOSE FORM*** *(for adding a purpose to a notification)* A purpose form must be completed for **each** new purpose

You must quote your Security number or the form will be returned

Data controller name:		
Registration number:		
Security number/user number:		
Purpose title:		See Notification Handbook Section 3.1.8 for full list
Write here a brief description only if none of the standard purposes apply.		
Data Subject Codes:		See Notification Handbook Section 3.1.9 for full list
Write here additional descriptions only if none of the standard descriptions apply.		
Data Class Codes:		See Notification Handbook Section 3.1.10 for full list
Write here additional descriptions only if none of the standard descriptions apply.		
Recipient Codes:		See Notification Handbook Section 3.1.11 for full list
Write here additional descriptions only if none of the standard descriptions apply.		

Declaration

To the best of my knowledge and belief, the particulars given in this form and on any continuation sheets are correct and complete. I confirm that I am the Data Controller named overleaf or that I am authorised to act on behalf of the Data Controller.

Signature   _____

Name   _____

Job Title   _____

Date   _____

Tel. No.   _____

Note:

Once you have notified you must keep your register entry up to date. When any part of your entry becomes inaccurate or incomplete you must inform us. This action must be taken as soon as practicable and in any event within a period of 28 days from the date on which your entry became inaccurate or incomplete. Failure to do so is a criminal offence.

Send this form with your Part 1 and Part 2 if making a new notification

or

If amending an existing notification send to:
Notification Changes Section, Information Commissioner's Office
Wycliffe House, Water Lane, Wilmslow, Cheshire SK9 5AF

Privacy Policies 23.9

Many websites have forms or notices called privacy policies setting out how personal data will be used (see **36 PRINCIPLES**). These are not in any statutory form but need to cover the issues of who is the data controller and how will that data be used.

Audit Manual 23.10

The Information Commissioner publishes a detailed Audit Manual containing information and forms which can be used in checking whether internal procedures are compliant with the legislation. It includes *inter alia* audit and meeting pro formas. It is on the Information Commissioner's website at www.informationcommissioner.gov.uk/dpaudit/whatis/index.htm. It includes meeting record sheets and acts as a useful prompt as to the issues to be addressed in undertaking a data protection audit.

Extracts from the Audit Manual appears in **APPENDIX 4**. The extracts included are Annex C to the Manual, which is the Information Commissioner's own internal checklists/forms, and 'Section 2 – The Audit Method'.

Further Information 23.11

The Information Commissioner's Audit Manual 2001 can be found at www.informationcommissioner.gov.uk/dpaudit/whatis/index.htm.

FAQs 23.12

How do I obtain forms under *DPA 1998*?

The Commissioner's website is at www.informationcommissioner.gov.uk from which certain forms can be downloaded.

Are there forms for employers to use to ensure compliance?

The Audit Manual (extracts of which appear in **APPENDIX 4**) on the Commissioner's website contains some forms, some industry sectors have designed their own forms and some companies have customised forms to their own requirements.

Is there a form for a privacy policy on a website?

No, but there are many examples of such policies on the internet.

Chapter 24 – Freedom of Information Act 2000

At A Glance

✓ When it comes into force the *Freedom of Information Act 2000 (FIA 2000)* will give individuals and businesses additional rights to information held about them by public bodies to complement the *Data Protection Act 1998 (DPA 1998)*.

✓ *FIA 2000* is due to be in force at the latest on 30 November 2005, but in November 2001 the Government announced that individuals' rights of access to data under the Act would come into force early in January 2005.

✓ Companies as well as individuals will be able to exercise rights under *FIA 2000*.

✓ The Information Commissioner is in charge of *FIA 2000* in a dual role which also encompasses *DPA 1998*.

✓ Public bodies may now want to align their subject access request procedures to accommodate the two regimes.

✓ Codes of practice and other documents on *FIA 2000* are accessible via the Commissioner's website.

Introduction   24.1

On 30 November 2000 *FIA 2000* received Royal Assent. The Information Commissioner is in charge of enforcing the legislation – a combined role of freedom of information and data protection. Elizabeth France, who was Data Protection Registrar and then Data Protection Commissioner under the 1984 Act became the first Information Commissioner. In October 2002 Richard Thomas, who had previously worked at law firm Clifford Chance, became the second Information Commissioner. Both *FIA 2000* and *DPA 1998* relate to information handling, and the dual role will allow the Commissioner to provide an integrated and coherent approach.

Provisions of FIA 2000   24.2

Basic provisions   24.3

FIA 2000 provides a statutory right of access to information held by public authorities. The Information Commissioner is an independent authority, with a statutory duty to promote good practice by public authorities and to disseminate information on good practice.

The implications of the Act will depend upon the organisation. Those in the public sector to whom *FIA 2000* will apply will need to consider carefully how their obligations to provide information to members of the public will now be expanded. Those in the private sector will find it has a much lesser impact, but it may be relevant when they wish to obtain information from public authorities.

Essential provisions   24.4

FIA 2000:

- gives a general right of access to information of all kinds held by public authorities (and those providing services for them);
- sets out exemptions from that right of access; and
- places a number of obligations on public authorities.

The Act relates to individuals' rights and not to business relationships in the private sector.

The Information Commissioner summarises the Act as follows:

'The *Freedom of Information Act* enables people to gain access to information held by public authorities in two ways:

- 'From 1 January 2005, people will have the right to make a request for any information held by a public authority (although this right is subject to a number of exemptions which permit the withholding of information) and the authority will have to comply with the Act in responding.

  - 'Prior to that, in the run up to January 2005, every public authority must make some information available as a matter of course through a publication scheme, with information included in the publication scheme being routinely made available to anyone who consults it. A publication scheme is both a public commitment to make certain information available and a guide to how that information can be obtained'.

Timing   24.5

FIA 2000 must be brought fully into force within five years of Royal Assent, although it may be sooner. The long stop date is 30 November 2005.

The *Freedom of Information Act 2000* is being brought into force in stages. From 1 January 2005 people will have the right to make a written request seeking specific information from a public authority. The public authority will be required to follow the provisions of the *Freedom of Information Act 2000* in dealing with that request.

Prior to that, in the run up to January 2005, each public authority is required to put in place a publication scheme setting out details of the information it makes available as a matter of routine. The requirement to adopt and maintain a publication scheme is being phased in across the public sector as shown in the table below.

Sector	Date
Central Government	30 November 2002
Local Government	28 February 2003
Police and prosecuting authorities	30 June 2003
Health service	31 October 2003
Education (except nursery schools)	29 February 2004
Remaining public authorities	30 June 2004

People will be entitled to request to see a copy of an authority's publication scheme from the dates indicated in the table above. A more detailed breakdown of which public authorities fall within these provisions is described below.

The timetable for implementing the *Freedom of Information Act 2000 (FOIA)* was announced by the Lord Chancellor on 13 November 2001. The Act will be implemented in full by 1 January 2005. The requirement for each public authority to adopt a publication scheme will come into force according to the following programme:

- **30 November 2002**: Central Government (except the Crown Prosecution Service and the Serious Fraud Office), Parliament, National Assembly for Wales, Non Departmental Public Bodies (NDPBs) subject to the Open Government Code (Code of Practice on Access to Government Information) (FOIA Schedule 1, Part I, sections 1, 2, 3 and 5; some of Part VI);

- **28 February 2003**: Local Government (except police authorities) (FOIA Schedule 1, Part II);

- **30 June 2003**: Police, police authorities, Crown Prosecution Service, Serious Fraud Office, Armed Forces (FOIA Schedule 1, Part V not relating to Northern Ireland and Part I, section 6);

- **31 October 2003**: Health Service (FOIA Schedule 1, Part III relating to England and Wales);

- **28 February 2004**: Schools (except for maintained nursery schools), Universities, remaining NDPBs (FOIA Schedule 1, Part IV relating to England and Wales and some of Part VI); and

- **30 June 2004**: Maintained Nursery Schools, remaining public authorities.

The individual right of access to information will come into force for all public authorities on 1 January 2005.

The Information Commissioner says:

> 'The aim of a phased approach is both to allow for growth of the Information Commissioner's Office, to cope with the new regulatory regime, and to allow public authorities, in particular those which have not been subject to the Open Government Code, a reasonable period in which to develop their own internal procedures for compliance. It is in the clear interest of public authorities and the Information Commissioner alike to begin work now on the development of publication schemes and preparations for responding to individual requests for information. These responsibilities are considered further under separate headings.'

In addition, by January 2005 Central Government will have been operating Electronic Records Management ('ERM') for a year. This is separate from *FIA 2000* and is supervised by the Public Record Office. It introduces a requirement that all newly created public records are stored and retrieved electronically by 2004. The Government says that 'This initiative will enable the fast retrieval of information which will be necessary to meet the demands of the Freedom of Information Act 2000'.

In the Annual IC's report to March 2003 The IC said:

> 'With a lengthy implementation timescale, our freedom of information work has yet to take off. But we have already approved large numbers of freedom of information publication schemes, have negotiated model schemes with leading representative organisations and are developing detailed plans to deal with a new caseload which is unpredictable in quantity, but guaranteed to be difficult and sensitive.'

This is, therefore, an area to watch in future. Many readers in public sector bodies will already have done much work on the FOIA.

Bodies Covered   24.6

Only public authorities are covered by *FIA 2000*. These include:

- Government departments;

- local authorities;

- NHS bodies, such as hospitals, as well as doctors, dentists, pharmacists and opticians;

- schools, colleges and universities;

- the Police; and

- the House of Commons and the House of Lords, the Northern Ireland Assembly and the National Assembly for Wales.

It also includes a long list of other public bodies, ranging from various official advisory and expert committees, to regulators and organisations such as the Post Office, the National Gallery and the Parole Board. A list is provided in *Schedule 1* to *FIA 2000*. Readers whose company is public or quasi-public should check the list to see if their employer is on it.

Rights granted   24.7

Section 7 of *DPA 1998* provides a subject access right. As far as public bodies are concerned, *FIA 2000* will extend these rights to allow access to all the types of information held by public bodies, whether personal or non-personal. However, some of the information requested need not be provided if one of the exemptions in *FIA 2000* applies.

Who can make a request?   24.8

Anyone will be able make a request for information, although the request must be in permanent form (ie. by email or on paper, but not by telephone). *FIA 2000* gives applicants two related rights:

- the right to be told whether the information exists; and

- the right to receive the information and, where possible, in the manner requested, for example as a copy or summary; alternatively the applicant may ask to inspect a record.

The 'Introduction to FIA 2000' produced by the Information Commissioner states that:

> 'It is important to note that applicants will not be able to exercise their right of access until the body concerned has been phased in. However, applicants will then still be able to request information recorded before the Act was passed.'

New responsibilities   **24.9**

Publication schemes   **24.10**

FIA 2000 places a duty on public authorities to adopt and maintain publication schemes, which must be approved by the Information Commissioner. Such schemes must set out the types of information the authority publishes, the form in which the information is published and details of any charges. The Commissioner may also approve model schemes for groups of similar bodies, for example schools.

The Information Commissioner will be working with groups of public authorities to develop guidance on what should be included in publication schemes.

Responding to requests   **24.11**

In general, public authorities will have to respond to requests within 20 working days. They may charge a fee, which will have to be calculated according to regulations relating to fees, which are yet to be drafted. If a fee is required, the 20 working days will be extended by up to three months until the fee is paid.

In cases where information is covered by an exemption, but the authority is then required to consider the public interest in releasing it, the authority must provide the information within a reasonable time.

Exemptions   **24.12**

There are 23 exemptions in *FIA 2000*, some of which are familiar under data protection legislation, for example that information need not be released if it would prejudice national security or law enforcement.

Under *FIA 2000*, some exemptions apply to a whole category or class of information, for example:

- information relating to investigations and proceedings conducted by public authorities;
- court records; and
- trade secrets.

Any information covered by these class-based exemptions is always exempt.

Other exemptions are subject to a prejudice test, for example, where disclosure would or would be likely to prejudice:

- the interests of the United Kingdom abroad; or
- the prevention or detection of crime.

Information only becomes exempt if disclosing it would or would be likely to prejudice the activity or interest described in the exemption. In most cases, where information is exempt the public authority must then consider the public interest in providing the information. This public interest test involves considering the circumstances of each particular case and the exemption that covers the information. The information may only be withheld if the public interest in withholding it is greater than the public interest in releasing it.

Role of the Information Commissioner   24.13

The Information Commissioner is an independent public official reporting directly to Parliament. She is responsible for implementing *FIA 2000*. This involves:

- promoting good practice;

- approving and assisting in the preparation of publication schemes;

- providing information as to the public's rights under *FIA 2000*; and

- enforcing compliance with *FIA 2000*.

Guidance and Codes of Practice   24.14

In June 2001 the Commissioner issued an overview of *FIA 2000*, which is accessible via www.informationcommissioner.gov.uk/dpr/foi.nsf

Two codes of practice issued under *FIA 2000* provide guidance to public authorities on:

- responding to requests for information and associated matters (a draft is available at www.lcd.gov.uk/foi/foidpunit.htm); and

- records management (draft available via: www.pro.gov.uk/recordsmanagement/).

These are discussed in detail at **24.15–24.17** below.

Home Office Draft Code of Practice: Discharge of Functions of Public Authorities   24.15

The Home Office Draft Code of Practice under *Part I* of *FIA 2000* is issued under *section 45* of *FIA 2000*. Whilst the Code mentioned below remains in draft and pending the introduction of the general right of access to information created by *FIA 2000*, the Home Office and its Agencies remain committed, under the Code of Practice on Access to Government Information (2nd edition 1997 at www.lcd.gov.uk/foi/ogcode981.htm), to:

- promote informed policy making and debate;

- provide timely and accessible information to explain the Department's policies, actions and decisions; and

- respond to reasonable requests for information.

It provides guidance to public authorities on desirable practices for them to follow under that part of the Act dealing with access to information held by them. The aims of the Code are to:

- facilitate the disclosure of information under *FIA 2000* by setting out good administrative practice which it is desirable for public authorities to follow when handling requests for information, including, where appropriate, the transfer of a request to a different authority;

- protect the interests of applicants by setting out standards for the provision of advice which it would be good practice to make available to them and to encourage the development of effective means of complaining about decisions taken under *FIA 2000*;

- ensure that the interests of third parties who may be affected by any decision to disclose information are considered by the authority by setting standards for consultation; and

- ensure that authorities consider the implications for the freedom of information before agreeing to confidentiality provisions in contracts and accepting information in confidence from a third party more generally.

The Code says that all public authorities should provide advice and assistance to those making requests for information and should publish their procedures for such requests. It is recommended that decisions be made within 20 working days where possible. Transfers to other bodies who in fact have the information requested should be made promptly. Where the disclosure of information may affect the legal rights of a third party such as the right to have certain information treated in confidence, or rights under *Article 8* of the *European Convention on Human Rights*, then the authority should seek consent from that third party.

The code and contracts 24.16

The Code's provisions on contracts are interesting. Many companies enter into contracts with public authorities. The Code says that when entering into contracts, public authorities should refuse to include:

> 'contractual terms which purport to restrict the disclosure of information held by the authority and relating to the contract beyond the restrictions permitted by the Act. Public authorities should not agree to hold information "in confidence" which is not in fact confidential in nature.'

When entering into contracts with non-public authority contractors, public authorities may be under pressure to accept confidentiality clauses so that information relating to the terms of the contract, its value and performance will be exempt from disclosure. Public authorities should not accept such clauses where this is commercially viable. This could have quite an impact in practice. Any acceptance of such confidentiality provisions must be for good reasons and capable of being justified to the Information Commissioner. In most cases it is for the public authority to disclose information under *FIA 2000*, and not the contractor. However, the public authority may need to protect from disclosure by the contractor information which would be exempt from disclosure under *FIA 2000*, by appropriate contractual terms. Apart from such cases, public authorities should not impose terms of secrecy on contractors.

The Code provides that a public authority should only accept information from third parties in confidence if it is necessary to obtain that information in connection with the exercise of any of the authority's functions. In addition, public authorities should not agree to hold information received from third parties 'in confidence' which is not confidential in nature. And again, acceptance of any confidentiality provisions must be for good reasons, capable of being justified to the Commissioner.

Public records   24.17

The Public Record Office ('PRO') has produced guidance on data protection and there will be a Code of Practice on records management under *FIA 2000*. A working draft of the Lord Chancellor's Code of Practice on the Management of Records Under Freedom of Information is available at www.pro.gov.uk/recordsmanagement/CodeOfPractice.htm.

There are currently two model action plans to help public authorities reach compliance with the Code of Practice. One is for central government departments and agencies; the other is for local authorities.

The PRO has also produced a Manual of Guidance on Access to Public Records. This explains the current criteria for extended retention or closure of public records, and contains specialist guidance on specific topics or types of records. It has been approved by the Lord Chancellor's Advisory Council on Public Records.

The *Government of Wales Act 1998* made provision for a Public Record Office of Wales. However, until this has been established, the PRO will continue to look after Welsh public records and a Memorandum of Understanding has been drawn up to formalise this agreement.

Further information and the documents referred to in this paragraph are available at www.pro.gov.uk/recordsmanagement/access/default.htm.

Publication Schemes   24.18

A lot of effort has been made, by the Information Commissioner's office, to approving publication schemes. In the IC's Annual Report to 31 March 2003 it was said: 'A key component of our work during the past 12 months has been the development and approval of model schemes'. The following schemes have been approved:

- port health authorities;

- parish councils;

- parish meetings;

- police authorities;

- police forces;

- magistrates court committees;

- fire authorities;

- internal drainage boards;

- district drainage commissioners; and

- passenger transport authorities.

Model schemes for the health sector wave in England have also been approved for the following:

- acute trusts;

- strategic health authorities;

- primary care trusts;

- opticians and optometrists;

- mental health trusts;

- general practitioners;

- dentists;

- community pharmacists; and

- ambulance trusts.

An equivalent models for Wales and Northern Ireland are expected to be approved shortly.

Adoption rates within the first wave of schemes has been good, with 257 schemes approved. Only one public authority in this wave is known to have not yet submitted a satisfactory scheme for approval. Within the second wave, some 456 primary local authorities (districts, counties and unitaries) have submitted and had schemes approved. Some 7,000 model schemes have been adopted, principally by parish councils and parish meetings. The Information Commissioner's Office estimates that some 5,000 of these bodies have failed to adopt schemes, although in the absence of a comprehensive list, it is impossible to be precise. In addition to parish councils and meetings, port health authorities have been slow to meet their obligations under the Act.

Environmental Information Regulations 1992   24.19

The *Environmental Information Regulations 1992 (SI 1992/3240)* sit alongside the *FIA 2000* in giving public access to information, but in this case is limited to environmental information.

Public authorities are obliged to provide access to information about the environment under the *Environmental Information Regulations 1992* (as amended by the *Environmental Information (Amendment) Regulations 1998 (SI 1998/1447)*. The Department for the Environment, Food and Rural Affairs (DEFRA) are currently responsible for overseeing these Regulations. Further information can be found at: http://www.defra.gov.uk/.

However, a new set of regulations are being drafted by DEFRA. It is anticipated that when these new regulations come into force, the responsibility for enforcing them will be given to the Information Commissioner.

The Regulations implement Council Directive 90/313/EEC on the freedom of access to information on the environment.

The Regulations apply where the information requested is not the subject of other statutory obligations of disclosure.

Regulation 3(1) contains the primary obligation for environmental information to be made available on request.

Further Information   24.20

Information published by the Information Commissioner can be obtained from the Freedom of Information part of the website www.informationcommissioner.gov.uk/dpr/foi.nsf

Information on the public records aspects is at www.pro.gov.uk/recordsmanagement/access/default.htm.

The *Freedom of Information Act 2000* is available from the Stationery Office (ISBN 0105436003, price £9.55). The Explanatory Notes are available separately. The Act can also be accessed free via the Stationery Office website at www.tso-online.co.uk and the Parliament website at www.parliament.uk.

A useful website on freedom of information in the EU is 'Statewatch' and includes access to relevant EU documents in the privacy law area and case law in this field. See www.statewatch.org/foi.htm.

The report of the Advisory Group on Openness in the Public Sector can be read at www.lcd.gov.uk/foi/foiadvgp.htm.

Details of the Public Record Office advice and guidance to records managers across Central Government on ERM can be read at www.pro.gov.uk/recordsmanagement/default.htm.

FAQs

What does *FIA 2000* do?

FIA 2000 gives a general right of access to all types of 'recorded' information held by public authorities, sets out exemptions from that right and places a number of obligations on public authorities.

Who does *FIA 2000* cover?

Only public authorities are covered by *FIA 2000*. These include Government Departments, local authorities, NHS bodies (such as hospitals, as well as doctors, dentists, pharmacists and opticians), schools, colleges and universities, the Police, the House of Commons and the House of Lords, the Northern Ireland Assembly and the National Assembly for Wales. It also includes a long list of other public bodies, ranging from various official advisory and expert committees, to regulators and organisations such as the Post Office, National Gallery and the Parole Board. A list is provided in *Schedule 1* of the Act. There is a provision in the Act for other authorities to be named later and for organisations to be designated by the Secretary of State as public authorities because they exercise functions of a public nature or provide a service under a contract which is a function of that authority.

When will *FIA 2000* come into force?

The Act will be brought fully into force by January 2005 (see 24.5 above).

What new rights are created by *FIA 2000*?

Individuals already have the right to access information about themselves, held on computer, and in some paper files, under *FIA 2000*. This is known as the 'subject access right', (advice on the Act is currently available from the Information Commissioner's website). As far as public bodies are concerned, the Act will extend these rights to allow access to all the types of information they hold, whether personal or non-personal. However, the public authority will not be required to release information to which any of the exemptions in the Act applies.

Anyone will be able make a request for information, although the request must be made in writing, which includes emails. The request must contain details of the applicant and the information sought. The Act gives applicants two related rights:

- to be told whether the information is held by the public authority

- to receive the information (and where possible, in the manner requested, ie. as a copy or summary, or the applicant may ask to inspect a record)

Public authorities will be obliged to provide information recorded both before and after the Act was passed.

Public authorities should also be aware that there is right of access to certain information under the Environmental Information Regulations. These are referred to briefly at the end of this paper.

Copyright The Information Commissioner 2002

Chapter 25 –
Health, Education and Social
Work

At A Glance

✓   Personal data relating to health, education and social work will often be classed as sensitive, personal data under the *Data Protection Act 1998* (*DPA 1998*).

✓   Limited exemption orders exist in these categories and are described in this chapter.

✓   Special rules on subject access and health records are examined in this chapter.

✓   Guidance has been issued on the issuing of school examination results to the media by the Information Commissioner.

✓   Other legislation with relevance to these areas is examined.

Introduction   25.1

A vast amount of personal data is held relating to individuals' health and in the education and social work context. Much of that data may be sensitive personal data (see **42 SENSITIVE PERSONAL DATA**). Special regulations have been made under *DPA 1998* in relation to health, education and social work. There is guidance on medical records and employment in Part 4 of the data protection employment code of practice, to be finalised in 2004.

Health   25.2

The *Data Protection (Subject Access Modification) (Health) Order 2000* (*SI 2000/413*) (the 'Health Order') exempts from subject access requirements any data relating to the physical or mental health condition of the data subject, where the application of *section 7* of *DPA 1998* would be likely to cause serious harm to the physical or mental health or condition of the data subject or any other person.

Data controllers have a legal obligation before they decide if this exemption applies to consult with a 'health professional' responsible for the clinical care of the data subject (if there is more than one, the most suitable health professional must be consulted). The Information Commissioner, in Guidance issued in October 2001, states:

> 'The Commissioner recognises that in many cases there will be more than one health professional responsible for the patient's clinical care at the time a subject access request is made. Data controllers should ensure that they have systems in place to enable the most suitable health professional to be identified and consulted to enable the data controller to comply with a subject access request within the statutory time limit of 40 days.
>
> Where a request for subject access is made by someone other than the data subject (ie. by someone with parental responsibility for a child or, in relation to Scotland, by such a person on behalf of someone under the age of 16, or by a person appointed by a court to manage the affairs of the data subject) the data controller should consider any expectation of confidentiality the data subject may have had at the time the information was provided or obtained, and any wishes expressed by the data subject with regard to the disclosure of personal data relating to his physical or mental health condition.
>
> In specific circumstances set out in the Health Order where certain personal data are processed by the Court, there is also an exemption from the subject information provisions.'

If the data controller already has a written opinion from the appropriate health professional obtained in the previous six months that an exemption to the right of subject access exists because the disclosure is likely to cause serious harm to the physical or mental health of the data subject, or any other person, then there will not be a right of subject access in such a case. Where this is relied upon, the data controller should consider whether it is reasonable in all the circumstances to re-consult the health professional. This exemption does not apply if the request relates to information which the data controller is satisfied either:

- has previously been seen by the data subject; or
- is already within the knowledge of the data subject.

Access to a record containing information as to the data subject's physical or mental health or condition cannot be denied on the grounds that the identity of a third party would be disclosed if the third party is a health professional who has compiled, or contributed to, the health record, or has been involved in the care of the data subject in his capacity as a health professional, unless serious harm to that health professional's physical or mental health or condition is likely to be caused by giving access.

Subject access and medical data   25.3

In September 2000 the Information Commissioner issued guidance (see **25.17** below) on subject access requests and information in health records. A 'health record' is defined in *section 68(2)* of *DPA 1998* as any record which consists of information relating to the physical or mental health or condition of an individual, and has been made by or on behalf of a health professional in connection with the care of that individual. Appendix 1 to the Information Commissioner's guidance provides further details on the definition. The definition would apply to material held on an X-ray or an MRI scan, for example. This means that when a subject access request is made, the information contained in such material must be supplied to the applicant. The Information Commissioner states:

> 'It is clear, therefore, that many of the records being held by NHS Trusts, surgeries and other health care institutions will constitute "health records" and will therefore fall within the scope of the 1998 Act's subject access provisions.'

The old *Health Records Act 1990* has now been repealed.

The *Data Protection (Subject Access Modification) (Health) Order 2000* (*SI 2000/413*) provides that information need not be disclosed if it would be likely to cause serious harm to the physical or mental health of the data subject or any other person, and describes the mechanisms for ensuring that decisions as to whether to disclose or withhold information are taken by the appropriate health professional.

Fees for access   25.4

In March 2001 the Information Commissioner issued guidance on charging fees for subject access requests for medical data, which is on her website (see 25.17 below). The subject access rights are modified by two orders made under *DPA 1998*. Firstly, the *Data Protection (Subject Access Modification) (Health) Order 2000* (*SI 2000/413*) mentioned above, and secondly the *Data Protection (Subject Access) (Fees and Miscellaneous Provisions) Regulations 2000* (*SI 2000/191*). *Regulation 6* of *SI 2000/191* provides that whereas the normal maximum subject access fee that may be charged is £10, for health records there is a fee of up to £50 for access to non-automated records. This had been planned to cease to have effect on 24 October 2001. However, the *Data Protection (Subject Access) (Fees and Miscellaneous Provisions) (Amendment) Regulations 2001* (*SI 2001/3223*) extended the right to continue to charge the £50 fee.

The Commissioner's March 2001 guidance says that the subject access fee should be set no higher than that necessary to deter vexatious requests:

> 'The right to obtain a copy of personal data is a fundamental one. The provisions in *DPA 1998* reflect those of the *Data Protection Directive* (*95/46/EC*) and specify that data subjects should be able to gain access to their data "without excessive expense"'.

A fee of up to £10 appears to the Commissioner to achieve this. However *SI 2001/3223* mentioned above shows that lobbying by the health sector has succeeded and a fee of £50 can be charged. Even that fee often will not reflect the true cost of the exercise. The Commissioner thinks that if fees could be charged on a cost recovery basis for health data, this would inevitably lead to arguments by other types of data controller that they too should be able to set subject access fees according to the effort taken to respond. It could also mean those with poor record-management practices, for whom it is more expensive to extract the data, could charge more – a perverse result.

Fees, reportedly as high as £1000 for some requests under the former *Access to Health Records Act 1990*, are likely to deter most data subjects from exercising their rights and to lead to 'widespread mistrust of the standards to which health organisations process personal data', according to the Commissioner.

The Commissioner says if individuals ask for their whole record it is possible for the data controller to ask data subjects for information which they reasonably need in order to locate the data requested. In addition, under *section 8* of *DPA 1998* information need not be provided in permanent form where this would involve disproportionate effort.

Response periods 25.5

40 days is quite a short period for many in the health service, as the *Data Protection (Subject Access Modification) (Social Work) Order 2000 (SI 2000/415)* requires consideration to be given by the appropriate health professional as to whether the disclosure of information might seriously harm the health of data subjects or other persons, particularly where, unusually, it may be necessary to consult more than one health professional. Perhaps those involved could make a case to the Secretary of State, the Commissioner says, although it is pointed out that others in industry also have to cope with the 40 day period.

On 30 July 2001 the Information Commissioner issued a paper entitled *Medical Records: Subject Access – Fees for Access* which confirms that the Commissioner believes higher fees are not justified. She also expresses the view that destroying X-rays after two years may breach other provisions of *DPA 1998* (the destruction might ease the burden of responding to subject access requests which have been growing in this sector with the rise in personal injury claims and conditional fee agreement).

Example – disclosure of medical data 25.6

In her first Annual Report (June 2001) the Information Commissioner gave one case example which related in part to confidential medical data.

A council employee sent into the office a large amount of employee personnel information found in a black bin liner in a skip at the council depot where he was employed. He alleged that the manager of the depot disposed of the personnel files of employees working there by placing them in black bin liners and then into skips to be transported to a public refuse tip. He said that two additional bags containing similar information had also been found.

The retrieved documents contained a large amount of personal data relating to the employees and their relatives, including pay and financial details, leave applications, medical information relating to sick leave and so on. Virtually all the documents retrieved were copies of manual documents, which did not come under the scope of *DPA 1998*.

However, there was one document (a sickness record relating to the complainant) which appeared to have been computer generated. On this basis the council concerned was notified that there had been a contravention of the Seventh Data Protection Principle in this case.

The council responded explaining that whilst systems and procedures were in place at the depot concerned these had not been strictly adhered to. As a result of the complaint all depots had been issued with shredders and management had been reminded of the procedures, which should be followed. In addition all employees were to receive data protection awareness training. Data protection liaison officers throughout the council were informed of the incident and asked to apply the lessons learned in their own areas.

Midwifery 25.7

The *Nursing and Midwifery Order 2002 (SI 2001/253)* in force 12 February 2002, as amended by the *Nursing and Midwifery Order 2002 (Consequential Amendments) Order 2002 (SI 2002/881)* is also relevant in this field. It was commented upon by the Information Commissioner when still in draft as it provides for a register of such staff. The comments were issued on 27 June 2001 and the Commissioner particularly objected to the publication of home addresses of such staff. 'The Draft Nursing and Midwifery Order 2001: Comments by the Information Commissioner' are on the Commissioner's website under Guidance/Codes of Practice and other responses. The Order also amended *DPA 1998*; in *section 69(1)* subsection *(e)* was substituted with 'a registered nurse or midwife'.

Health and Social Care Act 2001 25.8

In April 2000 the Information Commissioner issued her comments on the *Health and Social Care Act 2001 (HSCA 2001)* (then in Bill form). *Part 5 of HSCA 2001* deals with the control of patient information and the extension of prescribing rights as well as various other matters. *Section 60 of HSCA 2001* contains provisions relating to patient information and *DPA 1998*.

Section 60 of HSCA 2001 allows the Secretary of State to require or permit patient information to be shared for medical purposes where it is considered that this is in the interests of improving patient care or in the public interest. *Section 61 of HSCA 2001* provides for the establishment of a statutory committee that is to be consulted about regulations to be made under *section 60*.

Section 60 of HSCA 2001 should make it possible for patients to receive more information about their clinical care and for confidential patient information to be lawfully processed without informed consent to support prescribed activities such as cancer registries, the Government says in its explanatory note to *HSCA 2001*. *Section 60* of *HSCA 2001* does not amend *DPA 1998*, and any regulations must not derogate – and will not be able to derogate – from *DPA 1998*. *Section 60(2)(a)* of *HSCA 2001* enables regulations to be made that require specified communications about patients to be disclosed to them by NHS bodies, in certain circumstances. Such regulations may only provide for these communications to be disclosed to those persons to whom they relate or principally relate, or to a prescribed person on their behalf, for example a spouse. This is intended to support the NHS Plan commitment that clinicians will, in the future, be required to share information about patients with them.

What is 'patient information'? 25.9

Section 60(8) of *HSCA 2001* defines 'patient information' as any information that is, or is derived from, information concerning a patient's physical or mental health or condition, the diagnosis of their condition or their care or treatment.

In addition to information which directly identifies individuals, this would include information which is either anonymised (eg any information that cannot be tracked back to the individual) or coded (eg information that can be tracked back to an individual by persons in possession of a key to the code). It includes information recorded in any manner, whether electronically or manually. *Section 60(9)* of *HSCA 2001* provides that 'confidential patient information' for the purposes of the section is patient information that has been obtained by a person who owes an obligation of confidence to an individual where the identity of that individual is ascertainable from that information or from that information and other information which is in, or is likely to come into, the possession of the person processing the information.

Personal data in medical context 25.10

In her October 2001 Legal Guidance, when addressing the question of 'what is processing?', the Information Commissioner gives a medical example.

'It should be noted that the disclosure of personal data by a data controller amounts to processing under *DPA 1998*. For example:

The obtaining of clinical information linked to a National Health Service number by a person having access to the National Health Service Central Register will amount to processing of personal data by that person because that person will have access to information enabling him to identify the individuals concerned.

It will be incumbent upon anyone processing data to take such technical and organisational measures as are necessary to ensure that the data cannot be reconstituted to become personal data and to be prepared to justify any decision they make with regard to the processing of the data.'

The Health Service (Control of Patient Information) Regulations 2002   25.11

The *Health Service (Control of Patient Information) Regulations 2002 (SI 2002/1438)* deal with the processing of patient information, including confidential patient information. They make provision relating to the processing of patient information in connection with the construction and maintenance of databases by bodies (known as 'cancer registries') which undertake the surveillance of health and disease of patients referred for the diagnosis or treatment of neoplasia. *Regulation 3* makes provision for the processing of patient information for the recognition, control and prevention of communicable disease and other risks to public health. *Regulation 3(4)* makes provision for information on the operation of these Regulations to be passed to the Secretary of State. Bodies can be nominated to handle the data by regulation. *Regulation 4* provides that information may be processed in accordance with these Regulations notwithstanding any common law obligation of confidence. *Regulation 5* and the Schedule to the Regulations makes general provision in relation to the processing of patient information. Such processing is restricted to that approved by the Secretary of State and, in the case of processing for research purposes, the relevant ethics committee. *Regulation 6(1)* requires the Secretary of State to record and make public particulars relating to approvals which permit the transfer of confidential patient information. *Regulation 7* restricts the processing of information under the Regulations, for example by requiring the removal of particulars by which the persons to whom information relates can be identified if that is practical. *Regulation 8* provides for enforcement by civil penalty. The *Schedule* to *SI 2002/1438* sets out the circumstances in which confidential patient information may be processed for medical purposes under *regulation 5*. The provisions relate, for example, to the processing of confidential patient information in order to identify who should be invited to participate in medical research (*SI 2002/1438, Sch, para 3*) or to enable the auditing, monitoring and analysing the provision made by the health service (*SI 2002/1438, Sch, para 5*).

Education   25.12

A similar order to that relating to health (as described at **25.2** above) exists in relation to education – the *Data Protection (Subject Access Modification) (Education) Order 2000 (SI 2000/414)*.

SI 2000/414 applies to education records and allows for exemptions and modifications for such material, where disclosure of the information pursuant to a subject access request would be likely to cause serious harm to the physical or mental health or condition of the data subject, or to some other person or, in some circumstances, where disclosure would reveal that the data subject is, or may be at risk of, child abuse (as defined by *regulation 5(4)*). *SI 2000/414* does not apply to personal data to which the *Data Protection (Subject Access Modification) (Health) Order 2000 (SI 2000/413)* applies.

Disclosure of examination results by schools to the media   25.13

The Information Commissioner has issued some guidance on disclosure of examination results by schools to the media. The Information Commissioner's Office regularly receives enquiries about the data protection implications of schools disclosing the examination results of their students to the local media for publication. Therefore, in February 2001 an advice sheet was issued which explains the impact of *DPA 1998* on this use of personal data, and provides guidance on how such disclosures can be made within the remit of the Act. Schools should ensure that pupils and their parents are aware that examination results may be published. It may also be necessary to explain the form in which this will take place. Some pupils, for example, might object to their results being published if they know that they will be published in order of grades attained rather than alphabetically. The Commissioner does not think that pupils or their parents must give their consent to the publication of examination results, knowing from experience of complaints that in a small number of cases publication can cause distress. In informing pupils or their parents of the practice of publication of examination results, schools should therefore advise them of the right to object to publication.

The rights given to a data subject by *DPA 1998* are not affected by the data subject's age. The Commissioner generally advises that providing that people are able to understand their rights then it is them, and not their parents or guardians, who should be informed of uses and disclosures of data and who have the right to object to processing. In most cases, therefore, it is sufficient to provide the information described above to pupils. In a small number of cases, it may be that pupils are not capable of understanding their rights or of understanding the consequences of publication. In these cases, schools should provide the relevant information to parents or guardians.

Relevant person – education   25.14

For education records the *Data Protection (Subject Access Modification) (Education) Order 2000 (SI 2000/414)* referred to above defines a 'relevant person' as:

- an employee of the local education authority which maintains the school, a teacher or other employee of an education and library board, or in the case of a voluntary aided, foundation or foundation special school or special school not maintained by a local education authority, a teacher or other employee of the school;

- a person employed by an education authority (within the meaning of *paragraph 6 of Schedule 11 to DPA 1998*) in pursuance of its function relating to education and the information relates to him, or he supplied the information in his capacity as such employee; or

- the person making the request.

Social Work 25.15

The *Data Protection (Subject Access Modification) (Social Work) Order 2000* (*SI.2000/415*) provides for modifications and exemptions where the personal data relate to social work falling within any of the descriptions set out in the Order. *SI 2000/415* does not apply to personal data to which the *Data Protection (Subject Access Modification) (Health) Order 2000 (SI 2000/413)* (see **25.2** above) and the *Data Protection (Subject Access Modification) (Education) Order 2000 (SI 2000/414)* (see **25.12** above) apply.

It is not permissible to deny access to a social work record on the grounds that the identity of a third party would be disclosed where the third party is a 'relevant person' as defined by *DPA 1998*, unless serious harm to that person's physical or mental health or condition is likely to be caused by giving access.

Social work – conditions 25.16

If the information is 'social work' (defined by *SI 2000/415*)) and:

(a)   (except in relation to Scotland) the data subject is a child and the request is made by someone with parental responsibility who is enabled to make the request by some enactment or rule of law; or

(b)   in relation to Scotland, the data subject is a person under 16 and the request is made by someone with parental responsibility who is enabled to make the request by some enactment or rule of law; or

(c)   the data subject is incapable of managing his own affairs and the person making the request has been appointed by a court to manage those affairs;

the information should *not* be supplied if:

•   the information was supplied in expectation that it would not be disclosed to that person; or

•   the information results from an examination or investigation to which the data subject consented in the expectation that it would not be disclosed; or

•   the data subject has expressly indicated that the information should not be disclosed.

Further Information 25.17

The Commissioner has issued the following separate guidance relevant in this field:

•   Use and disclosure of health data (May 2002).

•   Schools: exam results, publication.

- Subject access – education records in England.

- Subject access – health records.

- Subject access – health records: fees for access.

- Subject access – medical records: Fees for access.

- Subject access – social services records.

- Employment Code of Practice Part IV: Medical records.

The guidance is available on the website of the Information Commissioner (www.informationcommissioner.gov.uk under Compliance Advice). Also see the Code of Practice Part 4 (draft), to be finalised in 2004, on Medical Records, Employment and Data Protection.

FAQs   25.18

How much fair processing information should be provided?

Concern has been expressed that the fair processing rules may require the provision of very large amounts of information in which patients have no real interest. In the Commissioner's view this concern is misplaced. In effect the fair processing information provided should achieve two basic purposes:

- It should provide sufficient information to allow the patients to exercise their rights in relation to their data. Hence patients should be told who will process their data, including any disclosures of personal data (which will allow them to make subject access requests), whether it must be supplied (which will allow them to opt-out if they wish), and what information is contained in their record (which will allow them to give meaningful consent to its processing.)

- It should provide sufficient information to allow the individual to assess the risks to him or her in providing their data, in consenting to their wider use, in choosing not to object to their processing etc. This should have at least two consequences for data controllers. It should become clear that fair processing notices do not need to contain a large amount of detail about routine, administrative uses of data. It should also become clear that researchers engaged in open-ended studies are not prevented by the Act from soliciting patient data on the grounds that their fair processing notices cannot be sufficiently detailed. Fair processing notices in this case should simply need to make clear that the research in question is indeed open-ended, leaving the individual to assess the risk.

It may also be helpful to bear in mind that the fair processing rules do not mean that patients must be provided with information that they are known to already possess.

When should fair processing information be provided?

It is likely that there will be a number of standard purposes for which the personal data of all patients entering a hospital or registering with a GP will be processed, information about which can be provided to patients at the outset of the episode of care. In particular, patients may need to be told about typical flows of data between different NHS bodies. This information is relatively timeless and it is appropriate that patients are given it at an early opportunity. It would certainly be good practice to remind patients of this information from time to time, for instance by ensuring that leaflets containing the relevant information are available to patients.

Some patients may subsequently have their personal data processed for a number of additional purposes eg information about a cancer diagnosis may be passed to a cancer registry, or information may be passed to social services. Those patients who will have their personal data processed for these additional purposes will need to be provided with this further information, in order to satisfy the fair processing requirements. This type of information is specific to particular patients at particular times and should be given in context, at a time when individuals are able to make sense of it.

How should the fair processing information be given?

The provision of 'fair processing information' by means of a poster in the surgery or waiting room or by a notice in the local paper etc is unlikely to be sufficient to meet the requirements of the Act since not all patients will see or be able to understand such information. Such methods may, however, be used to supplement other forms of communication. Methods by which the fair processing information may be provided include a standard information leaflet, information provided face to face in the course of a consultation, information included with an appointment letter from a hospital or clinic, or a letter sent to a patient's home. The effort involved in providing this information may be minimised by integrating the process with existing procedures. Many GP practices, for instance, already provide leaflets to patients about how the practice operates. Such leaflets could easily incorporate the fair processing information. Doctors may be able to easily provide specific information to patients in the course of consultations. Only where such an opportunity does not present itself will it be necessary to contact patients separately, for instance, if they are to be invited to participate in a programme of research involving the disclosure of their medical records to a researcher who may wish to interview patients with particular medical conditions.

Copyright The Information Commissioner 2002

Chapter 26 –
Human Rights Act 1998

At A Glance

✓   The *Human Rights Act 1998* (*HRA 1998*) came into force on 2 October 2000 and makes the *European Convention on Human Rights* (*ECHR*) part of English law.

✓   *Article 8* of *ECHR* provides for a right to respect for private and family life, which has implications for privacy law.

✓   *Article 10* of *ECHR* provides a right of freedom of expression.

✓   The Information Commissioner takes account of *HRA 1998* in her interpretation of the *Data Protection Act 1998* (*DPA 1998*).

✓   The High Court has ruled that a breach of *DPA 1998* occurred when a voter was prosecuted for refusing to go on the electoral roll because his local council refused to allow him to opt-out of his details being commercially sold on by the council (*Brian Robertson v Wakefield City Council (High Court, 16 November 2001)*).

Introduction
26.1

Since 2 October 2000 *HRA 1998* has applied in the UK. The Act guarantees certain rights which may have implications in the data protection field, in particular a right to respect for private life. Therefore correspondence which breaches data protection legislation may also breach *HRA 1998*.

Commissioner's Legal Guidance
26.2

In her Legal Guidance to *DPA 1998* the Commissioner says:

> 'As I am required to do, I have sought to interpret the Act in the light of the provisions of the Human Rights Act 1998, which came into force on 2 October 2000. This will need to be kept under review. The full effect of the Human Rights Act on our legal system, and on society as a whole, has yet to be felt. It is, however, clear that the role of information in our society makes it increasingly important to develop respect

among data controllers for the private lives of individuals and to ensure good information handling practice. The Human Rights Act, and in particular Articles 8 and 10 of the European Convention on Human Rights provide the legal framework within which interpretation of the Act, and the Data Protection Principles which underpin it, can be developed.'

In the 2003 Annual Report the IC comments on the case law in this area to date, which is of considerable interest:

'There is undoubtedly a body of "privacy" law being developed by the higher courts in the context of cases involving high profile celebrities and their claims for rights to privacy as against the rights of newspapers and other media to publish articles about their private lives. This inevitably involves the courts in consideration of two competing human rights, contained in the European Convention on Human Rights and enshrined in UK law by the *Human Rights Act 1998*, the right to respect for private and family life (*article 8*) and the right to freedom of expression (*article 10*)'.

Lawful Obtaining   26.3

Under the Eight Data Protection Principles data must be lawfully obtained. Data which is obtained in breach of confidence or in breach of an enforceable contractual agreement comes within this category, as does breach of *HRA 1998* by a data controller bound by that Act (this is an example given by the Information Commissioner in her Legal Guidance).

Convention Rights   26.4

In the Employment Practices Data Protection Code (2000 Draft), the Commissioner writes the following about *HRA 1998*:

' ... the Act gives effect to rights and freedoms guaranteed under the European Convention on Human Rights. Public authorities including the courts and tribunals such as the Data Protection Tribunal must not act in a way that is incompatible with a Convention right unless the need to apply primary legislation leaves them with no choice'.

The Convention rights most relevant to the area of data protection, those given by *Article 8* and *Article 10* of the *ECHR*, are set out at **26.5–26.6** below.

Article 8 26.5

Right to respect for private and family life

1. Everyone has the right to respect for his private and family life, his home and his correspondence.

2. There shall be no interference by a public authority with the exercise of this right except such as is in accordance with the law and is necessary in a democratic society in the interests of national security, public safety or the economic well-being of the country, for the prevention of disorder or crime, for the protection of health or morals, or for the protection of the rights and freedoms of others.

Article 10 26.6

Freedom of expression

1. Everyone has the right to freedom of expression. This right shall include freedom to hold opinions and to receive and impart information and ideas without interference by public authority and regardless of frontiers. This Article shall not prevent States from requiring the licensing of broadcasting, television or cinema enterprises.

2. The exercise of these freedoms, since it carries with it duties and responsibilities, may be subject to such formalities, conditions, restrictions or penalties as are prescribed by law and are necessary in a democratic society, in the interests of national security, territorial integrity or public safety, for the prevention of disorder or crime, for the protection of health or morals, for the protection of the reputation or rights of others, for preventing the disclosure of information received in confidence, or for maintaining the authority and impartiality of the judiciary.

Interception 26.7

The interception of communications can breach *HRA 1998* as well as *DPA 1998*. The *Telecommunications (Lawful Business Practice) (Interception of Communications) Regulations 2000 (SI 2000/2699)* set out the relevant law in this area and permit the carrying out of covert, directed surveillance of individuals by public authorities. It sets out arrangements for the authorisation of such surveillance and the grounds on which an authorisation can be given. An example given by the Commissioner is as follows.

A local authority sets up a secret camera in the office of the Deputy Director of Social Services, who it suspects of sexually harassing another member of staff. The surveillance has not been authorised in accordance with the provisions of *section 28* of the *Regulation of Investigatory Powers Act 2000*. The processing of personal data involved in the surveillance will be unlawful, putting the local authority in breach of the First Data Protection Principle. This is because the surveillance is not carried out in accordance with the law, in this case the *Regulation of Investigatory Powers Act 2000*. Furthermore, it contravenes *Article 8* of the *European Convention on Human Rights* as given effect by the *Human Rights Act 1998* in that there is an interference with the Deputy Director's exercise of his right to respect for his private life that is not in accordance with the law.

Commissioner's Views   26.8

DPA 1998 derives from the *ECHR* as it is based upon the Council of Europe *Convention on Data Protection*, which seeks to give particularity to the provisions of *Article 8* of *ECHR*. This makes it unlike many other statutes. When commenting on the proposed Social Security Fraud Bill in January 2001, the Commissioner noted that the exemptions contained in *DPA 1998* are based upon those provided for in *ECHR*.

Social Security Fraud Act 2000   26.9

In the context of the *Social Security Fraud Act 2000*, the Commissioner took advice from counsel about the compatibility of the proposals in the Bill with the European Court of Human Rights ('ECtHR').

Article 8(1) of *ECHR* provides that:

> 'Everyone has the right to respect for his private and family life, his home and his correspondence.'

This right is qualified by *Article 8(2)* of *ECHR* which states:

> 'There shall be no interference by a public authority with the exercise of this right except such as in accordance with the law and is necessary in a democratic society in the interests of national security, public safety or the economic well-being of the country, for the prevention of disorder or crime, for the protection of health or morals or for the protection of the rights or freedoms of others.'

It is useful to examine the Commissioner's comments which show her own and counsel's views of the impact of *HRA 1998* in this field. She said she:

> 'considers that the test of necessity may be failed for other reasons. c.1 of the Bill lists organisations which may be required to provide information

to "authorised officers". However, it seems … that in a significant number of cases the organisations described either do not have the information required or will have considerable difficulty in ensuring that the information they do possess relates to the subject of an officer's enquiries…'

In considering 'necessity' the ECtHR has considered the matter of proportionality. The Commissioner writes the following:

'It is hard to see how the proposed powers may be justified when they are compared, say with those of the police, who even where the matters under investigation are extremely serious, must either seek evidence from the suspect, must persuade others of their need for information or, as a last resort seek judicial authority for the collection of information without consent.

Wide information gathering can breach *HRA 1998*. The ECtHR has also found that for an interference with the right to privacy to be justified, there must be adequate, enforceable safeguards. The provisions from the Bill are now contained in the *Social Security Fraud Act 2000*, and include the powers criticised above for state bodies to cross-check data of claimants for DSS benefits. Whilst the above quotes are comments on only one piece of legislation, they do illustrate the Commissioner's views on the application of *HRA 1998* in this area.

Emails 26.10

In the area of subject access rights and emails, in her guidance the Information Commissioner is of the view that if an email were written in a private rather than an official capacity, then only exceptional circumstances will justify the disclosure of third party information without the consent of the individual concerned. 'Cases which involve possible breaches of *Article 8* provisions will be considered on their individual merits', the Commissioner says.

Traffic and billing data 26.11

The *Directive on the Processing of Personal Data and the Protection of Privacy in the Telecommunications Sector (97/66/EC)* recognises the importance of safeguarding traffic and billing data, and lays down strict rules about the retention and use of this information by telecoms providers. It is the Commissioner's view that access to traffic and billing data should also be made subject to prior judicial scrutiny, so that consideration could be given to *Article 8* of *ECHR*. The *Anti-terrorism, Crime and Security Act 2001* may, under its Code of Practice, lead to a requirement for the retention of traffic data for up to 12 months, however this is the traffic data rather than the contents of the traffic itself.

The *Directive on Privacy and Electronic Communications (2002/58/EC)* deals with certain privacy issues relating to 'traffic data'.

Human Rights and Monitoring   26.12

In 2001 the Institute of Management suggested that some monitoring by managers of staff email and telephone calls could breach *HRA 1998*. Ringing staff at
home to discuss work matters could, under UK human rights legislation, be construed as an invasion of privacy.

> 'An employer does not have the right to demand an employee's tele-
> phone number, unless it is specified in the contract that the employee
> has a duty to be available outside normal working hours.'

The Institute also warned that the unauthorised vetting of emails and phone calls
could be considered an invasion of privacy, even if employees are thought to be
sending personal messages through company lines.

The 'Employment Practices Data Protection Code: Monitoring at Work: An
Employer's Guide' (Draft 2002) has been drafted to be consistent with the
Human Rights Act 1998 and contains sections of guidance on monitoring at
work.

Case Law   26.13

In the case of *A v B plc and another, Times Law Reports, 2 November 2001,* on
10 September 2001 the High Court granted an interlocutory injunction to
prevent an unnamed first defendant from disclosing or publishing any information about the extra-marital sexual relationships a married professional foot-
baller had allegedly had with two women. However this was overturned by
the Court of Appeal. The court said that facts concerning the existence of a
sexual relationship and details of the sexual activity in the relationship,
whether within a marriage or outside of it, were confidential. Here there was
no public interest in the publication of the details and the information was not
already in the public domain. The information was confidential and publication would be a breach of the claimant's right of privacy enshrined in *HRA
1998*. The right to privacy prevailed over the newspaper's right to freedom of
expression.

A v B plc is consistent with earlier cases which have held that famous people
who choose to sunbathe on a public beach did not have any right to privacy
sufficient to prevent publication of photographs taken of them, whereas those
inviting guests to a very private wedding at which photography is banned and
tight security imposed with the aim of ensuring confidentiality would be protected. In the latter case, the courts have held that the individuals may then
restrain publication of illicit photographs taken there in breach of confidentiality and privacy rights. Similarly, the careless, or public, adulterer may find
their lack of discretion held against them where similar injunctions are sought,
whereas the discreet will find that their privacy rights prevail.

In the case of *Brian Robertson v Wakefield City Council (High Court, 16 November 2001)*, the High Court held a breach of *Article 8* of *ECHR*, as given effect by *HRA 1998*, when a voter was prosecuted for refusing to register to vote on the grounds that his local council allowed the electoral roll to be used for commercial purposes by third parties. They would not let him opt-out of such use. Mr Justice Maurice Kay said that there was a breach of *Article 8*, and also this resulted in a disproportionate and unjustified restriction on Mr Robertson's right to vote.

The judge also said on this issue that the British Government had not properly implemented the *Data Protection Directive (95/46/EC)* in *DPA 1998*. Mr Robertson argued through his solicitors that his details should only be used for electoral purposes for which he had consented, or other purposes justified in the public interest, and yet for years (at least since 1918) all local authorities have sold their electoral registers for commercial use.

In *Robertson* the judge said that in considering the various submissions he found it useful to contemplate a hypothetical situation with a resemblance to the case.

'Assume that the Government department which administers the State pension disclosed the names and addresses of all recipients of the State pension to private providers of residential care, knowing full well that the information would then be used to approach pensioners in their homes, by post or otherwise, as a marketing exercise. All that would have been disclosed would be names and addresses, together with, by implication, the fact that the persons named would be over 65. That, it seems to me, is a situation in which there would be a *prima facie* interference with the right to respect for family life. Moreover, that conclusion is reached by taking into account the expected consequences of disclosing the names and addresses. In my judgment the submission on behalf of the claimant is correct. It is necessary to examine not just the information which is disclosed but also the anticipated use to which it will be put. In the present case one therefore has to focus not only on the raw data – names and addresses and, by implication, the fact that those named are all over 18 (and, in some cases, recently so). Account also has to be taken of what is known and anticipated about the use to which it will be put. In these circumstances, I conclude that, quite apart from Mr. Blake's [counsel's] submission about European convergence (to which I shall return) there is a prima facie engagement with Article 8 [of ECHR].

The case of *Campbell v Express (October 2002, CA)* considered the *Human Rights Act 1998* (see **19 EXEMPTIONS**), as did *Douglas v Hello [2001] QB 967* (see **5 COMPENSATION, DAMAGES AND PREVENTION OF PROCESSING**).

(cont'd)

In a decision concerning CCTV footage, *Peck v The United Kingdom [2003], European Court of Human Rights (Application No. 44647/98)*, the Court held that:

'59. The monitoring of the actions of an individual in a public place by the use of photographic equipment which does not record the visual data does not, as such, give rise to an interference with the individual's private life (see, for example, *Herbecq and Another v Belgium*). On the other hand, the recording of the data and the systematic or permanent nature of the record may give rise to such considerations.

'60. ... the Court notes that [Mr Peck] did not complain that the collection of data through the CCTV camera monitoring of his movements and the creation of a permanent record of itself amounted to an interference with his private life ... Rather he argued that it was the disclosure of that record of his movements to the public in a manner in which he could never have foreseen which gave rise to such an interference.

'61. In this respect, the Court recalls the Lupker and Friedl cases decided by the Commission which concerned the unforeseen use by the authorities of photographs which had been previously voluntarily submitted to them ... In those cases, the Commission attached importance to whether the photographs amounted to an intrusion into the applicant's privacy (as, for instance, by entering and taking photographs in a person's home), whether the photograph related to private or public matters and whether the material thus obtained was envisaged for a limited use or was likely to be made available to the general public.

'62. [In the case of Mr Peck] the relevant moment was viewed to an extent which far exceeded any exposure to a passer-by or to security observation ... and to a degree surpassing that which the applicant could possibly have foreseen.

'63. Accordingly, the Court considers that the disclosure by the Council of the relevant footage constituted a serious interference with the applicant's right to respect for his private life'.

Representation of the People Regulations 2002 26.14

The *Robertson* case (see **26.13** above) led to the *Representation of the People (England and Wales)(Amendment) Regulations 2002 (SI 2002/1871)*. These provide for an edited version of the register of electors which does not contain the names of those persons who have requested the exclusion of their names from this version of the register. The request is made either in the form of return of the annual canvass under *section 10* of the *Representation of the People Act 1983* (RPA 1983), as substituted by *Schedule 1* to the *Representation of the People Act 2000* (RPA 2000), or in the form of application to be registered. The form to be used for the canvass is prescribed by *Part I* of the *Schedule* to the Regulations. Under *regulation 110* of the Regulations, the edited version of the register is available for sale without restriction and the fees payable are set out. The Regulations introduced new restrictions, not only on the sale of the full version of the register but also on its use arising from its being supplied free of charge. No full copy of the register may be sold except to bodies such as government departments and credit reference agencies. Such sales are subject to the fees and conditions set out in inserted *regulations 111* and *112*, in particular the restrictions on use. The purchasers are restricted to the uses which are authorised by *regulations 113* and *114*.

The way in which the full register is to be available for inspection is set out. This will be only under supervision. Only handwritten copies may be taken.

The IC's views on this were summarised in the 2003 Annual Report:

> 'In the past we have expressed concern about the widespread availability of the electoral register and its use for many different purposes. The *Representation of the Peoples Act 2000* established a framework where there would be two versions of the electoral register. There would be a full version available for use only for electoral and other limited purposes and another edited version that could be made available for sale for any purpose. Individuals should now be given the choice to 'opt out' of the edited version should they so wish. After some delay the necessary Regulations are now in place, meaning that for the first time individuals are being given a choice over the use and disclosure of the information they provide for electoral purposes. Whilst we have some concerns over the prominence and wording of this choice on some canvass forms, the provision of a choice is a welcome step forward. We look forward to seeing how well these arrangements work in practice, and in particular how well individuals understand and exercise the choice they now have'.

Further Information 26.15

See *A v B plc and another (10 September 2001, Times Law Reports 2 November 2001)* and *A v B plc [2002] 3 WLR 542* (Court of Appeal, 11 March 2002).

See the Information Commissioner's guidance 'Electoral Register – The use of the electoral register in light of the Robertson case'.

FAQs 26.16

Does compliance with *DPA 1998* achieve compliance with *HRA 1998*?

Not necessarily. Compliance with both pieces of legislation is necessary.

What rights does *HRA 1998* give in this area?

HRA 1998 confers rights in many areas including as to privacy of one's personal communications.

Has there been much case law on *HRA 1998* and data protection?

Not much except the *A v B* case mentioned in this chapter and the *Campbell* case.

Chapter 27 –
International Aspects

At A Glance

✓ The *Data Protection Act 1998* (*DPA 1998*) implements the *Data Protection Directive (95/46/EC)* in the UK.

✓ Internationally, in 1980 the Organisation for Economic Co-operation and Development ('OECD') agreed guidelines on data protection.

✓ Further international development of such guidelines may occur in due course.

✓ In September 2001 the Council of Europe agreed the Cybercrime Convention which has data protection implications.

Introduction   27.1

DPA 1998 implements the *Data Protection Directive (95/46/EC)*. However, the UK Information Commissioner liaises with international data protection bodies in the course of her work. In 1980 the OECD agreed guidelines in the data protection field, and the Information Commissioner has also been involved in a long running series of international conferences of data protection commissioners.

OECD Data Protection Guidelines   27.2

The Guidelines on the Protection of Privacy and Transborder Flows of Personal Data (the 'Privacy Guidelines') were adopted on 23 September 1980 as a Recommendation of the Council of the OECD. In adopting the Privacy Guidelines, the OECD member countries clearly intended to 'help to harmonise national privacy legislation and, while upholding such human rights, to prevent at the same time interruptions in international flows of data'. According to the OECD, since then the Recommendation has 'proved to represent international consensus on general guidance concerning the collection and management of personal information'.

The principles contained in the OECD Privacy Guidelines are reflected in legislation and practices for the protection of privacy worldwide. The principles were designed in a technology-neutral way to accommodate future developments; they are still applicable with regard to any technology used for collecting and processing data, including network technologies.

The last international conference of data protection commissioners examined whether the time was right for a review of the international instruments which address data protection and the preparation of a more global multi-lateral convention.

The Information Commissioner, in her First Annual Report (June 2001), states that 'the predominant view was that it would be more constructive for the moment to concentrate on pragmatic means of securing the implementation of and compliance with the acknowledged international principles declared in instruments such as the OECD Guidelines'. In September 2001 the OECD conference met again to discuss these issues in Paris.

The aim of the Privacy Guidelines which arose from the Council of Europe Convention is to provide protection for individuals whilst also allowing a free flow of information for trade purposes. The Commonwealth Centre for Electronic Governance, which has been recently set up, also works in these areas.

OECD Privacy Statement Generator   27.3

In 2000 the OECD adopted the *OECD Privacy Statement Generator* for websites at http://cs3-hq.oecd.org/scripts/pwv3/pwhome.htm. Privacy policies are also addressed in **37 PRIVACY POLICIES AND AUDITS**.

The Generator has been endorsed by the OECD's 29 member countries, and aims to:

- offer guidance on compliance with the Privacy Guidelines and to help organisations develop privacy policies and statements for display on their websites;

- provide guidance on conducting an internal review of existing personal data practices and on developing a privacy policy statement;

- give links to private sector organisations with expertise in developing a privacy policy; and

- offer links to governmental agencies, non-governmental organisations and private bodies that give information on applicable regulations.

The OECD say: 'The Generator makes use of a questionnaire to learn about your personal data practices. A Help Section provides explanatory notes and practical guidance. Warning flags appear where appropriate. Your answers are then fed into a pre-formatted draft policy statement. You must assess this statement: is it an accurate reflection of your personal data practices and policy? Note that the OECD does not guarantee that such a draft privacy policy statement meets applicable legal or self-regulatory requirements. The statement merely reflects the answers given to the Generator's questions. However, the draft statement will furnish an indication of the extent to which your privacy practices are consistent with the OECD Privacy Guidelines.'

The OECD feels that by making the Generator freely available online, it will help:

- foster awareness of privacy issues amongst website owners;

- increase awareness among visitors about privacy practices on the websites which they browse; and

- encourage user and consumer trust in global networks and electronic commerce.

Use of the OECD Generator does not, however, necessarily imply that a website complies with the OECD Privacy Guidelines. The Guidelines are accessible on the OECD website (see **27.6** below).

E-commerce Privacy Disputes and Other Work of OECD   27.4

The OECD began work in 2000 on creating methods of online alternative dispute resolution for addressing privacy and consumer disputes in the e-commerce area.

The OECD is also examining the special privacy problems arising from genetic research data.

Council of Europe Convention on Cybercrime   27.5

In 2001 the Council of Europe Ministers' Deputies approved the Convention on Cybercrime.

The Convention on Cybercrime is the first international treaty on crimes committed via the Internet and other computer networks, dealing particularly with infringements of copyright, computer-related fraud, child pornography and violations of network security. It also contains a series of powers and procedures relating to the search of computer networks and the interception of data. Its main objective, set out in the preamble, is to pursue a common criminal policy aimed at the protection of society against cybercrime, especially by adopting appropriate legislation and fostering international co-operation. The Convention is the product of four years of work by Council of Europe experts, but also by the United States, Canada, Japan and other countries which are not members of the organisation. It will be supplemented by an additional protocol making any publication of racist and xenophobic propaganda via computer networks a criminal offence.

The COE held a signing ceremony on 22 to 23 November 2001 in Hungary, where over 30 countries including the US, Canada and Japan signed the treaty. The COE in 2004 is beginning work on an optional protocol on 'criminalisation of acts of a racist or xenophobic nature committed through computer networks'.

Further Information   27.6

The OECD's website is at www.oecd.org.

The OECD Privacy Statement Generator for websites can be found at http://cs3-hq.oecd.org/scripts/pwv3/pwhome.htm.

Privacy International's Cybercrime page is at http://www.privacyinternational.org/issues/cybercrime/index.html.

FAQs   27.7

Is there international harmonisation of data protection laws?

Not extensively, although many nations follow the agreed OECD Privacy Guidelines mentioned in this chapter.

What happens when national and other states' laws disagree?

In the EU this often leads to one giving way,.eg under the recent *Directive on Privacy and Electronic Communications 2002 (2002/58/EC)* on the issue of spam emails, the UK gave way to the majority of other nations. Internationally, there may simply end up being two different legal decisions.

Chapter 28 –
Internet

At A Glance

✓ Personal data is often gathered on Internet websites and must be handled in accordance with the applicable sections of the *Data Protection Act 1998* (*DPA 1998*).

✓ The Information Commissioner has issued guidance for data controllers and for data subjects relating to the Internet, and in June 2001 also issued a list of Frequently Asked Questions in relation to the Internet and personal data.

✓ The Information Commissioner's Employment Practices Data Protection Code Part 3: Monitoring at Work also looks at Internet use by employees and the data protection implications thereof, including those relating to surveillance (see **15 EMAILS**, **29 LAWFUL BUSINESS PRACTICE REGULATIONS** and **40 REGULATION OF INVESTIGATORY POWERS ACT 2000**).

✓ Many companies have a privacy policy on their website.

Introduction   28.1

Many companies gather personal data through use of a website. They must comply with *DPA 1998*. Many display a privacy policy on the website (see **37 PRIVACY POLICIES AND AUDITS**). The Organisation for Economic Co-operation and Development ('OECD') has also issued some guidance on privacy policies also addressed in **37 PRIVACY POLICIES AND AUDITS**.

Information to be Given to Users of a Website   28.2

Some websites collect no personal data at all; they are simply online catalogues displaying the goods or services offered by a business. There may be no data protection implications and no need for a privacy policy or other notice on the website. However, in other cases, for the processing of personal data to be fair and compliant with the law, website operators who collect personal data directly from individuals must always ensure that individuals are aware of:

- the identity of the person or organisation responsible for operating the website and of anyone else who collects personal data through the site;

- the purposes for which they intend to process the personal data; and

- any other information needed to ensure fairness to individuals, taking into account the specific circumstances of the processing – this will include informing individuals of any disclosure of information about them to third parties, including disclosure to companies within the same group.

The Information Commissioner states that:

> 'Unless it is obvious, website operators must give this information to individuals before they collect any personal data from them. It should be remembered that visitors to a website will not necessarily enter it through its homepage. They may, for example, come directly to a particular page via a hypertext link. The above information should therefore be provided at any point at which personal data are collected.'

In some cases there will be more than one data controller collecting data, for example where there is banner advertising placed by a third party, or where a third party provides a secure payment mechanism. In such cases all data controllers should be identified, the Information Commissioner advises.

Where information collected is to be used or disclosed for direct marketing purposes, individuals should be provided with the opportunity to prevent this. Website operators may wish to adopt the Information Commissioner's padlock symbol (available at www.informationcommissioner.gov.uk/#info_padlock_signpost) (see **34 PADLOCK (USE OF THE SIGN CALLED PADLOCK)**). This alerts individuals to the fact that their information is being collected, and draws their attention to the explanation of how it is to be used. Further information about the symbol is available under News and Events on the Commissioner's website (www.informationcommissioner.gov.uk).

Using privacy statements is a good way to ensure individuals are given the information they need. It does not, however, remove the requirement for notification. The Commissioner says that although a privacy statement is important, it is not sufficient to provide the above information simply in the form 'click here to view our privacy statement'. At least the basic messages and choices should be displayed in an intelligible and prominent form wherever personal data are collected, even where a more detailed explanation is provided elsewhere by means of a privacy statement. Clearly, any basic messages or information given about choices should correspond with the contents of any privacy statement.

Help in designing a privacy statement is available. The OECD has developed a Privacy Policy Generator (see **27 INTERNATIONAL ASPECTS** and **37 PRIVACY POLICIES AND AUDITS**). This is available at www.oecd.org under 'OECD Tools'. The Information Commissioner advises that:

> 'As a matter of good practice and as an aid to encouraging confidence, a privacy statement should describe not only what a website operator does

with personal data but also what it does not do. It should also tell individuals something about their rights and how to exercise them. For example, individuals have a right to be told whether data about them are being processed and to have a copy of the data. They should be told how to go about this. The privacy statement must include the physical address of the website operator unless this is clearly available on the site.'

Is Opting-in or Opting-out Required? 28.3

A major issue for businesses gathering personal data is whether they can use information unless someone objects ('opting-out'), or whether they can only use it if the individual expressly agrees ('opting-in'). For many businesses, particularly where the data is not sensitive, the practice has been to give individuals a right to tick a box to indicate they object, and if they do not indicate this then to make use of the data as set out on the notice accompanying the box (opting-out). Commercially this is the easiest method for businesses keen to use personal data for particular marketing purposes.

One question posed by the Information Commissioner in her guidance is whether those supplying data to a website should be required to opt-in or opt-out to the further use of their data (see **33 OPT-IN AND OPT-OUT**). The Commissioner states:

'The general standard to ensure compliance with the *Data Protection Act 1998* is for a website to provide an individual with an opportunity to opt-out of the use or disclosure of their personal data for direct marketing, whether by email or other means. This requires a statement along the following lines:

"We would like to email you with offers relating to products of ours that we think you might be interested in. Click here if you object to receiving such offers."; and/or

"We would like to pass your details on to other businesses so they can email you with offers of goods/services that you might be interested in. Click here if you don't want your details to be passed on."

It should be easy for the individual to register his or her wishes. It would not be acceptable, for example, to expect an individual to visit another site to register his or her wishes, or to register his or her wishes by post.

In some cases an opt-out facility will not be sufficient. This is likely to be the case where the processing of sensitive personal data is involved. Where sensitive data about an individual are collected it will usually be necessary to obtain the data subject's explicit consent to the processing before collecting the information. Sensitive data, as defined in *DPA 1998*, are information as to a person's:

- racial or ethnic origin;

- political opinions;

- religious or similar beliefs;

- trade union membership;

- physical or mental health;

- sexual life;

- commission of criminal offences; and

- involvement in criminal proceedings.

Where explicit consent is required a statement along the following lines will be needed:

"We keep information you have provided us with about your health in order to send you offers of vitamin supplements we think you are likely to be interested in. Click here to show that you agree to this."

It should be noted that explicit consent cannot be obtained by the presence of a pre-crossed box. The individual must take some positive action to signify consent and must be free not to consent.'

In some other countries an opt-in clause is required which raises an interesting jurisdictional issue. It is understood that the general standard is 'opt-in' in Germany, Denmark, Finland, Sweden and Italy.

E-privacy Directive and the Privacy and Electronic Communications (EC Directive) Regulations 2003   28.4

The *Directive on Privacy and Electronic Communications (2002/58/EC)* ('*E-privacy Directive*') provides for an opt-in and was implemented in the UK on 11 December 2003 by the *Privacy and Electronic Communications (EC Directive) Regulations 2003 (SI 2003/2426)*. Where businesses have obtained data from staff already when they purchased they can then email them thereafter (*E-privacy Directive, arts 13.2, 13.3*). The Directive and Regulations are considered in more detail in **CHAPTER 13**. The Information Commissioner has issued detailed guidance on the Regulations and FAQs. The Regulations are included in **APPENDIX 7**. The guidance is contained in **APPENDIX 8**.

Marketing   28.5

Many companies ask for personal data from those visiting the site for marketing purposes. This is lawful as long as the individuals are told that their data will be used for such a function. If personal information is only required for marketing and is not strictly necessary for the supply of a product or service it should be made clear to visitors why the information is being requested, and its supply should be optional.

Wording along the following lines is suggested by the Information Commissioner:

> 'You do not have to answer the following questions but if you do so your answers will help us understand you better as a customer. We will then be able to bring to your attention offers that we believe you are likely to be interested in.'

Cookies 28.6

Many websites gather data through the use of 'cookies'. A cookie is a message given to a web browser by a web server. The message is then stored by the browser in a text file called cookie.txt. Each time the browser requests a page from the server, the message is sent back. A cookie's main objective is to identify users and personalise their visit by customising web pages for them, for example by welcoming them by name next time they visit the same site. A site using cookies will usually invite the user to provide personal information such as their name, email address and interests.

Internet users who have not disabled the cookie function will find that their Internet use can be tracked and a profile developed of them (without the collection of traditional identifiers) which is used in advertising to them later. The Information Commissioner advises that if the operator intends to link this profile to a name and postal address or even an email address, there is no doubt that the profile information is personal data subject to the requirements of *DPA 1998*. The Commissioner is of the opinion that in the context of the online world 'the information that identifies an individual is that which uniquely locates him or her in that world, by distinguishing him or her from others. Thus profiles that are based on cookies and that are used to deliver targeted marketing messages to particular individuals are personal data.'

There are many different methods in which cookies are used in websites. The important legal issue is to ensure visitors know what is going on, for example by way of an online notification or in the privacy statement. Advice from the Office of the Information Commissioner is that 'if a notification provided via an online privacy statement is to be relied upon it is important that at least some reference to the use of tracking technology is clearly displayed to all site visitors.'

The *E-privacy Directive (2002/58/EC)*, in recital 28, deals with cookies and says:

> 'However, such devices, for instance so-called 'cookies', can be a legitimate and useful tool, for example, in analysing the effectiveness of website design and advertising, and in verifying the identity of users engaged in online transactions. Where such devices, for instance cookies, are

intended for a legitimate purpose, such as to facilitate the provision of information society services, their use should be allowed on condition that users are provided with clear and precise information in accordance with *Directive 95/46/EC* about the purposes of cookies or similar devices so as to ensure that users are made aware of information being placed on the terminal equipment they are using. Users should have the opportunity to refuse to have a cookie or similar device stored on their terminal equipment. This is particularly important where users other than the original user have access to the terminal equipment and thereby to any data containing privacy-sensitive information stored on such equipment. Information and the right to refuse may be offered once for the use of various devices to be installed on the user's terminal equipment during the same connection and also covering any further use that may be made of those devices during subsequent connections. The methods for giving information, offering a right to refuse or requesting consent should be made as userfriendly as possible. Access to specific website content may still be made conditional on the well-informed acceptance of a cookie or similar device, if it is used for a legitimate purpose.'

The *Privacy and Electronic Communications (EC Directive) Regulations 2003* implement the Directive. Part 1 of the IC's Guidance on the Regulations suggests the following:

'Confidentiality of communications

'Regulation 6 is concerned with the use of electronic communications networks to store information or gain access to information stored in the terminal equipment of a subscriber or user. So-called "spyware" can enter a terminal without the knowledge of the subscriber or user in order to gain access to information, store information or trace the activities of the user. The regulation of the use of such devices reflects the growing concern about the use of covert surveillance mechanisms online. It is, however, recognised in the Directive that the use of such devices will not necessarily be harmful or unwarranted. The use of devices, such as cookies, has for some time been commonplace. Cookies are important to the provision of many online services. The use of such devices is not, therefore, prohibited by the Regulations but they do require that subscribers and users should, to some extent, be given the choice as to which of their online activities are monitored in this way.

'1. Cookies and personal data

'Although devices which process personal data give rise to greater privacy and security implications than those which process data from which the individual cannot be identified, the Regulations apply to all uses of such devices, not just those involving the processing of personal data. Where the use of a cookie type device does involve the processing of personal data, service providers will be required to ensure that they comply with the additional requirements of the Data Protection Act 1998. This includes the requirements of the third data protection principle which states that data controllers shall not process personal data that is excessive (see http://www.dataprotection.gov.uk/dpr/dpdoc.nsf, *Data Protection Act 1998: Legal Guidance*, paragraph 3.3). Where personal data is collected, the data controller should consider the extent to which that data can be effectively processed anonymously. This is likely to be of particular relevance where the data is to be processed for a purpose other than the provision of the service directly requested by the user, for example the counting of visitors to a website.

2 Information to be provided

'Cookies or similar devices shall not be used unless the subscriber or user of the relevant terminal equipment:

a) is provided with clear and comprehensive information about the purposes of the storage of, or access to, that information; and

b) is given the opportunity to refuse the storage of, or access to, that information.

'The Regulations are not prescriptive about the sort of information that should be provided but the text should be sufficiently full and intelligible to enable individuals to gain a clear appreciation of the potential consequences of allowing storage and access to the information collected by the device should they wish to do so. This is comparable with the transparency requirements of the first data protection principle (see http://www.dataprotection.gov.uk/dpr/dpdoc.nsf, Data Protection Act 1998: Legal Guidance, paragraph 3.1.7). The requirement that the user or subscriber should be "given the opportunity to refuse" the use of the cookie type device may be subject to differing interpretation. At the very least, however, the user or subscriber should be given a clear choice as to whether or not they wish to allow a service provider to engage in the continued storage of information on the terminal in question. The fact that an "opportunity to refuse" such storage or access must be provided imposes a greater obligation on the relevant party than that they should simply make such a refusal a possibility. The mechanism by which a subscriber or user may exercise their right to refuse continued storage should, therefore, be prominent, intelligible and readily available to all, not just the most computer literate or technically aware. Where the relevant information is to be included in a privacy policy, for example, the policy should be clearly signposted at least on those pages where a user may enter a website. The relevant information should be appear in the policy in a way that is suitably prominent and accessible and it should be worded so that all users and subscribers are capable of understanding, and acting upon it, without difficulty.

'The Interactive Advertising Bureau (IAB) is an industry body that develops standards and guidelines to support online business processes. It has produced a series of web pages (www.allaboutcookies.org) which explains to users how cookies work and can be managed. The IAB welcomes website owners who wish to link their cookie policies directly to these pages.

'Regulation 6(3) states that once a person has used such a device to store or access data in the terminal equipment of a user or subscriber, that person will not be required to provide the information described in Regulation 6(2) (and discussed above) on subsequent occasions, provided that these requirements were met in respect of the initial use. Although the Regulations do not require the provision of the relevant information on each occasion, they do not prevent this.

3 Responsibility for providing the information

'The Regulations do not define who should be responsible for providing the information outlined in Regulation 6(2). Where a person operates an online service and any use of a cookie type device will be for their purposes only, it is clear that that person will be responsible for providing the information in question. We recognise that it is possible for organisations to use cookie type devices on websites seemingly within the control of another organisation, for example through a third party advertisement on a website. In such cases the organisation to whom the site primarily refers will be obliged to alert users to the fact that a third party advertiser operates cookies. It will not be sufficient for that organisation to provide a statement to the effect that they cannot be held responsible for any use of such devices employed by other persons they allow to place content on their websites. In addition, the third party would also have a responsibility to provide the user with the relevant information.

4 Refusal of cookies

'The Regulations are also non-prescriptive about the way in which a user or subscriber should be able to refuse the use of a cookie type device. Again, although a standard approach would be beneficial, whether service providers choose to make their own switch off facilities available or else explain to the user or subscriber how they can use the facilities specific to their browser type is less important than that the mechanism is uncomplicated, easy to understand and accessible to all. There is, in addition, nothing to prevent service providers from requiring users to "opt in" to receipt of the cookie as opposed to providing them with the opportunity to "opt out".

5 Exemptions from the right to refuse a cookie

'The Regulations specify that service providers should not have to provide the information specified in Regulation 6(2) where that device is to be used:

a)   for the sole purpose of carrying out or facilitating the transmission of a communication over an electronic communications network; or

b) where such storage or access is strictly necessary for the provision of an information society service requested by the subscriber or user.

'In defining an "information society service" the Electronic Commerce (EC Directive) Regulations 2002 refer to "any service normally provided for remuneration, at a distance, by means of electronic equipment for the processing (including digital compression) and storage of data, and at the individual request of a recipient of a service". The term "strictly necessary" means that such storage of or access to information should be essential, as opposed to reasonably necessary, for this exemption to apply. It will also, however, be restricted to what is essential for the provision of the service requested by the user, rather than what might be essential for any other uses the service provider might wish to make of that data. It will also include what is required for compliance with any other legislation to which the service provider might be subject, for example, the security requirements of the seventh data protection principle (see http://www.dataprotection.gov.uk/dpr/dpdoc.nsf, Data Protection Act 1998: Legal Guidance, paragraph 3.7) Where the use of a cookie type device is deemed "important" as opposed to "strictly necessary" the user of the device is still obliged to provide information about the device to the potential service recipient so that they can decide whether or not they wish to proceed. The information provided to the user about the uses the collector intends to make of that data should be of sufficient clarity to enable the user to make a truly informed decision.

6 Wishes of subscribers and users

'Regulation 6 states that the relevant information and the opportunity to refuse the cookie type device should be provided to "the subscriber or user" but it does not specify whose wishes should take precedence in the event that they do not coincide. There may well be cases where a subscriber, for example an employer, provides an employee with a terminal at work along with access to certain services in order to carry out a particular task, where the effective completion of this task depends upon the use of a cookie type device. In such cases it would not seem unreasonable that the employer's wishes should take precedence. It also, however, seems likely that there will be circumstances where a user's wish should prevail. To continue the above example, an employer's wish to accept such a device should not prevail where this will involve the unwarranted collection of personal data of which that employee is the data subject'.

Profiling Visitors   28.7

The position is the same if a profile of visitors is built up although it can be hard to use Internet protocol ('IP') addresses to build up personalised profiles. These are often dynamic so that each time a user connects to his or her Internet Service

Provider ('ISP') he or she is allocated an IP address. The Information Commissioner states that:

> 'This IP address will be different each time. Thus it is only the ISP that can link the IP address to an individual. It is hard to see how the collection of dynamic IP addresses without other identifying information would bring a website operator within the scope of the *Data Protection Act 1998*. Static IP addresses are different. As with cookies they can be linked to a particular computer which may actually or by assumption be linked to an individual user. If static IP addresses were to form the basis for profiles that are used to deliver targeted marketing messages to particular individuals they, and the profiles, would be personal data subject to the *Data Protection Act 1998*. However, it is not easy for a website operator to distinguish between dynamic and static IP addresses. Thus the scope for using IP addresses for personalised profiling is limited.'

If dynamic or static IP addresses are collected simply to analyse aggregate patterns of website use they are not necessarily personal data. They will only become personal data if the website operator has some means of linking IP addresses to a particular individual, perhaps through other information held or from information that is publicly available on the Internet. ISPs will of course be able to make this link but the information they keep will not normally be available to a website operator.

Using Internet Information: Spiders etc 28.8

One of the Information Commissioner's FAQs is whether information on the Internet can be used by people for their own purposes. The Commissioner advises that:

> 'Website operators should exercise caution when obtaining personal data from a source other than the individual him or herself. It is by no means the case that the processing of personal data obtained via the Internet is free from restriction. Simply because individuals have put their email addresses in the public domain, perhaps by participating in a chat-room, does not mean they can be used for marketing or other purposes. Those who use "spiders" or other scavenging type programmes to harvest email addresses, or other personal data from the Internet, are likely to breach the Act unless the use they are making of the information is consistent with the purpose for which it was first made available. If email marketing lists are used there is a responsibility to ensure that the personal data on the list were obtained fairly in the first place, bearing in mind the intended use of the list. The user of the list must also respect any relevant conditions put on its use by the source.'

Lots of data subjects, of course, put up often highly personal information on the Internet at their own option. They display pictures of their children (whether with or without the child's consent is not always clear) and give other details. The

Information Commissioner advises that individuals should be wary of doing this. However, this does not absolve others from ensuring the information is used fairly with regard to the purpose for which it was posted on the Internet.

Web Bugs 28.9

Web bugs (see the definition below) may be used as can similar software. However, if they are invisible to the user it is hard to see how they can be used in compliance with *DPA 1998*.

The Commissioner says that 'individuals being monitored through the use of a web bug or similar device should be informed that monitoring is taking place, who the monitoring is being performed by and for what purposes the monitoring is taking place. The Information Commissioner suggests that data controllers who intend to place a web bug or similar device give the individual a simple means of refusing or disabling the device prior to any personal information being collected through it.'

A web bug is a graphics file, generally only 1x1 pixel in size, that is designed to monitor who is reading a web page or email message. As with the use of a cookie the use of such a device may well result in personal data being processed.

IC FAQs, Information Commissioner's website June 2001

Commissioner's Guidance 28.10

The Information Commissioner has issued some general guidance for data controllers and separately for data subjects which is reproduced with permission below. This may need to be revised in the light of the *Privacy and Electronic Communications (EC Directive) Regulations 2003*.

Internet: Protection of Privacy-Data Controllers

In using the Internet for their business dealings, data controllers must take into account the privacy rights of individuals and their own responsibilities under privacy and data protection legislation. The following points should be considered by data controllers in planning their Internet strategies.

Personal data placed on the Internet is available worldwide. In many countries the use of personal data is not protected by legislation. Because of this it is always advisable and will often be essential to obtain consent from individuals before publishing their personal data on your website.

(cont'd)

When collecting information via the Internet always inform the user of who you are, what personal data you are collecting, processing and storing and for what purpose. Do this before a user gives you *any* information, when they visit your site and wherever they are asked to provide information, for example via an on-line application form. It is good practice to ask for consent for the collection of all data and it is usually essential to get consent if you want to process sensitive personal data.

It is good practice for a data controller who sets up a website to provide a statement of its privacy policy. A 'privacy statement' helps individuals to decide whether or not to visit a site and, when they do visit, whether or not to provide any personal information to the data controller.

Always let individuals know when you intend to use 'cookies' or other covert software to collect information about them.

Never collect or retain personal data unless it is strictly necessary for your purposes. For example you should not require a person's name and full address to provide an on-line quotation. If extra information is required for marketing purposes this should be made clear and the provision of the information should be optional.

Design your systems in such a way as to avoid or minimise the use of personal data.

Upon a user's request you should correct, change or delete inaccurate details. If information is altered notify the third parties to whom the original information was communicated. Regularly delete data which is out of date or no longer required.

Stop processing data if the user objects to it because the processing is causing them damage or distress.

Only use personal data collected on-line for marketing purposes where the user has already been told that his or her information was to be used in this way. If a user asks you to stop using his or her data for marketing purposes you must do so and the individual should always be given the opportunity to opt of the use of his or her data for marketing. It is also good practice to get the individual's consent before using their information for marketing. It will always be necessary to get their consent where if the data is sensitive.

Use the most up-to-date technologies to protect the personal data collected or stored on your site. Especially sensitive or valuable information, such as financial details should be protected by reliable encryption technologies.

Internet: Protection of Privacy – Data Subjects

It is easy to see and understand the benefits the Internet offers individuals, allowing immediate access to global information and markets and facilitating direct global communications. It is however worth remembering a few points:

The Internet is not secure. There is a risk that information provided over the Internet might be intercepted by people you wouldn't want to read it.

Information you provide to a website or send via email may be made available anywhere in the world and may not be protected by data protection legislation.

Never provide information online unless you are confident you know what the website intends to use the information for.

Is more information being collected than is absolutely necessary? Be aware of this when accessing a site or making a transaction, especially if it not clear why this additional information is being requested. Don't be afraid to ask. Just because you are asked a question doesn't mean you have to answer it.

Show caution with your credit card and account numbers, for example, are your details security protected? Remember your information can be used and abused.

The best way to protect your privacy when using services over the Internet is to avoid giving your name or other personal details out over the Internet. If anonymity is impractical you may use a pseudonym (if permitted by law) so that only yourself and your ISP know your personal identity, for example when signing on to use a chatroom

Information may be collected from you on the Internet without your knowledge. Your ISP will have access to a lot of detailed information relating to you. Always choose a reliable ISP. Enquire what data they collect, process and store, in what way and for what purpose. Do this periodically. If you want to know what information your ISP or any other service or website provider (based in the European Economic Area) holds about you can make a subject access request.

Websites you visit may also implant software known as 'cookies' on your machine. Some of these cookies serve a useful purpose, for example they can be used to facilitate on line 'shopping baskets but some are used to track your movements on the Internet. Check your 'Cookie' files and consider deleting those you do not want.

Email addresses are personal data. If you find yourself on a directory or user list you can request to be omitted from it.

You can also ask not to be sent 'junk email or SPAM' and where the sender is based in the EEA they should comply with your request.

Consider using reliable encryption techniques for confidential email

Try and keep up to date with the latest privacy and security risks on the Internet. Try the Internet search engine facilities using the words 'privacy' and 'security'.

All guidance is current at the date of this book but is updated from time to time, and reference should always ideally be made to the Information Commissioner's website at www.informationcommissioner.gov.uk

Further Information 28.11

See also **15** EMAILS, **29** LAWFUL BUSINESS PRACTICE REGULATIONS and **40** REG-ULATION OF INVESTIGATORY POWERS ACT **2000**.

For privacy policies see **37** PRIVACY POLICIES AND AUDITS.

More information on the padlock symbol is available on the Information Commissioner's website under News and Events at www.informationcommissioner.gov.uk.

For information on employment and data protection issues, see the Information Commissioner's Employment Practices Data Protection Code.

FAQs 28.12

The Commissioner has issued the following additional Frequently Asked Questions relating to the Internet.

A: If we have collected information about someone other than directly from them, do we have to tell them that we have got it?

Where information is obtained from a third party, for example where one web-site operator obtains information about an individual from another website operator, there is still a duty to ensure that the subsequent processing of infor-mation about the individual is fair, ie. that the individual is aware of such mat-ters as the identity of the person or organisation that now holds the information and the purposes for which it is to be used. In some cases it may be possible for operators to inform individuals of the fact that information about them is to be obtained indirectly, and the purposes for which the data are to be used, before the data are obtained. This might be the case where the operator has already had contact with the individual, perhaps when he or she has registered with a website, and has informed him or her that there is an intention to obtain infor-mation from other sources. In other cases the source may already have provided a full explanation to the individual on behalf of the third party website opera-tor. This might be the case where two operators routinely exchange informa-tion about individuals, and their respective fair processing notices explain this.

Where individuals do not have the information necessary to make the process-ing of personal data about them fair, operators should provide the necessary information as soon as is practicable. If there is an intention to disclose per-sonal data, the explanation should certainly be provided no later than the time when the information is first disclosed.

The website operator does not have to contact the individual where it would involve 'disproportionate effort' to do so. If an operator believes this to be the case it will have to ensure that it can provide the necessary explanation to any individual who asks for it. It must also keep a record of the reasons why it concluded that providing the information would involve disproportionate effort. Website operators should be aware that the ease by which explanations can be provided on-line, for example by the automated sending of an email, means that the circumstances in which they can rely on this exemption are limited. However, the Commissioner would not normally seek to challenge a website operator's compliance with the Act if after obtaining a legitimate email marketing list, the operator provided the necessary explanation with its first marketing approach rather than separately, as long as the first marketing approach came soon after the list was obtained.

B: Our website is directed at children. Are there any special rules that we have to follow?

Websites that collect information from children may have to put more rigorous safeguards in place to ensure the processing of those children's information is fair. Website operators should recognise that children generally have a lower level of understanding than adults and notices explaining the way their data will be used should be appropriate to this level of understanding and should not attempt to exploit any lack of understanding. The consent of a parent or guardian is necessary where a child is asked to provide personal data unless it is reasonable to believe the child clearly understands what is involved and is capable of making an informed decision.

The Act does not lay down a precise age at which a child can act in his/her own right and the Commissioner does not consider it is valid to try and do so. Much depends on the capacity of the child and the complexity of the proposition that is being put to him/her. As a general rule the Commissioner considers the standard adopted by Trust UK (www.trustuk.org) in its accreditation criteria to be a reasonable one. This is that: "Personal data must only be collected from children with the explicit and verifiable consent of the child's parent/guardian unless that child is aged 12 years or over, the information collected is restricted to that necessary to enable the child to be sent further but limited on-line communications and it is clear that the child understands what is involved".

The above standard is based on the definition of a child as a person aged 16 years or under. There are certain practices that, if adopted, are likely to breach the requirements of the Act. These include collecting personal data relating to other people (for example parents) from children and enticing children to divulge personal data with the prospect of a game prize or similar inducement. If personal data collected from children are to be disclosed or transferred to third parties this should not take place without the explicit and verifiable

(cont'd)

375

consent of the child's parent/guardian unless it can be demonstrated that the child really appreciates what is going on and the consequences of his or her actions. Similarly, where a website operator wishes to publish personal data relating to a child on the Internet the verifiable consent of the child's parent/guardian should usually be obtained. Whether it is necessary to seek the parent or guardian's consent to publication, rather than that of the child, will again depend on the circumstances, in particular the age of the child, and whether or not the data controller can be certain that the child fully understands the implications of making their information available on the Internet. Where parental consent is required the website operator must have some way of verifying that this has been given. It will not usually be sufficient to simply ask children to confirm that their parents have agreed by means of a mouse click. It will in all likelihood be necessary to revert to postal communication. If parental consent is the required standard but the website operator concludes that the effort in verifying the consent is disproportionate, the proposed marketing activity or other course of action should not be pursued.

C: We collect personal information through our website. Do we have to use an encryption based transmission system?

A website operator is responsible for the security of its processing of personal data. It must adopt appropriate technical and organisational measures to protect the personal data. The processing of personal data includes its obtaining. A website operator is therefore required to obtain personal data in a way that is sufficiently secure. It is hard to see how this can be done without the use of a secure, encryption-based transmission system if the personal data are in any way sensitive or otherwise pose a risk to individuals, for example because they include credit card numbers.

Website operators should be aware that whilst the use of a secure, encryption-based transmission system will protect personal data whilst in transit, there is a potentially greater threat to the security of personal data once the data have been decrypted and they are held in unencrypted form on a website operator's server. Personal data that are in any way sensitive or otherwise pose a risk to individuals should not be held on a website server or, if they are, should be properly secured by encryption or similar techniques.

D: If we use another company to host our website, who is responsible for data protection?

Responsibility for compliance with the *Data Protection Act 1998* rests with the data controller, that is the person who determines the purposes for which and the manner in which the personal data are or are to be processed. This is likely to be the website operator rather than the host. A data controller does not have to own the equipment on which the processing actually takes place. A website operator that uses a separate processor, ie. a person who processes personal data on the operator's behalf, must have a written contract with the processor under which the processor is required to act only on instructions from the website operator and to have in place appropriate technical and organisational security measures.

E: Can we publish personal data on our website?

The eighth principle of the Act [Eight Data Protection Principle] states that personal data shall not be transferred outside the European Economic Area if the country to which the data are transferred does not ensure an adequate level of protection for the individual in each case. Placing personal data on the Internet potentially involves a transfer to any country worldwide. In many countries the processing of personal data is not protected by legislation so it will not always be possible for website providers to guarantee the protection of personal data placed on their website. However, all the circumstances of such a transfer can be taken into account when assessing the adequacy of protection provided for the data. In some cases the risks arising as a result of a transfer, even in the absence of protective legislation, may be negligible. This may be the case with information that is already in the public domain, for example publication of details of the sporting achievements of well-known athletes. It may also be a relevant factor if the information published does not enable the individual to be contacted, although the sensitivity of the information will have to be taken into account. In other cases it will be necessary to obtain the individual's consent for their data to be published on the Internet. This consent must be 'informed', in that the website operator must explain the possible consequences of publishing the data. Consent must also be 'freely given' in that the individual must be able to decline without penalty.

Although likely to lead to similar conclusions, in most cases the general requirement of fairness in the processing of personal data must also be addressed when considering publication on a website. For example, a yacht club may have traditionally published the names and contact details of its members in a handbook distributed to all members and placed in local libraries. The club now intends to publish these details on its website.

Although the information has always been publicly available, the implications for members of publication on the web are significantly different. Fairness requires that the individuals concerned are told that there is an intention to publish information about them on the website and that the wishes of individuals who object are respected. If the intention is that information about the club's membership is only made available to other club members, the club should employ technical means to prevent access by unauthorised individuals, for example, by preventing general access to the site or to the part of the site where information about the club's members is published through the use of password protection.

(cont'd)

F: If we want to use the personal data we have obtained through our website differently can we simply change our privacy statement?

The simple answer is no. Changing the privacy statement and other information on the site can only affect how you can use personal data that are obtained after the date of the change. Visitors who provided you with personal data prior to the change will have done so on the basis of the privacy statement and other information you provided at that time. You must honour the assurances you gave them.

If you want to use the personal data differently the safest course of action is to obtain your customers' consent to the new use. In other words you must explain the proposed new use to them and only proceed when they have given you a positive indication of their agreement. Failure to respond to an email message would not be sufficient. This is sometimes referred to as 'opt-in'. The opt-in approach will be necessary if the data you have obtained are to be used by you or others for a new purpose or are to be disclosed either for the first time or to different organisations from those referred to in your privacy statement. It will also be necessary if the personal data are sensitive or if they are subject to a duty of confidentiality which would be breached by the new use.

In some cases it will be sufficient to advise your customers of the new use and to give them an opportunity to object. This will be the case if the new use does not amount to use for a new purpose or where the nature and purpose of a new disclosure remains close to the terms described in the privacy statement. For example, your site was originally set up to sell books, your customers were advised only that you would use their information for marketing and they were given an opportunity to opt-out. In the absence of any indication to the contrary they would have assumed your marketing was confined to books. You are now expanding into the sale of CDs and want to market these. As this activity is close to but nevertheless outside the terms of your original privacy statement, you should at least advise those customers that did not opt-out originally of the new use and give them another opportunity to opt-out, either from all marketing or from the marketing of CDs. Those customers that opted out originally should not be contacted. If in the above example the new marketing is of financial services or holidays, for example, or if customer details are to be provided to a third party for their marketing, the standard has to be opt-in. This will certainly be the case if, for the first time and with no previous explanation the marketing is to be based on a profile of the individual's book buying habits.

In other cases the new use might fall within the original privacy statement. For example, the privacy statement might have referred to the intention to market a range of products even though at the time this was confined to books. Now it will include CDs. There is no need to advise customers specifically of this as the products are sufficiently closely related. Clearly the wishes of any customers that subsequently object to the receipt of the new marketing message should be respected.

If the new products are substantially different, for example if they now include financial services, the marketing of these would not have been within customers' expectations even though arguably the privacy statement might have covered it. It is the interpretation which customers are likely to have placed on the privacy statement rather than its precise wording that is important. Depending on how far removed from this likely interpretation the new use is, the standard may be opt-in rather than opt-out.

G: Can we disclose personal data if our web-based company is subject to a takeover or merger?

The Act [*DPA 1998*] would not necessarily prevent this. Essentially the position on disclosure is no different simply because a web-based company goes out of business or is otherwise subject to a takeover or merger. A disclosure could breach the Act where individuals have previously been assured that personal data about them will not be disclosed, where the personal data are subject to a duty of confidentiality or where once disclosed the personal data are processed in a manner that has a markedly different effect on individuals. In such cases the consent of individuals will be required before the disclosure takes place. Before making a disclosure of personal data careful consideration should be given as to how the data were originally obtained. If a disclosure is to take place, in order to prevent unfairness to individuals it may be necessary to place restrictions on the purposes for which and the manner in which the data may be processed. So long as individuals were not led to believe their data would never be disclosed, the new owner in effect takes over the existing business and the personal data will be used in substantially the same way as previously. The Act is likely to be satisfied if individuals are told of the change of ownership and have an opportunity to object to the new owner holding their details.

H: Do we have to notify the commissioner if we put personal data on our website or obtain personal data through it?

Website operators who are established in the UK and who process personal data will need to notify the Commissioner unless exempt. Failure to notify is a criminal offence for those required to do so. There are conditional exemptions from notification where personal data are only processed for certain core business purposes. These include advertising and marketing your own business and keeping accounts and records. The exemptions will not necessarily be lost because personal data are obtained through a website or used for marketing by electronic means. They are more likely to be lost through publishing personal data on a website.

Many website operators will need to notify under the Act. You should visit www.dpr.gov.uk for more information about this and to notify. The current fee for notification is £35 for one year.

(cont'd)

I: Does the Data Protection Act 1998 apply if our website is operated outside the UK?

Website operators not established in the UK but established elsewhere within the European Economic Area ('EEA') will be subject to the data protection laws of the countries where they are established. In some circumstances website operators established outside the EEA might be subject to UK data protection law. If a website operator established outside the EEA uses equipment in the United Kingdom to process personal data, the processing will be subject to the Act even though the operator is not established in the UK. This might be the case where the operator's site is hosted in the UK or where the operator places a 'cookie' on the computer of a UK Internet user in order to create a profile of that individual's on-line behaviour.

J: What is the position if i only use my website for domestic purposes?

Where personal data are processed only for an individual's personal, family or household affairs, including recreational purposes, the data are exempt from the Act's notification requirements and from the requirements of the data protection principles. However, the Information Commissioner retains her powers of investigation and enforcement to determine whether the scope of the exemption has been exceeded, for example because the site is also used for business purposes.

Chapter 29 –
Lawful Business Practice Regulations

At A Glance

✓ The *Telecommunications (Lawful Business Practice) (Interception of Communications) Regulations 2000 (SI 2000/2699)* ('*Lawful Business Practice Regulations*') are made under the *Regulation of Investigatory Powers Act 2000 (RIPA 2000)*.

✓ The Regulations permit interception of emails and telephone calls by employers and others without consent for a vast range of purposes.

✓ In addition, compliance with the *Data Protection Act 1998 (DPA 1998)* must be achieved.

✓ The Information Commissioner's Employment Practices Data Protection Code addresses these issues in relation to the employment aspects (see **16 EMPLOYMENT**).

✓ Since January 2004 the *Regulation of Investigatory Powers (Communications Data) Order 2003 (SI 2003/3172)* allows certain state bodies to share communications traffic data, but not the content of the emails or other traffic.

Introduction   29.1

The *Telecommunications (Lawful Business Practice) (Interception of Communications) Regulations 2000 (SI 2000/2699)* came into force on 24 October 2000 under *RIPA 2000*. *RIPA 2000* is considered in **40 REGULATION OF INVESTIGATORY POWERS ACT 2000**. Recording of telephone calls and emails is also considered in **38 RECORDING TELEPHONE CALLS AND EMAILS**. **15 EMAILS**, and **16 EMPLOYMENT** are also relevant in this field.

What the Regulations do   29.2

The *Telecommunications (Lawful Business Practice) (Interception of Communications) Regulations 2000 (SI 2000/2699)* authorise businesses to monitor or record communications on their telecommunications systems *without consent* for the purposes set out below. These cover most of the reasons why employers might want to intercept communications, except perhaps snooping on employees' personal relationships.

However, people must be notified of the surveillance and this includes both employees and third parties sending emails to a business. This can easily be achieved in an employment contract, staff handbook or email to members of staff. Interception without consent is permitted for the following reasons under the Regulations:

- to establish the existence of facts relevant to the business (eg keeping records of transactions and other communications in cases where it is necessary or desirable to know the specific facts of the conversation);

- to ascertain compliance with regulatory or self-regulatory practices or procedures relevant to the business (eg monitoring as a means to check that the business is complying with regulatory or self regulatory rules or guidelines);

- to ascertain or demonstrate standards which are or ought to be achieved by persons using the telecoms system (eg monitoring for purposes of quality control or staff training);

- to prevent or detect crime (eg monitoring or recording to detect fraud or corruption);

- to investigate or detect the unauthorised use of the telecoms systems (eg monitoring to ensure that employees do not breach company rules regarding use of the telecoms system); and

- to ensure the effective operation of the system (eg monitoring for viruses or other threats to the system; automated processes such as caching or load distribution).

The Regulations also authorise businesses to monitor (but not record) without consent in the following cases:

- for the purpose of determining whether or not they are communications relevant to the business (eg checking email accounts to access business communications in staff absence); and

- in the case of communications to a confidential anonymous counselling or support helpline (eg monitoring calls to confidential welfare helplines in order to protect or support helpline staff).

Staff whose communications may be intercepted without their consent should be told, according to the Department of Trade and Industry ('DTI'), who state:

> 'Businesses could place a note in staff contracts or in other readily available literature informing staff that interceptions may take place. The persons who use a system are the people who make direct use of it. Someone who calls from outside, or who receives a call outside, using another system is not a user of the system on which the interception is made.'

Interceptions Outside the Regulations   29.3

Some interceptions will be outside the scope of the *Telecommunications (Lawful Business Practice) (Interception of Communications) Regulations 2000 (SI 2000/2699)*. In those cases business must obtain consent of the sender and recipient.

Examples given by the DTI are:

- interceptions for purposes such as marketing or market research; and

- interceptions for any other purposes that fall outside the list described above.

The types of steps businesses can take to gain consent of staff and others are:

o   the business could insert a clause in staff contracts by which employees consented to calls being monitored or recorded;

o   the call operator could ask outsiders at the start of a call whether they consented to their call being monitored or recorded; and/or

o   the business could begin calls with a recorded message stating that calls might be monitored or recorded unless outsiders requested otherwise.

The DTI believes that, as a minimum, a business would need to give outsiders a clear opportunity to refuse consent to interception and to be able to continue with the call.

Overlap with DPA 1998   29.4

Consideration should be given to *DPA 1998*. If the interceptions involve obtaining, recording or otherwise processing personal data by means of automated equipment (for example recording calls or filtering emails) it also falls within the scope of *DPA 1998*. So too does the holding or processing of personal data after the interception has taken place.

The *Telecommunications (Lawful Business Practice) (Interception of Communications) Regulations 2000 (SI 2000/2699)* also specifically state that compliance must be achieved with *DPA 1998*. Part 4 of the Information Commissioner's Employment Practices Data Protection Code examines such interception in the context of employment relationships and advocates data controllers taking the least intrusive surveillance method possible to achieve their objective, in order to ensure compliance with *DPA 1998*. This is considered in **15 EMAILS** and **16 EMPLOYMENT**.

Interception of Emails by ISPs   29.5

On 22 July 2002 the High Court confirmed a decision of Ipswich Crown Court from September 2001 that Internet Service Providers ('ISPs') can lawfully intercept emails where requested by the police who are searching for evidence of a serious crime. The ISP involved was ntl. They received notification from the police that they were applying for access to all information relating to a particular email address over a period of ten days. They told ntl, which kept a server for ISP Virgin, that it should not 'conceal, destroy, alter or dispose of' the material involved, except with judicial or police permission. The company's systems, however, were designed automatically to destroy emails quickly after they were been accessed by the recipient. The only way to keep the information sought would be to intercept emails. ntl said that compliance with the notice would infringe *RIPA 2000*. It applied to the court for permission to delete or dispose of the material. The court refused and said that the interception and retention of the emails was lawful as the police had notified ntl that they were applying for a special production order under the *Police and Criminal Evidence Act 1984 (PACE 1984)*. Therefore, ntl had implicit 'lawful authority' to intercept and retain the emails. The High Court decision said: 'If [ntl] was not in a position to take that action without committing an offence, it would mean that the [*PACE 1984* provisions] would be almost totally worthless.'

Regulation of Investigatory Powers (Maintenance of Interception Capability) Order 2002

29.6

ISPs in the UK were obliged to start intercepting and storing electronic communications including emails, faxes and web-surfing data from 1 August 2002. The rules only apply to large ISPs. Any criminal organisation wishing to avoid interception simply has to find an ISP that has fewer than 10,000 customers. The interception capability is made under *RIPA 2000*. On 1 August 2002, the *Regulation of Investigatory Powers (Maintenance of Interception Capability) Order 2002 (SI 2002/1931)* came into force.

Regulation of Investigatory Powers (Communications Data) Order 2003

29.7

In January 2004 the *Regulation of Investigatory Powers (Communications Data) Order 2003 (SI 2003/3172)* came into force allowing some public authorities access to customer data held by telecoms companies and Internet service providers. The regulations are made under the *Regulation of Investigatory Powers Act 2000 (RIPA 2000)*. Earlier 2001 terrorism legislation required the retention of communications data by ISPs, as these were needed to fight terrorism. Once obtained, the *RIPA 2000* provisions allow access to many other agencies for purposes unconnected with terrorism. The data concerned is information, which includes information from telephone companies, ISPs and interactive TV providers and it describes the caller and the means of communication (eg subscriber details, billing data, email logs, personal details of customers and records showing the location where mobile phone calls were made). It does not include content.

In addition to the police, Inland Revenue, Customs and Excise, MI5, MI6 and GCHQ, the *Regulation of Investigatory Powers (Communications Data) Order 2003* gives some other agencies rights to access communications data. These are fewer in number than in the original proposal which critics called the 'Snoopers' Charter', but do include:

- the Financial Services Authority;
- the Office of Fair Trading;
- the Maritime and Coastguard Agency;
- the UK Atomic Energy Constabulary;
- the Scottish Drugs Enforcement Agency;
- the Radiocommunications Agency;
- NHS bodies, in connection with health and fraud;
- local authorities (but not parish councils); and
- the Office of the Police Ombudsman for Northern Ireland.

The *Regulation of Investigatory Powers (Communications Data) Order 2003* can be viewed at http://www.hmso.gov.uk/si/si2003/20033172.htm

Further Information 29.8

A copy of the *Telecommunications (Lawful Business Practice) (Interception of Communications) Regulations 2000 (SI 2000/2699)* is on the HMSO website, www.hmso.gov.uk, under Statutory Instruments 2000.

The *Regulation of Investigatory Powers (Communications Data) Order 2003* can be viewed at http://www.hmso.gov.uk/si/si2003/20033172.htm.

FAQs 29.9

Do employees have to consent to interception of their communications under the *Lawful Business Practice Regulations (SI 2000/2699)*?

No, they just have to be informed.

What is the best way to inform employees?

By a separate data protection agreement they ideally sign or in their staff handbook or by email – but keep records of such emails as sent.

If one complies with the Regulations does one also have to comply with *DPA 1998*?

Yes, the two run side by side, in addition to obligations under the *Human Rights Act 1998*.

Chapter 30 –
Manual Records

At A Glance

✓ The *Data Protection Act 1998* (*DPA 1998*) applies to manual records which form part of a structured set.

✓ Most manual data records are outside the *DPA 1998*, following the *Durant* case.

✓ A first transitional period for certain such manual records expired on 23 October 2001 after which time subject access requests for all such records became available.

✓ The precise meaning of 'manual records' is not always clear.

✓ The decision in *Durant v Financial Services Authority [2003] EWCA Civ 1746* clarified the law.

Introduction   30.1

The *Data Protection Act 1984* (*DPA 1984*) applied only to data on computer systems. *DPA 1998* also applies to certain, but not all, manual data. This chapter examines which data is caught by the 1998 Act. *DPA 1998* has applied to such data since it came into force on 1 March 2000. However, some businesses had manual data in relation to which processing was already underway on 24 October 1998 (the date when the *Data Protection Directive* (*95/46/EC*) should have been implemented). For those businesses the right of subject access to that manual data did not apply until three years later when the first transitional period under *DPA 1998* expired on 24 October 2001.

Types of Manual Data Caught   30.2

The legislation applies to information 'recorded as part of a relevant filing system or with the intention that it should form part of a relevant filing system' (*DPA 1998, s 1(1)(c)*).

Relevant filing system means any 'set of information relating to individuals to the extent that...the set is structured, either by reference to individuals or by reference to criteria relating to individuals, in such a way that specific information relating to a particular individual is readily accessible' *(DPA 1998, s 1(1))*. In the *Data Protection Directive (95/46/EC)* a 'personal data filing system' is defined as 'any structured set of personal data which are accessible according to specific criteria, whether centralised, decentralised or dispersed on a functional or geographical basis'. It also provides that the scope of protection of individuals does not cover 'unstructured files'.

Manual data following the Durant case – IC's guidance 30.3

In the Durant case the Court of Appeal took the view that the Act intended to cover manual files 'only if they are of sufficient sophistication to provide the same or similar ready accessibility as a computerised filing system'. Any manual filing system 'which, for example, requires the searcher to leaf through files to see what and whether information qualifying as personal data of the person who has the made the request [for access to his personal data] is to be found there, would bear no resemblance to a computerised search'. It would not, therefore, qualify as a relevant filing system.

The judgment concluded that:

> 'a 'relevant filing system' for the purposes of the Act, is limited to a system:
>
> 1. in which the files forming part of it are structured or referenced in such a way as to clearly indicate at the outset of the search whether specific information capable of amounting to personal data of an individual requesting it under section 7 is held within the system and, if so, in which file or files it is held; and
>
> 2. which has, as part of its own structure or referencing mechanism, a sufficiently sophisticated and detailed means of readily indicating whether and where in an individual file or files specific criteria or information about the applicant can be readily located.'

The judgment includes some helpful statements as to the effect of this interpretation, as follows, which are quoted in February 2002 guidance on the case by the Information Commissioner:

- 'the protection given by the legislation is for the privacy of personal data, not documents';

- 'if the [DPA] statutory scheme [for the handling of manual personal data] is to have any sensible and practical effect, it can only be in the context of filing systems that enable identification of relevant information with a minimum of time and costs, through clear referencing mechanisms within any filing system potentially containing personal data…';

- 'to qualify [as a relevant filing system] under ... the Act ... requires ... a file to which [a] search [for personal data] leads to be so structured and/or indexed as to enable easy location within it or any sub-files of specific information about the data subject that he has requested'; and

- ... it is only to the extent that manual filing systems are broadly equivalent to computerised systems in ready accessibility to ... personal data that they are within the system of data protection'.

In the Information Commissioner's view it follows, therefore, that when a subject access request is received for information held in manual form (other than information contained in an 'accessible record', the statutory right to be given access to personal data will only apply if the filing system is structured as a 'relevant filing system'. That is to say, the filing system is structured in such a way as to allow the recipient of the request to: either:

- know that there is a system in place which will allow the retrieval of file/s in the name of an individual (if such file/s exists); and know that the file/s will contain the category of personal data requested (if such data exists); or

- know that there is a system in place which will allow the retrieval of file/s covering topics about individuals (eg personnel type topics such as leave, sick notes, contracts etc); and know that the file/s are indexed/structured to allow the retrieval of information about a specific individual (if such information exists) (eg the topic file is subdivided in alphabetical order of individuals' names).

Where manual files fall within the definition of relevant filing system, the content will either be so sub-divided as to allow the searcher to go straight to the correct category and retrieve the information requested without a manual search, or will be so indexed as to allow a searcher to go directly to the relevant page/s.

For example, a set of legal files containing files divided into sections for legal aid, pleadings, orders, correspondence by year, instructions to counsel, counsel's advice, will not be a relevant filing system because the divisions/referencing do not assist a searcher in retrieving the required personal information without the need to leaf through the file contents.

It is important to note that the *Freedom of Information Act 2000* ('*FOIA 2000*') will, in 2005, amend the *DPA 1998* to expand the definition of 'data'. As a result of the expanded definition, public sector bodies caught by the *FOIA 2000* must ensure that the personal data they hold (including unstructured manual personal data *except* unstructured manual personnel records) must be accurate, up to date and accessible under *section* 7 of the *DPA 1998*. They should also note that the compensation and rectification provisions of the *DPA 1998* will apply in respect of such data, although so far as subject access fees are concerned, the charges under the *FOIA 2000* will apply.

Where information is filed in a system using individuals' names as file names, the system may not qualify as a relevant filing system if the indexing/referencing/sub-division is structured otherwise than to allow the retrieval of personal data without leafing through the file.

A filing system containing files about individuals, or topics about individuals, where the content of each file is structured purely in chronological order will not be a relevant filing system, as the files are not appropriately structured/indexed/divided or referenced to allow the retrieval of personal data without leafing through the file.

Personnel files and other manual files using individuals' names or unique identifiers as the file names, which are sub-divided/indexed to allow retrieval of personal data without a manual search (such as, sickness, absence, contact details, etc), are likely to be held in a 'relevant filing system' for the purposes of the *DPA 1998*. However, following the *Durant* judgment it is likely that very few manual files will be covered by the provisions of the *DPA 1998*. Most information about individuals held in manual form does not, therefore, fall within the data protection regime.

Paper Files   30.4

Transitional arrangements exempted manual records held in a 'relevant filing system' before 24 October 1998 from full compliance until 2007. However, the right of subject access to information held in paper files covered by *DPA 1998* is available from 24 October 2001 regardless of the date from which the information was held.

Commissioner's Guidance   30.5

In October 2001 the Information Commissioner issued her 'Legal Guidance on DPA 1998' which addresses manual data. This is likely to be revised in 2004 in the light of *Durant v Financial Services Authority [2003] EWCA Civ 1746* – see **30.8**

The advice in that guidance is that data controllers should examine all their non-automated information systems in order to determine how far *DPA 1998* applies to personal data processed in those systems. The Information Commissioner states:

> 'It is not wholly clear how this definition translates in practical terms in all conceivable situations. The Commissioner can only give general guidance; the final decision in cases of dispute is a question for the courts. Whether or not manual information falls within this definition will be a matter of fact in each case. It is not possible for the Commissioner to state categorically whether or not certain types of information or files are caught by *DPA 1998* although it is recognised that there are certain areas of business where the question of whether manual information falls within the definition will be of particular

significance, eg personnel files. In deciding whether manual information falls within the definition, data controllers should consider the following:

- There must be a set of information about individuals. The word "set" suggests a grouping together of things by reference to a distinct identifier ie a set of information with a common theme or element. Examples might include a set of information on customers or employees. Sets of information about individuals need not necessarily be grouped together in a file or files. They may be grouped together in some other way, for example, by prefix codes, or by attaching an identifying sticker within a file or files. Similarly, the information does not necessarily have to be grouped together in the same drawer of the filing cabinet or the same filing cabinet; nor does it necessarily have to be maintained centrally by an organisation. The set of information might be dispersed over different locations within the organisation, for example, different departments, branch offices, or via home workers.

- The set of information must be structured in such a way that specific information about a particular individual is readily accessible. What does or does not amount to such specific information will be a matter of fact in each individual case. *DPA 1998* does not define what is meant by "readily accessible". In deciding whether or not it is readily accessible, a suggested approach is to assume that a set or sets of manual information which are referenced to individuals (or criteria relating to individuals), are caught by *DPA 1998* if they are, as matter of fact, generally accessible at any time to one or more people within the data controller's organisation in connection with the day to day operation of that organisation.

In practice, data controllers may find that their manual files consist partly of information which forms, or is intended to form, part of a "relevant filing system", and partly of information which does not. It is essential for data controllers to keep in mind that it is the information and the ease with which it may be located which they should assess rather than whether it is in itself a file or filing system. In other words a file is not synonymous with "relevant filing system". Manual information which forms part of clearly highly structured files, for example, card indexes or records, is likely to fall within the definition.

The Commissioner recognises that data controllers may find that there are grey areas in determining whether or not certain manual information is subject to the requirements of *DPA 1998*. It is suggested that in those cases where data controllers are unsure whether or not manual information comes within the definition of data/"relevant filing system" they should evaluate how accessible the data are by making reasoned judgements. Data controllers should consider whether or not and, if so, the extent to which, a decision not to treat the information as being covered by *DPA 1998* will prejudice the individual concerned. Where the risk of prejudice is reasonably likely then data controllers would be expected to err on the side of caution and take steps to ensure compliance. Whether the Commissioner decides to enforce any particular case does not affect the rights of individuals to seek redress from the Courts under *DPA 1998* on the basis of a different or wider interpretation of "relevant filing system".

Where manual information falls within the definition, data controllers may not have to comply with the requirements of *DPA 1998* in full immediately as transitional relief may apply Where the data controller does not qualify for transitional relief manual data should have been processed in compliance with *DPA 1998* from 1 March 2000.'

Durant v Financial Services Authority   30.6

In *Durant v Financial Services Authority [2003] EWCA Civ 1746*, the Court of Appeal examined, for the first time, what manual data was caught by the Act in a decision in 2003. Mr Durant was a customer of Barclays Bank plc. There was litigation between them which Mr Durant lost in 1993. Since then he had sought disclosure of records in connection with the dispute, which he believes may assist him to re-open claims against Barclays. In July/August 2000 he asked the Financial Services Authority (FSA) (the regulator for financial services in the UK) to help him obtain disclosure. In addition, he wanted to know what documents the FSA had obtained from Barclays in its supervisory role. The FSA completed its investigation against Barclays and closed the investigation without informing Mr Durant of the outcome due to its obligation of confidentiality under the *Banking Act 1987*. Mr Durant complained about the matter to the FSA Complaints Commissioner who dismissed his complaint.

In September/October 2001 Mr Durant made two subject access requests under the *DPA 1998* to the FSA. In October 2001 the FSA provided copies of documents relating to him held in computerised form, some redacted so as not to disclose the names of others. However, it refused access to all the manual files on the basis that the information sought was not 'personal' and even if it was, it did not form part of a 'relevant filing system'.

The FSA acknowledged that some of its files contained information on which Mr Durant featured, that some of them identified him by reference to specific dividers within the file and that they contained documents, such as copies of telephone attendance notes, a report of forensic examinations document, transcripts of judgments, handwritten notes, internal memoranda, correspondence with Barclays Bank, correspondence with other individuals and correspondence between the FSA and Mr Durant.

The judges considered that four important issues of law concerning the right of access to personal data were raised:

1.   What makes 'data' 'personal' within the meaning of 'personal data'?

2.   What is meant by a 'relevant filing system'?

3.   Upon what basis should a data controller consider it 'reasonable in all the circumstances' within the meaning of *section 7(4)(b)* of the *DPA 1998* to comply with the request even though the personal data includes information about another and that other has not consented to disclosure?

4.   How much discretion does the court have as to whether to order compliance with a request if it finds the data controller has wrongly refused a request under *section 7(4)* of the *DPA 1998*?

The findings below were summarised by the Data Protection Office as follows:

Personal data

The judges found that in conformity with the 1981 Council of Europe Convention (Convention 108) and the 1995 General Data Protection Directive (95/46/EC) the purpose of *section 7* of the *DPA 1998* is to enable an individual to check whether a data controller's processing of his personal data unlawfully infringes his privacy and, if so, to take steps, for example under *section 14* or *section 10*, to protect it. It is not an automatic key to any information, readily accessible or not, of matters in which he may be named or involved. Nor is it to assist him, for example, to obtain discovery of documents that may assist him in litigation or complaints against third parties. It is likely in most cases that only information that named and directly refers to him will qualify.

> 'Mere mention of the data subject in a document held by a data controller does not necessarily amount to his personal data. Whether it does so in any particular instance depends on where it falls in a "continuum of relevance or proximity to the data subject as distinct, say, from transactions or matters in which he may have been involved to a greater or lesser degree."'

The judgment highlighted two notions that may assist:

> 'The first is whether the information is biographical in a significant sense, that is, going beyond the recording of the putative data subject's involvement in the matter or an event that has no personal connotations... The second is one of focus. The information should have the putative data subject as its focus rather than some other person with whom he may have been involved or some transaction or event in which he may have figured or have had an interest'.

These notions were summarised as information affecting a person's privacy whether in his personal or family life, business or professional capacity.

The mere fact that a document is retrievable by reference to his name does not entitle him to a copy of it under the Act.

The Court found that none of the personal data sought by Mr Durant amounted to personal data and, therefore, his claim fell at the first hurdle.

Relevant filing system

The judges noted that there was no material difference in the provisions of the Directive and of the Act. The court concluded that the intention 'is to provide as near as possible the same standard of sophistication of accessibility to personal data in manual filing systems as to computerised records'. It is right that the definition be broken down into three constituents:

1.   whether the material was a set of information relating to an individual;

2.   whether the material was structured either by reference to individuals or by reference to criteria relating to individuals; and

3.   whether it was structured in such a way that specific information relating to a particular individual was readily accessible.

The Court found that the Directive supported a restrictive interpretation of 'relevant filing system', and that 'the protection given by the legislation was for the privacy of personal data, not documents'.

The judgment summarised the meaning of 'a relevant filing system' as a 'system':

'1)   in which the files forming part of it are structured or referenced in such a way as to clearly indicate at the outset of the search whether specific information capable of amounting to personal data of an individual requesting it under *section* 7 is held within the system and, if so, in which file or files it is held; and

2)   which has, as part of its own structure or referencing mechanism, a sufficiently sophisticated and detailed means of readily indicating whether and where in an individual file or files specific criteria or information about the applicant can be readily located'.

Redaction

The Court found the protection that the Act gives to other individuals is qualified. The principle of proportionality means that the interest of the data subject in gaining access to his personal data must be balanced against that of the other individual in the protection of his privacy.

The balancing exercise only arises if the information relating to the other person forms part of the 'personal data' of the data subject. The provisions of the Act appear to create a presumption that information relating to a third party should not be disclosed without his consent. The presumption may, however, be rebutted if the data controller considers that it is reasonable 'in all the circumstances' to disclose it without such consent. The circumstances that go to the reasonableness of such a decision include, but are not confined to, those set out in *section 7(6)* of the *DPA 1998*.

It is appropriate to ask what, if any, legitimate interests the data subject has in disclosure of the identity of another individual named in or identifiable from personal data.

Section 7(4) of the *DPA 1998* contemplates a two stage thought process:

1. Is the information about the third party *necessarily* part of the personal data the data subject has requested?

2. If so, how critical is the third party information to the legitimate protection of the data subject's privacy, when balanced against the existence or otherwise of any obligation of confidence to the third party or any other sensitivity of the third party disclosure sought.

Where the third party is a recipient of the data and he or she might act on the data to the data subject's disadvantage, the data subject's right to protect their privacy may weigh heavily and obligations of confidence may be non-existent or of less weight. Equally, where the third party is the source of information, the data subject may have a strong case for their identification if they need to take action to correct some damaging inaccuracy, though consideration for the obligation of confidence to the source or some other sensitivity may have to be weighed in the balance.

The Court's discretion

The last issue to be considered by the Court was the extent of the Court's discretion under *section 7(9)* of the *DPA 1998* to order a data controller to comply with a request for information under that section where the data controller has failed to do so in breach of the Act.

The Court noted that the question of the exercise of discretion did not arise in this case but agreed with the observations of Mundy J in the case of *R (on the application of Alan Lord) v The Secretary of State for the Home Department [2003] EWHC 2073*, at paragraph 160, that 'the discretion conferred by that provision is general and untrammelled'.

Data Protection Commissioner's commentary

In December 2003 the Data Protection Commissioner commented as follows on this decision:

> 'The Commissioner welcomes the extent to which this judgment provides firm guidance and greater clarity as to the meaning of "personal data" and "relevant filing system". These have always been complex issues and any jurisprudence in this area is helpful. The Commissioner particularly welcomes the fact that the Court has reiterated the fundamental link between data protection and privacy rights'.

The Commissioner recognised that the interpretation suggested by Lord Justice Auld is more restrictive than the approach adopted by the Commissioner to date. In 2004 the guidance issued by the Commissioner's office will be reviewed and amended to reflect this difference of approach. All the Commissioner's responsibilities, including existing and future casework, will be carried out in accordance with this judgment.

Action 30.7

The following action is recommended.

- Audit manual records and list what is found.

- Ensure the audit covers data held off site (such as at home workers' homes) as well as on site.

- Ensure all employees know the right of subject access will now apply to all manual data which falls within *DPA 1998*.

- Prepare for subject access requests relating to information held in manual data.

Further Information 30.8

The Information Commissioner's Guidance is on the Information Commissioner's website at www.informationcommissioner.gov.uk.

FAQs 30.9

Is all manual data within *DPA 1998*?

No, just where it is part of a structured set strictly in accordance with *DPA 1998*.

When will the exemption for manual data expire?

It expired in October 2001.

Is manual data kept in employees' rooms within *DPA 1998*?

Yes, a check of all manual data to do with the data controller's business should be undertaken.

Chapter 31 –
Marketing

At A Glance

✓ Many forms of marketing have data protection implications.

✓ Individuals have a right under *section 11* of the *Data Protection Act 1998* (*DPA 1998*) to prevent the processing of their personal data for direct marketing purposes.

✓ Data must be fairly processed in accordance with *Schedule 2 to DPA 1998*.

✓ Marketing to employees must be handled with particular care.

✓ *Privacy and Electronic Communications (EC Directive) Regulations 2003 (SI 2003/2426)* set out the rules on email marketing.

Introduction   31.1

The process of marketing involves substantial amounts of personal data in most cases. Thus marketing must be approached with great care to ensure that the requirements of *DPA 1998* are met. (See also **12 DIRECT MAIL**, **13 DIRECT MARKETING** and **33 OPT-IN AND OPT-OUT**.) However, many other forms of marketing exist which may have data protection implications. Where marketing is done via the Internet, reference should be made to **28 INTERNET**, and in particular to the Information Commissioner's guidance in this field.

The *Privacy and Electronic Communications (EC Directive) Regulations 2003 (SI 2003/2426)* set out the rules on email marketing and are addressed in **CHAPTER 13**.

Right to Prevent Processing for the Purposes of Direct Marketing   31.2

Under *section 11* of *DPA 1998* an individual can, by written notice, require a data controller to cease, or not to begin, processing his personal data for the purpose of direct marketing. When a data controller receives such a notice, he must comply as soon as he can. There are no exceptions to this under *DPA 1998*. The data subject may apply to the court for an order if the data controller fails to comply with the notice.

'Direct marketing' is defined in *DPA 1998* for the purposes of this provision as meaning the communication, by whatever means, of any advertising or marketing material which is directed to particular individuals. In her Legal Guidance (October 2001) the Commissioner says that she regards the term 'direct market-ing' as covering a wide range of activities, applying not just to the offer for sale of goods or services, but also to the promotion of an organisation's aims and ideals.

Preference Services   31.3

An individual who wishes to prevent personally addressed marketing material being sent to him may register with the Mailing Preference Service. Contact details for the Mailing Preference Service can be found at **31.6** below.

Uninvited telesales calls and uninvited telemarketing faxes can be prevented by registering with the Telephone Preference Service on 0845 070 0707 and the Fax Preference Service on 0845 070 0702. 12 DIRECT MAIL and **13 DIRECT MARKET-ING** contain further information on this area.

Fair Processing   31.4

Under the First Data Protection Principle (see **21 FAIR PROCESSING**) data must be processed fairly and lawfully. Under *Schedule 2* to *DPA 1998* this is shown for data which is not sensitive personal data where:

- the data subject has given his consent to the processing;
- the processing is necessary:
    - for the performance of a contract to which the data subject is a party, or
    - for the taking of steps at the request of the data subject with a view to entering into a contract;
- the processing is necessary to comply with any legal obligation to which the data controller is subject, other than an obligation imposed by contract; or
- the processing is necessary in order to protect the vital interests of the data subject.

In most cases consent is the key issue. Consent is addressed in **33 OPT-IN AND OPT-OUT**. Sensitive personal data is dealt with in **42 SENSITIVE PERSONAL DATA**.

Marketing to Employees   31.5

Some employers distribute marketing material to their employees to sell them goods or services, or to give them details of third parties' goods or services such as insurance and charities. The Information Commissioner, in Part 2 of the Employment Practices Data Protection Code, says that marketing includes the promotion of aims and ideals as well as goods and services, and that employees have a right not to have their data used for this purpose. She proposes the following standards.

The benchmarks

1. Inform new workers if your organisation intends to use their personal information to deliver advertising or marketing messages to them. Give workers a clear opportunity to object ('opt-out') and respect any objections whenever received.

2. Do not disclose workers' details to other organisations for their marketing unless individual workers have positively and freely indicated their agreement ('opt-in').

3. If you intend to use details of existing workers for marketing for the first time, either in ways that were not explained when they first joined or that they would not expect, do not proceed until individual workers have positively and freely indicated their agreement ('opt-in').

Notes and examples

1. If your organisation uses workers' details for advertising or marketing you should explain this fully at the outset, making clear what personal details will be used. You should give workers a clear opportunity to object and respect any objections. An objection might be received, for example, in response to a human resources department telling workers that there is an intention to market to them unless they object. This arrangement is often described as offering an 'opt-out'. The worker's right to prevent information about him or her being used for marketing does not just apply to the marketing of products or services, but also to marketing or advertising in a broader sense, such as the promotion of another organisation's aims and ideals.

2. The disclosure of workers' details for marketing requires express approval from each individual, for example by the worker sending an email to the human resources department indicating agreement. This is often described as an 'opt-in'. It would arise, for example, where a company wants to pass workers' home addresses to a sister organisation so it can market them with its products. The positive indication of consent is required because the disclosure of workers' information is intrusive and could amount to a breach of the employer's duty of confidence unless consent is obtained.

3. This benchmark applies equally to former workers such as pensioners whose details are still kept for payroll purposes, if their details are to be

(cont'd)

399

used for marketing. An 'opt-in' will not be needed if the new use of workers' details is likely to be expected by them. For example, if the offering of discounts on your products and services to workers is accepted practice within the industry concerned, it may well be that they would expect to receive details of such offers personally addressed to them. In any event, enclosing details of particular offers within a communication that they will receive anyway, for example in a pay-slip, is acceptable as long as the offer includes an explanation of how to object.

Further Information   31.6

See also **12 DIRECT MAIL** and **13 DIRECT MARKETING**.

See **28 INTERNET** for Internet marketing.

Opting-in and opting-out are addressed in **33 OPT-IN AND OPT-OUT**.

Sensitive personal data are addressed in **42 SENSITIVE PERSONAL DATA** and fair processing in **21 FAIR PROCESSING**.

The Mailing Preference Service can be contacted at:

Mailing Preference Service
FREEPOST 22
London
W1E 7EZ
Tel: 020 7766 4410

The Direct Marketing Association (UK) Ltd's Guide to the DPA for Direct Marketing is available from www.dma.org.uk and costs £75 (members) and £150 (non-members).

FAQs   31.7

Is all marketing caught by *DPA 1998*?

Not unless it involves personal data. However, few mailing lists avoid any personal data. It is best to assume it does.

Are there special rules on marketing to employees?

There are no special laws but the Information Commissioner has set out his views in Part 2 of the Employment Practices Data Protection Code which is covered in the relevant part in this chapter.

Are all forms of marketing treated the same under *DPA 1998*?

No, there are special rules for fax marketing, as well as a new 2002 directive applicable to electronic marketing by way of 'spam' and the earlier *E-commerce Directive*.

Chapter 32 –
Offences

At A Glance

✓ Many offences are created by the *Data Protection Act 1998* (*DPA 1998*).

✓ In some circumstances individuals such as directors and company secretaries can be prosecuted for breach of the legislation.

✓ A specific offence of unlawfully selling personal data is also created.

✓ Enforced subject access is also an offence.

Introduction   32.1

The enforcement of the *Data Protection Act 1984* (*DPA 1984*) was characterised by the 'softly softly' approach of the Data Protection Registrar. Prosecutions were few and fines low. Although introducing more offences, *DPA 1998* is unlikely to result in a huge change to that approach. The Information Commissioner still principally intends to educate companies, and enforcement proceedings have so far been few.

Fines of up to £5,000 can be imposed, and this is likely to be per offence, so if high deterrent damages were to be awarded then the £5,000 fines could be cumulated. However, in the Commissioner's First Annual Report (June 2001), the Commissioner's fines displayed tended to be around £1,000–£3,000.

It must be remembered that offences bring bad publicity for commercial companies. An even greater cost can be the obligation to change their practices to comply with the legislation. Therefore companies must take the obligations imposed under *DPA 1998* seriously.

Criminal Offences   32.2

DPA 1998 includes various criminal offences which can be prosecuted by the Information Commissioner or by the Director of Public Prosecutions. Special rules apply in Scotland and Northern Ireland.

Someone accused of the offences of:

- intentionally obstructing a person in the execution of a search warrant issued in accordance with *DPA 1998*; or

- failing without reasonable excuse to give any person executing such a warrant such assistance as he may reasonably require for the execution of the warrant,

cannot elect a Crown Court trial and will be tried in the Magistrates' Court, or the Sheriff Court of Scotland.

In her Legal Guidance (October 2001), the Information Commissioner says that if someone is found guilty of one of the above offences, then the court can impose a fine not exceeding Level 5 on the standard scale of fines contained in the *Criminal Justice Act 1982* (as amended) and the *Criminal Procedure (Scotland) Act 1995*, which is at present £5,000.

All other offences under *DPA 1998* can be tried either way:

- in England and Wales either in the Magistrates' Court (summary trial) or the Crown Court (on indictment); or

- in Scotland on indictment in the Sheriff Court or High Court of Justiciary.

A person found guilty of any of these offences can be sentenced on summary conviction to a fine not exceeding the statutory maximum, which is currently £5,000, or upon conviction on indictment to an unlimited fine.

Legal proceedings

Prosecutions	2000/01	2001/02	2002/03
Number of offences brought to Court	23	66	91
Number of offences withdrawn/ or on which no evidence offered	—	16	11
Number of offences acquitted after trial	—	8	—
Number of offences to lie on file	—	9	—
Number of offences resulting in a finding of guilt	21	33	80
Cautions administered	12	13	11
Offences taken into consideration			601

(Source IC's 2003 Annual Report.)

Strict Liability 32.3

Liability without fault, that is without the usual *mens rea* or knowledge needed for criminal offences, exists for the offences of:

- processing without notification;
- processing before the expiry of the assessable processing time limits; and
- enforced subject access.

On conviction the court may order any data apparently connected with the crime to be forfeited, destroyed or erased. Anyone other than the offender who claims to own the material may apply to the court that such an order should not be made.

Personal Liability 32.4

An important issue for companies is the extent to which individuals can be personally liable for an offence under *DPA 1998*. Many personnel and human resources managers who are charged with achieving data protection compliance, and who are wrestling to ensure their departments are given sufficient resources in this field, will find it helpful to show their finance and other directors that personal liability can attach to individuals. Such liability may arise unless sufficient resources are devoted to data protection to ensure that *DPA 1998* is less likely to be breached.

Under *section 61* of *DPA 1998*, if a company commits a criminal offence under the Act, any director, manager, secretary or similar officer, or someone purporting to act in any such capacity, is personally guilty of the offence in addition to the corporate body if:

- the offence was committed with their consent or connivance; or
- the offence is attributable to any neglect on their part.

Where the affairs of a corporate body are managed by its members, any member who exercises the functions of management as if he were a director can also be guilty of the offence that results from any of their acts or omissions.

Government Liability 32.5

Much personal data is handled by state bodies. Their liability must also be considered. In the Legal Guidance the Information Commissioner states that Government departments are not liable to prosecution under *DPA 1998*. However, individual civil servants may be prosecuted if they are believed to be personally guilty of an offence under *section 55* of *DPA 1998*, which covers the unlawful obtaining or disclosure of personal data, or believed to be obstructing or failing to assist in the execution of a warrant issued in accordance with the Act (*DPA 1998, Sch 9, para 12*).

Offences

32.6

The offences included in *DPA 1998* are:

(*a*)   processing without notification (*DPA 1998, s 21(1)*);

(*b*)   failure to notify the Commissioner of changes to the notification register entry (*DPA 1998, s 21(2)*);

(*c*)   processing before expiry of assessable processing time limits or receipt of assessable processing notice within such time (*DPA 1998, s 22(6)*);

(*d*)   failure to comply with written request for particulars (*DPA 1998, s 24*);

(*e*)   failure to comply with an enforcement notice, information notice or special information notice (*DPA 1998, s 47(1)*);

(*f*)   knowingly or recklessly making a false statement in compliance with an information notice or special information notice (*DPA 1998, s 47(2)*);

(*g*)   intentional obstruction of, or failure to give reasonable assistance in, execution of a warrant (*DPA 1998, Sch 9*).

(*h*)   unlawful obtaining etc, of personal data (*DPA 1998, s 55(1)*); there is a defence to this offence if the person can show:

    (i)   that the obtaining, disclosing or procuring of the data:

        • was necessary to prevent or detect crime, or

        • was required or authorised by law,

    (ii)   that he acted in the reasonable belief that he had the legal right to obtain, disclose or procure the disclosure,

    (iii)   that he acted in the reasonable belief that the data controller would have consented to the obtaining, disclosing or procuring if the data controller had known, or

    (iv)   that in the particular circumstances the obtaining, disclosing or procuring was justified as being in the public interest.

Where employees use data belonging to their employer for personal or unrelated purposes outside their job, then they commit offences if they use their position to obtain, disclose, or procure the disclosure of personal data for their own purposes. Examples of individuals who have misused data in this way are given in the Commissioner's First Annual Report (June 2001).

Unlawful Selling 32.7

It is an offence for someone who obtains data in breach of *section 55(1)* of *DPA 1998* to then sell that data. Advertising data for sale is counted as offering it for sale.

Enforced Subject Access 32.8

Under *section 56* of *DPA 1998* it is an offence to require someone to exercise their right of subject access unless an exception applies (see **32.9** below).

Section 56 of *DPA 1998* states that:

'A person must not, in connection with:

(*a*)   the recruitment of another person as an employee;

(*b*)   the continued employment of another person; or

(*c*)   any contract for the provision of services to him by another person,

require that other person or a third party to supply him with a relevant record or to produce a relevant record to him.'

Statutory Exceptions 32.9

The statutory exceptions to liability for the offences set out at **32.6** above are:

- that the imposition of the requirement was required or authorised by law; or

- that in the particular circumstances the imposition of the requirements was justified as being in the public interest.

DPA 1998 provides that the imposition of the requirement is not to be regarded as being justified in the public interest on the ground that it would assist in the prevention or detection of crime.

The Information Commissioner says that:

'The term "relevant record" is defined in *section 56* of *DPA 1998* by reference to a table which lists data controllers and the subject matter of subject access requests that may be made to them by data subjects. Generally, the term relates to records of cautions, criminal convictions and to certain social security records relating to the data subject.'

Section 56 of *DPA 1998* does not come into force until the Criminal Records Bureau is up and running, which is likely to be in 2002. The Commissioner says that the 'practice of requiring subject access may still breach other provisions of the Act, or the *Human Rights Act 1998* or the *Rehabilitation of Offenders Act 1974.*'

Disclosure by the Commissioner   32.10

4 COMMISSIONER examined *section 59* of *DPA 1998*, which makes it an offence for the Commissioner or her staff to disclose information. Some of the provisions of *section 59* appear to curb the Commissioner's power too much and she has suggested the provisions be modified.

Further Information   32.11

4 COMMISSIONER deals with compensation, damages and prevention of processing.

Criminal issues are covered in **8 CRIME**; the chapter includes a summary of the prosecutions in the First Annual Report of the Information Commissioner (June 2001).

The powers of the Commissioner are covered in **4 COMMISSIONER**.

Enforcement remedies and powers are addressed in **17 ENFORCEMENT, REMEDIES AND POWERS**.

FAQs   32.12

What is the maximum fine for breach of *DPA 1998*?

£5,000, but this is per offence so a number of offences could lead to several such fines.

Is there an offence of unlawfully selling personal data?

Yes under *section 55* of *DPA 1998*.

Is forcing someone to exercise their right of subject access an offence?

Yes, under *section 56* of *DPA 1998*. There are many separate offences under the Act.

Chapter 33 –
Opt-in and Opt-out

At A Glance

✓ Data subjects must, in many cases, consent to the processing of their personal data.

✓ Consent can be obtained on forms, and one difficult question is whether opting-in or opting-out is required.

✓ The safest course is opting-out and this will normally be required at least where sensitive personal data is concerned.

✓ The decision in *Brian Robertson v Wakefield City Council (High Court, 16 November 2001)* held that current use of electoral registers for commercial purposes breached the *Human Rights Act 1998 (HRA 1998)*, and that the UK had not properly implemented the *Data Protection Directive (95/46/EC)* in this regard.

✓ The *Directive on Privacy and Electronic Communications (2002/58/EC)* ('E-privacy Directive'), and UK implementing regulations – the *Privacy and Electronic Communications (EC Directive) Regulations 2003* requires opting-in for marketing emails.

Introduction   33.1

The *Data Protection Act 1998 (DPA 1998)* requires that data subjects must in many cases consent to the processing of their data (see **21 FAIR PROCESSING**). For sensitive personal data explicit consent is required (see **42 SENSITIVE PERSONAL DATA**). Here consideration is given to ordinary personal data which does not fall into that category. For such data the issue is whether 'consent' has been given or not.

Many people will be familiar with the box one ticks when filling in forms to 'opt-out' of personal data being used for other purposes. Some companies now use an 'opt-in' box, to be ticked if the user consents to their personal data being so used. *DPA 1998* is not entirely clear as to which is legally required. If there is a lot of money at stake, which will be lost by not having personal data freely useable, then it is advisable for companies to remain using an opting-out method. In practice, data subjects will often do nothing – thus when opting-out is used the data controller can use the data for other purposes. If opting-in is chosen, and again the data subject does nothing, then the data cannot be used.

However, for those clients who want to be entirely sure they comply with *DPA 1998* and there is little financial loss likely to ensure from a failure of individuals to opt-in, then the safest course to achieve compliance with the legislation will be to change to opting-in. Those companies wanting to appear a standard bearer for good practice and privacy will also want to move to opting-in as well, for obvious reasons.

In *Brian Robertson v Wakefield City Council (High Court, 16 November 2001)*, Mr Justice Maurice Kay held that Wakefield Council's refusal to comply with a request from Mr Robertson to register to vote without his personal data being used for commercial purposes breached *Article 8* of the *European Convention on Human Rights* ('ECHR'), as given effect by *HRA 1998* (see **26 HUMAN RIGHTS ACT 1998**). In addition, the court held that the UK had not properly implemented the *Data Protection Directive (95/46/EC)* in *DPA 1998* in this regard.

Mr Robertson's lawyers argued that his data should only be used for the purposes for which it was provided, that is electoral purposes or where it is justified in the public interest, such as the use of data for political parties, by police, security forces or public authorities.

The case led to the *Representation of the People (England and Wales) (Amendment) Regulations 2002 (SI 2002/1871)*, and at the date of writing, the draft *Data Protection (Processing of Sensitive Personal Data) (Elected Representatives) Order*, which is likely to come into force later in 2002. The Regulations give voters rights to opt-out of their electoral registration details being resold except in certain cases.

Commissioner's Guidance   33.2

In the Frequently Asked Questions (June 2001) relating to the Internet issued by the Information Commissioner, the following position is taken:

> 'The general standard to ensure compliance with the *DPA 1998* is for a website to provide an individual with an opportunity to opt-out of the use or disclosure of their personal data for direct marketing, whether by email or other means. This requires a statement along the following lines:
>
> - "We would like to email you with offers relating to products of ours that we think you might be interested in. Click here if you object to receiving such offers."; and/or
>
> - "We would like to pass your details on to other businesses so they can email you with offers of goods/services that you might be interested in. Click here if you do not want your details to be passed on."'

It should be easy for the individual to register his or her wishes. It would not be acceptable, for example, to expect an individual to visit another site to register his or her wishes, or to register his or her wishes by post.

In some cases an opt-out facility will not be sufficient. This is likely to be the case where the processing of sensitive personal data is involved.

Some countries provide expressly for 'opt-in'. These are Germany, Denmark, Finland, Sweden and Italy.

Signifying Consent 33.3

In the Legal Guidance (October 2001) the Information Commissioner says that 'consent is not particularly easy to achieve and that data controllers should consider other conditions in *Schedule 2* (and *Schedule 3* if processing sensitive personal data) before looking at consent. No condition carries greater weight than any other. All the conditions provide an equally valid basis for processing. Merely because consent is the first condition to appear in both *Schedules 2* and *3*, does not mean that data controllers should consider consent first.' (The Schedules referred to above are in *DPA 1998*.)

The problem is in part caused by there being no definition of 'consent' in *DPA 1998*. However, *Article 2(h)* of the *Data Protection Directive (95/46/EC)* defines 'the data subject's consent' as:

'...any freely given specific and informed indication of his wishes by which the data subject signifies his agreement to personal data relating to him being processed'.

As can be seen above the word 'signify' is used. The Commissioner says that this means there must be some active communication between the parties. A data subject may 'signify' agreement other than in writing. 'Data controllers cannot infer consent from non-response to a communication, for example from a customer's failure to return or respond to a leaflet.' This statement from the Commissioner appears to be at odds with the email guidance referred to at **33.2** above.

Importantly the Commissioner goes on to say that 'where a data subject does not signify his agreement to personal data relating to him being processed, but is given an opportunity to object to such processing, although this does not amount to consent for the purposes of *DPA 1998*, it may provide the data controller with the basis to rely upon another *Schedule 2* to *DPA 1998* condition, for example, the legitimate interests condition, provided that the data subject is given the right to object before the data are obtained.'

Arguably there is no reason why the act of signifying cannot be undertaken passively although the verb 'sign' is an active verb, therefore the Commissioner's view is unsurprising. It may be possible to argue that the requirement for 'explicit consent' for processing sensitive personal data must be different from any other consent and that such a difference might exist between opting-in and opting-out. Many commercial contract terms are legally accepted under English law by failure to object – standard terms and conditions of supply for example, which are not required to be signed.

Appropriate consent 33.4

Consent must be appropriate to the particular circumstances. The Commissioner gives the example of processing intended to continue after the end of a trading relationship. Where such processing is intended, then the data controller must ensure that it obtains a consent which expressly covers such an eventuality.

Enduring consent 33.5

Consents do not last forever. In most cases the Information Commissioner says ' ... consent will endure for as long as the processing to which it relates continues. Data controllers should recognise that, depending upon the nature of the consent given and the circumstances of the processing, the individual may be able to withdraw consent.'

Sensitive Data 33.6

As mentioned above there is a distinction in *DPA 1998* between the nature of the consent required to satisfy the condition for processing and that which is required in the case of the condition for processing sensitive data. The consent must be 'explicit' in the case of sensitive data.

The Information Commissioner writes that:

> 'The use of the word "explicit" and the fact that the condition requires explicit consent "to the processing of the personal data" suggests that the consent of the data subject should be absolutely clear. In appropriate cases it should cover the specific detail of the processing, the particular type of data to be processed (or even the specific information), the purposes of the processing and any special aspects of the processing which may affect the individual, for example, disclosures which may be made of the data.'

Direct Marketing Association 33.7

The Direct Marketing Association ('DMA') issued a booklet 'A Guide to the Data Protection Act 1998 for Direct Marketing'. Here, the author Colin Fricker states ' ... not ticking an opt-out box on a completed and returned order form might, depending on the clarity and wording of any "notification", constitute consent (except in regard to sensitive data)'.

The E-privacy Directive and Privacy and Electronic Communications (EC Directive) Regulations 2003 33.8

Article 13 of the *E-privacy Directive (2002/58/EC)*, 'Use of unsolicited communications', provides:

'1. The use of automated systems without human intervention (automatic calling machines), facsimile machines (fax) or electronic mail for the purposes of direct marketing may only be allowed in respect of subscribers who have given their prior consent.'

However, for existing customers a more liberal regime has been negotiated:

'2. Notwithstanding paragraph 1, where a natural or legal person obtains from its customers their electronic contact details for electronic mail, in the context of the sale of a product or a service, in accordance with Directive 95/46/EC, the same natural or legal person may use these electronic contact details for direct marketing of its own similar products or services provided that customers clearly and distinctly are given the opportunity to object, free of charge and in an easy manner, to such use of electronic contact details when they are collected and on the occasion of each message in case the customer has not initially refused such use.'

Article 13(4) provides that the practice of sending email for purposes of direct marketing, disguising or concealing the identity of the sender on whose behalf the communication is made, or without a valid address to which the recipient may send a request that such communications cease, shall be prohibited.

The *Privacy and Electronic Communications (EC Directive) Regulations 2003* implemented the Directive in the UK from 11 December 2003. The Regulations are considered in **CHAPTER 13** and a copy of the Regulations and the Part 1 of the IC's guidance notes on the regulations including FAQs is in **APPENDIX 8**.

The IC's guidance says:

'The Data Protection Directive defines "the data subject's consent" as "any freely given specific and informed indication of his wishes by which the data subject signifies his agreement to personal data relating to him being processed". In our view, therefore, there must be some form of communication whereby the individual knowingly indicates consent. This may involve clicking an icon, sending an email or subscribing to a service. The crucial consideration is that the individual must fully understand that by the action in question they will be signifying consent'.

The guidance continues:

411

'We are concerned that the terms "opt-in" and "opt-out" can be misunderstood. They are commonly taken to refer to the use of tick-boxes. In this context, "opt-in" refers to a box that you tick to indicate agreement and "opt-out" refers to a box that you tick to indicate objection. Marketers have traditionally favoured the latter, ie where the default (an unticked "opt-out" box) indicates a failure to register an objection. The fact that someone has had an opportunity to object which they have not taken only means that they have not objected. It does not mean that they have consented. By itself, the failure to register an objection will be unlikely to constitute valid consent. However, in context, a failure to indicate objection may be part of the mechanism whereby a person indicates consent. For example, if you receive a clear and prominent message along the following lines, the fact that a suitably prominent opt-out box has not been ticked may help establish that consent has been given: eg "By submitting this registration form, you will be indicating your consent to receiving email marketing messages from us unless you have indicated an objection to receiving such messages by ticking the above box". In summary, the precise mechanisms by which valid informed consent is obtained may vary. The crucial consideration is that individuals must fully appreciate that they are consenting and must fully appreciate what they are consenting to'.

Reading the guidance above would leave most readers unclear as to what is meant by consent. If it is not clear to lawyers it is even less clear to businesses, grappling with the legislation on a day to day basis. One of the most common questions asked for data protection lawyers is about how consent should be given and yet there is no effective judicial guidance on this. A test case would be useful on it in due course, and meanwhile companies have to decide how cautious or bullish to be.

Conclusion   33.9

The safest course is to have an option to opt-in. However, where this is not commercially viable and the information is not sensitive data, opting-out will be sufficient as long as it is clearly stated. This may be an area for businesses to take legal advice appropriate to their individual circumstances.

Further Information   33.10

'A Guide to the Data Protection Act 1998 for Direct Marketing' (2000) by Colin Fricker is available from the DMA (www.dma.co.uk).

26 HUMAN RIGHTS ACT 1998 gives information on the *Representation of the People (England and Wales) Amendment) Regulations 2002 (SI 2002/1871)*, which is the legislation introduced following the Robertson case (see **33.1** above).

FAQs

When we send out forms to potential customers should we ask them to opt-in or opt-out?

Views vary because *DPA 1998* is unclear. Assuming it is not sensitive personal data they are giving, the legal requirement is that consent be given. A cautious approach would say an active consent is needed, and not just a pre-ticked box. If however this will cause significant commercial loss, a more risky approach might be advisable given the value of obtaining and use of such data.

On the Internet should we have opting-out or opting-in?

Given that the *E-privacy Directive (2002/58/EC)* will require opting-in, it is best to adopt this approach now and ensure that all appropriate consents are obtained in advance in preparation for the new rules.

Chapter 34 – Padlock (Use of the Sign Called 'Padlock')

At A Glance

✓   The Information Commissioner has issued a system known as the 'information padlock' which businesses can use when personal data is gathered.

✓   Use of the symbol is not compulsory and has not been widely used to date.

✓   Some companies, however, display it on their marketing materials when they gather personal data.

Introduction   34.1

The *Data Protection Act 1998* (*DPA 1998*) requires that in many cases individuals be told how their personal data will be used. Such information therefore often appears on application forms and similar materials.

No precise form of words is prescribed, but the Information Commissioner suggests businesses may like to use a symbol or padlock device on places where such data is gathered so that individuals can see that personal data about them is being gathered on that website or in that place.

When to Use the Symbol   34.2

The Information Commissioner issued a leaflet concerning the symbol in which it is stated that the principles of 'good information handling' lay clear obligations on data controllers. However, individuals can take steps to prevent any mishandling of their information by ensuring that they are aware of the purpose(s) for which information is being collected from them, at the time it is collected.

The Commissioner writes: 'To assist in this, the Information Commissioner and the National Consumer Council have devised an 'information padlock' symbol to act as a signpost which will, at a glance, tell data subjects that personal information about them is being collected to be processed. The symbol is available to data controllers to use on their media to signpost individuals towards information regarding the use of their personal data.'

Where to site the signpost 34.3

The following information is contained in the leaflet mentioned above:

> 'The "information padlock" signpost is intended for use by all data controllers. It should be clearly positioned at any point where information is requested – this could be within any medium, such as an advertisement coupon, application form or Internet site. If an option box is used, the signpost should be placed next to it.
>
> Wherever the signpost appears, an explanation of why the information is requested should be detailed, or directions given to where such an explanation is provided. The signpost can be reproduced in any colour and may be reversed-out if necessary. No minimum or maximum size is recommended, but the symbol should always be clear to any reader.
>
> Electronic copies of the signpost and this leaflet can be downloaded from the [Information] Commissioner's website at [www.informationcommissioner.gov.uk].'

Printed copies of the symbol for use as bromides are also available, details of which are given in the leaflet (for availability, see **34.5** below).

The Padlock 34.4

This symbol alerts people to the fact that their information is being collected, and directs them to sources which will clearly explain how their information is to be used.

Further Information 34.5

The Information Commissioner's leaflet on the padlock and the padlock symbol itself are on the Information Commissioner's website (www.informationcommissioner.gov.uk under News and Events).

FAQs **34.6**

Is use of the padlock compulsory?

No, it is entirely voluntary, but may help users know when their data is being gathered. No one has to use it.

When is the use of the padlock recommended?

It can be usefully included on application forms and other places where personal data is gathered.

Chapter 35 –
Personal Data

At A Glance

✓ The *Data Protection Act 1998* (*DPA 1998*) applies to those processing 'personal data'.

✓ For the data to be personal it must relate to an individual and must apply to living individuals only, not companies or the deceased.

✓ 2004 Guidance following *Durant v FSA* addresses the definition of personal data.

✓ The issue of whether data can be made anonymous also needs to be addressed.

Introduction   35.1

DPA 1998 regulates personal data which is processed. *Section 1* of *DPA 1998* defines personal data as data

'which relate to a living individual who can be identified:

(*a*)   from those data; or

(*b*)   from those data and other information which is in the possession of, or is likely to come into the possession of, the data controller,

and includes any expression of opinion about the individual and any indication of the intentions of the data controller or any other person in respect of the individual'.

Which Personal Data is Caught?   35.2

Data will be personal data where the individual can be identified either from the data itself, from that data and other information held by the data controller, or information which is likely to come into the possession of the data controller. Under the *Data Protection Act 1984* (*DPA 1984*) personal data was information relating to a living individual who could be identified from the information, or from that and other information in the possession of the data user.

However, *Durant v Financial Services Authority [2003] EWCA Civ 1746* held that the mere mention of a data subject in a document held by a data controller in manual form does not necessarily comprise 'personal data'. In the light of this case, the IC intends to revise its guidance and when that is issued this may affect the definitions considered in this Chapter. The court held in *Durant* that the data had to be 'biographical to a significant extent' before it would be personal data. It had to be something which 'affects his privacy, whether in his personal or family life, business or professional capacity'.

> 'I reach the conclusion that it is not necessary or appropriate for me to have regard to [Parliamentary] material in reaching my conclusion. I do not need *Pepper v Hart Pepper v Hart [1993] AC 593* in relation to the problem that has arisen in this case… I am at this stage concerned with information that is recorded in paper files, not on computer, and I have to look, although I am adopting a purposive approach, at the wording and the definition. Data means in this context information which in (c) is recorded as part of a relevant filing system or with the intention that it should form part of a relevant filing system. In order to understand the phrase 'relevant filing system' I need to look at the definition of that phrase on the next page of the statute where I am told it means'.

A list of names and addresses of individual customers would be personal data, as the individuals can be identified from the data. In such cases there is no doubt the information is personal data. An exemption may apply but subject to that, *DPA 1998* will apply. However, it can often be unclear whether some types of data are personal data.

Article 2 of the Data Protection Directive (95/46/EC), which *DPA 1998* implements in the UK, defines an identifiable person as 'one who can be identified, indirectly, in particular by reference to an identification number or to one or more factors specific to his physical, physiological, mental, economic, cultural or social identity'. If images of distinguishable individuals' features are processed and an individual can be identified from it, this will amount to personal data (see the Information Commissioner's CCTV Code of Practice (reproduced in **APPENDIX 1**).

The individual must be a living individual. A database of people who have just died with perhaps the size of their estates, details from their wills etc will not be personal data of the individuals (although disclosure of legacies to individual beneficiaries may itself be personal data about those individuals).

Animals are not living individuals under English law.

It is not clear at what point an unborn child becomes a living individual; whether at conception, after most abortions are prohibited in law, or after birth. A hospital, for example, taking DNA samples from unborn children in a mass screening of those whose mothers have had a test for other purposes would need to consider if the data held about the foetuses is personal data.

Data will still be personal data even if the individual cannot be identified from the data if an identification can be made by other information the data controller has or could obtain. Having a list of people identified by a code number is still personal data if the data controller also has a separate system to identify, for example, who numbers 12345 or 34567 are.

Similarly, photographs of people's homes with an accompanying post code may be sufficient to make the photographs personal data because it is possible to purchase a CD-ROM of post codes from which the data controller, or indeed any third party, could then make the necessary connection. If the data controller swore an affidavit that it would never put such a CD-ROM into its possession, could it avoid the data becoming personal data? The 'other information' would never come into the possession of the controller so it is possible that the *DPA 1998* could then be circumnavigated, in relation to that data controller.

The Information Commissioner, in the Legal Guidance published in October 2001 (see **35.15** below) states:

> 'The definition in *DPA 1998* is not without difficulty and the Commissioner recognises that, potentially, the definition has a very broad scope. This, in turn, will have a considerable impact on data controllers in terms of compliance with the Data Protection Principles, in particular, the First Data Protection Principle.
>
> It is important not to look at the definition of personal data in isolation as it is the Commissioner's view that for the scope of the definition to be understood properly, it should be considered in the context of the definitions of "data", "data controller" and "data subject" in *DPA 1998*.'

In February 2004 the Information Commissioner issued further guidance on *Durant v Financial Services Authority [2003] EWCA Civ 1746* and its implications for the definition of personal data under the *DPA 1998*.

A full text of the judgment of the case is available from the Court Service website at www.courtservice.gov.uk. This provides that the *DPA 1998* applies only to 'personal data' and, therefore, a clear understanding of what is meant by this term is essential for compliance with its provisions. The Court of Appeal concluded that:

> 'personal data is information that affects [a person's] privacy, whether in his personal or family life, business or professional capacity.
>
> 'The concept of privacy is therefore clearly central to the definition of personal data. This suggests to the Commissioner that you should take into account whether or not the information in question is capable of having an adverse impact on the individual. The Court identified two notions that may assist in determining whether information "is information that affects [an individual's] privacy":

'The first is whether the information is biographical in a significant sense, that is, going beyond the recording of [the individual's] involvement in a matter or an event which has no personal connotations...

'The second concerns focus. "The information should have the [individual] as its focus rather than some other person with whom he may have been involved or some transaction or event in which he may have figured or have had an interest ..."'

In *Durant v Financial Services Authority [2003] EWCA Civ 1746* the Court of Appeal did not consider the issue of the identifiability of an individual in the definition of 'personal data' set out in *section 1(1)* of the *DPA 1998*. This is often the starting point in developing an understanding of personal data. Instead, the Court of Appeal in this case concentrated on the meaning of 'relate to' in that definition, identifiability not being an issue in the case.

Where an individual's name appears in information the name will only be 'personal data' where its inclusion in the information affects the named individual's privacy. Simply because an individual's name appears on a document, the information contained in that document will not necessarily be personal data about the named individual. It is more likely that an individual's name will be 'personal data' where the name appears together with other information about the named individual such as address, telephone number or information regarding his hobbies.

Provided the information in question can be linked to an identifiable individual, the following are examples of personal data:

* information about the medical history of an individual;

* an individual's salary details;

* information concerning an individual's tax liabilities;

* information comprising an individual's bank statements; and

* information about individuals' spending preferences.

These types of information may be contrasted with the following examples of information which will not normally be personal data:

* mere reference to a person's name where the name is not associated with any other personal information;

* incidental mention in the minutes of a business meeting of an individual's attendance at that meeting in an official capacity; or

* where an individual's name appears on a document or email indicating only that it has been sent or copied to that particular individual, the content of that document or email does not amount to personal data about the individual unless there is other information about the individual within it.

The following comments of Lord Justice Auld indicate some practical implications of the Court of Appeal's interpretation of 'personal data':

- 'not all information retrieved from a computer search against an individual's name or unique identifier is personal data';

- '[*section 7 DPA*] is not an automatic key to any information, readily accessible or not, of matters in which [the party making the request for information] may be named or involved';

- 'the mere fact that a document is retrievable by reference to [the applicant for information's] name does not entitle him to a copy of it under the Act'.

Information that has as its focus something other than the individual will not be 'personal data'. For example, information that focuses on a property (eg a structural survey) is not 'personal data', nor is information about the performance of an office department or a branch of a chain of stores. While such information may include information 'about' an individual, where the focus of the information is something other than the individual, such information will not 'relate to' the individual and, therefore, is not personal data. However, there are many circumstances where information, eg about a house or a car, could be personal data because that information is directly linked to an individual. One example would be a valuation of a house where this was being used in order to determine the assets of a particular individual in a matrimonial dispute. Another example would be the details of a car photographed by a speed camera where those details are used to direct a notice of intention to prosecute to the registered keeper of the vehicle.

The guidance then considers 'Manual Data' definitions in the light of the case – see **CHAPTER 30** for a summary of that part of the 2004 Guidance.

CCTV   35.3

CCTV pictures of individuals are 'personal data' under *DPA 1998*. *Article 14* of the Data Protection Directive (95/46/EC) provides that the Directive applies to 'the techniques used to capture, transmit, record, store or communicate sound and image data relating to natural persons'.

Codes of Practice   35.4

The Information Commissioner has issued a CCTV Code of Practice under *DPA 1998* (reproduced in **APPENDIX 2**) (for further information see **2 CCTV**). Similarly, the Employment Practices Data Protection Code provides similar guidance in the employment field.

Examples of personal data   35.5

The following is a non-exhaustive list of personal data.

- Names and addresses of individuals.

- Still photographs of individuals.

- Moving pictures of individuals.

- Email addresses of individuals, particularly if they give a person's name – for example john.smith@lexisnexis.com or susan@singlelaw.com.

- Information about individuals identified by reference number where the number in another listing reveals the identity of the individual.

The Information Commissioner has issued specific guidance on provisions under *DPA 1998*, including guidance as to the definition of personal data. The section below is based largely on that guidance.

What Determines Whether Data Relate to an Individual?   35.6

This will be a question of fact. One question is 'whether a data controller can form a connection between the data and the individual'. Data does not have to relate solely to one individual and the same data may relate to two or more people and still be personal data about each of them. For example, joint tenants of a property, or holders of a joint bank account, or even individuals who use the same telephone or email address. Information may relate to an individual in a business capacity and not just to their private life. Information about the business of a sole trader will amount to personal data as information about the business will be about the sole trader. Information about an individual in a partnership will be personal data if it relates to a specific partner. This will be more likely in a small partnership.

Although *DPA 1998* refers to individuals and not other legal entities such as limited companies, there will be situations where information about a limited company or other legal entity amounts to personal data because it relates to a specific individual, for example, the performance of a department. Information relating solely to the legal entity will not be personal data.

Does DPA 1998 Only Relate to Living Individuals?   35.7

DPA 1998 is only concerned with living individuals and so if the subject of the information is deceased, then the information cannot be personal data.

Identifying the Individual   35.8

The Information Commissioner recognises that an individual may be 'identified' without necessarily knowing the name and address of that particular individual. The Commissioner's view is that it is sufficient if the data are capable of being processed by the data controller to enable the data controller to distinguish the data subject from any other individual. This would be the case if a data subject could be treated differently from other individuals.

Future possession of data   35.9

In the majority of cases the ability to 'identify' an individual will be achieved by knowing the name and address of an individual or by the data controller being in possession of some other information. The definition also allows for an individual to be identified from data together with information 'likely to come into the possession of' the data controller. It will be for a data controller to satisfy himself whether it is likely that such information will come into his or her possession to render data personal data. This will depend largely on the nature of the processing undertaken by a data controller, the Commissioner says.

This issue is clearly relevant in the context of personal data which a data controller wishes to make anonymous (see **35.12** below).

Example – identifying an individual   35.10

The following example is given by the Information Commissioner.

> If information about a particular web user is built up over a period of time, perhaps through the use of tracking technology, with the intention that it may later be linked to a name and address, that information is personal data. Information may be compiled about a particular web user, but there might not be any intention of linking it to a name and address or email address. There might merely be an intention to target that particular user with advertising, or to offer discounts when they re-visit a particular website, on the basis of the profile built up, without any ability to locate that user in the physical world. The Commissioner takes the view that such information is, nevertheless, personal data. In the context of the online world the information that identifies an individual is that which uniquely locates him in that world, by distinguishing him from others.

What is Meant by the Expression 'Possession' in this Context?   35.11

The concept of possession is very wide. In the Information Commissioner's view possession does not necessarily mean that the identifying data are in the physical control of the data controller, or likely to come under the data controller's physical control. A data controller enters into a contract with a data processor for the processing of personal data. The arrangement is that the data processor may receive some of the identifying data from a third party and some from the data controller. The data are processed in accordance with the terms of the contract. The data controller determines the purposes for which, and the manner in which the personal data are to be processed by the data processor but may not have sight of all or any of the information which identifies a living individual. The data controller would, however, be deemed to be in possession of those data. The data controller could not argue in such a situation that the identifying data are not in his or her 'possession' and therefore is unable to absolve themselves of responsibilities as a data controller.

Can Personal Data be Made Anonymous? 35.12

The issue of information in the possession of, or likely to come into the possession of, a data controller has an impact on a data controller who seeks to make anonymous the personal data they are processing by stripping those data of all personal identifiers.

On this matter the Information Commissioner says:

> 'The fact that personal data may be anonymised is referred to in *Directive 95/46/EC* (the "Directive"), at *Recital 26*, and in the matter of *R v The Department of Health ex parte Source Informatics Limited [2000]1 All ER 786*. In that case it was acknowledged by the Court of Appeal that the Directive does not apply to anonymised data. In anonymising personal data the data controller will be processing such data and, in respect of such processing, will still need to comply with the provisions of the Act.'

The Commissioner recognises that the aim of anonymisation is to provide better data protection, although some people use it to avoid the onerous obligations of *DPA 1998*. The Commissioner believes it is essentially a good thing but very hard to achieve. The fact that the data controller is in the possession of this data set which, if linked to the data which have been stripped of all personal identifiers, will enable a living individual to be identified, means that all the data, including the data stripped of personal identifiers, remain personal data in the hands of that data controller and cannot be said to have been anonymised. The fact that the data controller may have no intention of linking these two data sets is immaterial.

A data controller who destroys the original data set retaining only the information which has been stripped of all personal identifiers and who assesses that it is not likely that information will come into his possession to enable him to reconstitute the data, ceases to be a data controller in respect of the retained data. This is because it will then not come within the definition of personal data under *section 1(1)* of *DPA 1998*, in the view of the Information Commissioner.

Whether or not data which have been stripped of all personal identifiers are personal data in the hands of a person to whom they are disclosed will depend upon that person being in possession of, or likely to come into the possession of, other information which would enable that person to identify a living individual (data is only 'personal data' when it can be identified as such – *DPA 1998, s 1(1)*).

It should be noted that the disclosure of personal data by a data controller amounts to processing under *section 1(1)* of *DPA 1998*.

Examples   35.13

The obtaining of clinical information linked to a National Health Service number by a person having access to the National Health Service Central Register will amount to processing of personal data by that person because that person will have access to information enabling him to identify the individuals concerned.

It will be a duty upon someone processing data to take steps to ensure that the data cannot be reconstituted to become personal data and to be prepared to justify any decision made on processing of the data.

In the case of data collected by the Office of National Statistics, where there is a disclosure of samples of anonymised data, it is conceivable that a combination of information in a particular geographic area may be unique to an individual or family who could therefore be identifiable from that information. In recognition of this fact, disclosures of information are done in such a way that any obvious identifiers are removed and the data presented so as to avoid particular individuals being distinguished.

If data have been stripped of all personal identifiers such that the data controller is no longer able to single out an individual and treat that individual differently, the data cease to be personal data. Whether this has been achieved may be open to challenge. Data controllers may therefore be required to justify the grounds for their view that the data are no longer personal data. When a subject access request is received, a data controller must be able to identify the data relating to the data subject making the request, to enable him to provide information specific to that data subject. In making a subject access request, a data subject might provide the data controller with sufficient information to enable their data to be distinguished from data relating to other individuals, in a situation where the data controller would not otherwise be able to do so from the information in his possession, which he may have stripped of all personal identifiers. In this case the data relating to the individual making the request become personal data, but the information provided by the data subject does not render the other data being held personal data, unless the data controller believes that it is likely that information will come into his possession to render the other data personal data.

If there are any doubts as to whether data are personal data the Commissioner's advice would be to treat the data as personal data, having particular regard to whether those data are *sensitive* personal data. In respect of such data, if a subject access request is received and the data controller cannot satisfy himself as to the identity of the person making the subject access request, or as to his ability to locate the information to which the subject access request relates because the data have been stripped of identifiers, then the data controller would not be obliged to comply with that subject access request, advising the data subject accordingly.

Expressions of Opinion or Intention   35.14

The definition of personal data contained in *DPA 1998* now expressly includes any indication of the intentions of the data controller or any other person in respect of an individual. This aspect of the definition was not included in the definition of 'personal data' in *DPA 1984*. The consequence of this may mean, for example, that an employer who processes appraisals of employees would have to disclose not only his opinions of the employees but also any intention to offer or decline promotion on the basis of those opinions subject to any exemption available at any particular time.

This is a major change which not all personnel or human resources departments have as yet noted.

Further Information   35.15

The Information Commissioner's Legal Guidance is on the website (www.informationcommissioner.gov.uk).

FAQs   35.16

Can information about 'companies' be personal data under *DPA 1998*?

No, only data about living individuals can be personal data under *DPA 1998*.

Are pictures personal data?

Yes, photographs and moving pictures are caught in the definition of personal data, as the guidance from the Information Commissioner makes clear.

Is there any guidance on the definition of personal data?

Yes, the Information Commissioner has issued guidance on this topic which is on the Information Commissioner's website (www.informationcommissioner.gov.uk). Reference should always be made to the *Durant* case because it affects much of the existing guidance described in this chapter, which will be revised by the IC in due course. See in particular **CHAPTER 30** and **CHAPTER 35**, which summarise the February 2004 guidance of the IC on this area, and the additional CCTV guidance at the end of **APPENDIX 1**.

Chapter 36 – Principles

At A Glance

✓   The Eight Data Protection Principles set out a code by which data controllers must gather and handle personal data.

✓   The Principles must be complied with even if the data controller has failed to register its holding of personal data.

✓   The Principles address issues such as fair processing of the data, use of the data for the purposes for which it was gathered and export of the data.

✓   Guidance is available from the Information Commissioner on the Principles and their application.

The Principles   36.1

The Eight Data Protection Principles must be followed by data controllers in their handling of personal data and the obtaining of such data. The Principles are slightly different from the eight previous Principles in the *Data Protection Act 1984* (*DPA 1984*), which they replaced.

First Principle: Fair and Lawful Processing   36.2

The First Principle provides that 'Personal data shall be processed fairly and lawfully and, in particular, shall not be processed unless:

●   at least one of the conditions in *Schedule 2* of the *Data Protection Act 1998* (*DPA 1998*) is met; and

●   in the case of sensitive personal data, at least one of the conditions in *Schedule 3* to *DPA 1998* is also met.'

Fair and lawful processing is covered in **21 FAIR PROCESSING**. 'Fair' essentially means with the data subject's consent. 'Lawful' is not defined. The Information Commissioner suggests that it may broadly be described by the courts as 'something which is contrary to some law or enactment or is done without lawful

429

justification or excuse' (see *R v R [1991] 4 All ER 481*). The term applies equally to the public and private sector and to breaches of both statute and common law, whether criminal or civil. According to the Commissioner, an example of information unlawfully obtained might be information which is obtained as a result of a breach of confidence or in breach of an enforceable contractual agreement. Since 2 October 2000 it applies to a breach of the *Human Rights Act 1998* (*HRA 1998*) by a data controller bound by that Act (see **26 HUMAN RIGHTS ACT 1998**).

Areas of law relevant to lawfulness listed by the Commissioner in her Legal Guidance (October 2001) are:

- confidentiality arising from the relationship of the data controller with the data subject;

- the *ultra vires* rule and the rule relating to the excess of delegated powers, under which the data controller may only act within the limits of its legal powers;

- legitimate expectation, that is, the expectation of the individual as to how the data controller will use the information relating to him or her; and

- *Article 8* of the *European Convention on Human Rights* (the right to respect for private and family life, home and correspondence).

Confidentiality 36.3

Some relationships imply confidentiality, such as those existing between banker and client. In *A v B plc [2002] 3 WLR 543* (CA 11 March 2002) the Court of Appeal overturning the court below held that a lover in a secret affair was not legally restrained from revealing all to the newspapers, whereas a married partner would be as the nature of the relationships differed. In marriage an obligation of confidentiality was implied at common law. The Information Commissioner says that 'the effect of an obligation of confidence is that a data controller is restricted from using the information for a purpose other than that for which it was provided or disclosing it without the individual's permission. It would be unlawful for a data controller to do this unless there was some overriding reason in the public interest for this to happen. Where such personal data are processed for a purpose other than that for which the information was provided, the processing is likely to be unlawful processing.'

Public bodies and other organisations have data for certain statutory functions. They must act solely in accordance with their powers.

The Commissioner advises:

'Where a public body obtains information of a confidential nature in order to carry out its statutory functions then processes that information for other purposes, there is likely to be a breach of the obligation of confidence to that individual, unless there is a good reason or some legal justification for using the information in that way.'

In *Brian Robertson v Wakefield City Council (High Court, 16 November 2001)*, the court held that refusing to allow Mr Robertson to register to vote without his data being used by way of the electoral roll being sold on for commercial purposes was a breach of *HRA 1998*. Allowing such sales showed that the UK had not properly implemented the *Data Protection Directive (95/46/EC)* through *DPA 1998*.

In the case of *Campbell v Mirror Group Newspapers plc* Naomi Campbell, the internationally renowned fashion model, sought damages for breach of confidentiality and compensation under *section 13* of *DPA 1998* in relation to newspaper articles with photographs which had been published by the defendants in The Mirror in February 2001.

The Mirror denied that it had acted in breach of confidence, that the information published was sensitive personal data and that the defendants were in breach of any duty under *DPA 1998*. They did not dispute that she was entitled to damages and/or compensation, including aggravated damages or compensation, assuming that she established breach of confidence and/or breach of duty under the Act against the defendants. The Mirror argued that if information published was confidential, its publication 'was legitimate in that the public interest in favour of publication outweighed any public interest in the protection' of Miss Naomi Campbell's rights of confidentiality. The Mirror said that she was an internationally famous supermodel 'so well-known as to be recognised immediately by appearance and name by a high proportion of the general public' and well-known for her commercial ventures and as a figurehead for charitable causes. She had not only been 'for many years the subject of extensive media attention and coverage relating to her private and personal life, activities and conduct', but also she had courted such attention and coverage including voluntarily disclosing otherwise inaccessible details about her private and personal life and feelings. Although she had discussed with the media that she had undergone therapy for behavioural problems and anger management, she had falsely and publicly asserted that she had not fallen prey to drug abuse thereby misleading the public.

The Court referred to the case of *Douglas v Hello! Ltd [2001] QB 967*. The Court of Appeal overturning Ms Campbell's win of £3,500 damages in the High Court for breach of *DPA 1998* said:

> 'The primary information that had been conveyed to the appellants [The Mirror Group Newspapers Plc] was that Miss Campbell was regularly attending Narcotics Anonymous. The fact she was a drug addict was a secondary inference from this primary fact, albeit an inescapable inference. We find the suggestion that The Mirror should have published the secondary inference without publishing the primary fact to be lacking in realism. What is it suggested The Mirror should have published? Naomi Campbell is a drug addict.

> The Mirror has discovered she is receiving treatment for her addiction? Such a story, without any background detail to support it, would have bordered on the absurd. We consider that the detail given, and indeed

the photographs, were a legitimate, if not an essential, part of the jour-nalistic package designed to demonstrate that Miss Campbell had been deceiving the public when she said she did not take drugs.

Given that it was legitimate for the appellants to publish the fact she was a drug addict and receiving treatment, it does not seem it was particu-larly significant to add the fact the treatment consisted of attendance at meetings of Narcotics Anonymous. We consider that the detail given, and indeed the photographs, were a legitimate, if not an essential, part of the journalistic package designed to demonstrate that Miss Campbell had been deceiving the public when she said she did not take drugs. Given that is was legitimate for the [newspaper] to publish the fact she was a drug addict and receiving treatment, it does not seem it was particularly significant to add the fact the treatment consisted of attendance at meet-ings of Narcotics Anonymous.'

The Court of Appeal said that Miss Campbell is an internationally famous model. She has courted, rather than shunned, publicity. In part, this has been to promote other ventures in which she is involved. In interviews she volunteered informa-tion about aspects of her private life and behaviour, including limited details about her relationships with male friends. She acknowledged she had behavioural problems, including difficulty in keeping her temper. When talking to the media, Miss Campbell went out of her way to aver that, in contrast to many models, she did not take drugs, stimulants or tranquillisers. This was untrue. She had, in fact, become addicted to drugs. On one occasion it became known Miss Campbell had entered a clinic, the Cottonwood de Tucson Centre in Arizona.

The explanation she gave was [that] she was having therapy aimed at dealing with behaviour and anger problems. The reality is she was also being treated for drug abuse. The judges agreed the initial Mirror story had been sympathetic to the model but a follow-up article was not, following her complaint her privacy had been invaded. She also complained that clinical details of her treatment had been published. The court held:

'We do not consider the information that she was receiving therapy from NA was to be equated with disclosure of details of medical treat-ment.'

They said it was also inevitable Miss Campbell's identity would be known to oth-ers attending meetings of NA with her. They continued:

'We do not consider a reasonable person on reading Miss Campbell was a drug addict would find it offensive that the Mirror also disclosed she was at NA.'

Disclosure of her NA sessions was not 'of sufficient significance to shock the con-science and justify the intervention of the court'. The judges insisted The Mirror was entitled to tell of Miss Campbell's addiction and treatment under *Article 10* of the *Human Rights Act 1998*. The information published was justified in order to provide a factual account of her drug addiction that had the detail necessary to carry credibility. Provided publication of confidential information is justifiable in the public interest, the journalist must be given reasonable latitude as to the manner in which that information is conveyed to the public or his right to freedom of expression will be unnecessarily inhibited. The court applied *A v B plc [2002] 3 WLR 542* (a confidentiality case – referred to above).

In the *Campbell* case the court said that on the data protection legislation the court said that the exemption in *section 32* of *DPA 1998* did apply. Where a data controller was responsible for the publication of hard copies which reproduced data previously processed by means of equipment operating automatically, the publication formed part of the processing and fell within *DPA 1998*. *Section 32(1) to (3)* of *DPA 1998* provided widespread exemption from the Act, provided that the data controller reasonably believed that publication would be in the public interest and that compliance was incompatible with the special purpose of journalist. The subsections must be given their natural meaning, and must apply both before and after publication. Miss Campbell had sought to argue that the exemption in *section 32(1)* depended on the processing being undertaken with a view to publication, therefore the processing could not include the publication. However the Court of Appeal said that it was the data which was exempt. Where under *section 32* the data became exempt as a result of a reasonable belief of the journalist that the publication would be in the public interest, the data remained subject to the exemption after that. Here the *section 32* exemption applied. In 2004 the Campbell (and Hello!) case will go to the House of Lords.

Second Principle: Purposes   36.4

The Second Data Protection Principle of *DPA 1998* requires that personal data should be obtained only for one or more specified and lawful purposes, and shall not be further processed in any manner incompatible with that purpose or those purposes. The purpose may, by *Schedule 1, Part II, paras 5–6* of *DPA 1998*, be specified in a notice given for that purpose or in a notification ('registration') given to the Commissioner under *DPA 1998*.

The Second Principle states that 'personal data shall be obtained only for one or more specified and lawful purposes, and shall not be further processed in any manner incompatible with that purpose or those purposes'.

In deciding whether any disclosure of personal data is compatible with the purpose or purposes for which the data were obtained, consideration will be given to the purpose or purposes for which the personal data are intended to be processed by any person to whom they are disclosed, the Commissioner says. Such decisions cannot be made retrospectively by data controllers once the data are obtained.

For the purposes of the Second Principle, the further processing of personal data in compliance with the conditions set out in *section 33* of *DPA 1998* is not to be regarded as incompatible with the purposes for which they were obtained. If the data controller has complied with *Schedule I, Part II, Para I* of *DPA 1998* then this is likely to indicate that a data subject has not been deceived or misled as to the purposes for which their personal data are to be processed.

In practice, letting users know in a lot of detail what will be done with their data is much better than simply saying their data may be used generally for all manner of things. A general notification may not satisfy the Commissioner.

Third Principle: Adequate, Relevant and not Excessive 36.5

The Third Principle requires that personal data must be adequate, relevant and not excessive in relation to the purposes for which it is processed. Concerning this, the Information Commissioner states in her October 2001 Legal Guidance:

> 'In complying with this Principle, data controllers should seek to identify the minimum amount of information that is required in order properly to fulfil their purpose and this will be a question of fact in each case. If it is necessary to hold additional information about certain individuals, such information should only be collected and recorded in those cases.
>
> This guidance has been endorsed by the Data Protection Tribunal in the context of *DPA 1984* in the case of *Runnymede Borough Council CCRO and Others v The Data Protection Registrar (November 1990)*. Where a data controller holds an item of information on all individuals which will be used or useful only in relation to some of them, the information is likely to be excessive and irrelevant in relation to those individuals in respect of whom it will not be used or useful and should not be held in those cases.
>
> It is not acceptable to hold information on the basis that it might possibly be useful in the future without a view of how it will be used. This is to be distinguished from holding information in the case of a particular foreseeable contingency which may never occur, for example, where an employer holds details of blood groups of employees engaged in hazardous occupations.'

Practical guidance 36.6

The Information Commissioner suggests data controllers should consider for all data in this context:

- the number of individuals on whom information is held;
- the number of individuals for whom it is used;
- the nature of the personal data;
- the length of time it is held;

- the way it was obtained;
- the possible consequences for individuals of the holding or erasure of the data;
- the way in which it is used; and
- the purpose for which it is held.

Fourth Principle: Accurate and Up-to-date 36.7

Personal data should be accurate and, where necessary, kept up-to-date. It is a matter of fact whether data is incorrect or misleading in each case. *Schedule 1, Part II, para 7 of DPA 1998* states that the Fourth Data Protection Principle is not to be taken as contravened where the data controller has taken reasonable steps to ensure the accuracy of the data.

'Necessary' 36.8

An interesting issue is when is it 'necessary' to keep the data up-to-date. The Information Commissioner's Legal Guidance indicates that if the data are intended to be used merely as an historical record of a transaction between the data controller and the data subject, updating would be inappropriate. To change the data so as to bring it up to date would defeat the purpose of maintaining the historical record. However, according to the Commissioner 'sometimes it is important for the purpose that the data reflect the data subject's current circumstances, for example, if the data are used to decide whether to grant credit or confer or withhold some other benefit. In those cases either steps should be taken to ensure that the data are kept up-to-date, or when the data are used, account should be taken of the fact that circumstances may have changed.'

A data controller will need to consider the following questions.

- Is there a record of when the data were recorded or last updated?
- Are all those involved with the data – including people to whom they are disclosed as well as employees of the data controller – aware that the data do not necessarily reflect the current position?
- Are steps taken to update the personal data – for example, by checking back at intervals with the original source or with the data subject? If so, how effective are these steps?
- Is the fact that the personal data are out of date likely to cause damage or distress to the data subject?

Fifth Principle: Data not to be Kept Longer than Purposes Require
36.9

Personal data processed for any purpose or purposes shall not be kept for longer than is necessary for that purpose or those purposes.

Some Acts of Parliament deal with this issue in particular for certain types of data, such as the *Police and Criminal Evidence Act 1984*. Reference should be made here to the CCTV Code of Practice (see **2 CCTV**) which makes recommendations for retention periods.

If personal data have been recorded because of a relationship between the data controller and the data subject, the need to keep the information should be considered when the relationship ceases to exist. For example, the data subject may be an employee who has left the employment of the data controller. The end of the relationship will not necessarily cause the data controller to delete all the personal data. It may well be necessary to keep some of the information so that the data controller will be able to confirm details of the data subject's employment for, say, the provision of references in the future or to enable the employer to provide the relevant information in respect of the data subject's pension arrangements. The Information Commissioner makes the point that 'it may well be necessary in some cases to retain certain information to enable the data controller to defend legal claims, which may be made in the future. Unless there is some other reason for keeping them, the personal data should be deleted when the possibility of a claim arising no longer exists ie when the relevant statutory time limit has expired.'

Sixth Principle: Data Processed in Accordance with Data Subjects' Rights
36.10

Personal data shall be processed in accordance with the rights of data subjects under *DPA 1998*. This provision is contravened if, but only if, a person contravenes:

- *section 7* of *DPA 1998* by failing to supply information which has been duly requested in accordance with that section;

- *sections 10–11* of *DPA 1998* by failing to comply with a notice duly given under that section; or

- *section 12* of *DPA 1998* by failing to give a notice under that section.

Seventh Principle: Security
36.11

Appropriate technical and organisational measures shall be taken against unauthorised or unlawful processing of personal data and against accidental loss or destruction of, or damage to, personal data.

Security measures should be taken at all stages (see **5 CONFIDENTIALITY AND DATA SECURITY: SEVENTH PRINCIPLE**). The *Data Protection Directive (95/46/EC)* provides that such measures should be taken both at the time of the design of the processing system and at the time of the processing itself, particularly in order to maintain security and thereby to prevent any unauthorised processing. Data controllers are, therefore, encouraged to consider the use of privacy-enhancing techniques as part of their obligations under the Seventh Principle.

In the Legal Guidance the Information Commissioner suggests as follows.

Some of the security controls that the data controller is likely to need to consider are set out below. (This is not a comprehensive list but is illustrative only.)

Security management

- Does the data controller have a security policy setting out management commitment to information security within the organisation?

- Is responsibility for the organisation's security policy clearly placed on a particular person or department?

- Are sufficient resources and facilities made available to enable that responsibility to be fulfilled?

Controlling access to information

- Is access to the building or room controlled or can anybody walk in?

- Can casual passers-by read information off screens or documents?

- Are passwords known only to authorised people and are the passwords changed regularly?

- Do passwords give access to all levels of the system or only to those personal data with which that employee should be concerned?

- Is there a procedure for cleaning media (such as tapes and disks) before they are reused or are new data merely written over old? In the latter case, is there a possibility of the old data reaching somebody who is not authorised to receive it? (eg as a result of the disposal of redundant equipment).

- Is printed material disposed of securely, for example, by shredding?

- Is there a procedure for authenticating the identity of a person to whom personal data may be disclosed over the telephone prior to the disclosure of the personal data?

- Is there a procedure covering the temporary removal of personal data from the data controller's premises, for example, for staff to work on at home? What security measures are individual members of staff required to take in such circumstances?

(cont'd)

- Are responsibilities for security clearly defined between a data processor and its customers?

Ensuring business continuity

- Are the precautions against burglary, fire or natural disaster adequate?

- Is the system capable of checking that the data are valid and initiating the production of back-up copies? If so, is full use made of these facilities?

- Are back-up copies of all the data stored separately from the live files?

- Is there protection against corruption by viruses or other forms of intrusion?

Staff selection and training

- Is proper weight given to the discretion and integrity of staff when they are being considered for employment or promotion or for a move to an area where they will have access to personal data?

- Are the staff aware of their responsibilities? Have they been given adequate training and is their knowledge kept up-to-date?

- Do disciplinary rules and procedures take account of the requirements of *DPA 1998*? Are these rules enforced?

- Does an employee found to be unreliable have his or her access to personal data withdrawn immediately?

- Are staff made aware that data should only be accessed for business purposes and not for their own private purposes?

Detecting and dealing with breaches of security

- Do systems keep audit trails so that access to personal data is logged and can be attributed to a particular person?

- Are breaches of security properly investigated and remedied; particularly when damage or distress could be caused to an individual?

DPA 1998 introduces express obligations upon data controllers when the processing of personal data is carried out by a data processor on behalf of the data controller. In order to comply with the Seventh Principle the data controller must:

- choose a data processor providing sufficient guarantees in respect of the technical and organisational security measures they take;

- take reasonable steps to ensure compliance with those measures; and

- ensure that the processing by the data processor is carried out under a contract, which is made or evidenced in writing, under which the data processor is to act only on instructions from the data controller. The contract must require the data processor to comply with obligations equivalent to those imposed on the data controller by the Seventh Principle.

Further advice may be found in BS 7799 and 1S0/IEC Standard 17799.

Eighth Principle: Data Export   **36.12**

Personal data shall not be transferred to a country or territory outside the European Economic Area, unless that country or territory ensures an adequate level of protection of the rights and freedoms of data subjects in relation to the processing of personal data.

This would appear to prevent a data export, however *Schedule 4* to *DPA 1998* sets out exceptions. **20 EXPORT OF DATA, 41 'SAFE HARBOR' AGREEMENT** and **44 TRANSBORDER DATA FLOWS** examine this Principle in more detail.

Schedule 4 of *DPA 1998* sets out when the Eighth Principle will not apply, and often seems to be overlooked by companies. It provides that this is the case where:

(*a*)   the data subject has given their consent to the transfer;

(*b*)   the transfer is necessary:

         (i)   for the performance of a contract between the data subject and the data controller, or

         (ii)   for the taking of steps at the request of the data subject with a view to the data subject entering into a contract with the data controller;

(*c*)   the transfer is necessary:

         (i)   for the conclusion of a contract between the data controller and a person other than the data subject which:

                 (A)   is entered into at the request of the data subject, or

                 (B)   is in the interests of the data subject, or

         (ii)   for the performance of such a contract;

(*d*)   the transfer is necessary for reasons of substantial public interest.

         The Secretary of State may specify by order the circumstances in which a transfer is to be taken to be necessary for reasons of substantial public interest. No order to this effect has been made to date;

(*e*)   the transfer:

         (i)   is necessary for the purpose of, or in connection with, any legal proceedings (including prospective legal proceedings);

         (ii)   is necessary for the purpose of obtaining legal advice; or

         (iii)   is otherwise necessary for the purposes of establishing, exercising or defending legal rights;

(*f*)   the transfer is necessary in order to protect the vital interests of the data subject;

(*g*)   the transfer is part of the personal data on a public register and any conditions subject to which the register is open to inspection are complied with by any person to whom the data are or may be disclosed after the transfer;

(*h*)   the transfer is made on terms which are of a kind approved by the Information Commissioner as ensuring adequate safeguards for the rights and freedoms of data subjects. It is not the practice of the Commissioner to consider or approve individual draft contracts submitted to her; or

(*j*)   the transfer has been authorised by the Commissioner as being made in such a manner as to ensure adequate safeguards for the rights and freedoms of data subjects.

Model Clauses for export to (i) data controllers and (ii) data processors appear in APPENDIX 3.

Information Commissioner's Audit Manual and Networks of Privacy Offices – EPON   36.13

All businesses which process personal data need to ensure on a regular basis that they are compliant with the Principles. Extracts from the Information Commissioner's Audit Manual which can be used by companies undertaking their own internal data protection compliance audit are in APPENDIX 4 to this book. The Information Commissioner's website gives access to a data protection audit process with forms which businesses can use in assessing their compliance with the legislation.

Privacy Laws and Business organises a network of data protection or privacy officers, European Privacy Offices Network ('EPON'), who meet three times a year to discuss privacy and data protection issues, form working groups and exchange information.

37 PRIVACY POLICIES AND AUDITS looks at audits in more detail and in particular the Commissioner's Audit Manual.

Further Information   36.14

With regard to CCTV and employers and employees, reference should be made to the Information Commissioner's CCTV Code (reproduced in APPENDIX 1) and Employment Practices Data Protection Code respectively – available online at www.informationcommissioner.gov.uk.

Details of the Privacy Laws and Business network of privacy officers are at www.privacylaws.com. Email: sandra@privacylaws.com. Tel: 020 8423 1300. Fax: 020 8423 4536.

FAQs 36.15

What is the legal status of the Data Protection Principles?

Breach of the Principles can lead to enforcement action being taken by the Information Commissioner. The Principles have full legal effect, notwithstanding that they are called 'principles'.

Do individuals have right under the Principles?

Individual can sue for damages for breach of *DPA 1998* pursuant to its provisions.

Can the Information Commissioner award compensation for breach of the Principles?

No, but private actions for damages can be brought.

Chapter 37 –
Privacy Policies and Audits

At A Glance

✓ Many companies which handle personal data choose to set up a privacy policy which gives data subjects access to information about how their data will be used.

✓ Auditing systems to ensure compliance should be the first stage before setting up such a policy. The Information Commissioner has produced an Audit Manual to provide guidance on this, extracts of which are appended to this book.

✓ There is no legal obligation to set up such a policy, although there are obligations to notify data subjects of certain matters in one form or another such as who is the data controller.

✓ Many websites which gather personal data have privacy policies.

✓ The Organisation for Economic Co-operation and Development ('OECD') has an online tool for the setting up of a privacy policy.

✓ An example of a simple Internet privacy policy is given in this chapter.

Introduction   37.1

The *Data Protection Act 1998* (*DPA 1998*) obliges data controllers to notify data subjects of important information about who the data controller is, how the data will be used etc. That information must be provided to individuals in whatever is the best form as regards the data concerned. There will be less space on a short paper form on which individuals provide personal data than there will be on a website where a lengthy document can be accommodated.

In practice, putting such information into one document known as a 'privacy policy' is a good idea. However, it is not a substitute for general compliance. The data controller must, for example, ensure that the information can be accessed. A privacy policy hidden in an obscure part of a website is worse than useless. The information should at least be visible when individuals supply the information concerned. In addition, before a privacy policy or general data protection policy can be set up, an audit should be done of the business' systems.

Websites 37.2

The information to be given on a website where data is gathered is:

- the identity of the person or organisation responsible for operating the website and of anyone else who collects personal data through the site;

- the purposes for which they intend to process the personal data; and

- any other information needed to ensure fairness to individuals, taking into account the specific circumstances of the processing. This will include informing individuals of any disclosure of information about them to third parties, including disclosure to companies within the same group.

The Information Commissioner says that

> 'Unless it is obvious, website operators must give this information to individuals before they collect any personal data from them. It should be remembered that visitors to a website will not necessarily enter it through its homepage. They may, for example, come directly to a particular page via a hypertext link. The above information should therefore be provided at any point at which personal data are collected.'
>
> *Information Commissioner FAQs – Internet*

28 INTERNET considers the data protection issues relating to the Internet in particular.

Developing a Privacy Policy 37.3

Before a privacy policy can be set up it is useful to carry out some kind of an audit. Lots of information is available on the Information Commissioner's website. Under the Compliance Advice section of the Commissioner's website, guidance is given to businesses in achieving compliance with *DPA 1998*.

The Commissioner's Audit Manual 37.4

The Information Commissioner has issued a comprehensive Audit Manual to be used by businesses to achieve compliance under *DPA 1998*. It covers the following.

Part 1: Introduction

1. Aims of Data Protection Compliance Audits

2. Why Should Organisations Audit?

3. Audit Objectives

4. What is an Audit?

5. Audit Categories

6. Audit Benefits

Part 2: The Audit Method

1. Audit Categories

2. Adequacy Audit Outcomes

3. Compliance Audit

Part 3: The Audit Process

1. Audit Planning

2. Audit Preparation

3. Conduct of the Compliance Audit

4. Compliance Audit Reporting

5. Audit Follow-up

Part 4: Guide to Auditing

1. The Role of an Auditor

2. Auditing Tasks

3. Human Aspects

4. Audit Techniques

5. Practical Considerations

Annex A: Risk Assessment.

Annex B: Sampling Criteria.

Annex C: Audit Pro formas.

Annex D: Meeting Pro formas.

Annex E: Adequacy Audit Checklist.

Annex F: Compliance Audit Checklists: Organisational & Management Issues.

Annex G: Compliance Audit Checklists: The Eight Data Protection Principles.

Annex H: Compliance Audit Checklists: Other Data Protection Issues.

Annex J: Process Audit Checklist.

Extracts from the Manual are appended to this book.

The Manual was piloted by Privacy Laws and Business in public and private sector organisations. It follows common auditing principles and is based on a two stage risk assessment:

(a)   an adequacy audit to assess whether a business' policy, code of practice, guidelines and procedures meet the requirements of *DPA 1998*; and

(b)   a compliance audit to check that the business is in compliance, giving guidance to data controllers in assessing the risks, and using pro formas and audit checklists.

Guidance and Training 37.5

Training 37.6

Privacy Laws and Business, who wrote the Audit Manual for the Information Commissioner (see **37.4** above) also provide audit workshops (see www.privacy laws.com) and they publish a regular UK and EU newsletter of data protection developments. In addition, many companies offer courses and conferences on data protection legal issues, including LexisNexis Butterworths Tolley.

Online seminars 37.7

On 30 October 2001 the Information Commissioner announced a series of online seminars to help individuals and organisations who hold personal information (data controllers) to understand *DPA 1998*. These consisted of a voice-over recording accompanied by a Powerpoint presentation. The seminars can be downloaded from the Information Commissioner's website at www.informationcommissioner.gov.uk/seminars.htm. The then Information Commissioner Elizabeth France said that the seminars will be of particular use to data protection officers, and that further specialist seminars will be added to the programme over the coming months to build up a comprehensive training package.

OECD guidance 37.8

The OECD has issued guidance on how to set up a privacy policy at http://cs3-hq.oecd.org/scripts/pwv3/PWPart1.htm.

Step I 37.9

The OECD suggest first reviewing internal systems by asking the following questions.

- Do you collect personal data?

- What kinds of personal data do you collect?

- How are they collected? From individuals, from third parties, from public bodies or authorities? Are individuals aware that their personal data are being collected?

- Who in your organisation is responsible for deciding what personal data are collected and how?

- Why do you collect personal data?

- How are they used?

- Who controls personal data once they are collected?

- Are personal data disclosed to third parties, and if so, why?

- How and where are they stored?

- Do you have standards, guidelines and regulations which apply to your collection and use of personal data?

- Do you allow visitors access to the personal data you have about them?

- What happens if a visitor has a query about their personal data? What if they are not satisfied with how you deal with their query?

Step 2 37.10

OECD suggest that the second step would then be a review of laws which apply to the company concerned which of course differ around the world.

Step 3 37.11

Once this is done, the next step is to use the OECD's generator answering the questions there. After a data controller has completed the questionnaire as accurately as possible, a draft privacy policy statement is automatically generated. It proposes pre-formatted sentences based on the answers given and choices made.

Step 4 37.12

The fourth step is to ensure that:

- the draft privacy statement accurately reflects your organisation's personal data practices;

- the draft privacy statement complies with applicable national, regional and international laws or (self) regulatory schemes; and

- errors are corrected and that the privacy statement reads smoothly.

Step 5 37.13

The final step is to place the privacy policy on the website. The OECD states:

> 'Regulations to which you may be subject may require a specific location for such a statement, such as on your homepage, or at the point(s) where personal data are collected. In the absence of specific regulatory requirements, you may wish to consider creating a link between your homepage and your privacy statement, or between pages where you collect personal data and your privacy statement. The OECD Privacy Guidelines recommend that individuals should be able to gain access to information about personal data practices without unreasonable effort as to time, knowledge and expense. You may also wish to create links to relevant web sites to make visitors aware of any relevant regulation.'

They end with the following warning:

> '**REMEMBER:** Once your privacy statement is publicly posted, you may be legally liable if you fail to abide by your privacy policy statement or if that statement does not comply with local laws.'

Example of a Simple Internet Privacy Policy 37.14

The OECD online privacy policy statement was revised using the OECD Generator. This example is not intended to be a 'model' statement. It is intended only to provide an indication of what you can expect your final privacy statement to look like.

Below is an example of a simple privacy policy for a fictional company, EFG Limited.

Privacy policy

EFG's commitment to privacy

EFG Limited is committed to protecting the privacy of those using our site and the confidentiality of the personal information with which our subscribers provide us.

Data Protection Act 1998

We are registered under the *Data Protection Act 1998* and comply with the Act in all our dealings with your personal data.

Your personal information is safe with us.

EFG will never sell personal information or share personal information with third parties unrelated to it. At EFG we use the information we collect to serve our customers in the following ways.

- If you become a subscriber to EFG or a user of other EFG services your name, email address, address and other information on the subscription form are kept by us and used to remind you when your next subscription is due and to send you the EFG Report.

- We may also use your contact information to let you know about enhancements to the site and your subscription entitlements. If you would rather not receive this information please inform us by email at privacy@efg.co.uk.

- We do not use cookies (defined below) for collecting user information from the site and we will not collect any information about you except that required for system administration of the web server.

Cookies

Message given to a web browser by a web server. The message is then stored by the browser in a text file called *cookietxt*. Each time the browser requests a page from the server, this message is sent back. A cookie's main objective is to identify users and personalise their visit by customising web pages for them, for example by welcoming them by name next time they visit the same site. A site using cookies will usually invite you to provide personal information such as your name, email address and interests.

Further information

For further information on data protection and privacy contact:

The Data Protection Manager, EFG Limited, _____

Telephone (+44) (0)20 7_____. Facsimile (+44) (0)20 7.

Email privacy@efg.co.uk.

Information on the *Data Protection Act 1998* is also on the Information Commissioner's website at www.informationcommissioner.gov.uk.

Use of this Site is subject to our Terms and Conditions

Privacy and Electronic Communications Directive and the Privacy and Electronic Communications (EC Directive) Regulations 2003
37.15

The *Directive on Privacy and Electronic Communications (2002/58/EC)* ('*E-privacy Directive*') requires that data subjects be told if cookies will be used, and this should therefore be added to privacy policies. The UK Regulations implementing this are the *Privacy and Electronic Communications (EC Directive) Regulations 2003 (SI 2003/2426)*. The IC's guidance on the Regulations, Part 2 has a section on cookies which is described in **CHAPTER 28 INTERNET.**

See **33 OPT-IN AND OPT-OUT** for an extract from the Directive in this regard.

Further Information
37.16

The OECD's guidance on forming a privacy policy is at http://cs3-hq.oecd.org/scripts/pwv3/PWPart1.htm

OECD says that further guidance on carrying out an internal review can be found on the websites of SIIA, USCIB,or CSA Model Code CAN/CSA-Q830.

They say businesses may also wish to consult the following websites:

- www.jipdec.or.jp/security/privacy/index-e.html
- www.research.att.com/projects/p3p/propgen
- www.the-dma.org
- www.truste.org/wizard

Details of Privacy Laws and Business who wrote the Information Commissioner's Audit Manual and their network of privacy officers is at www.privacylaws.com. Tel: 020 8423 1300. Fax 020 8423 4536.

FAQs

Is there a legal obligation to have a privacy policy on a website?

No, but in the EU, where data is gathered data subjects must be told the statutory information such as who is the data controller and how their data will be used. A privacy policy is a useful way of doing this.

Do companies need formal data protection policies?

Companies need to comply with *DPA 1998*. Many larger businesses find it useful to have a formal written policy as this can save time and ensure all staff are educated in the correct manner.

What assistance is available in relation to data protection audits?

Businesses such as Privacy Laws and Business and law firms such as the writer's firm Singletons can provide advice on practical and legal issues. The Information Commissioner has had produced an Audit Manual which helps companies comply.

Chapter 38 – Recording Telephone Calls and Emails

At A Glance

✓ The *Regulation of Investigatory Powers Act 2000* (*RIPA 2000*) regulates the interception of communications.

✓ The *Telecommunications (Lawful Business Practice) (Interception of Communications) Regulations 2000* (*SI 2000/2699*) regulate this area. These are known as the 'Lawful Business Practice Regulations'.

✓ In most cases recording is permitted if the other person is aware that it is occurring or may occur.

✓ The Government's Office of Telecommunications ('Oftel') has provided guidance for consumers in this field.

✓ Employers can include statements to this effect in employment contracts.

Introduction   38.1

The legislation relating to the recording of telephone calls and emails is contained in *RIPA 2000* (see **40 REGULATION OF INVESTIGATORY POWERS ACT 2000**). In addition, businesses must comply with the requirements set out in the *Data Protection Act 1998* (*DPA 1998*). In this respect, the Information Commissioner's Employment Practices Data Protection Code should be considered (see **16 EMPLOYMENT** and **28 INTERNET**). The *Lawful Business Practice Regulations* (*SI 2000/2699*) were made under *RIPA 2000*, and set out the law in this field. They are considered in **38.2** below, and in more detail in **29 LAWFUL BUSINESS PRACTICE REGULATIONS**.

Lawful Business Practice Regulations   38.2

The *Telecommunications (Lawful Business Practice) (Interception of Communications) Regulations 2000* (*SI 2000/2699*) provide that the interception has to be by or with the consent of a person carrying on a business for purposes relevant to that person's business, and using that business's own telecommunication system. The term 'carrying on a business' includes the activities of government departments, public authorities and others exercising statutory functions.

Interceptions are authorised for:

- the monitoring or recording of communications:
  - to establish the existence of facts, to ascertain compliance with regulatory or self-regulatory practices or procedures or to ascertain or demonstrate standards which are or ought to be achieved (quality control and training),
  - in the interests of national security (in which case only certain specified public officials may make the interception),
  - to prevent or detect crime,
  - to investigate or detect unauthorised use of telecommunication systems, or
  - to secure, or as an inherent part of, effective system operation;
- the monitoring of received communications to determine whether they are business or personal communications; and
- the monitoring of communications made to anonymous telephone helplines.

Interceptions are authorised only if the controller of the telecommunications system on which they are effected has made all reasonable efforts to inform potential users that interceptions may be made.

The *Lawful Business Practice Regulations (SI 2000/2699)* do not authorise interceptions to which the persons making and receiving the communications have consented; they are not prohibited by *DPA 1998*.

Interception of Emails by ISPs – ntl case 38.3

On 22nd July 2002 the High Court confirmed a decision of Ipswich Crown Court that Internet Service Providers ('ISPs') can lawfully intercept emails where requested by the police who are searching for evidence of a serious crime. The ISP was ntl. They received notification from police that they were applying for access to all information relating to a particular email address over a period of 10 days. They told ntl, which kept a server for ISP Virgin, that it should not 'conceal, destroy, alter or dispose of' the material involved, except with judicial or police permission. The company's systems, however, were designed automatically to destroy emails quickly after they were been accessed by the recipient. The only way to keep the information sought would be to intercept emails. ntl said that compliance with the notice would infringe *RIPA 2000*. It applied to the court for permission to delete or dispose of the material. The court refused and said that the interception and retention of the emails was lawful as the police had notified ntl that they were applying for a special production order under the *Police and Criminal Evidence Act 1984 (PACE 1984)*. Therefore, ntl had implicit 'lawful authority' to intercept and retain the emails. The High Court decision said 'If

[ntl] was not in a position to take that action without committing an offence, it would mean that the [*PACE 1984* provisions] would be almost totally worthless.

Regulation of Investigatory Powers (Maintenance of Interception Capability) Order 2002   38.4

ISPs in the UK were obliged to start intercepting and storing electronic communications including emails, faxes and web surfing data from 1 August 2002. At the date of writing the basis for compensation to be paid to them had not yet been ascertained for maintaining their interception capabilities. The new rules only apply to large ISPs. Any criminal organisation wishing to avoid interception simply has to find an ISP that has fewer than 10,000 customers. The interception capability is made under *RIPA 2000*. On 1 August 2002, the *Regulation of Investigatory Powers (Maintenance of Interception Capability) Order 2002 (SI 2002/1931)* came into force.

Regulation of Investigatory Powers (Communications Data) Order 2003   38.5

The *Regulation of Investigatory Powers (Communications Data) Order 2003* made under *RIPA* allows many Government agencies access to traffic data; but not the content of the data itself. It came into force on 5 January 2004.

In addition to the police, Inland Revenue, Customs and Excise, MI5, MI6 and GCHQ, the new Order gives certain other agencies rights to access communications data. These are fewer in number than in the original proposal which critics called the 'Snoopers' Charter', but do include:

- the Financial Services Authority;
- the Office of Fair Trading;
- the Maritime and Coastguard Agency;
- the UK Atomic Energy Constabulary;
- the Scottish Drugs Enforcement Agency;
- the Radiocommunications Agency;
- NHS bodies, in connection with health and fraud;
- local authorities (but not parish councils); and
- the Office of the Police Ombudsman for Northern Ireland.

The *Order* can be viewed at http://www.hmso.gov.uk/si/si2003/20033172.htm

Data Protection Act 1998 and Monitoring: Part 3 of the Employment Code 38.6

Part 3: Monitoring at Work of the Information Commissioner's Employment Practices Data Protection Code sets out benchmarks which deal specifically with the monitoring of electronic communications. This includes the monitoring of telephone, fax, email and Internet communications. In Part 3 of the Code the following terms are used to distinguish between different types of communication.

- *Private communications*: communications, whether sent for business purposes or not, that contain information that the worker would not wish to be generally known.

- *Personal communications*: communications that are sent in the course of the worker's private life and are not business communications even if sent from work.

Some communications may be both private and personal. Both types may contain personal information about the worker or others.

The benchmarks

General

- Establish a policy on the use of electronic communications and communicate it to workers.

- Ensure that where monitoring involves the interception of a communication it is not outlawed by the *Regulation of Investigatory Powers Act 2000.*

- Make an impact assessment to determine what, if any, monitoring of electronic communications is justified by the benefits.

- Limit the scope of monitoring to what is strictly required to deliver those benefits.

Telephone monitoring

- Ensure that the assessment of whether monitoring is justified takes account of the specific circumstances of telephone monitoring.

- Ensure that those making calls to or receiving calls from workers, as well as workers themselves, are aware of any monitoring and the purpose behind it, unless this is obvious.

- Ensure that workers are aware of the extent to which you receive information about the use of telephone lines in their homes, or mobile phones provided for their personal use, for which your business pays partly or fully. Do not make use of information about personal calls for monitoring.

Email and Internet access monitoring

- Ensure that the assessment of whether monitoring is justified takes account of the specific circumstances of email and/or Internet access monitoring.

- Make those sending emails to workers, as well as workers themselves, aware of any monitoring and the purpose behind it, unless this is obvious.

- If it is necessary to check the email accounts of workers in their absence, make sure that they are aware that this will happen.

- Inform workers of the extent to which information about their Internet access and emails is retained in the system and for how long.

- In reviewing the results of any monitoring take into account the possibility of unintentional access of websites by workers.

Notes and examples

It is important that an employer establishes, documents and communicates a policy on the use of electronic communications systems. However workers will base their expectations of privacy not only on the employer's stated policy but also on its practice. For example, if the employer's policy imposes a ban on personal telephone calls but in practice the employer 'turns a blind eye' to a limited number of personal calls, the employer will not be able to depend on there being a complete ban as its justification for carrying out monitoring. The capabilities of electronic systems should be used to remind workers of their responsibilities.

These can be set so that workers cannot proceed to access the Internet or email services without acknowledging the acceptance of certain conditions.

Except in limited circumstances that are unlikely to apply to the monitoring of communications by employers, interception, without the consent of sender and recipient, is against the law unless it is authorised by the *Lawful Business Practice Regulations*. This is the case for both public and private sector businesses.

An interception occurs when, in the course of its transmission, the contents of a communication are made available to someone other than the sender or intended recipient. It therefore includes access to emails before they have been opened by the intended recipient, but does not include stored records of emails that have been received and opened.

An impact assessment should be made to determine whether monitoring is justified and if so to determine its scope and nature. In making the impact assessment the following should be considered.

(cont'd)

- Can monitoring be limited to that necessary to ensure the security of the system, eg protection from intrusion and from malicious code (such as viruses or Trojans), or detection of the misuse of passwords?

- Can established methods of supervision of workers rather than electronic monitoring be relied on?

- Can the investigation of specific incidents or problems be relied on, for example accessing stored emails to follow up an allegation of racial harassment involving the use of the email system, rather than undertaking continuous monitoring.

- Can monitoring be limited to workers who complaints have been received about, or who there are other grounds to suspect of wrong-doing?

- Can monitoring be targeted at areas of highest risk, ie can it be directed at a few individuals whose jobs mean they pose a particular risk to the business rather than at all workers?

- Can monitoring be automated? This can reduce the extent to which extraneous information is made available to any person other than the parties to a communication. For example, monitoring to protect the security of a computer system can generally be automated. Monitoring to detect references to matters of particular sensitivity, for example the name of a company involved in a merger negotiation, might also be automated. Automated monitoring systems are becoming increasingly sophisticated and their capabilities should be exploited to assist data protection compliance, for example through the ability to target monitoring at suspicious patterns of activity.

- Can spot-checks or audit be undertaken instead of using continuous monitoring? In some cases though continuous automated monitoring might be less intrusive for workers, than spot-check or audit that involve human intervention.

Do not introduce monitoring or the recording of the content of calls in all cases. Consider whether an acceptable reduction in risk can be achieved by the use of an itemised call record. If the itemised call record is inadequate for this purpose, assess whether it can be used to help ensure that monitoring is strictly limited and targeted. For example, there might be evidence that commercial secrets are being passed to a competitor. By examining itemised call records it might be possible to narrow down those under suspicion and target monitoring accordingly.

Monitoring external calls will mean collecting information about those people who make calls to or receive calls from the organisation as well as about workers. These people are also entitled to be told that monitoring is taking place and why. Provide this information, where reasonably practicable, through the use of recorded messages on telephone systems. Don't forget that those who might be making personal calls to workers are less likely to expect that their calls may be monitored, or to understand why, than, for example, customers who might expect some recording to take place. If there is no better way of providing information, instruct workers to inform callers that their calls may be recorded and to explain why this is the case.

Where employers pay for mobile phones which workers may use for personal calls or for land lines in their homes, they may receive itemised bills directly or via their workers. If bills are received directly, workers should be made aware of the extent of information about personal use received by the employer. In either case, information about personal calls should not be used for monitoring. It may be used for billing or in exceptional circumstances where there is evidence of criminal activity accessed as part of a specific investigation.

An impact assessment should be made in order to determine whether email monitoring is justified and if so to determine its scope and nature. In making the privacy assessment the following should be considered.

- Can analysis of email traffic rather than monitoring the content of messages be used? If the traffic record alone is not sufficient, can the traffic record be used to narrow the scope of content monitoring, for example by only examining the content of messages that are being sent to a rival organisation?

- Is it feasible to use an automated monitoring and detection process, that for example detects malicious code such as viruses or Trojans, or limits the size of attachments that can be received?

- Are there secure lines of communication, for example for the transmission of sensitive information from the worker to an occupational health advisor or for trade union communications, that will not be subject to monitoring? Some systems can be set up so that messages to and from particular individuals or sections of the organisation are not subject to monitoring or are monitored differently to others

- Is there a system that allows workers to mark personal communications as such?

- Can facilities be provided that allow messages to be sent that do not bear the employer's 'official' heading? This should reduce the risk of employers' liabilities in respect of personal emails sent using the employer's equipment.

- Can emails that are marked personal, or which there are other grounds to believe are personal, be excluded from monitoring or treated differently? Apart from automated monitoring which rejects or returns unacceptable messages for security reasons messages that are both personal and private should only be opened in exceptional circumstances, for example where a worker is suspected of using email to harass other employees.

(cont'd)

- Is there a ban on personal use of the email system or a restriction on the types of messages that can be sent?

  Such a ban or restriction does not in itself justify the employer knowingly opening messages that are clearly personal. However an employer designing monitoring is entitled to work on the assumption that messages in the system are either all likely to be business ones or if personal are only likely to be of a particular type. If personal use is prohibited it may be possible to detect personal messages or take action against the sender or recipient without opening them.

- Are workers provided with a separate email account or an encryption capability. Are they allowed access to web-based mail services for personal use?

- Are systems for recording information about email use reliable? Employers should bear in mind that emails and associated records can be falsified. Without special measures their value as evidence in court may be limited.

An impact assessment should be made in order to determine whether Internet access monitoring is justified and if so to determine its scope and nature. In making the privacy assessment the following should be considered.

- Can monitoring be designed to prevent rather than detect misuse, for example by blocking access to inappropriate sites or material by using web-filtering software?

  (**Note:** Web filtering systems are becoming increasingly sophisticated and may be able to deliver real protection to employers with little intrusion on workers. For example, products are available that, it is claimed, can undertake complex analysis of images and thereby prevent the display of sexually explicit material.)

- Is it possible to prevent misuse of systems by recording the time spent accessing the Internet rather by monitoring the sites visited or the contents viewed?

- If this is not possible, is it possible to limit the use of the information collected. For example, if the issue is that a worker has been spending too much time on the Internet for purposes that are not work-related, is it necessary for the worker's manager to be told exactly what sites have been visited.

- Can private Internet access be separated from business access, perhaps by having a different log-on for private use and then limiting the collection of information on private use to the length and time of the session.

- Can monitoring be done on an aggregated basis, for example examining logs of which sites have been accessed from which departments and only focussing on specific workers if it is apparent there is a problem.

Monitoring external emails will mean collecting information about those people who send emails to or receive emails from the organisation, as well as about workers. These people are also entitled to be told that monitoring is taking place and why. In practice this may not be easy to achieve. Employers would not, for example, be expected to inform external senders of emails that messages will be virus checked even though this may involve processing their personal data. However, if information about external contacts is to be used in ways they would not expect they should be told. If email responses are solicited, for example, if job applicants are asked to send in their applications by email it should be possible to provide any necessary information beforehand, for example in the job advert. If emails are unsolicited the information could be provided in any response.

The purpose for doing this should be to ensure the business responds properly to its customers and other contacts. Only check email accounts, and use personal information contained in them, for other purposes if there is reason to believe the intrusion is justified by the benefit to the business. Only in exceptional circumstances should emails that are clearly personal and may also be private be opened, for example if the worker is suspected of criminal activity.

There are a variety of ways in which workers can be told about the retention of information about their email or Internet usage. This might be done by giving them an information pack addressing this when they are given access to the office's Internet or email systems, or by displaying on-line information on their computer. It is important to ensure that workers are aware of retention periods and, in particular, that they are not misled into believing that information will be either deleted or retained when this is not the case.

Websites can be visited unwittingly through unintended responses of search engines, unclear hypertext links, misleading banner advertising or miskeying.

Further Information   38.7

For the employment issues see **16 EMPLOYMENT**, **28 INTERNET** and **29 LAWFUL BUSINESS PRACTICE REGULATIONS**.

For information on *RIPA 2000* see **40 REGULATION OF INVESTIGATORY POWERS ACT 2000**.

The Home Office has a special section of its website devoted to *RIPA 2000*. This can be found via www.homeofficegov.uk, and includes drafts of codes of practice made under *RIPA 2000* and consultations.

The DTI consultation on the *Lawful Business Practice Regulations* (*SI 2000/2699*) is on the Internet at www.dti.gov.uk/cii/regulatory/telecomms/telecommsregulations/lawful_business_practice_regulations.shtml.

Oftel's guidance on recording of calls is at
www.oftel.gov.uk/consumer/advice/FAQs/prvfaq3.htm.

FAQs 38.8

Oftel, the Telecoms Regulator, provide a helpful summary of the laws in this
field for consumers at www.oftel.gov.uk/consumer/advice/FAQs/prvfaq3.htm.
This guidance is below.

Recording and monitoring telephone calls or emails

A general overview of interception, recording and monitoring of communications

The interception, recording and monitoring of telephone calls is governed by
a number of different pieces of UK legislation. The requirements of all relevant legislation must be complied with. The main ones are:

- *RIPA 2000;*

- *Telecommunications (Lawful Business Practice) (Interception of Communications)
  Regulations 2000 (SI 2000/2699);*

- *DPA 1998;*

- *Telecommunications (Data Protection and Privacy) Regulations 1999 (SI
  1999/2093); and*

- *Human Rights Act 1998.*

*It is not possible to provide comprehensive detail of that legislation here. Any person con-
sidering interception, recording or monitoring of telephone calls or emails is strongly
advised to seek his/her own independent legal advice and should not seek to rely on the
general information provided below. It should be borne in mind that criminal offences and
civil actions may occur when the relevant legislation is not complied with. Accordingly,
Oftel accepts no liability for reliance by any person on the following information.*

Can I record telephone conversations on my home phone?

Yes. The relevant law, *RIPA 2000*, does not prohibit individuals from recording their own communications provided that the recording is for their own
use. Recording or monitoring are only prohibited where some of the contents
of the communication – which can be a phone conversation or an email – are
made available to a third party, ie someone who was neither the caller or
sender nor the intended recipient of the original communication. For further
information see the Home Office website where *RIPA 2000* is posted.

**Do I have to let people know that I intend to record their telephone
conversations with me?**

No, provided you are not intending to make the contents of the communication available to a third party. If you are you will need the consent of the person you are recording.

Can a business or other organisation record or monitor my phone calls or email correspondence with them?

Yes they can, but only in a limited set of circumstances relevant for that business which have been defined by the *Lawful Business Practice Regulations* (*SI 2000/2699*). The main ones are:

- to provide evidence of a business transaction;

- to ensure that a business complies with regulatory procedures;

- to see that quality standards or targets are being met in the interests of national security;

- to prevent or detect crime to investigate the unauthorised use of a telecom system; and

- to secure the effective operation of the telecom system.

In addition, businesses can monitor, but not record, phone calls or emails which have been received to see whether they are relevant to the business, for example open an employee's voicemail or mailbox systems while they are away to see if there are any business communications stored there. Further information can be found on the Department of Trade and Industry ('DTI') website.

However, any interception of employees' communications must be proportionate and in accordance with the Data Protection Principles. The Data Protection Commissioner is consulting on a Draft Code of Practice on the Use of Personal Data in Employer/Employee Relationships. It is proposed that where the standards in the Code of Practice are, in the Commissioner's opinion, necessary for compliance with *DPA 1998*, they may be directly enforceable as a breach of the Data Protection Principles. Accordingly, this Code of Practice and *DPA 1998* must also be considered by any business before it intercepts employees' communications. For further information see the Information Commissioner's website.

Do businesses have to tell me if they are going to record or monitor my phone calls or emails?

No. As long as the recording or monitoring is done for one of the above purposes, then the only obligation on businesses is to inform their own employees. If businesses want to record for any other purpose, such as market research, they will have to obtain your consent.

Can a helpline record my calls?

No. If you phone an anonymous helpline that offers its services for free your conversation may be monitored but not recorded.

What do I do if my calls have been recorded unlawfully?

Under *RIPA 2000* it is a tort to record or monitor a communication unlawfully. This means that if you think you have suffered from unlawful interception of your phone calls or emails you have the right to seek redress by taking civil action against the offender in the courts.

Crown Copyright

Chapter 39 – Registration/Notification

At A Glance

✓   Data controllers have to notify the Information Commissioner of their holding of personal data and pay an annual fee, which is currently £35. This process is called notification, or sometimes registration.

✓   Some EU states provide for a notification or deposit of contract terms under which data is exported from the European Economic Area ('EEA').

✓   The Information Commissioner's website has an online notification form, as well as a question and answer section to check whether notification is necessary.

✓   Chapter 8 of the Information Commissioner's Legal Guidance (October 2001) provides information on Notification.

✓   Some companies who deal little with personal data do not have an obligation to notify as they benefit from various exemptions under the *Data Protection Act 1998 (DPA 1998)*.

Introduction   39.1

The first obligation of those handling personal data is to notify (register) with the Data Protection Office. *Part III* of *DPA 1998* contains the relevant law. Regular fees must be paid to keep a notification in effect. All those who are registered appear on the website at www.dpr.gov.uk. Further information on notification appears in Chapter 8 of the Commissioner's Legal Guidance (October 2001).

The European Commission, in providing general information on the *Data Protection Directive (95/46/EC)*, describes the notification obligation as follows.

'In order to ensure that the public are properly informed about data processing operations, and also so as to allow the supervisory authorities to perform their tasks, the Directive devises a system of notification for processing operations. National data protection authorities are required to keep a public register indicating details of the data controllers and of the processing undertaken.'

Some countries in the EU have opted to provide a deposit system for those entering into agreements for the export of personal data from the EEA within the Eighth Data Protection Principle under the Commission's model clauses for data export (see **APPENDIX 3**). The model clauses are considered in **20 EXPORT OF DATA** and **44 TRANSBORDER DATA FLOWS**. The UK has not adopted this optional requirement.

Duty to Notify   39.2

Section 16 of *DPA 1998* sets out the registrable particulars which those notifying must give. They include information such as the name and address of the person and a description of the data (see **39.3** below). Under the *Data Protection Act 1984* (*DPA 1984*) someone who was exempt from registration was exempt from compliance with the Act. Under *DPA 1998* the link has gone. Every data controller has to comply with *DPA 1998*, even if they are exempt from notification.

When is it necessary to notify and what information is provided?   39.3

Those who process personal data have to notify under *DPA 1998*. An online questionnaire on the Data Protection Register website (www.dpr.gov.uk/notify/4.html) can be completed by data processors, and will tell them whether they must register or not.

The notification includes a requirement to supply 'registrable particulars'. In relation to a data controller, these are:

- their name and address;

- if they have nominated a representative, the name and address of the representative;

- a description of the personal data being or to be processed and of the category(ies) of data subject to which they relate;

- a description of the purposes(s) for which the data are being or are to be processed;

- a description of any recipient(s) to whom the data controller intends or may wish to disclose the data;

- the name or a description of any countries or territories outside the European Economic Area to which the data controller transfers or intends or may wish to transfer the data; and

- where the personal data are of a type which is exempt from the prohibition against processing personal data without notification and where the notification does not extend to such data, a statement of that fact.

The Information Commissioner says in the Legal Guidance (October 2001):

'When a notification is made by a data controller he must also provide, in addition to the registrable particulars, a general description of the security measures taken to protect the personal data; this information will not appear on the register.'

Online notification 39.4

It is possible to register/notify online by completion of a form on the Commissioner's website. The form can currently be found at www.dpr.gov.uk/cgi-bin/dprproc?page=7.html.

Registration under DPA 1984 39.5

Many businesses are registered under *DPA 1984*. They are allowed to complete their earlier registration period before having to re-register, even if their registration expired after the first transitional period to 23 October 2001 (by the *Data Protection (Notification and Notification Fees) (Amendment) Regulations 2001 (SI 2001/3214)* which altered the original law). However, they still have to comply with the rest of *DPA 1998*, including the Data Protection Principles, until they re-register under *DPA 1998* and thereafter. They are still obliged to notify the Commissioner of certain changes in processing.

Differences from DPA 1984 39.6

The principal differences between *DPA 1984* and notification under *DPA 1998* are as follows.

- Data processors do not need to notify under *DPA 1998*.

- Register entries will still contain a description of the processing of personal data. However, this description is in very general terms. The detailed coding system no longer exists.

- Businesses do not need to describe sources of personal data in the entry.

- Registration of disclosures are replaced by notification of recipients.

- Businesses only need to describe transfers of personal data outside the EEA.

- Businesses have to provide a statement about their security measures.

- There is now no need to provide an address for the receipt of subject access requests.

- *DPA 1998* provides some exemptions from notification.

- The notification period is one year.

- A data controller can only have one register entry.

- Headteachers and governing bodies of schools may notify in the name of the school (for many one notification rather than two registrations will be possible).

In the 2003 Annual Report the IC said the following as regards notifications:

'The maintenance of the statutory register of data controllers has continued to be a significant administrative task for us. This has been a particularly busy year. The activities of the self-styled notification agencies referred to elsewhere in this report have created considerable extra work. We have received a large number of calls, emails and letters from those confused by the "official looking" notices they have received, or angry that they have been taken in and paid far more than the £35 statutory fee. There have been thousands of complaints about these businesses, including many from those who have responded and paid a substantial fee, sometimes when notification was not even required.

'We have sought to address the activities of these businesses by working closely with the Office of Fair Trading, Trading Standards and local police forces to ensure that appropriate action is taken. The Office of Fair Trading has obtained injunctions against three such agencies and undertakings from several more. Convictions under *section 14* of the *Trade Description Act 1968* have been obtained by Brent and Harrow trading standards service against one particularly active company and its director.

'This has been the last full year in which we have dealt with the consequences of the move from the standard 3 year period of registration under the 1984 Act to the 1 year period of notification under the 1998 Act. Some 55,000 of the 1984 Act entries expired. During the year nearly 110,500 new notification applications were received and the register grew from 198,519 to 211,251.

'We anticipate a very significant reduction in the number of fresh applications for notification, and expect that the major focus will be on renewals. We are also writing to all those who notified via an agency to alert them to the fact that they can renew direct with us and to instruct us to send all communications regarding their entry direct to them in future rather than the agency who submitted their original application. We hope to upgrade the platform on which our current notification system is based. We also intend to undertake a detailed study in preparation for commissioning a new computer system to handle the notification process. Among the priorities is to facilitate public access to the up-to-date register'.

Fees   39.7

The notification fee is £35 (no VAT) for each year. The Data Protection Office does not send invoices but will acknowledge receipt of payments. Under *DPA*

1984 a fee of £75 had to be paid every three years. Payment can be by direct debit, cheque or BACS.

The *Data Protection (Notification and Notification Fees) Regulations 2000 (SI 2000/188)* include the provision for the £35 fee. The Regulations can be found at www.legislation.hmso.gov.uk/si/si2000/20000188.htm.

Notification by Different Groups   39.8

Notification by partnerships   39.9

Regulation 5 of the *Data Protection (Notification and Notification Fees) Regulations 2000 (SI 2000/188)* provides that where a partnership is concerned the notification can be in the name of the firm.

Notification by schools   39.10

Regulation 6 of the *Data Protection (Notification and Notification Fees) Regulations 2000 (SI 2000/188)* says that schools can register the name of the school on behalf of both the headteacher and the governing body. The name and address to be given is that of the school.

Notification Offences   39.11

It is an offence to process personal data without notification unless:

- the personal data fall within either of the national security or domestic purposes exemptions;

- the personal data are exempt under the transitional exemptions;

- the personal data fall within the 'relevant filing system' or 'accessible record' or public register exceptions referred to above;

- the processing operation falls within the exemptions referred to in the *Data Protection (Notification and Notification Fees) Regulations 2000 (SI 2000/188)*, as amended by the *Data Protection (Notification and Notification Fees) (Amendment) Regulations 2001 (SI 2001/3214)*; or

- the processing is of a description which the Notification Regulations provide is exempt from the requirements to notify on the ground that it is unlikely to prejudice the rights and freedoms of data subjects. No such provision was included in the Regulations.

This is a strict liability offence, so even if the controller had no idea that *DPA 1998* existed, a prosecution could still follow.

Example   39.12

In the First Annual Report of the Information Commissioner (June 2001) one case study relating to failure to notify is discussed. An employee appropriated client data from his employer's database, then left that firm and established his own company. The appropriate data was retained on computer. He was convicted of unlawfully using the data for his own purposes and his new business was convicted of being an unregistered data user.

It is important to tell the Information Commissioner if a change occurs as otherwise an offence can be committed. The *Data Protection (Notification and Notification Fees) Regulations 2000 (SI 2000/188)*, as amended by the *Data Protection (Notification and Notification Fees) (Amendment) Regulations 2001 (SI 2001/3214)*, provided that such notification must be given as soon as is practicable, and in any event within a period of 28 days from the date upon which the entry becomes inaccurate or incomplete as a statement of the data controller's registrable particulars, or in respect of measures taken with regard to compliance with the Seventh Data Protection Principle. A defence is available to persons charged with such an offence if they can show that they exercised all due diligence to comply with the duty.

Further Information   39.13

Further information on notification under *DPA 1998* can be found on the Commissioner's website www.informationcommissioner.gov.uk

The Commissioner has issued Notification Exemptions – A Self Assessment Guide, which contains questions to help data controllers to determine if notification is required.

Other documents in the notification field on the website of the Information Commissioner are:

- Notification Handbook – A Complete Guide To Notification.

- Form to alter or remove a register entry (see **23 FORMS**).

- Purpose form – to add a purpose to a register entry (see **23 FORMS**).

Background information on the *Data Protection Directive* is on the Commission's website at www.europa.eu.int/comm/internal_market/en/dataprot/backinfo/info.htm

FAQs

The Information Commissioner has issued the following frequently asked questions on notification.

Q. What is notification?

A. The Commissioner maintains a public register of data controllers. Each register entry includes the name and address of the data controller and a general description of the processing of personal data by the data controller. Individuals can consult the register to find out what processing of personal data is being carried out by a particular data controller. Notification is the process by which a data controller's details are added to the register.

Q. Why do data controllers have to notify?

A. *DPA 1998* requires every data controller who is processing personal data to notify unless they are exempt.

Q. How can I find out if I am exempt?

A. The conditions required to be satisfied for each notification exemption are described in the publications 'Notification Handbook – A Complete Guide to Notification' and 'Notification Exemptions – A Self Assessment Guide', which can both be found at www.dpr.gov.uk

Q. Is there any link between notification and compliance?

A. No. The principal purpose of the notification process and the public register is openness. It is an important aspect of data protection legislation that the public should be able to find out who is carrying out the processing of personal data and other information about the processing, such as for what purposes the processing is carried out. However, notification does not equate to compliance with the Data Protection Principles.

The link between compliance and registration (or notification), which existed under *DPA 1984*, is no longer a feature of data protection legislation under *DPA 1998*. The Commissioner is able to enforce the Data Protection Principles against any data controller who is not otherwise exempt from compliance, regardless of their notification status, where she is satisfied that any of the Principles have been, or are being, contravened. It remains open to the Commissioner to investigate and prosecute those data controllers who are required to notify but who have not.

Chapter 40 – Regulation of Investigatory Powers Act 2000

At A Glance

✓ The *Regulation of Investigatory Powers Act 2000* (*RIPA 2000*) sets out legislation on interception of communications in the UK.

✓ *RIPA 2000* is supplemented by the *Telecommunications (Lawful Business Practice) (Interception of Communications) Regulations 2000 (SI 2000/2699)* ('*Lawful Business Practice Regulations 2000*').

✓ The Home Office has issued three Codes of Practice under *RIPA 2000*.

✓ The *Anti-terrorism, Crime and Security Act 2001* includes provisions for a code of practice under *RIPA 2000* which would require businesses to retain 'traffic data' about the use made of telecoms systems.

Introduction 40.1

RIPA 2000 governs the interception of communications in the UK. This chapter provides a summary of the Act and the latest developments under it. The *Lawful Business Practice Regulations 2000 (SI 2000/2699)* made under *RIPA 2000* are examined in **29 LAWFUL BUSINESS PRACTICE REGULATIONS. 38 RECORDING TELEPHONE CALLS AND EMAILS** contains information on recording telephone calls and emails, and includes Oftel's guidance to consumers on this topic.

Telecoms and email monitoring is a growth area. The Privacy Foundation in the US has found that one in three out of 40 million employees using email or the Internet are monitored. and that 100 million workers on a worldwide basis are monitored by one means or another. The report is at www.sonic.net/~undoc/extent.htm

This area should be watched closely. The *Anti-terrorism, Crime and Security Act 2002* widened the ability to intercept and therefore increased powers of police and others in this field.

Summary of RIPA 2000 40.2

The provisions of *RIPA 2000* are summarised at **40.3–40.6** below.

Part I: Interception and access to communications data   40.3

Part I of *RIPA 2000* updates the previous interception law (the *Interception of Communications Act 1985*) to cover all communications service providers. This includes Internet Service Providers ('ISPs'). Interception must be personally authorised by the Secretary of State and is only allowed when the strict criteria laid down in *RIPA 2000* are met. The forms authorising such access are on the Home Office's website. Under *section 12* of *RIPA 2000* the Secretary of State may require *individual* communication service providers to maintain a reasonable intercept capability, by means of a notice. However, this must be subject to a consultation process involving industry, and any draft notice must be approved by both Houses of Parliament. This part of the Act was very controversial, as many small ISPs felt they could not afford the cost of a compulsory scheme. The Government has announced that it will set aside £20m from April 2001 to 2004 to ease the introduction of the new arrangements.

RIPA 2000 also includes a provision to establish a Technical Advisory Board, which will be made up of both Government and industry members, to oversee the notices served on communications service providers requiring the maintenance of an intercept capability. The Government will be working in conjunction with industry on the proper composition of the board.

Part I of *RIPA 2000* also introduces comprehensive statutory controls for the first time, governing access to communications data, such as billing information. Access must be properly authorised for specified purposes only, and is subject to independent oversight.

Part II: Surveillance and covert human intelligence sources   40.4

Part II of *RIPA 2000* regulates techniques, such as the use of agents or informants, which have been used for many years by law enforcement, security and intelligence agencies, but which have up until now been authorised on a non-statutory basis. The *Human Rights Act 1998* requires there to be a statutory framework in place for authorising these activities (see **26 HUMAN RIGHTS ACT 1998**.) This part of *RIPA 2000* also provides a legal basis for the surveillance activities presently carried out by a wide range of Government departments in pursuance of their duties.

Part II of the Act was brought into force on 25 September 2000 to ensure that current surveillance operations were properly regulated and fully compliant with the *Human Rights Act 1998* for its commencement on 2 October 2000.

Part III: Encryption   40.5

Part III of *RIPA 2000* establishes a power to require any person served with an appropriate notice to disclose protected, that is encrypted, information in an intelligible form ('plain text'). The power is ancillary to all statutory and non-statutory powers and functions of public authorities. Its use requires proper and specific permission. A number of statutory requirements must be met before any such permission can be given to exercise the disclosure power. There are extra requirements where a decryption key – rather than plain text – is desired. *RIPA 2000* sets out statutory safeguards for the protection of all information obtained under the *Part III* power. In addition, there are associated offences.

This requirement was heavily criticised as the Bill progressed through Parliament.

Part IV: Oversight and complaints   40.6

Part IV of *RIPA 2000* sets out the oversight and complaints mechanisms for the powers in the legislation. This includes:

* independent Commissioners (who must be judicial figures) with a statutory responsibility to oversee the exercise of the powers; and

* an independent Tribunal to hear complaints.

Part IV also deals with codes of practice, covering all parts of *RIPA 2000*, which will be admissible as evidence in criminal and civil proceedings. Three draft codes have now been issued (see **40.8** below).

Forms   40.7

The Home Office website, at www.homeoffice.gov.uk, provides full details of the forms which are used to authorise interceptions by public bodies such as the police. For example, the authorisation form provides for the grounds of interception to be stated, as set out below.

Grounds on which the action is necessary: (*delete as inapplicable*)
In the interests of national security.
For the purpose of preventing or detecting crime or of preventing disorder.
In the interests of the economic well-being of the United Kingdom.
In the interests of public safety.
For the purpose of protecting public health.
For the purpose of assessing or collecting any tax, duty, levy or other imposition, contribution or charge payable to a government department.

Codes of Practice 40.8

In 2002 three Codes of Practice governing the day-to-day operation of the law enforcement powers set out by *RIPA 2000* came into force. They are:

- Interception of Communications Code of Practice, in force 1 July 2002;

- Covert Human Intelligence Sources Code of Practice, in force 1 August 2002; and

- Covert Surveillance Code of Practice, in force 1 August 2002.

The Codes have been issued to:

o   law enforcement and security agencies;

o   public authorities;

o   MPs; and

o   key representatives from industry, telecommunications operators and ISPs.

A further code on traffic data is also proposed but not yet published. Under *section 11* of the *Anti-terrorism, Crime and Security Act 2002*, the Home Secretary was granted powers to create a code of practice governing the retention of customer data, including detailed logs of Internet and email use. Also of note are the provisions of the *Directive on Privacy and Electronic Communications (2002/58/EC)* (*'E-privacy Directive'*), which must be implemented by 31 October 2003.

Accessing communications data code 40.9

The Home Office has issued a draft Code of Practice on Accessing Communications Data for public consultation. The Code will govern the conduct of law enforcement and public bodies when obtaining information relating to the use of postal or telecommunication services, for example telephone billing information. The consultation period expired on 2 November 2001.

Data may only be sought by the police and others under *RIPA 2000* for certain stated purposes such as:

- in the interests of national security;

- for the purpose of preventing or detecting crime or preventing disorder; or

- in the interests of public safety.

Communications Data and Regulation of Investigatory Powers (Communications Data) Order 2003 40.10

Communications data, such as telephone billing information, is useful to the police. This type of data does not include the contents of the communication.

Chapter II, Part I of *RIPA 2000* only deals with access to communications data. The Home Office say that, for example:

'a list of telephone numbers can be reasonably seen as just that and therefore is defined as communications data, it does not give any indication of what might have been said during a conversation'.

The *Regulation of Investigatory Powers (Communications Data) Order 2003 (SI 2003/3174)* came into force on 5 January 2004 and allows access and data sharing of certain traffic data, but not content.

In addition to the police, Inland Revenue, Customs and Excise, MI5, MI6 and Government Communications Headquarters, the new Order gives certain other agencies rights to access communications data. These are fewer in number than in the original proposal, which critics had called the 'Snoopers' Charter' and include:

- the Financial Services Authority;
- the Office of Fair Trading;
- the Maritime and Coastguard Agency;
- the UK Atomic Energy Constabulary;
- the Scottish Drugs Enforcement Agency;
- the Radiocommunications Agency;
- NHS bodies, in connection with health and fraud;
- local authorities (but not parish councils); and
- the Office of the Police Ombudsman for Northern Ireland.

The Order can be viewed at http://www.hmso.gov.uk/si/si2003/20033172.htm.

Communications Content   40.11

In contrast to what is stated at **40.10** above, what is said during the telephone call is communications content. The Government say that it remains strict policy that the content of communications can *only* be obtained under an interception warrant personally authorised by the Secretary of State.

Anti-terrorism legislation   40.12

The *Anti-terrorism, Crime and Security Act 2001* addresses the question of communications data and is available at www.parliament.the-stationery-office.co.uk/pa/pabills.htm. On communications data, *Part 11* contains provisions to allow communications service providers to retain data about their customers' communications for access by law enforcement agencies and for national security purposes, and to enable a code of practice to be drawn up in consultation with industry. The code of practice allows communications service providers to retain data about their customers' communications for access by law enforcement agencies. Previously communications service providers were obliged to erase this data when they no longer need it for billing purposes. These provisions fall within *RIPA 2000* which sets out the limits on the purposes for which the law enforcement, security and intelligence agencies may request access to data relating to specific communications. There is also a reserve power to review the arrangements and issue directions if necessary. If still needed, it must be reviewed by an affirmative order every two years. As soon as the power is exercised, there is no need for further review.

Part 2 of the Act contains provisions to allow communications service providers to retain data about their customers' communications for national security purposes. Retained data can then be accessed by the security, intelligence and law enforcement agencies under the terms of the proposed code of practice relating to the retention of traffic data which is not yet issued.

This Act led to the *Regulation of Investigatory Powers (Communications Data) Order 2003* (see **40.10** above).

Obligations imposed on the Secretary of State   40.13

Section 71 of *RIPA 2000* requires the Secretary of State to prepare, publish and consider any representations made to him on the content of the Codes before they are laid before Parliament for approval by affirmative resolution. The Codes of Practice are published on the official *RIPA 2000* website at www.homeoffice.gov.uk/ripa/ripact.htm.

Part I of *RIPA 2000* updates the previous interception law (the *Interception of Communications Act 1985*) to encompass all communications service providers, including Internet Service Providers (ISPs). Interception must be personally authorised by the Secretary of State and only when the strict criteria laid down in *RIPA 2000* are met.

Code of Practice on the interception of communications   40.14

This Code of Practice, published on 7 August 2002, sets out the powers and duties conferred or imposed under *Chapter 1* of *Part 1* of *RIPA 2000* regarding the regulation of the interception of communications. It gives guidance to intelligence agencies and others on warrants and the disclosure, copying, retention and other safeguards necessary for materials obtained through warranted interception. It is primarily intended for used by those public authorities listed in *section 6(2)* of *RIPA 2000*, but will also prove useful to postal and telecommunication operators and other interested bodies.

Regulation of Investigatory Powers (Maintenance of Interception Capability) Order 2002 40.15

ISPs in the UK were obliged to start intercepting and storing electronic communications including emails, faxes and web-surfing data from 1 August 2002. At the date of writing the basis for compensation to be paid to them had not yet been ascertained for maintaining their interception capabilities. The new rules only apply to large ISPs. Any criminal organisation wishing to avoid interception simply has to find an ISP that has fewer than 10,000 customers. The interception capability is made under *RIPA 2000*. On 1 August 2002, the *Regulation of Investigatory Powers (Maintenance of Interception Capability) Order 2002 (SI 2002/1931)* came into force.

Powers given to the Secretary of State 40.16

Section 12 of *RIPA 2000* provides a power allowing the Secretary of State to impose obligations upon providers of publicly available communication services to maintain a reasonable intercept capability. The Secretary of State will do this through an order to be approved by both Houses of Parliament. This order will be subject to a consultation process involving industry before it is laid.

Interception Requirements 40.17

Under *RIPA 2000* a small proportion of communication service providers ('CSPs') may be required to maintain a reasonable intercept capability to assist investigations into serious crime and counterthreats to the nation's security or economic well-being. *RIPA 2000* will also establish a Technical Advisory Board, made up of an equal number of Government and CSP representatives under an independent chairman, to act as ombudsman and to advise the Home Secretary on matters concerning interception of communications via CSPs.

The Government has launched a consultation to hear CSPs' views on the form and detail of the interception requirements to ensure that they will be 'effective, technologically relevant and industry-friendly'. CSPs are also invited to nominate representatives for the Technical Advisory Board to ensure that the industry's interests are fully represented in these matters.

Section 12 40.18

Chapter I of *Part I* of *RIPA 2000* updates the previous interception law, the *Interception of Communications Act 1985*, to encompass all communications service providers, including ISPs. Its provisions were implemented on 2 October 2000 to coincide with the *Human Rights Act 1998*. However, implementing the interception provisions of *RIPA 2000* does not mean that UK CSPs not currently required to have an intercept capability will immediately be required to install one.

Section 12 of DPA 1998 provides a power enabling the Secretary of State to serve a notice requiring individual CSPs to maintain a reasonable intercept capability. This has led to much criticism, particularly about the cost of this. The notice will specify the services for which an interception capability is required, the steps and time-scale for meeting this requirement, and the division of costs between the government and CSPs. Before this can happen, an order must be approved by both Houses of Parliament.

RIPA 2000 specifies that interception warrants must be authorised personally by the Secretary of State, and may only be authorised where this is necessary as being in the interests of national security; for the purpose of preventing or detecting serious crime; or for the purpose of safeguarding the economic well-being of the United Kingdom.

Implementation Timetable 40.19

The following is a general indication of the implementation timetable of the various parts of *RIPA 2000*. For further details refer to the *Regulation of Investigatory Powers Act 2000 (Commencement No. 1 and Transitional Provisions) Order 2000 (SI 2000/2543)*.

Part I Chapter I (Interception of Communications): With the exception of *section 1(3)*, this part of the Act came into force on 2 October 2000. *Section 1(3)* and the *Telecommunications (Lawful Business Practice) (Interception of Communications) Regulations 2000 (SI 2000/2699)* referred to in *section 4(2)* came into force on 24 October 2000.

Part I Chapter II (Access to Communications Data): Implemented in 2002.

Part II (Surveillance and Covert Human Intelligence Sources): This part of the Act was brought into force on 25 September 2000.

Part III (the investigation of electronic data protected by encryption): The intention was for this part of the Act to be implemented during the second half of 2001.

Part IV (Scrutiny etc of Investigatory Powers and of the functions of the Intelligence Services), Part V and the Schedules: Implemented on various dates as set out in the *Regulation of Investigatory Powers Act 2000 (Commencement No. 1 and Transitional Provisions) Order 2000 (SI 2000/2543)*.

Discussion documents 40.20

The following discussion documents are available on the Parliament website.

- *Regulation of Investigatory Powers (British Broadcasting Corporation) Order 2001* and *Designation of Public Authorities for the Purposes of Intrusive Surveillance Order 2001* (First Standing Committee) House of Commons.

- *Regulation of Investigatory Powers (British Broadcasting Corporation) Order 2001 (SI 2001/1057)* and *Designation of Public Authorities for the Purposes of Intrusive Surveillance Order 2000* House of Lords, Hansard.

- First Standing Committee on Delegated Legislation – discussion of the *Regulation of Investigatory Powers (Notification of Authorisations etc) Order (SI 2000/2563)* and the *Investigatory Powers Tribunal Rules 2000 (SI 2000/2665)* on 30 October 2000.

- The *Regulation of Investigatory Powers (Notification of Authorisations etc) Order 2000 (SI 2000/2563)* – House of Lords, Hansard, 27 October 2000.

- The *Investigatory Powers Tribunal Rules 2000 (SI 2000/2665)* – House of Lords, Hansard, 27 October 2000.

- The *Regulation of Investigatory Powers (Communications Data) Order 2003 (SI 2003/3174).*

Secondary legislation   40.21

The following Statutory Instruments are available on the HMSO website.

- The *Wireless Telegraphy (Interception and Disclosure of Messages)(Designation) Regulations 2000 (SI 2000/2409).*

- The *Regulation of Investigatory Powers (Prescription of Offices, Ranks and Positions) Order 2000 (SI 2000/2417).*

- The *Regulation of Investigatory Powers (Authorisations Extending to Scotland) Order 2000 (SI 2000/2418).*

- The *Regulation of Investigatory Powers Act 2000 (Commencement No. 1 and Transitional Provisions) Order 2000 (SI 2000/2543).*

- The *Regulation of Investigatory Powers (Notification of Authorisations etc.) Order 2000 (SI 2000/2563).*

- The *Investigatory Powers Tribunal Rules 2000 (SI 2000/2665).*

- The *Telecommunications (Lawful Business Practice) (Interception of Communications) Regulations 2000 (SI 2000/2699).*

- The *Regulation of Investigatory Powers (Source Records) Regulations 2000 (SI 2000/2725).*

- The *Regulation of Investigatory Powers (Juveniles) Order 2000 (SI 2000/2793).*

- The *Regulation of Investigatory Powers (Cancellation of Authorisations) Regulations 2000 (SI 2000/2794).*

- The *Regulation of Investigatory Powers (British Broadcasting Corporation) Order 2001 (SI 2001/1057).*

- The *Regulation of Investigatory Powers (Designation of Public Authorities for the Purposes of Intrusive Surveillance) Order 2001 (SI 2001/1126)*.

- The *Regulation of Investigatory Powers Act 2000 (Commencement No. 2) Order 2001 (SI 2001/2727)*.

- The *Regulation of Investigatory Powers (Maintenance of Interception Capability) Order 2002 (SI 2002/1931)*.

- The *Regulation of Investigatory Powers (Covert Human Intelligence Sources: Code of Practice) Order 2002 (SI 2002/1932)*.

- The *Regulation of Investigatory Powers (Covert Surveillance: Code of Practice) Order 2002 (SI 2002/1933)*.

Case Law   40.22

In the decision in the case of *PG and JH v United Kingdom, The Times, 19 October 2001* the European Court of Human Rights held that covert listening devices at police stations were a breach of *Articles 8* and *13* of the *European Convention on Human Rights*, which provide the right to respect for a private life (*Article 8*) and the right to an effective remedy (*Article 13*). However there was no *Article 6* breach of the right to a fair hearing.

The case arose from the armed robbery of a Securicor van in the UK about which the police had been tipped off, and so had set up surveillance. The Chief Constable had given authorisation for a listening device to be used to obtain more evidence. The two applicants in the case (known as 'P.G' and 'J.H.') were arrested in a stolen car in which there were two black balaclavas, five cable ties, two pairs of gloves and two army kit bags. Devices were placed in the cells of those arrested to hear what they said. Again, authorisation from the chief constable was obtained. In 1996 the accused were sentenced to 15 years in jail for armed robbery. Evidence derived from the surveillance was used in court. At the time the surveillance took place *RIPA 2000* was not in force.

E-privacy Directive and the Privacy and Electronic Communications (EC Directive) Regulations 2003   40.23

The *Directive on Privacy and Electronic Communications (2002/58/EC)* ('E-privacy Directive') was implemented on the 11 December 2003 by the *Privacy and Electronic Communications (EC Directive) Regulations 2003*. It deals in part with the retention of traffic data which can of course be used by police to track criminals but also has data protection implications.

This provides in relevant part:

'1.   Traffic data relating to subscribers and users processed and stored by the provider of a public communications network or publicly available electronic communications service must be erased or made anonymous when it is no longer needed for the purpose of the transmission of a communication without prejudice to paragraphs 2, 3 and 5 of this Article and Article 15(1).

2. Traffic data necessary for the purposes of subscriber billing and interconnection payments may be processed. Such processing is permissible only up to the end of the period during which the bill may lawfully be challenged or payment pursued.

3. For the purpose of marketing electronic communications services or for the provision of value added services, the provider of a publicly available electronic communications service may process the data referred to in paragraph 1 to the extent and for the duration necessary for such services or marketing, if the subscriber or user to whom the data relate has given his/her consent. Users or subscribers shall be given the possibility to withdraw their consent for the processing of traffic data at any time.

4. The service provider must inform the subscriber or user of the types of traffic data which are processed and of the duration of such processing for the purposes mentioned in paragraph 2 and, prior to obtaining consent, for the purposes mentioned in paragraph 3.

5. Processing of traffic data, in accordance with paragraphs 1, 2, 3 and 4, must be restricted to persons acting under the authority of providers of the public communications networks and publicly available electronic communications services handling billing or traffic management, customer enquiries, fraud detection, marketing electronic communications services or providing a value added service, and must be restricted to what is necessary for the purposes of such activities.

6. Paragraphs 1, 2, 3 and 5 shall apply without prejudice to the possibility for competent bodies to be informed of traffic data in conformity with applicable legislation with a view to settling disputes, in particular interconnection or billing disputes.'

Article 9 deals with devices known as location devices which can be used to track people – they can be for example tagging of criminals devices or technology in milk floats or heavy goods vehicles to track where staff are at any time. It provides that where location data other than traffic data, relating to users or subscribers of public communications networks or publicly available electronic communications services, can be processed:

'such data may only be processed when they are made anonymous, or with the consent of the users or subscribers to the extent and for the duration necessary for the provision of a value added service. The service provider must inform the users or subscribers, prior to obtaining their consent, of the type of location data other than traffic data which will be processed, of the purposes and duration of the processing and whether the data will be transmitted to a third party for the purpose of providing the value added service. Users or subscribers shall be given the possibility to withdraw their consent for the processing of location data other than traffic data at any time.'

Traffic Data   40.24

The *Privacy and Electronic Communications (EC Directive) Regulations 2003* deal with 'traffic data". The IC's Guidance on the Regulations (Part 2) provides some advice on this subject.

Traffic data means any data which are processed:

- for the conveyance of a communication on an electronic communications network; or
- for the billing in respect of that communication (billing data under the *Telecommunications (Data Protection and Privacy) Regulations 1999*).

It includes data relating to the routing, duration or time of a communication.

Retention   40.25

Data processed to establish communications could potentially contain personal information which should only be stored for limited purposes and retention periods in accordance with the second and fifth principles of the *DPA 1998*. The Regulations provide for the protection of individual and corporate subscribers with regard to the processing of traffic data. Where such data are no longer required for the purpose of the transmission of a communication, on the termination of that communication, that data must be erased or dealt with in such a way that they cease to be personal data in the case of an individual subscriber, or in the case of a corporate subscriber, modified so that they cease to be data that would be personal data in the case of an individual.

Data required by the communications network or service provider for the purpose of calculating the subscriber's bill or for interconnection charges can only be retained until the end of the period, during which the bill may lawfully be challenged or payment pursued. In terms of contract law, this would normally mean that a limitation period of six years plus appeals applied. However, the Commissioner's view is that this provision merely permits retention of such data where circumstances require it, for example where a challenge is made to the bill during the time a communications network or service provider would normally retain the data for their own billing purposes. It does not permit the wholesale retention of such traffic data in every case. Regard must be had to the fifth data protection principle, which provides that personal data shall not be kept for longer than is necessary for the purpose for which they are processed.

Purposes for processing   40.26

Traffic data may be processed for only the restricted purposes outlined in the Regulations.

Value added services   40.27

A value added service means any service which requires the processing of traffic data or location data beyond that which is necessary for the transmission of a communication or the billing of that communication, for example a service which locates the driver of a broken down vehicle. There is no restriction on the type of service that can be provided but such processing may only take place with the prior consent of the subscriber or user.

The marketing of the service provider's own electronic communications services   40.28

Under the Regulations, the consent of the subscriber or user must be obtained before the service provider can market its own electronic communications services. Such marketing need not necessarily be carried out over the telephone and might include, by way of an example, an analysis of a subscriber's usage patterns to provide that subscriber with the best tariff available. Such processing may only be undertaken by the communications provider or by a person acting under his authority. Given that ultimate responsibility for compliance with the Regulations regarding the processing of traffic, data will lie with the communications provider, the requirements of the seventh data protection principle should be observed. The provisions concerning contracts are of particular relevance. Although the Act applies only to the processing of personal data, there is nothing to stop service providers imposing such contracts as regards the processing of traffic data relating to corporate subscribers.

Consent to process for the above purposes   40.29

Where traffic data is processed for the above purposes the prior consent of the subscriber or user of the line or account must be obtained. In the case of a corporate subscriber, it is reasonable for the communications provider to accept at face value the assurances of a person holding himself out as capable of giving consent on the part of the company unless the communications provider has reasonable grounds to believe otherwise.

The Regulations do not prescribe how service providers should obtain this consent. However, in order to obtain valid informed consent, the subscriber or user should be given sufficient clear information in order for them to have a broad appreciation of how the data are going to be used and the consequences of giving consent to such use. In light of this, the service provider will not be able to rely on a blanket 'catch all' statement on a bill or a website, but will be required to obtain specific informed consent for each value added service requested and for the marketing of their own electronic communications services.

Where, for example, a value added service is provided by a communications provider in conjunction with a third party, in the interests of transparency the consent to process for such a purpose should be obtained by the person who will be seen to be responsible for providing that service. Whether this will be the service provider, the third party or both will depend on the specific circumstances. The point is that the way in which a service is provided should be consistent with the expectations of the subscriber or user. Where the user provides consent to one party for the purpose of the provision of a particular service, they should not then be surprised when they are contacted by another party relating to the provision of that service.

The Regulations also specifically require that the subscriber or user is provided with information regarding the types of traffic data which are to be processed and the duration of such processing. Any such consent given by the subscriber or user to process related traffic data may be withdrawn at any time by that subscriber or user.

General provisions relating to the processing of traffic data   40.30

The Regulations allow the processing of traffic data by a public communications provider in the course of its business for the following purposes:

- the management of billing or traffic;
- customer enquiries; and
- the prevention and detection of fraud.

The processing of traffic data is to be restricted to what is necessary for these activities and by persons acting under proper authority.

Disputes   40.31

Nothing is to prevent the furnishing of traffic data to a person who has been given statutory authority to resolve disputes, for example OFCOM.

Location Data   40.32

Location data means any data processed in an electronic communications network indicating the geographical position of the terminal equipment of a user of a public electronic communications service, including information relating to:

- the latitude, longitude or altitude of the terminal equipment;
- the direction of travel of the user; or
- the time the location information was recorded.

Restrictions on processing   40.33

Location data relating to a subscriber or user of a public electronic communications network may only be processed where:

- the subscriber or user cannot be identified from that data; or
- where it is necessary for the provisions of a value added service with the consent of the relevant user or subscriber.

Location data shall only be processed by the communications provider in question, the third party provider of the value added service or a person acting on behalf of either of the above. Where the processing is carried out for the purposes of the provision of a value added service, the processing of location data should be restricted to what is necessary for those purposes.

Again, as ultimate responsibility for compliance with the Regulations regarding the processing of location data lies with the communications provider, the requirements of the seventh data principle of the *Data Protection Act* should be observed, particularly as regards the processing of personal data carried out by a data processor. Although the Act applies only to the processing of personal data, there is nothing to stop service providers imposing such contracts with regard to the processing of location data from which an individual cannot be identified.

Consent to process

The public communications provider must obtain the prior consent of the user or subscriber to process location data for the purposes of providing a value added service (where the user or subscriber can be identified from that data). Before consent can be obtained the communications provider must provide the user or subscriber with the following information:

- the types of location data that will be processed;
- the purposes and duration of the processing of those data; and
- whether the data will be transmitted to a third party for the purposes of providing the value added service.

In the case of a corporate subscriber, a person holding himself out as capable of making decisions on the part of the company is likely to be able to give consent, unless the communications provider has reasonable grounds to believe otherwise. The Regulations do not prescribe how service providers should obtain this consent. However, in order to obtain valid informed consent, the subscriber or user should be given sufficient clear information in order for them to have a broad appreciation of how the data are going to be used and the consequences of giving consent to such use. In light of this, the service provider will not be able to rely on a blanket 'catch all' statement on a bill or a website, but rather will be required to obtain specific informed consent for each value added service requested and for the marketing of their own electronic communications services.

Where a valued added service is provided by a public communications provider in conjunction with a third party, in the interests of transparency it is likely that the consent to process location data for such a purpose should be obtained by the person who will be seen to be responsible for providing the service. Whether this will be the service provider or the third party will depend on the specific circumstances. The point is that the way in which a service is provided should be consistent with the expectations of the subscriber or user. Where the user provides consent to one party for the purpose of the provision of a particular service, they should not then be surprised when they are contacted by another party relating to the provision of that service.

Where a user or subscriber has given informed consent to the processing of location data, the user or subscriber shall be able to withdraw that consent at any time and the communications provider should make the user or subscriber aware of that fact. The user or subscriber should also be provided with an opportunity to withdraw their consent on the occasion of each connection to the network or on each transmission of a communication. Although the obligation is to provide for a permanent withdrawal of consent, there is nothing in the Regulations that will prevent the service provider from also offering the user the chance to suspend their consent for a limited, specified period of time. If the user chooses to accept such an option, there is similarly nothing to prevent the provider from 'reactivating' their consent after the specified period of time has elapsed, providing the intention to do so was made sufficiently clear at the time at which the user opted for a time bound suspension.

Further Information   40.34

The Home Office's website provides the fullest information on *RIPA 2000*. A useful page is www.homeoffice.gov.uk/ripa/ripact.htm, which also contains access to the three 2002 Codes of Practice.

See also **3 CODES OF PRACTICE** and **38 RECORDING TELEPHONE CALLS AND EMAILS**.

15 EMAILS and **16 EMPLOYMENT** examine monitoring in relation to email and employment respectively.

The Privacy Foundation of the US has a website at www.privacyfoundation.org

Information on *RIPA 2000* can be obtained by post from the following address.

RIPA Implementation Team
Room 735
Home Office
50 Queen Anne's Gate
London
SW1H 9AT

FAQs

What has *RIPA 2000* to do with data protection?

Interception of individuals' personal data can have security implications. The *Lawful Business Practice Regulations 2000* which allow limited interception are made under *RIPA 2000*.

What are the data protection implications of the *Regulation of Investigatory Powers (Maintenance of Interception Capability) Order 2002*?

The Order, which came into force on 1 August 2002, requires ISPs to retain and intercept communications data. Such retention may be expensive for them but should aid law enforcement.

What are the three Codes of Practice in force from August 2002?

They are (i) the Interception Code of Practice (ii) the Covert Human Intelligence Source Code of Practice and (iii) the Covert Surveillance Code of Practice.

Chapter 41 –
'Safe Harbor' Agreement

At A Glance

✓   The Eighth Data Protection Principle prohibits the export of personal data from the European Economic Area ('EEA') except where strict conditions are met.

✓   The EU and US agreed a Safe Harbor Agreement in July 2000 which permits such exports where the US recipient has signed the Safe Harbor Agreement

✓   The agreement is not the only lawful manner in which personal data can be exported to the US. The Eighth Principle permits exports on other conditions, such as when the EU Model Clauses for data export apply.

✓   The US has a safe harbor website on which information of relevance appears. The US Safe Harbor website FAQs are given at the end of this Chapter.

Introduction 41.1

The Eighth Data Protection Principle requires that personal data should not be exported without compliance with the requirements of that principle as set down in *DPA 1998*. On July 2000 the US agreed its 'Safe Harbor' agreement with the EU to permit exports of personal data to the US by those companies registering in the US as prepared to comply with the US Safe Harbor Agreement. Only those who register and meet the requirements can benefit from the Safe Harbor Agreement This is not the only lawful means of such data export, and often instead the EU Model Clauses can be used (see **APPENDIX 3**, and also the Frequently Asked Questions on the Model Clauses in **APPENDIX 2**) or other requirements of the Eighth Principle satisfied.

Coverage 41.2

The Model Clauses apply to e-commerce but not to financial services. They are intended to aid businesses shipping personal data between the EEA and the US. On 25 August 2000, the EU published its decision adopting the Safe Harbor Agreement (OJ L215/7) under the *Data Protection Directive (95/46/EC)*. The US

Government has said that failure to comply with data protection laws will be considered a deceptive business practice and a prosecutable offence. The US Commerce Department runs a register of industry self-regulators, and monitors those companies to ensure that they comply with privacy rules. Regulators are required to reapply for membership of the list each year. The Federal Trade Commission ('FTC') and the US judicial system will be able to impose sanctions on companies that violate the rules.

The US safe harbor website is at www.export.gov/safeharbor/

How to Comply with the Rules   41.3

Companies are able to comply with the rules in four ways:

- by reporting to a data protection authority in Europe;
- by subjecting themselves to monitoring by US lawmakers;
- by joining a self-regulatory body, which will be monitored by the US FTC; or
- if a company is not online, by committing itself to obey a new European panel of data privacy officials.

Companies like Amazon.com, for example, will also be obliged to insert a link on their websites to their data privacy regulator in order to inform customers of the protection being provided.

Enforcement   41.4

Enforcement is expected to take place in the US under US law, and the Department of Commerce expects it to be largely private sector enforcement: 'The effect of these statutes is to give an organisation's safe harbor commitments the force of law *vis-a-vis* that organisation.'

The Department of Commerce states the following.

> 'Private Sector Enforcement: As part of their safe harbor obligations, organisations are required to have in place a dispute resolution system that will investigate and resolve individual complaints and disputes and procedures for verifying compliance. They are also required to remedy problems arising out of a failure to comply with the principles. Sanctions that dispute resolution bodies can apply must be severe enough to ensure compliance by the organisation; they must include publicity for findings of non-compliance and deletion of data in certain circumstances. They may also include suspension from membership in a privacy program (and thus effectively suspension from the safe harbor) and injunctive orders.

The dispute resolution, verification, and remedy requirements can be satisfied in different ways. For example, an organisation could comply with a private sector developed privacy seal program that incorporates and satisfies the safe harbor principles. If the seal program, however, only provides for dispute resolution and remedies but not verification, then the organisation would have to satisfy the verification requirement in an alternative way.

Organisations can also satisfy the dispute resolution and remedy requirements through compliance with government supervisory authorities or by committing to co-operate with data protection authorities located in Europe.

Government Enforcement: Depending on the industry sector, the comparable US government agencies, overarching government enforcement of company relies in whole or in part the safe harbor principles, its failure must be actionable under federal or ptive acts or it is not eligible to join nisations that are subject to the juris-mmission or the Department of rriers and ticket agents may partici-deral Trade Commission and the h respect to air carriers and ticket he European Commission that they organisations that state that they are in compliance with the safe harbor framework but then fail to live up to their statements.

Under the Federal Trade Commission Act, for example, a company's failure to abide by commitments to implement the safe harbor principles might be considered deceptive and actionable by the Federal Trade Commission. This is the case even where an organisation adhering to the safe harbor principles relies entirely on self-regulation to provide the enforcement required by the safe harbor enforcement principle. The FTC has the power to rectify such misrepresentations by seeking administrative orders and civil penalties of up to $12,000 per day for violations.

Failure to Comply with the Safe Harbor Requirements: If an organisation persistently fails to comply with the safe harbor requirements, it is no longer entitled to benefit from the safe harbor. Persistent failure to comply arises where an organisation refuses to comply with a final determination by any self-regulatory or government body or where such a body determines that an organisation frequently fails to comply with the requirements to the point where its claim to comply is no longer credible. In these cases, the organisation must promptly notify the Department of Commerce of such facts. Failure to do so may be actionable under the False Statements Act (18 U.S.C. § 1001).

The Department of Commerce will indicate on the public list it maintains of organisations self certifying adherence to the safe harbor requirements any notification it receives of persistent failure to comply and will make clear which organisations are assured and which organisations are no longer assured of safe harbor benefits.

An organisation applying to participate in a self-regulatory body for the purposes of re-qualifying for the safe harbor must provide that body with full information about its prior participation in the safe harbor.'

Further Information 41.5

The US safe harbor website is at www.export.gov/safeharbor/.

Documents relating to safe harbor, including Frequently Asked Questions, are at www.export.gov/safeharbor/sh_documents.html.

The list of companies registered under safe harbor is at http://web.ita.doc.gov/safeharbor/shlist.nsf/webPages/safe+harbor+list.

The European Commission's Decision, published August 2000, adopting the Safe Harbor Agreement is at http://europa.eu.int/comm/trade/pdf/safeharbour.pdf.

See **20 EXPORT OF DATA** and **44 TRANSBORDER DATA FLOWS**. For export of employee data see **16 EMPLOYMENT**. **36 PRINCIPLES** also covers the Eighth Principle. **APPENDICES 2** and **3** give the Commission's Frequently Asked Questions about the Model Clauses and the Model Clauses for export to data controllers and data processors respectively. For amendments to the Model Clauses see http://europa.eu.int/comm/internal_market/en/dataprot/news/annotateddecision.pdf

FAQs 41.6

The US Department of Commerce summarise the requirements thus.

What do the safe harbor principles require?

Organisations must comply with the seven safe harbor principles. The principles require the following.

Notice: Organisations must notify individuals about the purposes for which they collect and use information about them. They must provide information about how individuals can contact the organisation with any inquiries or complaints, the types of third parties to which it discloses the information and the choices and means the organisation offers for limiting its use and disclosure.

Choice: Organisations must give individuals the opportunity to choose ('opt-out') whether their personal information will be disclosed to a third party or used for a purpose incompatible with the purpose for which it was originally collected or subsequently authorised by the individual. For sensitive information, affirmative or explicit ('opt-in') choice must be given if the information is to be disclosed to a third party or used for a purpose other than its original purpose, or the purpose authorised subsequently by the individual.

Onward Transfer (Transfers to Third Parties): To disclose information to a third party, organisations must apply the notice and choice principles. Where an organisation wishes to transfer information to a third party that is acting as an agent, it may do so if it makes sure that the third party subscribes to the safe harbor principles or is subject to the Directive or another adequacy finding. As an alternative, the organisation can enter into a written agreement with such third party requiring that the third party provide at least the same level of privacy protection as is required by the relevant principles.

Access: Individuals must have access to personal information about them that an organisation holds and be able to correct, amend, or delete that information where it is inaccurate, except where the burden or expense of providing access would be disproportionate to the risks to the individual's privacy in the case in question, or where the rights of persons other than the individual would be violated.

Security: Organisations must take reasonable precautions to protect personal information from loss, misuse and unauthorised access, disclosure, alteration and destruction.

Data integrity: Personal information must be relevant for the purposes for which it is to be used. An organisation should take reasonable steps to ensure that data is reliable for its intended use, accurate, complete, and current.

Enforcement: In order to ensure compliance with the safe harbor principles, there must be:

(a) readily available and affordable independent recourse mechanisms so that each individual's complaints and disputes can be investigated and resolved, and damages awarded where the applicable law or private sector initiatives so provide;

(b) procedures for verifying that the commitments companies make to adhere to the safe harbor principles have been implemented; and

(c) obligations to remedy problems arising out of a failure to comply with the principles.

Sanctions must be sufficiently rigorous to ensure compliance by the organisation. Organisations that fail to provide annual self-certification letters will no

(cont'd)

longer appear in the list of participants and safe harbor benefits will no longer be assured.

To provide further guidance, the Department of Commerce has issued a set of frequently asked questions and answers ('FAQs') that clarify and supplement the safe harbor principles.

These cover the following topics and are accessible under Documents on the safe harbor website at www.export.gov/safeharbor/sh_documents.html.

(*a*)   Sensitive Data.

(*b*)   Journalistic Exceptions.

(*c*)   Secondary Liability.

(*d*)   Investment Banking and Audits.

(*e*)   The Role of Data Protection Authorities.

(*f*)   Self-Certification.

(*g*)   Verification.

(*h*)   Access.

(*j*)   Human Resources.

(*k*)   Article 17 Contracts.

(*l*)   Dispute Resolution and Enforcement.

(*m*)   Choice – Timing of Opt-out.

(*n*)   Travel Information.

(*o*)   Pharmaceutical and Medical Products.

(*p*)   Public Record and Publicly Available Information.

Safe Harbor FAQs 41.7

FAQ 1 – Sensitive data

Must an organisation always provide explicit (opt in) choice with respect to sensitive data?

No, such choice is not required where the processing is:

- in the vital interests of the data subject or another person;

- necessary for the establishment of legal claims or defences;

- required to provide medical care or diagnosis;

- carried out in the course of legitimate activities by a foundation, association or any other non-profit body with a political, philosophical, religious or trade-union aim and on condition that the processing relates solely to the members of the body or to the persons who have regular contact with it in connection with its purposes and that the data are not disclosed to a third party without the consent of the data subjects;

- necessary to carry out the organisation's obligations in the field of employment law; or

- related to data that are manifestly made public by the individual.

FAQ 2 – Journalistic exceptions

Given US constitutional protections for freedom of the press and the Directive's exemption for journalistic material, do the Safe Harbor Principles apply to personal information gathered, maintained, or disseminated for journalistic purposes?

Where the rights of a free press embodied in the First Amendment of the US Constitution intersect with privacy protection interests, the First Amendment must govern the balancing of these interests with regard to the activities of US persons or organisations. Personal information that is gathered for publication, broadcast or other forms of public communication of journalistic material, whether used or not, as well as information found in previously published material disseminated from media archives, is not subject to the requirements of the Safe Harbor Principles.

FAQ 3 – secondary liability

Are Internet service providers (ISPs), telecommunications carriers or other organisations liable under the Safe Harbor Principles when on behalf of another organisation they merely transmit, route, switch or cache information that may violate their terms?

No. As is the case with the Directive itself, the safe harbor does not create secondary liability. To the extent that an organisation is acting as a mere conduit

(cont'd)

---

for data transmitted by third parties and does not determine the purposes and means of processing those personal data, it would not be liable.

FAQ 4 – investment banking and audits

The activities of auditors and investment bankers may involve processing personal data without the consent or knowledge of the individual. Under what circumstances is this permitted by the notice, choice, and access principles?

Investment bankers or auditors may process information without knowledge of the individual only to the extent and for the period necessary to meet statutory or public interest requirements and in other circumstances in which the application of these principles would prejudice the legitimate interests of the organisation. These legitimate interests include the monitoring of companies' compliance with their legal obligations and legitimate accounting activities, and the need for confidentiality connected with possible acquisitions, mergers, joint ventures or other similar transactions carried out by investment bankers or auditors.

FAQ 5 – the role of the data protection authorities

How will companies that commit to co-operate with European Union data protection authorities (DPAs) make those commitments and how will they be implemented?

Under the safe harbor, US organisations receiving personal data from the EU must commit to employ effective mechanisms for assuring compliance with the Safe Harbor Principles. More specifically as set out in the enforcement principle, they must provide

(a)   recourse for individuals to whom the data relate;

(b)   follow up procedures for verifying that the attestations and assertions they have made about their privacy practices are true; and

(c)   obligations to remedy problems arising out of failure to comply with the principles and consequences for such organisations.

An organisation may satisfy points (a) and (c) of the enforcement principle if it adheres to the requirements of this FAQ for co-operating with the DPAs.

An organisation may commit to cooperate with the DPAs by declaring in its safe harbor certification to the Department of Commerce that the organisation:

●   elects to satisfy the requirement in points (a) and (c) of the Safe Harbor Enforcement Principle by committing to co-operate with the DPAs;

●   will co-operate with the DPAs in the investigation and resolution of complaints brought under the safe harbor; and

- will comply with any advice given by the DPAs where the DPAs take the view that the organisation needs to take specific action to comply with the Safe Harbor Principles, including remedial or compensatory measures for the benefit of individuals affected by any non-compliance with the principles, and will provide the DPAs with written confirmation that such action has been taken.

The co-operation of the DPAs will be provided in the form of information and advice in the following way:

- The advice of the DPAs will be delivered through an informal panel of DPAs established at the European Union level, which will *inter alia* help ensure a harmonised and coherent approach.

- The panel will provide advice to the US organisations concerned on unresolved complaints from individuals about the handling of personal information that has been transferred from the EU under the safe harbor. This advice will be designed to ensure that the Safe Harbor Principles are being correctly applied and will include any remedies for the individual(s) concerned that the DPAs consider appropriate.

- The panel will provide such advice in response to referrals from the organisations concerned and/or to complaints received directly from individuals against organisations which have committed to co-operate with DPAs for safe harbor purposes, while encouraging and, if necessary, helping such individuals in the first instance to use the in-house complaint handling arrangements that the organisation may offer.

- Advice will be issued only after both sides in a dispute have had a reasonable opportunity to comment and to provide any evidence they wish. The panel will seek to deliver advice as quickly as this requirement for due process allows. As a general rule, the panel will aim to provide advice within 60 days after receiving a complaint or referral and more quickly where possible.

- The panel will make public the results of its consideration of complaints submitted to it, if it sees fit.

- The delivery of advice through the panel will not give rise to any liability for the panel or for individual DPAs.

As noted above, organisations choosing this option for dispute resolution must undertake to comply with the advice of the DPAs. If an organisation fails to comply within 25 days of the delivery of the advice and has offered no satisfactory explanation for the delay, the panel will give notice of its intention either to submit the matter to the Federal Trade Commission or another US federal or state body with statutory powers to take enforcement action in cases of deception or misrepresentation, or to conclude that the agreement to co-operate has been seriously breached and must, therefore, be considered null and

(cont'd)

void. In the latter case, the panel will inform the Department of Commerce (or its designee) so that the list of safe harbor participants can be duly amended. Any failure to fulfil the undertaking to co-operate with the DPAs, as well as failures to comply with the Safe Harbor Principles, will be actionable as a deceptive practice under *Section 5* of the *Federal Trade Commission Act 1914* or other similar statute.

Organisations choosing this option will be required to pay an annual fee which will be designed to cover the operating costs of the panel, and they may additionally be asked to meet any necessary translation expenses arising out of the panel's consideration of referrals or complaints against them. The annual fee will not exceed $500 and will be less for smaller companies.

The option of co-operating with the DPAs will be available to organisations joining the safe harbor during a three-year period. The DPAs will reconsider this arrangement before the end of that period if the number of US organisations choosing this option proves to be excessive.

FAQ 6 – self-certification

How does an organisation self-certify that it adheres to the Safe Harbor Principles?

Safe harbor benefits are assured from the date on which an organisation self-certifies to the Department of Commerce (or its designee) its adherence to the principles in accordance with the guidance set forth below.

To self-certify for the safe harbor, organisations can provide to the Department of Commerce (or its designee) a letter, signed by a corporate officer on behalf of the organisation that is joining the safe harbor, that contains at least the following information:

(1)   name of organisation, mailing address, email address, telephone and fax numbers;

(2)   description of the activities of the organisation with respect to personal information received from the EU; and

(3)   description of the organisation's privacy policy for such personal information, including:

- where the privacy policy is available for viewing by the public;

- its effective date of implementation;

- a contact office for the handling of complaints, access requests and any other issues arising under the safe harbor;

- the specific statutory body that has jurisdiction to hear any claims against the organisation regarding possible unfair or deceptive practices and violations of laws or regulations governing privacy (and that is listed in the annex to the principles);

- name of any privacy programs in which the organisation is a member;

- method of verification (eg in-house, third party); and

- the independent recourse mechanism that is available to investigate unresolved complaints.

Where the organisation wishes its safe harbor benefits to cover human resources information transferred from the EU for use in the context of the employment relationship, it may do so where there is a statutory body with jurisdiction to hear claims against the organisation arising out of human resources information that is listed in the annex to the principles. In addition, the organisation must indicate this in its letter and declare its commitment to co-operate with the EU authority or authorities concerned in conformity with FAQ 9 and FAQ 5, as applicable, and that it will comply with the advice given by such authorities.

The department (or its designee) will maintain a list of all organisations that file such letters, thereby assuring the availability of safe harbor benefits, and will update such list on the basis of annual letters and notifications received pursuant to FAQ 11. Such self-certification letters should be provided not less than annually, otherwise the organisation will be removed from the list and safe harbor benefits will no longer be assured. Both the list and the self-certification letters submitted by the organisations will be made publicly available. All organisations that self-certify for the safe harbor must also state in their relevant published privacy policy statements that they adhere to the Safe Harbor Principles.

The undertaking to adhere to the Safe Harbor Principles is not time-limited in respect of data received during the period in which the organisation enjoys the benefits of the safe harbor. Its undertaking means that it will continue to apply the principles to such data for as long as the organisation stores, uses or discloses them, even if it subsequently leaves the safe harbor for any reason.

An organisation that will cease to exist as a separate legal entity as a result of a merger or a takeover must notify the Department of Commerce (or its designee) of this in advance. The notification should also indicate whether the acquiring entity or the entity resulting from the merger will:

(1) continue to be bound by the Safe Harbor Principles by the operation of law governing the takeover or merger; or

(2) elect to self-certify its adherence to the Safe Harbor Principles or put in place other safeguards, such as a written agreement that will ensure adherence to the Safe Harbor Principles.

Where neither (1) nor (2) applies, any data that has been acquired under the safe harbor must be promptly deleted.

(cont'd)

An organisation does not need to subject all personal information to the Safe Harbor Principles, but it must subject to the Safe Harbor Principles all personal data received from the EU after it joins the safe harbor.

Any misrepresentation to the general public concerning an organisation's adherence to the Safe Harbor Principles may be actionable by the Federal Trade Commission or other relevant government body. Misrepresentations to the Department of Commerce (or its designee) may be actionable under the *False Statements Act (18 USC § 1001)*.

FAQ 7 – verification

How do organisations provide follow up procedures for verifying that the attestations and assertions they make about their safe harbor privacy practices are true and those privacy practices have been implemented as represented and in accordance with the Safe Harbor Principles?

To meet the verification requirements of the Enforcement Principle, an organisation may verify such attestations and assertions either through self-assessment or outside compliance reviews.

Under the self-assessment approach, such verification would have to indicate that an organisation's published privacy policy regarding personal information received from the EU is accurate, comprehensive, prominently displayed, completely implemented and accessible. It would also need to indicate that its privacy policy conforms to the Safe Harbor Principles; that individuals are informed of any in-house arrangements for handling complaints and of the independent mechanisms through which they may pursue complaints; that it has in place procedures for training employees in its implementation, and disciplining them for failure to follow it; and that it has in place internal procedures for periodically conducting objective reviews of compliance with the above. A statement verifying the self-assessment should be signed by a corporate officer or another authorised representative of the organisation at least once a year and made available upon request by individuals or in the context of an investigation or a complaint about non-compliance.

Organisations should retain their records on the implementation of their safe harbor privacy practices and make them available upon request in the context of an investigation or a complaint about non-compliance to the independent body responsible for investigating complaints or to the agency with unfair and deceptive practices jurisdiction.

Where the organisation has chosen outside compliance review, such a review needs to demonstrate that its privacy policy regarding personal information received from the EU conforms to the Safe Harbor Principles, that it is being complied with and that individuals are informed of the mechanisms through which they may pursue complaints. The methods of review may include without limitation auditing, random reviews, use of 'decoys' or use of technology tools as appropriate. A statement verifying that an outside compliance review has been successfully completed should be signed either by the reviewer or by the corporate officer or another authorised representative of the organisation at least once a year and made available upon request by individuals or in the context of an investigation or a complaint about compliance.

FAQ 8 – access

Access principle

Individuals must have access to personal information about them that an organisation holds and must be able to correct, amend or delete that information where it is inaccurate, except where the burden or expense of providing access would be disproportionate to the risks to the individual's privacy in the case in question or where the legitimate rights of persons other than the individual would be violated.

Is the right of access absolute?

No. Under the Safe Harbor Principles, the right of access is fundamental to privacy protection. In particular, it allows individuals to verify the accuracy of information held about them. Nonetheless, the obligation of an organisation to provide access to the personal information it holds about an individual is subject to the principle of proportionality or reasonableness and has to be tempered in certain instances. Indeed, the Explanatory Memorandum to the 1980 OECD Privacy Guidelines makes clear that an organisation's access obligation is not absolute. It does not require the exceedingly thorough search mandated, for example, by a subpoena, nor does it require access to all the different forms in which the information may be maintained by the organisation.

Rather, experience has shown that in responding to individuals' access requests, organisations should first be guided by the concern(s) that led to the requests in the first place. For example, if an access request is vague or broad in scope, an organisation may engage the individual in a dialogue so as to better understand the motivation for the request and to locate responsive information. The organisation might inquire about which part(s) of the organisation the individual interacted with and/or about the nature of the information (or its use) that is the subject of the access request. Individuals do not, however, have to justify requests for access to their own data.

Expense and burden are important factors and should be taken into account, but they are not controlling in determining whether providing access is reasonable. For example, if the information is used for decisions that will significantly affect the individual (eg the denial or grant of important benefits, such as insurance, a mortgage or a job), then consistent with the other provisions of these FAQs, the organisation would have to disclose that information even if it is relatively difficult or expensive to provide.

(cont'd)

If the information requested is not sensitive or not used for decisions that will significantly affect the individual (eg, non-sensitive marketing data that is used to determine whether or not to send the individual a catalogue), but is readily available and inexpensive to provide, an organisation would have to provide access to factual information that the organisation stores about the individual. The information concerned could include facts obtained from the individual, facts gathered in the course of a transaction or facts obtained from others that pertain to the individual.

Consistent with the fundamental nature of access, organisations should always make good faith efforts to provide access. For example, where certain information needs to be protected and can be readily separated from other information subject to an access request, the organisation should redact the protected information and make available the other information. If an organisation determines that access should be denied in any particular instance, it should provide the individual requesting access with an explanation of why it has made that determination and a contact point for any further inquiries.

What is confidential commercial information and may organisations deny access in order to safeguard it?

Confidential commercial information (as that term is used in the Federal Rules of Civil Procedure on discovery) is information which an organisation has taken steps to protect from disclosure, where disclosure would help a competitor in the market. The particular computer program an organisation uses, such as a modeling program, or the details of that program may be confidential commercial information. Where confidential commercial information can be readily separated from other information subject to an access request, the organisation should redact the confidential commercial information and make available the non-confidential information. Organisations may deny or limit access to the extent that granting it would reveal its own confidential commercial information as defined above, such as marketing inferences or classifications generated by the organisation or the confidential commercial information of another where such information is subject to a contractual obligation of confidentiality in circumstances where such an obligation of confidentiality would normally be undertaken or imposed.

In providing access, may an organisation disclose to individuals personal information about them derived from its data bases or is access to the data base itself required?

Access can be provided in the form of disclosure by an organisation to the individual and does not require access by the individual to an organisation's data base.

Does an organisation have to restructure its data bases to be able to provide access?

Access needs to be provided only to the extent that an organisation stores the information. The access principle does not itself create any obligation to retain, maintain, reorganise or restructure personal information files.

These replies make clear that access may be denied in certain circumstances. In what other circumstances may an organisation deny individuals access to their personal information?

Such circumstances are limited and any reasons for denying access must be specific. An organisation can refuse to provide access to information to the extent that disclosure is likely to interfere with the safeguarding of important countervailing public interests, such as national security; defense or public security. In addition, where personal information is processed *solely* for research or statistical purposes, access may be denied. Other reasons for denying or limiting access are:

- interference with execution or enforcement of the law, including the prevention, investigation or detection of offences or the right to a fair trial;

- interference with private causes of action, including the prevention, investigation or detection of legal claims or the right to a fair trial;

- disclosure of personal information pertaining to other individual(s) where such references cannot be redacted;

- breaching a legal or other professional privilege or obligation;

- breaching the necessary confidentiality of future or ongoing negotiations, such as those involving the acquisition of publicly quoted companies;

- prejudicing employee security investigations or grievance proceedings;

- prejudicing the confidentiality that may be necessary for limited periods in connection with employee succession planning and corporate re-organisations; or

- prejudicing the confidentiality that may be necessary in connection with monitoring, inspection or regulatory functions connected with sound economic or financial management; or

- other circumstances in which the burden or cost of providing access would be disproportionate or the legitimate rights or interests of others would be violated.

An organisation which claims an exception has the burden of demonstrating its applicability (as is normally the case). As noted above, the reasons for denying or limiting access and a contact point for further inquires should be given to individuals.

(cont'd)

Can an organisation charge a fee to cover the cost of providing access?

Yes. The OECD Guidelines recognise that organisations may charge a fee, provided that it is not excessive. Thus, organisations may charge a reasonable fee for access. Charging a fee may be useful in discouraging repetitive and vexatious requests.

Organisations that are in the business of selling publicly available information may thus charge the organisation's customary fee in responding to requests for access. Individuals may alternatively seek access to their information from the organisation that originally compiled the data.

Access may not be refused on cost grounds if the individual offers to pay the costs.

Is an organisation required to provide access to personal information derived from public records?

To clarify first, public records are those records kept by government agencies or entities at any level that are open to consultation by the public in general. It is not necessary to apply the Access Principle to such information as long as it is not combined with other personal information, apart from when small amounts of non-public record information are used for indexing or organising public record information. However, any conditions for consultation established by the relevant jurisdiction are to be respected. Where public record information is combined with other non-public record information (other than as specifically noted above), however, an organisation must provide access to all such information, assuming it is not subject to other permitted exceptions.

Does the Access Principle have to be applied to publicly available personal information?

As with public record information, it is not necessary to provide access to information that is already publicly available to the public at large, as long as it is not combined with non-publicly available information.

How can an organisation protect itself against repetitious or vexatious requests for access?

An organisation does not have to respond to such requests for access. For these reasons, organisations may charge a reasonable fee and may set reasonable limits on the number of times within a given period that access requests from a particular individual will be met. In setting such limitations, an organisation should consider such factors as the frequency with which information is updated, the purpose for which the data are used, and the nature of the information.

How can an organisation protect itself against fraudulent requests for access?

An organisation is not required to provide access unless it is supplied with sufficient information to allow it to confirm the identity of the person making the request.

Is there a time within which responses must be provided to access requests?

Yes, organisations should respond without excessive delay and within a reasonable time period. This requirement may be satisfied in different ways as the explanatory memorandum to the 1980 OECD Privacy Guidelines states. For example, a data controller who provides information to data subjects at regular intervals may be exempted from obligations to respond at once to individual requests.

FAQ 9 – human resources

Is the transfer from the EU to the United States of personal information collected in the context of the employment relationship covered by the safe harbor?

Yes, where a company in the EU transfers personal information about its employees (past or present) collected in the context of the employment relationship, to a parent, affiliate or unaffiliated service provider in the United States participating in the safe harbor, the transfer enjoys the benefits of the safe harbor. In such cases, the collection of the information and its processing prior to transfer will have been subject to the national laws of the EU country where it was collected and any conditions for or restrictions on its transfer according to those laws will have to be respected.

The Safe Harbor Principles are relevant only when individually identified records are transferred or accessed. Statistical reporting relying on aggregate employment data and/or the use of anonymised or pseudonymised data does not raise privacy concerns.

How do the notice and choice principles apply to such information?

A US organisation that has received employee information from the EU under the safe harbor may disclose it to third parties and/or use it for different purposes only in accordance with the notice and choice principles. For example, where an organisation intends to use personal information collected through the employment relationship for non–employment related purposes, such as marketing communications, the US organisation must provide the affected individuals with choice before doing so, unless they have already authorised the use of the information for such purposes. Moreover, such choices must not be used to restrict employment opportunities or take any punitive action against such employees.

(cont'd)

It should be noted that certain generally applicable conditions for transfer from some Member States may preclude other uses of such information even after transfer outside the EU and such conditions will have to be respected.

In addition, employers should make reasonable efforts to accommodate employee privacy preferences. This could include, for example, restricting access to the data, anonymising certain data or assigning codes or pseudonyms when the actual names are not required for the management purpose at hand.

To the extent and for the period necessary to avoid prejudicing the legitimate interests of the organisation in making promotions, appointments or other similar employment decisions, an organisation does not need to offer notice and choice.

How does the access principle apply?

The FAQs on access provide guidance on reasons which may justify denying or limiting access on request in the human resources context. Of course, employers in the European Union must comply with local regulations and ensure that European Union employees have access to such information as is required by law in their home countries, regardless of the location of data processing and storage. The safe harbor requires that an organisation processing such data in the United States will co-operate in providing such access either directly or through the EU employer.

How will enforcement be handled for employee data under the Safe Harbor Principles?

In so far as information is used only in the context of the employment relationship, primary responsibility for the data *vis-à-vis* the employee remains with the company in the EU. It follows that, where European employees make complaints about violations of their data protection rights and are not satisfied with the results of internal review, complaint and appeal procedures (or any applicable grievance procedures under a contract with a trade union), they should be directed to the state or national data protection or labor authority in the jurisdiction where the employee works. This also includes cases where the alleged mishandling of their personal information has taken place in the United States, is the responsibility of the US organisation that has received the information from the employer and not of the employer and thus involves an alleged breach of the Safe Harbor Principles, rather than of national laws implementing the Directive. This will be the most efficient way to address the often overlapping rights and obligations imposed by local labor law and labor agreements, as well as data protection law.

A US organisation participating in the safe harbor that uses EU human resources data transferred from the Europe Union in the context of the employment relationship and that wishes such transfers to be covered by the safe harbor must, therefore, commit to co-operate in investigations by and to comply with the advice of competent EU authorities in such cases. The DPAs that have agreed to co-operate in this way will notify the European Commission and the Department of Commerce. If a US organisation participating in the safe harbor wishes to transfer human resources data from a Member State where the DPA has not so agreed, the provisions of FAQ 5 will apply.

FAQ 10 – Article 17 contracts

When data is transferred from the EU to the United States only for processing purposes, will a contract be required, regardless of participation by the processor in the safe harbor?

Yes. Data controllers in the European Union are always required to enter into a contract when a transfer for mere processing is made, whether the processing operation is carried out inside or outside the EU. The purpose of the contract is to protect the interests of the data controller, ie the person or body who determines the purposes and means of processing, who retains full responsibility for the data *vis-à-vis* the individual(s) concerned. The contract thus specifies the processing to be carried out and any measures necessary to ensure that the data are kept secure.

A US organisation participating in the safe harbor and receiving personal information from the EU merely for processing thus does not have to apply the principles to this information, because the controller in the EU remains responsible for it *vis-à-vis* the individual in accordance with the relevant EU provisions (which may be more stringent than the equivalent Safe Harbor Principles).

Because adequate protection is provided by safe harbor participants, contracts with safe harbor participants for mere processing do not require prior authorisation (or such authorisation will be granted automatically by the Member States) as would be required for contracts with recipients not participating in the safe harbor or otherwise not providing adequate protection.

FAQ 11 – dispute resolution and enforcement

How should the dispute resolution requirements of the enforcement principle be implemented, and how will an organisation's persistent failure to comply with the principles be handled?

The enforcement principle sets out the requirements for safe harbor enforcement. How to meet the requirements of point (b) of the Principle is set out in the FAQ on verification (FAQ 7). This FAQ 11 addresses points (a) and (c), both of which require independent recourse mechanisms. These mechanisms may take different forms, but they must meet the enforcement principle's requirements. Organisations may satisfy the requirements through the following:

(cont'd)

(1) compliance with private sector developed privacy programs that incorporate the Safe Harbor Principles into their rules and that include effective enforcement mechanisms of the type described in the enforcement principle;

(2) compliance with legal or regulatory supervisory authorities that provide for handling of individual complaints and dispute resolution; or

(3) commitment to co-operate with data protection authorities located in the European Union or their authorised representatives. This list is intended to be illustrative and not limiting. The private sector may design other mechanisms to provide enforcement, so long as they meet the requirements of the enforcement principle and the FAQs. Please note that the enforcement principle's requirements are additional to the requirement set forth in paragraph 3 of the introduction to the principles that self- regulatory efforts must be enforceable under *Article 5* of the *Federal Trade Commission Act* or similar statute.

Recourse mechanisms

Consumers should be encouraged to raise any complaints they may have with the relevant organisation before proceeding to independent recourse mechanisms. Whether a recourse mechanism is independent is a factual question that can be demonstrated in a number of ways, for example, by transparent composition and financing or a proven track record. As required by the enforcement principle, the recourse available to individuals must be readily available and affordable. Dispute resolution bodies should look into each complaint received from individuals unless they are obviously unfounded or frivolous. This does not preclude the establishment of eligibility requirements by the organisation operating the recourse mechanism, but such requirements should be transparent and justified (for example, to exclude complaints that fall outside the scope of the program or are for consideration in another forum), and should not have the effect of undermining the commitment to look into legitimate complaints. In addition, recourse mechanisms should provide individuals with full and readily available information about how the dispute resolution procedure works when they file a complaint. Such information should include notice about the mechanism's privacy practices, in conformity with the Safe Harbor Principles. They should also co-operate in the development of tools such as standard complaint forms to facilitate the complaint resolution process.

Remedies and sanctions

The result of any remedies provided by the dispute resolution body should be that the effects of non-compliance are reversed or corrected by the organisation, in so far as feasible, and that future processing by the organisation will be in conformity with the principles and, where appropriate, that processing of the personal data of the individual who has brought the complaint will cease. Sanctions need to be rigorous enough to ensure compliance by the organisation with the principles. A range of sanctions of varying degrees of severity will allow dispute resolution bodies to respond appropriately to varying degrees of non-compliance. Sanctions should include both publicity for findings of non-compliance and the requirement to delete data in certain circumstances. Other sanctions could include suspension and removal of a seal, compensation for individuals for losses incurred as a result of non-compliance and injunctive orders. Private sector dispute resolution bodies and self-regulatory bodies must notify failures of safe harbor organisations to comply with their rulings to the governmental body with applicable jurisdiction or to the courts, as appropriate, and to notify the Department of Commerce (or its designee).

FTC action

The FTC has committed to reviewing on a priority basis referrals received from privacy self-regulatory organisations, such as BBBOnline and TRUSTe, and EU Member States alleging non-compliance with the Safe Harbor Principles to determine whether *Section 5* of the *FTC Act* prohibiting unfair or deceptive acts or practices in commerce has been violated. If the FTC concludes that it has reason[s] to believe *Section 5* has been violated, it may resolve the matter by seeking an administrative cease and desist order prohibiting the challenged practicesor by filing a complaint in a federal district court, which if successful could result in a federal court order to the same effect. The FTC may obtain civil penalties for violations of an administrative cease and desist order and may pursue civil or criminal contempt for violation of a federal court order. The FTC will notify the Department of Commerce of any such actions it takes. The Department of Commerce encourages other government bodies to notify it of the final disposition of any such referrals or other rulings determining adherence to the Safe Harbor Principles.

Persistent failure to comply

If an organisation persistently fails to comply with the principles, it is no longer entitled to benefit from the safe harbor. Persistent failure to comply arises where an organisation that has self-certified to the Department of Commerce (or its designee) refuses to comply with a final determination by any self-regulatory or government body or where such a body determines that an organisation frequently fails to comply with the principles to the point where its claim to comply is no longer credible. In these cases, the organisation must promptly notify the Department of Commerce (or its designee) of such facts. Failure to do so may be actionable under the *False Statements Act (18 USC § 1001)*.

The Department (or its designee) will indicate on the public list it maintains of organisations self-certifying adherence to the Safe Harbor Principles any notification it receives of persistent failure to comply, whether it is received from the organisation itself, from a self-regulatory body or from a government body, but only after first providing 30 days' notice and an opportunity to

(cont'd)

respond to the organisation that has failed to comply. Accordingly, the public list maintained by the Department of Commerce (or its designee) will make clear which organisations are assured and which organisations are no longer assured of safe harbor benefits.

An organisation applying to participate in a self-regulatory body for the purposes of re-qualifying for the safe harbor must provide that body with full information about its prior participation in the safe harbor.

Dispute resolution bodies are not required to conform with the enforcement principle. They may also derogate from the Principles where they encounter conflicting obligations or explicit authorisations in the performance of their specific tasks.

Dispute resolutions bodies have discretion about the circumstances in which they use these sanctions. The sensitivity of the data concerned is one factor to be taken into consideration in deciding whether deletion of data should be required, as is whether an organisation has collected, used or disclosed information in blatant contravention of the principles.

FAQ 12 – choice – timing of opt out

Does the choice principle permit an individual to exercise choice only at the beginning of a relationship or at any time?

Generally, the purpose of the choice principle is to ensure that personal information is used and disclosed in ways that are consistent with the individual's expectations and choices. Accordingly, an individual should be able to exercise 'opt out' (or choice) of having personal information used for direct marketing at any time subject to reasonable limits established by the organisation, such as giving the organisation time to make the opt out effective. An organisation may also require sufficient information to confirm the identity of the individual requesting the 'opt out'. In the United States, individuals may be able to exercise this option through the use of a central 'opt out' program such as the Direct Marketing Association's Mail Preference Service. Organisations that participate in the Direct Marketing Association's Mail Preference Service should promote its availability to consumers who do not wish to receive commercial information. In any event, an individual should be given a readily available and affordable mechanism to exercise this option.

Similarly, an organisation may use information for certain direct marketing purposes when it is impracticable to provide the individual with an opportunity to opt out before using the information, if the organisation promptly gives the individual such opportunity at the same time (and upon request at any time) to decline (at no cost to the individual) to receive any further direct marketing communications and the organisation complies with the individual's wishes.

FAQ 13 – travel information

When can airline passenger reservation and other travel information, such as frequent flyer or hotel reservation information and special handling needs, such as meals to meet religious requirements or physical assistance, be transferred to organisations located outside the EU?

Such information may be transferred in several different circumstances. Under *Article 26* of the Directive, personal data may be transferred 'to a third country which does not ensure an adequate level of protection within the meaning of *Article 25(2)*' on the condition that it:

(1)   is necessary to provide the services requested by the consumer or to fulfill the terms of an agreement, such as a 'frequent flyer' agreement; or

(2)   has been unambiguously consented to by the consumer. US organisations subscribing to the safe harbor provide adequate protection for personal data and may, therefore, receive data transfers from the EU without meeting those conditions or other conditions set out in *Article 26* of the Directive.

Since the safe harbor includes specific rules for sensitive information, such information (which may need to be collected, for example, in connection with customers' needs for physical assistance) may be included in transfers to safe harbor participants. In all cases, however, the organisation transferring the information has to respect the law in the EU Member State in which it is operating, which may *inter alia* impose special conditions for the handling of sensitive data.

FAQ 14 – pharmaceutical and medical products

If personal data are collected in the EU and transferred to the United States for pharmaceutical research and/or other purposes, do Member State laws or the Safe Harbor Principles apply?

Member State law applies to the collection of the personal data and to any processing that takes place prior to the transfer to the United States. The Safe Harbor Principles apply to the data once they have been transferred to the United States. Data used for pharmaceutical research and other purposes should be anonymised when appropriate.

Personal data developed in specific medical or pharmaceutical research studies often play a valuable role in future scientific research. Where personal data collected for one research study are transferred to a US organisation in the safe harbor, may the organisation use the data for a new scientific research activity?

Yes, if appropriate notice and choice have been provided in the first instance. Such a notice should provide information about any future specific uses of the

(cont'd)

data, such as periodic follow-up, related studies or marketing. It is understood that not all future uses of the data can be specified, since a new research use could arise from new insights on the original data, new medical discoveries and advances, and public health and regulatory developments. Where appropriate, the notice should, therefore, include an explanation that personal data may be used in future medical and pharmaceutical research activities that are unanticipated. If the use is not consistent with the general research purpose(s) for which the data were originally collected, or to which the individual has consented subsequently, new consent must be obtained.

What happens to an individual's data if a participant decides voluntarily, or at the request of the sponsor, to withdraw from the clinical trial?

Participants may decide or be asked to withdraw from a clinical trial at any time. Any data collected previous to withdrawal may still be processed along with other data collected as part of the clinical trial, however, if this was made clear to the participant in the notice at the time he or she agreed to participate.

Pharmaceutical and medical device companies are allowed to provide personal data from clinical trials conducted in the EU to regulators in the United States for regulatory and supervision purposes. Are similar transfers allowed to parties other than regulators, such as company locations and other researchers?

Yes, consistent with the principles of notice and choice.

To ensure objectivity in many clinical trials, participants, and often investigators, as well, cannot be given access to information about which treatment each participant may be receiving. Doing so would jeopardize the validity of the research study and results. Will participants in such clinical trials (referred to as 'blinded' studies) have access to the data on their treatment during the trial?

No, such access does not have to be provided to a participant if this restriction has been explained when the participant entered the trial and the disclosure of such information would jeopardise the integrity of the research effort. Agreement to participate in the trial under these conditions is a reasonable forgoing of the right of access. Following the conclusion of the trial and analysis of the results, participants should have access to their data if they request it. They should seek it primarily from the physician or other health care provider from whom they received treatment within the clinical trial, or secondarily from the sponsoring company.

Does a pharmaceutical or medical device firm have to apply the Safe Harbor Principles with respect to notice, choice, onward transfer, and access in its product safety and efficacy monitoring activities, including the reporting of adverse events and the tracking of patients/subjects using certain medicines or medical devices (eg a pacemaker)?

No, to the extent that adherence to the principles interferes with compliance with regulatory requirements. This is true both with respect to reports by, for example, health care providers, to pharmaceutical and medical device companies, and with respect to reports by pharmaceutical and medical device companies to government agencies, like the Food and Drug Administration.

Invariably, research data are uniquely key-coded at their origin by the principal investigator so as not to reveal the identity of individual data subjects. Pharmaceutical companies sponsoring such research do not receive the key. The unique key code is held only by the researcher, so that he or she can identify the research subject under special circumstances (eg if follow-up medical attention is required). Does a transfer from the EU to the United States of data coded in this way constitute a transfer of personal data that is subject to the Safe Harbor Principles?

No. This would not constitute a transfer of personal data that would be subject to the principles.

FAQ 15 – public record and publicly available information

Is it necessary to apply the notice, choice and onward transfer principles to public record information or publicly available information?

It is not necessary to apply the notice, choice or onward transfer principles to public record information, as long as it is not combined with non-public record information and as long as any conditions for consultation established by the relevant jurisdiction are respected.

Also, it is generally not necessary to apply the notice, choice or onward transfer principles to publicly available information unless the European transferor indicates that such information is subject to restrictions that require application of those principles by the organisation for the uses it intends. Organisations will have no liability for how such information is used by those obtaining such information from published materials.

Where an organisation is found to have intentionally made personal information public in contravention of the principles so that it or others may benefit from these exceptions, it will cease to qualify for the benefits of the safe harbor.

Chapter 42 –
Sensitive Personal Data

At A Glance

✓ Handlers of sensitive personal data are subject to strict obligations under the *Data Protection Act 1998 (DPA 1998)*, as set out in *Schedule 3 to DPA 1998*.

✓ Sensitive personal data includes data about race, political beliefs, union activities, sex life, commission of offences etc.

✓ Explicit consent must in many cases be obtained before such data is processed.

✓ The Commissioner's Legal Guidance and Employment Practices Data Protection Code provide useful guidance in this field.

Introduction   42.1

Sensitive personal data is subject to much stricter regulation under *DPA 1998* than ordinary personal data. The category of sensitive personal data includes information such as race, religion and sex life. *Schedule 3 to DPA 1998* contains the requirements for the processing of data of this nature. In particular, sensitive personal data must not be processed unless:

- the data subject has given explicit consent;

- it is processed in performance of a legal right of employment law;

- it is a matter of life or death; or

- it comes under certain other categories.

What is Sensitive Personal Data?   42.2

Section 2 of DPA 1998 defines sensitive personal data as information as to:

(*a*) the racial or ethnic origin of the data subject;

(*b*) political opinions;

(*c*)   religious beliefs or beliefs of a similar nature;

(*d*)   membership of a trade union or non-membership;

(*e*)   physical or mental health or condition;

(*f*)   sexual life;

(*g*)   the commission or alleged commission of any offence; or

(*h*)   any proceedings for an offence committed or alleged to have been committed by him or her, the disposal of any such proceedings or the sentence of any court to such proceedings.

Examples   42.3

(*a*)   A list of which politicians are homosexual or which members of a royal family carry a defective gene would be sensitive personal data.

(*b*)   An interesting issue is whether a name alone can be sensitive personal data. 'Seamus O'Hara' may appear to be of Celtic origin but may be from a Kenyan tribe.

(*c*)   A photograph of someone may reveal sensitive personal data about them, such as whether they are clearly physically handicapped or their ethnic origin. That would appear to make photographs of individuals sensitive personal data, but the information is hardly confidential as every time that person walks down the street their ethnic origin is clear (to the extent that appearance does reveal such origin).

The law in this area is complex and advice should be sought.

Case example   42.4

In *Campbell v Mirror Group Newspapers plc, QBD, 27 March 2002* the court had to look at whether a picture of Naomi Campbell the model leaving a Narcotics Anonymous meeting was sensitive personal data within *section 2 of DPA 1998*.

The court said that section 2 states:

'In this Act "sensitive personal data" means personal data consisting of information as to–

(a) The racial or ethnic origin of the data subject ...

(e) his physical or mental health or condition.

'In my judgment the contention, that the published photographs of the claimant are sensitive personal data because they consist of information as to her racial or ethnic origin, has no materiality or

> relevance to the circumstances of this case. The claimant is proud to be a leading black fashion model and it is part of her lifestyle and profession to be photographed as a black woman. She has suffered no damage or distress because the photographs disclose that she is black. However, it should not be understood that I am ruling that images whether photographic or otherwise that disclose whether from physical characteristic or dress racial or ethnic origins cannot amount to sensitive personal data. In my judgment the information as to the nature of and details of the therapy that the claimant was receiving at Narcotics Anonymous including the photographs with captions was clearly information as to her physical or mental health or condition, that is her drug addiction and therefore "sensitive personal data".'

Conditions for Processing Sensitive Personal Data

42.5

Schedule 3 to *DPA 1998* sets out the detailed conditions of the processing of sensitive personal data. This is addressed in depth in Chapter 3.1.3 of the Information Commissioner's Legal Guidance (October 2001). For employment and the CCTV processing of personal data reference should be made to the Information Commissioner's Codes of Practice in those areas. Processing of sensitive personal data may take place where one of the conditions set out at **42.6–42.12** is satisfied.

Explicit consent

42.6

The data subject gives their explicit consent to the process. The *Data Protection Directive (95/46/EC)*, implemented by *DPA 1998* in the UK, says that consent must be freely given and that it should be a specific and informed indication of the data subject's wishes by which 'the data subject signifies his agreement to personal data relating to him being processed.'

> 'The consent must be "explicit" in the case of sensitive data. The use of the word "explicit" and the fact that the condition requires explicit consent "to the processing of the personal data" suggests that the consent of the data subject should be absolutely clear. In appropriate cases it should cover the specific detail of the processing, the particular type of data to be processed (or even the specific information), the purposes of the processing and any special aspects of the processing which may affect the individual, for example, disclosures which may be made of the data.'
>
> *Information Commissioner's Legal Guidance, October 2001*

Employment 42.7

The processing of sensitive personal data is also allowed where the processing is necessary (not just desirable) in order to exercise or perform a function imposed by law on the data controller 'in connection with employment'. The Employment Practices Data Protection Code gives further information on this in the context of employment (see **16 EMPLOYMENT**).

Vital interests 42.8

Sensitive personal data may be processed where this is necessary to protect the vital interests of the data subject. However, this has been interpreted to mean where it is a matter of life or death.

Associations 42.9

Processing of sensitive personal data is allowed where it is carried out by non-profit-making associations for political, philosophical, religious or trade union purposes with appropriate safeguards. It must only relate to members of or those with a contract with the body, and cannot not involve disclosure of the personal data to a third party without the third party's consent.

Data subject has made the information public 42.10

If the data subject has deliberately taken steps to make the sensitive personal data public then it can be processed. For example, if a famous person sells the stories of their extramarital gay affairs to the press, or if a well-known actor discloses that he is HIV positive.

Other exceptions 42.11

There are other exceptions in certain cases, such as where the processing of the sensitive personal data is necessary for legal advice or litigation, the administration of justice or for medical purposes.

Processing is also allowed where the data is gathered on race or ethnic origins to assess an equal opportunities policy.

Secondary legislation 42.12

The *Data Protection (Processing of Sensitive Personal) Data Order 2000 (SI 2000/417)* includes rules on processing personal data, because *paragraph 10 of Schedule 3 to DPA 1998* allows further categories to be laid down. These are not described here, but they include various law enforcement rights, rights to process for pensions and insurance matters, and rights for maintaining archives.

Commissioner's Legal Guidance   42.13

The issues addressed in this chapter are also considered in detail in the Information Commissioner's Legal Guidance (October 2001). This gives examples of sensitive personal data, as well as describing in detail the rules considered above.

Example   42.14

'To illustrate this point, in a common scenario where negotiations are taking place between an individual and an insurance company with a view to entering into a contract of insurance, various disclosures have to be made which may include sensitive personal data about a third party to enable the insurer to assess the risk and calculate the premium. Examples could be a group insurance policy for holiday insurance where medical details of individuals who are not party to the negotiations are disclosed, or car insurance where conviction details of named drivers would have to be revealed by the proposer. No contract exists at this stage and the insurance company may decide not to accept the risk and enter into a contract of insurance.

Reliance by the insurance company, as data controller, upon paragraph (c) of this condition as a basis for processing the sensitive personal data of a third party would not be acceptable to the Commissioner prior to the existence of the contract and the data controller would have to rely upon another condition for processing sensitive data in Schedule 3 or under the Sensitive Data Order unless, on a case by case analysis, the data controller has reasonable grounds for believing that an agency relationship exists between the individual with whom he is dealing and the data subject. (ie a relationship exists whereby one party, the "agent," has the authority or capacity to create legal relations between a person acting as "principal" and a third party).'

Conclusion   42.15

Many businesses process sensitive personal data, and these businesses need to ensure that they put in place adequate systems to cope with this. **37 PRIVACY POLICIES AND AUDITS** provides guidance in this area.

Further Information   42.16

Chapter 3 of the Commissioner's Legal Guidance deals with sensitive personal data. It can be found on the Commissioner's website at www.informationcommissioner.gov.uk.

For employee issues see **16 EMPLOYMENT** and the Information Commissioner's Employment Practices Data Protection Code.

For information on CCTV see **2 CCTV**.

FAQs   42.17

(Extracted from Part 2: Records Management of the Employment Practices Data Protection Code)

Employment: When can sensitive personal data be processed?

The Act sets out a series of rules, at least one of which has to be met before an employer can collect, store, use, disclose or otherwise process sensitive personal data. The rules which are most likely to be relevant to employment records are where:

- The processing is necessary for the purposes of exercising or performing any right or obligation which is conferred or imposed by law on the data controller in connection with employment.

  Note: This condition can have quite wide application in the context of employment records. Employers' rights and obligations may be conferred or imposed by statute or common law, which in this context means decisions in relevant legal cases. For example, they will include obligations to:

  - ensure the health, safety and welfare at work of workers;

  - ensure a safe working environment;

  - not discriminate on the grounds of race, sex or disability;

  - consider reasonable adjustments to the workplace to accommodate workers with disabilities;

  - maintain records of statutory sick pay and maternity pay;

  - not dismiss workers when it is unfair to do so;

  - supply information on accidents where industrial injuries benefit may be payable;

  - protect customers' property or funds in the employer's possession;

  - ensure continuity of employment under *TUPE Regulations 1981*.

  Thus an employer may be able to keep information about a worker's physical or mental health in connection with sickness absence or criminal convictions if this can be shown to be necessary to enable the employer to meet its obligations in relation to the safety of its workers or others to whom it owes a duty of care. This condition might also be relied on to enable an employer to keep sickness records more generally

---

on the basis that these are necessary if the employer is to ensure that it does not dismiss workers on the grounds of absence when it would be unfair to do so.

- The processing –

  ○ is necessary for the purpose of, or in connection with, any legal proceedings (including prospective legal proceedings),

  ○ is necessary for the purpose of obtaining legal advice, or

  ○ is otherwise necessary for the purposes of establishing, exercising or defending legal rights.

Note: This condition will apply in the context of tribunal or court proceedings. It might, for example, be relied on to enable an employer to process sensitive personal data to defend him or herself against a claim for unfair dismissal.

- The processing –

  ○ is of information in categories relating to racial or ethnic origin, religious beliefs or other beliefs of a similar nature, physical or mental health or condition,

  ○ is necessary for the purpose of identifying or keeping under review the existence or absence of equality of opportunity or treatment,

  ○ contains safeguards for the data subject.

Note: This condition will be relevant to equal opportunities monitoring related to racial origin, religion and disability. Processing must be 'necessary', emphasising that wherever practicable monitoring should be based on anonymous or aggregated information.

- The information has been made public as a result of steps deliberately taken by the data subject.

Note: An example would be where a worker's trade union membership is known because the worker has appeared on local television as a spokesperson for the trade union.

- The processing is necessary:

  ○ for the exercise of any functions conferred on any person by or under an enactment or

  ○ for the exercise of any functions of the Crown, a Minister of the Crown or a government department.

Note: This condition will be mainly relevant to public sector bodies that may have specific legal duties placed on them in relation to the qualifications, attributes, background or probity of their workers. It will

(cont'd)

also be relevant when a public sector body concludes that in order to discharge its wider statutory functions it is necessary for it to process sensitive personal data such as criminal convictions relating to workers, or in exceptional cases, their family or close associates.

- The processing is necessary for medical purposes including preventative medicine and medical research and is undertaken by a health professional or someone else subject to an equivalent duty of confidentiality.

  Note: This condition is only likely to apply where information is held by a company doctor or similar person. It will be relevant in the context of an occupational health scheme, but not where information is in the hands of human resources professionals or other managers.

- The processing is in the substantial public interest, is necessary for the prevention or detection of any unlawful act and must necessarily be carried out without the explicit consent of the data subject being sought, so as not to prejudice those purposes.

  Note: This condition will cover situations where allegations of work-related criminal offences by workers arise, for example, as a result of audit investigations or complaints from customers.

- The processing is in the substantial public interest, is necessary for research purposes, does not support decisions about individuals and is unlikely to cause substantial damage or distress.

  Note: This condition most likely to be relevant in the context of research into occupational disease or illness.

- The data subject has given his or her explicit consent to the processing.

  Note: Employers seeking to rely on this condition must bear in mind that:

  o The consent must be explicit. This means the worker must have been told clearly what personal data are involved and the use that will be made of them. The worker must have given a positive indication of agreement eg a signature;

  o The consent must be freely given. This means the worker must have a real choice whether or not to consent and there must be no significant detriment that arises from not consenting.

  o The extent to which consent can be relied upon in the context of employment is limited because of the need for any consent to be freely given. For example if the direct consequence of not consenting is dismissal, being passed over for promotion or the denial of a significant benefit that would be given to a consenting worker, consent is unlikely to be freely given.

Chapter 43 –
Subject Access Requests

At A Glance

✓   *Section 7* of the *Data Protection Act 1998* (*DPA 1998*) gives individuals a right of access to much of the data held about them.

✓   The data controller must respond within 40 days to a subject access request, but may require the individual to provide further details in appropriate cases.

✓   A maximum charge of £10 can be imposed (£50 in cases of health records).

✓   There are a number of exemptions from subject access which need to be considered.

✓   Chapter 4.1 of the Commissioner's Legal Guidance examines subject access.

✓   Important security issues arise in ensuring that those seeking access are who they say they are.

✓   Those responding to subject access requests need to ensure they do not disclose third party data. The Commissioner has issued specific guidance on this aspect.

✓   Under the *Freedom of Information Act 2000* (*FIA 2000*) when fully in force similar rights will be given as against state bodies.

Introduction 43.1

Individuals are entitled to access to the personal data held about them by data controllers. This is known as subject access. *Section 7* of *DPA 1998* contains these rights. There are some exclusions to the rights of subject access (see **19 EXEMPTIONS**). Employment issues are addressed in **16 EMPLOYMENT**. Special rules in the health, education and social work sectors are covered in **25 HEALTH, EDUCATION AND SOCIAL WORK**. It is important that those receiving subject access requests check that individuals making such a request are who they claim to be, as otherwise *DPA 1998* can be breached (see **5 COMPENSATION, DAMAGES AND PREVENTION OF PROCESSING**).

Right of Access to Personal Data   43.2

Individuals are entitled to be told by data controllers whether the controller is processing their data or not. If their data is being processed, then the data controller must give a description of the personal data, the purposes for which it is processed and the recipients to whom it is disclosed. Data subjects are entitled to have their personal data communicated to them in intelligible form.

Where processing of the data is by automated means to evaluate the individual's performance at work, creditworthiness, reliability, conduct or similar matters, and decisions will be made about the individual solely based on this information, then the individual is entitled to be informed by the data controller of 'the logic involved in that decision-taking' (see **1 AUTOMATED DECISION-TAKING**).

An amendment to the entitlement to be informed of the logic behind a decision is to be brought in by *paragraph 1* of *Schedule 6* to *FIA 2000* (this is not yet in force – see **24 FREEDOM OF INFORMATION ACT 2000**) which will provide that where a data controller:

- reasonably requires further information in order to satisfy himself as to the identity of the person making a subject access request and to locate the information which that person seeks; and

- has informed him of that requirement,

then the data controller is not obliged to comply with the request unless he is supplied with that further information.

The amendment does not address the situation where the data subject may have failed to provide the requisite fee. The Information Commissioner's Legal Guidance provides that unless a reasonable interval has elapsed between compliance with the previous request and the making of the current request, data controllers do not need to comply with a request where they have already complied with an identical or similar request by the same individual.

In defining a reasonable interval, the following factors should be considered:

- the nature of the data;

- the purpose for which the data are processed; and

- the frequency with which the data are altered.

The information given in response to a subject access request should be all that which is contained in the personal data at the time the request was received. The Commissioner says that:

> 'routine amendments and deletions of the data may continue between the date of the request and the date of the reply. To this extent, the information revealed to the data subject may differ from the data which

were held at the time the request was received, even to the extent that data are no longer held. But, having received a request, the data controller must not make any special amendment or deletion which would not otherwise have been made. The information must not be tampered with in order to make it acceptable to the data subject.'

Guidance 43.3

The Commissioner has issued specific guidance on subject access as follows.

- Subject access – education records in England.

- Subject access and emails.

- Subject access and health records: fees for access.

- Subject access and health records.

- Subject access – local authority housing records.

- Subject access – medical records: Fees for access.

- Subject access to social services records.

- Subject access to social services records.

- Subject access and third party information.

Procedure and Fee to Obtain Access 43.4

Data subjects wanting access to data held about them must apply in writing to the data controller. It is usually necessary to pay a fee. *Regulation 3* of the *Data Protection (Subject Access) (Fees and Miscellaneous Provisions) Regulations 2000 (SI 2000/1910)* provides that the maximum subject access fee is £10. Requests must generally be complied with within 40 days of receipt of a request or, if later, within 40 days of receipt of both the fee and all the information required by the data controller to satisfy him or herself as to the identity of the person making the request, and to locate the information required by that person. For the health sector, reference should be made to **25 HEALTH, EDUCATION AND SOCIAL WORK**, where the rules vary and a fee of £50 may be charged. For educational records there is a sliding scale in operation. There is a special period of seven working days for credit matters (see **7 CREDIT REFERENCES AND ACCESS TO CREDIT FILES**).

Further information on subject access is given in the Commissioner's Legal Guidance on the Commissioner's website (www.informationcommissioner. gov.uk).

Credit Reference Agencies 43.5

Where the data controller is a credit reference agency and the request has been limited to data about an individual's financial standing, then under specific regulations made under the *Consumer Credit Act 1974* and applicable to the credit sector, the maximum fee is £2, and requests must be complied with within seven working days.

Under *section 9* of *DPA 1998*, where the data controller is a credit reference agency and an individual makes a subject access request, this is taken to be limited to information about his financial standing, unless the request shows a contrary intention. Responding to such requests may also require a statement to be given under *section 159* of the *Consumer Credit Act 1974*. Credit issues are dealt with in **7 CREDIT REFERENCES AND ACCESS TO CREDIT FILES**.

Confidentiality and Disclosure   43.6

Sometimes a subject access request might result in the disclosure of information about someone other than the data subject. In such cases, *DPA 1998* sets out only two circumstances when the data controller would then have to comply with the subject access request:

- where the other individual has consented; or
- where it is reasonable in all the circumstances to comply with the request without the consent of the individual.

Confidentiality issues are addressed in **6 CONFIDENTIALITY AND SECURITY: SEVENTH PRINCIPLE**.

DPA 1998 provides that in considering when it is reasonable to comply with such a request, factors to be considered include:

- confidentiality owed to the other individual;
- steps the data controller has taken to obtain consent;
- whether the other individuals is capable of giving consent; and
- any express refusal of consent by the other individual.

Enforced Subject Access   43.7

It is an offence under *DPA 1998* for someone to require another person to provide them with a copy of a relevant record, that is their personal data held by a data controller. In particular, the offence can be committed in connection with recruitment and employment, and where a person is providing goods or services to the public as a condition of their offering goods or services to that person. If a law imposes such a requirement or if it is in the public interest, then it is justified and allowed. *Section 56* of *DPA 1998* sets out the relevant law. Enforced subject access is also considered in **32 OFFENCES**.

Emails   43.8

Separate guidance has been issued by the Information Commissioner on subject access and emails; this is addressed in **15 EMAILS**.

Access to Information Held by the Commissioner and Fees   43.9

Separately, data subjects can ask the Commissioner who is registered under *DPA 1998*. This is free if it is searched for on the Internet on the Data Protection Register website at www.dpr.gov.uk. If instead a different form of request is made, then under the *Data Protection (Fees Under Section 19(7)) Regulations 2000* (*SI 2000/187*) a fee of £2 is paid for a duly certified copy of the data controller's entry on the register. This is not, of course, the personal data held by that controller. It is just the registered particulars of the controller himself.

Case Law   43.10

In *Norman Baker MP v Secretary of State for the Home Department (1 October 2001)*, under *DPA 1998* it was decided that the security service and Secretary of State were wrong to say that a blanket exemption (under *DPA 1998, s 28* national security exemption provisions) applied when a *section 7* of *DPA 1998* subject access request was refused.

The security service had said *that* subject access requests would only be permitted *in* the categories of:

• staff administration;

• building security CCTV; and

• commercial agreements,

in which three categories in any event the security service held no data relating to the data subject, Mr Baker. This was held to be wrong in law by the Data Protection Tribunal.

The Tribunal asked:

'When does national security take precedence over human rights?

Where the context is national security, judges and tribunals should supervise with the lightest touch appropriate; there is no area (foreign affairs apart) where judges have traditionally deferred more to the executive view than that of national security; and for good and sufficient reason.'

They found, however, that there were no reasonable grounds for the Secretary of State to issue the certificate which he did. It was held that this led to the failure to disclose whether any information except in the three categories mentioned above.

Section 28 of *DPA 1998* provides an exemption from a number of provisions of *DPA 1998* if exemption from any such provision is required for the purpose of safeguarding national security. Such an exemption is, in effect, the Commissioner says, 'asserted by means of certificates, signed by a Minister of the Crown, certifying that exemption from all or any of the provisions is or was required for the requisite purpose. Such a certificate is conclusive evidence of that fact'. Any person directly affected by the issuing of such a certificate may appeal to the Data Protection Tribunal against the certificate.

The Tribunal is specially constituted to hear such appeals and is subject to different rules than in the case of appeals against enforcement and information notices (the *Data Protection Tribunal (National Security Appeals) Rules 2000 (SI 2000/206)*). The first appeal to be heard by this Tribunal was the *Baker* case. As this was the first appeal, the parties consented to the proceedings taking place in public (subject to certain restrictions to protect the identity of some witnesses).

Third Party Data   43.11

It is crucial that those responding to subject access requests do not disclose third party data in the process. The Commissioner has issued separate guidance on subject access and third party data which is available on her website at www.informationcommissioner.gov.uk.

For third party data in the credit area see **7 CREDIT REFERENCES AND ACCESS TO CREDIT FILES**.

The Commissioner has also given guidance on subject access and emails which is considered in **15 EMAILS**. This also emphasises the point of not giving individuals access to third party data in responding to such requests.

Advice to Data Subjects   43.12

The Information Commissioner has issued some guidance to data subjects exercising their rights under *section 7* of *DPA 1998* by way of Frequently Asked Questions as set out at the end of this chapter.

Freedom of Information Act 2000   43.13

FIA 2000 will give both individuals and companies rights of access to data held by Government bodies held about them when the Act is fully in force. The response period will be 20 working days. **24 FREEDOM OF INFORMATION ACT 2000** examines the Act.

Further Information 43.14

The following guidance on subject access is on the Information Commissioner's website.

- Subject access – education records in England.
- Subject access & emails.
- Subject access & health records: fees for access.
- Subject access & health records.
- Subject access – local authority housing records.
- Subject access – medical records: Fees for access.
- Subject access to social services records.
- Subject access to social services records.
- Subject access and third party information.

The case *Norman Baker MP v Secretary of State for the Home Department (1 October 2001)* is not yet reported at the date of writing, but is available the full judgment on the Information Commissioner's website at www.informationcommissioner. gov.uk under Tribunal Decisions.

Confidentiality issues are addressed in **6 CONFIDENTIALITY AND DATA SECURITY: SEVENTH PRINCIPLE.**

7 CREDIT REFERENCES AND ACCESS TO CREDIT FILES covers credit issues

15 EMAILS considers subject access requests relating to information in emails.

19 EXEMPTIONS provides further information on the exemptions from subject access which are many and complicated.

24 FREEDOM OF INFORMATION ACT 2000 examines FIA 2000 which contains similar rights of access to data.

32 OFFENCES, considered the offence of enforced subject access.

For employment issues see **16 EMPLOYMENT** and the Commissioner's Employment Practices Data Protection Code.

Special rules in the health, education and social work sectors are covered in **25 HEALTH, EDUCATION AND SOCIAL WORK.**

Automated decision taking is covered in **1 AUTOMATED DECISION-TAKING.**

Frequently Asked Questions

Q. How can I find out what information is held about me?

A. A request for a copy of information held about you is known as a 'subject access request'. Requests must be made to the person or organisation ('data controller') who you think processes (for example, holds discloses and/or uses) the information to which you want access. Requests must be made in writing and must be accompanied by the appropriate fee (as to which see below).

You are entitled to be told if any personal data are held about you and, if so:

● to be given a description of the data;

● to be told for what purposes the data are processed; and

● to be told the recipients or the classes of recipients to whom the data may have been disclosed.

This information should include what sort of data are held, the purposes for which the data are processed and the type of organisation or people to whom the data may be disclosed.

You are also entitled:

● to be given a copy of the information with any unintelligible terms explained;

● to be given any information available to the controller about the source of the data; and

● to be given an explanation as to how any automated decisions taken about you have been made

Q. How much does it cost to gain access?

A. Data controllers may charge a fee of up to £10 for responding to a subject access request.

Unless you specifically ask to be given an explanation as to how any automated decisions about you have been made, the data controller is not obliged to provide such information. If you do specifically include a request for such information in your request then the data controller must provide it within the single £10 fee. If you do not, then the data controller is entitled to charge a separate fee of no more than £10 for the separate provision of such information. You should also be aware of the fact that data controllers may not be required to provide such information if, or to the extent that, the information amounts to a trade secret.

Different fee structures apply to some 'accessible records' such as health, education or social services files.

Q. What else do I need to do?

A. Data controllers may ask for the information they reasonably need to verify the identity of the person making the request and to locate the data. This means you may need to provide the data controller with proof of your identity and information such as whether you were a customer or employee of the data controller concerned.

Q. What is the timescale for gaining access to the information?

A. *DPA 1998* requires data controllers to comply with subject access requests promptly and, in any event, within forty days from receipt of the request or, if later, forty days from the day on which the data controller has both the required fee and the necessary information to confirm your identity and to locate the data.

The Act requires the information to be provided promptly. This means a deliberate delay on the part of a data controller is not acceptable and the Commissioner might make an adverse assessment of a data controller where the data controller delayed requesting payment of any required fee, or the provision of any further details required to identify or locate the required information, where such delays resulted in the response to the subject access request being provided after forty days from receipt of the original subject access request.

There are different periods for requests for copies of credit files (seven days) and for school pupil records, which is fifteen school days.

If a data controller already has in place a system for the provision of information for one purpose (eg a data controller who provides information to a commercial organisation within a certain timescale) then the Commissioner would expect that data controller to be able to deal with a subject access request for the same or similar information promptly.

Q. What can I do if access is not given to me?

A. Although there are some limited circumstances in which access can be withheld, access should normally be provided to you. If you feel your request has not been complied with you may take further action, as follows.

1. Write back to the data controller setting out why you think that the information should have been provided to you. If you receive a response with which you are not satisfied, then the options available are as follows:

    (*a*) You may apply to the court alleging a failure to comply with the subject access provisions of the 1998 Act. The court may make an order requiring compliance with those provisions and may also award compensation for any damage you have suffered as a result and any associated distress.

(cont'd)

(b)   You may write to the Information Commissioner. The Commissioner may do one of the following:

(i)   make an assessment as to whether it is likely or unlikely that the data controller in question has complied with the 1998 Act.

(ii)   issue enforcement proceedings if she is satisfied that the data controller has contravened one of the Data Protection Principles.

(iii)   recommend that you apply to court alleging a failure to comply with the subject access provisions of the 1998 Act.

Further information on individual rights is available, see paper entitled 'Using the law to protect your information", which can be found at www.information commissioner.gov.uk under Guidance & other publications/Your rights. More specialist information on access to credit health social services, school pupils and local authority housing records is also available.

Q. How can I obtain a copy of my credit file?

A. Credit grantors exchange information with each other about their customers. They also have access to the electoral roll and to publicly available financial information, which will have a bearing on an individual's credit worthiness, including County Court Judgments and Scottish decrees. This information is held by credit reference agencies. In order to get a copy of the information which relates to your financial standing (ie your credit file), you should write to the two main credit reference agencies. These are:

Equifax Plc
Credit File Advice Service
PO Box 3001
Glasgow
G81 2DT

Experian Ltd
Consumer Help Service
PO Box 8000
Nottingham
NG1 5GX

You should send a fee of £2 and provide your full name and address, including postcode, and any other addresses you have lived at during the last 6 years and details of any other names you have used or been known by in that time. Unless the agencies require any further information to locate your file, they have 7 working days from the receipt of your letter in which to provide you with a copy of your file. For further information look at the paper 'No Credit' at www.informationcommissioner.gov.uk under Guidance & other publications/Your rights.

Copyright the Information Commissioner

Chapter 44 –
Transborder Data Flows

At A Glance

✓ Personal data under the *Data Protection Directive (95/46/EC)* may be exported from the European Economic Area ('EEA') only where the conditions set out in the legislation are met.

✓ 'Transborder data flows' is the term used by the Commissioner relating to such exports.

✓ Two documents containing guidance have been issued by the Commissioner on transborder data flows and data export.

✓ Data may be exported either under the Model Clauses issued by the Commission to an approved country, under the US/EU Safe Harbor Agreement or otherwise in compliance with the Eighth Data Protection Principle.

Introduction   44.1

The export of personal data from the EEA requires careful consideration. The Eighth Data Protection Principle only allows such export where there are adequate levels of protection. In many cases the consent of the data subject can be obtained. In other cases the countries have been approved (see **20 EXPORT OF DATA**). The US and EU have agreed a Safe Harbor Agreement, under which certain companies who are registered may export their data (see **41 'SAFE HARBOR' AGREEMENT**). The Information Commissioner has issued two documents providing advice and guidance on the Eighth Principle:

• a lengthy 'The Eighth Data Protection Principle and Transborder Dataflows' (available at www.informationcommissioner.gov.uk under Legal Guidance – International Transfers); and

• a shorter advice document on transborder data flows (available at www.informationcommissioner.gov.uk under Compliance – International Transfers Summary – Eighth Principle).

The Eighth Principle   44.2

The Eighth Data Protection Principle states:

> 'Personal data shall not be transferred to a country or territory outside
> the European Economic Area unless that country or territory ensures an
> adequate level of protection for the rights and freedoms of data subjects
> in relation to the processing of personal data'.
>
> *(Schedule 1 of the Data Protection Act 1998).*

However, *DPA 1998* does allow the export of data outside the EEA where the
transfer is necessary to perform a contract. In addition, a contract can include provisions protecting the data and thus the export may be permitted. There are
detailed rules on this in the advice from the Commissioner in this field.

Schedule 1, Paragraphs 13–15   44.3

Paragraphs 13–15 of *Schedule 1* to *DPA 1998* provide some guidance on the
Eighth Data Protection Principle. These paragraphs state that an adequate level of
protection is:

> 'one which is adequate in all the circumstances of the case, having regard
> in particular to:
>
> * the nature of the personal data;
>
> * the country or territory of origin of the information contained in
>   the data;
>
> * the country or territory of the final destination of that information;
>
> * the purposes for which and period during which the data are
>   intended to be processed;
>
> * the law in force in the country or territory in question;
>
> * the international obligations of that country or territory;
>
> * any relevant codes of conduct or other rules which are enforceable
>   in that country or territory (whether generally or by arrangement
>   in particular cases); and
>
> * any security measures taken in respect of the data in that country
>   or territory.'

Paragraph 14 of *Schedule 1* to *DPA 1998* says that the Eighth Data Protection
Principle does not apply to a transfer falling within *Schedule 4* except where the
Secretary of State provides. *Schedule 4* to *DPA 1998* is summarised at **44.6** below.

Paragraph 15   **44.4**

Paragraph 15 of *Schedule 1* to *DPA 1998* provides that where a 'community find-ing' has been made, then the question is determined in accordance with such finding. There are no such findings to date. Such a finding by *paragraph 15(2)* would be that a country outside the EEA does or does not ensure an adequate level of protection.

Examples   **44.5**

In her advice the Commissioner gives the following useful examples.

> (*a*) The sporting achievements of well-known athletes are gathered from published material in the UK and put on a website. It is difficult to see that there could be a problem with adequacy. The personal data are already in the public domain, so there is no obvious reason why a data subject might object to their transfer and there is little if any scope for misuse.
>
> (*b*) A customer list from company A in the UK is transferred to company B outside the UK to enable company A to send a mailing to customers of company B. If the data transferred are no more than names and addresses, there is nothing particularly sensitive about company A's line of business, the names and addresses are for one time use and must be returned or destroyed within a short time scale, company B is known to company A as reliable and there is a contract between them governing use of the data, the Commissioner is unlikely to call into question com-pany A's decision that adequate protection exists. Other factors that might weigh in company A's decision include the nature of the country in which company B is located, whether company A and B are members of the same group, if so whether there is any group policy on data pro-tection and the terms of such a policy or any contract that is in place.
>
> (*c*) An employee travels abroad with a laptop containing personal data con-nected with his/her employment. His/her employer in the UK remains the data controller. Provided the data remain in the possession of the employee and the employer has an effective procedure which addresses security and other risks posed by the use of laptops, including the addi-tional risks posed by international travel, a conclusion that there is ade-quate protection is likely to be reasonable.
>
> (*d*) Company A, an insurer based in the UK, reinsures some of its business with company B in Jersey. In the course of this it transfers personal data to Jersey. Jersey has a data protection law that is similar to the UK *Data Protection Act 1984*. The main relevant differences between the two Acts relate to international transfers and sensitive data. Provided the contract
>
> *(cont'd)*

> between companies A and B prevents any further international transfer of the personal data by B and either no sensitive data are transferred or consent to the transfer (which is likely to be required anyway to comply with *Schedule 3*) is obtained, a conclusion of adequacy is likely to be reasonable.
>
> (e) A UK-based bank has a branch in India which collects personal data on local customers. The data are transferred to the UK where they are processed and then transferred from the UK back to India. The customers' expectations will be that their data are treated in accordance with Indian law. Given the source of the data and that the Bank has no reason to suppose the data will be misused after transfer, a conclusion of adequacy is reasonable.

Schedule 4 44.6

Schedule 4 to *DPA 1998* sets out the transfers to which the Eighth Data Protection Principle does not apply.

(a) The data subject has given their consent to the transfer. Paragraph 8.2 of the advice at Annex 1 gives some examples of the Commissioner's of what might and might not be a valid consent and model wording.

(b) The transfer is necessary:

    (i) for the performance of a contract between the data subject and the data controller; or

    (ii) for the taking of steps at the request of the data subject with a view to their entering into a contract with the data controller.

(c) The transfer is necessary:

    (i) for the conclusion of a contract between the data controller and a person other than the data subject which:

        ● is entered into at the request of the data subject;

        ● is in the interests of the data subject; or

    (ii) for the performance of such a contract.

(d) The transfer is necessary for reasons of substantial public interest. The Secretary of State may by order specify the circumstances in which a transfer is taken to be necessary for reasons of substantial public interest. No such orders are in force to date.

(e) The transfer:

    (i) is necessary for the purpose of, or in connection with, any legal proceedings (including prospective legal proceedings);

    (ii) is necessary for the purpose of obtaining legal advice; or

(iii) is otherwise necessary for the purposes of establishing, exercising or defending legal rights.

(*f*) The transfer is necessary in order to protect the vital interests of the data subject.

(*g*) The transfer is part of the personal data on a public register, and any conditions, subject to which the register is open to inspection, are complied with by any person to whom the data are or may be disclosed after the transfer.

(*h*) The transfer is made on terms which are of a kind approved by the Commissioner as ensuring adequate safeguards for the rights and freedoms of data subjects.

(*j*) The transfer has been authorised by the Commissioner as being made in such a manner as to ensure adequate safeguards for the rights and freedoms of data subjects.

Consent 44.7

The Commissioner provides guidance in the advice as to what constitutes 'consent' for these purposes, in addition to the general guidance on consent in the Legal Guidance issued under *DPA 1998*.

Consent: Transfers can be made with the consent of the data subject. Consent must be freely given. It can be made a condition for the provision of a non-essential service but consent is unlikely to be valid if the data subject has no real choice but to give his/her consent. For example, if an existing employee is required to agree to the international transfer of personal data any consent given is unlikely to be valid if the penalty for not agreeing is dismissal. Consent must also be specific and informed. The data subject must know and have understood what he/she is agreeing to. The reasons for the transfer and as far as possible the countries involved should be specified. If the data controller is aware of any particular risks involved in the transfer it should bring these to the data subject's attention. Although all the circumstances of a particular case would need to be considered, it is possible to give some general examples.

'By signing below you accept that we can transfer any of the information we keep about you to any country when a business need arises.'	Unlikely to produce valid consent.
'By signing below you accept that we may pass details of your mortgage application to XYZ Ltd in Singapore who we have chosen to arrange mortgages on our behalf. You should be aware that Singapore does not have a data protection law.'	Likely to produce valid consent.

(cont'd)

'By signing below you agree that we may pass relevant personnel records to our subsidiary companies in any country to which you are transferred. Your records will continue to be handled in accordance with our code of good practice although you might no longer have rights under data protection law.'	Likely to produce valid consent in the case of an employee of a multinational group who accepts a job involving international postings and where the multinational has a group-wide data protection code.
'By signing below you agree that we may pass information about you and your policy to other insurance companies with which we reinsure our business. These companies may be located in countries outside the UK that do not have laws to protect your information. Details of the companies and countries involved in your case will be provided on request.'	Likely to be acceptable where it is not practicable to list all the reinsurers and the countries in which they are located because the list is too long, because it changes regularly or because different reinsurers from the list are used in different cases.

Transit and Transfer   44.8

When an email is sent it will often be routed through 'servers' in a number of different countries before ending up in the place of destination. Does this constitute an export of data? The Commissioner says no. This is the difference between a transit and a transfer. Transfers are caught, but transits are not. What matters, therefore, is where the data came from and where it ended up.

For example, if an English company sends a list of prospective employees to another English company, there is no export of data even if the data went to France by email en route. Conversely, if the English company sends the data to its US subsidiary then it would be caught.

In her advice at Annex 1, paragraph 4.3, the Commissioner says:

> 'Putting personal data on a website will almost certainly involve transfers to countries outside the UK. The transfers are to any countries from which the website is accessed.'

As there are rarely, if ever, technical means whereby a UK company can stop people accessing the site where they are outside the UK, all information on a website will therefore be 'exported'. It is possible that only those with user names and passwords can get on to the site, and that those would only be used to UK/EEA residents and thus any export prevented. This would be hard to achieve without checking the location of those users. In addition, many UK residents now take their laptops on holiday and would expect to be able to access the data whilst in a hotel in the US, for example. In such a case, it is not the individual taking their laptop to the US who is exporting the data (although they may be exporting data held generally on the laptop by so doing), but the company with the website, unless they were to say that their EEA authorised users must not, in the terms and conditions, use the site abroad. Even then they may be required to check that this did not occur.

It is therefore safest to assume that all data put on the website is exported.

The EEA   44.9

There are no restrictions on the export of personal data within the EEA. The EEA states are listed on the table below.

Countries to which data can be freely exported
Austria
Belgium
Denmark
Finland
France
Germany
Greece
Iceland
Ireland
Italy
Liechtenstein
Luxembourg
Netherlands
Norway
Portugal
Spain
Sweden

The list above is of those countries to which there is no restriction on export. They comprise the EEA and are all subject to the legal requirements of the *Data Protection Directive (95./46/EC)*. The Channel Islands and the Isle of Man are not part of the EEA, however, so those exporting data there need to take legal advice and may not be entitled to do so.

Designated Territories   44.10

DPA 1998 does allow the Commissioner to designate certain foreign countries as having adequate measures for export of data in place.

The European Commission, as at January 2004, had approved the following countries as having adequate national data protection safeguards to permit export without restriction, subject always, of course, to the general provisions of the *DPA 1998* as they would apply in the UK:

Guernsey

● Commission Decision of 21 November 2003 on the adequate protection of personal data in Guernsey (OJ L 308, 25 November 2003).

Argentina

● Commission Decision C(2003) 1731 of 30 June 2003 (OJ L 168, 5 July 2003).

Canada

● Commission Decision 2002/2/EC of 20 December 2001 on the adequate protection of personal data provided by the Canadian *Personal Information Protection and Electronic Documents Act* (OJ L 2/13 of 4 January 2002).

● See also Frequently Asked Questions on the Commission's adequacy finding on the Canadian *Personal Information Protection and Electronic Documents Act* (March 2002).

Switzerland

● Commission Decision 2000/518/EC of 26 July 2000 (OJ L 215/1 of 25 August 2000).

Hungary

● Commission Decision 2000/519/EC of 26 July 2000 (OJ L 215/4 of 25.8.2000).

The adequacy list is at
http://europa.eu.int/comm/internal_market/privacy/adequacy_en.htm

In 2003 and 2004 the EU and US were debating transfer of air passengers' personal data for security purposes (see Brussels, 16 December 2003 COM(2003) 826 final Communication from the Commission to the Council and the Parliament Transfer of Air Passenger Name Record (PNR) Data: A Global EU Approach).

The advice document at Annex 1 on compliance lists the following countries as having full data protection laws in place and therefore likely to be so designated in future, although it must be stressed this is not yet the case.

Australia

Canada (now designated)

Guernsey (now designated)

Hong Kong

Hungary (now designated)

Isle of Man

Israel

Japan

Jersey

New Zealand

Poland

Slovak Republic

Slovenia

Switzerland (now designated)

Taiwan

Model Clauses   44.11

In 2001 the European Commission issued standard clauses for the transfer of personal data to third countries to data controllers and in 2002 to data processors. These are considered in **20 EXPORT OF DATA**. The Model Clauses can be accessed from www.europa.eu.int/comm/internal_market/en/media/dataprot/news/callcom.htm and are in **APPENDIX 3** of this book. In **APPENDIX 2** the Commission's Frequently Asked Questions on the Clauses appear.

ICC Clauses   44.12

In 2001 industry issued its own version of some standard clauses for data export and is seeking approval of them from the European Commission. The International Chamber of Commerce ('ICC'), which was involved in the process, says that its clauses, unlike those of the EU, would avoid imposing what it regards as excessive obligations on companies.

Seven associations submitted alternative model contract clauses to EC internal market.

Business associations behind the move are: the ICC, the Federation of European Direct Marketing ('FEDMA'), the EU Committee of the American Chamber of Commerce in Belgium ('Amcham'), the Japan Business Council in Europe

('JBCE'), the Confederation of British Industry ('CBI'), the International Communications Round Table ('ICRT'), and the European Information and Communications Technology Industry Association ('EICTA').

The ICC says that the alternative clauses are intended to provide just as high a level of data protection as the Commission's clauses, but using more flexible mechanisms that reflect business realities. For example, the clauses provide an alternative to the 'joint and several liability' regime – or shared liability between exporters and importers – contained in the Commission's clauses (to which many companies have taken exception), and include a 'due diligence' responsibility on exporters in dealing with importers. A further safeguard allows exporters to carry out audits to check that the data supplied is not being misused. Further information is available on the ICC website at www.iccwbo.org/home/news_archives/2001/dataflow.asp

EU General Guidance   44.13

The European Commission has issued FAQs (to be found at www.europa.eu.int/comm/internal_market/en/dataprot/backinfo/info.htm) on data protection in general as it applies to transfer of data outside of the EEA. It has also issued FAQs on the Model Clauses for data export (see **APPENDIX 2**).

Further Information   44.14

The Information Commissioner has issued two documents on this topic:

- the Eighth Data Protection Principle and Transborder Dataflows (under Legal Guidance – 'International Transfers' at www.informationcommissioner.gov.uk); and

- a shorter advice document on transborder data flows (which is available under Compliance – 'International Transfers Summary – Eighth Data Protection Principle').

The ICC's alternative clauses are described at www.iccwbo.org/home/news_archives/2001/dataflow.asp.

See also **20 EXPORT OF DATA** and **41 'SAFE HARBOR' AGREEMENT**.

The Commission's Frequently Asked Questions on its new model clauses for data export are at www.europa.eu.int/comm/internal_market/en/media/dataprot/news/clausesfaq.htm.

And see:http://europa.eu.int/comm/internal_market/en/media/dataprot/wpdocs/wp40en.htm.

The US authorities have a safe harbor website which is at www.export.gov/safe-harbor/.

The International Chamber of Commerce's information on data export is at www.iccwbo.org/home/news_archives/2001/dataflow.asp.

FAQS   44.15

See **APPENDIX 2** for FAQs.

Chapter 45 – Transitional Provisions (Timing)

At A Glance

✓ The *Data Protection Act 1998* (*DPA 1998*) came into force on 1 March 2000.

✓ A first transitional period operated to 24 October 2001 for some of the provisions of *DPA 1998* in a very limited way (eg subject access requests for manual data being processed on 24 October 1998 became possible for such data from 24 October 2001).

✓ A second transitional period runs thereafter.

Introduction   45.1

DPA 1998 has applied from 1 March 2000. In areas where it changed the law radically, in many cases businesses were given an additional three years to bring their practices into line. This particularly applies in areas previously exempt such as manual data. This three year period ran from 24 October 1998 (when the *Data Protection Directive* (*95/46/EC*) should have been brought into force, not the 1 March 2000 implementation date). On 24 October 2001, for example, subject access requests for all manual data which falls within *DPA 1998* became possible (see **30 MANUAL RECORDS**).

Transitional Provisions   45.2

The transitional provisions under *DPA 1998* are extremely important, exempting certain areas relating to:

- manual data;

- processing otherwise than by reference to the data subject;

- payrolls and accounts;

- unincorporated members' clubs and mailing lists;

- back-up data;

- exemption for all eligible automated data from certain requirements; and

- historical research.

The Information Commissioner's Legal Guidance (Chapter 6) sets out a summary of the transitional provisions under *DPA 1998* to which reference should be made.

Processing 'Underway' 45.3

Many of the transitional exemptions apply where processing of data was 'underway' on 24 October 1998. It is therefore crucial to know in relation to particular data whether this is the case or not. The Information Commissioner recognises that the meaning of this is not very clear. The questions that the Commissioner suggests can be asked include whether the processing is for a new purpose, whether the data being processed is in the same category, and if the recipients of the data remain the same.

For processing which was already under way on 24 October 1998, manual data (with some exceptions) was effectively exempt from all the provisions of *DPA 1998* until 24 October 2001. Following this date a further transitional period exists until 24 October 2007 during which some, but not all, of the provisions of *DPA 1998* will apply.

Examples 45.4

Examples given by the Information Commissioner include where:

- existing data is amended;

- additional personal data is added on existing data subjects;

- personal data is added on new data subjects; or

- essential program and software changes are carried out to enable existing operations to continue.

In such cases, unless these examples produce a different effect on the processing operation, 'it is unlikely that these things alone will mean that this is not processing already under way'.

Adding to manual systems 45.5

This means that data controllers can add names to, for example, a paper card index system without this being 'new data processing'. The effect would have been that such manual records would remain outside the provisions of *DPA 1998* until 24 October 2001.

Takeovers   45.6

Where there is a change in the legal entity which is the data controller, the Information Commissioner believes that as long as the processing is existing processing the change in legal entity will not mean the processing is not underway on the relevant date (Information Commissioner's Introduction to DPA 1998, p28). However if the new entity takes on new functions then new processing takes place and *DPA 1998* would apply from 1 March 2000.

The First Transitional Period   45.7

The first transitional period ran to 23 October 2001. During this period, for example, credit reference agency records which came within *DPA 1998* for the first time under *DPA 1998*, would remain as under *DPA 1984* where the processing was already under way at 24 October 1998. The exemption was from the Data Protection Principles 1–8, *Part II* of the right – individual's rights in most cases and *Part III* of *DPA 1998*– notification.

The Second Transitional Period   45.8

From 24 October 2001 to 23 October 2007 a very limited exception for manual data which was being processed at 24 October 1998 applies. This also covers credit reference agency records and accessible records. This does not apply where manual data are added on or after 24 October 1998. There are all sorts of caveats and exceptions to this which must be considered in practice. Legal advice should be sought.

Further Information   45.9

For manual records and their transitional period see **30 MANUAL RECORDS**.

The Commissioner's Legal Guidance (October 2001) covers the transitional provisions in some depth – see www.informationcommissioner.gov.uk.

FAQs   45.10

> **When did *DPA 1998* come into force?**
>
> 1 March 2000.
>
> **When did the first transitional period end?**
>
> 23 October 2001 – eg manual data in relation to which processing was already underway on 24 October 1998 (when the directive should have been implemented) did not come within subject access provisions of *DPA 1998* until that date.

Appendix I – CCTV Code of Practice

Foreword

Closed circuit television (CCTV) surveillance is an increasing feature of our daily lives. There is an ongoing debate over how effective CCTV is in reducing and preventing crime, but one thing is certain, its deployment is commonplace in a variety of areas to which members of the public have free access. We might be caught on camera while walking down the high street, visiting a shop or bank or travelling through a railway station or airport. The House of Lords Select Committee on Science and Technology expressed their view that if public confidence in CCTV systems was to be maintained there needed to be some tighter control over their deployment and use (Fifth Report – Digital Images as Evidence).

There was no statutory basis for systematic legal control of CCTV surveillance over public areas until 1 March 2000 when the Data Protection Act came into force. The definitions in this new Act are broader than those of the Data Protection Act 1984 and so more readily cover the processing of images of individuals caught by CCTV cameras than did the previous data protection legislation. The same legally enforceable information handling standards as have previously applied to those processing personal data on computer now cover CCTV. An important new feature of the recent legislation is a power for me to issue a Commissioner's Code of Practice (section 51(3)(b) of DPA 1998) setting out guidance for the following of good practice. In my 14th Annual Report to Parliament I signalled my intention to use this power to provide guidance on the operation of CCTV as soon as those new powers became available to me. This Code of Practice is the first Commissioner's Code to be issued under the Data Protection Act 1998.

This code deals with surveillance in areas to which the public have largely free and unrestricted access because, as the House of Lords Committee highlighted, there is particular concern about a lack of regulation and central guidance in this area. Although the Data Protection Act 1998 covers other uses of CCTV this Code addresses the area of widest concern. Many of its provisions will be relevant to other uses of CCTV and will be referred to as appropriate when we develop other guidance. There are some existing standards that have been developed by representatives of CCTV system operators and, more particularly, the British Standards Institute. While such standards are helpful, they are not legally enforceable. The changes in data protection legislation mean that for the first time legally enforceable standards will apply to the collection and processing of images relating to individuals.

This Code of Practice has the dual purpose of assisting operators of CCTV systems to understand their legal obligations while also reassuring the public about the safeguards that should be in place. It sets out the measures which must be adopted to comply with the Data Protection Act 1998, and goes on to set out guidance for the following of good data protection practice. The Code makes clear the standards which must be followed to ensure compliance with the Data Protection Act 1998 and then indicates those which are not a strict legal requirement but do represent the following of good practice.

Before issuing this Code I consulted representatives of relevant data controllers and data subjects, and published a draft copy of the Code on my website. I am grateful to all those consultees who responded and have taken account of their comments in producing this version.

Our experience of the Codes of Practice which were put forward under the 1984 Act was that they needed to remain relevant to the day to day activities of data controllers. They need to be 'living' documents, which are updated as practices, and understanding of the law develops.

This code will therefore be kept under review to ensure that it remains relevant in the context of changing technology, use and jurisprudence. In this context it is likely that the Human Rights Act 1998, which comes into force on 2 October 2000, and provides important legal safeguards for individuals, will lead to developments in legal interpretation which will require review of the Code.

It is my intention that this Code of Practice should help those operating CCTV schemes monitoring members of the public to do so in full compliance of the Data Protection Act 1998 and in adherence to high standards of good practice. There does seem to be public support for the widespread deployment of this surveillance technology, but public confidence has to be earned and maintained. Compliance with this Code will not only help CCTV scheme operators' process personal data in compliance with the law but also help to maintain that public confidence without which they cannot operate.

Elizabeth France
Data Protection Commissioner
July 2000

Introduction

This is a code of practice issued by the Data Protection Commissioner in accordance with her powers under section 51 (3)(b) of the Data Protection Act 1998 (the '1998 Act'). It is intended to provide guidance as to good practice for users of CCTV (closed circuit television) and similar surveillance equipment.

It is not intended that the contents of this Code should apply to:

- targeted and intrusive surveillance activities, which are covered by the provisions of the forthcoming Regulation of Investigatory Powers Act 2000;

- use of surveillance techniques by employers to monitor their employees' compliance with their contracts of employment[1];

- security equipment (including cameras) installed in homes by individuals for home security purposes[2];

- use of cameras and similar equipment by the broadcast media for the purposes of journalism, or for artistic or literary purposes.

This Code of Practice is drafted in two parts.

Part I

This sets out:

- the standards which must be met if the requirements of the 1998 Act are to be complied with. These are based on the Data Protection Principles which say that data must be

  o   fairly and lawfully processed;

  o   processed for limited purposes and not in any manner incompatible with those purposes;

  o   adequate, relevant and not excessive;

  o   accurate;

  o   not kept for longer than is necessary;

  o   processed in accordance with individuals' rights;

    o   secure;

    o   not transferred to countries without adequate protection;

    o   guidance on good practice;

    o   examples of how to implement the standards and good practice.

The Data Protection Commissioner has the power to issue Enforcement Notices where she considers that there has been a breach of one or more of the Data Protection Principles. An Enforcement Notice[3] would set out the remedial action that the Commissioner requires to ensure future compliance with the requirements of the Act. The Data Protection Commissioner will take into account the extent to which users of CCTV and similar surveillance equipment have complied with this Code of Practice when determining whether they have met their legal obligations when exercising her powers of enforcement.

Part II – Glossary

This sets out the interpretation of the 1998 Act on which Part I is based. Part I is cross-referenced to Part II to try to clarify the reasoning behind the standard or guidance.

It is intended that this Code of Practice will be revised on a regular basis in order to take account of developments in the interpretation of the provisions of the data protection legislation, developments in the technology involved in the recording of images, and developments in the use of such technologies, the use of sound recording, facial recognition techniques and the increased use of digital technology.

Please note that italicised text indicates good practice.

Initial Assessment Procedures

Before installing and using CCTV and similar surveillance equipment, users will need to establish the purpose or purposes for which they intend to use the equipment.[4] This equipment may be used for a number of different purposes – for example, prevention, investigation and detection of crime, apprehension and prosecution of offenders (including use of images as evidence in criminal proceedings), public and employee safety, monitoring security of premises etc.

Standards

1.	Establish who is the person(s) or organisation(s) legally responsible for the proposed scheme.[5]
2.	Assess the appropriateness of, and reasons for, using CCTV or similar surveillance equipment (First Data Protection Principle).
3.	*Document this assessment process and the reasons for the installation of the scheme.*
4.	Establish the purpose of the Scheme (First and Second Data Protection Principle).[6]
5.	*Document the purpose of the scheme.*
6.	Ensure that the notification lodged with the Office of the Data Protection Commissioner covers the purposes for which this equipment is used.[7]
7.	*Establish and document the person(s) or organisation(s) who are responsible for ensuring the day-to-day compliance with the requirements of this Code of Practice (if different from above).*
8.	*Establish and document security and disclosure policies.*

Siting the cameras

It is essential that the location of the equipment is carefully considered, because the way in which images are captured will need to comply with the First Data Protection Principle. Detailed guidance on the interpretation of the First Data Protection Principle is provided in Part II, but the standards to be met under this Code of Practice are set out below.

Standards

1. The equipment should be sited in such a way that it only monitors those spaces which are intended to be covered by the equipment (First and Third Data Protection Principles).

2. If domestic areas such as gardens or areas not intended to be covered by the scheme border those spaces which are intended to be covered by the equipment, then the user should consult with the owners of such spaces if images from those spaces might be recorded. In the case of back gardens, this would be the resident of the property overlooked (First and Third Data Protection Principles).

3. Operators must be aware of the purpose(s) for which the scheme has been established (Second and Seventh Data Protection Principles).

4. Operators must be aware that they are only able to use the equipment in order to achieve the purpose(s) for which it has been installed (First and Second Data Protection Principles).

5. If cameras are adjustable by the operators, this should be restricted so that operators cannot adjust or manipulate them to overlook spaces which are not intended to be covered by the scheme (First and Third Data Protection Principles).

6. If it is not possible physically to restrict the equipment to avoid recording images from those spaces not intended to be covered by the scheme, then operators should be trained in recognising the privacy implications of such spaces being covered (First and Third Data Protection Principles).

   For example – individuals sunbathing in their back gardens may have a greater expectation of privacy than individuals mowing the lawn of their front garden.

   For example – it may be appropriate for the equipment to be used to protect the safety of individuals when using ATMs, but images of PIN numbers, balance enquiries etc should not be captured.

7. Signs should be placed so that the public are aware that they are entering a zone which is covered by surveillance equipment (First Data Protection Principle).

8. The signs should be clearly visible and legible to members of the public (First Data Protection Principle)

9. The size of signs will vary according to circumstances:

   For example – *a sign on the entrance door to a building society office may only need to be A4 size because it is at eye level of those entering the premises.*

   For example – signs at the entrances of car parks alerting drivers to the fact that the car park is covered by such equipment will usually need to be large, for example, probably A3 size as they are likely to be viewed from further away, for example by a driver sitting in a car.

10. e signs should contain the following information.

    (a) Identity of the person or organisation responsible for the scheme.

(cont'd)

(b)   The purposes of the scheme.

(c)   Details of whom to contact regarding the scheme.

(First Data Protection Principle)

For example – Where an image of a camera is not used on a sign – the following wording is recommended:

'Images are being monitored for the purposes of crime prevention and public safety. This scheme is controlled by the Greentown Safety Partnership.

For further information contact 01234–567–890'

For example – Where an image of a camera is used on a sign – the following wording is recommended:

'This scheme is controlled by the Greentown Safety Partnership.

For further information contact 01234–567–890'

11.   In exceptional and limited cases, if it is assessed that the use of signs would not be appropriate, the user of the scheme must ensure that they have:

- Identified specific criminal activity.

- Identified the need to use surveillance to obtain evidence of that criminal activity.

- Assessed whether the use of signs would prejudice success in obtaining such evidence.

- Assessed how long the covert monitoring should take place to ensure that it is not carried out for longer than is necessary.

- *Documented (a) to (d) above.*[8]

12.   Information so obtained must only be obtained for prevention or detection of criminal activity, or the apprehension and prosecution of offenders.[9] It should not be retained and used for any other purpose. If the equipment used has a sound recording facility, this should not be used to record conversations between members of the public (First and Third Data Protection Principles).

Quality of the images

It is important that the images produced by the equipment are as clear as possible in order that they are effective for the purpose(s) for which they are intended. This is why it is essential that the purpose of the scheme is clearly identified. For example if a system has been installed to prevent and detect crime, then it is essential that the images are adequate for that purpose. The Third, Fourth and Fifth Data Protection Principles are concerned with the quality of personal data, and they are outlined in more detail in Part II. The standards to be met under this Code of Practice are set out below.

Standards

1.   Upon installation an initial check should be undertaken to ensure that the equipment performs properly.

2.   If tapes are used, it should be ensured that they are good quality tapes (Third and Fourth Data Protection Principles).

(cont'd)

555

3. The medium on which the images are captured should be cleaned so that images are not recorded on top of images recorded previously (Third and Fourth Data Protection Principles).

4. The medium on which the images have been recorded should not be used when it has become apparent that the quality of images has deteriorated. (Third Data Protection Principle).

5. If the system records features such as the location of the camera and/or date and time reference, these should be accurate (Third and Fourth Data Protection Principles).

6. *If their system includes such features, users should ensure that they have a documented procedure for ensuring their accuracy.*

7. Cameras should be situated so that they will capture images relevant to the purpose for which the scheme has been established (Third Data Protection Principle)

   For example – if the purpose of the scheme is the prevention and detection of crime and/or apprehension and prosecution of offenders, the cameras should be sited so that images enabling identification of perpetrators are captured.

   For example – if the scheme has been established with a view to monitoring traffic flow, the cameras should be situated so that they do not capture the details of the vehicles or drivers.

8. If an automatic facial recognition system is used to match images captured against a database of images, then both sets of images should be clear enough to ensure an accurate match (Third and Fourth Data Protection Principles).

9. If an automatic facial recognition system is used, procedures should be set up to ensure that the match is also verified by a human operator, who will assess the match and determine what action, if any, should be taken (First and Seventh Data Protection Principles).[10]

10. *The result of the assessment by the human operator should be recorded whether or not they determine there is a match.*

11. When installing cameras, consideration must be given to the physical conditions in which the cameras are located (Third and Fourth Data Protection Principles).

    For example – infrared equipment may need to be installed in poorly lit areas.

12. Users should assess whether it is necessary to carry out constant real time recording, or whether the activity or activities about which they are concerned occur at specific times (First and Third Data Protection Principles)

    For example – it may be that criminal activity only occurs at night, in which case constant recording of images might only be carried out for a limited period e.g. 10.00 pm to 7.00 am

13. Cameras should be properly maintained and serviced to ensure that clear images are recorded (Third and Fourth Data Protection Principles)

14. Cameras should be protected from vandalism in order to ensure that they remain in working order (Seventh Data Protection Principle)

15. *A maintenance log should be kept.*

16. If a camera is damaged, there should be clear procedures for:

    (*a*) Defining the person responsible for making arrangements for ensuring that the camera is fixed.

    (*b*) Ensuring that the camera is fixed within a specific time period (Third and Fourth Data Protection Principle).

    (*c*) Monitoring the quality of the maintenance work.

Processing the images

Images, which are not required for the purpose(s) for which the equipment is being used, should not be retained for longer than is necessary. While images are retained, it is essential that their integrity be maintained, whether it is to ensure their evidential value or to protect the rights of people whose images may have been recorded. It is therefore important that access to and security of the images is controlled in accordance with the requirements of the 1998 Act. The Seventh Data Protection Principle sets out the security requirements of the 1998 Data Protection Act. This is discussed in more depth at Part II. However, the standards required by this Code of Practice are set out below.

Standards

1. Images should not be retained for longer than is necessary (Fifth Data Protection Principle)

    For example – publicans may need to keep recorded images for no longer than seven days because they will soon be aware of any incident such as a fight occurring on their premises.

    For example – images recorded by equipment covering town centres and streets may not need to be retained for longer than 31 days unless they are required for evidential purposes in legal proceedings.

    For example – images recorded from equipment protecting individuals' safety at ATMs might need to be retained for a period of three months in order to resolve customer disputes about cash withdrawals. The retention period of three months is based on the interval at which individuals receive their account statements.

2. Once the retention period has expired, the images should be removed or erased (Fifth Data Protection Principle).

3. If the images are retained for evidential purposes, they should be retained in a secure place to which access is controlled (Fifth and Seventh Data Protection Principles).

4. On removing the medium on which the images have been recorded for the use in legal proceedings, the operator should ensure that they have documented:

    (*a*) The date on which the images were removed from the general system for use in legal proceedings.

    (*b*) The reason why they were removed from the system.

    (*c*) Any crime incident number to which the images may be relevant.

    (*d*) The location of the images.

    For example – if the images were handed to a police officer for retention, the name and station of that police officer.

    (*e*) The signature of the collecting police officer, where appropriate (see below)(Third and Seventh Data Protection Principles).

5. Monitors displaying images from areas in which individuals would have an expectation of privacy should not be viewed by anyone other than

    authorised employees of the user of the equipment (Seventh Data Protection Principle).

6. Access to the recorded images should be restricted to a manager or designated member of staff who will decide whether to allow requests for access by third parties in accordance with the user's documented disclosure policies (Seventh Data Protection Principle).[11]

(cont'd)

7. Viewing of the recorded images should take place in a restricted area, for example, in a manager's or designated member of staff's office. Other employees should not be allowed to have access to that area when a viewing is taking place (Seventh Data Protection Principle).

8. Removal of the medium on which images are recorded, for viewing purposes, should be documented as follows:

   (a) *The date and time of removal*

   (b) The name of the person removing the images

   (c) The name(s) of the person(s) viewing the images. If this should include third parties, this include the organisation of that third party

   (d) The reason for the viewing

   (e) The outcome, if any, of the viewing

   (f) The date and time the images were returned to the system or secure place, if they have been retained for evidential purposes

9. All operators and employees with access to images should be aware of the procedure which need to be followed when accessing the recorded images (Seventh Data Protection Principle).

10. All operators should be trained in their responsibilities under this Code of Practice i.e. they should be aware of:

    (*a*) The user's security policy e.g. procedures to have access to recorded images.

    (*b*) The user's disclosure policy.[12]

    (*c*) Rights of individuals in relation to their recorded images.[13]

    (Seventh Data Protection Principle)

Access to and disclosure of images to third parties

It is important that access to, and disclosure of, the images recorded by CCTV and similar surveillance equipment is restricted and carefully controlled, not only to ensure that the rights of individuals are preserved, but also to ensure that the chain of evidence remains intact should the images be required for evidential purposes. Users of CCTV will also need to ensure that the reason(s) for which they may disclose copies of the images are compatible with the reason(s) or purpose(s) for which they originally obtained those images. These aspects of this Code are to be found in the Second and Seventh Data Protection Principles, which are discussed in more depth at Part II. However, the standards required by this Code are set out below.

Standards

All employees should be aware of the restrictions set out in this code of practice in relation to access to, and disclosure of, recorded images.

1. Access to recorded images should be restricted to those staff who need to have access in order to achieve the purpose(s) of using the equipment (Seventh Data Protection Principle).[14]

(cont'd)

2. All access to the medium on which the images are recorded should be documented (Seventh Data Protection Principle).[15]

3. Disclosure of the recorded images to third parties should only made in limited and pre-scribed circumstances (Second and Seventh Data Protection Principles).

    For example – if the purpose of the system is the prevention and detection of crime, then disclosure to third parties should be limited to the following.

    - Law enforcement agencies where the images recorded would assist in a specific criminal enquiry.

    - Prosecution agencies.

    - Relevant legal representatives.

    - The media, where it is decided that the public's assistance is needed in order to assist in the identification of victim, witness or perpetrator in relation to a criminal incident. As part of that decision, the wishes of the victim of an incident should be taken into account.

    - People whose images have been recorded and retained (unless disclosure to the individual would prejudice criminal enquiries or criminal proceedings).

4. All requests for access or for disclosure should be recorded. If access or disclosure is denied, the reason should be documented (Seventh Data Protection Principle)

5. If access to or disclosure of the images is allowed, then the following should be documented:

    (*a*) The date and time at which access was allowed or the date on which disclosure was made

    (*b*) The identification of any third party who was allowed access or to whom disclosure was made

    (*c*) The reason for allowing access or disclosure

    (*d*) The extent of the information to which access was allowed or which was disclosed.[16]

6. Recorded images should not be made more widely available – for example they should not be routinely made available to the media or placed on the Internet (Second, Seventh and Eighth Data Protection Principles).

7. If it is intended that images will be made more widely available, that decision should be made by the manager or designated member of staff. The reason for that decision should be documented (Seventh Data Protection Principle).

8. If it is decided that images will be disclosed to the media (other than in the circumstances outlined above), the images of individuals will need to be disguised or blurred so that they are not readily identifiable (First, Second and Seventh Data Protection Principles).

9. *If the system does not have the facilities to carry out that type of editing, an editing company may need to be hired to carry it out.*

10. If an editing company is hired, then the manager or designated member of staff needs to ensure that:

    (*a*) There is a contractual relationship between the data controller and the editing company.

    (*b*) That the editing company has given appropriate guarantees regarding the security measures they take in relation to the images.

    (*c*) The manager has checked to ensure that those guarantees are met

    (cont'd)

> (*d*)   The written contract makes it explicit that the editing company can only use the images in accordance with the instructions of the manager or designated member of staff.
>
> (*e*)   The written contract makes the security guarantees provided by the editing company explicit.
>
> 11.   If the media organisation receiving the images undertakes to carry out the editing, then (a) to (e) will still apply.
>
> *(Seventh Data Protection Principle)*

Access by data subjects

This is a right, which is provided by section 7 of the 1998 Act. A detailed explanation of the interpretation of this right is given in Part II. The standards of this Code of Practice are set out below.

Standards

> 1.   All staff involved in operating the equipment must be able to recognise a request for access to recorded images by data subjects (Sixth and Seventh Data Protection Principles).
>
> 2.   *Data subjects should be provided with a standard subject access request form which:*
>
>   (*a*)   *Indicates the information required in order to locate the images requested.*
>
>   **For example** *– an individual may have to provide dates and times of when they visited the premises of the user of the equipment.*
>
>   (*b*)   *Indicates the information required in order to identify the person making the request.*
>
>   **For example** *–if the individual making the request is unknown to the user of the equipment, a photograph of the individual may be requested in order to locate the correct image.*
>
>   (*c*)   *Indicates the fee that will be charged for carrying out the search for the images requested. A maximum of £10.00 may be charged for the search.*
>
>   (d)   Asks whether the individual would be satisfied with merely viewing the images recorded.
>
>   (e)   Indicates that the response will be provided promptly and in any event within 40 days of receiving the required fee and information.
>
>   (f)   Explains the rights provided by the 1998 Act.
>
> 3.   Individuals should also be provided with a leaflet which describes the types images which are recorded and retained, the purposes for which those images are recorded and retained, and information about the disclosure policy in relation to those images (Sixth Data Protection Principle).[17]
>
> 4.   This should be provided at the time that the standard subject access request form is provided to an individual (Sixth Data Protection Principle).[18]
>
> 5.   *All subject access requests should be dealt with by a manager or designated member of staff.*
>
> 6.   *The manager or designated member of staff should locate the images requested.*
>
> 7.   The manager or designated member of staff should determine whether disclosure to the individual would entail disclosing images of third parties (Sixth Data Protection Principle).[19]
>
> *(cont'd)*

8. The manager or designated member of staff will need to determine whether the images of third parties are held under a duty of confidence (First and Sixth Data Protection Principle).[20]

   For example – it may be that members of the public whose images have been recorded when they were in town centres or streets have less expectation that their images are held under a duty of confidence than individuals whose images have been recorded in more private space such as the waiting room of a doctor's surgery.

9. If third party images are not to be disclosed, the manager or designated member of staff shall arrange for the third party images to be disguised or blurred (Sixth Data Protection Principle).[21]

10. *If the system does not have the facilities to carry out that type of editing, a third party or company may be hired to carry it out.*

11. If a third party or company is hired, then the manager or designated member of staff needs to ensure that:

    (*a*) There is a contractual relationship between the data controller and the third party or company.

    (*b*) That the third party or company has given appropriate guarantees regarding the security measures they take in relation to the images.

    (*c*) The manager has checked to ensure that those guarantees are met.

    (*d*) The written contract makes it explicit that the third party or company can only use the images in accordance with the instructions of the manager or designated member of staff.

    (*e*) The written contract makes the security guarantees provided by the third party or company explicit

    (Seventh Data Protection Principle)

12. *If the manager or designated member of staff decides that a subject access request from an individual is not to be complied with, the following should be documented:*

    (a) *The identity of the individual making the request*

    (b) The date of the request

    (c) The reason for refusing to supply the images requested

    (d) The name and signature of the manager or designated member of staff making the decision.[22]

13. All staff should be aware of individuals' rights under this section of the Code of Practice (Seventh Data Protection Principle)

Other rights

A detailed explanation of the other rights under Sections 10, 12 and 13 of the Act are provided in Part II of this Code. The standards of this Code are set out below.

Standards

1. All staff involved in operating the equipment must be able to recognise a request from an individual to:

    (*a*) Prevent processing likely to cause substantial and unwarranted damage to that individual.[23]

    (*b*) Prevent automated decision taking in relation to that individual.[24]

2. *All staff must be aware of the manager or designated member of staff who is responsible for responding to such requests.*

3. In relation to a request to prevent processing likely to cause substantial and unwarranted damage, the manager or designated officer's response should indicate whether he or she will comply with the request or not.[25]

4. The manager or designated member of staff must provide a written response to the individual within 21 days of receiving the request setting out their decision on the request.[26]

5. If the manager or designated member of staff decide that the request will not be complied with, they must set out their reasons in the response to the individual.[27]

6. *A copy of the request and response should be retained.*

7. If an automated decision is made about an individual, the manager or designated member of staff must notify the individual of that decision.[28]

8. If, within 21 days of that notification, the individual requires, in writing, the decision to be reconsidered, the manager or designated staff member shall reconsider the automated decision.[29]

9. On receipt of a request to reconsider the automated decision, the manager or designated member of staff shall respond within 21 days setting out the steps that they intend to take to comply with the individual's request.[30]

10. *The manager or designated member of staff shall document:*

    (*a*) *The original decision.*

    (*b*) *The request from the individual.*

    (*c*) *Their response to the request from the individual.*

Monitoring compliance with this code of practice

Standards

1. The contact point indicated on the sign should be available to members of the public during office hours. Employees staffing that contact point should be aware of the policies and procedures governing the use of this equipment.

2. *Enquiries should be provided on request with one or more of the following:*

    (*a*) *The leaflet which individuals receive when they make a subject access request as general information*

(cont'd)

(b)   A copy of this code of practice

(c)   A subject access request form if required or requested

(d)   The complaints procedure to be followed if they have concerns about the use of the system

(e)   The complaints procedure to be followed if they have concerns about non-compliance with the provisions of this Code of Practice

3.   *A complaints procedure should be clearly documented.*

4.   A record of the number and nature of complaints or enquiries received should be maintained together with an outline of the action taken.

5.   A report on those numbers should be collected by the manager or designated member of staff in order to assess public reaction to and opinion of the use of the system.

6.   A manager or designated member of staff should undertake regular reviews of the documented procedures to ensure that the provisions of this Code are being complied with (Seventh Data Protection Principle).

7.   A report on those reviews should be provided to the data controller(s) in order that compliance with legal obligations and provisions with this Code of Practice can be monitored.

8.   An internal annual assessment should be undertaken which evaluates the effectiveness of the system.

9.   The results of the report should be assessed against the stated purpose of the scheme. If the scheme is not achieving its purpose, it should be discontinued or modified.

10.   The result of those reports should be made publicly available.

Part II
Glossary
The Data Protection Act 1998

1. Definitions

There are several definitions in sections 1 and 2 of the 1998 Act which users of CCTV systems or similar surveillance equipment must consider in order to determine whether they need to comply with the requirements of the 1998 Act, and if so, to what extent the 1998 Act applies to them:

(a) Data Controller

'A person who (either alone or jointly or in common with other persons) determines the purposes for which and the manner in which any personal data are, or are to be, processed.'

For example: if a police force and local authority enter into a partnership to install CCTV in a town centre with a view to:

- preventing and detecting crime;

- apprehending and prosecuting offenders; and

- protecting public safety.

They will both be data controllers for the purpose of the scheme.

For example, if a police force, local authority and local retailers decide to install a CCTV scheme in a town centre or shopping centre, for the purposes of:

- prevention or detection crime;

- apprehending or prosecuting offenders; and

- protecting public safety.

All will be data controllers for the purposes of the scheme. It is the data controllers who should set out the purposes of the scheme (as outlined above) and who should set out the policies on the use of the images (as outlined in the Standards section of this Code of Practice).

The data controller(s) may devolve day-to-day running of the scheme to a manager, but that manager is not the data controller – he or she can only manage the scheme according to the instructions of the data controller(s), and according to the policies set out by the data controller(s).

If the manager of the scheme is an employee of one or more of the data controllers, then the manager will not have any personal data protection responsibilities as a data controller. However, the manager should be aware that if he or she acts outside the instructions of the data controller(s) in relation to obtaining or disclosing the images, they may commit a criminal offence contrary to section 55 of the 1998 Act, as well as breach their contract of employment.

If the manager is a third party such as a security company employed by the data controller to run the scheme, then the manager may be deemed a data processor. This is "any person (other than an employee of the data controller) who processes the personal data on behalf of the data controller. If the data controller(s) are considering using a data processor, they will need to consider their compliance with the Seventh Data Protection Principle in terms of this relationship.

(b) Personal Data

'Data which relate to a living individual who can be identified:

- from those data, or

- from those data and other information which is in the possession of, or is likely to come into the possession of, the data controller.'

The provisions of the 1998 Act are based on the requirements of a European Directive[31], which at, Article 2, defines, personal data as follows:

'Personal data' shall mean any information relating to an identified or identifiable natural person; an identifiable person is one who can be identified, directly or indirectly, in particular by reference to an identification number or to one or more factors specific to his physical, physiological, mental, economic, cultural or social identity.

The definition of personal data is not therefore limited to circumstances where a data controller can attribute a name to a particular image. If images of distinguishable individuals' features are processed and an individual can be identified from these images, they will amount to personal data.

(c) Sensitive Personal Data

Section 2 of the 1998 Act separates out distinct categories of personal data, which are deemed sensitive. The most significant of these categories for the purposes of this code of practice are information about:[32]

- the commission or alleged commission of any offences

- any proceedings for any offence committed, or alleged to have been committed, the disposal of such proceedings or the sentence of any court in such proceedings.

This latter bullet point will be particularly significant for those CCTV schemes which are established by retailers in conjunction with the local police force, which use other information to identify known and convicted shoplifters from images, with a view to reducing the amount of organised shoplifting in a retail centre.

It is essential that data controllers determine whether they are processing sensitive personal data because it has particular implications for their compliance with the First Data Protection Principle.

(d) Processing

Section 1 of the 1998 Act sets out the type of operations that can constitute processing:

'In relation to information or data, means obtaining, processing, recording or holding the information or data or carrying out any operation or set of operations on the information or data, including:

- organisation, adaptation or alteration of the information or data,

- retrieval, consultation or use of the information or data,

- disclosure of the information or data by transmission, dissemination or otherwise making available, or

- alignment, combination, blocking, erasure or destruction of the information or data.'

The definition is wide enough to cover the simple recording and holding of images for a limited period of time, even if no further reference is made to those images. It is also wide enough to cover real-time transmission of the images. Thus if the images of individuals passing in front of a camera are shown in real time on a monitor, this constitutes "transmission, dissemination or otherwise making available. Thus even the least sophisticated capturing and use of images falls within the definition of processing in the 1998 Act.

2. Purposes for which personal data/images are processed

Before considering compliance with the Data Protection Principles, a user of CCTV or similar surveillance equipment, will need to determine two issues:

- What type of personal data are being processed i.e. are there any personal data which fall within the definition of sensitive personal data as defined by section 2 of the 1998 Act.

- For what purpose(s) are both personal data and sensitive personal data being processed?

Users of surveillance equipment should be clear about the purposes for which they intend to use the information/images captured by their equipment. The equipment may be used for a number of purposes:

- Prevention, investigation and/or detection of crime.

- Apprehension and/or prosecution of offenders (including images being entered as evidence in criminal proceedings).

- Public and employee safety.
- Staff discipline.
- Traffic flow monitoring.

Using information captured by a surveillance system will not always require the processing of personal data or the processing of sensitive personal data. For example, use of the system to monitor traffic flow in order to provide the public with up to date information about traffic jams, will not necessarily require the processing of personal data.

3. Data protection principles

First Data Protection Principle

This requires that

'Personal data shall be processed fairly and lawfully, and, in particular, shall not be processed unless:

- at least one of the conditions in Schedule 2 is met, and

- in the case of sensitive personal data, at least one of the conditions in Schedule 3 is also met.'

To assess compliance with this Principle, it is recommended that the data controller address the following questions:

(a) Are personal data and/or sensitive personal data processed?

The definition of sensitive personal data[33] has been discussed above and it is essential that the data controller has determined whether they are processing information/images, which fall into that category in order to assess which criteria to consider when deciding whether there is a legitimate basis for the processing of that information/images.

(b) Has a condition for processing been met?

The First Data Protection Principle requires that the *data controller* have a legitimate basis for processing. It is for the data controller to be clear about which grounds to rely on in this respect. These are set out in Schedules 2 and 3 to the Act.

Users of schemes which monitor spaces to which the public have access, such as town centres, may be able to rely on Paragraph 5 (d) of Schedule 2 because the processing is for the exercise of any other function of a public nature exercised in the public interest by any person. This could include purposes such as prevention and detection of crime, apprehension and prosecution of offenders or public/employee safety.

Users of schemes which monitor spaces in shops or retail centres to which the public have access may be able to rely on Paragraph 6(1) of Schedule 2 because the processing is necessary for the purposes of legitimate interests pursued by the data controller or the third party or third parties to whom the data are disclosed, except where the processing is unwarranted in any particular case by reason of prejudice to the rights and freedoms or legitimate interests of the data subject.

It should be noted that while this criterion may provide a general ground for processing, in an individual case, the interests of the data controller i.e. the user of the surveillance equipment might not outweigh the rights of an individual.

If the data controller has determined that he or she is processing sensitive personal data, then the data controller will also need to determine whether he or she has a legitimate basis for doing so under Schedule 3. It should be noted that Schedule 3 does not contain the grounds cited above in relation to Schedule 2.

Users of surveillance equipment in town centres, particularly where the local authority or police force (or a partnership of the two) are the data controllers may be able to rely on Paragraph 7(l)(b) of Schedule 3 because the processing is necessary for the exercise of any functions conferred on any person by or under an enactment. It may be that the use of such information/images by a public authority in order to meet the objectives of the Crime and Disorder Act 1998 would satisfy this criterion.

Users of information/images recorded in a shop or retail centre may be able to rely on one of the grounds contained in the Order made under Schedule 3(10) of the 1998 Act.[34]

For example-

'(1) The processing:

(*a*)   is in the substantial public interest;

(*b*)   is necessary for the purposes of the prevention and detection of any unlawful act; and

(*c*)   must necessarily be carried out without the explicit consent of the data subject so as not to prejudice those purposes.'

It is for the data controller to be sure that he or she has legitimate grounds for their processing and therefore it is essential that the data controller has identified:

- what categories of data are processed, and
- why.

(c) Are the information/images processed lawfully?

The fact that the data controller has a legitimate basis for processing does not mean that this element of the First Data Protection Principle is automatically satisfied. The data controller will also need to consider whether the information/images processed are subject to any other legal duties or responsibilities such as the common law duty of confidentiality. Public sector bodies will need to consider their legal powers under administrative law in order to determine whether there are restrictions or prohibitions on their ability to process such data. They will also need to consider the implications of the Human Rights Act 1998.

(d) Are the information/images processed fairly?

The fact that a data controller has a legitimate basis for processing the information/images will not automatically mean that this element of the First Data Protection Principle is satisfied.

The interpretative provisions[35] of the Act set out what is required in order to process fairly. In order to process fairly, the following information, at least, must be provided to the individuals at the point of obtaining their images:

- the identity of the data controller

- the identity of a representative the data controller has nominated for the purposes of the Act

- the purpose or purposes for which the data are intended to be processed, and

- any information which is necessary, having regard to the specific circumstances in which the data are or are to be processed, to enable processing in respect of the individual to be fair.

(e) Circumstances in which the requirement for signs may be set aside

The Act does not make specific reference to the use of covert processing of (sensitive) personal data but it does provide a limited exemption from the requirement of fair processing. Because fair processing (as indicated above) requires that individuals are made aware that they are entering an area where their images may be captured, by the use of signs, it follows that the use of covert processing i.e. removal or failure to provide signs, is prima facie a breach of the fairness requirement of the First Data Protection Principle. However, a breach of this requirement will not arise if an exemption can be relied on. Such an exemption may be found at section 29(l) of the Act, which states that:

'Personal data processed for any of the following purposes:

- prevention or detection of crime

- apprehension or prosecution of offenders

are exempt from the first data protection principle (except to the extent to which it requires compliance with the conditions in Schedules 2 and 3) ... in any case to the extent to which the application of those provisions to the data would be likely to prejudice any of the matters mentioned ... '

This means that if the data controller processes images for either or both of the purposes listed in the exemption, he or she may be able to obtain and process images without signs without breaching the fairness requirements of the First Data Protection Principle.

Second Data Protection Principle

This requires that:

'Personal data shall be obtained only for one or more specified and lawful purposes, and shall not be further processed in any manner incompatible with that purpose or those purposes.'

In order to ascertain whether the data controller can comply with this Data Protection Principle, it is essential that he or she is clear about the purpose(s) for which the images are processed.

Specified purposes may be those, which have been notified to the Commissioner or to the individuals.

There are a number of issues to be considered when determining lawfulness:

- Whether the data controller has a legitimate basis (see First Data Protection Principle) for the processing.

- Whether the images are processed in accordance with any other legal duties to which the data controller may be subject e.g. the common law duty of confidence, administrative law in relation to public sector powers etc.

It is quite clear from the interpretative provisions to the Principle that the requirement of compatibility is particularly significant when considering making a disclosure to a third party or developing a policy on disclosures to third parties. If the data controller intends to make a disclosure to a third party, regard must be had to the purpose(s) for which the third party may process the data.

This means, for example, that if the purpose(s) for which images are processed is:

- Prevention or detection of crime
- Apprehension or prosecution of offenders

The data controller may only disclose to third parties who intend processing the data for compatible purposes. Thus, for example, where there is an investigation into criminal activity, disclosure of footage relating to that criminal activity to the media in order to seek assistance from the public in identifying either the perpetrator, the victim or witnesses, may be appropriate. However, it would be an incompatible use if images from equipment installed to prevent or detect crime were disclosed to the media merely for entertainment purposes. For example, it might be appropriate to disclose to the media images of drunken individuals stumbling around a town centre on a Saturday night to show proper use of policing resources to combat anti-social behaviour. However, it would not be appropriate for the same images to be provided to a media company merely for inclusion in a 'humorous' video.

If it is determined that a particular disclosure is compatible with the purposes for which the data controller processes images, then the extent of disclosure will need to be considered. If the footage, which is to be disclosed contains images of unrelated third parties, the data controller will need to ensure that those images are disguised in such a way that they cannot be identified.

If the data controller does not have the facilities to carry out such editing, he or she may agree with the media organisation that it will ensure that those images are disguised. This will mean that the media organisation is carrying out processing, albeit of a limited nature on behalf of the data controller which is likely to render it a data processor. In which case the data controller will need to ensure that the relationship with the media organisation complies with the Seventh Data Protection Principle.

Third Data Protection Principle

This requires that:

'Personal data shall be adequate, relevant and not excessive in relation to the purpose or purposes for which they are processed.'

This means that consideration must be given to the situation of the cameras so that they do not record more information than is necessary for the purpose for which they were installed. For example cameras installed for the purpose of recording acts of vandalism in a car park should not overlook private residences. Furthermore, if the recorded images on the tapes are blurred or indistinct, it may well be that this will constitute inadequate data. For example, if the purpose of the system is to collect evidence of criminal activity, blurred or indistinct images from degraded tapes or poorly maintained equipment will not provide legally sound evidence, and may therefore be inadequate for its purpose.

Fourth Data Protection Principle

This requires that:

'Personal data shall be accurate and, where necessary, kept up to date.'

This principle requires that the personal information that is recorded and stored must be accurate. This is particularly important if the personal information taken from the system is to be used as evidence in cases of criminal conduct or in disciplinary disputes with employees. The Commissioner recommends that efforts are made to ensure the clarity of the images, such as using only good quality tapes in recording the information, cleaning the tapes prior to re-use and not simply recording over existing images, and replacing tapes on a regular basis to avoid degradation from over-use.

If the data controller's system uses features such as time references and even location references, then these should be accurate. This means having a documented procedure to ensure the accuracy of such features are checked and if necessary, amended or altered.

Care should be exercised when using digital-enhancement and compression technologies to produce stills for evidence from tapes because these technologies often contain pre-programmed presumptions as to the likely nature of sections of the image. Thus the user cannot be certain that the images taken from the tape are an accurate representation of the actual scene. This may create evidential difficulties if they are to be relied on either in court or an internal employee disciplinary hearing.

Fifth Data Protection Principle

This requires that:

> 'Personal data processed for any purpose or purposes shall not be kept for longer than is necessary for that purpose or those purposes.'

This principle requires that the information shall not be held for longer than is necessary for the purpose for which it is to be used. The tapes that have recorded the relevant activities should be retained until such time as the proceedings are completed and the possibility of any appeal has been exhausted. After that time, the tapes should be erased. Apart from those circumstances, stored or recorded images should not be kept for any undue length of time. A policy on periods for retention of the images should be developed which takes into account the nature of the information and the purpose for which it is being collected. For example where images are being recorded for the purposes of crime prevention in a shopping area, it may be that the only images that need to be retained are those relating to specific incidents of criminal activity; the rest could be erased after a very short period. The Commissioner understands that generally town centre schemes do not retain recorded images for more than 28 days unless the images are required for evidential purposes.

Sixth Data Protection Principle

This requires that:

> 'Personal data shall be processed in accordance with the rights of data subjects under this Act.'

The Act provides individuals with a number of rights in relation to the processing of their personal data. Contravening the following rights will amount to a contravention of the Sixth Data Protection Principle:

- The right to be provided, in appropriate cases, with a copy of the information constituting the personal data held about them – Section 7.[36]

- The right to prevent processing which is likely to cause damage or distress – Section 10.[37]

- Rights in relation to automated decision-taking – Section 12.[38]

Seventh Data Protection Principle[39]

This requires that:

'Appropriate technical and organisational measures shall be taken against unauthorised or unlawful processing of personal data and against accidental loss or destruction of, or damage to, personal data.'

In order to assess the level of security the data controller needs to take to ensure compliance with this Principle, he or she needs to assess:

- the harm that might result from unauthorised or unlawful processing or accidental loss, destruction or damage of the personal data.[40] While it is clear that breach of this Principle may have a detrimental effect on the purpose(s) of the scheme e.g. the evidence or images might not stand up in court, or the public may lose confidence in your use of surveillance equipment due to inappropriate disclosure, the harm test required by the Act also requires primarily the effect on the people recorded to be taken into account;

- the nature of the data to be protected must be considered. Sensitive personal data was defined at the beginning of this part of the Code, but there may be other aspects, which need to be considered. For example, a town centre scheme may coincidentally record the image of a couple kissing in a parked car, or a retailer's scheme may record images of people in changing rooms (in order to prevent items of clothing being stolen). Whilst these images may not fall within the sensitive categories as set in Section 2 (described above), it is clear that the people whose images have been captured will consider that information or personal data should be processed with greater care.

Eighth Data Protection Principle

This requires that:

'Personal data shall not be transferred to a country or territory outside the European Economic Area unless that country or territory ensures an adequate level of protection for the rights and freedoms of data subjects in relation to the processing of personal data.'

This Principle places limitations on the ability to transfer personal data to countries and territories outside of the EEA.[41] It is unlikely that the data controller would want, in general, to make such transfers of personal data overseas, but the data controller should refrain from putting the images on the Internet or on their website. In order to ensure that this Principle is not breached, the data controller should consider the provisions of Schedule 4 of the 1998 Act.

4. Right of subject access

Upon making a request in writing (which includes transmission by electronic means) and upon paying the fee to the data controller an individual is entitled:

- To be told by the data controller whether they or someone else on their behalf is processing that individual's personal data.

- If so, to be given a description of:

  (*a*)   the personal data,

  (*b*)   the purposes for which they are being processed, and

  (*c*)   those to whom they are or may be disclosed.

- To be told, in an intelligible manner, of:

    (*a*)   all the information, which forms any such personal data. This information must be supplied in permanent form by way of a copy, except where the supply of such a copy is not possible or would involve disproportionate effort or the individual agrees otherwise. If any of the information in the copy is not intelligible without explanation, the individual should be given an explanation of that information, e.g. where the data controller holds the information in coded form which cannot be understood without the key to the code, and

    (*b*)   any information as to the source of those data. However, in some instances the data controller is not obliged to disclose such information where the source of the data is, or can be identified as, an individual.

A data controller may charge a fee (subject to a maximum) for dealing with subject access. A data controller must comply with a subject access request promptly, and in any event within forty days of receipt of the request or, if later, within forty days of receipt of:

- the information required (i.e. to satisfy himself as to the identity of the person making the request and to locate the information which that person seeks); and

- the fee.

However, unless the data controller has received a request in writing, the prescribed fee and, if necessary, the said information the data controller need not comply with the request. If the data controller receives a request without the required fee and/or information, they should request whichever is outstanding as soon as possible in order that they can comply with the request promptly and in any event within 40 days. A data controller does not need to comply with a request where they have already complied with an identical or similar request by the same individual unless a reasonable interval has elapsed between compliance with the previous request and the making of the current request. In deciding what amounts to a reasonable interval, the following factors should be considered: the nature of the data, the purpose for which the data are processed and the frequency with which the data are altered.

The information given in response to a subject access request should be all that which is contained in the personal data at the time the request was received. However, routine amendments and deletions of the data may continue between the date of the request and the date of the reply. To this extent, the information revealed to the individual may differ from the personal data which were held at the time the request was received, even to the extent that data are no longer held. But, having received a request, the data controller must not make any special amendment or deletion which would not otherwise have been made. The information must not be tampered with in order to make it acceptable to the individual.

A particular problem arises for data controllers who may find that in complying with a subject access request they will disclose information relating to an individual other than the individual who has made the request, who can be identified from that information, including the situation where the information enables that other individual to be identified as the source of the information. The Act recognises this problem and sets out only two circumstances in which the data controller is obliged to comply with the subject access request in such circumstances, namely:

- where the other individual has consented to the disclosure of the information, or

- where it is reasonable in all the circumstances to comply with the request without the consent of the other individual.

The Act assists in interpreting whether it is reasonable in all the circumstances to comply with the request without the consent of the other individual concerned. In deciding this question regard shall be had, in particular, to:

- any duty of confidentiality owed to the other individual,

- any steps taken by the data controller with a view to seeking the consent of the other individual,

- whether the other individual is capable of giving consent, and

- any express refusal of consent by the other individual.

If a data controller is satisfied that the individual will not be able to identify the other individual from the information, taking into account any other information which, in the reasonable belief of the data controller, is likely to be in (or to come into) the possession of the individual, then the data controller must provide the information.

If an individual believes that a data controller has failed to comply with a subject access request in contravention of the Act they may apply to Court for an order that the data controller complies with the request. An order may be made if the Court is satisfied that the data controller has failed to comply with the request in contravention of the Act.

5. Exemptions to subject access rights

There are a limited number of exemptions to an individuals right of access. One of potential relevance to CCTV images is found at section 29 of the Act. This provides an exemption from the subject access rights, which is similar to that discussed in relation to the exemption to the fairness requirements of the First Data Protection Principle. This means that where personal data are held for the purposes of:

- prevention or detection of crime,

- apprehension or prosecution of offenders,

the data controller will be entitled to withhold personal data from an individual making a subject access request, where it has been adjudged that to disclose the personal data would be likely to prejudice one or both of the above purposes. Like the exemption to the fairness requirements of the First Data Protection Principle, this judgement must be made on a case-by-case basis, and in relation to each element of the personal data held about the individual. It is likely that this exemption may only be appropriately relied upon where the data controller has recorded personal data about an individual in accordance with guidance set out in relation to the fairness requirements of the First Data Protection Principle.[42]

6. Other rights

Right to prevent processing likely to cause damage or distress

Under section 10 of the Act, an individual is entitled to serve a notice on a data controller requiring the data controller not to begin, or to cease, processing personal data relating to that individual. Such a notice could only be served on the grounds that the processing in question is likely to cause substantial, unwarranted damage or distress to that individual or another person. There are certain limited situations where this right to serve a notice does not apply. These are where the individual has consented; the processing is in connection with performance of a contract with the data subject, or in compliance with a legal obligation on the data controller, or in order to protect the vital interests of the individual. If a data controller receives such a notice they must respond within 21 days indicating either compliance with the notice or why the notice is not justified.

Rights in relation to automated decision-taking

Under section 12 of the Act individuals also have certain rights to prevent automated decision taking where a decision, which significantly affects them is based solely on automated processing. The Act draws particular attention to decisions taken aimed at evaluating matters such as the individual's performance at work and their reliability or conduct. The Act does provide exemption for certain decisions reached by automated means and these cover decisions which have been taken in the course of contractual arrangements with the individual, where a decision is authorised or required by statute, where the decision is to grant a request of the individual or where steps have been taken to safeguard the legitimate interests of individuals. This latter point may include matters such as allowing them to make representations about a decision before it is implemented.

Where no notice has been served by an individual and a decision which significantly affects the individual based solely on automated processing will be made, then there is still an obligation on the data controller to notify the individual that the decision was taken on the basis of automated processing as soon as reasonably practicable. The individual may, within 21 days of receiving such a notification, request the data controller to reconsider the decision or take another decision on a new basis. Having received such a notice the data controller has 21 days in which to respond, specifying the steps that they intend to take to comply with the notice.

In the context of CCTV surveillance it may be the case that certain automated decision-making techniques are deployed, such as with automatic facial recognition. It is important therefore that any system takes account of an individual's rights in relation to automated decision taking. It should be noted that these rights are founded on decisions, which are taken solely on the basis of automated processing. If a decision whether to take particular action in relation to a particular identified individual is taken further to human intervention, then such a decision would not be based solely on automated processing.

The individual's rights to prevent processing in certain circumstances and in connection with automated decision taking are underpinned by an individual's right to seek a court order should any notice served by the individual not be complied with.

Compensation for failure to comply with certain requirements

Under section 13 of the Act, individuals who suffer unwarranted damage or damage and distress as a result of any contravention of the requirements of the Act are entitled to go to court to seek compensation in certain circumstances. This right to claim compensation for a breach of the Act is in addition to an individual's right to request the Data Protection Commissioner to make an assessment as to whether processing is likely or unlikely to comply with the Act.

1. It is intended that employers' use of personal data to monitor employee compliance with contracts of employment will be covered by the Data Protection Commissioner's forthcoming code of practice on use of employee personal data.
2. It is likely that the use of cameras by individuals to protect their own property is excluded from the provisions of the Act under the exemption at section 36 of the Act.
3. The Commissioner's powers to issue an Enforcement Notice may be found in section 40 of the Act.
4. The First Data Protection Principle requires data controllers to have a legitimate basis for processing personal data, in this case images of individuals. The Act sets out criteria for processing, one of which must be met in order to demonstrate that there is a legitimate basis for processing the images.
5. Section 4(4) of the Act places all data controllers under a duty to comply with the data protection principles in relation to all personal data with respect to which he is the data controller as defined by section 1(1) of the Act. See the section on definitions.
6. The First Data Protection Principle requires data controllers to have a legitimate basis for processing, one of which must be met in order to demonstrate that there is a legitimate basis for processing the images.
7. Section 17 of the Act prohibits the processing of personal data unless the data controller has notified the Data Protection Commissioner. The notification scheme requires that the purpose(s) of the processing be identified.

8. Section 29 of the Act sets out the circumstances in which the fair processing requirements of the First Data Protection Principle are set aside.

9. It may be that the particular problem identified is theft from cars in a car park. Following the appropriate assessment, surveillance equipment is installed but signs are not. If the equipment co-incidentally records images relating to other criminality for example a sexual assault, it will not be inappropriate for those images to be used in the detection of that crime or in order to apprehend and prosecute the offender. However, it might be inappropriate for images so obtained to be used in civil proceedings or disciplinary proceedings eg the car park attendant is recorded committing a minor disciplinary misdemeanour.

10. Users of such systems should be aware of the affect of section 12 of the 1998 Act regarding individuals' rights in relation to automated decision taking.

11. See the section on access to and disclosure of images to third parties.

12. See the section on access to and disclosure of images to third parties.

13. See the section on individual's rights.

14. See the section on the seventh data protection principle.

15. See the section on access to and disclosure of images to third parties.

16. See the section on access to and disclosure of images to third parties.

17. See the section on the right of subject access.

18. See the section on the right of subject access.

19. See the section on the right of subject access.

20. See the section on the right of subject access.

21. See the section on the right of subject access.

22. See the section on the right of subject access.

23. Section 10 of the Act provides individuals with the right to prevent processing likely to cause damage or distress. See the section on other rights.

24. Users of such a system should be aware of the effects of section 12 of the Act regarding individuals' rights in relation to automated decision taking.

25. Section 10 of the Act provides individuals with the right to prevent processing likely to cause substantial damage or distress. See the section on other rights.

26. Section 10 of the Act provides individuals with the right to prevent processing likely to cause substantial damage or distress. See the section on other rights.

27. Section 10 of the Act provides individuals with the right to prevent processing likely to cause substantial damage or distress. See the section on other rights.

28. Users of such systems should be aware of the effect of section 12 of the 1998 Act regarding individuals' rights in relation to automated decision taking.

29. Users of such systems should be aware of the effect of section 12 of the 1998 Act regarding individuals' rights in relation to automated decision taking.

30. Users of such systems should be aware of the effect of section 12 of the 1998 Act regarding individuals' rights in relation to automated decision taking.

31. European Directive 95/46/EC on the protection of individuals with regard to the processing of personal data and on the free movement of such data.

32. Section 2 of Act sets out the full list of categories of sensitive personal data. This part of the Code only refers to some of the categories, which may have particular relevance for users of CCTV. For a full list, please see the relevant section of the Act.

33. Section 2 of Act sets out the full list of categories of sensitive personal data. This part of the Code only refers to some of the categories, which may have particular relevance for users of CCTV. For a full list, please see the relevant section of the Act.

34. The Data Protection (Processing of Sensitive Personal Data) Order 2000 (SI 2000/417).

35. Schedule 1 Part II Sections 1–4 of the Act.

36. See the section on the right of subject access.

37. Section 2 of the Act sets out the full list of categories of sensitive personal data. This part of the Code only refers to some of the categories, which may have particular relevance for users of CCTV. For a full list, please see the relevant section of the Act.

38. Users of such systems should be aware of the effect of section 12 of the 1998 Act regarding individuals' rights in relation to automated decision taking.

39. British Standard Institute – BS 7958:1991 'Closed Circuit Television (CCTV) – Management and Operation Code of Practice' provides guidance on issues of security, tape management etc.

40. Schedule 1, Part II, Paragraph 9 of the Act.

41. Schedule 1, Part II, Paragraphs 13–15 of the Act.

42. See the subsection on circumstances in which the requirements for signs may be set aside.

CCTV Systems and the Data Protection Act 1998 (DPA)

Guidance Note on when the Act applies

1. Why is there a need for additional guidance?

There has been a recent court case which affects whether particular CCTV activities are covered by the DPA. This Guidance Note makes clearer which CCTV activities are covered by the DPA. It is particularly aimed at helping users of basic CCTV systems such as small businesses.

2. What CCTV activities are covered by the DPA?

The court case dealt with when information relates to an individual and is then covered by the DPA. (The case is Durant-v- Financial Services Authority and was heard by the Court of Appeal. Guidance on the general effect of this case is available via our website.) The court decided that for information to relate to an individual, it had to affect their privacy. To help judge this, the Court decided that two matters were important:

- that a person had to be the focus of the information
- the information tells you something significant about them.

So, whether you are covered or not will depend on how you use your CCTV system.

3. I only use a very basic CCTV system, how am I affected?

If you have just a basic CCTV system, your use may no longer be covered by the DPA. This depends on what happens in practice. For example, small retailers would not be covered who:

- only have a couple cameras,
- can't move them remotely,
- just record on video tape whatever the cameras pick up, and
- only give the recorded images to the police to investigate an incident in their shop.

The shopkeepers would need to make sure that they do not use the images for their own purposes such as checking whether a member of staff is doing their job properly, because if they did, then that person would be the focus of attention and they would be trying to learn things about them so the use would then be covered by the DPA. (We have published an Employment Practices Code. Part 3 includes guidance on what you have to do to comply with the DPA if you are monitoring your staff. This is available from our website.)

4. It sounds like many users of basic CCTV systems are not covered by the DPA, is there an easy way to tell?

Think about what you are trying to achieve by using CCTV. Is it there for you to learn about individuals' activities for your own business purposes (such as monitoring a member of staff giving concern)? If so, then it will still be covered. However if you can answer 'no' to all the following 3 questions you will not be covered:

- Do you ever operate the cameras remotely in order to zoom in/out or point in different directions to pick up what particular people are doing?
- Do you ever use the images to try to observe someone's behaviour for your own business purposes such as monitoring staff members?
- Do you ever give the recorded images to anyone other than a law enforcement body such as the police?

5. How are more sophisticated CCTV systems affected?

In many CCTV schemes, such as are used in town centres or by large retailers, CCTV systems are more sophisticated. They are used to focus on the activities of particular people either by directing cameras at an individual's activities, looking out for particular individuals or examining recorded CCTV images to find things out about the people in them such as identifying a criminal or a witness or assessing how an employee is performing. These activities will still be covered by the DPA but some of the images they record will no longer be covered. So if only a general scene is recorded without any incident occurring and with no focus on any particular individual's activities, these images are not covered by the DPA. In short, organisations using CCTV for anything other than the most basic of surveillance will have to comply with the DPA but not all their images will be covered in all circumstances. The simple rule of thumb is that you need to decide whether the image you have taken is aimed at learning about a particular person's activities.

6. What should I do next?

If some of your CCTV activities are still covered you still need to comply with the DPA by making sure you have notified the Commissioner, having signs, deciding how long you retain images and making sure your equipment works properly. The Information Commissioner has issued a CCTV Code of Practice (Copies of the CCTV Code of Practice and other publications are available on our website www.informationcommissioner.gov.uk) and this together with a checklist for users of small CCTV systems provides detailed guidance for those using CCTV systems. The only difference is that you will no longer have to give individuals access to those images that are just general scenes neither focusing on a particular individual nor being used to learn information about individuals.

If you are a user of a basic system and are not covered, you do not have to comply with the DPA though you may find the guidance on compliance in the CCTV Code of Practice helpful as this gives good practice advice to help make sure the images are up to the job of preventing and detecting crime. If you have already notified the Information Commissioner of your CCTV activities you will not have to renew this when it is due. Just let us know when you get your renewal reminder.

7. Will you be issuing further guidance on CCTV?

The Information Commissioner is already conducting an extensive review of the existing CCTV Code of Practice to make sure it has kept up to date with technological and other developments. This review will also take into account the changes to the interpretation of the DPA covered by this paper. The revised code should be published later in the year.

8. Confused?

Just give us a call, our Data Protection Helpline staff will be happy to help. The number is 01625 545745. If you have a query about an existing notification entry our Notification staff can help you- their number is 01625 545740

Appendix 2 – European Commission Frequently Asked Questions on Model Clauses for Data Export

Commission decision on standard contractual clauses for the transfer of personal data to third countries (2001/497/EC)

Frequently asked questions

1. Are the standard contractual clauses compulsory for companies interested in transferring data outside the EU?

2. Do these clauses set a minimum standard for individual contracts or future model contracts?

3. Can companies still rely on different contracts approved at national level?

4. Will the Commission consider issuing in future other standard contractual clauses?

5. When using the standard contractual clauses do companies still need a national authorisation to proceed with the transfer?

6. Is the deposit of the contract before the Member States compulsory? And can the transfer take place before the deposit?

7. How can companies protect their confidential information if they have to deposit a copy of these clauses with the Supervisory Authorities and provide the data subject with a copy on request?

8. Can Member States block or suspend data transfers using the standard contractual clauses?

9. What is meant by 'restrictions necessary in a democratic society' in Article 3 (a)?

10. What is covered by the term 'legislation' in Clause 5 (a)? And what specific action should the Data Importer take to ascertain that he is not prevented from fulfilling his obligations under the contract?

11. Can companies implement the standard contractual clauses in a wider contract and add specific clauses?

12. Does joint and several liability mean that the liability of the parties is strict?

13. Does joint and several liability mean that the Data Importer can be sued for the Data Exporters' violation before the transfer has taken place?

14. Does joint and several liability mean that the Data Importer will never be sued?

15. Does joint and several liability mean that the Data Exporter is responsible in relation to the individual for breach of contract by the Data Importer?

16. Does joint and several liability mean that the Data Exporter has to pay for any damages caused to individuals as a consequence of the violations committed by the Data Importer in a third country?

17. Does compliance with the "Mandatory Data Protection Principles" mean compliance with the provisions of the Directive 95/46/EC?

18. The model contract allow the Data Subject the right of access to his or her personal information. Is the right of access absolute and does it apply to both the Data Exporter and the Data Importer?

19. Can Data Importers be exempted from the application of the mandatory principles to fulfil their obligations under national law?

20. Are the parties liable for damages caused to individuals in such cases?

21. Can US based organisations that have joined the Safe Harbor use the standard contractual clauses to receive data from the EU?

22. Can U.S. based companies that have not joined the Safe Harbor use the relevant Safe Harbor rules under the contract?

23. What is an onward transfer?

24. Do the restrictions on onward transfers apply to onward transfers to recipients that have been found to provide for adequate protection?

These Frequently Asked Questions are very different from the FAQs of the Safe Harbor Decision. The FAQs of the Safe Harbor were part of Safe Harbor system issued by the U.S. Department of Commerce and therefore were part of the Commission Decision approved by the European Commission. These FAQs on the standard contractual clauses, on the contrary, do not form part of the draft Commission decision, have not been approved by the European Commission and do not have any legal value.

They are aimed at providing additional information to companies and individuals about the draft decision the Commission is likely to approve before the summer break, and they summarise those questions the Commission's services have been receiving from interested parties during the last months (see also letters received and replies from the Commission) and, in particular, in the meetings hold with representatives of business associations. These FAQs will be improved or updated if and when the need arises.

Directive 95/46/EC on the protection of individuals with regard to the processing of personal data and on the free movement of such data, requires Member

States to permit transfers of personal data only to third countries where there is adequate protection for such data, unless one of a limited number of specific exemptions applies. Where this is not the case, the transfer must not be allowed.[1]

Without such rules, the high standards of data protection established by the Directive would quickly be undermined, given the ease with which data can be moved around on international networks.

Article 26 (4) allows the Commission, with the support of a Management Committee composed of Member States representatives, to issue standard contractual clauses for the purpose of fulfilling the requirements set down by the directive when transferring data to third countries.

The present FAQs summarise the main issues of the draft Commission decision and provide information to individuals and companies on how to best make use of the standard contractual clauses. They are not part of the Commission decision, have not gone through a consultative process either with the Article 29 Working Party or the Management Committee and do not have a legal status of their own.

1. Are the standard contractual clauses compulsory for companies interested in transferring data outside the EU?

    No. The standard contractual clauses are neither compulsory for businesses nor are they the only way of lawfully transferring data to third countries.

    First of all, organisations do not need contractual clauses if they want to transfer personal data to recipients in countries which have been recognised as adequate by the Commission. This is the case of transfers to Switzerland,[2] Hungary[3] or US based companies adhering to the Safe Harbor Privacy Principles issued by the US Department of Commerce.[4]

    Secondly, even if the country of destination does not offer an adequate level of protection, data may be transferred in specific circumstances. These are listed in Article 26 (1) and include cases where:

    1. the data subject has given his consent unambiguously to the proposed transfer; or

    2. the transfer is necessary for the performance of a contract between the data subject and the controller or the implementation of pre-contractual measures taken in response to the data subject's request; or

    3. the transfer is necessary for the conclusion or performance of a contract concluded in the interest of the data subject between the controller and a third party; or

    4. the transfer is necessary or legally required on important p public interest grounds, or for the establishment, exercise or defence of legal claims; or

    5. the transfer is necessary in order to protect the vital interests of the data subject; or

6.   The transfer is made from a register which according to laws or regulations is intended to provide information to the public and which is open to consultation either by the public in general or by any person who can demonstrate legitimate interest, to the extent that the conditions laid down in law for consultation are fulfilled in the particular case.

Finally, under Article 26 (2) national authorities may authorise on a case by case basis specific transfers to a country not as offering an adequate protection where the exporter in the EU adduces adequate safeguards with respect to the protection of privacy by fundamental rights and freedoms of individuals and as regards the exercise of the corresponding rights.. This could be done for example by contractual arrangements between the exporter and the importer of data, subject to the prior approval of national authorities.

2.   Do these clauses set a minimum standard for individual contracts or future model contracts?

No. The standard contractual clauses do not have any effect on individual contracts or future model contractual clauses.

Once adopted this decision will simply oblige Member States to recognise the contractual clauses annexed to the decision as providing adequate safeguards and fulfilling the requirements set down in Articles 26 of the directive for data transfers to non-EU countries that do not provide for an adequate level of protection for personal data.

3.   Can companies still rely on different contracts approved at national level?

Yes. The standard contractual clauses do not prejudice past or future contractual arrangements authorised by national Data Protection Authorities pursuant to national legislation.

Authorisations at national level may be granted if Data Protection Authorities consider that the safeguards adduced by Data Exporters to protect the individuals privacy are sufficient in relation to the specific contract.[5] The content of these national contracts may be different from the Commission's standard contractual clauses. These contracts need to be notified to the Commission and the other Member States.

4.   Will the Commission consider issuing in future other standard contractual clauses?

Yes. The Commission intends to start work on other standard contractual clauses, in particular to deal with low risk transfers that may allow for a lighter approach to be followed. A first decision is likely to concern the transfer of data to a subcontractor for the mere processing, a category of transfers excluded from the scope of the draft Decision (see recital 9). We welcome input from businesses, in particular the submission of drafts from Industry Associations and encourage them to signal their needs in this respect.

5.   When using the standard contractual clauses do companies still need a national authorisation to proceed with the transfer?

Member States are obliged to recognise the standard contractual clauses as fulfilling the requirements set down by the directive for the export of data and consequently may not refuse the transfer. In most cases there is no need for a prior national authorisation to proceed with the transfer but some Member States maintain a license system. In this case however, the authorisation is automatically given and its requirement can in no way delay or hinder the performance of the contract.

6.   Is the deposit of the contract before the Member States compulsory? And can the transfer take place before the deposit?

The answer may vary from one Member State to another, as this is an option under the standard contractual clauses. Some Member States have already announced that they will request the deposit of the contract. Others may request the presentation of the contract or decide that no deposit or presentation will be necessary. Should the deposit or presentation of the contract be requested at national level, Member States will determine the procedure dealing with this question.

The deposit of the contract is only a formality to facilitate the work of the national data protection authorities and should not unduly delay the performance of the contract.

7.   How can companies protect their confidential information if they have to deposit a copy of these clauses with the Supervisory Authorities and provide the data subject with a copy on request?

In the case of standard contractual clauses, the clauses relating to the individual's data are those already in the public domain, and published in annex to the decision. All other clauses relating to the company's business can remain confidential. Moreover, data protection authorities and the European Commission are bound by a duty of confidentiality when exercising their duties.

8.   Can Member States block or suspend data transfers using the standard contractual clauses?

Yes, but only in the exceptional circumstances referred to in Article 3 of the Commission Decision. These include cases where:

(*a*)   It is established that the law to which the Data Importer is subject imposes upon him to derogate from the relevant data protection rules beyond the restrictions necessary in a democratic society as provided for in Article 13 of Directive 95/46/EC where those derogations are likely to have a substantial adverse effect on the guarantees provided by the standard contractual clauses, or

(*b*)   A competent authority has established that the Data Importer has not respected the contractual clauses, or

(*c*)   There is a substantial likelihood that the standard contractual clauses in the annex are not being or will not be complied with and the continuing transfer would create an imminent risk of grave harm to the Data Subjects

It is expected that this safeguard clause will be very rarely used as it caters for exceptional cases only. As provided for in Article 3 (3) of the draft decision, the European Commission will be informed of any use made by the Member States of this safeguard clause and will forward the information received to other Member States. The Commission may take appropriate measures in accordance with the procedure laid down in Article 31 (2) of Directive 95/46/EC

It is also important to highlight the fact that prior to the transfer it is the national law implementing the directive that apply and not the standard contractual clauses. In other words, transfers outside the EU can be lawfully made only if the data have been collected and further processed in accordance with the national laws applicable by the data controller established in the EU.

Therefore, companies interested in using the standard contractual clauses would still need to comply with the conditions for the lawfulness of the disclosure of the personal data in the Member State where the data exporter is established. Where a disclosure of data to a third party recipient inside a Member State would not be lawful, the mere circumstance that the recipient may be situated in a third country does not change this legal evaluation.

9. What is meant by "restrictions necessary in a democratic society" in Article 3 (a)?

Exceptions to the basic data protection principles must be limited to those which are necessary for the protection of fundamental values in a democratic society. These criteria cannot be laid down for all countries and all times but should be considered in the light of the given situation in the country in question. The interests protected are listed in article 13 of the directive and include all such measures that are necessary to safeguard:

(*a*)   national security;

(*b*)   defence;

(*c*)   public security;

(*d*)   the prevention, investigation, detection and prosecution of criminal offences, or of breaches of ethics for regulated professions;

(*e*)   an important economic or financial interest of the State including monetary, budgetary and taxation matters;

(*f*)   a monitoring, inspection or regulatory function connected, even occasionally, with the exercise of official authority in cases referred to in (c), (d) and (e);

(*g*)   the protection of the data subject or of the rights and freedoms of others.

The condition "necessary in a democratic society" derives from Articles 8–11 of the European Convention of Human Rights and extensive case law has been developed by the Commission of Human Rights on this issue. The same principle also occurs in the Council of Europe Convention 108.

10. What is covered by the term "legislation" in Clause 5 (a)? And what specific action should the Data Importer take to ascertain that he is not prevented from fulfilling his obligations under the contract?

    The term "legislation" in Clause 5 (a) also covers case law, rule or regulation that may impede on the performance of the contract. The Data Importer should take reasonable care to determine if there are any such rules that might prevent him from fulfilling his obligation.

11. Can companies implement the standard contractual clauses in a wider contract and add specific clauses ?

    Yes. Parties are free to agree to add other clauses as long as they do not contradict, directly or indirectly, the standard contractual clauses approved by the Commission or prejudice fundamental rights or freedoms of the data subjects. It is possible, for example, to include additional guarantees or procedural safeguards for the individuals (e.g. on-line procedures or relevant provisions contained in a privacy policy, etc.). All these other clauses that parties may decide to add would not be covered by the third party beneficiary rights and would benefit from confidentiality rights where appropriate.

    Member States may also further specify or complete the Appendix annexed to the contract.

    In all cases, the standard clauses have to be fully respected if they are to deploy the legal effect of providing for an adequate safeguard for the transfer of personal data as required by the EU directive.

    Recital 10 of the Draft decision states that Member States retain the power to particularise the information the parties are required to provide in the Appendix. What does it mean?

    The Appendix to the contract contains the minimum information that should be included in the contract. This said, it may be necessary to add additional requirements laid down in national law and necessary to make the transfer from a specific Member State lawful (see FAQ 6). For this reason Member States retain the power to add such specifications, relating for example to If a Member State decides to particularise the Appendix to the contract , it is that modified Appendix that must be used when data is transferred from that Member State.

    The Commission recognises that it may be useful, in future and on the basis of experience, to amend the Appendix in order to ensure that the information requirements are as similar as possible throughout the Union.

12. Does joint and several liability mean that the liability of the parties is strict?

    No. A party can be exempted from liability if it proofs that it is not responsible for the event causing the damage. It does not need to prove that the other party is responsible for the damage but at the same time it cannot be exempted from liability simply by alleging that the other party is responsible for the event causing the damage. In other words, exemption from liability is possible, for instance, in cases of force majeur or to the extent that there is a participation of the data subject in the event causing the damage.

13. Does joint and several liability mean that the Data Importer can be sued for the Data Exporters' violation before the transfer has taken place?

No. This case is excluded from the third party beneficiary's rights (Clause 3). Data subjects can however exercise their rights in the European Union against the Data Exporter for unlawful processing in the European Community.

14. Does joint and several liability mean that the Data Importer will never be sued?

Not necessarily. The data subjects may decide to sue the Data Exporter, the Data Importer or both. Although an action against the Data Exporter before a European court seems the preferable way for an individual to obtain compensation, he or she may decide to take action against the Data Importer, if, for example the Data Exporter has disappeared or filed for bankruptcy. In these cases, the Data Importer may be sued before the Data Exporter's Courts (clause 7) or before the Courts of his own country if so permitted under private international law.

15. Does joint and several liability mean that the Data Exporter is responsible in relation to the individual for breach of contract by the Data Importer?

No. Data Exporters are jointly and severally liable vis-à-vis the data subjects only for damages caused to individuals resulting from the violation of those provisions covered by third party beneficiary's rights (Clause 3). In the cases where the violation of the clauses does not result in damages for individuals, every party is solely responsible vis-à-vis the data subjects.

16. Does joint and several liability mean that the Data Exporter has to pay for any damages caused to individuals as a consequence of the violations committed by the Data Importer in a third country?

Yes, but only to the extent that the provision violated is covered by the third party beneficiary's rights (clause 3). Subsequently the Data Exporter has a right to recover any cost, charge, damage, expenses or loss from the Data Importer, to the extent that the latter is liable (see clause 6 (3)[6]).

Indemnification has been considerably eased by some of the provisions contained in the standard contractual clauses. In fact, the Data Importer agrees and warrants to deal promptly and properly with all inquires from the Data Subjects, the Data Exporter or the Supervisory Authority (Clause 5, letter c) and to submit its data processing facilities for audit at the request of the Data Exporter (clause 5, letter d).

It is therefore expected as a practical way to proceed that Data Exporters in the case of data subjects' complaints for damages caused by Data Importers' violations of the clauses will be able to convince their contractual counterparts to provide any necessary compensations himself in the first place and therefore to avoid subsequent indemnification. As it was already explained before, parties are free to include any additional clauses on mutual assistance or indemnification they consider pertinent.

In conclusion, "joint and several liability does not need to leave one party paying for the damages resulting from the unlawful processing of the other party because clause 6 (3) provides for mutual indemnification" (see recital 18).

17. Does compliance with the "Mandatory Data Protection Principles" mean compliance with the provisions of the Directive 95/46/EC?

No. The mandatory data protection principles reflect a set of substantive data protection principles that guarantees an adequate, not an equivalent level of protection. They have been construed on the basis of the Working Party's opinion 12/98.[7]

18. The model contract allow the Data Subject the right of access to his or her personal information. Is the right of access absolute and does it apply to both the Data Exporter and the Data Importer?

Both the Data Exporter and the Data Importer agree and warrant to respond properly and reasonably to inquiries from the Data Subjects about the processing of the data transferred. As indicated in Clause 4 c), the Data Exporter will respond to the extent reasonably possible as the questions posed by the Data Subjects would relate to the processing of personal data carried out by the Data Importer.

Clause 5 c) stipulates that the Data Importer warrants to deal promptly and properly with all reasonable inquiries from the Data Exporter. Therefore, if a Data Exporter receives an access request from a Data Subject concerning processing operations carried out by the Data Importer, the Data Exporter is expected to enforce clause 5 c) against the Data Importer, if necessary, to give satisfaction to the access request posed by the Data Subject.

19. Can Data Importers be exempted from the application of the mandatory principles to fulfil their obligations under national law?

Yes, as provided for in the closing paragraph of the mandatory principles they may do so as long as they are not confronted with mandatory requirements that go beyond what is necessary in a democratic society, namely because they constitute a necessary measure to safeguard national security, defence, public security, the prevention, investigation, detection and prosecution of criminal offences or of breaches of ethics for the regulated professions; an important economic or financial interest of the State or the protection of the Data Subjects or the rights and freedoms of others.

20. Are the parties liable for damages caused to individuals in such cases?

No, the exemption from the Mandatory Principles is complete.

The Data Importer (and the Data Exporter via application of Clause 6), however, would be liable for damages caused to individuals in case of compliance with mandatory requirements of national legislation that go beyond what is necessary in a democratic society on the basis of one of the interests mentioned above. In fact, at the signature of the contract, the Data Importer warrants that he has no reason to believe the legislation applicable to him prevents him from fulfilling his obligations under the contract and he undertakes to notify the Data Exporter and the Data Protection Authority of any change of this situation.

21. Can US based organisations that have joined the Safe harbor use the standard contractual clauses to receive data from the EU?

As a general rule, standard contractual clauses are not necessary if the data recipient is covered by a system providing adequate data protection such as the Safe Harbor. However, if the transfer concerns data that is not covered by their Safe Harbor commitments, use of the standard contract clauses is one way of providing the necessary safeguards.

22. Can U.S. based companies that have not joined the Safe Harbor use the relevant Safe Harbor rules under the contract?

Yes, provided that they also apply the three mandatory data protection principles in the Annex (applicable to all countries of destination): the purpose limitation, restrictions on onward transfers and the right of access, rectification, deletion and objection.

23. What is an onward transfer

There is an onward transfer every time personal data is transferred from the Data Importer to another natural or legal person that autonomously determines the purpose and means of processing.

Processing means any operation which is performed on personal data, such as collection, recording, organisation, storage, adaptation or alteration, retrieval, consultation, use disclosure, dissemination, alignment or combination, blocking, erasure or destruction.

24. Do the restrictions on onward transfers apply to onward transfers to recipients that have been found to provide for adequate protection?

No, the restrictions on onward transfers apply only to those cases where the recipient does not benefit from an adequacy finding. So far transfers to Switzerland, Hungary and US based organisations that have adhered to the Safe Harbor benefit from an adequacy finding.

The restrictions on onward transfers also do not apply when the recipient is established in a Member State of the EU or in an EEA Member State (Norway, Iceland and Liechtenstein).

[1] See Articles 25 and 26
[2] Commission decision 2000/518/EC (OJ L 215 of 25.08.2000, p. 1–3)
[3] Commission decision 2000/519/EC (OJ L 215 of 25.08.2000, p. 4–6)
[4] Commission decision 2000/520/EC (OJ L 215 of 25.08.2000, p. 7–47)
[5] See Article 26 (2) of Directive 95/46/EC.
[6] The parties agree that if one party is held liable for a violation by the other party of any of the provisions referred to in Clause 3, the second party will indemnify the first party from any cost, charge, damages, expenses or loss incurred by the first party to the extent to which the second party is liable
[7] WP12: Transfers of personal data to third countries : Applying Articles 25 and 26 of the EU data protection directive, adopted by the Working Party on 24 July 1998, available in the web site "europa.eu.int/comm/internal_markt/en/media.dataprot/wpdocs/wp12/en" hosted by the European Commission.

Appendix 3 – Model Clauses for Data Export

I For Data Controllers

COMMISSION DECISION

(2001/497/EC)

of 15 June 2001

on Standard Contractual Clauses for the transfer of personal data to third countries under Directive 95/46/EC

(notified under document number C(2001) 1539)

(Text with EEA relevance)

THE COMMISSION OF THE EUROPEAN COMMUNITIES,

Having regard to the Treaty establishing the European Community,

Having regard to Directive 95/46/EC of the European Parliament and of the Council of 24 October 1995 on the protection of individuals with regard to the processing of personal data and on the free movement of such data[1], and in particular Article 26(4) thereof,

Whereas:

1. Pursuant to Directive 95/46/EC, Member States are required to provide that a transfer of personal data to a third country may only take place if the third country in question ensures an adequate level of data protection and the Member States' laws, which comply with the other provisions of the Directive, are respected prior to the transfer.

2. However, Article 26(2) of Directive 95/46/EC provides that Member States may authorise, subject to certain safeguards, a transfer or a set of transfers of personal data to third countries which do not ensure an adequate level of protection. Such safeguards may in particular result from appropriate contractual clauses.

3. Pursuant to Directive 95/46/EC, the level of data protection should be assessed in the light of all the circumstances surrounding the data transfer operation or set of data transfer operations. The Working Party on Protection of Individuals with regard to the Processing of Personal Data established under that Directive[2] has issued guidelines to aid with the assessment[3].

4. Article 26(2) of Directive 95/46/EC, which provides flexibility for an organisation wishing to transfer data to third countries, and Article 26(4), which provides for standard contractual clauses, are essential for maintaining the necessary flow of personal data between the Community and third countries without unnecessary burdens for economic operators. Those articles are particularly important in view of the fact that the Commission is unlikely to adopt adequacy findings under Article 25(6) for more than a limited number of countries in the short or even medium term.

5.   The standard contractual clauses are only one of several possibilities under Directive 95/46/EC, together with Article 25 and Article 26(1) and (2), for lawfully transferring personal data to a third country. It will be easier for organisations to transfer personal data to third countries by incorporating the standard contractual clauses in a contract. The standard contractual clauses relate only to data protection. The data exporter and the data importer are free to include any other clauses on business related issues, such as clauses on mutual assistance in cases of disputes with a data subject or a supervisory authority, which they consider as being pertinent for the contract as long as they do not contradict the standard contractual clauses.

6.   This Decision should be without prejudice to national authorisations. Member States may grant in accordance with national provisions implementing Article 26(2) of Directive 95/46/EC. The circumstances of specific transfers may require that data controllers provide different safeguards within the meaning of Article 26(2). In any case, this Decision only has the effect of requiring the Member States not to refuse to recognise as providing adequate safeguards the contractual clauses described in it and does not therefore have any effect on other contractual clauses.

7.   The scope of this Decision is limited to establishing that the clauses in the Annex may be used by a controller established in the Community in order to adduce sufficient safeguards within the meaning of Article 26(2) of Directive 95/46/EC. The transfer of personal data to third countries is a processing operation in a Member State, the lawfulness of which is subject to national law. The Data Protection Supervisory Authorities of the Member States, in the exercise of their functions and powers under Article 28 of Directive 95/46/EC, should remain competent to assess whether the Data Exporter has complied with national legislation implementing the provisions of Directive 95/46/EC and, in particular, any specific rules as regards the obligation of providing information under that Directive.

8.   This Decision does not cover the transfer of personal data by controllers established in the Community to recipients established outside the territory of the Community who act only as processors. Those transfers do not require the same safeguards because the processor acts exclusively on behalf of the controller. The Commission intends to address that type of transfer in a subsequent decision.

9.   It is appropriate to lay down the minimum information that the parties must specify in the contract dealing with the transfer. Member States should retain the power to particularise the information the parties are required to provide. The operation of this Decision should be reviewed in the light of experience.

10.   The Commission will also consider in the future whether standard contractual clauses submitted by business organisations or other interested parties offer adequate safeguards in accordance with Directive 95/46/EC.

11.   While the parties should be free to agree on the substantive data protection rules to be complied with by the Data Importer, there are certain data protection principles which should apply in any event.

12.   Data should be processed and subsequently used or further communicated only for specified purposes and should not be kept longer than necessary.

13.   In accordance with Article 12 of Directive 95/46/EC, the Data Subject should have the right of access to all data relating to him and as appropriate to rectification, erasure or blocking of certain data.

14.   Further transfers of personal data to another controller established in a third country should be permitted only subject to certain conditions, in particular to ensure that data subjects are given proper information and have the opportunity to object, or in certain cases to withhold their consent.

15.   In addition to assessing whether transfers to third countries are in accordance with national law, Supervisory Authorities should play a key role in this contractual mechanism in ensuring that personal data are adequately protected after the transfer. In specific circumstances, the Supervisory Authorities of the Member States should retain the power to prohibit or suspend a data transfer or a set of transfers based on the standard contractual clauses in those exceptional cases where it is established that a transfer on contractual basis is likely to have a substantial adverse effect on the guarantees providing adequate protection to the data subject.

16.   The standard contractual clauses should be enforceable not only by the organisations which are parties to the contract, but also by the Data Subjects, in particular, where the Data Subjects suffer damage as a consequence of a breach of the contract.

17.   The governing law of the contract should be the law of the Member State in which the Data Exporter is established, enabling a third-party beneficiary to enforce a contract. Data Subjects should be allowed to be represented by associations or other bodies if they so wish and if authorised by national law.

18.   To reduce practical difficulties which Data Subjects could experience when trying to enforce their rights under the standard contractual clauses, the Data Exporter and the Data Importer should be jointly and severally liable for damages resulting from any violation of those provisions which are covered by the third-party beneficiary clause.

19.   The Data Subject is entitled to take action and receive compensation from the Data Exporter, the Data Importer or from both for any damage resulting from any act incompatible with the obligations contained in the standard contractual clauses. Both parties may be exempted from that liability if they prove that neither of them was responsible.

20. Joint and several liability does not extend to those provisions not covered by the third-party beneficiary clause and does not need to leave one party paying for the damage resulting from the unlawful processing of the other party. Although mutual indemnification between the parties is not a requirement for the adequacy of the protection for the Data Subjects and may therefore be deleted, it is included in the standard contractual clauses for the sake of clarification and to avoid the need for the parties to negotiate indemnification clauses individually.

21. In the event of a dispute between the Parties and the Data Subject which is not amicably resolved and where the Data Subject invokes the third-party beneficiary clause, the parties agree to provide the Data Subject with the choice between mediation, arbitration or litigation. The extent to which the Data Subject will have an effective choice will depend on the availability of reliable and recognised systems of mediation and arbitration. Mediation by the Supervisory Authorities of a Member State should be an option where they provide such a service.

22. The Working Party on the Protection of Individuals with regard to the processing of Personal Data established under Article 29 of Directive 95/46/EC has delivered an Opinion on the level of protection provided under the standard contractual clauses annexed to this Decision, which has been taken into account in the preparation of this Decision[4].

23. The measures provided for in this Decision are in accordance with the opinion of the Committee established under Article 31 of Directive 95/46/EC,

HAS ADOPTED THIS DECISION:

Article 1   The standard contractual clauses set out in the Annex are considered as offering adequate safeguards with respect to the protection of the privacy and fundamental rights and freedoms of individuals and as regards the exercise of the corresponding rights as required by Article 26(2) of Directive 95/46/EC.

Article 2   This Decision concerns only the adequacy of protection provided by the standard contractual clauses for the transfer of personal data set out in the Annex. It does not affect the application of other national provisions implementing Directive 95/46/EC that pertain to the processing of personal data within the Member States.

This Decision shall not apply to the transfer of personal data by controllers established in the Community to recipients established outside the territory of the Community who act only as processors.

Article 3   For the purposes of this Decision:

(a)   the definitions in Directive 95/46/EC shall apply;

(b)   'special categories of data' means the data referred to in Article 8 of that Directive;

(c)   'supervisory authority' means the authority referred to in Article 28 of that Directive;

(d)   'data exporter' means the controller who transfers the personal data;

(e)   'data importer' means the controller who agrees to receive from the data exporter personal data for further processing in accordance with the terms of this Decision.

Article 4

1.   Without prejudice to their powers to take action to ensure compliance with national provisions adopted pursuant to chapters II, III, V and VI of Directive 95/46/EC, the competent authorities in the Member States may exercise their existing powers to prohibit or suspend data flows to third countries in order to protect individuals with regard to the processing of their personal data in cases where:

   (a)   it is established that the law to which the data importer is subject imposes upon him requirements to derogate from the relevant data protection rules which go beyond the restrictions necessary in a democratic society as provided for in Article 13 of Directive 95/46/EC where those requirements are likely to have a substantial adverse effect on the guarantees provided by the standard contractual clauses; or

   (b)   a competent authority has established that the data importer has not respected the contractual clauses; or

   (c)   there is a substantial likelihood that the standard contractual clauses in the Annex are not being or will not be complied with and the continuation of transfer would create an imminent risk of grave harm to the data subjects.

2.   The prohibition or suspension pursuant to paragraph 1 shall be lifted as soon as the reasons for the prohibition or suspension no longer exist.

3.   When Member States adopt measures pursuant to paragraphs 1 and 2, they shall without delay inform the Commission which will forward the information to the other Member States.

Article 5   The Commission shall evaluate the operation of this Decision on the basis of available information three years after its notification to the Member States. It shall submit a report on the findings to the Committee established under Article 31 of Directive 95/46/EC. It shall include any evidence that could affect the evaluation concerning the adequacy of the standard contractual clauses in the Annex and any evidence that this Decision is being applied in a discriminatory way.

Article 6   This Decision shall apply from 3 September 2001.

Article 7   This Decision is addressed to the Member States.

Done at Brussels,

For the Commission
Frederik BOLKESTEIN
Member of the Commission

ANNEX

Standard contractual clauses

for the purposes of Article 26(2) of Directive 95/46/EC for the transfer of personal data to third countries which do not ensure an adequate level of protection

Name of the data exporting organisation..

....

Address ....

Tel...; *Fax*....................................; *e-mail*: ....

Other information needed to identify the organisation..

('the data exporter')

and

Name of the data importing organisation: ....

....

Address ....

Tel...; *Fax*....................................; *e-mail*: ....

Other information needed to identify the organisation..

('the data importer')

HAVE AGREED on the following contractual clauses ('the **Clauses**') in order to adduce adequate safeguards with respect to the protection of privacy and fundamental rights and freedoms of individuals for the transfer by the Data Exporter to the Data Importer of the personal data specified in Appendix 1.

Clause 1   Definitions

For the purposes of the Clauses:

(a)   '*personal data*', '*special categories of data*', '*process/processing*', '*controller*', '*processor*', '*Data Subject*' and '*Supervisory Authority*' shall have the same meaning as in Directive 95/46/EC of 24 October 1995 on the protection of individuals with regard to the processing of personal data and on the free movement of such data ('the Directive');

(b)   'the **Data Exporter**' shall mean the Controller who transfers the Personal Data;

(c)   'the **Data Importer**' shall mean the Controller who agrees to receive from the Data Exporter personal data for further processing in accordance with the terms of these Clauses and who is not subject to a third country's system ensuring adequate protection.

Clause 2   Details of the Transfer

The details of the transfer, and in particular the categories of personal data and the purposes for which they are transferred, are specified in Appendix 1 which forms an integral part of the Clauses.

Clause 3   Third-party beneficiary clause

The Data Subjects can enforce this Clause, Clause 4 (b), (c) and (d), Clause 5 (a), (b), (c) and (e), Clause 6 (1) and (2), and Clauses 7, 9 and 11 as third-party beneficiaries. The parties do not object to the Data Subjects being represented by an association or other bodies if they so wish and if permitted by national law.

Clause 4   Obligations of the data exporter

The Data Exporter agrees and warrants:

(a)   that the processing, including the transfer itself, of the personal data by him has been and, up to the moment of the transfer, will continue to be carried out in accordance with all the relevant provisions of the Member State in which the Data Exporter is established (and where applicable has been notified to the relevant Authorities of that State) and does not violate the relevant provisions of that State;

(b)   that if the transfer involves special categories of Data the Data Subject has been informed or will be informed before the transfer that his data could be transmitted to a third country not providing adequate protection;

(c)   to make available to the Data Subjects upon request a copy of the Clauses; and

(d)   to respond in a reasonable time and to the extent reasonably possible to enquiries from the Supervisory Authority on the processing of the relevant Personal Data by the Data Importer and to any enquiries from the Data Subject concerning the processing of his Personal Data by the Data Importer.

Clause 5   Obligations of the data importer

The Data Importer agrees and warrants:

(a)   that he has no reason to believe that the legislation applicable to him prevents him from fulfilling his obligations under the contract and that in the event of a change in that legislation which is likely to have a substantial adverse effect on the guarantees provided by the Clauses, he will notify the change to the Data Exporter and to the Supervisory Authority where the Data Exporter is established, in which case the Data Exporter is entitled to suspend the transfer of data and/or terminate the contract;

(b)   to process the Personal Data in accordance with the Mandatory Data Protection Principles set out in Appendix 2;

   or, if explicitly agreed by the parties by ticking below and subject to compliance with the Mandatory Data Protection Principles set out in Appendix 3, to process in all other respects the data in accordance with:

   •   the relevant provisions of national law (attached to these Clauses) protecting the fundamental rights and freedoms of natural persons, and in particular their right to privacy with respect to the processing of personal data applicable to a Data Controller in the country in which the Data Exporter is established, or,

   •   the relevant provisions of any Commission decision under Article 25(6) of Directive 95/46/EC finding that a third country provides adequate protection in certain sectors of activity only, if the Data Importer is based in that third country and is not covered by those provisions, in so far those provisions are of a nature which makes them applicable in the sector of the transfer;

(c)   to deal promptly and properly with all reasonable inquiries from the Data Exporter or the Data Subject relating to his processing of the Personal Data subject to the transfer and to cooperate with the competent Supervisory Authority in the course of all its inquiries and abide by the advice of the Supervisory Authority with regard to the processing of the data transferred;

(d)   at the request of the Data Exporter to submit its data processing facilities for audit which shall be carried out by the Data Exporter or an inspection body composed of independent members and in possession of the required professional qualifications, selected by the Data Exporter, where applicable, in agreement with the Supervisory Authority;

(e)   to make available to the Data Subject upon request a copy of the Clauses and indicate the office which handles complaints.

Clause 6   Liability

1.   The Parties agree that a Data Subject who has suffered damage as a result of any violation of the provisions referred to in Clause 3 is entitled to receive compensation from the parties for the damage suffered. The Parties agree that they may be exempted from this liability only if they prove that neither of them is responsible for the violation of those provisions.

2.   The Data Exporter and the Data Importer agree that they will be jointly and severally liable for damage to the Data Subject resulting from any violation referred to in paragraph 1. In the event of such a violation, the Data Subject may bring an action before a court against either the Data Exporter or the Data Importer or both.

3.   The parties agree that if one party is held liable for a violation referred to in paragraph 1 by the other party, the latter will, to the extent to which it is liable, indemnify the first party for any cost, charge, damages, expenses or loss it has incurred*.

[* paragraph 3 is optional]

Clause 7 Mediation and jurisdiction

1. The parties agree that if there is a dispute between a Data Subject and either party which is not amicably resolved and the Data Subject invokes the third-party beneficiary provision in Clause 3, they accept the decision of the Data Subject:

    (a) to refer the dispute to mediation by an independent person or, where applicable, by the Supervisory Authority;

    (b) to refer the dispute to the courts in the Member State in which the Data Exporter is established.

2. The Parties agree that by agreement between a Data Subject and the relevant party a dispute can be referred to an arbitration body, if that party is established in a country which has ratified the New York Convention on enforcement of arbitration awards.

3. The parties agree that paragraphs 1 and 2 apply without prejudice to the Data Subject's substantive or procedural rights to seek remedies in accordance with other provisions of national or international law.

Clause 8 Cooperation with supervisory authorities

The parties agree to deposit a copy of this contract with the Supervisory Authority if it so requests or if such deposit is required under national law.

Clause 9 Termination of the clauses

The parties agree that the termination of the Clauses at any time, in any circumstances and for whatever reason does not exempt them from the obligations and/or conditions under the Clauses as regards the processing of the data transferred.

Clause 10 Governing law

The Clauses shall be governed by the law of the Member State in which the Data Exporter is established, namely ....

Clause 11 Variation of the contract

The parties undertake not to vary or modify the terms of the Clauses.

On behalf of the Data Exporter:

Name (written out in full): ....

Position: ....

Address: ....

Other information necessary in order for the contract to be binding (if any): ....

....

Signature..

(stamp of organisation)

On behalf of the Data Importer:

Name (written out in full): ....

Position: ....

Address: ....

Other information necessary in order for the contract to be binding (if any): ....

....

Signature..

(stamp of organisation)

APPENDIX 1 to the Standard Contractual Clauses

This Appendix forms part of the Clauses and must be completed and signed by the parties

(*The Member States may complete or specify, according to their national procedures, any additional necessary information to be contained in this Appendix)

Data exporter

The data exporter is (please specify briefly your activities relevant to the transfer):

....

....

....

Data importer

The data importer is (please specify briefly your activities relevant to the transfer):

....

....

....

Data importer

The personal data transferred concern the following categories of data subjects (please specify):

....

....

....

Purposes of the transfer

The transfer is necessary for the following purposes (please specify):

....

....

....

Categories of data

The personal data transferred fall within the following categories of data (please specify):

....

....

....

Sensitive data (if appropriate)

The personal data transferred fall within the following categories of sensitive data (please specify):

....

....

....

Recipients

The personal data transferred may be disclosed only to the following recipients or categories of recipients (please specify):

....

....

....

Storage limit

The personal data transferred may be stored for no more than (please indicate): .... (months/years)

Data exporter	Data importer
Name	....
Authorised Signature	....

APPENDIX 2 to the Standard Contractual Clauses

Mandatory Data Protection Principles referred to in the first paragraph of Clause 5(b).

These data protection principles should be read and interpreted in the light of the provisions (principles and relevant exceptions) of Directive 95/46/EC[5].

They shall apply subject to the mandatory requirements of the national legislation applicable to the Data Importer which do not go beyond what is necessary in a democratic society on the basis of one of the interests listed in Article 13(1) of Directive 95/46/EC, that is, if they constitute a necessary measure to safeguard national security, defence, public security, the prevention, investigation, detection and prosecution of criminal offences or of breaches of ethics for the regulated professions, an important economic or financial interest of the State or the protection of the Data Subject or the rights and freedoms of others.

(1)   *Purpose limitation:* data must be processed and subsequently used or further communicated only for the specific purposes in Appendix 1 to the Clauses. Data must not be kept longer than necessary for the purposes for which they are transferred.

(2)   *Data quality and proportionality:* data must be accurate and, where necessary, kept up to date. The data must be adequate, relevant and not excessive in relation to the purposes for which they are transferred and further processed.

(3)   *Transparency:* data subjects must be provided with information as to the purposes of the processing and the identity of the data controller in the third country, and other information insofar as this is necessary to ensure fair processing, unless such information has already been given by the data exporter.

(4)   *Security and confidentiality:* technical and organisational security measures must be taken by the data controller that are appropriate to the risks, such as unauthorised access, presented by the processing. Any person acting under the authority of the data controller, including a processor, must not process the data except on instructions from the controller.

(5)   *Rights of access, rectification, erasure and blocking of data:* as provided for in Article 12 of Directive 95/46/EC, the Data Subject must have a right of access to all data relating to him that are processed and, as appropriate, the right to the rectification, erasure or blocking of data the processing of which does not comply with the principles set out in this Appendix, in particular because the data are incomplete or inaccurate. He should also be able to object to the processing of the data relating to him on compelling legitimate grounds relating to his particular situation.

(6)   *Restrictions on onward transfers:* Further transfers of personal data from the Data Importer to another controller established in a third country not providing adequate protection or not covered by a Decision adopted by the Commission pursuant to Article 25(6) of Directive 95/46/EC (onward transfer) may take place only if either:

    (a)   Data Subjects have, in the case of special categories of data, given their unambiguous consent to the onward transfer or, in other cases, have been given the opportunity to object.

        The minimum information to be provided to Data Subjects must contain in a language understandable to them:

- the purposes of the onward transfer,

- the identification of the Data Exporter established in the Community,

- the categories of further recipients of the data and the countries of destination, and

- an explanation that, after the onward transfer, the data may be processed by a controller established in a country where there is not an adequate level of protection of the privacy of individuals;

    or

    (b)   the Data Exporter and the Data Importer agree to the adherence to the Clauses of another controller which thereby becomes a party to the Clauses and assumes the same obligations as the Data Importer.

(7)   *Special categories of data:* where data revealing racial or ethnic origin, political opinions, religious or philosophical beliefs or trade union memberships and data concerning health or sex life and data relating to offences, criminal convictions or security measures are processed, additional safeguards should be in place within the meaning of Directive 95/46/EC, in particular, appropriate security measures such as strong encryption for transmission or such as keeping a record of access to sensitive data.

(8)   *Direct marketing:* where data are processed for the purposes of direct marketing, effective procedures should exist allowing the data subject at any time to 'opt-out' from having his data used for such purposes.

(9)   *Automated individual decisions:* data subjects are entitled not to be subject to a decision which is based solely on automated processing of data, unless other measures are taken to safeguard the individual's legitimate interests as provided for in Article 15(2) of Directive 95/46/EC. Where the purpose of the transfer is the taking of an automated decision as referred to in Article 15 of Directive 95/46/EC, which produces legal effects

concerning the individual or significantly affects him and which is based solely on automated processing of data intended to evaluate certain personal aspects relating to him, such as his performance at work, creditworthiness, reliability, conduct, etc., the individual should have the right to know the reasoning for this Decision.

APPENDIX 3 to the standard contractual clauses

Mandatory Data Protection Principles referred to in the second paragraph of Clause 5(b).

(1) *Purpose limitation:* data must be processed and subsequently used or further communicated only for the specific purposes in Appendix 1 to the Clauses. Data must not be kept longer than necessary for the purposes for which they are transferred.

(2) *Rights of access, rectification, erasure and blocking of data:* As provided for in Article 12 of Directive 95/46/EC, the Data Subject must have a right of access to all data relating to him that are processed and, as appropriate, the right to the rectification, erasure or blocking of data the processing of which does not comply with the principles set out in this Appendix, in particular because the data is incomplete or inaccurate. He should also be able to object to the processing of the data relating to him on compelling legitimate grounds relating to his particular situation.

(3) *Restrictions on onward transfers:* Further transfers of personal data from the Data Importer to another controller established in a third country not providing adequate protection or not covered by a Decision adopted by the Commission pursuant to Article 25(6) of Directive 95/46/EC (onward transfer) may take place only if either:

    (a) Data subjects have, in the case of if special categories of data, given their unambiguous consent to the onward transfer, or, in other cases, have been given the opportunity to object.

The minimum information to be provided to Data Subjects must contain in a language understandable to them:

- the purposes of the onward transfer,

- the identification of the Data Exporter established in the Community,

- the categories of further recipients of the data and the countries of destination, and,

- an explanation that, after the onward transfer, the data may be processed by a controller established in a country where there is not an adequate level of protection of the privacy of individuals;

    or

    (b) the Data Exporter and the Data Importer agree to the adherence to the Clauses of another controller which thereby becomes a party to the Clauses and assumes the same obligations as the Data Importer.

---

1. OJ L 281, 23.11.1995, p. 31.
2. The web address of the Working Party is: http://www.europa.eu.int/comm/internal_market/en/media/dataprot/wpdocs/index.htm.
3. WP 4 (5020/97) 'First orientations on Transfers of Personal Data to Third Countries – Possible Ways Forward in Assessing Adequacy', a discussion document adopted by the Working Party on 26 June 1997;
WP 7 (5057/97) Working document: 'Judging industry self-regulation: when does it make a meaningful contribution to the level of data protection in a third country?', adopted by the Working Party on 14 January 1998;
WP 9 (5005/98) Working Document: 'Preliminary views on the use of contractual provisions in the context of transfers of personal data to third countries', adopted by the Working Party on 22 April 1998;
WP 12: Transfers of personal data to third countries: Applying Articles 25 and 26 of the EU data protection directive, adopted by the Working Party on 24 July 1998, available in the web site 'europa.eu.int/comm/internal_markt/en/media.dataprot/wpdocs/wp12/en' hosted by the European Commission.
4. Opinion No 1/2001 adopted by the Working Party on 26 January 2001 (DG MARKT 5102/00 WP 38), available in the web site 'Europa' hosted by the European Commission.
5. Directive 95/46/EC of the European Parliament and of the Council of 24 of October 1995 on the protection of individuals with regard to the processing of personal data and on the free movement of such data, *Official Journal of the European Communities*, L 281, 23.11.1995, p. 31.

2 For Data Processors

COMMISSION DECISION

(2002/16/EC)

of 27 December 2001

on standard contractual clauses for the transfer of personal data to processors established in third countries, under Directive 95/46/EC

(notified under document number C(2001)4540)

(Text with EEA relevance)

THE COMMISSION OF THE EUROPEAN COMMUNITIES,

Having regard to the Treaty establishing the European Community,

Having regard to Directive 95/46/EC of the European Parliament and of the Council of 24 October 1995 on the protection of individuals with regard to the processing of personal data and on the free movement of such data[1], and in particular Article 26(4)thereof,

Whereas:

1. Pursuant to Directive 95/46/EC Member States are required to provide that a transfer of personal data to a third country may only take place if the third country in question ensures an adequate level of data protection and the Member States' laws, which comply with the other provisions of the Directive, are respected prior to the transfer.

2. However, Article 26(2)of Directive 95/46/EC provides that Member States may authorise, subject to certain safeguards, a transfer or a set of transfers of personal data to third countries which do not ensure an adequate level of protection. Such safeguards may in particular result from appropriate contractual clauses.

3. Pursuant to Directive 95/46/EC the level of data protection should be assessed in the light of all the circumstances surrounding the data transfer operation or set of data transfer operations. The Working Party on the Protection of Individuals with regard to the Processing of Personal Data established under that Directive[2] has issued guidelines to aid with the assessment[3].

4. The standard contractual clauses relate only to data protection. The data exporter and the data importer are free to include any other clauses on business related issues which they consider as being pertinent for the contract as long as they do not contradict the standard contractual clauses.

5. This Decision should be without prejudice to national authorisations Member States may grant in accordance with national provisions implementing Article 26(2)of Directive 95/46/EC. This Decision only has the effect of requiring the Member States not to refuse to recognise as providing adequate safeguards the contractual clauses set out in it and does not therefore have any effect on other contractual clauses.

6. The scope of this Decision is limited to establishing that the clauses which it sets out may be used by a data controller established in the Community in order to adduce adequate safeguards within the meaning of Article 26(2)of Directive 95/46/EC for the transfer of personal data to a processor established in a third country.

7. This Decision should implement the obligation provided for in Article 17(3)of Directive 95/46/EC and does not prejudice the content of the contracts or legal acts established pursuant to that provision. However, some of the standard contractual clauses, in particular as regards the data exporter's obligations, should be included in order to increase clarity as to the provisions which may be contained in a contract between a controller and a processor.

8. Supervisory authorities of the Member States play a key role in this contractual mechanism in ensuring that personal data are adequately protected after the transfer. In exceptional cases where data exporters refuse or are unable to instruct the data importer properly, with an imminent risk of grave harm to the data subjects, the standard contractual clauses should allow the supervisory authorities to audit data importers and, where

appropriate, take decisions which are binding on data importers. The supervisory authorities should have the power to prohibit or suspend a data transfer or a set of transfers based on the standard contractual clauses in those exceptional cases where it is established that a transfer on contractual basis is likely to have a substantial adverse effect on the warranties and obligations providing adequate protection for the data subject.

9. The Commission may also consider in the future whether standard contractual clauses for the transfer of personal data to data processors established in third countries not offering an adequate level of data protection, submitted by business organisations or other interested parties, offer adequate safeguards in accordance with Article 26(2)of Directive 95/46/EC.

10. A disclosure of personal data to a data processor established outside the Community is an international transfer protected under Chapter IV of Directive 95/46/EC. Consequently, this Decision does not cover the transfer of personal data by controllers established in the Community to controllers established outside the Community who fall within the scope of Commission Decision 2001/497/EC of 15 June 2001 on standard contractual clauses for the transfer of personal data to third countries, under Directive 95/46/EC[4].

11. The standard contractual clauses should provide for the technical and organisational security measures ensuring a level of security appropriate to the risks represented by the processing and the nature of the data to be protected that a data processor established in a third country not providing adequate protection must apply. Parties should make provision in the contract for those technical and organisational measures which, having regard to applicable data protection law, the state of the art and the cost of their implementation, are necessary in order to protect personal data against accidental or unlawful destruction or accidental loss, alteration, unauthorised disclosure or access or any other unlawful forms of processing.

12. In order to facilitate data flows from the Community, it is desirable that processors providing data processing services to several data controllers in the Community be allowed to apply the same technical and organisational security measures irrespective of the Member State from which the data transfer originates, in particular in those cases where the data importer receives data for further processing from different establishments of the data exporter in the Community, in which case the law of the designated Member State of establishment should apply.

13. It is appropriate to lay down the minimum information that the parties must specify in the contract dealing with the transfer. Member States should retain the power to particularise the information the parties are required to provide. The operation of this Decision should be reviewed in the light of experience.

14. The data importer should process the transferred personal data only on behalf of the data exporter and in accordance with his instructions and the obligations contained in the clauses. In particular the data importer should not disclose the personal data to a third party unless in accordance with certain conditions. The data exporter should instruct the data importer throughout the duration of the data processing Services to process the data in accordance with his instructions, the applicable data protection laws and the obligations contained in the clauses. The transfer of personal data to processors established outside the Community does not prejudice the fact that the processing activities should be governed in any case by the applicable data protection law.

15. The standard contractual clauses should be enforceable not only by the organisations which are parties to the contract, but also by the data subjects, in particular where the data subjects suffer damage as a consequence of a breach of the contract.

16. The data subject should be entitled to take action and, where appropriate, receive compensation from the data exporter who is the data controller of the personal data transferred. Exceptionally, the data subject should also be entitled to take action, and, where appropriate, receive compensation from the data importer in those cases, arising out of a breach by the data importer of any of his obligations referred to in the second paragraph of clause 3, where the data exporter has factually disappeared or has ceased to exist in law or has become insolvent.

17. In the event of a dispute between a data subject, who invokes the third-party beneficiary clause and the data importer, which is not amicably resolved, the data importer should agree to provide the data subject with the choice between mediation, arbitration or litigation. The extent to which the data subject will have an effective choice should depend on the availability of reliable and recognised systems of mediation and arbitration. Mediation by the data protection supervisory authorities of the Member State in which the data exporter is established should be an option where they provide such a service.

18. The contract should be governed by the law of the Member State in which the data exporter is established enabling a third-party beneficiary to enforce a contract. Data subjects should be allowed to be represented by associations or other bodies if they so wish and if authorised by national law.

19. The Working Party on the Protection of Individuals with regard to the processing of Personal Data established under Article 29 of Directive 95/46/EC has delivered an opinion on the level of protection provided under the standard contractual clauses annexed to this Decision, which has been taken into account in the preparation of this Decision[5].

20. The measures provided for in this Decision are in accordance with the opinion of the Committee established under Article 31 of Directive 95/46/EC,

HAS ADOPTED THIS DECISION:

Article 1   The standard contractual clauses set out in the Annex are considered as offering adequate safeguards with respect to the protection of the privacy and fundamental rights and freedoms of individuals and as regards the exercise of the corresponding rights as required by Article 26(2)of Directive 95/46/EC.

Article 2   This Decision concerns only the adequacy of protection provided by the standard contractual clauses set out in the Annex for the transfer of personal data to processors. It does not affect the application of other national provisions implementing Directive 95/46/EC that pertain to the processing of personal data within the Member States.

This Decision shall apply to the transfer of personal data by controllers established in the Community to recipients established outside the territory of the Community who act only as processors.

Article 3   For the purposes of this Decision:

(a)   the definitions in Directive 95/46/EC shall apply;

(b)   'special categories of data 'means the data referred to in Article 8 of that Directive;

(c)   'supervisory authority 'means the authority referred to in Article 28 of that Directive;

(d)   'data exporter 'means the controller who transfers the personal data;

(e)   'data importer 'means the processor established in a third country who agrees to receive from the data exporter personal data intended for processing on the data exporter's behalf after the transfer in accordance with his instructions and the terms of this Decision and who is not subject to a third country's system ensuring adequate protection;

(f)   'applicable data protection law 'means the legislation protecting the fundamental rights and freedoms of natural persons and, in particular, their right to privacy with respect to the processing of personal data applicable to a data controller in the Member State in which the data exporter is established;

(g)   'technical and organisational security measures 'means those measures aimed at protecting personal data against accidental or unlawful destruction or accidental loss, alteration, unauthorised disclosure or access, in particular where the processing involves the transmission of data over a network, and against all other unlawful forms of processing.

Article 4

1.   Without prejudice to their powers to take action to ensure compliance with national provisions adopted pursuant to Chapters II,III,V and VI of Directive 95/46/EC, the competent authorities in the Member States may exercise their existing powers to prohibit or suspend data flows to third countries in order to protect individuals with regard to the processing of their personal data in cases where:

(a)   it is established that the law to which the data importer is subject imposes upon him requirements to derogate from the applicable data protection law which go beyond the restrictions necessary in a democratic society as provided for in Article 13 of Directive 95/46/EC where those requirements are likely to have a substantial adverse effect on the guarantees provided by the applicable data protection law and the standard contractual clauses; or

(b)   a competent authority has established that the data importer has not respected the contractual clauses in the Annex; or

(c)   there is a substantial likelihood that the standard contractual clauses in the Annex are not being or will not be complied with and the continuing transfer would create an imminent risk of grave harm to the data subjects.

2.   The prohibition or suspension pursuant to paragraph 1 shall be lifted as soon as the reasons for the suspension or prohibition no longer exist.

3.   When Member States adopt measures pursuant to paragraphs 1 and 2, they shall, without delay, inform the Commission which will forward the information to the other Member States.

Article 5   The Commission shall evaluate the operation of this Decision on the basis of available information three years after its notification to the Member States. It shall submit a report on the findings to the Committee established under Article 31 of Directive 95/46/EC. It shall include any evidence that could affect the evaluation concerning the adequacy of the standard contractual clauses in the Annex and any evidence that this Decision is being applied in a discriminatory way.

Article 6   This Decision shall apply from 3 April 2002.

Article 7   This Decision is addressed to the Member States.

Done at Brussels, 27 December 2001

For the Commission
Frederik BOLKESTEIN
Member of the Commission

ANNEX

Standard Contractual Clauses (processors)

For the purposes of Article 26(2) of Directive 95/46/EC for the transfer of personal data to processors established in third countries which do not ensure an adequate level of data protection

Name of the data exporting organisation ....

Address ....

Tel ....; *Fax* ....; *e-mail:* ....

Other information needed to identify the organisation ....

('the data exporter')

and

Name of the data exporting organisation ....

Address ....

Tel ....; *Fax* ....; *e-mail:* ....

Other information needed to identify the organisation ....

('the data importer')

HAVE AGREED on the following Contractual Clauses (the Clauses) in order to adduce adequate safeguards with respect to the protection of privacy and fundamental rights and freedoms of individuals for the transfer by the data exporter to the data importer of the personal data specified in Appendix 1.

Clause 1

(a) '*personal data*', '*special categories of data*', '*process/processing*', '*controller*', '*processor*', '*Data Subject*' and '*Supervisory Authority*' shall have the same meaning as in Directive 95/46/EC of the European Parliament and of the Council of 24 October 1995 on the protection of individuals with regard to the processing of personal data and on the free movement of such data ('the Directive')[6];

(b) 'the **Data Exporter**' shall mean the Controller who transfers the Personal Data;

(c) 'the **Data Importer**' shall mean the Processor who agrees to receive from the Data Exporter personal data intended for processing on his behalf after the transfer in accordance with his instructions and the terms of these Clauses and who is not subject to a third country's system ensuring adequate protection.

(d) 'the **applicable data protection law**' shall mean the legislation protecting the fundamental rights and freedoms of natural persons and, in particular, their right to privacy with respect to the processing of personal data applicable to a data controller in the Member States in which the Data Exporter is established.

(e) '**technical and organisational security measures**' shall mean those measures aimed at protecting personal data against accidental or unlawful destruction or accidental loss, alteration, unauthorised disclosure or access, in particular where the processing involves the transmission of data over a network, and against all other unlawful forms of processing.

Clause 2   Details of the Transfer

The details of the transfer, and in particular the special categories of personal data where applicable are specified in Appendix 1 which forms an integral part of the Clauses.

Clause 3   Third-party beneficiary clause

The Data Subject can enforce against the Data Exporter this Clause, Clause 4(b) to (h), Clause 5(a) to (e) and (g), Clause 6(1) and (2), and Clauses 7, Clause 8(2) and Clauses 9, 10 and 11 as third-party beneficiaries.

The Data Subject can enforce against the Data Importer this Clause, Clause 5(a) to (e) and (g), Clause 6(1) and (2), Clause 7, Clause 8(2), and Clauses 9.10 and 11, in cases where the Data Exporter has factually disappeared or has ceased to exist in law.

The parties do not object to a Data Subject being represented by an association or other body if the Data Subject so expressly wishes and if permitted by national law.

Clause 4   Obligations of the data exporter

The Data Exporter agrees and warrants:

(a)   that the processing, including the transfer itself, of the personal data by him has been and will continue to be carried out in accordance with the relevant provisions of the applicable data protection law (and, where applicable, has been notified to the relevant Authorities of the Member State where the Data Exporter is established) and does not violate the relevant provisions of that State;

(b)   that he has instructed and throughout the duration of the personal data processing services will instruct the Data Importer to process the personal data transferred only on the Data Exporter's behalf and in accordance with the applicable data protection law and these clauses;

(c)   that the Data Importer shall provide sufficient guarantees in respect of the technical and organisational security measures specified in Appendix 2 to this contract;

(d)   that after assessment of the requirements of the applicable data protection law, the security measures are appropriate to protect personal data against accidental or unlawful destruction or accidental loss, alteration, unauthorised disclosure or access, in particular where the processing involves the transmission of data over a network, and against all other unlawful forms of processing, and that these measures ensure a level of security appropriate to the risks presented by the processing and the nature of the data to be protected having regard to the state of the art and the cost of their implementation;

(e)   that he will ensure compliance with the security measures;

(f)   that, if the transfer involves special categories of data, the data subject has been informed or will be informed before, or as soon as possible after, the transfer that his data could be transmitted to a third country not providing adequate protection;

(g)   that he agrees to forward the notification received from the data importer pursuant to Clause 5(b) to the data protection supervisory authority if he decides to continue the transfer or to lift his suspension;

(h)   to make available to the data subjects upon request a copy of the Clauses set out in this Annex, with the exception of Appendix 2 which shall be replaced by a summary description of the security measures.

Clause 5   Obligations of the data importer[7]

The data importer agrees and warrants:

(a)   to process the personal data only on behalf of the data exporter and in compliance with his instructions and the clauses; if he cannot provide such compliance for whatever reason, he agrees to inform promptly the data exporter of his inability to comply, in which case the data exporter is entitled to suspend the transfer of data and/or terminate the contract;

(b)   that he has no reason to believe that the legislation applicable to him prevents him from fulfilling the instructions received from the data exporter and his obligations under the contract and that in the event of a change in this legislation which is likely to have a substantial adverse effect on the warranties and obligations provided by the Clauses, he will promptly notify the change to the data exporter as soon as he is aware, in which case the data exporter is entitled to suspend the transfer of data and/or terminate the contract;

(c)   that he has implemented the technical and organisational measures specified in Appendix 2 before processing the personal data transferred;

(d)   that he shall promptly notify the data exporter about:

   (i)   any legally binding request for disclosure of the personal data by a law enforcement authority unless otherwise prohibited, such as a prohibition under criminal law to preserve the confidentiality of a law enforcement investigation;

   (ii)   any accidental or unauthorised access; and

   (iii) any request received directly from the data subjects without responding to that request, unless he has been otherwise authorised to do so:

(e)   to deal promptly and properly with all inquiries from the data exporter relating to his processing of the personal data subject to the transfer and to abide by the advice of the supervisory authority with regard to the processing of the data transferred;

(f)   at the request of the data exporter to submit his data processing facilities for audit of the processing activities covered by the clauses which shall be carried out by the data exporter or an inspection body composed of independent members and in possession of the required professional qualifications bound by a duty of confidentiality, selected by the data exporter, where applicable, in agreement with the supervisory authority;

(g)   to make available to the data subject upon request a copy of the Clauses set out in the Annex, with the exception of Appendix 2 which shall be replaced by a summary description of the security measures in those cases where the data subject is unable to obtain a copy from the data exporter.

Clause 6   Liability

1.   The parties agree that a data subject, who has suffered damage as a result of any violation of the provisions referred to in Clause 3 is entitled to receive compensation from the data exporter for the damage suffered.

2.   If a data subject is not able to bring the action referred to in paragraph 1 arising out of a breach by the data importer of any of his obligations referred to in Clause 3 against the data exporter because the data exporter has disappeared factually or has ceased to exist in law or became insolvent, the data importer agrees that the data subject may issue a claim against the data importer as if he were the data exporter.

3.   The parties agree that if one party is held liable for a violation of the clauses committed by the other party, the latter will, to the extent to which it is liable, indemnify the first party for any cost, charge, damages, expenses or loss it has incurred.

Indemnification is contingent upon:

(a)   the data exporter promptly notifying the data importer of a claim; and

(b)   the data importer being given the possibility to cooperate with the data exporter in the defence and settlement of the claim[8].

Clause 7   Mediation and jurisdiction

1.   The data importer agrees that if the data subject invokes against him third-party beneficiary rights and/or claims compensation for damages under the clauses, the data importer will accept the decision of the data subject;

(a)   to refer the dispute to mediation, by an independent person or, where applicable, by the supervisory authority;

(b)   to refer the dispute to the courts in the Member State in which the data exporter is established.

2.   The data importer agrees that, by agreement with the data subject, the resolution of a specific dispute can be referred to an arbitration body if the data importer is established in a country which has ratified the New York Convention on enforcement of arbitration awards.

3.   The parties agree that the choice made by the data subject will not prejudice his substantive or procedural rights to seek remedies in accordance with other provisions of national or international law.

Clause 8   Cooperation with supervisory authorities

1.   The data exporter agrees to deposit a copy of this contract with the supervisory authority if it so requests or if such deposit id required under the applicable data protection law.

2.   The parties agree that the supervisory authority has the right to conduct an audit of the data importer which has the same scope and is subject to the same conditions as would apply to an audit of the data exporter under the applicable data protection law.

Clause 9   Governing Law

The Clauses shall be governed by the law of the Member State in which the data exporter is established, namely ....

Clause 10   Variation in the contract

The parties undertake not to vary or modify the terms of the Clauses.

Clause 11   Obligation after the termination of personal data processing services

1.   The parties agree that on the termination of the provision of data processing services, the data importer shall, at the choice of the data exporter, return all the personal data transferred and the copies thereof to the data exporter or shall destroy all the personal data and certify to the data exporter that he has done so, unless legislation imposed upon the data importer prevents him from returning or destroying all or part of the personal data transferred. In that case, the data importer warrants that he will guarantee the confidentiality of the personal data transferred and will not actively process the personal data transferred anymore.

2.   The data importer warrants that upon request of the data exporter and/or of the supervisory authority, he will submit his data processing facilities for an audit of the measures referred to in paragraph 1.

On behalf of the Data Exporter:

Name (written out in full): ....

Position: ....

Address: ....

Other information necessary in order for the contract to be binding (if any): ....

....

Signature ....

(stamp of organisation)

On behalf of the Data Importer:

Name (written out in full): ....

Position: ....

Address: ....

Other information necessary in order for the contract to be binding (if any): ....

....

Signature ....

(stamp of organisation)

APPENDIX 1 to the Standard Contractual Clauses

This Appendix forms part of the Clauses and must be completed and signed by the parties

(*The Member States may complete or specify, according to their national procedures, any additional necessary information to be contained in this Appendix)

Data exporter

The data exporter is (please specify briefly your activities relevant to the transfer):

....

....

....

Data importer

The data importer is (please specify briefly activities relevant to the transfer):

....

....

....

Data subjects

The personal data transferred concern the following categories of data subjects (please specify):

....

....

....

Categories of data

The personal data transferred concern the following categories of data (please specify):

....

....

....

Special categories of data (if appropriate)

The personal data transferred concern the following categories of sensitive data (please specify):

....

....

....

Processing operations

The personal data transferred will be subject to the following basic processing activities (please specify):

....

....

....

Data exporter	Data importer
Name	....
Authorised Signature	....

APPENDIX 2 to the Standard Contractual Clauses

This Appendix forms part of the Clauses and must be completed and signed by the parties

Description of the technical and organisational security measures implemented by the data importer in accordance with Clauses 4(d) and 5(c) (or document/legislation attached):

....

....

....

....

....

....

[1] OJ L 281,23.11.1995,p.31.

[2] The web address of the Working Party is:
http://europa.eu.int/comm/internal_market/en/dataprot/wpdocs/index.htm.

[3] WP 4 (5020/97):'First orientations on Transfers of Personal Data to Third Countries —Possible Ways Forward in Assessing Adequacy ',a discussion document adopted by the Working Party on 26 June 1997.
WP 7 (5057/97):Working document:'Judging industry self-regulation:when does it make a meaningful contribution to the level of data protection in a third country?',adopted by the Working Party on 14 January 1998.
WP 9(5005/98):Working Document:'Preliminary views on the use of contractual provisions in the context of transfers of personal data to third countries ',adopted by the Working Party on 22 April 1998.
WP 12:Transfers of personal data to third countries:Applying Articles 25 and 26 of the EU data protection directive,adopted by the Working Party on 24 July 1998,available on the website 'http://europa.eu.int/comm/internal_market/en/dataprot/wpdocs/wp12en.htm 'hosted by the European Commission.

[4] OJ L 181,4.7.2001,p.19.

[5] Opinion No 7/2001 adopted by the Working Party on 13 September 2001 (DG MARKT ....),available on the website 'Europa 'hosted by the European Commission.

[6] Parties may reproduce definitions and meanings contained in Directive 95/46/EC within this Clause if they considered it better for the contract to stand alone.

[7] Mandatory requirements of the national legislation applicable to the data importer which do not go beyond what is necessary in a democratic society on the basis of one of the interests listed in Article 13(1) of Directive 95/46/EC, that is, if they constitute a necessary measure to safeguard national security defence, public security, the prevention, investigation, detection and prosecution of criminal offences or of breaches of ethics for the regulated professions, an important economic or financial interest of the State or the protection of the data subject or the rights and freedoms of others, are not in contradiction with the standard contractual clauses. Some examples of such mandatory requirements which do not go beyond what is necessary in a democratic society are, inter alia, internationally recognised sanctions, tax-reporting requirements or anti-money-laundering reporting requirements.

[8] Paragraph 3 is optional.

Appendix 4 – The Information Commissioner's Audit Manual

The Information Commissioner's Audit Manual (June 2001) is available in full on the IC website at www.informationcommissioner.gov.uk. A few selected extracts appear in this appendix.

Part 2: The Audit Method

The purpose of this part of the Audit Manual is to explain the background to the two-part audit methodology that is used by the Commissioner as the basis for conducting assessments of how organisations handle the processing of personal data. We will also describe the options available to the Auditor when conducting the different categories of Data Protection Audits and outline the key concepts behind the methodology.

1. Audit Categories

Section 5 of Part 1 has already discussed the concepts of First, Second and Third Party Audits. The best way to understand the differences between them is by reference to Figure 2.1 below:

It can be seen from Figure 2.1 that ideally, External and Supplier Audits (i.e. Third and Second Party) are conducted in two parts, namely an Adequacy Audit followed by a Compliance Audit. Internal Audits (i.e. First Party) are conducted as a single Compliance Audit. It is important to realise that Adequacy and Compliance Audits fulfil different purposes in this methodology.

1.1 Purpose of Adequacy Audits

The purpose of the Adequacy Audit is to check that any documented Policies, Codes of Practice, Guidelines and Procedures meet the requirements of the Data Protection Act 1998. This part of the audit is performed first and is a desktop exercise that can usually be conducted off-site.

It is possible, of course, for an Adequacy Audit to be conducted by Internal Auditors provided they have the necessary specialist understanding of the requirements of the Data Protection Act.

1.2 Purpose of Compliance Audits

The purpose of the Compliance Audit is to check that the organisation is in fact operating in accordance with its documented Policies, Codes of Practice, Guidelines and Procedures. It is the most important part of an audit and has to be conducted on-site.

An obvious question raised by Figure 2.1 is why an Internal Audit only involves a Compliance Audit? The reasons for this are that the following assumptions are made:

- It is more effective carrying out scheduled Internal Audits on data protection systems that have been formally documented and are fully operational.

- The data protection system will in theory meet the requirements of the Data Protection Act 1998 because it should have been designed specifically with this objective.

Fig 2.1: The Three Audit Categories

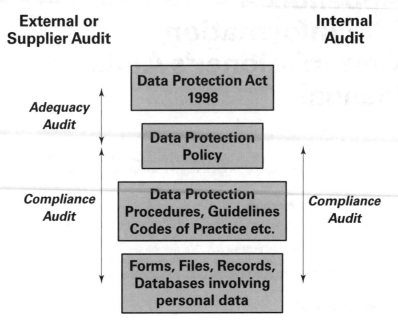

- If the data protection system is mature it may well have been subjected to an earlier Adequacy Audit by independent third parties as part of the implementation process.

Therefore, it is normal practice for Internal Audits not to include an Adequacy Audit. **There is of course no reason why organisations cannot conduct Adequacy Audits as part of their Internal Audit programmes should they so wish, and in fact this might prove quite beneficial for new systems where outside help has not been involved.**

1.3 Audit Evidence

It should be apparent from the previous sections that Internal and External audits are looking for evidence concerning different aspects of a data protection system. These different aspects relate back to the original Audit Objectives detailed in Section 3 of Part 1 and are summarised in the table below:

Audit Objective	Evidence Sought	Adequacy Audit	Compliance Audit
The system **EXISTS** and is **ADEQUATE**	Documentation, e.g. Data Protection Policy, Procedures etc.	Yes	Yes (assumed)
The system is **USED**	Records of Subject Access Requests, Complaints etc.	No	Yes
The system **WORKS**	Corrective Actions, System updates and improvements	No	Yes

The above table should help to make the distinction between Adequacy and Compliance Audits even clearer, i.e.

- The Adequacy Audit™s prime concern is that there is a documented data protection system that adequately addresses all aspects of the Data Protection Act.

- The Compliance Audit is concerned with how the data protection system is being used and how effective it is.

2. Adequacy Audit Outcomes

It is very important for Second and Third Party Audits that the Adequacy Audit is conducted first as the results of the Adequacy Audit will determine what happens next in the process. The two possible outcomes of an Adequacy Audit are:

2.1 Satisfactory Adequacy Audit

If the Adequacy Audit indicates that the organisation has a documented data protection system in place with perhaps only a small number of gaps or deficiencies, the Auditor can continue with a Compliance Audit as described in section 3.

2.2 Unsatisfactory Adequacy Audit

The Adequacy Audit may indicate that the organisation has very little data protection documentation in place with inadequate procedures and major gaps in areas such as data protection awareness training. If an Auditor uncovered such major deficiencies at this preliminary stage, they must make a policy decision as how to proceed. In these circumstances there are three options:

- The organisation may still wish to go ahead with a Compliance Audit to help formulate potential solutions to address the key gaps and weaknesses already identified in its systems

- The Auditor can inform the organisation that there is little point in conducting the Compliance Audit until the major deficiencies have been addressed.

- The Auditor can refer the organisation to the Commissioner or others providing data protection advice and guidance in order to rectify the deficiencies in the data protection system.

3. Compliance Audit

There are 2 basic methodologies that are commonly used for conducting Compliance Audits and these can either be used separately or in combination on each audit.

3.1 Functional or Vertical Audit

This type of audit involves checking all aspects of the data protection system within a particular area, function or department. A Functional Audit concentrates on processes, procedures and records restricted to the department itself and does not cross inter-departmental boundaries. It is recommended that Auditors question data protection staff during Functional Audits because they should be most familiar with how departmental systems implement the organisation'!'"s overall data protection policies.

A typical example of when it would be appropriate to conduct a Functional Audit would be where it was required to assess the compliance of a Human Resources department. In this case most of the procedures, personnel files etc. associated with the Human Resources function are likely to reside wholly within the department itself. The Functional Audit could then restrict itself to checking all the activities involving the gathering and processing of personal data within the department.

The way that such a Functional Audit would be undertaken is illustrated graphically in Figure 2.2 which represents the structure of a typical organisation as being divided into separate, vertical, functional departments. It shows how the Functional Audit would only affect the Human Resources department but would also have to examine the Data Protection Policy, Organisational Resources and Records that directly relate to the Human Resources function.

3.2 Process or Horizontal Audit

This type of audit involves tracking a particular process from one end to the other. A Process Audit will cross a number of interfaces between areas, functions or departments. It is the key to understanding how an organisation functions and is best conducted with front-line, operational staff.

A typical example of when it would be appropriate to conduct a Process Audit would be where it was required to assess the processing of Data Subject Access Requests. In this case the processing of these requests is likely to involve the co-operation of a number of different departments within the organisation. The Process Audit would follow the progress of the Subject Access Request as it was processed by the various departments and staff involved.

Another example could be the process for approving a new application form that involved the collection of personal data. The form could typically originate with the Marketing Department, but might need to be checked by Sales, Operations, Finance, Legal and IT and should certainly require some form of data protection sign off.

The way that such a Process Audit would be undertaken is illustrated graphically in Figure 2.3, which shows how processes like Subject Access Requests may cut horizontally across many different inter-departmental boundaries. Section 3.3.2 of Part 3 describes how the Auditor has the choice of either starting at the beginning of a process and tracing forward, or starting at the end and tracing backwards.

Data Protection System					
Organisation & Resources					
SALES	MARKETING	OPERATIONS	FINANCE	HUMAN RESOURCES	CUSTOMER SERVICES
Records					

Fig 2.2: Functional or Vertical Audit

610

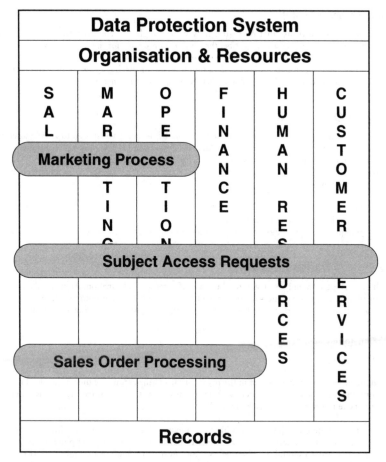

Fig 2.3: Process of Horizontal Audit

3.3 Interactions with Staff

It is very important to realise that no matter how well thought out and documented an organisation™s data protection procedures might be, they still rely on people for their operation.

It is impossible therefore, for an Auditor to do a thorough job unless they speak to the staff involved in the activities being audited, and this dialogue should occur in two distinct ways.

3.3.1 STAFF QUESTIONING

Whether conducting Functional or Process Audits it will be necessary to ask staff to answer a series of questions based on the Checklists provided in Annexes F, G, H and J. The purpose of this questioning is to obtain sufficient evidence to decide whether what is actually taking place complies with what the data protection system says should occur in practice. In this situation the Auditor is effectively behaving like an interviewer.

It is therefore important that a good rapport is established with the interviewee so that the required information can be obtained as quickly as possible. The Auditor will also need to have a good questioning techniques, and tips about this and the other human aspects of auditing will be found in Part 4.

3.3.2 STAFF AWARENESS INTERVIEWS

As well as speaking to members of staff to obtain specific items of information, Auditors need to assess the general level of staff awareness of data protection issues and their commitment to protecting the privacy of personal data. Perhaps the best way of assessing staff awareness during an audit is by means of either:

- One-to-one interviews
- Focus groups

– depending upon the number of staff in the organisation and the amount of time available. The Audit Manual provides guidance for conducting these sessions in Section 3.3 of Part 3, and also supplies a series of suitable interview questions in Annex D.4.

In circumstances where it is just not possible to conduct staff interviews then Auditors may wish to prepare Data Protection Awareness Questionnaires based on the material supplied in Annex D.4. However, this approach should only be used as a last resort as it is inferior to direct face-to-face contact.

Annex C: Audit Pro formas

This annex contains examples of all the Audit pro formas mentioned in Part 3 of the Audit Manual that are used by the Information Commissioner˝!˝"'s own staff when carrying out Data Protection Audits.

By placing these documents in the public domain the Commissioner hopes that organisations adopt them as models thus saving time and effort in designing forms for themselves.

These Audit pro formas will be of particular interest to those organisations setting up their own internal audit programmes. Of course, the pro formas included here are not meant to be rigidly prescriptive but are intended to illustrate the key elements that need to be covered. Ultimately, these pro formas are templates for organisations to adapt to the exact style and content that best suits their own needs.

IC	INTERNAL AUDIT SCHEDULE										Sheet of sheets		
Year: 2000	**DATA PROTECTION AUDIT PROGRAMME**												
Department or Function	Audit Freq.	Jan	Feb	Mar	Apr	May	Jun	Jul	Aug	Sep	Oct	Nov	Dec

Version 1   Form C.1

page C.2

613

IC	PRE-AUDIT QUESTIONNAIRE	Audit Reference	
Name of Organisation			
Department			
Address			
Postcode		**Telephone**	
Fax		**E-mail**	
Contact Name			
Position/Job Title			
Products and/or services provided			
Number of sites/ locations to be covered			
Number of full-time staff		**Number of part-time staff/sub-contractors**	

DATA PROTECTION QUESTIONS

Question 1	Does your organisation process personal data on individuals?
Question 2	What personal information are collected? E.g. name, address, telephone number etc.
Question 3	Why do you hold this personal data?
Question 4	Please provide details of databases/filing systems containing personal data:

Version 1   Form C.2

IC	PRE-AUDIT QUESTIONNAIRE	Audit Reference	

DATA PROTECTION QUESTIONS

Question 5	Do you hold any sensitive personal information (e.g. medical/health data, ethnic origin etc.)? If so, for what purpose?

Question 6	How are thess personal data collected?

Question 7	Who are these personal data collected from?

Question 8	Once personal data have been collected, do you disclose these data to anyone? (If the answer is yes, please provide examples and reasons):

Question 9	How does your organisation store personal information? E.g. on computer or manual files or both.

Question 10	Who has access to this information?

Completed by		Date	

Version 1   Form C.2

IC	AUDIT MANAGEMENT CHECKLIST	Audit Reference	

Name of Organisation:	

PREPARATORY MEETING

Names of participants:	

Questionnaire completed?	☐ Yes ☐ No	Meeting Date:	

ADEQUACY AUDIT

Date data received:		Date audit completed:	

Documentation received	☐ DP Policy ☐ Procedures ☐ Codes of practice ☐ Other

Audit outcome:	☐ Satisfactory ☐ Unsatisfactory

Compliance Audit scheduled?	☐ Yes ☐ No	Scheduled Compliance Audit date:	

COMPLIANCE AUDIT

Actual Audit date:		Audit duration (days):	

Audit Team Leader	

Audit Team Members	

Documentation check before leaving for the audit:

☐ Pre-Audit Questionnaire   ☐ Audit Plan
☐ System Audit Checklists   ☐ Process Audit Checklists
☐ Interview/Focus Group Record Sheets   ☐ Non-compliance Records
☐ Observation Notes   ☐ Compliance Audit Reports

Names of participants at the Opening Meeting:	

Number of Major Non-compliances raised:		Number of Minor Non-compliances raised:	
Number of Observations made:		Number of staff One-to-One interviews held:	
Number of staff Focus Groups held:		Compliance Audit Report completed?	☐ Yes ☐ No
Names of participants at the Closing Meeting:			

IC	**AUDIT MANAGEMENT CHECKLIST**	**Audit Reference**	
Name of Organisation:			

AUDIT FOLLOW-UP

Audit Follow-up scheduled?	☐ Yes　　☐ No	**Scheduled Audit Follow-up date:**	
Audit Team Leader			
Audit Team Members			
All Major Non-compliances cleared?	☐ Yes　　☐ No	**All Minor Non-compliances cleared?**	☐ Yes　　☐ No
Audit closed?	☐ Yes　　☐ No	**Audit completion date:**	

NOTES

Completed by		**Date**	

Version 1　　　　　　　　　　　　　　　　　　　　　　　　　　　　　　Form C.3

IC	ADEQUACY AUDIT REPORT	Audit Reference	
Organisation			
Department		**Adequacy Audit Date**	

DOCUMENTATION REVIEW SUMMARY

NON-COMPLIANCES AND/OR POINTS TO BE CLARIFIED

Document reference	Item for clarification

AUDIT OUTCOME

☐ **Satisfactory:** Organisation can proceed with Compliance Audit without further action.

☐ **Unsatisfactory:** Organisation can only proceed with Compliance Audit after the above points have been clarified.

☐ **Unsatisfactory:** Compliance Audit not appropriate with current status of organisation's Data Protection System.

PROPOSED COMPLIANCE AUDIT

Estimated Compliance audit duration:		days	Estimated number of Auditors required:	
Proposed Compliance audit date:				
DP AUDITOR NAME:	**SIGNATURE:**			**DATE:**

Version 1   Form C.4

page C.7

618

IC	AUDIT PLAN		Audit Reference	
Organisation			Page	
Department			Audit Date	

Date	Time	Area/Function	Auditor	Activity/DP Issue Assessed

AUDIT PLAN COMPILED BY:	SIGNATURE:	DATE:

Version 1   Form C.5

IC	NON-COMPLIANCE RECORD	Audit Reference	
Organisation		NC Reference	
Department		Audit Date	

DETAILS OF NON-COMPLIANCE

Non-compliance Category	DP Auditor Name	Signature	Date
☐ Minor ☐ Major			

CORRECTIVE ACTION PROGRAMME

	Function	Signature	Date
	DP Auditor		
	DP Representative		
	Follow-up Date		

CORRECTIVE ACTION FOLLOW-UP

	Function	Signature	Date
	DP Auditor		
	DP Representative		

Version 1   Form C.6

page C.9

620

IC	**OBSERVATION NOTE**	Audit Reference	
Organisation		Obs. Reference	
Department		Audit Date	

DETAILS OF OBSERVATION

	DP Auditor Name	Signature	Date

FOLLOW-UP ACTION (If relevant)

	Function	Signature	Date
	DP Auditor		
	DP Representative		
	Follow-up Date		

Version 1   Form C.7

IC	COMPLIANCE AUDIT REPORT	Audit Reference	
Organisation		Page	1
Department		Audit Date	

AUDIT SUMMARY

	Function	Signature	Date
	DP Auditor		

Version 1   Form C.8

IC	COMPLIANCE AUDIT REPORT	Audit Reference	
Organisation		Page	2
Department		Audit Date	

SUMMARY OF OBSERVATIONS

Obs. Ref.	Details of Observation

SUMMARY OF AGREED CORRECTIVE ACTIONS

NC Ref.	Action by	Corrective action to be taken	Date

AGREED AUDIT FOLLOW-UP

	Function	Signature	Date
	DP Auditor		
	DP Representative		

AUDIT CLOSED

	DP Auditor		
	DP Representative		

Version 1

Form C.8

Appendix 5 – Data Protection Act 1998

Key

Text which appears [_____] is newly inserted or substituted and is not yet in force (see notes below text for date of enforcement.

Text which appears in [ ] has been inserted by subsequent legislation.

DATA PROTECTION ACT 1998

1998 CHAPTER 29

An Act to make new provision for the regulation of the processing of information relating to individuals, including the obtaining, holding, use or disclosure of such information.

[16th July 1998]

BE IT ENACTED by the Queen's most Excellent Majesty, by and with the advice and consent of the Lords Spiritual and Temporal, and Commons, in this present Parliament assembled, and by the authority of the same, as follows:—

Part I
Preliminary

1 Basic interpretative provisions

(1) In this Act, unless the context otherwise requires—

"data" means information which—

    (a)   is being processed by means of equipment operating automatically in response to instructions given for that purpose,

    (b)   is recorded with the intention that it should be processed by means of such equipment,

    (c)   is recorded as part of a relevant filing system or with the intention that it should form part of a relevant filing system, *or*

    (d)   does not fall within paragraph (a), (b) or (c) but forms part of an accessible record as defined by section 68; [or

    (e)   is recorded information held by a public authority and does not fall within any of paragraphs (a) to (d);]

"data controller" means, subject to subsection (4), a person who (either alone or jointly or in common with other persons) determines the purposes for which and the manner in which any personal data are, or are to be, processed;

"data processor", in relation to personal data, means any person (other than an employee of the data controller) who processes the data on behalf of the data controller;

"data subject" means an individual who is the subject of personal data;

"personal data" means data which relate to a living individual who can be identified—

    (a)   from those data, or

    (b)   from those data and other information which is in the possession of, or is likely to come into the possession of, the data controller,

and includes any expression of opinion about the individual and any indication of the intentions of the data controller or any other person in respect of the individual;

"processing", in relation to information or data, means obtaining, recording or holding the information or data or carrying out any operation or set of operations on the information or data, including—

    (a)   organisation, adaptation or alteration of the information or data,

    (b)   retrieval, consultation or use of the information or data,

    (c)   disclosure of the information or data by transmission, dissemination or otherwise making available, or

    (d)   alignment, combination, blocking, erasure or destruction of the information or data;

["public authority" has the same meaning as in the Freedom of Information Act 2000;]

"relevant filing system" means any set of information relating to individuals to the extent that, although the information is not processed by means of equipment operating automatically in response to instructions given for that purpose, the set is structured, either by reference to individuals or by reference to criteria relating to individuals, in such a way that specific information relating to a particular individual is readily accessible.

(2) In this Act, unless the context otherwise requires—

(a)   "obtaining" or "recording", in relation to personal data, includes obtaining or recording the information to be contained in the data, and

(b)   "using" or "disclosing", in relation to personal data, includes using or disclosing the information contained in the data.

(3) In determining for the purposes of this Act whether any information is recorded with the intention—

(a)   that it should be processed by means of equipment operating automatically in response to instructions given for that purpose, or

(b)   that it should form part of a relevant filing system,

it is immaterial that it is intended to be so processed or to form part of such a system only after being transferred to a country or territory outside the European Economic Area.

(4) Where personal data are processed only for purposes for which they are required by or under any enactment to be processed, the person on whom the obligation to process the data is imposed by or under that enactment is for the purposes of this Act the data controller.

[(5) In paragraph (e) of the definition of "data" in subsection (1), the reference to information "held" by a public authority shall be construed in accordance with section 3(2) of the Freedom of Information Act 2000.

(6) Where section 7 of the Freedom of Information Act 2000 prevents Parts I to V of that Act from applying to certain information held by a public authority, that information is not to be treated for the purposes of paragraph (e) of the definition of "data" in subsection (1) as held by a public authority.]

NOTES

Amendment

Sub-s (1): in definition "data" word "or" at the end of para (c) repealed by the Freedom of Information Act 2000, ss 68(1), (2), 86, Sch 8, Pt III.

Date in force: 30 November 2005 (unless the Secretary of State by order appoints an earlier date): see the Freedom of Information Act 2000, s 87(3).

Sub-s (1): in definition "data" para (e) and the word "or" immediately preceding it inserted by the Freedom of Information Act 2000, s 68(1), (2)(a).

Date in force: 30 November 2005 (unless the Secretary of State by order appoints an earlier date): see the Freedom of Information Act 2000, s 87(3).

Sub-s (1): definition "public authority" inserted by the Freedom of Information Act 2000, s 68(1), (2)(b).

Date in force: 30 November 2005 (unless the Secretary of State by order appoints an earlier date): see the Freedom of Information Act 2000, s 87(3).

2 Sensitive personal data

In this Act "sensitive personal data" means personal data consisting of information as to—

(a)   the racial or ethnic origin of the data subject,

(b)   his political opinions,

(c)   his religious beliefs or other beliefs of a similar nature,

(d)   whether he is a member of a trade union (within the meaning of the Trade Union and Labour Relations (Consolidation) Act 1992,

(e)   his physical or mental health or condition,

(f)   his sexual life,

(g)   the commission or alleged commission by him of any offence, or

(h)   any proceedings for any offence committed or alleged to have been committed by him, the disposal of such proceedings or the sentence of any court in such proceedings.

3 The special purposes

In this Act "the special purposes" means any one or more of the following—

(a)   the purposes of journalism,

(b)   artistic purposes, and

(c)   literary purposes.

4 The data protection principles

(1) References in this Act to the data protection principles are to the principles set out in Part I of Schedule 1.

(2) Those principles are to be interpreted in accordance with Part II of Schedule 1.

(3) Schedule 2 (which applies to all personal data) and Schedule 3 (which applies only to sensitive personal data) set out conditions applying for the purposes of the first principle; and Schedule 4 sets out cases in which the eighth principle does not apply.

(4) Subject to section 27(1), it shall be the duty of a data controller to comply with the data protection principles in relation to all personal data with respect to which he is the data controller.

5 Application of Act

(1) Except as otherwise provided by or under section 54, this Act applies to a data controller in respect of any data only if—

(a)   the data controller is established in the United Kingdom and the data are processed in the context of that establishment, or

(b)   the data controller is established neither in the United Kingdom nor in any other EEA State but uses equipment in the United Kingdom for processing the data otherwise than for the purposes of transit through the United Kingdom.

(2) A data controller falling within subsection (1)(b) must nominate for the purposes of this Act a representative established in the United Kingdom.

(3) For the purposes of subsections (1) and (2), each of the following is to be treated as established in the United Kingdom—

(a)   an individual who is ordinarily resident in the United Kingdom,

(b)   a body incorporated under the law of, or of any part of, the United Kingdom,

(c)   a partnership or other unincorporated association formed under the law of any part of the United Kingdom, and

(d)   any person who does not fall within paragraph (a), (b) or (c) but maintains in the United Kingdom—

    (i)   an office, branch or agency through which he carries on any activity, or

    (ii)   a regular practice;

and the reference to establishment in any other EEA State has a corresponding meaning.

6   The Commissioner and the Tribunal

[(1) For the purposes of this Act and of the Freedom of Information Act 2000 there shall be an officer known as the Information Commissioner (in this Act referred to as "the Commissioner").]

(2) The Commissioner shall be appointed by Her Majesty by Letters Patent.

[(3) For the purposes of this Act and of the Freedom of Information Act 2000 there shall be a tribunal known as the Information Tribunal (in this Act referred to as "the Tribunal").]

(4) The Tribunal shall consist of—

(a)   a chairman appointed by the Lord Chancellor after consultation with the [Secretary of State],

(b)   such number of deputy chairmen so appointed as the Lord Chancellor may determine, and

(c)   such number of other members appointed by the [Secretary of State] as he may determine.

(5) The members of the Tribunal appointed under subsection (4)(a) and (b) shall be—

(a)   persons who have a 7 year general qualification, within the meaning of section 71 of the Courts and Legal Services Act 1990,

(b)   advocates or solicitors in Scotland of at least 7 years' standing, or

(c)   members of the bar of Northern Ireland or solicitors of the Supreme Court of Northern Ireland of at least 7 years' standing.

(6) The members of the Tribunal appointed under subsection (4)(c) shall be—

(a)   persons to represent the interests of data subjects,

[(aa)   persons to represent the interests of those who make requests for information under the Freedom of Information Act 2000,]

(b)   persons to represent the interests of data controllers [and

(bb)   persons to represent the interests of public authorities].

(7) Schedule 5 has effect in relation to the Commissioner and the Tribunal.

Transfer of Functions

The Secretary of State: functions of the Secretary of State under sub-s (4)(a) and (b) are transferred, in so far as they are exercisable in or as regards Scotland, to the Scottish Ministers, by the Scotland Act 1998 (Transfer of Functions to the Scottish Ministers etc) Order 1999, SI 1999/1750, art 2, Sch 1.

Part II
Rights of Data Subjects and Others

7 Right of access to personal data

(1) Subject to the following provisions of this section and to *sections 8 and 9* [sections 8, 9 and 9A], an individual is entitled—

(a)   to be informed by any data controller whether personal data of which that individual is the data subject are being processed by or on behalf of that data controller,

(b)   if that is the case, to be given by the data controller a description of—

    (i)   the personal data of which that individual is the data subject,

    (ii)   the purposes for which they are being or are to be processed, and

    (iii)   the recipients or classes of recipients to whom they are or may be disclosed,

(c)   to have communicated to him in an intelligible form—

    (i)   the information constituting any personal data of which that individual is the data subject, and

    (ii)   any information available to the data controller as to the source of those data, and

(d)   where the processing by automatic means of personal data of which that individual is the data subject for the purpose of evaluating matters relating to him such as, for example, his performance at work, his creditworthiness, his reliability or his conduct, has constituted or is likely to constitute the sole basis for any decision significantly affecting him, to be informed by the data controller of the logic involved in that decision-taking.

(2) A data controller is not obliged to supply any information under subsection (1) unless he has received—

(a) a request in writing, and

(b) except in prescribed cases, such fee (not exceeding the prescribed maximum) as he may require.

[(3) Where a data controller—

(a) reasonably requires further information in order to satisfy himself as to the identity of the person making a request under this section and to locate the information which that person seeks, and

(b) has informed him of that requirement,

the data controller is not obliged to comply with the request unless he is supplied with that further information.]

(4) Where a data controller cannot comply with the request without disclosing information relating to another individual who can be identified from that information, he is not obliged to comply with the request unless—

(a) the other individual has consented to the disclosure of the information to the person making the request, or

(b) it is reasonable in all the circumstances to comply with the request without the consent of the other individual.

(5) In subsection (4) the reference to information relating to another individual includes a reference to information identifying that individual as the source of the information sought by the request; and that subsection is not to be construed as excusing a data controller from communicating so much of the information sought by the request as can be communicated without disclosing the identity of the other individual concerned, whether by the omission of names or other identifying particulars or otherwise.

(6) In determining for the purposes of subsection (4)(b) whether it is reasonable in all the circumstances to comply with the request without the consent of the other individual concerned, regard shall be had, in particular, to—

(a) any duty of confidentiality owed to the other individual,

(b) any steps taken by the data controller with a view to seeking the consent of the other individual,

(c) whether the other individual is capable of giving consent, and

(d) any express refusal of consent by the other individual.

(7) An individual making a request under this section may, in such cases as may be prescribed, specify that his request is limited to personal data of any prescribed description.

(8) Subject to subsection (4), a data controller shall comply with a request under this section promptly and in any event before the end of the prescribed period beginning with the relevant day.

(9) If a court is satisfied on the application of any person who has made a request under the foregoing provisions of this section that the data controller in question has failed to comply with the request in contravention of those provisions, the court may order him to comply with the request.

(10) In this section—

"prescribed" means prescribed by the [Secretary of State] by regulations;

"the prescribed maximum" means such amount as may be prescribed;

"the prescribed period" means forty days or such other period as may be prescribed;

"the relevant day", in relation to a request under this section, means the day on which the data controller receives the request or, if later, the first day on which the data controller has both the required fee and the information referred to in subsection (3).

(11) Different amounts or periods may be prescribed under this section in relation to different cases.

NOTES

Amendment

Sub-s (1): words "sections 8 and 9" in italics repealed and subsequent words in square brackets substituted by the Freedom of Information Act 2000, s 69(1).

Date in force: 30 November 2005 (unless the Secretary of State by order appoints an earlier date): see the Freedom of Information Act 2000, s 87(3).

8 Provisions supplementary to section 7

(1) The [Secretary of State] may by regulations provide that, in such cases as may be prescribed, a request for information under any provision of subsection (1) of section 7 is to be treated as extending also to information under other provisions of that subsection.

(2) The obligation imposed by section 7(1)(c)(i) must be complied with by supplying the data subject with a copy of the information in permanent form unless—

(a)   the supply of such a copy is not possible or would involve disproportionate effort, or

(b)   the data subject agrees otherwise;

and where any of the information referred to in section 7(1)(c)(i) is expressed in terms which are not intelligible without explanation the copy must be accompanied by an explanation of those terms.

(3) Where a data controller has previously complied with a request made under section 7 by an individual, the data controller is not obliged to comply with a subsequent identical or similar request under that section by that individual unless a reasonable interval has elapsed between compliance with the previous request and the making of the current request.

(4) In determining for the purposes of subsection (3) whether requests under section 7 are made at reasonable intervals, regard shall be had to the nature of the data, the purpose for which the data are processed and the frequency with which the data are altered.

(5) Section 7(1)(d) is not to be regarded as requiring the provision of information as to the logic involved in any decision-taking if, and to the extent that, the information constitutes a trade secret.

(6) The information to be supplied pursuant to a request under section 7 must be supplied by reference to the data in question at the time when the request is received, except that it may take account of any amendment or deletion made between that time and the time when the information is supplied, being an amendment or deletion that would have been made regardless of the receipt of the request.

(7) For the purposes of section 7(4) and (5) another individual can be identified from the information being disclosed if he can be identified from that information, or from that and any other information which, in the reasonable belief of the data controller, is likely to be in, or to come into, the possession of the data subject making the request.

9 Application of section 7 where data controller is credit reference agency

(1) Where the data controller is a credit reference agency, section 7 has effect subject to the provisions of this section.

(2) An individual making a request under section 7 may limit his request to personal data relevant to his financial standing, and shall be taken to have so limited his request unless the request shows a contrary intention.

(3) Where the data controller receives a request under section 7 in a case where personal data of which the individual making the request is the data subject are being processed by or on behalf of the data controller, the obligation to supply information under that section includes an obligation to give the individual making the request a statement, in such form as may be prescribed by the [Secretary of State] by regulations, of the individual's rights—

(a)   under section 159 of the Consumer Credit Act 1974 , and

(b)   to the extent required by the prescribed form, under this Act.

[9A Unstructured personal data held by public authorities]

[(1) In this section "unstructured personal data" means any personal data falling within paragraph (e) of the definition of "data" in section 1(1), other than information which is recorded as part of, or with the intention that it should form part of, any set of information relating to individuals to the extent that the set is structured by reference to individuals or by reference to criteria relating to individuals.

(2) A public authority is not obliged to comply with subsection (1) of section 7 in relation to any unstructured personal data unless the request under that section contains a description of the data.

(3) Even if the data are described by the data subject in his request, a public authority is not obliged to comply with subsection (1) of section 7 in relation to unstructured personal data if the authority estimates that the cost of complying with the request so far as relating to those data would exceed the appropriate limit.

(4) Subsection (3) does not exempt the public authority from its obligation to comply with paragraph (a) of section 7(1) in relation to the unstructured personal data unless the estimated cost of complying with that paragraph alone in relation to those data would exceed the appropriate limit.

(5) In subsections (3) and (4) "the appropriate limit" means such amount as may be prescribed by the [Secretary of State] by regulations, and different amounts may be prescribed in relation to different cases.

(6) Any estimate for the purposes of this section must be made in accordance with regulations under section 12(5) of the Freedom of Information Act 2000.]

10 Right to prevent processing likely to cause damage or distress

(1) Subject to subsection (2), an individual is entitled at any time by notice in writing to a data controller to require the data controller at the end of such period as is reasonable in the circumstances to cease, or not to begin, processing, or processing for a specified purpose or in a specified manner, any personal data in respect of which he is the data subject, on the ground that, for specified reasons—

(a)   the processing of those data or their processing for that purpose or in that manner is causing or is likely to cause substantial damage or substantial distress to him or to another, and

(b)   that damage or distress is or would be unwarranted.

(2) Subsection (1) does not apply—

(a)   in a case where any of the conditions in paragraphs 1 to 4 of Schedule 2 is met, or

(b)   in such other cases as may be prescribed by the [Secretary of State] by order.

(3) The data controller must within twenty-one days of receiving a notice under subsection (1) ("the data subject notice") give the individual who gave it a written notice—

(a)   stating that he has complied or intends to comply with the data subject notice, or

(b)   stating his reasons for regarding the data subject notice as to any extent unjustified and the extent (if any) to which he has complied or intends to comply with it.

(4) If a court is satisfied, on the application of any person who has given a notice under subsection (1) which appears to the court to be justified (or to be justified to any extent), that the data controller in question has failed to comply with the notice, the court may order him to take such steps for complying with the notice (or for complying with it to that extent) as the court thinks fit.

(5) The failure by a data subject to exercise the right conferred by subsection (1) or section 11(1) does not affect any other right conferred on him by this Part.

11 Right to prevent processing for purposes of direct marketing

(1) An individual is entitled at any time by notice in writing to a data controller to require the data controller at the end of such period as is reasonable in the circumstances to cease, or not to begin, processing for the purposes of direct marketing personal data in respect of which he is the data subject.

(2) If the court is satisfied, on the application of any person who has given a notice under subsection (1), that the data controller has failed to comply with the notice, the court may order him to take such steps for complying with the notice as the court thinks fit.

[(2A) This section shall not apply in relation to the processing of such data as are mentioned in paragraph (1) of regulation 8 of the Telecommunications (Data Protection and Privacy) Regulations 1999 (processing of telecommunications billing data for certain marketing purposes) for the purposes mentioned in paragraph (2) of that regulation.]

(3) In this section "direct marketing" means the communication (by whatever means) of any advertising or marketing material which is directed to particular individuals.

12 Rights in relation to automated decision-taking

(1) An individual is entitled at any time, by notice in writing to any data controller, to require the data controller to ensure that no decision taken by or on behalf of the data controller which significantly affects that individual is based solely on the processing by automatic means of personal data in respect of which that individual is the data subject for the purpose of evaluating matters relating to him such as, for example, his performance at work, his creditworthiness, his reliability or his conduct.

(2) Where, in a case where no notice under subsection (1) has effect, a decision which significantly affects an individual is based solely on such processing as is mentioned in subsection (1)—

(a)   the data controller must as soon as reasonably practicable notify the individual that the decision was taken on that basis, and

(b)   the individual is entitled, within twenty-one days of receiving that notification from the data controller, by notice in writing to require the data controller to reconsider the decision or to take a new decision otherwise than on that basis.

(3) The data controller must, within twenty-one days of receiving a notice under subsection (2)(b) ("the data subject notice") give the individual a written notice specifying the steps that he intends to take to comply with the data subject notice.

(4) A notice under subsection (1) does not have effect in relation to an exempt decision; and nothing in subsection (2) applies to an exempt decision.

(5) In subsection (4) "exempt decision" means any decision—

(a)   in respect of which the condition in subsection (6) and the condition in subsection (7) are met, or

(b)   which is made in such other circumstances as may be prescribed by the [Secretary of State] by order.

(6) The condition in this subsection is that the decision—

(a)   is taken in the course of steps taken—

    (i)   for the purpose of considering whether to enter into a contract with the data subject,

    (ii)   with a view to entering into such a contract, or

    (iii)   in the course of performing such a contract, or

(b)   is authorised or required by or under any enactment.

(7) The condition in this subsection is that either—

(a)   the effect of the decision is to grant a request of the data subject, or

(b)   steps have been taken to safeguard the legitimate interests of the data subject (for example, by allowing him to make representations).

(8) If a court is satisfied on the application of a data subject that a person taking a decision in respect of him ("the responsible person") has failed to comply with subsection (1) or (2)(b), the court may order the responsible person to reconsider the decision, or to take a new decision which is not based solely on such processing as is mentioned in subsection (1).

(9) An order under subsection (8) shall not affect the rights of any person other than the data subject and the responsible person.

[12A   Rights of data subjects in relation to exempt manual data]

[(1) A data subject is entitled at any time by notice in writing—

(a)   to require the data controller to rectify, block, erase or destroy exempt manual data which are inaccurate or incomplete, or

(b)   to require the data controller to cease holding exempt manual data in a way incompatible with the legitimate purposes pursued by the data controller.

(2) A notice under subsection (1)(a) or (b) must state the data subject's reasons for believing that the data are inaccurate or incomplete or, as the case may be, his reasons for believing that they are held in a way incompatible with the legitimate purposes pursued by the data controller.

(3) If the court is satisfied, on the application of any person who has given a notice under subsection (1) which appears to the court to be justified (or to be justified to any extent) that the data controller in question has failed to comply with the notice, the court may order him to take such steps for complying with the notice (or for complying with it to that extent) as the court thinks fit.

(4) In this section "exempt manual data" means—

(a)   in relation to the first transitional period, as defined by paragraph 1(2) of Schedule 8, data to which paragraph 3 or 4 of that Schedule applies, and

(b)   in relation to the second transitional period, as so defined, data to which paragraph 14 of that Schedule applies.

(5) For the purposes of this section personal data are incomplete if, and only if, the data, although not inaccurate, are such that their incompleteness would constitute a contravention of the third or fourth data protection principles, if those principles applied to the data.]

> **NOTES**
>
> **Amendment**
>
> Temporarily inserted by the Data Protection Act 1998, s 72, Sch 13, para 1, until 23 October 2007.
>
> Date in force: 1 March 2000: see SI 2000/183, art 2(1).

13 Compensation for failure to comply with certain requirements

(1) An individual who suffers damage by reason of any contravention by a data controller of any of the requirements of this Act is entitled to compensation from the data controller for that damage.

(2) An individual who suffers distress by reason of any contravention by a data controller of any of the requirements of this Act is entitled to compensation from the data controller for that distress if—

(a) the individual also suffers damage by reason of the contravention, or

(b) the contravention relates to the processing of personal data for the special purposes.

(3) In proceedings brought against a person by virtue of this section it is a defence to prove that he had taken such care as in all the circumstances was reasonably required to comply with the requirement concerned.

14 Rectification, blocking, erasure and destruction

(1) If a court is satisfied on the application of a data subject that personal data of which the applicant is the subject are inaccurate, the court may order the data controller to rectify, block, erase or destroy those data and any other personal data in respect of which he is the data controller and which contain an expression of opinion which appears to the court to be based on the inaccurate data.

(2) Subsection (1) applies whether or not the data accurately record information received or obtained by the data controller from the data subject or a third party but where the data accurately record such information, then—

(a) if the requirements mentioned in paragraph 7 of Part II of Schedule 1 have been complied with, the court may, instead of making an order under subsection (1), make an order requiring the data to be supplemented by such statement of the true facts relating to the matters dealt with by the data as the court may approve, and

(b) if all or any of those requirements have not been complied with, the court may, instead of making an order under that subsection, make such order as it thinks fit for securing compliance with those requirements with or without a further order requiring the data to be supplemented by such a statement as is mentioned in paragraph (a).

(3) Where the court

(a) makes an order under subsection (1), or

(b) is satisfied on the application of a data subject that personal data of which he was the data subject and which have been rectified, blocked, erased or destroyed were inaccurate,

it may, where it considers it reasonably practicable, order the data controller to notify third parties to whom the data have been disclosed of the rectification, blocking, erasure or destruction.

(4) If a court is satisfied on the application of a data subject—

(a) that he has suffered damage by reason of any contravention by a data controller of any of the requirements of this Act in respect of any personal data, in circumstances entitling him to compensation under section 13, and

(b) that there is a substantial risk of further contravention in respect of those data in such circumstances,

the court may order the rectification, blocking, erasure or destruction of any of those data.

(5) Where the court makes an order under subsection (4) it may, where it considers it reasonably practicable, order the data controller to notify third parties to whom the data have been disclosed of the rectification, blocking, erasure or destruction.

(6) In determining whether it is reasonably practicable to require such notification as is mentioned in subsection (3) or (5) the court shall have regard, in particular, to the number of persons who would have to be notified.

15 Jurisdiction and procedure

(1) The jurisdiction conferred by sections 7 to 14 is exercisable by the High Court or a county court or, in Scotland, by the Court of Session or the sheriff.

(2) For the purpose of determining any question whether an applicant under subsection (9) of section 7 is entitled to the information which he seeks (including any question whether any relevant data are exempt from that section by virtue of Part IV) a court may require the information constituting any data processed by or on behalf of the data controller and any information as to the logic involved in any decision-taking as mentioned in section 7(1)(d) to be made available for its own inspection but shall not, pending the determination of that question in the applicant's favour, require the information sought by the applicant to be disclosed to him or his representatives whether by discovery (or, in Scotland, recovery) or otherwise.

Part III
Notification by Data Controllers

16 Preliminary

(1) In this Part "the registrable particulars", in relation to a data controller, means—

(a)   his name and address,

(b)   if he has nominated a representative for the purposes of this Act, the name and address of the representative,

(c)   a description of the personal data being or to be processed by or on behalf of the data controller and of the category or categories of data subject to which they relate,

(d)   a description of the purpose or purposes for which the data are being or are to be processed,

(e)   a description of any recipient or recipients to whom the data controller intends or may wish to disclose the data,

(f)   the names, or a description of, any countries or territories outside the European Economic Area to which the data controller directly or indirectly transfers, or intends or may wish directly or indirectly to transfer, the data,

[(ff)   where the data controller is a public authority, a statement of that fact,] and

(g)   in any case where—

(i)   personal data are being, or are intended to be, processed in circumstances in which the prohibition in subsection (1) of section 17 is excluded by subsection (2) or (3) of that section, and

(ii)   the notification does not extend to those data,

a statement of that fact.

(2) In this Part—

"fees regulations" means regulations made by the [Secretary of State] under section 18(5) or 19(4) or (7);

"notification regulations" means regulations made by the [Secretary of State] under the other provisions of this Part;

"prescribed", except where used in relation to fees regulations, means prescribed by notification regulations.

(3) For the purposes of this Part, so far as it relates to the addresses of data controllers—

(a)   the address of a registered company is that of its registered office, and

(b)   the address of a person (other than a registered company) carrying on a business is that of his principal place of business in the United Kingdom.

NOTES

Amendment

Sub-s (1): para (ff) inserted by the Freedom of Information Act 2000, s 71.

Date in force: 30 November 2005 (unless the Secretary of State by order appoints an earlier date): see the Freedom of Information Act 2000, s 87(3).

---

17 Prohibition on processing without registration

(1) Subject to the following provisions of this section, personal data must not be processed unless an entry in respect of the data controller is included in the register maintained by the Commissioner under section 19 (or is treated by notification regulations made by virtue of section 19(3) as being so included).

(2) Except where the processing is assessable processing for the purposes of section 22, subsection (1) does not apply in relation to personal data consisting of information which falls neither within paragraph (a) of the definition of "data" in section 1(1) nor within paragraph (b) of that definition.

(3) If it appears to the [Secretary of State] that processing of a particular description is unlikely to prejudice the rights and freedoms of data subjects, notification regulations may provide that, in such cases as may be prescribed, subsection (1) is not to apply in relation to processing of that description.

(4) Subsection (1) does not apply in relation to any processing whose sole purpose is the maintenance of a public register.

18 Notification by data controllers

(1) Any data controller who wishes to be included in the register maintained under section 19 shall give a notification to the Commissioner under this section.

(2) A notification under this section must specify in accordance with notification regulations—

(a) the registrable particulars, and

(b) a general description of measures to be taken for the purpose of complying with the seventh data protection principle.

(3) Notification regulations made by virtue of subsection (2) may provide for the determination by the Commissioner, in accordance with any requirements of the regulations, of the form in which the registrable particulars and the description mentioned in subsection (2)(b) are to be specified, including in particular the detail required for the purposes of section 16(1)(c), (d), (e) and (f) and subsection (2)(b).

(4) Notification regulations may make provision as to the giving of notification—

(a) by partnerships, or

(b) in other cases where two or more persons are the data controllers in respect of any personal data.

(5) The notification must be accompanied by such fee as may be prescribed by fees regulations.

(6) Notification regulations may provide for any fee paid under subsection (5) or section 19(4) to be refunded in prescribed circumstances.

19 Register of notifications

(1) The Commissioner shall—

(a) maintain a register of persons who have given notification under section 18, and

(b) make an entry in the register in pursuance of each notification received by him under that section from a person in respect of whom no entry as data controller was for the time being included in the register.

(2) Each entry in the register shall consist of—

(a) the registrable particulars notified under section 18 or, as the case requires, those particulars as amended in pursuance of section 20(4), and

(b) such other information as the Commissioner may be authorised or required by notification regulations to include in the register.

(3) Notification regulations may make provision as to the time as from which any entry in respect of a data controller is to be treated for the purposes of section 17 as having been made in the register.

(4) No entry shall be retained in the register for more than the relevant time except on payment of such fee as may be prescribed by fees regulations.

(5) In subsection (4) "the relevant time" means twelve months or such other period as may be prescribed by notification regulations; and different periods may be prescribed in relation to different cases.

(6) The Commissioner—

(a) shall provide facilities for making the information contained in the entries in the register available for inspection (in visible and legible form) by members of the public at all reasonable hours and free of charge, and

(b) may provide such other facilities for making the information contained in those entries available to the public free of charge as he considers appropriate.

(7) The Commissioner shall, on payment of such fee, if any, as may be prescribed by fees regulations, supply any member of the public with a duly certified copy in writing of the particulars contained in any entry made in the register.

20 Duty to notify changes

(1) For the purpose specified in subsection (2), notification regulations shall include provision imposing on every person in respect of whom an entry as a data controller is for the time being included in the register maintained under section 19 a duty to notify to the Commissioner, in such circumstances and at such time or times and in such form as may be prescribed, such matters relating to the registrable particulars and measures taken as mentioned in section 18(2)(b) as may be prescribed.

(2) The purpose referred to in subsection (1) is that of ensuring, so far as practicable, that at any time—

(a)   the entries in the register maintained under section 19 contain current names and addresses and describe the current practice or intentions of the data controller with respect to the processing of personal data, and

(b)   the Commissioner is provided with a general description of measures currently being taken as mentioned in section 18(2)(b).

(3) Subsection (3) of section 18 has effect in relation to notification regulations made by virtue of subsection (1) as it has effect in relation to notification regulations made by virtue of subsection (2) of that section.

(4) On receiving any notification under notification regulations made by virtue of subsection (1), the Commissioner shall make such amendments of the relevant entry in the register maintained under section 19 as are necessary to take account of the notification.

21 Offences

(1) If section 17(1) is contravened, the data controller is guilty of an offence.

(2) Any person who fails to comply with the duty imposed by notification regulations made by virtue of section 20(1) is guilty of an offence.

(3) It shall be a defence for a person charged with an offence under subsection (2) to show that he exercised all due diligence to comply with the duty.

22 Preliminary assessment by Commissioner

(1) In this section "assessable processing" means processing which is of a description specified in an order made by the [Secretary of State] as appearing to him to be particularly likely—

(a)   to cause substantial damage or substantial distress to data subjects, or

(b)   otherwise significantly to prejudice the rights and freedoms of data subjects.

(2) On receiving notification from any data controller under section 18 or under notification regulations made by virtue of section 20 the Commissioner shall consider—

(a)   whether any of the processing to which the notification relates is assessable processing, and

(b)   if so, whether the assessable processing is likely to comply with the provisions of this Act.

(3) Subject to subsection (4), the Commissioner shall, within the period of twenty-eight days beginning with the day on which he receives a notification which relates to assessable processing, give a notice to the data controller stating the extent to which the Commissioner is of the opinion that the processing is likely or unlikely to comply with the provisions of this Act.

(4) Before the end of the period referred to in subsection (3) the Commissioner may, by reason of special circumstances, extend that period on one occasion only by notice to the data controller by such further period not exceeding fourteen days as the Commissioner may specify in the notice.

(5) No assessable processing in respect of which a notification has been given the Commissioner as mentioned in subsection (2) shall be carried on unless either—

(a)   the period of twenty-eight days beginning with the day on which the notification is received by the Commissioner (or, in a case falling within subsection (4), that period as extended under that subsection) has elapsed, or

(b)   before the end of that period (or that period as so extended) the data controller has received a notice from the Commissioner under subsection (3) in respect of the processing.

(6) Where subsection (5) is contravened, the data controller is guilty of an offence.

(7) The [Secretary of State] may by order amend subsections (3), (4) and (5) by substituting for the number of days for the time being specified there a different number specified in the order.

23   Power to make provision for appointment of data protection supervisors

(1) The [Secretary of State] may by order—

(a)   make provision under which a data controller may appoint a person to act as a data protection supervisor responsible in particular for monitoring in an independent manner the data controller's compliance with the provisions of this Act, and

(b)   provide that, in relation to any data controller who has appointed a data protection supervisor in accordance with the provisions of the order and who complies with such conditions as may be specified in the order, the provisions of this Part are to have effect subject to such exemptions or other modifications as may be specified in the order.

(2) An order under this section may—

(a)   impose duties on data protection supervisors in relation to the Commissioner, and

(b)   confer functions on the Commissioner in relation to data protection supervisors.

24   Duty of certain data controllers to make certain information available

(1) Subject to subsection (3), where personal data are processed in a case where—

(a)   by virtue of subsection (2) or (3) of section 17, subsection (1) of that section does not apply to the processing, and

(b)   the data controller has not notified the relevant particulars in respect of that processing under section 18,

the data controller must, within twenty-one days of receiving a written request from any person, make the relevant particulars available to that person in writing free of charge.

(2) In this section "the relevant particulars" means the particulars referred to in paragraphs (a) to (f) of section 16(1).

(3) This section has effect subject to any exemption conferred for the purposes of this section by notification regulations.

(4) Any data controller who fails to comply with the duty imposed by subsection (1) is guilty of an offence.

(5) It shall be a defence for a person charged with an offence under subsection (4) to show that he exercised all due diligence to comply with the duty.

25   Functions of Commissioner in relation to making of notification regulations

(1) As soon as practicable after the passing of this Act, the Commissioner shall submit to the Secretary of State proposals as to the provisions to be included in the first notification regulations.

(2) The Commissioner shall keep under review the working of notification regulations and may from time to time submit to the [Secretary of State] proposals as to amendments to be made to the regulations.

(3) The [Secretary of State] may from time to time require the Commissioner to consider any matter relating to notification regulations and to submit to him proposals as to amendments to be made to the regulations in connection with that matter.

(4) Before making any notification regulations, the [Secretary of State] shall—

(a)   consider any proposals made to him by the Commissioner under [subsection (2) or (3)], and

(b)   consult the Commissioner.

26   Fees regulations

(1) Fees regulations prescribing fees for the purposes of any provision of this Part may provide for different fees to be payable in different cases.

(2) In making any fees regulations, the [Secretary of State] shall have regard to the desirability of securing that the fees payable to the Commissioner are sufficient to offset—

(a)   the expenses incurred by the Commissioner and the Tribunal in discharging their functions [under this Act] and any expenses of the Secretary of State in respect of the Commissioner or the Tribunal [so far as attributable to their functions under this Act], and

(b)   to the extent that the [Secretary of State] considers appropriate—

(i)   any deficit previously incurred (whether before or after the passing of this Act) in respect of the expenses mentioned in paragraph (a), and

(ii)   expenses incurred or to be incurred by the [Secretary of State] in respect of the inclusion of any officers or staff of the Commissioner in any scheme under section 1 of the Superannuation Act 1972.

Part IV
Exemptions

27 Preliminary

(1) References in any of the data protection principles or any provision of Parts II and III to personal data or to the processing of personal data do not include references to data or processing which by virtue of this Part are exempt from that principle or other provision.

(2) In this Part "the subject information provisions" means—

(a) the first data protection principle to the extent to which it requires compliance with paragraph 2 of Part II of Schedule 1, and

(b) section 7.

(3) In this Part "the non-disclosure provisions" means the provisions specified in subsection (4) to the extent to which they are inconsistent with the disclosure in question.

(4) The provisions referred to in subsection (3) are—

(a) the first data protection principle, except to the extent to which it requires compliance with the conditions in Schedules 2 and 3,

(b) the second, third, fourth and fifth data protection principles, and

(c) sections 10 and 14(1) to (3).

(5) Except as provided by this Part, the subject information provisions shall have effect notwithstanding any enactment or rule of law prohibiting or restricting the disclosure, or authorising the withholding, of information.

28 National security

(1) Personal data are exempt from any of the provisions of—

(a) the data protection principles,

(b) Parts II, III and V, and

(c) Sections 54A and 55

if the exemption from that provision is required for the purpose of safeguarding national security.

(2) Subject to subsection (4), a certificate signed by a Minister of the Crown certifying that exemption from all or any of the provisions mentioned in subsection (1) is or at any time was required for the purpose there mentioned in respect of any personal data shall be conclusive evidence of that fact.

(3) A certificate under subsection (2) may identify the personal data to which it applies by means of a general description and may be expressed to have prospective effect.

(4) Any person directly affected by the issuing of a certificate under subsection (2) may appeal to the Tribunal against the certificate.

(5) If on an appeal under subsection (4), the Tribunal finds that, applying the principles applied by the court on an application for judicial review, the Minister did not have reasonable grounds for issuing the certificate, the Tribunal may allow the appeal and quash the certificate.

(6) Where in any proceedings under or by virtue of this Act it is claimed by a data controller that a certificate under subsection (2) which identifies the personal data to which it applies by means of a general description applies to any personal data, any other party to the proceedings may appeal to the Tribunal on the ground that the certificate does not apply to the personal data in question and, subject to any determination under subsection (7), the certificate shall be conclusively presumed so to apply.

(7) On any appeal under subsection (6), the Tribunal may determine that the certificate does not so apply.

(8) A document purporting to be a certificate under subsection (2) shall be received in evidence and deemed to be such a certificate unless the contrary is proved.

(9) A document which purports to be certified by or on behalf of a Minister of the Crown as a true copy of a certificate issued by that Minister under subsection (2) shall in any legal proceedings be evidence (or, in Scotland, sufficient evidence) of that certificate.

(10) The power conferred by subsection (2) on a Minister of the Crown shall not be exercisable except by a Minister who is a member of the Cabinet or by the Attorney General or the [Advocate General for Scotland].

(11) No power conferred by any provision of Part V may be exercised in relation to personal data which by virtue of this section are exempt from that provision.

(12) Schedule 6 shall have effect in relation to appeals under subsection (4) or (6) and the proceedings of the Tribunal in respect of any such appeal.

29 Crime and taxation

(1) Personal data processed for any of the following purposes—

(a)   the prevention or detection of crime,

(b)   the apprehension or prosecution of offenders, or

(c)   the assessment or collection of any tax or duty or of any imposition of a similar nature,

are exempt from the first data protection principle (except to the extent to which it requires compliance with the conditions in Schedules 2 and 3) and section 7 in any case to the extent to which the application of those provisions to the data would be likely to prejudice any of the matters mentioned in this subsection.

(2) Personal data which—

(a)   are processed for the purpose of discharging statutory functions, and

(b)   consist of information obtained for such a purpose from a person who had it in his possession for any of the purposes mentioned in subsection (1),

are exempt from the subject information provisions to the same extent as personal data processed for any of the purposes mentioned in that subsection.

(3) Personal data are exempt from the non-disclosure provisions in any case in which—

(a)   the disclosure is for any of the purposes mentioned in subsection (1), and

(b)   the application of those provisions in relation to the disclosure would be likely to prejudice any of the matters mentioned in that subsection.

(4) Personal data in respect of which the data controller is a relevant authority and which—

(a)   consist of a classification applied to the data subject as part of a system of risk assessment which is operated by that authority for either of the following purposes—

     (i)   the assessment or collection of any tax or duty or any imposition of a similar nature, or

     (ii)   the prevention or detection of crime, or apprehension or prosecution of offenders, where the offence concerned involves any unlawful claim for any payment out of, or any unlawful application of, public funds, and

(b)   are processed for either of those purposes,

are exempt from section 7 to the extent to which the exemption is required in the interests of the operation of the system.

(5) In subsection (4)—

"public funds" includes funds provided by any Community institution;

"relevant authority" means—

     (a)   a government department,

     (b)   a local authority, or

     (c)   any other authority administering housing benefit or council tax benefit.

30 Health, education and social work

(1) The [Secretary of State] may by order exempt from the subject information provisions, or modify those provisions in relation to, personal data consisting of information as to the physical or mental health or condition of the data subject.

(2) The [Secretary of State] may by order exempt from the subject information provisions, or modify those provisions in relation to—

(a)   personal data in respect of which the data controller is the proprietor of, or a teacher at, a school, and which consist of information relating to persons who are or have been pupils at the school, or

(b)   personal data in respect of which the data controller is an education authority in Scotland, and which consist of information relating to persons who are receiving, or have received, further education provided by the authority.

(3) The [Secretary of State] may by order exempt from the subject information provisions, or modify those provisions in relation to, personal data of such other descriptions as may be specified in the order, being information—

(a)   processed by government departments or local authorities or by voluntary organisations or other bodies designated by or under the order, and

(b)   appearing to him to be processed in the course of, or for the purposes of, carrying out social work in relation to the data subject or other individuals;

but the [Secretary of State] shall not under this subsection confer any exemption or make any modification except so far as he considers that the application to the data of those provisions (or of those provisions without modification) would be likely to prejudice the carrying out of social work.

(4) An order under this section may make different provision in relation to data consisting of information of different descriptions.

(5) In this section—

"education authority" and "further education" have the same meaning as in the Education (Scotland) Act 1980 ("the 1980 Act"), and

"proprietor"—

(a)   in relation to a school in England or Wales, has the same meaning as in the Education Act 1996,

(b)   in relation to a school in Scotland, means—

(i)   *in the case of a self-governing school, the board of management within the meaning of the Self-Governing Schools etc (Scotland) Act 1989,*

(ii)   in the case of an independent school, the proprietor within the meaning of the 1980 Act,

(iii)   in the case of a grant-aided school, the managers within the meaning of the 1980 Act, and

(iv)   in the case of a public school, the education authority within the meaning of the 1980 Act, and

(c)   in relation to a school in Northern Ireland, has the same meaning as in the Education and Libraries (Northern Ireland) Order 1986 and includes, in the case of a controlled school, the Board of Governors of the school.

31 Regulatory activity

(1) Personal data processed for the purposes of discharging functions to which this subsection applies are exempt from the subject information provisions in any case to the extent to which the application of those provisions to the data would be likely to prejudice the proper discharge of those functions.

(2) Subsection (1) applies to any relevant function which is designed—

(a)   for protecting members of the public against—

(i)   financial loss due to dishonesty, malpractice or other seriously improper conduct by, or the unfitness or incompetence of, persons concerned in the provision of banking, insurance, investment or other financial services or in the management of bodies corporate,

(ii)   financial loss due to the conduct of discharged or undischarged bankrupts, or

(iii)   dishonesty, malpractice or other seriously improper conduct by, or the unfitness or incompetence of, persons authorised to carry on any profession or other activity,

(b)   for protecting charities against misconduct or mismanagement (whether by trustees or other persons) in their administration,

(c)   for protecting the property of charities from loss or misapplication,

(d)   for the recovery of the property of charities,

(e)   for securing the health, safety and welfare of persons at work, or

(f)   for protecting persons other than persons at work against risk to health or safety arising out of or in connection with the actions of persons at work.

(3) In subsection (2) "relevant function" means—

(a)   any function conferred on any person by or under any enactment,

(b)   any function of the Crown, a Minister of the Crown or a government department, or

(c)   any other function which is of a public nature and is exercised in the public interest.

(4) Personal data processed for the purpose of discharging any function which—

(a)   is conferred by or under any enactment on—

    (i)   the Parliamentary Commissioner for Administration,

    (ii)   the Commission for Local Administration in England, the Commission for Local Administration in Wales or the Commissioner for Local Administration in Scotland,

    (iii)   the Health Service Commissioner for England, the Health Service Commissioner for Wales or the Health Service Commissioner for Scotland,

    (iv)   the Welsh Administration Ombudsman,

    (v)   the Assembly Ombudsman for Northern Ireland, or

    (vi)   the Northern Ireland Commissioner for Complaints, and

(b)   is designed for protecting members of the public against—

    (i)   maladministration by public bodies,

    (ii)   failures in services provided by public bodies, or

    (iii)   a failure of a public body to provide a service which it was a function of the body to provide,

are exempt from the subject information provisions in any case to the extent to which the application of those provisions to the data would be likely to prejudice the proper discharge of that function.

[(4A) Personal data processed for the purpose of discharging any function which is conferred by or under Part XVI of the Financial Services and Markets Act 2000 on the body established by the Financial Services Authority for the purposes of that Part are exempt from the subject information provisions in any case to the extent to which the application of those provisions to the data would be likely to prejudice the proper discharge of the function.]

(5) Personal data processed for the purpose of discharging any function which—

(a)   is conferred by or under any enactment on the Office of Fair Trading, and

(b)   is designed—

    (i)   for protecting members of the public against conduct which may adversely affect their interests by persons carrying on a business,

    (ii)   for regulating agreements or conduct which have as their object or effect the prevention, restriction or distortion of competition in connection with any commercial activity, or

    (iii)   for regulating conduct on the part of one or more undertakings which amounts to the abuse of a dominant position in a market,

are exempt from the subject information provisions in any case to the extent to which the application of those provisions to the data would be likely to prejudice the proper discharge of that function.

32 Journalism, literature and art

(1) Personal data which are processed only for the special purposes are exempt from any provision to which this subsection relates if—

(a)   the processing is undertaken with a view to the publication by any person of any journalistic, literary or artistic material,

(b)   the data controller reasonably believes that, having regard in particular to the special importance of the public interest in freedom of expression, publication would be in the public interest, and

(c)   the data controller reasonably believes that, in all the circumstances, compliance with that provision is incompatible with the special purposes.

(2) Subsection (1) relates to the provisions of—

(a)   the data protection principles except the seventh data protection principle,

(b)   section 7,

(c)   section 10,

(d)   section 12,

[(dd)   section 12A,] and

(e)   section 14(1) to (3).

(3) In considering for the purposes of subsection (1)(b) whether the belief of a data controller that publication would be in the public interest was or is a reasonable one, regard may be had to his compliance with any code of practice which—

(a)   is relevant to the publication in question, and

(b)   is designated by the [Lord Chancellor] by order for the purposes of this subsection.

(4) Where at any time ("the relevant time") in any proceedings against a data controller under section 7(9), 10(4), 12(8)[, 12A(3)] or 14 or by virtue of section 13 the data controller claims, or it appears to the court, that any personal data to which the proceedings relate are being processed—

(a)   only for the special purposes, and

(b)   with a view to the publication by any person of any journalistic, literary or artistic material which, at the time twenty-four hours immediately before the relevant time, had not previously been published by the data controller,

the court shall stay the proceedings until either of the conditions in subsection (5) is met.

(5) Those conditions are—

(a)   that a determination of the Commissioner under section 45 with respect to the data in question takes effect, or

(b)   in a case where the proceedings were stayed on the making of a claim, that the claim is withdrawn.

(6) For the purposes of this Act "publish", in relation to journalistic, literary or artistic material, means make available to the public or any section of the public.

33   Research, history and statistics

(1) In this section—

"research purposes" includes statistical or historical purposes;

"the relevant conditions", in relation to any processing of personal data, means the conditions—

(a)   that the data are not processed to support measures or decisions with respect to particular individuals, and

(b)   that the data are not processed in such a way that substantial damage or substantial distress is, or is likely to be, caused to any data subject.

(2) For the purposes of the second data protection principle, the further processing of personal data only for research purposes in compliance with the relevant conditions is not to be regarded as incompatible with the purposes for which they were obtained.

(3) Personal data which are processed only for research purposes in compliance with the relevant conditions may, notwithstanding the fifth data protection principle, be kept indefinitely.

(4) Personal data which are processed only for research purposes are exempt from section 7 if—

(a)   they are processed in compliance with the relevant conditions, and

(b)   the results of the research or any resulting statistics are not made available in a form which identifies data subjects or any of them.

(5) For the purposes of subsections (2) to (4) personal data are not to be treated as processed otherwise than for research purposes merely because the data are disclosed—

(a)   to any person, for research purposes only,

(b)   to the data subject or a person acting on his behalf,

(c)   at the request, or with the consent, of the data subject or a person acting on his behalf, or

(d)   in circumstances in which the person making the disclosure has reasonable grounds for believing that the disclosure falls within paragraph (a), (b) or (c).

[33A   Manual data held by public authorities]

[(1) Personal data falling within paragraph (e) of the definition of "data" in section 1(1) are exempt from—

(a)   the first, second, third, fifth, seventh and eighth data protection principles,

(b)   the sixth data protection principle except so far as it relates to the rights conferred on data subjects by sections 7 and 14,

(c)   sections 10 to 12,

(d)   section 13, except so far as it relates to damage caused by a contravention of section 7 or of the fourth data protection principle and to any distress which is also suffered by reason of that contravention,

(e)   Part III, and

(f)   section 55.

(2) Personal data which fall within paragraph (e) of the definition of "data" in section 1(1) and relate to appointments or removals, pay, discipline, superannuation or other personnel matters, in relation to—

(a)   service in any of the armed forces of the Crown,

(b)   service in any office or employment under the Crown or under any public authority, or

(c)   service in any office or employment, or under any contract for services, in respect of which power to take action, or to determine or approve the action taken, in such matters is vested in Her Majesty, any Minister of the Crown, the National Assembly for Wales, any Northern Ireland Minister (within the meaning of the Freedom of Information Act 2000) or any public authority,

are also exempt from the remaining data protection principles and the remaining provisions of Part II.]

> **NOTES**
>
> **Amendment**
>
> Inserted by the Freedom of Information Act 2000, s 70(1).
>
> Date in force: 30 November 2005 (unless the Secretary of State by order appoints an earlier date): see the Freedom of Information Act 2000, s 87(3).

34   Information available to the public by or under enactment

Personal data are exempt from—

(a)   the subject information provisions,

(b)   the fourth data protection principle and [sections 12A and 14(1) to (3)], and

(c)   the non-disclosure provisions,

if the data consist of information which the data controller is obliged by or under any enactment [other than an enactment contained in the Freedom of Information Act 2000] to make available to the public, whether by publishing it, by making it available for inspection, or otherwise and whether gratuitously or on payment of a fee.

> **NOTES**
>
> **Amendment**
>
> Words "other than an enactment contained in the Freedom of Information Act 2000" in square brackets inserted by the Freedom of Information Act 2000, s 72.
>
> Date in force: 30 November 2005 (unless the Secretary of State by order appoints an earlier date): see the Freedom of Information Act 2000, s 87(3).

35   Disclosures required by law or made in connection with legal proceedings etc

(1) Personal data are exempt from the non-disclosure provisions where the disclosure is required by or under any enactment, by any rule of law or by the order of a court.

(2) Personal data are exempt from the non-disclosure provisions where the disclosure is necessary—

(a)   for the purpose of, or in connection with, any legal proceedings (including prospective legal proceedings), or

(b)   for the purpose of obtaining legal advice,

or is otherwise necessary for the purposes of establishing, exercising or defending legal rights.

[35A   Parliamentary privilege]

[Personal data are exempt from—

(a)   the first data protection principle, except to the extent to which it requires compliance with the conditions in Schedules 2 and 3,

(b)   the second, third, fourth and fifth data protection principles,

(c)   section 7, and

(d)   sections 10 and 14(1) to (3),

if the exemption is required for the purpose of avoiding an infringement of the privileges of either House of Parliament.]

> **NOTES**
>
> **Amendment**
>
> Inserted by the Freedom of Information Act 2000, s 73, Sch 6, para 2.
>
> Date in force: 30 November 2005 (unless the Secretary of State by order appoints an earlier date): see the Freedom of Information Act 2000, s 87(3).

36   Domestic purposes

Personal data processed by an individual only for the purposes of that individual's personal, family or household affairs (including recreational purposes) are exempt from the data protection principles and the provisions of Parts II and III.

37   Miscellaneous exemptions

Schedule 7 (which confers further miscellaneous exemptions) has effect.

38   Powers to make further exemptions by order

(1)   The [Secretary of State] may by order exempt from the subject information provisions personal data consisting of information the disclosure of which is prohibited or restricted by or under any enactment if and to the extent that he considers it necessary for the safeguarding of the interests of the data subject or the rights and freedoms of any other individual that the prohibition or restriction ought to prevail over those provisions.

(2)   The [Secretary of State] may by order exempt from the non-disclosure provisions any disclosures of personal data made in circumstances specified in the order, if he considers the exemption is necessary for the safeguarding of the interests of the data subject or the rights and freedoms of any other individual.

39   Transitional relief

Schedule 8 (which confers transitional exemptions) has effect.

Part V
Enforcement

40   Enforcement notices

(1)   If the Commissioner is satisfied that a data controller has contravened or is contravening any of the data protection principles, the Commissioner may serve him with a notice (in this Act referred to as "an enforcement notice") requiring him, for complying with the principle or principles in question, to do either or both of the following—

(a)   to take within such time as may be specified in the notice, or to refrain from taking after such time as may be so specified, such steps as are so specified, or

(b)   to refrain from processing any personal data, or any personal data of a description specified in the notice, or to refrain from processing them for a purpose so specified or in a manner so specified, after such time as may be so specified.

(2)   In deciding whether to serve an enforcement notice, the Commissioner shall consider whether the contravention has caused or is likely to cause any person damage or distress.

(3)   An enforcement notice in respect of a contravention of the fourth data protection principle which requires the data controller to rectify, block, erase or destroy any inaccurate data may also require the data controller to rectify,

block, erase or destroy any other data held by him and containing an expression of opinion which appears to the Commissioner to be based on the inaccurate data.

(4) An enforcement notice in respect of a contravention of the fourth data protection principle, in the case of data which accurately record information received or obtained by the data controller from the data subject or a third party, may require the data controller either—

(a)   to rectify, block, erase or destroy any inaccurate data and any other data held by him and containing an expression of opinion as mentioned in subsection (3), or

(b)   to take such steps as are specified in the notice for securing compliance with the requirements specified in paragraph 7 of Part II of Schedule 1 and, if the Commissioner thinks fit, for supplementing the data with such statement of the true facts relating to the matters dealt with by the data as the Commissioner may approve.

(5) Where—

(a)   an enforcement notice requires the data controller to rectify, block, erase or destroy any personal data, or

(b)   the Commissioner is satisfied that personal data which have been rectified, blocked, erased or destroyed had been processed in contravention of any of the data protection principles,

an enforcement notice may, if reasonably practicable, require the data controller to notify third parties to whom the data have been disclosed of the rectification, blocking, erasure or destruction; and in determining whether it is reasonably practicable to require such notification regard shall be had, in particular, to the number of persons who would have to be notified.

(6) An enforcement notice must contain—

(a)   a statement of the data protection principle or principles which the Commissioner is satisfied have been or are being contravened and his reasons for reaching that conclusion, and

(b)   particulars of the rights of appeal conferred by section 48.

(7) Subject to subsection (8), an enforcement notice must not require any of the provisions of the notice to be complied with before the end of the period within which an appeal can be brought against the notice and, if such an appeal is brought, the notice need not be complied with pending the determination or withdrawal of the appeal.

(8) If by reason of special circumstances the Commissioner considers that an enforcement notice should be complied with as a matter of urgency he may include in the notice a statement to that effect and a statement of his reasons for reaching that conclusion; and in that event subsection (7) shall not apply but the notice must not require the provisions of the notice to be complied with before the end of the period of seven days beginning with the day on which the notice is served.

(9) Notification regulations (as defined by section 16(2)) may make provision as to the effect of the service of an enforcement notice on any entry in the register maintained under section 19 which relates to the person on whom the notice is served.

(10) This section has effect subject to section 46(1).

41   Cancellation of an enforcement notice

(1) If the Commissioner considers that all or any of the provisions of an enforcement notice need not be complied with in order to ensure compliance with the data protection principle or principles to which it relates, he may cancel or vary the notice by written notice to the person on whom it was served.

(2) A person on whom an enforcement notice has been served may, at any time after the expiry of the period during which an appeal can be brought against that notice, apply in writing to the Commissioner for the cancellation or variation of that notice on the ground that, by reason of a change of circumstances, all or any of the provisions of that notice need not be complied with in order to ensure compliance with the data protection principle or principles to which that notice relates.

42   Request for assessment

(1) A request may be made to the Commissioner by or on behalf of any person who is, or believes himself to be, directly affected by any processing of personal data for an assessment as to whether it is likely or unlikely that the processing has been or is being carried out in compliance with the provisions of this Act.

(2) On receiving a request under this section, the Commissioner shall make an assessment in such manner as appears to him to be appropriate, unless he has not been supplied with such information as he may reasonably require in order to—

(a)   satisfy himself as to the identity of the person making the request, and

(b)   enable him to identify the processing in question.

(3) The matters to which the Commissioner may have regard in determining in what manner it is appropriate to make an assessment include—

(a)   the extent to which the request appears to him to raise a matter of substance,

(b)   any undue delay in making the request, and

(c)   whether or not the person making the request is entitled to make an application under section 7 in respect of the personal data in question.

(4) Where the Commissioner has received a request under this section he shall notify the person who made the request—

(a)   whether he has made an assessment as a result of the request, and

(b)   to the extent that he considers appropriate, having regard in particular to any exemption from section 7 applying in relation to the personal data concerned, of any view formed or action taken as a result of the request.

43   Information notices

(1) If the Commissioner—

(a)   has received a request under section 42 in respect of any processing of personal data, or

(b)   reasonably requires any information for the purpose of determining whether the data controller has complied or is complying with the data protection principles,

he may serve the data controller with a notice (in this Act referred to as "an information notice") requiring the data controller, within such time as is specified in the notice, to furnish the Commissioner, in such form as may be so specified, with such information relating to the request or to compliance with the principles as is so specified.

(2) An information notice must contain—

(a)   in a case falling within subsection (1)(a), a statement that the Commissioner has received a request under section 42 in relation to the specified processing, or

(b)   in a case falling within subsection (1)(b), a statement that the Commissioner regards the specified information as relevant for the purpose of determining whether the data controller has complied, or is complying, with the data protection principles and his reasons for regarding it as relevant for that purpose.

(3) An information notice must also contain particulars of the rights of appeal conferred by section 48.

(4) Subject to subsection (5), the time specified in an information notice shall not expire before the end of the period within which an appeal can be brought against the notice and, if such an appeal is brought, the information need not be furnished pending the determination or withdrawal of the appeal.

(5) If by reason of special circumstances the Commissioner considers that the information is required as a matter of urgency, he may include in the notice a statement to that effect and a statement of his reasons for reaching that conclusion; and in that event subsection (4) shall not apply, but the notice shall not require the information to be furnished before the end of the period of seven days beginning with the day on which the notice is served.

(6) A person shall not be required by virtue of this section to furnish the Commissioner with any information in respect of—

(a)   any communication between a professional legal adviser and his client in connection with the giving of legal advice to the client with respect to his obligations, liabilities or rights under this Act, or

(b)   any communication between a professional legal adviser and his client, or between such an adviser or his client and any other person, made in connection with or in contemplation of proceedings under or arising out of this Act (including proceedings before the Tribunal) and for the purposes of such proceedings.

(7) In subsection (6) references to the client of a professional legal adviser include references to any person representing such a client.

(8) A person shall not be required by virtue of this section to furnish the Commissioner with any information if the furnishing of that information would, by revealing evidence of the commission of any offence other than an offence under this Act, expose him to proceedings for that offence.

(9) The Commissioner may cancel an information notice by written notice to the person on whom it was served.

(10) This section has effect subject to section 46(3).

44 Special information notices

If the Commissioner—

(a) has received a request under section 42 in respect of any processing of personal data, or

(b) has reasonable grounds for suspecting that, in a case in which proceedings have been stayed under section 32, the personal data to which the proceedings relate—

(i) are not being processed only for the special purposes, or

(ii) are not being processed with a view to the publication by any person of any journalistic, literary or artistic material which has not previously been published by the data controller,

he may serve the data controller with a notice (in this Act referred to as a "special information notice") requiring the data controller, within such time as is specified in the notice, to furnish the Commissioner, in such form as may be so specified, with such information as is so specified for the purpose specified in subsection (2).

(2) That purpose is the purpose of ascertaining—

(a) whether the personal data are being processed only for the special purposes, or

(b) whether they are being processed with a view to the publication by any person of any journalistic, literary or artistic material which has not previously been published by the data controller.

(3) A special information notice must contain—

(a) in a case falling within paragraph (a) of subsection (1), a statement that the Commissioner has received a request under section 42 in relation to the specified processing, or

(b) in a case falling within paragraph (b) of that subsection, a statement of the Commissioner's grounds for suspecting that the personal data are not being processed as mentioned in that paragraph.

(4) A special information notice must also contain particulars of the rights of appeal conferred by section 48.

(5) Subject to subsection (6), the time specified in a special information notice shall not expire before the end of the period within which an appeal can be brought against the notice and, if such an appeal is brought, the information need not be furnished pending the determination or withdrawal of the appeal.

(6) If by reason of special circumstances the Commissioner considers that the information is required as a matter of urgency, he may include in the notice a statement to that effect and a statement of his reasons for reaching that conclusion; and in that event subsection (5) shall not apply, but the notice shall not require the information to be furnished before the end of the period of seven days beginning with the day on which the notice is served.

(7) A person shall not be required by virtue of this section to furnish the Commissioner with any information in respect of—

(a) any communication between a professional legal adviser and his client in connection with the giving of legal advice to the client with respect to his obligations, liabilities or rights under this Act, or

(b) any communication between a professional legal adviser and his client, or between such an adviser or his client and any other person, made in connection with or in contemplation of proceedings under or arising out of this Act (including proceedings before the Tribunal) and for the purposes of such proceedings.

(8) In subsection (7) references to the client of a professional legal adviser include references to any person representing such a client.

(9) A person shall not be required by virtue of this section to furnish the Commissioner with any information if the furnishing of that information would, by revealing evidence of the commission of any offence other than an offence under this Act, expose him to proceedings for that offence.

(10) The Commissioner may cancel a special information notice by written notice to the person on whom it was served.

45 Determination by Commissioner as to the special purposes

(1) Where at any time it appears to the Commissioner (whether as a result of the service of a special information notice or otherwise) that any personal data—

(a) are not being processed only for the special purposes, or

(b) are not being processed with a view to the publication by any person of any journalistic, literary or artistic material which has not previously been published by the data controller,

he may make a determination in writing to that effect.

(2) Notice of the determination shall be given to the data controller; and the notice must contain particulars of the right of appeal conferred by section 48.

(3) A determination under subsection (1) shall not take effect until the end of the period within which an appeal can be brought and, where an appeal is brought, shall not take effect pending the determination or withdrawal of the appeal.

46 Restriction on enforcement in case of processing for the special purposes

(1) The Commissioner may not at any time serve an enforcement notice on a data controller with respect to the processing of personal data for the special purposes unless—

(a) a determination under section 45(1) with respect to those data has taken effect, and

(b) the court has granted leave for the notice to be served.

(2) The court shall not grant leave for the purposes of subsection (1)(b) unless it is satisfied—

(a) that the Commissioner has reason to suspect a contravention of the data protection principles which is of substantial public importance, and

(b) except where the case is one of urgency, that the data controller has been given notice, in accordance with rules of court, of the application for leave.

(3) The Commissioner may not serve an information notice on a data controller with respect to the processing of personal data for the special purposes unless a determination under section 45(1) with respect to those data has taken effect.

47 Failure to comply with notice

(1) A person who fails to comply with an enforcement notice, an information notice or a special information notice is guilty of an offence.

(2) A person who, in purported compliance with an information notice or a special information notice—

(a) makes a statement which he knows to be false in a material respect, or

(b) recklessly makes a statement which is false in a material respect,

is guilty of an offence.

(3) It is a defence for a person charged with an offence under subsection (1) to prove that he exercised all due diligence to comply with the notice in question.

48 Rights of appeal

(1) A person on whom an enforcement notice, an information notice or a special information notice has been served may appeal to the Tribunal against the notice.

(2) A person on whom an enforcement notice has been served may appeal to the Tribunal against the refusal of an application under section 41(2) for cancellation or variation of the notice.

(3) Where an enforcement notice, an information notice or a special information notice contains a statement by the Commissioner in accordance with section 40(8), 43(5) or 44(6) then, whether or not the person appeals against the notice, he may appeal against—

(a) the Commissioner's decision to include the statement in the notice, or

(b) the effect of the inclusion of the statement as respects any part of the notice.

(4) A data controller in respect of whom a determination has been made under section 45 may appeal to the Tribunal against the determination.

(5) Schedule 6 has effect in relation to appeals under this section and the proceedings of the Tribunal in respect of any such appeal.

49 Determination of appeals

(1) If on an appeal under section 48(1) the Tribunal considers—

(a) that the notice against which the appeal is brought is not in accordance with the law, or

(b) to the extent that the notice involved an exercise of discretion by the Commissioner, that he ought to have exercised his discretion differently, the Tribunal shall allow the appeal or substitute such other notice or decision as could have been served or made by the Commissioner; and in any other case the Tribunal shall dismiss the appeal.

(2) On such an appeal, the Tribunal may review any determination of fact on which the notice in question was based.

(3) If on an appeal under section 48(2) the Tribunal considers that the enforcement notice ought to be cancelled or varied by reason of a change in circumstances, the Tribunal shall cancel or vary the notice.

(4) On an appeal under subsection (3) of section 48 the Tribunal may direct—

(a)   that the notice in question shall have effect as if it did not contain any such statement as is mentioned in that subsection, or

(b)   that the inclusion of the statement shall not have effect in relation to any part of the notice,

and may make such modifications in the notice as may be required for giving effect to the direction.

(5) On an appeal under section 48(4), the Tribunal may cancel the determination of the Commissioner.

(6) Any party to an appeal to the Tribunal under section 48 may appeal from the decision of the Tribunal on a point of law to the appropriate court; and that court shall be—

(a)   the High Court of Justice in England if the address of the person who was the appellant before the Tribunal is in England or Wales,

(b)   the Court of Session if that address is in Scotland, and

(c)   the High Court of Justice in Northern Ireland if that address is in Northern Ireland.

(7) For the purposes of subsection (6)—

(a)   the address of a registered company is that of its registered office, and

(b)   the address of a person (other than a registered company) carrying on a business is that of his principal place of business in the United Kingdom.

50   Powers of entry and inspection

Schedule 9 (powers of entry and inspection) has effect.

Part VI
Miscellaneous and General

Functions of Commissioner

51   *General duties of Commissioner*

(1) It shall be the duty of the Commissioner to promote the following of good practice by data controllers and, in particular, so to perform his functions under this Act as to promote the observance of the requirements of this Act by data controllers.

(2) The Commissioner shall arrange for the dissemination in such form and manner as he considers appropriate of such information as it may appear to him expedient to give to the public about the operation of this Act, about good practice, and about other matters within the scope of his functions under this Act, and may give advice to any person as to any of those matters.

(3) Where—

(a)   the [Secretary of State] so directs by order, or

(b)   the Commissioner considers it appropriate to do so,

the Commissioner shall, after such consultation with trade associations, data subjects or persons representing data subjects as appears to him to be appropriate, prepare and disseminate to such persons as he considers appropriate codes of practice for guidance as to good practice.

(4) The Commissioner shall also—

(a)   where he considers it appropriate to do so, encourage trade associations to prepare, and to disseminate to their members, such codes of practice, and

(b)   where any trade association submits a code of practice to him for his consideration, consider the code and, after such consultation with data subjects or persons representing data subjects as appears to him to be appropriate, notify the trade association whether in his opinion the code promotes the following of good practice.

(5) An order under subsection (3) shall describe the personal data or processing to which the code of practice is to relate, and may also describe the persons or classes of persons to whom it is to relate.

(6) The Commissioner shall arrange for the dissemination in such form and manner as he considers appropriate of—

(a)   any Community finding as defined by paragraph 15(2) of Part II of Schedule 1,

(b)   any decision of the European Commission, under the procedure provided for in Article 31(2) of the Data Protection Directive, which is made for the purposes of Article 26(3) or (4) of the Directive, and

(c)   such other information as it may appear to him to be expedient to give to data controllers in relation to any personal data about the protection of the rights and freedoms of data subjects in relation to the processing of personal data in countries and territories outside the European Economic Area.

(7) The Commissioner may, with the consent of the data controller, assess any processing of personal data for the following of good practice and shall inform the data controller of the results of the assessment.

(8) The Commissioner may charge such sums as he may with the consent of the [Secretary of State] determine for any services provided by the Commissioner by virtue of this Part.

(9) In this section—

"good practice" means such practice in the processing of personal data as appears to the Commissioner to be desirable having regard to the interests of data subjects and others, and includes (but is not limited to) compliance with the requirements of this Act;

"trade association" includes any body representing data controllers.

52   Reports and codes of practice to be laid before Parliament

(1) The Commissioner shall lay annually before each House of Parliament a general report on the exercise of his functions under this Act.

(2) The Commissioner may from time to time lay before each House of Parliament such other reports with respect to those functions as he thinks fit.

(3) The Commissioner shall lay before each House of Parliament any code of practice prepared under section 51(3) for complying with a direction of the [Secretary of State], unless the code is included in any report laid under subsection (1) or (2).

53   Assistance by Commissioner in cases involving processing for the special purposes

(1) An individual who is an actual or prospective party to any proceedings under section 7(9), 10(4), 12(8)[, 12A(3)] or 14 or by virtue of section 13 which relate to personal data processed for the special purposes may apply to the Commissioner for assistance in relation to those proceedings.

(2) The Commissioner shall, as soon as reasonably practicable after receiving an application under subsection (1), consider it and decide whether and to what extent to grant it, but he shall not grant the application unless, in his opinion, the case involves a matter of substantial public importance.

(3) If the Commissioner decides to provide assistance, he shall, as soon as reasonably practicable after making the decision, notify the applicant, stating the extent of the assistance to be provided.

(4) If the Commissioner decides not to provide assistance, he shall, as soon as reasonably practicable after making the decision, notify the applicant of his decision and, if he thinks fit, the reasons for it.

(5) In this section—

(a)   references to "proceedings" include references to prospective proceedings, and

(b)   "applicant", in relation to assistance under this section, means an individual who applies for assistance.

(6) Schedule 10 has effect for supplementing this section.

54   International co-operation

(1) The Commissioner—

(a) shall continue to be the designated authority in the United Kingdom for the purposes of Article 13 of the Convention, and

(b) shall be the supervisory authority in the United Kingdom for the purposes of the Data Protection Directive.

(2) The [Secretary of State] may by order make provision as to the functions to be discharged by the Commissioner as the designated authority in the United Kingdom for the purposes of Article 13 of the Convention.

(3) The [Secretary of State] may by order make provision as to co-operation by the Commissioner with the European Commission and with supervisory authorities in other EEA States in connection with the performance of their respective duties and, in particular, as to—

(a) the exchange of information with supervisory authorities in other EEA States or with the European Commission, and

(b) the exercise within the United Kingdom at the request of a supervisory authority in another EEA State, in cases excluded by section 5 from the application of the other provisions of this Act, of functions of the Commissioner specified in the order.

(4) The Commissioner shall also carry out any data protection functions which the [Secretary of State] may by order direct him to carry out for the purpose of enabling Her Majesty's Government in the United Kingdom to give effect to any international obligations of the United Kingdom.

(5) The Commissioner shall, if so directed by the [Secretary of State], provide any authority exercising data protection functions under the law of a colony specified in the direction with such assistance in connection with the discharge of those functions as the [Secretary of State] may direct or approve, on such terms (including terms as to payment) as the [Secretary of State] may direct or approve.

(6) Where the European Commission makes a decision for the purposes of Article 26(3) or (4) of the Data Protection Directive under the procedure provided for in Article 31(2) of the Directive, the Commissioner shall comply with that decision in exercising his functions under paragraph 9 of Schedule 4 or, as the case may be, paragraph 8 of that Schedule.

(7) The Commissioner shall inform the European Commission and the supervisory authorities in other EEA States—

(a) of any approvals granted for the purposes of paragraph 8 of Schedule 4, and

(b) of any authorisations granted for the purposes of paragraph 9 of that Schedule.

(8) In this section—

"the Convention" means the Convention for the Protection of Individuals with regard to Automatic Processing of Personal Data which was opened for signature on 28th January 1981;

"data protection functions" means functions relating to the protection of individuals with respect to the processing of personal information.

Unlawful obtaining etc of personal data

55 Unlawful obtaining etc of personal data

(1) A person must not knowingly or recklessly, without the consent of the data controller—

(a) obtain or disclose personal data or the information contained in personal data, or

(b) procure the disclosure to another person of the information contained in personal data.

(2) Subsection (1) does not apply to a person who shows—

(a) that the obtaining, disclosing or procuring—

    (i) was necessary for the purpose of preventing or detecting crime, or

    (ii) was required or authorised by or under any enactment, by any rule of law or by the order of a court,

(b) that he acted in the reasonable belief that he had in law the right to obtain or disclose the data or information or, as the case may be, to procure the disclosure of the information to the other person,

(c) that he acted in the reasonable belief that he would have had the consent of the data controller if the data controller had known of the obtaining, disclosing or procuring and the circumstances of it, or

(d) that in the particular circumstances the obtaining, disclosing or procuring was justified as being in the public interest.

(3) A person who contravenes subsection (1) is guilty of an offence.

(4) A person who sells personal data is guilty of an offence if he has obtained the data in contravention of subsection (1).

(5) A person who offers to sell personal data is guilty of an offence if—

(a)   he has obtained the data in contravention of subsection (1), or

(b)   he subsequently obtains the data in contravention of that subsection.

(6) For the purposes of subsection (5), an advertisement indicating that personal data are or may be for sale is an offer to sell the data.

(7) Section 1(2) does not apply for the purposes of this section; and for the purposes of subsections (4) to (6), "personal data" includes information extracted from personal data.

(8) References in this section to personal data do not include references to personal data which by virtue of section 28 [or 33A] are exempt from this section.

Records obtained under data subject's right of access

56   Prohibition of requirement as to production of certain records

(1) A person must not, in connection with—

(a)   the recruitment of another person as an employee,

(b)   the continued employment of another person, or

(c)   any contract for the provision of services to him by another person,

require that other person or a third party to supply him with a relevant record or to produce a relevant record to him.

(2) A person concerned with the provision (for payment or not) of goods, facilities or services to the public or a section of the public must not, as a condition of providing or offering to provide any goods, facilities or services to another person, require that other person or a third party to supply him with a relevant record or to produce a relevant record to him.

(3) Subsections (1) and (2) do not apply to a person who shows—

(a)   that the imposition of the requirement was required or authorised by or under any enactment, by any rule of law or by the order of a court, or

(b)   that in the particular circumstances the imposition of the requirement was justified as being in the public interest.

(4) Having regard to the provisions of Part V of the Police Act 1997 (certificates of criminal records etc), the imposition of the requirement referred to in subsection (1) or (2) is not to be regarded as being justified as being in the public interest on the ground that it would assist in the prevention or detection of crime.

(5) A person who contravenes subsection (1) or (2) is guilty of an offence.

(6) In this section "a relevant record" means any record which—

(a)   has been or is to be obtained by a data subject from any data controller specified in the first column of the Table below in the exercise of the right conferred by section 7, and

(b)   contains information relating to any matter specified in relation to that data controller in the second column,

and includes a copy of such a record or a part of such a record.

Data controller	Subject-matter
1 Any of the following persons— (a) a chief officer of police of a police force in England and Wales. (b) a chief constable of a police force in Scotland. (c) the [Chief Constable of the Police Service of Northern Ireland]. (d) the Director General of the National Criminal Intelligence Service. (e) the Director General of the National Crime Squad.	(a) Convictions. (b) Cautions.
2 The Secretary of State.	(a) Convictions. (b) Cautions. (c) His functions under [section 92 of the Powers of Criminal Courts (Sentencing) Act 2000], section 205(2) or 208 of the Criminal Procedure (Scotland) Act 1995 or section 73 of the Children and Young Persons Act (Northern Ireland) 1968 in relation to any person sentenced to detention. (d) His functions under the Prison Act 1952, the Prisons (Scotland) Act 1989 or the Prison Act (Northern Ireland) 1953 in relation to any person imprisoned or detained. (e) His functions under the Social Security Contributions and Benefits Act 1992, the Social Security Administration Act 1992 or the Jobseekers Act 1995. (f) His functions under Part V of the Police Act 1997.
3 The Department of Health and Social Services for Northern Ireland.	Its functions under the Social Security Contributions and Benefits (Northern Ireland) Act 1992, the Social Security Administration (Northern Ireland) Act 1992 or the Jobseekers (Northern Ireland) Order 1995.

[(6A) A record is not a relevant record to the extent that it relates, or is to relate, only to personal data falling within paragraph (e) of the definition of "data" in section 1(1).]

(7) In the Table in subsection (6)—

"caution" means a caution given to any person in England and Wales or Northern Ireland in respect of an offence which, at the time when the caution is given, is admitted;

"conviction" has the same meaning as in the Rehabilitation of Offenders Act 1974 or the Rehabilitation of Offenders (Northern Ireland) Order 1978.

(8) The [Lord Chancellor] may by order amend—

(a)   the Table in subsection (6), and

(b)   subsection (7).

(9) For the purposes of this section a record which states that a data controller is not processing any personal data relating to a particular matter shall be taken to be a record containing information relating to that matter.

(10) In this section "employee" means an individual who—

(a)   works under a contract of employment, as defined by section 230(2) of the Employment Rights Act 1996, or

(b)   holds any office,

whether or not he is entitled to remuneration; and "employment" shall be construed accordingly.

NOTES

Amendment

Sub-s (6A): inserted by the Freedom of Information Act 2000, s 68(4).

Date in force: 30 November 2005 (unless the Secretary of State by order appoints an earlier date): see the Freedom of Information Act 2000, s 87(3).

57   Avoidance of certain contractual terms relating to health records

(1) Any term or condition of a contract is void in so far as it purports to require an individual—

(a)   to supply any other person with a record to which this section applies, or with a copy of such a record or a part of such a record, or

(b)   to produce to any other person such a record, copy or part.

(2) This section applies to any record which—

(a)   has been or is to be obtained by a data subject in the exercise of the right conferred by section 7, and

(b)   consists of the information contained in any health record as defined by section 68(2).

Information provided to Commissioner or Tribunal

58   *Disclosure of information*

No enactment or rule of law prohibiting or restricting the disclosure of information shall preclude a person from furnishing the Commissioner or the Tribunal with any information necessary for the discharge of their functions under this Act [or the Freedom of Information Act 2000].

59   Confidentiality of information

(1) No person who is or has been the Commissioner, a member of the Commissioner's staff or an agent of the Commissioner shall disclose any information which—

(a)   has been obtained by, or furnished to, the Commissioner under or for the purposes of [the information Acts],

(b)   relates to an identified or identifiable individual or business, and

(c)   is not at the time of the disclosure, and has not previously been, available to the public from other sources,

unless the disclosure is made with lawful authority.

(2) For the purposes of subsection (1) a disclosure of information is made with lawful authority only if, and to the extent that—

(a)   the disclosure is made with the consent of the individual or of the person for the time being carrying on the business,

(b)   the information was provided for the purpose of its being made available to the public (in whatever manner) under any provision of [the information Acts],

(c)   the disclosure is made for the purposes of, and is necessary for, the discharge of—

(i)   any functions under [the information Acts], or

(ii)   any Community obligation,

(d)   the disclosure is made for the purposes of any proceedings, whether criminal or civil and whether arising under, or by virtue of, [the information Acts] or otherwise, or

(e)   having regard to the rights and freedoms or legitimate interests of any person, the disclosure is necessary in the public interest.

(3) Any person who knowingly or recklessly discloses information in contravention of subsection (1) is guilty of an offence.

[(4) In this section "the information Acts" means this Act and the Freedom of Information Act 2000.]

See Further

See further, in relation to the extension of disclosure powers under sub-s (1) above: the Anti-terrorism, Crime and Security Act 2001, s 17, Sch 4, Pt 1, para 42.

General provisions relating to offences

60   *Prosecutions and penalties*

(1) No proceedings for an offence under this Act shall be instituted—

(a)   in England or Wales, except by the Commissioner or by or with the consent of the Director of Public Prosecutions;

(b)   in Northern Ireland, except by the Commissioner or by or with the consent of the Director of Public Prosecutions for Northern Ireland.

(2) A person guilty of an offence under any provision of this Act other than [section 54A and] paragraph 12 of Schedule 9 is liable—

(a)   on summary conviction, to a fine not exceeding the statutory maximum, or

(b)   on conviction on indictment, to a fine.

(3) A person guilty of an offence under [section 56A and] paragraph 12 of Schedule 9 is liable on summary conviction to a fine not exceeding level 5 on the standard scale.

(4) Subject to subsection (5), the court by or before which a person is convicted of—

(a)   an offence under section 21(1), 22(6), 55 or 56,

(b)   an offence under section 21(2) relating to processing which is assessable processing for the purposes of section 22, or

(c)   an offence under section 47(1) relating to an enforcement notice,

may order any document or other material used in connection with the processing of personal data and appearing to the court to be connected with the commission of the offence to be forfeited, destroyed or erased.

(5) The court shall not make an order under subsection (4) in relation to any material where a person (other than the offender) claiming to be the owner of or otherwise interested in the material applies to be heard by the court, unless an opportunity is given to him to show cause why the order should not be made.

61   Liability of directors etc

(1) Where an offence under this Act has been committed by a body corporate and is proved to have been committed with the consent or connivance of or to be attributable to any neglect on the part of any director, manager, secretary or similar officer of the body corporate or any person who was purporting to act in any such capacity, he as well as the body corporate shall be guilty of that offence and be liable to be proceeded against and punished accordingly.

(2) Where the affairs of a body corporate are managed by its members subsection (1) shall apply in relation to the acts and defaults of a member in connection with his functions of management as if he were a director of the body corporate.

(3) Where an offence under this Act has been committed by a Scottish partnership and the contravention in question is proved to have occurred with the consent or connivance of, or to be attributable to any neglect on the part of, a partner, he as well as the partnership shall be guilty of that offence and shall be liable to be proceeded against and punished accordingly.

Amendments of Consumer Credit Act 1974

62   Amendments of Consumer Credit Act 1974

(1) In section 158 of the Consumer Credit Act 1974 (duty of agency to disclose filed information)—

(a)   in subsection (1)—

(i)   in paragraph (a) for "individual" there is substituted "partnership or other unincorporated body of persons not consisting entirely of bodies corporate", and

(ii)   for "him" there is substituted "it",

(b)   in subsection (2), for "his" there is substituted "the consumer's", and

(c)   in subsection (3), for "him" there is substituted "the consumer".

(2) In section 159 of that Act (correction of wrong information) for subsection (1) there is substituted—

"(1) Any individual (the "objector") given—

(a)   information under section 7 of the Data Protection Act 1998 by a credit reference agency, or

(b)   information under section 158,

who considers that an entry in his file is incorrect, and that if it is not corrected he is likely to be prejudiced, may give notice to the agency requiring it either to remove the entry from the file or amend it.".

(3) In subsections (2) to (6) of that subsection—

(a)   for "consumer", wherever occurring, there is substituted "objector", and

(b)   for "Director", wherever occurring, there is substituted "the relevant authority".

(4) After subsection (6) of that section there is inserted—

"(7) The Data Protection Commissioner may vary or revoke any order made by him under this section.

(8) In this section "the relevant authority" means—

(a)   where the objector is a partnership or other unincorporated body of persons, the Director, and

(b)   in any other case, the Data Protection Commissioner.".

(5) In section 160 of that Act (alternative procedure for business consumers)—

(a)   in subsection (4)—

(i)   for "him" there is substituted "to the consumer", and

(ii)   in paragraphs (a) and (b) for "he" there is substituted "the consumer" and for "his" there is substituted "the consumer's", and

(b)   after subsection (6) there is inserted—

"(7) In this section "consumer" has the same meaning as in section 158.".

General

63 Application to Crown

(1) This Act binds the Crown.

(2) For the purposes of this Act each government department shall be treated as a person separate from any other government department.

(3) Where the purposes for which and the manner in which any personal data are, or are to be, processed are determined by any person acting on behalf of the Royal Household, the Duchy of Lancaster or the Duchy of Cornwall, the data controller in respect of those data for the purposes of this Act shall be—

(a)   in relation to the Royal Household, the Keeper of the Privy Purse,

(b)   in relation to the Duchy of Lancaster, such person as the Chancellor of the Duchy appoints, and

(c)   in relation to the Duchy of Cornwall, such person as the Duke of Cornwall, or the possessor for the time being of the Duchy of Cornwall, appoints.

(4) Different persons may be appointed under subsection (3)(b) or (c) for different purposes.

(5) Neither a government department nor a person who is a data controller by virtue of subsection (3) shall be liable to prosecution under this Act, but [sections 54A and] 55 and paragraph 12 of Schedule 9 shall apply to a person in the service of the Crown as they apply to any other person.

[63A   Application to Parliament]

[(1) Subject to the following provisions of this section and to section 35A, this Act applies to the processing of personal data by or on behalf of either House of Parliament as it applies to the processing of personal data by other persons

(2) Where the purposes for which and the manner in which any personal data are, or are to be, processed are determined by or on behalf of the House of Commons, the data controller in respect of those data for the purposes of this Act shall be the Corporate Officer of that House.

(3) Where the purposes for which and the manner in which any personal data are, or are to be, processed are determined by or on behalf of the House of Lords, the data controller in respect of those data for the purposes of this Act shall be the Corporate Officer of that House.

(4) Nothing in subsection (2) or (3) is to be taken to render the Corporate Officer of the House of Commons or the Corporate Officer of the House of Lords liable to prosecution under this Act, but section 55 and paragraph 12 of Schedule 9 shall apply to a person acting on behalf of either House as they apply to any other person.]

> **NOTES**
>
> **Amendment**
>
> Inserted by the Freedom of Information Act 2000, s 73, Sch 6, para 3.
>
> Date in force: 30 November 2005 (unless the Secretary of State by order appoints an earlier date): see the Freedom of Information Act 2000, s 87(3).

64 Transmission of notices etc by electronic or other means

(1) This section applies to

(a) a notice or request under any provision of Part II,

(b) a notice under subsection (1) of section 24 or particulars made available under that subsection, or

(c) an application under section 41(2),

but does not apply to anything which is required to be served in accordance with rules of court.

(2) The requirement that any notice, request, particulars or application to which this section applies should be in writing is satisfied where the text of the notice, request, particulars or application—

(a) is transmitted by electronic means,

(b) is received in legible form, and

(c) is capable of being used for subsequent reference.

(3) The [Secretary of State] may by regulations provide that any requirement that any notice, request, particulars or application to which this section applies should be in writing is not to apply in such circumstances as may be prescribed by the regulations.

65 Service of notices by Commissioner

(1) Any notice authorised or required by this Act to be served on or given to any person by the Commissioner may—

(a) if that person is an individual, be served on him—

    (i) by delivering it to him, or

    (ii) by sending it to him by post addressed to him at his usual or last-known place of residence or business, or

    (iii) by leaving it for him at that place;

(b) if that person is a body corporate or unincorporate, be served on that body—

    (i) by sending it by post to the proper officer of the body at its principal office, or

    (ii) by addressing it to the proper officer of the body and leaving it at that office;

(c) if that person is a partnership in Scotland, be served on that partnership—

    (i) by sending it by post to the principal office of the partnership, or

    (ii) by addressing it to that partnership and leaving it at that office.

(2) In subsection (1)(b) "principal office", in relation to a registered company, means its registered office and "proper officer", in relation to any body, means the secretary or other executive officer charged with the conduct of its general affairs.

(3) This section is without prejudice to any other lawful method of serving or giving a notice.

66 Exercise of rights in Scotland by children

(1) Where a question falls to be determined in Scotland as to the legal capacity of a person under the age of sixteen years to exercise any right conferred by any provision of this Act, that person shall be taken to have that capacity where he has a general understanding of what it means to exercise that right.

(2) Without prejudice to the generality of subsection (1), a person of twelve years of age or more shall be presumed to be of sufficient age and maturity to have such understanding as is mentioned in that subsection.

67   Orders, regulations and rules

(1) Any power conferred by this Act on the [Secretary of State] to make an order, regulations or rules shall be exercisable by statutory instrument.

(2) Any order, regulations or rules made by the [Secretary of State] under this Act may—

(a)   make different provision for different cases, and

(b)   make such supplemental, incidental, consequential or transitional provision or savings as the [Secretary of State] considers appropriate;

and nothing in section 7(11), 19(5), 26(1) or 30(4) limits the generality of paragraph (a).

(3) Before making—

(a)   an order under any provision of this Act other than section 75(3),

(b)   any regulations under this Act other than notification regulations (as defined by section 16(2)),

the [Secretary of State] shall consult the Commissioner.

(4) A statutory instrument containing (whether alone or with other provisions) an order under—

section 10(2)(b),

section 12(5)(b),

section 22(1),

section 30,

section 32(3),

section 38,

section 56(8),

paragraph 10 of Schedule 3, or

paragraph 4 of Schedule 7,

shall not be made unless a draft of the instrument has been laid before and approved by a resolution of each House of Parliament.

(5) A statutory instrument which contains (whether alone or with other provisions)—

(a)   an order under—

    section 22(7),

    section 23,

    section 51(3),

    section 54(2), (3) or (4),

    paragraph 3, 4 or 14 of Part II of Schedule 1,

    paragraph 6 of Schedule 2,

    paragraph 2, 7 or 9 of Schedule 3,

    paragraph 4 of Schedule 4,

    paragraph 6 of Schedule 7,

(b)   regulations under section 7 which—

    (i)   prescribe cases for the purposes of subsection (2)(b),

    (ii)   are made by virtue of subsection (7), or

    (iii) relate to the definition of "the prescribed period",

(c)   regulations under section 8(1) *or 9(3)* [*, 9(3) or 9A(5)*],

(d)   regulations under section 64,

(e)   notification regulations (as defined by section 16(2)), or

(f)   rules under paragraph 7 of Schedule 6,

and which is not subject to the requirement in subsection (4) that a draft of the instrument be laid before and approved by a resolution of each House of Parliament, shall be subject to annulment in pursuance of a resolution of either House of Parliament.

(6) A statutory instrument which contains only—

(a)   regulations prescribing fees for the purposes of any provision of this Act, or

(b)   regulations under section 7 prescribing fees for !he purposes of any other enactment,

shall be laid before Parliament after being made.

NOTES

Amendment

Sub-s (5): in para (c) words "or 9(3)" in italics repealed and subsequent words in square brackets substituted by the Freedom of Information Act 2000, s 69(3).

Date in force: 30 November 2005 (unless the Secretary of State by order appoints an earlier date): see the Freedom of Information Act 2000, s 87(3).

---

68   Meaning of "accessible record"

(1) In this Act "accessible record" means—

(a)   a health record as defined by subsection (2),

(b)   an educational record as defined by Schedule 11, or

(c)   an accessible public record as defined by Schedule 12.

(2) In subsection (1)(a) "health record" means any record which—

(a)   consists of information relating to the physical or mental health or condition of an individual, and

(b)   has been made by or on behalf of a health professional in connection with the care of that individual.

69   Meaning of "health professional"

(1) In this Act "health professional" means any of the following—

(a)   a registered medical practitioner,

(b)   a registered dentist as defined by section 53(1) of the Dentists Act 1984,

(c)   a registered optician as defined by section 36(1) of the Opticians Act 1989,

(d)   a registered pharmaceutical chemist as defined by section 24(1) of the Pharmacy Act 1954 or a registered person as defined by Article 2(2) of the Pharmacy (Northern Ireland) Order 1976,

(e)   *a registered nurse, midwife or health visitor,*

[(e)   a registered nurse or midwife,]

(f)   a registered osteopath as defined by section 41 of the Osteopaths Act 1993,

(g)   a registered chiropractor as defined by section 43 of the Chiropractors Act 1994,

(h)   any person who is registered as a member of a profession to which [the Health Professions Order 2001] for the time being extends,

(i)   a clinical psychologist [or child psychologist],

(j)   a music therapist employed by a health service body, and

(k)   a scientist employed by such a body as head of a department.

(2) In subsection (1)(a) "registered medical practitioner" includes any person who is provisionally registered under section 15 or 21 of the Medical Act 1983 and is engaged in such employment as is mentioned in subsection (3) of that section.

(3) In subsection (1) "health service body" means—

(a)   a [strategic Health Authority or a] Health Authority established under section 8 of the National Health Service Act 1977,

(b)   a Special Health Authority established under section 11 of that Act,

[(bb)   a Primary Care Trust established under section 16A of that Act,] [(bbb) a Local Health Board established under section 16BA of that Act,]

(c) a Health Board within the meaning of the National Health Service (Scotland) Act 1978,

(d) a Special Health Board within the meaning of that Act,

(e) the managers of a State Hospital provided under section 102 of that Act,

(f) a National Health Service trust first established under section 5 of the National Health Service and Community Care Act 1990 or section 12A of the National Health Service (Scotland) Act 1978,

[(fa) an NHS foundation trust]

(g) a Health and Social Services Board established under Article 16 of the Health and Personal Social Services (Northern Ireland) Order 1972,

(h) a special health and social services agency established under the Health and Personal Social Services (Special Agencies) (Northern Ireland) Order 1990, or

(i) a Health and Social Services trust established under Article 10 of the Health and Personal Social Services (Northern Ireland) Order 1991.

70 Supplementary definitions

(1) In this Act, unless the context otherwise requires—

"business" includes any trade or profession;

"the Commissioner" means [the Information Commissioner];

"credit reference agency" has the same meaning as in the Consumer Credit Act 1974;

"the Data Protection Directive" means Directive 95/46/EC on the protection of individuals with regard to the processing of personal data and on the free movement of such data;

"EEA State" means a State which is a contracting party to the Agreement on the European Economic Area signed at Oporto on 2nd May 1992 as adjusted by the Protocol signed at Brussels on 17th March 1993;

"enactment" includes an enactment passed after this Act [and any enactment comprised in, or in any instrument made under, an Act of the Scottish Parliament];

"government department" includes a Northern Ireland department and any body or authority exercising statutory functions on behalf of the Crown;

"Minister of the Crown" has the same meaning as in the Ministers of the Crown Act 1975;

"public register" means any register which pursuant to a requirement imposed—

(a) by or under any enactment, or

(b) in pursuance of any international agreement,

is open to public inspection or open to inspection by any person having a legitimate interest;

"pupil"—

(a) in relation to a school in England and Wales, means a registered pupil within the meaning of the Education Act 1996,

(b) in relation to a school in Scotland, means a pupil within the meaning of the Education (Scotland) Act 1980, and

(c) in relation to a school in Northern Ireland, means a registered pupil within the meaning of the Education and Libraries (Northern Ireland) Order 1986;

"recipient", in relation to any personal data, means any person to whom the data are disclosed, including any person (such as an employee or agent of the data controller, a data processor or an employee or agent of a data processor) to whom they are disclosed in the course of processing the data for the data controller, but does not include any person to whom disclosure is or may be made as a result of, or with a view to, a particular inquiry by or on behalf of that person made in the exercise of any power conferred by law;

"registered company" means a company registered under the enactments relating to companies for the time being in force in the United Kingdom;

"school"—

(a) in relation to England and Wales, has the same meaning as in the Education Act 1996,

(b) in relation to Scotland, has the same meaning as in the Education (Scotland) Act 1980, and

(c) in relation to Northern Ireland, has the same meaning as in the Education and Libraries (Northern Ireland) Order 1986;

"teacher" includes—

(a)   in Great Britain, head teacher, and

(b)   in Northern Ireland, the principal of a school;

"third party", in relation to personal data, means any person other than—

(a)   the data subject,

(b)   the data controller, or

(c)   any data processor or other person authorised to process data for the data controller or processor;

"the Tribunal" means [the Information Tribunal].

(2)   For the purposes of this Act data are inaccurate if they are incorrect or misleading as to any matter of fact.

71   Index of defined expressions

The following Table shows provisions defining or otherwise explaining expressions used in this Act (other than provisions defining or explaining an expression only used in the same section or Schedule)—

accessible record	section 68
address (in Part III)	section 16(3)
business	section 70(1)
the Commissioner	section 70(1)
credit reference agency	section 70(1)
data	section 1(1)
data controller	sections 1(1) and (4) and 63(3)
data processor	section 1(1)
the Data Protection Directive	section 70(1)
data protection principles	section 4 and Schedule 1
data subject	section 1(1)
disclosing (of personal data)	section 1(2)(b)
EEA State	section 70(1)
enactment	section 70(1)
enforcement notice	section 40(1)
fees regulations (in Part III)	section 16(2)
government department	section 70(1)
health professional	section 69
inaccurate (in relation to data)	section 70(2)
information notice	section 43(1)
Minister of the Crown	section 70(1)
the non-disclosure provisions (in Part IV)	section 27(3)
notification regulations (in Part III)	section 16(2)
obtaining (of personal data)	section 1(2)(a)
personal data	section 1(1)
prescribed (in Part III)	section 16(2)
processing (of information or data)	section 1(1) and paragraph 5 of Schedule 8
[public authority	section 1(1)]
public register	section 70(1)
publish (in relation to journalistic, literary or artistic material)	section 32(6)
pupil (in relation to a school)	section 70(1)
recipient (in relation to personal data)	section 70(1)
recording (of personal data)	section 1(2)(a)
registered company	section 70(1)
registrable particulars (in Part III)	section 16(1)
relevant filing system	section 1(1)
school	section 70(1)
sensitive personal data	section 2
special information notice	section 44(1)
the special purposes	section 3
the subject information provisions (in Part IV)	section 27(2)
teacher	section 70(1)
third party (in relation to processing of personal data)	section 70(1)
the Tribunal	section 70(1)
using (of personal data)	section 1(2)(b).

NOTES

Amendment

Table: entry "public authority" inserted by the Freedom of Information Act 2000, s 68(5).

Date in force: 30 November 2005 (unless the Secretary of State by order appoints an earlier date): see the Freedom of Information Act 2000, s 87(3).

---

72 Modifications of Act

During the period beginning with the commencement of this section and ending with 23rd October 2007, the provisions of this Act shall have effect subject to the modifications set out in Schedule 13.

73 Transitional provisions and savings

Schedule 14 (which contains transitional provisions and savings) has effect.

74 Minor and consequential amendments and repeals and revocations

(1) Schedule 15 (which contains minor and consequential amendments) has effect.

(2) The enactments and instruments specified in Schedule 16 are repealed or revoked to the extent specified.

75 Short title, commencement and extent

(1) This Act may be cited as the Data Protection Act 1998.

(2) The following provisions of this Act—

(a)   sections 1 to 3,

(b)   section 25(1) and (4),

(c)   section 26,

(d)   sections 67 to 71,

(e)   this section,

(f)   paragraph 17 of Schedule 5,

(g)   Schedule 11,

(h)   Schedule 12, and

(i)   so much of any other provision of this Act as confers any power to make subordinate legislation,

shall come into force on the day on which this Act is passed.

(3) The remaining provisions of this Act shall come into force on such day as the [Secretary of State] may by order appoint; and different days may be appointed for different purposes.

(4) The day appointed under subsection (3) for the coming into force of section 56 must not be earlier than the first day on which sections 112, 113 and 115 of the Police Act 1997 (which provide for the issue by the Secretary of State of criminal conviction certificates, criminal record certificates and enhanced criminal record certificates) are all in force.

(5) Subject to subsection (6), this Act extends to Northern Ireland.

(6) Any amendment, repeal or revocation made by Schedule 15 or 16 has the same extent as that of the enactment or instrument to which it relates.

SCHEDULE I
The Data Protection Principles

Section 4(1) and (2)

Part I
The Principles

1   Personal data shall be processed fairly and lawfully and, in particular, shall not be processed unless—

(a)   at least one of the conditions in Schedule 2 is met, and

(b)   in the case of sensitive personal data, at least one of the conditions in Schedule 3 is also met.

2   Personal data shall be obtained only for one or more specified and lawful purposes, and shall not be further processed in any manner incompatible with that purpose or those purposes.

3   Personal data shall be adequate, relevant and not excessive in relation to the purpose or purposes for which they are processed.

4   Personal data shall be accurate and, where necessary, kept up to date.

5   Personal data processed for any purpose or purposes shall not be kept for longer than is necessary for that purpose or those purposes.

6   Personal data shall be processed in accordance with the rights of data subjects under this Act.

7   Appropriate technical and organisational measures shall be taken against unauthorised or unlawful processing of personal data and against accidental loss or destruction of, or damage to, personal data.

8   Personal data shall not be transferred to a country or territory outside the European Economic Area unless that country or territory ensures an adequate level of protection for the rights and freedoms of data subjects in relation to the processing of personal data.

Part II
Interpretation of the Principles in Part I

The first principle

1   (1)   In determining for the purposes of the first principle whether personal data are processed fairly, regard is to be had to the method by which they are obtained, including in particular whether any person from whom they are obtained is deceived or misled as to the purpose or purposes for which they are to be processed.

(2)   Subject to paragraph 2, for the purposes of the first principle data are to be treated as obtained fairly if they consist of information obtained from a person who—

(a)   is authorised by or under any enactment to supply it, or

(b)   is required to supply it by or under any enactment or by any convention or other instrument imposing an international obligation on the United Kingdom.

2   (1)   Subject to paragraph 3, for the purposes of the first principle personal data are not to be treated as processed fairly unless—

(a)   in the case of data obtained from the data subject, the data controller ensures so far as practicable that the data subject has, is provided with, or has made readily available to him, the information specified in sub-paragraph (3), and

(b)   in any other case, the data controller ensures so far as practicable that, before the relevant time or as soon as practicable after that time, the data subject has, is provided with, or has made readily available to him, the information specified in sub-paragraph (3).

(2)   In sub-paragraph (1)(b) "the relevant time" means—

(a)   the time when the data controller first processes the data, or

(b)   in a case where at that time disclosure to a third party within a reasonable period is envisaged—

(i)   if the data are in fact disclosed to such a person within that period, the time when the data are first disclosed,

(ii)   if within that period the data controller becomes, or ought to become, aware that the data are unlikely to be disclosed to such a person within that period, the time when the data controller does become, or ought to become, so aware, or

(iii)   in any other case, the end of that period.

(3) The information referred to in sub-paragraph (1) is as follows, namely—

(a)   the identity of the data controller,

(b)   if he has nominated a representative for the purposes of this Act, the identity of that representative,

(c)   the purpose or purposes for which the data are intended to be processed, and

(d)   any further information which is necessary, having regard to the specific circumstances in which the data are or are to be processed, to enable processing in respect of the data subject to be fair.

3 (1) Paragraph 2(1)(b) does not apply where either of the primary conditions in sub-paragraph (2), together with such further conditions as may be prescribed by the [Secretary of State] by order, are met.

(2) The primary conditions referred to in sub-paragraph (1) are—

(a)   that the provision of that information would involve a disproportionate effort, or

(b)   that the recording of the information to be contained in the data by, or the disclosure of the data by, the data controller is necessary for compliance with any legal obligation to which the data controller is subject, other than an obligation imposed by contract.

4 (1) Personal data which contain a general identifier falling within a description prescribed by the [Secretary of State] by order are not to be treated as processed fairly and lawfully unless they are processed in compliance with any conditions so prescribed in relation to general identifiers of that description.

(2) In sub-paragraph (1) "a general identifier" means any identifier (such as, for example, a number or code used for identification purposes) which—

(a)   relates to an individual, and

(b)   forms part of a set of similar identifiers which is of general application.

The second principle

5 The purpose or purposes for which personal data are obtained may in particular be specified—

(a)   in a notice given for the purposes of paragraph 2 by the data controller to the data subject, or

(b)   in a notification given to the Commissioner under Part III of this Act.

6

In determining whether any disclosure of personal data is compatible with the purpose or purposes for which the data were obtained, regard is to be had to the purpose or purposes for which the personal data are intended to be processed by any person to whom they are disclosed.

The fourth principle

7 The fourth principle is not to be regarded as being contravened by reason of any inaccuracy in personal data which accurately record information obtained by the data controller from the data subject or a third party in a case where—

(a)   having regard to the purpose or purposes for which the data were obtained and further processed, the data controller has taken reasonable steps to ensure the accuracy of the data, and

(b)   if the data subject has notified the data controller of the data subject's view that the data are inaccurate, the data indicate that fact.

The sixth principle

8 A person is to be regarded as contravening the sixth principle if, but only if—

(a)   he contravenes section 7 by failing to supply information in accordance with that section,

(b)   he contravenes section 10 by failing to comply with a notice given under subsection (1) of that section to the extent that the notice is justified or by failing to give a notice under subsection (3) of that section,

(c)   he contravenes section 11 by failing to comply with a notice given under subsection (1) of that section, …

(d)   he contravenes section 12 by failing to comply with a notice given under subsection (1) or (2)(b) of that section or by failing to give a notification under subsection (2)(a) of that section or a notice under subsection (3) of that section [or

(e)   he contravenes section 12A by failing to comply with a notice given under subsection (1) of that section to the extent that the notice is justified].

The seventh principle

9   Having regard to the state of technological development and the cost of implementing any measures, the measures must ensure a level of security appropriate to—

(a)   the harm that might result from such unauthorised or unlawful processing or accidental loss, destruction or damage as are mentioned in the seventh principle, and

(b)   the nature of the data to be protected.

10   The data controller must take reasonable steps to ensure the reliability of any employees of his who have access to the personal data.

11   Where processing of personal data is carried out by a data processor on behalf of a data controller, the data controller must in order to comply with the seventh principle—

(a)   choose a data processor providing sufficient guarantees in respect of the technical and organisational security measures governing the processing to be carried out, and

(b)   take reasonable steps to ensure compliance with those measures.

12   Where processing of personal data is carried out by a data processor on behalf of a data controller, the data controller is not to be regarded as complying with the seventh principle unless—

(a)   the processing is carried out under a contract—

      (i)   which is made or evidenced in writing, and

      (ii)   under which the data processor is to act only on instructions from the data controller, and

(b)   the contract requires the data processor to comply with obligations equivalent to those imposed on a data controller by the seventh principle.

The eighth principle

13   An adequate level of protection is one which is adequate in all the circumstances of the case, having regard in particular to—

(a)   the nature of the personal data,

(b)   the country or territory of origin of the information contained in the data,

(c)   the country or territory of final destination of that information,

(d)   the purposes for which and period during which the data are intended to be processed,

(e)   the law in force in the country or territory in question,

(f)   the international obligations of that country or territory,

(g)   any relevant codes of conduct or other rules which are enforceable in that country or territory (whether generally or by arrangement in particular cases), and

(h)   any security measures taken in respect of the data in that country or territory.

14   The eighth principle does not apply to a transfer falling within any paragraph of Schedule 4, except in such circumstances and to such extent as the [Secretary of State] may by order provide.

15   (1) Where—

(a)   in any proceedings under this Act any question arises as to whether the requirement of the eighth principle as to an adequate level of protection is met in relation to the transfer of any personal data to a country or territory outside the European Economic Area, and

(b)   a Community finding has been made in relation to transfers of the kind in question,

that question is to be determined in accordance with that finding.

(2) In sub-paragraph (1) "Community finding" means a finding of the European Commission, under the procedure provided for in Article 31(2) of the Data Protection Directive, that a country or territory outside the European Economic Area does, or does not, ensure an adequate level of protection within the meaning of Article 25(2) of the Directive.

NOTES

Amendment

Para 8: in sub-para (c) word omitted temporarily repealed by the Data Protection Act 1998, s 72, Sch 13, para 5, until 23 October 2007.

Date in force: 1 March 2000: see SI 2000/183, art 2(1).

Para 8: sub-para (e) temporarily inserted by the Data Protection Act 1998, s 72, Sch 13, para 5, until 23 October 2007.

Date in force: 1 March 2000: see SI 2000/183, art 2(1).

SCHEDULE 2
Conditions Relevant for Purposes of the First Principle: Processing of any Personal Data

Section 4(3)

1 The data subject has given his consent to the processing.

2 The processing is necessary—

(a)   for the performance of a contract to which the data subject is a party, or

(b)   for the taking of steps at the request of the data subject with a view to entering into a contract.

3 The processing is necessary for compliance with any legal obligation to which the data controller is subject, other than an obligation imposed by contract.

4 The processing is necessary in order to protect the vital interests of the data subject.

5 The processing is necessary—

(a)   for the administration of justice,

[(aa)   for the exercise of any functions of either House of Parliament,]

(b)   for the exercise of any functions conferred on any person by or under any enactment,

(c)   for the exercise of any functions of the Crown, a Minister of the Crown or a government department, or

(d)   for the exercise of any other functions of a public nature exercised in the public interest by any person.

6 (1) The processing is necessary for the purposes of legitimate interests pursued by the data controller or by the third party or parties to whom the data are disclosed, except where the processing is unwarranted in any particular case by reason of prejudice to the rights and freedoms or legitimate interests of the data subject.

(2) The [Secretary of State] may by order specify particular circumstances in which this condition is, or is not, to be taken to be satisfied.

NOTES

Amendment

Para 5: sub-para (aa) inserted by the Freedom of Information Act 2000, s 73, Sch 6, para 4.

Date in force: 30 November 2005 (unless the Secretary of State by order appoints an earlier date): see the Freedom of Information Act 2000, s 87(3).

SCHEDULE 3
Conditions Relevant for Purposes of the First Principle: Processing of Sensitive Personal Data

Section 4(3)

1   The data subject has given his explicit consent to the processing of the personal data.

2   (1)   The processing is necessary for the purposes of exercising or performing any right or obligation which is conferred or imposed by law on the data controller in connection with employment.

(2)   The [Secretary of State] may by order—

(a)   exclude the application of sub-paragraph (1) in such cases as may be specified, or

(b)   provide that, in such cases as may be specified, the condition in subparagraph (1) is not to be regarded as satisfied unless such further conditions as may be specified in the order are also satisfied.

3   The processing is necessary—

(a)   in order to protect the vital interests of the data subject or another person, in a case where—

   (i)   consent cannot be given by or on behalf of the data subject, or

   (ii)   the data controller cannot reasonably be expected to obtain the consent of the data subject, or

(b)   in order to protect the vital interests of another person, in a case where consent by or on behalf of the data subject has been unreasonably withheld.

4   The processing—

(a)   is carried out in the course of its legitimate activities by any body or association which—

   (i)   is not established or conducted for profit, and

   (ii)   exists for political, philosophical religious or trade-union purposes,

(b)   is carried out with appropriate safeguards for the rights and freedoms of data subjects,

(c)   relates only to individuals who either are members of the body or association or have regular contact with it in connection with its purposes, and

(d)   does not involve disclosure of the personal data to a third party without the consent of the data subject.

5   The information contained in the personal data has been made public as a result of steps deliberately taken by the data subject.

6   The processing—

(a)   is necessary for the purpose of, or in connection with, any legal proceedings (including prospective legal proceedings),

(b)   is necessary for the purpose of obtaining legal advice, or

(c)   is otherwise necessary for the purposes of establishing, exercising or defending legal rights.

7   (1)   The processing is necessary—

(a)   for the administration of justice,

[(aa)   for the exercise of any functions of either House of Parliament,]

(b)   for the exercise of any functions conferred on any person by or under an enactment, or

(c)   for the exercise of any functions of the Crown, a Minister of the Crown or a government department.

(2)   The [Secretary of State] may by order—

(a)   exclude the application of sub-paragraph (1) in such cases as may be specified, or

(b)   provide that, in such cases as may be specified, the condition in subparagraph (1) is not to be regarded as satisfied unless such further conditions as may be specified in the order are also satisfied.

8   (1)   The processing is necessary for medical purposes and is undertaken by—

(a)   a health professional, or

(b)   a person who in the circumstances owes a duty of confidentiality which is equivalent to that which would arise if that person were a health professional.

(2) In this paragraph "medical purposes" includes the purposes of preventative medicine, medical diagnosis, medical research, the provision of care and treatment and the management of healthcare services.

9 (1) The processing—

(a)   is of sensitive personal data consisting of information as to racial or ethnic origin,

(b)   is necessary for the purpose of identifying or keeping under review the existence or absence of equality of opportunity or treatment between persons of different racial or ethnic origins, with a view to enabling such equality to be promoted or maintained, and

(c)   is carried out with appropriate safeguards for the rights and freedoms of data subjects.

(2) The [Lord Chancellor] may by order specify circumstances in which processing falling within sub-paragraph (1)(a) and (b) is, or is not, to be taken for the purposes of sub-paragraph (1)(c) to be carried out with appropriate safeguards for the rights and freedoms of data subjects.

10   The personal data are processed in circumstances specified in an order made by the [Lord Chancellor] for the purposes of this paragraph.

NOTES

Amendment

Para 7: sub-para (1)(aa) inserted by the Freedom of Information Act 2000, s 73, Sch 6, para 5.

Date in force: 30 November 2005 (unless the Secretary of State by order appoints an earlier date): see the Freedom of Information Act 2000, s 87(3).

SCHEDULE 4
Cases where the Eighth Principle does not Apply

Section 4(3)

1   The data subject has given his consent to the transfer.

2   The transfer is necessary—

(a)   for the performance of a contract between the data subject and the data controller, or

(b)   for the taking of steps at the request of the data subject with a view to his entering into a contract with the data controller.

3   The transfer is necessary—

(a)   for the conclusion of a contract between the data controller and a person other than the data subject which—

    (i)   is entered into at the request of the data subject, or

    (ii)   is in the interests of the data subject, or

(b)   for the performance of such a contract.

4   (1)   The transfer is necessary for reasons of substantial public interest.

(2) The [Secretary of State] may by order specify—

(a)   circumstances in which a transfer is to be taken for the purposes of subparagraph (1) to be necessary for reasons of substantial public interest, and

(b)   circumstances in which a transfer which is not required by or under an enactment is not to be taken for the purpose of sub-paragraph (1) to be necessary for reasons of substantial public interest.

5   The transfer—

(a)   is necessary for the purpose of, or in connection with, any legal proceedings (including prospective legal proceedings),

(b)   is necessary for the purpose of obtaining legal advice, or

(c)   is otherwise necessary for the purposes of establishing, exercising or defending legal rights.

6   The transfer is necessary in order to protect the vital interests of the data subject.

7 The transfer is of part of the personal data on a public register and any conditions subject to which the register is open to inspection are complied with by any person to whom the data are or may be disclosed after the transfer.

8 The transfer is made on terms which are of a kind approved by the Commissioner as ensuring adequate safeguards for the rights and freedoms of data subjects.

9 The transfer has been authorised by the Commissioner as being made in such a manner as to ensure adequate safeguards for the rights and freedoms of data subjects.

SCHEDULE 5
[The Information Commissioner] and [the Information Tribunal]

Section 6(7)

Part I
The Commissioner

Status and capacity

1 (1) The corporation sole by the name of the Data Protection Registrar established by the Data Protection Act 1984 shall continue in existence by the name of the [Information Commissioner].

(2) The Commissioner and his officers and staff are not to be regarded as servants or agents of the Crown.

Tenure of office

2 (1) Subject to the provisions of this paragraph, the Commissioner shall hold office for such term not exceeding five years as may be determined at the time of his appointment.

(2) The Commissioner may be relieved of his office by Her Majesty at his own request.

(3) The Commissioner may be removed from office by Her Majesty in pursuance of an Address from both Houses of Parliament.

(4) The Commissioner shall in any case vacate his office—

(a)   on completing the year of service in which he attains the age of sixty-five years, or

(b)   if earlier, on completing his fifteenth year of service.

(5) Subject to sub-paragraph (4), a person who ceases to be Commissioner on the expiration of his term of office shall be eligible for re-appointment, but a person may not be re-appointed for a third or subsequent term as Commissioner unless, by reason of special circumstances, the person's re-appointment for such a term is desirable in the public interest.

Salary etc

3 (1) There shall be paid—

(a)   to the Commissioner such salary, and

(b)   to or in respect of the Commissioner such pension,

as may be specified by a resolution of the House of Commons.

(2) A resolution for the purposes of this paragraph may—

(a)   specify the salary or pension,

(b)   provide that the salary or pension is to be the same as, or calculated on the same basis as, that payable to, or to or in respect of, a person employed in a specified office under, or in a specified capacity in the service of, the Crown, or

(c)   specify the salary or pension and provide for it to be increased by reference to such variables as may be specified in the resolution.

(3) A resolution for the purposes of this paragraph may take effect from the date on which it is passed or from any earlier or later date specified in the resolution.

(4) A resolution for the purposes of this paragraph may make different provision in relation to the pension payable to or in respect of different holders of the office of Commissioner.

(5) Any salary or pension payable under this paragraph shall be charged on and issued out of the Consolidated Fund.

(6) In this paragraph "pension" includes an allowance or gratuity and any reference to the payment of a pension includes a reference to the making of payments towards the provision of a pension.

Officers and staff

4 (1) The Commissioner—

(a)   shall appoint a deputy commissioner [or two deputy commissioners], and

(b)   may appoint such number of other officers and staff as he may determine.

[(1A) The Commissioner shall, when appointing any second deputy commissioner, specify which of the Commissioner's functions are to be performed, in the circumstances referred to in paragraph 5(1), by each of the deputy commissioners.]

(2) The remuneration and other conditions of service of the persons appointed under this paragraph shall be determined by the Commissioner.

(3) The Commissioner may pay such pensions, allowances or gratuities to or in respect of the persons appointed under this paragraph, or make such payments towards the provision of such pensions, allowances or gratuities, as he may determine.

(4) The references in sub-paragraph (3) to pensions, allowances or gratuities to or in respect of the persons appointed under this paragraph include references to pensions, allowances or gratuities by way of compensation to or in respect of any of those persons who suffer loss of office or employment.

(5) Any determination under sub-paragraph (1)(b), (2) or (3) shall require the approval of the [Secretary of State].

(6) The Employers' Liability (Compulsory Insurance) Act 1969 shall not require insurance to be effected by the Commissioner.

5 (1) The deputy commissioner [or deputy commissioners] shall perform the functions conferred by this Act [or the Freedom of Information Act 2000] on the Commissioner during any vacancy in that office or at any time when the Commissioner is for any reason unable to act.

(2) Without prejudice to sub-paragraph (1), any functions of the Commissioner under this Act [or the Freedom of Information Act 2000] may, to the extent authorised by him, be performed by any of his officers or staff.

Authentication of seal of the Commissioner

6 The application of the seal of the Commissioner shall be authenticated by his signature or by the signature of some other person authorised for the purpose.

Presumption of authenticity of documents issued by the Commissioner

7 Any document purporting to be an instrument issued by the Commissioner and to be duly executed under the Commissioner's seal or to be signed by or on behalf of the Commissioner shall be received in evidence and shall be deemed to be such an instrument unless the contrary is shown.

Money

8 The [Secretary of State] may make payments to the Commissioner out of money provided by Parliament.

9 (1) All fees and other sums received by the Commissioner in the exercise of his functions under this Act[, under section 159 of the Consumer Credit Act 1974 or under the Freedom of Information Act 2000] shall be paid by him to the [Secretary of State].

(2) Sub-paragraph (1) shall not apply where the [Secretary of State], with the consent of the Treasury, otherwise directs.

(3) Any sums received by the [Secretary of State] under sub-paragraph (1) shall be paid into the Consolidated Fund.

Accounts

10 (1) It shall be the duty of the Commissioner—

(a) to keep proper accounts and other records in relation to the accounts,

(b) to prepare in respect of each financial year a statement of account in such form as the [Secretary of State] may direct, and

(c) to send copies of that statement to the Comptroller and Auditor General on or before 31st August next following the end of the year to which the statement relates or on or before such earlier date after the end of that year as the Treasury may direct.

(2) The Comptroller and Auditor General shall examine and certify any statement sent to him under this paragraph and lay copies of it together with his report thereon before each House of Parliament.

(3) In this paragraph "financial year" means a period of twelve months beginning with 1st April.

Application of Part I in Scotland

11 Paragraphs 1(1), 6 and 7 do not extend to Scotland.

Part II
The Tribunal

Tenure of office

12 (1) Subject to the following provisions of this paragraph, a member of the Tribunal shall hold and vacate his office in accordance with the terms of his appointment and shall, on ceasing to hold office, be eligible for re-appointment.

(2) Any member of the Tribunal may at any time resign his office by notice in writing to the Lord Chancellor ... . [(in the case of the chairman of a deputy chairman) or to the Secretary of State (in the case of any other member)].

(3) A person who is the chairman or deputy chairman of the Tribunal shall vacate his office on the day on which he attains the age of seventy years; but this sub-paragraph is subject to section 26(4) to (6) of the Judicial Pensions and Retirement Act 1993 (power to authorise continuance in office up to the age of seventy-five years).

Salary etc

13 The [Secretary of State] shall pay to the members of the Tribunal out of money provided by Parliament such remuneration and allowances as he may determine.

Officers and staff

14 The [Secretary of State] may provide the Tribunal with such officers and staff as he thinks necessary for the proper discharge of its functions.

Expenses

15 Such expenses of the Tribunal as the [Secretary of State] may determine shall be defrayed by the [Secretary of State] out of money provided by Parliament.

Part III ...

...

SCHEDULE 6
Appeal Proceedings

Sections 28(12), 48(5)

Hearing of appeals

1   For the purpose of hearing and determining appeals or any matter preliminary or incidental to an appeal the Tribunal shall sit at such times and in such places as the chairman or a deputy chairman may direct and may sit in two or more divisions.

Constitution of Tribunal in national security cases

2   (1)   The Lord Chancellor shall from time to time designate, from among the chairman and deputy chairmen appointed by him under section 6(4)(a) and (b), those persons who are to be capable of hearing appeals under section 28(4) or (6) [or under section 60(1) or (4) of the Freedom of Information Act 2000].

(2)   A designation under sub-paragraph (1) may at any time be revoked by the Lord Chancellor.

3   In any case where the application of paragraph 6(1) is excluded by rules under paragraph 7, the Tribunal shall be duly constituted for an appeal under section 28(4) or (6) if it consists of three of the persons designated under paragraph 2(1), of whom one shall be designated by the Lord Chancellor to preside.

[3   The Tribunal shall be duly constituted—

(a)   for an appeal under section 28(4) or (6) in any case where the application of paragraph 6(1) is excluded by rules under paragraph 7, or

(b)   for an appeal under section 60(1) or (4) of the Freedom of Information Act 2000,

if it consists of three of the persons designated under paragraph 2(1), of whom one shall be designated by the Lord Chancellor to preside.]

Constitution of Tribunal in other cases

4   (1)   Subject to any rules made under paragraph 7, the Tribunal shall be duly constituted for an appeal under section 48(1), (2) or (4) if it consists of—

(a)   the chairman or a deputy chairman (who shall preside), and

(b)   an equal number of the members appointed respectively in accordance with paragraphs (a) and (b) of section 6(6).

[(1A)   Subject to any rules made under paragraph 7, the Tribunal shall be duly constituted for an appeal under section 57(1) or (2) of the Freedom of Information Act 2000 if it consists of—

(a)   the chairman or a deputy chairman (who shall preside), and

(b)   an equal number of the members appointed respectively in accordance with paragraphs (aa) and (bb) of section 6(6).]

(2)   The members who are to constitute the Tribunal in accordance with subparagraph (1) [or (1A)] shall be nominated by the chairman or, if he is for any reason unable to act, by a deputy chairman.

Determination of questions by full Tribunal

5   The determination of any question before the Tribunal when constituted in accordance with paragraph 3 or 4 shall be according to the opinion of the majority of the members hearing the appeal.

Ex parte proceedings

6   (1)   Subject to any rules made under paragraph 7, the jurisdiction of the Tribunal in respect of an appeal under section 28(4) or (6) shall be exercised ex parte by one or more persons designated under paragraph 2(1).

(2)   Subject to any rules made under paragraph 7, the jurisdiction of the Tribunal in respect of an appeal under section 48(3) shall be exercised ex parte by the chairman or a deputy chairman sitting alone.

Rules of procedure

7   (1)   The [Secretary of State] may make rules for [regulating—

(a)   the exercise of the rights of appeal conferred—

    (i)   by sections 28(4) and (6) and 48, and

    (ii)   by sections 57(1) and (2) and section 60(1) and (4) of the Freedom of Information Act 2000, and

(b)   the practice and procedure of the Tribunal].

(2) Rules under this paragraph may in particular make provision—

(a)   with respect to the period within which an appeal can be brought and the burden of proof on an appeal,

[(aa)   for the joinder of any other person as a party to any proceedings on an appeal under the Freedom of Information Act 2000,

(ab)   for the hearing of an appeal under this Act with an appeal under the Freedom of Information Act 2000,]

(b)   for the summoning (or, in Scotland, citation) of witnesses and the administration of oaths,

(c)   for securing the production of documents and material used for the processing of personal data,

(d)   for the inspection, examination, operation and testing of any equipment or material used in connection with the processing of personal data,

(e)   for the hearing of an appeal wholly or partly in camera,

(f)   for hearing an appeal in the absence of the appellant or for determining an appeal without a hearing,

(g)   for enabling an appeal under section 48(1) against an information notice to be determined by the chairman or a deputy chairman,

(h)   for enabling any matter preliminary or incidental to an appeal to be dealt with by the chairman or a deputy chairman,

(i)   for the awarding of costs or, in Scotland, expenses,

(j)   for the publication of reports of the Tribunal's decisions, and

(k)   for conferring on the Tribunal such ancillary powers as the [Secretary of State] thinks necessary for the proper discharge of its functions.

(3) In making rules under this paragraph which relate to appeals under section 28(4) or (6) the [Secretary of State] shall have regard, in particular, to the need to secure that information is not disclosed contrary to the public interest.

Obstruction etc

8 (1) If any person is guilty of any act or omission in relation to proceedings before the Tribunal which, if those proceedings were proceedings before a court having power to commit for contempt, would constitute contempt of court, the Tribunal may certify the offence to the High Court or, in Scotland, the Court of Session.

(2) Where an offence is so certified, the court may inquire into the matter and, after hearing any witness who may be produced against or on behalf of the person charged with the offence, and after hearing any statement that may be offered in defence, deal with him in any manner in which it could deal with him if he had committed the like offence in relation to the court.

NOTES

Amendment

Para 3: substituted by the Freedom of Information Act 2000, s 61(1), Sch 4, para 2.

Date in force: 30 November 2005 (unless the Secretary of State by order appoints an earlier date): see the Freedom of Information Act 2000, s 87(3).

Para 4: sub-para (1A) inserted by the Freedom of Information Act 2000, s 61(1), Sch 4, para 3(1), (2).

Date in force: 30 November 2005 (unless the Secretary of State by order appoints an earlier date): see the Freedom of Information Act 2000, s 87(3).

Para 4: in sub-para (2) words "or (1A)" in square brackets inserted by the Freedom of Information Act 2000, s 61(1), Sch 4, para 3(1), (3).

Date in force: 30 November 2005 (unless the Secretary of State by order appoints an earlier date): see the Freedom of Information Act 2000, s 87(3).

SCHEDULE 7
Miscellaneous Exemptions

Confidential references given by the data controller

1 Personal data are exempt from section 7 if they consist of a reference given or to be given in confidence by the data controller for the purposes of—

(a)   the education, training or employment, or prospective education, training or employment, of the data subject,

(b)   the appointment, or prospective appointment, of the data subject to any office, or

(c)   the provision, or prospective provision, by the data subject of any service.

Armed forces

2 Personal data are exempt from the subject information provisions in any case to the extent to which the application of those provisions would be likely to prejudice the combat effectiveness of any of the armed forces of the Crown.

Judicial appointments and honours

3 Personal data processed for the purposes of—

(a)   assessing any person's suitability for judicial office or the office of Queen's Counsel, or

(b)   the conferring by the Crown of any honour [or dignity],

are exempt from the subject information provisions.

Crown employment and Crown or Ministerial appointments

4 [(1)] The [Secretary of State] may by order exempt from the subject information provisions personal data processed for the purposes of assessing any person's suitability for—

(a)   employment by or under the Crown, or

(b)   any office to which appointments are made by Her Majesty, by a Minister of the Crown or by a [Northern Ireland authority].

[(2) In this paragraph "Northern Ireland authority" means the First Minister, the deputy First Minister, a Northern Ireland Minister or a Northern Ireland department.]

Management forecasts etc

5 Personal data processed for the purposes of management forecasting or management planning to assist the data controller in the conduct of any business or other activity are exempt from the subject information provisions in any case to the extent to which the application of those provisions would be likely to prejudice the conduct of that business or other activity.

Corporate finance

6 (1) Where personal data are processed for the purposes of, or in connection with, a corporate finance service provided by a relevant person—

(a)   the data are exempt from the subject information provisions in any case to the extent to which either—

   (i)   the application of those provisions to the data could affect the price of any instrument which is already in existence or is to be or may be created, or

   (ii)   the data controller reasonably believes that the application of those provisions to the data could affect the price of any such instrument, and

(b)   to the extent that the data are not exempt from the subject information provisions by virtue of paragraph (a), they are exempt from those provisions if the exemption is required for the purpose of safeguarding an important economic or financial interest of the United Kingdom.

(2) For the purposes of sub-paragraph (1)(b) the [Secretary of State] may by order specify—

(a)   matters to be taken into account in determining whether exemption from the subject information provisions is required for the purpose of safeguarding an important economic or financial interest of the United Kingdom, or

(b)   circumstances in which exemption from those provisions is, or is not, to be taken to be required for that purpose.

(3) In this paragraph—

"corporate finance service" means a service consisting in—

(a)   underwriting in respect of issues of, or the placing of issues of, any instrument,

(b)   advice to undertakings on capital structure, industrial strategy and related matters and advice and service relating to mergers and the purchase of undertakings, or

(c)   services relating to such underwriting as is mentioned in paragraph (a);

"instrument" means any instrument listed in section B of the Annex to the Council Directive on investment services in the securities field (93/22/EEC) … ;

"price" includes value;

"relevant person" means—

[(a)   any person who, by reason of any permission he has under Part IV of the Financial Services and Markets Act 2000, is able to carry on a corporate finance service without contravening the general prohibition, within the meaning of section 19 of that Act,

(b)   an EEA firm of the kind mentioned in paragraph 5(a) or (b) of Schedule 3 to that Act which has qualified for authorisation under paragraph 12 of that Schedule, and may lawfully carry on a corporate finance service,

(c)   any person who is exempt from the general prohibition in respect of any corporate finance service—

        (i)   as a result of an exemption order made under section 38(1) of that Act, or

        (ii)   by reason of section 39(1) of that Act (appointed representatives),

(cc)   any person, not falling within paragraph (a), (b) or (c) who may lawfully carry on a corporate finance service without contravening the general prohibition,]

(d)   any person who, in the course of his employment, provides to his employer a service falling within paragraph (b) or (c) of the definition of "corporate finance service", or

(e)   any partner who provides to other partners in the partnership a service falling within either of those paragraphs.

Negotiations

7 Personal data which consist of records of the intentions of the data controller in relation to any negotiations with the data subject are exempt from the subject information provisions in any case to the extent to which the application of those provisions would be likely to prejudice those negotiations.

Examination marks

8 (1) Section 7 shall have effect subject to the provisions of sub-paragraphs (2) to (4) in the case of personal data consisting of marks or other information processed by a data controller—

(a)   for the purpose of determining the results of an academic, professional or other examination or of enabling the results of any such examination to be determined, or

(b)   in consequence of the determination of any such results.

(2) Where the relevant day falls before the day on which the results of the examination are announced, the period mentioned in section 7(8) shall be extended until—

(a)   the end of five months beginning with the relevant day, or

(b)   the end of forty days beginning with the date of the announcement,

whichever is the earlier.

(3) Where by virtue of sub-paragraph (2) a period longer than the prescribed period elapses after the relevant day before the request is complied with, the information to be supplied pursuant to the request shall be supplied both by reference to the data in question at the time when the request is received and (if different) by reference to the data as from time to time held in the period beginning when the request is received and ending when it is complied with.

(4) For the purposes of this paragraph the results of an examination shall be treated as announced when they are first published or (if not published) when they are first made available or communicated to the candidate in question.

(5) In this paragraph—

"examination" includes any process for determining the knowledge, intelligence, skill or ability of a candidate by reference to his performance in any test, work or other activity;

"the prescribed period" means forty days or such other period as is for the time being prescribed under section 7 in relation to the personal data in question;

"relevant day" has the same meaning as in section 7.

Examination scripts etc

9 (1) Personal data consisting of information recorded by candidates during an academic, professional or other examination are exempt from section 7.

(2) In this paragraph "examination" has the same meaning as in paragraph 8.

Legal professional privilege

10 Personal data are exempt from the subject information provisions if the data consist of information in respect of which a claim to legal professional privilege [or, in Scotland, to confidentiality of communications] could be maintained in legal proceedings.

Self-incrimination

11 (1) A person need not comply with any request or order under section 7 to the extent that compliance would, by revealing evidence of the commission of any offence other than an offence under this Act, expose him to proceedings for that offence.

(2) Information disclosed by any person in compliance with any request or order under section 7 shall not be admissible against him in proceedings for an offence under this Act.

SCHEDULE 8
Transitional Relief

Section 39

Part I
Interpretation of Schedule

1 (1) For the purposes of this Schedule, personal data are "eligible data" at any time if, and to the extent that, they are at that time subject to processing which was already under way immediately before 24th October 1998.

(2) In this Schedule—

"eligible automated data" means eligible data which fall within paragraph (a) or (b) of the definition of "data" in section 1(1);

"eligible manual data" means eligible data which are not eligible automated data;

"the first transitional period" means the period beginning with the commencement of this Schedule and ending with 23rd October 2001;

"the second transitional period" means the period beginning with 24th October 2001 and ending with 23rd October 2007.

Part II
Exemptions Available Before 24th October 2001

Manual data

2 (1) Eligible manual data, other than data forming part of an accessible record, are exempt from the data protection principles and Parts II and III of this Act during the first transitional period.

(2) This paragraph does not apply to eligible manual data to which paragraph 4 applies.

3 (1) This paragraph applies to—

(a)   eligible manual data forming part of an accessible record, and

(b)   personal data which fall within paragraph (d) of the definition of "data" in section 1(1) but which, because they are not subject to processing which was already under way immediately before 24th October 1998, are not eligible data for the purposes of this Schedule.

(2) During the first transitional period, data to which this paragraph applies are exempt from—

(a)   the data protection principles, except the sixth principle so far as relating to sections 7 and 12A,

(b)   Part II of this Act, except—

    (i)   section 7 (as it has effect subject to section 8) and section 12A, and

    (ii)   section 15 so far as relating to those sections, and

(c)   Part III of this Act.

4 (1) This paragraph applies to eligible manual data which consist of information relevant to the financial standing of the data subject and in respect of which the data controller is a credit reference agency.

(2) During the first transitional period, data to which this paragraph applies are exempt from—

(a)   the data protection principles, except the sixth principle so far as relating to sections 7 and 12A,

(b)   Part II of this Act, except—

    (i)   section 7 (as it has effect subject to sections 8 and 9) and section 12A, and

    (ii)   section 15 so far as relating to those sections, and

(c)   Part III of this Act.

Processing otherwise than by reference to the data subject

5 During the first transitional period, for the purposes of this Act (apart from paragraph 1), eligible automated data are not to be regarded as being "processed" unless the processing is by reference to the data subject.

Payrolls and accounts

6 (1) Subject to sub-paragraph (2), eligible automated data processed by a data controller for one or more of the following purposes—

(a)   calculating amounts payable by way of remuneration or pensions in respect of service in any employment or office or making payments of, or of sums deducted from, such remuneration or pensions, or

(b)   keeping accounts relating to any business or other activity carried on by the data controller or keeping records of purchases, sales or other transactions for the purpose of ensuring that the requisite payments are made by or to him in respect of those transactions or for the purpose of making financial or management forecasts to assist him in the conduct of any such business or activity,

are exempt from the data protection principles and Parts II and III of this Act during the first transitional period.

(2) It shall be a condition of the exemption of any eligible automated data under this paragraph that the data are not processed for any other purpose, but the exemption is not lost by any processing of the eligible data for any other purpose if the data controller shows that he had taken such care to prevent it as in all the circumstances was reasonably required.

(3) Data processed only for one or more of the purposes mentioned in subparagraph (1)(a) may be disclosed—

(a)   to any person, other than the data controller, by whom the remuneration or pensions in question are payable,

(b)   for the purpose of obtaining actuarial advice,

(c)   for the purpose of giving information as to the persons in any employment or office for use in medical research into the health of, or injuries suffered by, persons engaged in particular occupations or working in particular places or areas,

(d)   if the data subject (or a person acting on his behalf) has requested or consented to the disclosure of the data either generally or in the circumstances in which the disclosure in question is made, or

(e)   if the person making the disclosure has reasonable grounds for believing that the disclosure falls within paragraph (d).

(4) Data processed for any of the purposes mentioned in sub-paragraph (1) may be disclosed—

(a)   for the purpose of audit or where the disclosure is for the purpose only of giving information about the data controller's financial affairs, or

(b)   in any case in which disclosure would be permitted by any other provision of this Part of this Act if sub-paragraph (2) were included among the non-disclosure provisions.

(5) In this paragraph "remuneration" includes remuneration in kind and "pensions" includes gratuities or similar benefits.

Unincorporated members' clubs and mailing lists

7   Eligible automated data processed by an unincorporated members' club and relating only to the members of the club are exempt from the data protection principles and Parts II and III of this Act during the first transitional period.

8   Eligible automated data processed by a data controller only for the purposes of distributing, or recording the distribution of, articles or information to the data subjects and consisting only of their names, addresses or other particulars necessary for effecting the distribution, are exempt from the data protection principles and Parts II and III of this Act during the first transitional period.

9   Neither paragraph 7 nor paragraph 8 applies to personal data relating to any data subject unless he has been asked by the club or data controller whether he objects to the data relating to him being processed as mentioned in that paragraph and has not objected.

10   It shall be a condition of the exemption of any data under paragraph 7 that the data are not disclosed except as permitted by paragraph 11 and of the exemption under paragraph 8 that the data are not processed for any purpose other than that mentioned in that paragraph or as permitted by paragraph 11, but—

(a)   the exemption under paragraph 7 shall not be lost by any disclosure in breach of that condition, and

(b)   the exemption under paragraph 8 shall not be lost by any processing in breach of that condition,

if the data controller shows that he had taken such care to prevent it as in all the circumstances was reasonably required.

11   Data to which paragraph 10 applies may be disclosed—

(a)   if the data subject (or a person acting on his behalf) has requested or consented to the disclosure of the data either generally or in the circumstances in which the disclosure in question is made,

(b)   if the person making the disclosure has reasonable grounds for believing that the disclosure falls within paragraph (a), or

(c)   in any case in which disclosure would be permitted by any other provision of this Part of this Act if paragraph 10 were included among the non-disclosure provisions.

Back-up data

12   Eligible automated data which are processed only for the purpose of replacing other data in the event of the latter being lost, destroyed or impaired are exempt from section 7 during the first transitional period.

Exemption of all eligible automated data from certain requirements

13   (1) During the first transitional period, eligible automated data are exempt from the following provisions—

(a)   the first data protection principle to the extent to which it requires compliance with—

    (i)   paragraph 2 of Part II of Schedule 1,

    (ii)   the conditions in Schedule 2, and

    (iii) the conditions in Schedule 3,

(b)   the seventh data protection principle to the extent to which it requires compliance with paragraph 12 of Part II of Schedule 1;

(c)   the eighth data protection principle,

(d)   in section 7(1), paragraphs (b), (c)(ii) and (d),

(e)   sections 10 and 11,

(f)   section 12, and

(g)   section 13, except so far as relating to—

    (i)   any contravention of the fourth data protection principle,

    (ii)   any disclosure without the consent of the data controller,

    (iii) loss or destruction of data without the consent of the data controller, or

    (iv) processing for the special purposes.

(2) The specific exemptions conferred by sub-paragraph (1)(a), (c) and (e) do not limit the data controller's general duty under the first data protection principle to ensure that processing is fair.

Part III
Exemptions Available After 23rd October 2001 but Before 24th October 2007

14 (1) This paragraph applies to—

(a)   eligible manual data which were held immediately before 24th October 1998, and

(b)   personal data which fall within paragraph (d) of the definition of "data" in section 1(1) but do not fall within paragraph (a) of this subparagraph,

but does not apply to eligible manual data to which the exemption in paragraph 16 applies.

(2) During the second transitional period, data to which this paragraph applies are exempt from the following provisions—

(a)   the first data protection principle except to the extent to which it requires compliance with paragraph 2 of Part II of Schedule 1,

(b)   the second, third, fourth and fifth data protection principles, and

(c)   section 14(1) to (3).

[14A (1) This paragraph applies to personal data which fall within paragraph (e) of the definition of "data" in section 1(1) and do not fall within paragraph 14(1)(a), but does not apply to eligible manual data to which the exemption in paragraph 16 applies

(2) During the second transitional period, data to which this paragraph applies are exempt from—

(a)   the fourth data protection principle, and

(b)   section 14(1) to (3).]

NOTES

Amendment

Para 14A: inserted by the Freedom of Information Act 2000, s 70(3).

Date in force: 30 November 2005 (unless the Secretary of State by order appoints an earlier date): see the Freedom of Information Act 2000, s 87(3).

Part IV
Exemptions after 23rd October 2001 for Historical Research

15   In this Part of this Schedule "the relevant conditions" has the same meaning as in section 33.

16   (1) Eligible manual data which are processed only for the purpose of historical research in compliance with the relevant conditions are exempt from the provisions specified in sub-paragraph (2) after 23rd October 2001.

(2) The provisions referred to in sub-paragraph (1) are—

(a)   the first data protection principle except in so far as it requires compliance with paragraph 2 of Part II of Schedule 1,

(b)   the second, third, fourth and fifth data protection principles, and

(c)   section 14(1) to (3).

17   (1) After 23rd October 2001 eligible automated data which are processed only for the purpose of historical research in compliance with the relevant conditions are exempt from the first data protection principle to the extent to which it requires compliance with the conditions in Schedules 2 and 3.

(2) Eligible automated data which are processed—

(a)   only for the purpose of historical research,

(b)   in compliance with the relevant conditions, and

(c)   otherwise than by reference to the data subject,

are also exempt from the provisions referred to in sub-paragraph (3) after 23rd October 2001.

(3) The provisions referred to in sub-paragraph (2) are—

(a)   the first data protection principle except in so far as it requires compliance with paragraph 2 of Part II of Schedule 1,

(b)   the second, third, fourth and fifth data protection principles, and

(c)   section 14(1) to (3).

18   For the purposes of this Part of this Schedule personal data are not to be treated as processed otherwise than for the purpose of historical research merely because the data are disclosed—

(a)   to any person, for the purpose of historical research only,

(b)   to the data subject or a person acting on his behalf,

(c)   at the request, or with the consent, of the data subject or a person acting on his behalf, or

(d)   in circumstances in which the person making the disclosure has reasonable grounds for believing that the disclosure falls within paragraph (a), (b) or (c).

Part V
Exemption from Section 22

19   Processing which was already under way immediately before 24th October 1998 is not assessable processing for the purposes of section 22.

SCHEDULE 9
Powers of Entry and Inspection

Section 50

Issue of warrants

1   (1) If a circuit judge [or a District Judge (Magistrates' Courts)] is satisfied by information on oath supplied by the Commissioner that there are reasonable grounds for suspecting—

(a)   that a data controller has contravened or is contravening any of the data protection principles, or

(b)   that an offence under this Act has been or is being committed, and that evidence of the contravention or of the commission of the offence is to be found on any premises specified in the information, he may, subject to subparagraph (2) and paragraph 2, grant a warrant to the Commissioner.

(2) A judge shall not issue a warrant under this Schedule in respect of any personal data processed for the special purposes unless a determination by the Commissioner under section 45 with respect to those data has taken effect.

(3) A warrant issued under sub-paragraph (1) shall authorise the Commissioner or any of his officers or staff at any time within seven days of the date of the warrant to enter the premises, to search them, to inspect, examine, operate and test any equipment found there which is used or intended to be used for the processing of personal data and to inspect and seize any documents or other material found there which may be such evidence as is mentioned in that sub-paragraph.

2   (1)   A judge shall not issue a warrant under this Schedule unless he is satisfied—

(a)   that the Commissioner has given seven days' notice in writing to the occupier of the premises in question demanding access to the premises, and

(b)   that either—

     (i)   access was demanded at a reasonable hour and was unreasonably refused, or

     (ii)   although entry to the premises was granted, the occupier unreasonably refused to comply with a request by the Commissioner or any of the Commissioner's officers or staff to permit the Commissioner or the officer or member of staff to do any of the things referred to in paragraph 1(3), and

(c)   that the occupier, has, after the refusal, been notified by the Commissioner of the application for the warrant and has had an opportunity of being heard by the judge on the question whether or not it should be issued.

(2) Sub-paragraph (1) shall not apply if the judge is satisfied that the case is one of urgency or that compliance with those provisions would defeat the object of the entry.

3   A judge who issues a warrant under this Schedule shall also issue two copies of it and certify them clearly as copies.

Execution of warrants

4   A person executing a warrant issued under this Schedule may use such reasonable force as may be necessary.

5   A warrant issued under this Schedule shall be executed at a reasonable hour unless it appears to the person executing it that there are grounds for suspecting that the evidence in question would not be found if it were so executed.

6   If the person who occupies the premises in respect of which a warrant is issued under this Schedule is present when the warrant is executed, he shall be shown the warrant and supplied with a copy of it; and if that person is not present a copy of the warrant shall be left in a prominent place on the premises.

7   (1)   A person seizing anything in pursuance of a warrant under this Schedule shall give a receipt for it if asked to do so.

(2) Anything so seized may be retained for so long as is necessary in all the circumstances but the person in occupation of the premises in question shall be given a copy of anything that is seized if he so requests and the person executing the warrant considers that it can be done without undue delay.

Matters exempt from inspection and seizure

8   The powers of inspection and seizure conferred by a warrant issued under this Schedule shall not be exercisable in respect of personal data which by virtue of section 28 are exempt from any of the provisions of this Act.

9   (1)   Subject to the provisions of this paragraph, the powers of inspection and seizure conferred by a warrant issued under this Schedule shall not be exercisable in respect of—

(a)   any communication between a professional legal adviser and his client in connection with the giving of legal advice to the client with respect to his obligations, liabilities or rights under this Act, or

(b)   any communication between a professional legal adviser and his client, or between such an adviser or his client and any other person, made in connection with or in contemplation of proceedings under or arising out of this Act (including proceedings before the Tribunal) and for the purposes of such proceedings.

(2) Sub-paragraph (1) applies also to—

(a)   any copy or other record of any such communication as is there mentioned, and

(b)   any document or article enclosed with or referred to in any such communication if made in connection with the giving of any advice or, as the case may be, in connection with or in contemplation of and for the purposes of such proceedings as are there mentioned.

(3) This paragraph does not apply to anything in the possession of any person other than the professional legal adviser or his client or to anything held with the intention of furthering a criminal purpose.

(4) In this paragraph references to the client of a professional legal adviser include references to any person representing such a client.

10   If the person in occupation of any premises in respect of which a warrant is issued under this Schedule objects to the inspection or seizure under the warrant of any material on the grounds that it consists partly of matters in respect of which those powers are not exercisable, he shall, if the person executing the warrant so requests, furnish that person with a copy of so much of the material as is not exempt from those powers.

Return of warrants

11   A warrant issued under this Schedule shall be returned to the court from which it was issued—

(a)   after being executed, or

(b)   if not executed within the time authorised for its execution;

and the person by whom any such warrant is executed shall make an endorsement on it stating what powers have been exercised by him under the warrant.

Offences

12   Any person who—

(a)   intentionally obstructs a person in the execution of a warrant issued under this Schedule, or

(b)   fails without reasonable excuse to give any person executing such a warrant such assistance as he may reasonably require for the execution of the warrant,

is guilty of an offence.

Vessels, vehicles etc

13   In this Schedule "premises" includes any vessel, vehicle, aircraft or hovercraft, and references to the occupier of any premises include references to the person in charge of any vessel, vehicle, aircraft or hovercraft.

Scotland and Northern Ireland

14   In the application of this Schedule to Scotland—

(a)   for any reference to a circuit judge there is substituted a reference to the sheriff,

(b)   for any reference to information on oath there is substituted a reference to evidence on oath, and

(c)   for the reference to the court from which the warrant was issued there is substituted a reference to the sheriff clerk.

15   In the application of this Schedule to Northern Ireland—

(a)   for any reference to a circuit judge there is substituted a reference to a county court judge, and

(b)   for any reference to information on oath there is substituted a reference to a complaint on oath.

SCHEDULE 10
Further Provisions Relating to Assistance under Section 53

Section 53(6)

1 In this Schedule "applicant" and "proceedings" have the same meaning as in section 53.

2 The assistance provided under section 53 may include the making of arrangements for, or for the Commissioner to bear the costs of—

(a) the giving of advice or assistance by a solicitor or counsel, and

(b) the representation of the applicant, or the provision to him of such assistance as is usually given by a solicitor or counsel—

(i) in steps preliminary or incidental to the proceedings, or

(ii) in arriving at or giving effect to a compromise to avoid or bring an end to the proceedings.

3 Where assistance is provided with respect to the conduct of proceedings—

(a) it shall include an agreement by the Commissioner to indemnify the applicant (subject only to any exceptions specified in the notification) in respect of any liability to pay costs or expenses arising by virtue of any judgment or order of the court in the proceedings,

(b) it may include an agreement by the Commissioner to indemnify the applicant in respect of any liability to pay costs or expenses arising by virtue of any compromise or settlement arrived at in order to avoid the proceedings or bring the proceedings to an end, and

(c) it may include an agreement by the Commissioner to indemnify the applicant in respect of any liability to pay damages pursuant to an undertaking given on the grant of interlocutory relief (in Scotland, an interim order) to the applicant.

4 Where the Commissioner provides assistance in relation to any proceedings, he shall do so on such terms, or make such other arrangements, as will secure that a person against whom the proceedings have been or are commenced is informed that assistance has been or is being provided by the Commissioner in relation to them.

5 In England and Wales or Northern Ireland, the recovery of expenses incurred by the Commissioner in providing an applicant with assistance (as taxed or assessed in such manner as may be prescribed by rules of court) shall constitute a first charge for the benefit of the Commissioner—

(a) on any costs which, by virtue of any judgment or order of the court, are payable to the applicant by any other person in respect of the matter in connection with which the assistance is provided, and

(b) on any sum payable to the applicant under a compromise or settlement arrived at in connection with that matter to avoid or bring to an end any proceedings.

6 In Scotland, the recovery of such expenses (as taxed or assessed in such manner as may be prescribed by rules of court) shall be paid to the Commissioner, in priority to other debts—

(a) out of any expenses which, by virtue of any judgment or order of the court, are payable to the applicant by any other person in respect of the matter in connection with which the assistance is provided, and

(b) out of any sum payable to the applicant under a compromise or settlement arrived at in connection with that matter to avoid or bring to an end any proceedings.

SCHEDULE 11
Educational Records

Section 68(1)(b)

Meaning of "educational record"

1 For the purposes of section 68 "educational record" means any record to which paragraph 2, 5 or 7 applies.

England and Wales

2 This paragraph applies to any record of information which—

(a) is processed by or on behalf of the governing body of, or a teacher at, any school in England and Wales specified in paragraph 3,

(b)   relates to any person who is or has been a pupil at the school, and

(c)   originated from or was supplied by or on behalf of any of the persons specified in paragraph 4,

other than information which is processed by a teacher solely for the teacher's own use.

3 The schools referred to in paragraph 2(a) are—

(a)   a school maintained by a local education authority, and

(b)   a special school, as defined by section 6(2) of the Education Act 1996, which is not so maintained.

4 The persons referred to in paragraph 2(c) are—

(a)   an employee of the local education authority which maintains the school,

(b)   in the case of—

      (i)   a voluntary aided, foundation or foundation special school (within the meaning of the School Standards and Framework Act 1998), or

      (ii)   a special school which is not maintained by a local education authority,

      a teacher or other employee at the school (including an educational psychologist engaged by the governing body under a contract for services),

(c)   the pupil to whom the record relates, and

(d)   a parent, as defined by section 576(1) of the Education Act 1996, of that pupil.

Scotland

5 This paragraph applies to any record of information which is processed—

(a)   by an education authority in Scotland, and

(b)   for the purpose of the relevant function of the authority,

other than information which is processed by a teacher solely for the teacher's own use.

6 For the purposes of paragraph 5—

(a)   "education authority" means an education authority within the meaning of the Education (Scotland) Act 1980 ("the 1980 Act") *or, in relation to a self-governing school, the board of management within the meaning of the Self-Governing Schools etc (Scotland) Act 1989 ("the 1989 Act"),*

(b)   "the relevant function" means, in relation to each of those authorities, their function under section 1 of the 1980 Act and section 7(1) of the 1989 Act, and

(c)   information processed by an education authority is processed for the purpose of the relevant function of the authority if the processing relates to the discharge of that function in respect of a person—

      (i)   who is or has been a pupil in a school provided by the authority, or

      (ii)   who receives, or has received, further education (within the meaning of the 1980 Act) so provided.

Northern Ireland

7 (1) This paragraph applies to any record of information which—

(a)   is processed by or on behalf of the Board of Governors of, or a teacher at, any grant-aided school in Northern Ireland,

(b)   relates to any person who is or has been a pupil at the school, and

(c)   originated from or was supplied by or on behalf of any of the persons specified in paragraph 8,

other than information which is processed by a teacher solely for the teacher's own use.

(2) In sub-paragraph (1) "grant-aided school" has the same meaning as in the Education and Libraries (Northern Ireland) Order 1986.

8 The persons referred to in paragraph 7(1) are—

(a)   a teacher at the school,

(b)   an employee of an education and library board, other than such a teacher,

(c)   the pupil to whom the record relates, and

(d)   a parent (as defined by Article 2(2) of the Education and Libraries (Northern Ireland) Order 1986) of that pupil.

England and Wales: transitory provisions

9 (1) Until the appointed day within the meaning of section 20 of the School Standards and Framework Act 1998, this Schedule shall have effect subject to the following modifications.

(2) Paragraph 3 shall have effect as if for paragraph (b) and the "and" immediately preceding it there were substituted—

"(aa)   a grant-maintained school, as defined by section 183(1) of the Education Act 1996,

(ab)   a grant-maintained special school, as defined by section 337(4) of that Act, and

(b)   a special school, as defined by section 6(2) of that Act, which is neither a maintained special school, as defined by section 337(3) of that Act, nor a grant-maintained special school.".

(3) Paragraph 4(b)(i) shall have effect as if for the words from "foundation", in the first place where it occurs, to "1998)" there were substituted "or grant-maintained school".

SCHEDULE 12
Accessible Public Records

Section 68(1)(c)

Meaning of "accessible public record"

1 For the purposes of section 68 "accessible public record" means any record which is kept by an authority specified—

(a)   as respects England and Wales, in the Table in paragraph 2,

(b)   as respects Scotland, in the Table in paragraph 4, or

(c)   as respects Northern Ireland, in the Table in paragraph 6,

and is a record of information of a description specified in that Table in relation to that authority.

Housing and social services records: England and Wales

2 The following is the Table referred to in paragraph 1(a).

TABLE OF AUTHORITIES AND INFORMATION

The authorities	The accessible information
Housing Act local authority.	Information held for the purpose of any of the authority's tenancies.
Local social services authority.	Information held for any purpose of the authority's social services functions.

3 (1) The following provisions apply for the interpretation of the Table in paragraph 2.

(2) Any authority which, by virtue of section 4(e) of the Housing Act 1985, is a local authority for the purpose of any provision of that Act is a "Housing Act local authority" for the purposes of this Schedule, and so is any housing action trust established under Part III of the Housing Act 1988.

(3) Information contained in records kept by a Housing Act local authority is "held for the purpose of any of the authority's tenancies" if it is held for any purpose of the relationship of landlord and tenant of a dwelling which subsists, has subsisted or may subsist between the authority and any individual who is, has been or, as the case may be, has applied to be, a tenant of the authority.

(4) Any authority which, by virtue of section 1 or 12 of the Local Authority Social Services Act 1970, is or is treated as a local authority for the purposes of that Act is a "local social services authority" for the purposes of this Schedule; and information contained in records kept by such an authority is "held for any purpose of the authority's social services functions" if it is held for the purpose of any past, current or proposed exercise of such a function in any case.

(5) Any expression used in paragraph 2 or this paragraph and in Part II of the Housing Act 1985 or the Local Authority Social Services Act 1970 has the same meaning as in that Act.

Housing and social services records: Scotland

4   The following is the Table referred to in paragraph 1(b).

TABLE OF AUTHORITIES AND INFORMATION

The authorities	The accessible information
Local authority. Scottish Homes.	Information held for any purpose of any of the body's tenancies.
Social work authority.	Information held for any purpose of the authority's functions under the Social Work (Scotland) Act 1968 and the enactments referred to in section 5(1B) of that Act.

5   (1)   The following provisions apply for the interpretation of the Table in paragraph 4.

(2)   "Local authority" means—

(a)   a council constituted under section 2 of the Local Government etc (Scotland) Act 1994,

(b)   a joint board or joint committee of two or more of those councils, or

(c)   any trust under the control of such a council.

(3)   Information contained in records kept by a local authority *or Scottish Homes* is held for the purpose of any of their tenancies if it is held for any purpose of the relationship of landlord and tenant of a dwelling-house which subsists, has subsisted or may subsist between the authority *or, as the case may be, Scottish Homes* and any individual who is, has been or, as the case may be, has applied to be a tenant of theirs.

(4)   "Social work authority" means a local authority for the purposes of the Social Work (Scotland) Act 1968; and information contained in records kept by such an authority is held for any purpose of their functions if it is held for the purpose of any past, current or proposed exercise of such a function in any case.

Housing and social services records: Northern Ireland

6   The following is the Table referred to in paragraph 1(c).

TABLE OF AUTHORITIES AND INFORMATION

The authorities	The accessible information
The Northern Ireland Housing Executive.	Information held for the purpose of any of the Executive's tenancies.
A Health and Social Services Board.	Information held for the purpose of any past, current or proposed exercise by the Board of any function exercisable, by virtue of directions under Article 17(1) of the Health and Personal Social Services (Northern Ireland) Order 1972, by the Board on behalf of the Department of Health and Social Services with respect to the administration of personal social services under— (a) the Children and Young Persons Act (Northern Ireland) 1968; (b) the Health and Personal Social Services (Northern Ireland) Order 1972; (c) Article 47 of the Matrimonial Causes (Northern Ireland) Order 1978; (d) Article 11 of the Domestic Proceedings (Northern Ireland) Order 1980; (e) the Adoption (Northern Ireland) Order 1987; or (f) the Children (Northern Ireland) Order 1995.
An HSS trust.	Information held for the purpose of any past, current or proposed exercise by the trust of any function exercisable, by virtue of an authorisation under Article 3(1) of the Health and Personal Social Services (Northern Ireland) Order 1994, by the trust on behalf of a Health and Social Services Board with respect to the administration of personal social services under any statutory provision mentioned in the last preceding entry.

7   (1)   This paragraph applies for the interpretation of the Table in paragraph 6.

(2)   Information contained in records kept by the Northern Ireland Housing Executive is "held for the purpose of any of the Executive's tenancies" if it is held for any purpose of the relationship of landlord and tenant of a dwelling which subsists, has subsisted or may subsist between the Executive and any individual who is, has been or, as the case may be, has applied to be, a tenant of the Executive.

SCHEDULE 13
Modifications of Act having Effect before 24th October 2007

Section 72

1   After section 12 there is inserted—

"12A   Rights of data subjects in relation to exempt manual data

(1)   A data subject is entitled at any time by notice in writing—

(a)   to require the data controller to rectify, block, erase or destroy exempt manual data which are inaccurate or incomplete, or

(b)   to require the data controller to cease holding exempt manual data in a way incompatible with the legitimate purposes pursued by the data controller.

(2)   A notice under subsection (1)(a) or (b) must state the data subject's reasons for believing that the data are inaccurate or incomplete or, as the case may be, his reasons for believing that they are held in a way incompatible with the legitimate purposes pursued by the data controller.

(3)   If the court is satisfied, on the application of any person who has given a notice under subsection (1) which appears to the court to be justified (or to be justified to any extent) that the data controller in question has failed to comply with the notice, the court may order him to take such steps for complying with the notice (or for complying with it to that extent) as the court thinks fit.

(4)   In this section "exempt manual data" means—

(a)   in relation to the first transitional period, as defined by paragraph 1(2) of Schedule 8, data to which paragraph 3 or 4 of that Schedule applies, and

(b)   in relation to the second transitional period, as so defined, data to which paragraph 14 [or 14A] of that Schedule applies.

(5)   For the purposes of this section personal data are incomplete if, and only if, the data, although not inaccurate, are such that their incompleteness would constitute a contravention of the third or fourth data protection principles, if those principles applied to the data.".

2   In section 32—

(a)   in subsection (2) after "section 12" there is inserted—

"(dd)   section 12A,", and

(b)   in subsection (4) after "12(8)" there is inserted ", 12A(3)".

3   In section 34 for "section 14(1) to (3)" there is substituted "sections 12A and 14(1) to (3)."

4   In section 53(1) after "12(8)" there is inserted ", 12A(3)".

5   In paragraph 8 of Part II of Schedule 1, the word "or" at the end of paragraph (c) is omitted and after paragraph (d) there is inserted

"or

(e)   he contravenes section 12A by failing to comply with a notice given under subsection (1) of that section to the extent that the notice is justified.".

NOTES

Amendment

Para 1: in section 12A(4)(b), as set out, words "or 14A" in square brackets inserted by the Freedom of Information Act 2000, s 70(4).

Date in force: 30 November 2005 (unless the Secretary of State by order appoints an earlier date): see the Freedom of Information Act 2000, s 87(3).

SCHEDULE 14
Transitional Provisions and Savings

Section 73

Interpretation

1 In this Schedule—

"the 1984 Act" means the Data Protection Act 1984;

"the old principles" means the data protection principles within the meaning of the 1984 Act;

"the new principles" means the data protection principles within the meaning of this Act.

Effect of registration under Part II of 1984 Act

2 (1) Subject to sub-paragraphs (4) and (5) any person who, immediately before the commencement of Part III of this Act—

(a)   is registered as a data user under Part II of the 1984 Act, or

(b)   is treated by virtue of section 7(6) of the 1984 Act as so registered,

is exempt from section 17(1) of this Act until the end of the registration period … .

(2) In sub-paragraph (1) "the registration period", in relation to a person, means—

(a)   where there is a single entry in respect of that person as a data user, the period at the end of which, if section 8 of the 1984 Act had remained in force, that entry would have fallen to be removed unless renewed, and

(b)   where there are two or more entries in respect of that person as a data user, the period at the end of which, if that section had remained in force, the last of those entries to expire would have fallen to be removed unless renewed.

(3) Any application for registration as a data user under Part II of the 1984 Act which is received by the Commissioner before the commencement of Part III of this Act (including any appeal against a refusal of registration) shall be determined in accordance with the old principles and the provisions of the 1984 Act.

(4) If a person falling within paragraph (b) of sub-paragraph (1) receives a notification under section 7(1) of the 1984 Act of the refusal of his application, sub-paragraph (1) shall cease to apply to him—

(a)   if no appeal is brought, at the end of the period within which an appeal can be brought against the refusal, or

(b)   on the withdrawal or dismissal of the appeal.

(5) If a data controller gives a notification under section 18(1) at a time when he is exempt from section 17(1) by virtue of sub-paragraph (1), he shall cease to be so exempt.

(6) The Commissioner shall include in the register maintained under section 19 an entry in respect of each person who is exempt from section 17(1) by virtue of sub-paragraph (1); and each entry shall consist of the particulars which, immediately before the commencement of Part III of this Act, were included (or treated as included) in respect of that person in the register maintained under section 4 of the 1984 Act.

(7) Notification regulations under Part III of this Act may make provision modifying the duty referred to in section 20(1) in its application to any person in respect of whom an entry in the register maintained under section 19 has been made under sub-paragraph (6).

(8) Notification regulations under Part III of this Act may make further transitional provision in connection with the substitution of Part III of this Act for Part II of the 1984 Act (registration), including provision modifying the application of provisions of Part III in transitional cases.

Rights of data subjects

3 (1) The repeal of section 21 of the 1984 Act (right of access to personal data) does not affect the application of that section in any case in which the request (together with the information referred to in paragraph (a) of subsection (4) of that section and, in a case where it is required, the consent referred to in paragraph (b) of that subsection) was received before the day on which the repeal comes into force.

(2) Sub-paragraph (1) does not apply where the request is made by reference to this Act.

(3) Any fee paid for the purposes of section 21 of the 1984 Act before the commencement of section 7 in a case not falling within sub-paragraph (1) shall be taken to have been paid for the purposes of section 7.

4   The repeal of section 22 of the 1984 Act (compensation for inaccuracy) and the repeal of section 23 of that Act (compensation for loss or unauthorised disclosure) do not affect the application of those sections in relation to damage or distress suffered at any time by reason of anything done or omitted to be done before the commencement of the repeals.

5   The repeal of section 24 of the 1984 Act (rectification and erasure) does not affect any case in which the application to the court was made before the day on which the repeal comes into force.

6   Subsection (3)(b) of section 14 does not apply where the rectification, blocking, erasure or destruction occurred before the commencement of that section.

Enforcement and transfer prohibition notices served under Part V of 1984 Act

7   (1)   If, immediately before the commencement of section 40—

(a)   an enforcement notice under section 10 of the 1984 Act has effect, and

(b)   either the time for appealing against the notice has expired or any appeal has been determined,

then, after that commencement, to the extent mentioned in sub-paragraph (3), the notice shall have effect for the purposes of sections 41 and 47 as if it were an enforcement notice under section 40.

(2)   Where an enforcement notice has been served under section 10 of the 1984 Act before the commencement of section 40 and immediately before that commencement either—

(a)   the time for appealing against the notice has not expired, or

(b)   an appeal has not been determined,

the appeal shall be determined in accordance with the provisions of the 1984 Act and the old principles and, unless the notice is quashed on appeal, to the extent mentioned in sub-paragraph (3) the notice shall have effect for the purposes of sections 41 and 47 as if it were an enforcement notice under section 40.

(3)   An enforcement notice under section 10 of the 1984 Act has the effect described in sub-paragraph (1) or (2) only to the extent that the steps specified in the notice for complying with the old principle or principles in question are steps which the data controller could be required by an enforcement notice under section 40 to take for complying with the new principles or any of them.

8   (1)   If, immediately before the commencement of section 40—

(a)   a transfer prohibition notice under section 12 of the 1984 Act has effect, and

(b)   either the time for appealing against the notice has expired or any appeal has been determined,

then, on and after that commencement, to the extent specified in sub-paragraph (3), the notice shall have effect for the purposes of sections 41 and 47 as if it were an enforcement notice under section 40.

(2)   Where a transfer prohibition notice has been served under section 12 of the 1984 Act and immediately before the commencement of section 40 either—

(a)   the time for appealing against the notice has not expired, or

(b)   an appeal has not been determined,

the appeal shall be determined in accordance with the provisions of the 1984 Act and the old principles and, unless the notice is quashed on appeal, to the extent mentioned in sub-paragraph (3) the notice shall have effect for the purposes of sections 41 and 47 as if it were an enforcement notice under section 40.

(3)   A transfer prohibition notice under section 12 of the 1984 Act has the effect described in sub-paragraph (1) or (2) only to the extent that the prohibition imposed by the notice is one which could be imposed by an enforcement notice under section 40 for complying with the new principles or any of them.

Notices under new law relating to matters in relation to which 1984 Act had effect

9   The Commissioner may serve an enforcement notice under section 40 on or after the day on which that section comes into force if he is satisfied that, before that day, the data controller contravened the old principles by reason of any act or omission which would also have constituted a contravention of the new principles if they had applied before that day.

10   Subsection (5)(b) of section 40 does not apply where the rectification, blocking, erasure or destruction occurred before the commencement of that section.

11   The Commissioner may serve an information notice under section 43 on or after the day on which that section comes into force if he has reasonable grounds for suspecting that, before that day, the data controller contravened the old principles by reason of any act or omission which would also have constituted a contravention of the new principles if they had applied before that day.

12   Where by virtue of paragraph 11 an information notice is served on the basis of anything done or omitted to be done before the day on which section 43 comes into force, subsection (2)(b) of that section shall have effect as if the reference to the data controller having complied, or complying, with the new principles were a reference to the data controller having contravened the old principles by reason of any such act or omission as is mentioned in paragraph 11.

Self-incrimination, etc

13   (1) In section 43(8), section 44(9) and paragraph 11 of Schedule 7, any reference to an offence under this Act includes a reference to an offence under the 1984 Act.

(2) In section 34(9) of the 1984 Act, any reference to an offence under that Act includes a reference to an offence under this Act.

Warrants issued under 1984 Act

14   The repeal of Schedule 4 to the 1984 Act does not affect the application of that Schedule in any case where a warrant was issued under that Schedule before the commencement of the repeal.

Complaints under section 36(2) of 1984 Act and requests for assessment under section 42

15   The repeal of section 36(2) of the 1984 Act does not affect the application of that provision in any case where the complaint was received by the Commissioner before the commencement of the repeal.

16   In dealing with a complaint under section 36(2) of the 1984 Act or a request for an assessment under section 42 of this Act, the Commissioner shall have regard to the provisions from time to time applicable to the processing, and accordingly—

(a)   in section 36(2) of the 1984 Act, the reference to the old principles and the provisions of that Act includes, in relation to any time when the new principles and the provisions of this Act have effect, those principles and provisions, and

(b)   in section 42 of this Act, the reference to the provisions of this Act includes, in relation to any time when the old principles and the provisions of the 1984 Act had effect, those principles and provisions.

Applications under Access to Health Records Act 1990 or corresponding Northern Ireland legislation

17   (1) The repeal of any provision of the Access to Health Records Act 1990 does not affect—

(a)   the application of section 3 or 6 of that Act in any case in which the application under that section was received before the day on which the repeal comes into force, or

(b)   the application of section 8 of that Act in any case in which the application to the court was made before the day on which the repeal comes into force.

(2) Sub-paragraph (1)(a) does not apply in relation to an application for access to information which was made by reference to this Act.

18   (1) The revocation of any provision of the Access to Health Records (Northern Ireland) Order 1993 does not affect—

(a)   the application of Article 5 or 8 of that Order in any case in which the application under that Article was received before the day on which the repeal comes into force, or

(b)   the application of Article 10 of that Order in any case in which the application to the court was made before the day on which the repeal comes into force.

(2) Sub-paragraph (1)(a) does not apply in relation to an application for access to information which was made by reference to this Act.

Applications under regulations under Access to Personal Files Act 1987 or corresponding Northern Ireland legislation

19   (1) The repeal of the personal files enactments does not affect the application of regulations under those enactments in relation to—

(a)   any request for information,

(b)   any application for rectification or erasure, or

(c)   any application for review of a decision,

which was made before the day on which the repeal comes into force.

(2) Sub-paragraph (1)(a) does not apply in relation to a request for information which was made by reference to this Act.

(3) In sub-paragraph (1) "the personal files enactments" means—

(a)   in relation to Great Britain, the Access to Personal Files Act 1987, and

(b)   in relation to Northern Ireland, Part II of the Access to Personal Files and Medical Reports (Northern Ireland) Order 1991.

Applications under section 158 of Consumer Credit Act 1974

20   Section 62 does not affect the application of section 158 of the Consumer Credit Act 1974 in any case where the request was received before the commencement of section 62, unless the request is made by reference to this Act.

SCHEDULE 15
Minor and Consequential Amendments

Section 74(1)

Public Records Act 1958 (c 51)

1   (1) ...

(2) *That Schedule shall continue to have effect with the following amendment (originally made by paragraph 14 of Schedule 2 to the Data Protection Act 1984).*

(3) *After paragraph 4(1)(n) there is inserted—*

"(nn)   records of the Data Protection Tribunal".

...

2   ...

3   *In Schedule 4 to that Act (tribunals exercising administrative functions), in the entry relating to the Data Protection Tribunal, for "section 3 of the Data Protection Act 1984" there is substituted "section 6 of the Data Protection Act 1998".*

...

4   ...

House of Commons Disqualification Act 1975 (c 24)

5   (1) *Part II of Schedule 1 to the House of Commons Disqualification Act 1975 (bodies whose members are disqualified) shall continue to include the entry "The Data Protection Tribunal" (originally inserted by paragraph 12(1) of Schedule 2 to the Data Protection Act 1984).*

(2) ...

Northern Ireland Assembly Disqualification Act 1975 (c 25)

6   (1) *Part II of Schedule 1 to the Northern Ireland Assembly Disqualification Act 1975 (bodies whose members are disqualified) shall continue to include the entry "The Data Protection Tribunal" (originally inserted by paragraph 12(3) of Schedule 2 to the Data Protection Act 1984).*

(2) ...

Representation of the People Act 1983 (c 2)

7   In Schedule 2 of the Representation of the People Act 1983 (provisions which may be included in regulations as to registration etc), in paragraph 11A(2)—

691

(a)   for "data user" there is substituted "data controller", and

(b)   for "the Data Protection Act 1984" there is substituted "the Data Protection Act 1998".

Access to Medical Reports Act 1988 (c 28)

8   In section 2(1) of the Access to Medical Reports Act 1988 (interpretation), in the definition of "health professional", for "the Data Protection (Subject Access Modification) Order 1987" there is substituted "the Data Protection Act 1998".

Football Spectators Act 1989 (c 37)

9   (1)   Section 5 of the Football Spectators Act 1989 (national membership scheme: contents and penalties) is amended as follows.

(2) In subsection (5), for "paragraph 1(2) of Part II of Schedule 1 to the Data Protection Act 1984" there is substituted "paragraph 1(2) of Part II of Schedule 1 to the Data Protection Act 1998".

(3) In subsection (6), for "section 28(1) and (2) of the Data Protection Act 1984" there is substituted "section 29(1) and (2) of the Data Protection Act 1998".

Education (Student Loans) Act 1990 (c 6)

10   Schedule 2 to the Education (Student Loans) Act 1990 (loans for students) so far as that Schedule continues in force shall have effect as if the reference in paragraph 4(2) to the Data Protection Act 1984 were a reference to this Act.

Access to Health Records Act 1990 (c 23)

11   For section 2 of the Access to Health Records Act 1990 there is substituted—

"Health professionals.   2 In this Act "health professional" has the same meaning as in the Data
                                          Protection Act 1998."

12   In section 3(4) of that Act (cases where fee may be required) in paragraph (a), for "the maximum prescribed under section 21 of the Data Protection Act 1984" there is substituted "such maximum as may be prescribed for the purposes of this section by regulations under section 7 of the Data Protection Act 1998".

13   In section 5(3) of that Act (cases where right of access may be partially excluded) for the words from the beginning to "record" in the first place where it occurs there is substituted "Access shall not be given under section 3(2) to any part of a health record".

Access to Personal Files and Medical Reports (Northern Ireland) Order 1991 (1991/1707 (NI 14))

14   In Article 4 of the Access to Personal Files and Medical Reports (Northern Ireland) Order 1991 (obligation to give access), in paragraph (2) (exclusion of information to which individual entitled under section 21 of the Data Protection Act 1984) for "section 21 of the Data Protection Act 1984" there is substituted "section 7 of the Data Protection Act 1998".

15   In Article 6(1) of that Order (interpretation), in the definition of "health professional", for "the Data Protection (Subject Access Modification) (Health) Order 1987" there is substituted "the Data Protection Act 1998".

Tribunals and Inquiries Act 1992 (c 53)

16   In Part 1 of Schedule 1 to the Tribunals and Inquiries Act 1992 (tribunals under direct supervision of Council on Tribunals), for paragraph 14 there is substituted—

"Data protection   14

                                          (a) The Data Protection Commissioner appointed under section 6 of the
                                          Data Protection Act 1998;

                                          (b) the Data Protection Tribunal constituted under that section, in
                                          respect of its jurisdiction under section 48 of that Act."

Access to Health Records (Northern Ireland) Order 1993 (1993/1250 (NI 4))

17 For paragraphs (1) and (2) of Article 4 of the Access to Health Records (Northern Ireland) Order 1993 there is substituted—

"(1) In this Order "health professional" has the same meaning as in the Data Protection Act 1998.".

18 In Article 5(4) of that Order (cases where fee may be required) in subparagraph (a), for "the maximum prescribed under section 21 of the Data Protection Act 1984" there is substituted "such maximum as may be prescribed for the purposes of this Article by regulations under section 7 of the Data Protection Act 1998".

19 In Article 7 of that Order (cases where right of access may be partially excluded) for the words from the beginning to "record" in the first place where it occurs there is substituted "Access shall not be given under Article 5(2) to any part of a health record".

NOTES

Amendment

Para 1: sub-para (1) repealed by the Freedom of Information Act 2000, s 86, Sch 8, Pt II.

Date in force: 30 January 2001: see the Freedom of Information Act 2000, s 87(2)(d).

Para 1: sub-paras (2), (3) repealed by the Freedom of Information Act 2000, s 86, Sch 8, Pt III.

Date in force: 30 November 2005 (unless the Secretary of State by order appoints an earlier date): see the Freedom of Information Act 2000, s 87(3).

Para 3: repealed by the Freedom of Information Act 2000, s 86, Sch 8, Pt III.

Date in force: 30 November 2005 (unless the Secretary of State by order appoints an earlier date): see the Freedom of Information Act 2000, s 87(3).

Para 5: sub-para (1) repealed by the Freedom of Information Act 2000, s 86, Sch 8, Pt III.

Date in force: 30 November 2005 (unless the Secretary of State by order appoints an earlier date): see the Freedom of Information Act 2000, s 87(3).

Para 6: sub-para (1) repealed by the Freedom of Information Act 2000, s 86, Sch 8, Pt III.

Date in force: 30 November 2005 (unless the Secretary of State by order appoints an earlier date): see the Freedom of Information Act 2000, s 87(3).

SCHEDULE 16
Repeals and Revocations

Section 74(2)

Part I
Repeals

Chapter	Short title	Extent of repeal
1984 c 35.	The Data Protection Act 1984.	The whole Act.
1986 c 60.	The Financial Services Act 1986.	Section 190.
1987 c 37.	The Access to Personal Files Act 1987.	The whole Act.
1988 c 40.	The Education Reform Act 1988.	Section 223.
1988 c 50.	The Housing Act 1988.	In Schedule 17, paragraph 80.
1990 c 23.	The Access to Health Records Act 1990.	In section 1(1), the words from "but does not" to the end.
		In section 3, subsection (1)(a) to (e) and, in subsection (6)(a), the words "in the case of an application made otherwise than by the patient".
		Section 4(1) and (2).
		In section 5(1)(a)(i), the words "of the patient or" and the word "other".
		In section 10, in subsection (2) the words "or orders" and in subsection (3) the words "or an order under section 2(3) above".

Chapter	Short title	Extent of repeal
		In section 11, the definitions of "child" and "parental responsibility".
1990 c 37.	The Human Fertilisation and Embryology Act 1990.	Section 33(8).
1990 c 41.	The Courts and Legal Services Act 1990.	In Schedule 10, paragraph 58.
1992 c 13.	The Further and Higher Education Act 1992.	Section 86.
1992 c 37.	The Further and Higher Education (Scotland) Act 1992.	Section 59.
1993 c 8.	The Judicial Pensions and Retirement Act 1993.	In Schedule 6, paragraph 50.
1993 c 10.	The Charities Act 1993.	Section 12.
1993 c 21.	The Osteopaths Act 1993.	Section 38.
1994 c 17.	The Chiropractors Act 1994.	Section 38.
1994 c 19.	The Local Government (Wales) Act 1994.	In Schedule 13, paragraph 30.
1994 c 33.	The Criminal Justice and Public Order Act 1994.	Section 161.
1994 c 39.	The Local Government etc (Scotland) Act 1994.	In Schedule 13, paragraph 154.

Part II
Revocations

Number	Title	Extent of revocation
SI 1991/1142.	The Data Protection Registration Fee Order 1991.	The Whole Order.
SI 1991/1707 (NI 14).	The Access to Personal Files and Medical Reports (Northern Ireland) Order 1991.	Part II. The Schedule.
SI 1992/3218.	The Banking Co-ordination (Second Council Directive) Regulations 1992.	In Schedule 10, paragraphs 15 and 40.
SI 1993/1250 (NI 4).	The Access to Health Records (Northern Ireland) Order 1993.	In Article 2(2), the definitions of "child" and "parental responsibility". In Article 3(1), the words from "but does not include" to the end. In Article 5, paragraph (1)(a) to (d) and, in paragraph (6)(a), the words "in the case of an application made otherwise than by the patient". Article 6(1) and (2). In Article 7(1)(a)(i), the words "of the patient or" and the word "other".
SI 1994/429 (NI 2).	The Health and Personal Social Services (Northern Ireland) Order 1994.	In Schedule 1, the entries relating to the Access to Personal Files and Medical Reports (Northern Ireland) Order 1991.
SI 1994/1696.	The Insurance Companies (Third Insurance Directives) Regulations 1994.	In Schedule 8, paragraph 8.
SI 1995/755 (NI 2).	The Children (Northern Ireland) Order 1995.	In Schedule 9, paragraphs 177 and 191.
SI 1995/3275.	The Investment Services Regulations 1995.	In Schedule 10, paragraphs 3 and 15.
SI 1996/2827.	The Open-Ended Investment Companies (Investment Companies with Variable Capital) Regulations 1996.	In Schedule 8, paragraphs 3 and 26.

Appendix 6 – List of Statutory Instruments

- *Data Protection Act 1998 (Commencement) Order 2000 (SI 2000/183)*

- *Data Protection (Corporate Finance Exemption) Order 2000 (SI 2000/184)*

- *Data Protection (Conditions under Paragraph 3 of Part II of Schedule 1) Order 2000 (SI 2000/185)*

- *Data Protection (Functions of Designated Authority) Order 2000 (SI 2000/186)*

- *Data Protection (Fees under section 19(7)) Regulations 2000 (SI 2000/187)*

- *Data Protection (Notification and Notification Fees) Regulations 2000 (SI 2000/188)*

- *Data Protection Tribunal (Enforcement Appeals) Rules 2000 (SI 2000/189)*

- *Data Protection (International Co-operation) Order 2000 (SI 2000/190)*

- *Data Protection (Subject Access) (Fees and Miscellaneous Provisions) Regulations 2000 (SI 2000/191)*

- *Data Protection Tribunal (National Security Appeals) Rules 2000 (SI 2000/206)*

- *Consumer Credit (Credit Reference Agency) Regulations 2000 (SI 2000/290)*

- *Data Protection (Subject Access Modification) (Health) Order 2000 (2000/413)*

- *Data Protection (Subject Access Modification) (Education) Order 2000 (2000/414)*

- *Data Protection (Subject Access Modification) (Social Work) Order 2000 (SI 2000/415)*

- *Data Protection (Crown Appointments) Order 2000 (SI 2000/416)*

- *Data Protection (Processing of Sensitive Personal Data) Order 2000 (SI 2000/417)*

- *Data Protection (Miscellaneous Subject Access) Exemptions) Order 2000 (SI 2000/419)* (amended by SI 2000/1865)

- *Data Protection Tribunal (National Security Appeals) (Telecommunications) Rules 2000 (SI 2000/731)*

- *Data Protection (Designated Codes of Practice) (No. 2) Order 2000 (SI 2000/1864)* (replaced SI 2000/418)

- *Data Protection (Miscellaneous Subject Access Exemptions) (Amendment) Order 2000 (SI 2000/1865)* (amended SI 2000/419)

- *Utilities Act 2000 (Supply of Information) Regulations 2000 (SI 2000/2956)*

- *Freedom of Information Act 2000 (Commencement No 1) Order 2001 (SI 2001/1637)*

- *Data Protection (Notification and Notification Fees) (Amendment) Regulations 2001 (SI 2001/3214)*

- *Data Protection (Subject Access) (Fees and Miscellaneous Provisions) (Amendment) Regulations 2001 (SI 2001/3223)*

- *Police Act 1997 (Criminal Records) Regulations 2002 (SI 2002/233)*

- *Nursing and Midwifery Order 2001 (SI 2002/253)*

- *Health Service (Control of Patient Information) Regulations 2002 (SI 2002/1438)*

- *Representation of the People (England and Wales)(Amendment) Regulations 2002 (SI 2002/1871)*

- *Regulation of Investigatory Powers (Maintenance of Interception Capability) Order 2002 (SI 2002/1931)*

- Regulation of Investigatory Powers (Covert Surveillance: Code of Practice) Order 2002 *(SI 2002)*
- *Information Tribunal (Enforcement Appeals) (Amendment) Rules 2002 (SI 2002/2722)*
- *Data Protection (Processing of Sensitive Personal Data) (Elected Representatives) Order 2002 (SI 2002/2905)*
- *Privacy and Electronic Communications (EC Directive) Regulations 2003 (SI 2003/2426)*
- *Regulation of Investigatory Powers (Communications Data) Order 2003 (SI 2003/2174)*
- *Regulation of Investigatory Powers (Directed Surveillance and Covert Human Intelligence Sources) Order 2003 (SI 2003/3171)*
- *Regulation of Investigatory Powers (Intrusive Surveillance) Order 2003 (SI 2003/3174)*

Appendix 7 – Privacy and Electronic Communications (EC Directive) Regulations 2003

Privacy and Electronic Communications (EC Directive) Regulations 2003

2003 No 2426

Made	*18th September 2003*
Laid before Parliament	*18th September 2003*
Coming into force	*11th December 2003*

The Secretary of State, being a Minister designated for the purposes of section 2(2) of the European Communities Act 1972 in respect of matters relating to electronic communications, in exercise of the powers conferred upon her by that section, hereby makes the following Regulations:

1 Citation and commencement

These Regulations may be cited as the Privacy and Electronic Communications (EC Directive) Regulations 2003 and shall come into force on 11th December 2003.

2 Interpretation

(1) In these Regulations—

"bill" includes an invoice, account, statement or other document of similar character and "billing" shall be construed accordingly;

"call" means a connection established by means of a telephone service available to the public allowing two-way communication in real time;

"communication" means any information exchanged or conveyed between a finite number of parties by means of a public electronic communications service, but does not include information conveyed as part of a programme service, except to the extent that such information can be related to the identifiable subscriber or user receiving the information;

"communications provider" has the meaning given by section 405 of the Communications Act 2003;

"corporate subscriber" means a subscriber who is—

(a)   a company within the meaning of section 735(1) of the Companies Act 1985;

(b)   a company incorporated in pursuance of a royal charter or letters patent;

(c)   a partnership in Scotland;

(d)   a corporation sole; or

(e)   any other body corporate or entity which is a legal person distinct from its members;

"the Directive" means Directive 2002/58/EC of the European Parliament and of the Council of 12 July 2002 concerning the processing of personal data and the protection of privacy in the electronic communications sector (Directive on privacy and electronic communications);

"electronic communications network" has the meaning given by section 32 of the Communications Act 2003;

"electronic communications service" has the meaning given by section 32 of the Communications Act 2003;

697

"electronic mail" means any text, voice, sound or image message sent over a public electronic communications network which can be stored in the network or in the recipient's terminal equipment until it is collected by the recipient and includes messages sent using a short message service;

"enactment" includes an enactment comprised in, or in an instrument made under, an Act of the Scottish Parliament;

"individual" means a living individual and includes an unincorporated body of such individuals;

"the Information Commissioner" and "the Commissioner" both mean the Commissioner appointed under section 6 of the Data Protection Act 1998;

"information society service" has the meaning given in regulation 2(1) of the Electronic Commerce (EC Directive) Regulations 2002;

"location data" means any data processed in an electronic communications network indicating the geographical position of the terminal equipment of a user of a public electronic communications service, including data relating to—

(f)   the latitude, longitude or altitude of the terminal equipment;

(g)   the direction of travel of the user; or

(h)   the time the location information was recorded;

"OFCOM" means the Office of Communications as established by section 1 of the Office of Communications Act 2002;

"programme service" has the meaning given in section 201 of the Broadcasting Act 1990;

"public communications provider" means a provider of a public electronic communications network or a public electronic communications service;

"public electronic communications network" has the meaning given in section 151 of the Communications Act 2003;

"public electronic communications service" has the meaning given in section 151 of the Communications Act 2003;

"subscriber" means a person who is a party to a contract with a provider of public electronic communications services for the supply of such services;

"traffic data" means any data processed for the purpose of the conveyance of a communication on an electronic communications network or for the billing in respect of that communication and includes data relating to the routing, duration or time of a communication;

"user" means any individual using a public electronic communications service; and

"value added service" means any service which requires the processing of traffic data or location data beyond that which is necessary for the transmission of a communication or the billing in respect of that communication.

(2) Expressions used in these Regulations that are not defined in paragraph (1) and are defined in the Data Protection Act 1998 shall have the same meaning as in that Act.

(3) Expressions used in these Regulations that are not defined in paragraph (1) or the Data Protection Act 1998 and are defined in the Directive shall have the same meaning as in the Directive.

(4) Any reference in these Regulations to a line shall, without prejudice to paragraph (3), be construed as including a reference to anything that performs the function of a line, and "connected", in relation to a line, is to be construed accordingly.

3   Revocation of the Telecommunications (Data Protection and Privacy) Regulations 1999

The Telecommunications (Data Protection and Privacy) Regulations 1999 and the Telecommunications (Data Protection and Privacy) (Amendment) Regulations 2000 are hereby revoked.

4   Relationship between these Regulations and the Data Protection Act 1998

Nothing in these Regulations shall relieve a person of his obligations under the Data Protection Act 1998 in relation to the processing of personal data.

5   Security of public electronic communications services

(1) Subject to paragraph (2), a provider of a public electronic communications service ("the service provider") shall take appropriate technical and organisational measures to safeguard the security of that service.

(2) If necessary, the measures required by paragraph (1) may be taken by the service provider in conjunction with the provider of the electronic communications network by means of which the service is provided, and that network provider shall comply with any reasonable requests made by the service provider for these purposes.

(3) Where, notwithstanding the taking of measures as required by paragraph (1), there remains a significant risk to the security of the public electronic communications service, the service provider shall inform the subscribers concerned of—

(a)   the nature of that risk;

(b)   any appropriate measures that the subscriber may take to safeguard against that risk; and

(c)   the likely costs to the subscriber involved in the taking of such measures.

(4) For the purposes of paragraph (1), a measure shall only be taken to be appropriate if, having regard to—

(a)   the state of technological developments, and

(b)   the cost of implementing it,

it is proportionate to the risks against which it would safeguard.

(5) Information provided for the purposes of paragraph (3) shall be provided to the subscriber free of any charge other than the cost to the subscriber of receiving or collecting the information.

6 Confidentiality of communications

(1) Subject to paragraph (4), a person shall not use an electronic communications network to store information, or to gain access to information stored, in the terminal equipment of a subscriber or user unless the requirements of paragraph (2) are met.

(2) The requirements are that the subscriber or user of that terminal equipment—

(a)   is provided with clear and comprehensive information about the purposes of the storage of, or access to, that information; and

(b)   is given the opportunity to refuse the storage of or access to that information.

(3) Where an electronic communications network is used by the same person to store or access information in the terminal equipment of a subscriber or user on more than one occasion, it is sufficient for the purposes of this regulation that the requirements of paragraph (2) are met in respect of the initial use.

(4) Paragraph (1) shall not apply to the technical storage of, or access to, information—

(a)   for the sole purpose of carrying out or facilitating the transmission of a communication over an electronic communications network; or

(b)   where such storage or access is strictly necessary for the provision of an information society service requested by the subscriber or user.

7 Restrictions on the processing of certain traffic data

(1) Subject to paragraphs (2) and (3), traffic data relating to subscribers or users which are processed and stored by a public communications provider shall, when no longer required for the purpose of the transmission of a communication, be—

(a)   erased;

(b)   in the case of an individual, modified so that they cease to constitute personal data of that subscriber or user; or

(c)   in the case of a corporate subscriber, modified so that they cease to be data that would be personal data if that subscriber was an individual.

(2) Traffic data held by a public communications provider for purposes connected with the payment of charges by a subscriber or in respect of interconnection payments may be processed and stored by that provider until the time specified in paragraph (5).

(3) Traffic data relating to a subscriber or user may be processed and stored by a provider of a public electronic communications service if—

(a)   such processing and storage are for the purpose of marketing electronic communications services, or for the provision of value added services to that subscriber or user; and

(b)   the subscriber or user to whom the traffic data relate has given his consent to such processing or storage; and

(c)   such processing and storage are undertaken only for the duration necessary for the purposes specified in sub-paragraph (a).

(4) Where a user or subscriber has given his consent in accordance with paragraph (3), he shall be able to withdraw it at any time.

(5) The time referred to in paragraph (2) is the end of the period during which legal proceedings may be brought in respect of payments due or alleged to be due or, where such proceedings are brought within that period, the time when those proceedings are finally determined.

(6) Legal proceedings shall not be taken to be finally determined—

(a)   until the conclusion of the ordinary period during which an appeal may be brought by either party (excluding any possibility of an extension of that period, whether by order of a court or otherwise), if no appeal is brought within that period; or

(b)   if an appeal is brought, until the conclusion of that appeal.

(7) References in paragraph (6) to an appeal include references to an application for permission to appeal.

8   Further provisions relating to the processing of traffic data under regulation 7

(1) Processing of traffic data in accordance with regulation 7(2) or (3) shall not be undertaken by a public communications provider unless the subscriber or user to whom the data relate has been provided with information regarding the types of traffic data which are to be processed and the duration of such processing and, in the case of processing in accordance with regulation 7(3), he has been provided with that information before his consent has been obtained.

(2) Processing of traffic data in accordance with regulation 7 shall be restricted to what is required for the purposes of one or more of the activities listed in paragraph (3) and shall be carried out only by the public communications provider or by a person acting under his authority.

(3) The activities referred to in paragraph (2) are activities relating to—

(a)   the management of billing or traffic;

(b)   customer enquiries;

(c)   the prevention or detection of fraud;

(d)   the marketing of electronic communications services; or

(e)   the provision of a value added service.

(4) Nothing in these Regulations shall prevent the furnishing of traffic data to a person who is a competent authority for the purposes of any provision relating to the settling of disputes (by way of legal proceedings or otherwise) which is contained in, or made by virtue of, any enactment.

9   Itemised billing and privacy

(1) At the request of a subscriber, a provider of a public electronic communications service shall provide that subscriber with bills that are not itemised.

(2) OFCOM shall have a duty, when exercising their functions under Chapter 1 of Part 2 of the Communications Act 2003, to have regard to the need to reconcile the rights of subscribers receiving itemised bills with the rights to privacy of calling users and called subscribers, including the need for sufficient alternative privacy-enhancing methods of communications or payments to be available to such users and subscribers.

10   Prevention of calling line identification—outgoing calls

(1) This regulation applies, subject to regulations 15 and 16, to outgoing calls where a facility enabling the presentation of calling line identification is available.

(2) The provider of a public electronic communications service shall provide users originating a call by means of that service with a simple means to prevent presentation of the identity of the calling line on the connected line as respects that call.

(3) The provider of a public electronic communications service shall provide subscribers to the service, as respects their line and all calls originating from that line, with a simple means of preventing presentation of the identity of that subscriber's line on any connected line.

(4) The measures to be provided under paragraphs (2) and (3) shall be provided free of charge.

11   Prevention of calling or connected line identification—incoming calls

(1) This regulation applies to incoming calls.

(2) Where a facility enabling the presentation of calling line identification is available, the provider of a public electronic communications service shall provide the called subscriber with a simple means to prevent, free of charge for reasonable use of the facility, presentation of the identity of the calling line on the connected line.

(3) Where a facility enabling the presentation of calling line identification prior to the call being established is available, the provider of a public electronic communications service shall provide the called subscriber with a simple means of rejecting incoming calls where the presentation of the calling line identification has been prevented by the calling user or subscriber.

(4) Where a facility enabling the presentation of connected line identification is available, the provider of a public electronic communications service shall provide the called subscriber with a simple means to prevent, without charge, presentation of the identity of the connected line on any calling line.

(5) In this regulation "called subscriber" means the subscriber receiving a call by means of the service in question whose line is the called line (whether or not it is also the connected line).

12   Publication of information for the purposes of regulations 10 and 11

Where a provider of a public electronic communications service provides facilities for calling or connected line identification, he shall provide information to the public regarding the availability of such facilities, including information regarding the options to be made available for the purposes of regulations 10 and 11.

13   Co-operation of communications providers for the purposes of regulations 10 and 11

For the purposes of regulations 10 and 11, a communications provider shall comply with any reasonable requests made by the provider of the public electronic communications service by means of which facilities for calling or connected line identification are provided.

14   Restrictions on the processing of location data

(1) This regulation shall not apply to the processing of traffic data.

(2) Location data relating to a user or subscriber of a public electronic communications network or a public electronic communications service may only be processed—

(a)   where that user or subscriber cannot be identified from such data; or

(b)   where necessary for the provision of a value added service, with the consent of that user or subscriber.

(3) Prior to obtaining the consent of the user or subscriber under paragraph (2)(b), the public communications provider in question must provide the following information to the user or subscriber to whom the data relate—

(a)   the types of location data that will be processed;

(b)   the purposes and duration of the processing of those data; and

(c)   whether the data will be transmitted to a third party for the purpose of providing the value added service.

(4) A user or subscriber who has given his consent to the processing of data under paragraph (2)(b) shall—

(a)   be able to withdraw such consent at any time, and

(b)   in respect of each connection to the public electronic communications network in question or each transmission of a communication, be given the opportunity to withdraw such consent, using a simple means and free of charge.

(5) Processing of location data in accordance with this regulation shall—

(a)   only be carried out by—

(i)   the public communications provider in question;

(ii)   the third party providing the value added service in question; or

(iii)   a person acting under the authority of a person falling within (i) or (ii); and

(b)   where the processing is carried out for the purposes of the provision of a value added service, be restricted to what is necessary for those purposes.

15 Tracing of malicious or nuisance calls

(1) A communications provider may override anything done to prevent the presentation of the identity of a calling line where—

(a) a subscriber has requested the tracing of malicious or nuisance calls received on his line; and

(b) the provider is satisfied that such action is necessary and expedient for the purposes of tracing such calls.

(2) Any term of a contract for the provision of public electronic communications services which relates to such prevention shall have effect subject to the provisions of paragraph (1).

(3) Nothing in these Regulations shall prevent a communications provider, for the purposes of any action relating to the tracing of malicious or nuisance calls, from storing and making available to a person with a legitimate interest data containing the identity of a calling subscriber which were obtained while paragraph (1) applied.

16 Emergency calls

(1) For the purposes of this regulation, "emergency calls" means calls to either the national emergency call number 999 or the single European emergency call number 112.

(2) In order to facilitate responses to emergency calls—

(a) all such calls shall be excluded from the requirements of regulation 10;

(b) no person shall be entitled to prevent the presentation on the connected line of the identity of the calling line; and

(c) the restriction on the processing of location data under regulation 14(2) shall be disregarded.

17 Termination of automatic call forwarding

(1) Where—

(a) calls originally directed to another line are being automatically forwarded to a subscriber's line as a result of action taken by a third party, and

(b) the subscriber requests his provider of electronic communications services ("the subscriber's provider") to stop the forwarding of those calls,

the subscriber's provider shall ensure, free of charge, that the forwarding is stopped without any avoidable delay.

(2) For the purposes of paragraph (1), every other communications provider shall comply with any reasonable requests made by the subscriber's provider to assist in the prevention of that forwarding.

18 Directories of subscribers

(1) This regulation applies in relation to a directory of subscribers, whether in printed or electronic form, which is made available to members of the public or a section of the public, including by means of a directory enquiry service.

(2) The personal data of an individual subscriber shall not be included in a directory unless that subscriber has, free of charge, been—

(a) informed by the collector of the personal data of the purposes of the directory in which his personal data are to be included, and

(b) given the opportunity to determine whether such of his personal data as are considered relevant by the producer of the directory should be included in the directory.

(3) Where personal data of an individual subscriber are to be included in a directory with facilities which enable users of that directory to obtain access to that data solely on the basis of a telephone number—

(a) the information to be provided under paragraph (2)(a) shall include information about those facilities; and

(b) for the purposes of paragraph (2)(b), the express consent of the subscriber to the inclusion of his data in a directory with such facilities must be obtained.

(4) Data relating to a corporate subscriber shall not be included in a directory where that subscriber has advised the producer of the directory that it does not want its data to be included in that directory.

(5) Where the data of an individual subscriber have been included in a directory, that subscriber shall, without charge, be able to verify, correct or withdraw those data at any time.

(6) Where a request has been made under paragraph (5) for data to be withdrawn from or corrected in a directory, that request shall be treated as having no application in relation to an edition of a directory that was produced before the producer of the directory received the request.

(7) For the purposes of paragraph (6), an edition of a directory which is revised after it was first produced shall be treated as a new edition.

(8) In this regulation, "telephone number" has the same meaning as in section 56(5) of the Communications Act 2003 but does not include any number which is used as an internet domain name, an internet address or an address or identifier incorporating either an internet domain name or an internet address, including an electronic mail address.

19   Use of automated calling systems

(1) A person shall neither transmit, nor instigate the transmission of, communications comprising recorded matter for direct marketing purposes by means of an automated calling system except in the circumstances referred to in paragraph (2).

(2) Those circumstances are where the called line is that of a subscriber who has previously notified the caller that for the time being he consents to such communications being sent by, or at the instigation of, the caller on that line.

(3) A subscriber shall not permit his line to be used in contravention of paragraph (1).

(4) For the purposes of this regulation, an automated calling system is a system which is capable of—

(a)   automatically initiating a sequence of calls to more than one destination in accordance with instructions stored in that system; and

(b)   transmitting sounds which are not live speech for reception by persons at some or all of the destinations so called.

20   Use of facsimile machines for direct marketing purposes

(1) A person shall neither transmit, nor instigate the transmission of, unsolicited communications for direct marketing purposes by means of a facsimile machine where the called line is that of—

(a)   an individual subscriber, except in the circumstances referred to in paragraph (2);

(b)   a corporate subscriber who has previously notified the caller that such communications should not be sent on that line; or

(c)   a subscriber and the number allocated to that line is listed in the register kept under regulation 25.

(2) The circumstances referred to in paragraph (1)(a) are that the individual subscriber has previously notified the caller that he consents for the time being to such communications being sent by, or at the instigation of, the caller.

(3) A subscriber shall not permit his line to be used in contravention of paragraph (1).

(4) A person shall not be held to have contravened paragraph (1)(c) where the number allocated to the called line has been listed on the register for less than 28 days preceding that on which the communication is made.

(5) Where a subscriber who has caused a number allocated to a line of his to be listed in the register kept under regulation 25 has notified a caller that he does not, for the time being, object to such communications being sent on that line by that caller, such communications may be sent by that caller on that line, notwithstanding that the number allocated to that line is listed in the said register.

(6) Where a subscriber has given a caller notification pursuant to paragraph (5) in relation to a line of his—

(a)   the subscriber shall be free to withdraw that notification at any time, and

(b)   where such notification is withdrawn, the caller shall not send such communications on that line.

(7) The provisions of this regulation are without prejudice to the provisions of regulation 19.

21   Unsolicited calls for direct marketing purposes

(1) A person shall neither use, nor instigate the use of, a public electronic communications service for the purposes of making unsolicited calls for direct marketing purposes where—

(a)   the called line is that of a subscriber who has previously notified the caller that such calls should not for the time being be made on that line; or

(b)   the number allocated to a subscriber in respect of the called line is one listed in the register kept under regulation 26.

(2) A subscriber shall not permit his line to be used in contravention of paragraph (1).

(3) A person shall not be held to have contravened paragraph (1)(b) where the number allocated to the called line has been listed on the register for less than 28 days preceding that on which the call is made.

(4) Where a subscriber who has caused a number allocated to a line of his to be listed in the register kept under regulation 26 has notified a caller that he does not, for the time being, object to such calls being made on that line by that caller, such calls may be made by that caller on that line, notwithstanding that the number allocated to that line is listed in the said register.

(5) Where a subscriber has given a caller notification pursuant to paragraph (4) in relation to a line of his—

(a)   the subscriber shall be free to withdraw that notification at any time, and

(b)   where such notification is withdrawn, the caller shall not make such calls on that line.

22   Use of electronic mail for direct marketing purposes

(1) This regulation applies to the transmission of unsolicited communications by means of electronic mail to individual subscribers.

(2) Except in the circumstances referred to in paragraph (3), a person shall neither transmit, nor instigate the transmission of, unsolicited communications for the purposes of direct marketing by means of electronic mail unless the recipient of the electronic mail has previously notified the sender that he consents for the time being to such communications being sent by, or at the instigation of, the sender.

(3) A person may send or instigate the sending of electronic mail for the purposes of direct marketing where—

(a)   that person has obtained the contact details of the recipient of that electronic mail in the course of the sale or negotiations for the sale of a product or service to that recipient;

(b)   the direct marketing is in respect of that person's similar products and services only; and

(c)   the recipient has been given a simple means of refusing (free of charge except for the costs of the transmission of the refusal) the use of his contact details for the purposes of such direct marketing, at the time that the details were initially collected, and, where he did not initially refuse the use of the details, at the time of each subsequent communication.

(4) A subscriber shall not permit his line to be used in contravention of paragraph (2).

23   Use of electronic mail for direct marketing purposes where the identity or address of the sender is concealed

A person shall neither transmit, nor instigate the transmission of, a communication for the purposes of direct marketing by means of electronic mail—

(a)   where the identity of the person on whose behalf the communication has been sent has been disguised or concealed; or

(b)   where a valid address to which the recipient of the communication may send a request that such communications cease has not been provided.

24   Information to be provided for the purposes of regulations 19, 20 and 21

(1) Where a public electronic communications service is used for the transmission of a communication for direct marketing purposes the person using, or instigating the use of, the service shall ensure that the following information is provided with that communication—

(a)   in relation to a communication to which regulations 19 (automated calling systems) and 20 (facsimile machines) apply, the particulars mentioned in paragraph (2)(a) and (b);

(b)   in relation to a communication to which regulation 21 (telephone calls) applies, the particulars mentioned in paragraph (2)(a) and, if the recipient of the call so requests, those mentioned in paragraph (2)(b).

(2) The particulars referred to in paragraph (1) are—

(a)   the name of the person;

(b)   either the address of the person or a telephone number on which he can be reached free of charge.

25 Register to be kept for the purposes of regulation 20

(1) For the purposes of regulation 20 OFCOM shall maintain and keep up-to-date, in printed or electronic form, a register of the numbers allocated to subscribers, in respect of particular lines, who have notified them (notwithstanding, in the case of individual subscribers, that they enjoy the benefit of regulation 20(1)(a) and (2)) that they do not for the time being wish to receive unsolicited communications for direct marketing purposes by means of facsimile machine on the lines in question.

(2) OFCOM shall remove a number from the register maintained under paragraph (1) where they have reason to believe that it has ceased to be allocated to the subscriber by whom they were notified pursuant to paragraph (1).

(3) On the request of—

(a)   a person wishing to send, or instigate the sending of, such communications as are mentioned in paragraph (1), or

(b)   a subscriber wishing to permit the use of his line for the sending of such communications,

for information derived from the register kept under paragraph (1), OFCOM shall, unless it is not reasonably practicable so to do, on the payment to them of such fee as is, subject to paragraph (4), required by them, make the information requested available to that person or that subscriber.

(4) For the purposes of paragraph (3) OFCOM may require different fees—

(a)   for making available information derived from the register in different forms or manners, or

(b)   for making available information derived from the whole or from different parts of the register,

but the fees required by them shall be ones in relation to which the Secretary of State has notified OFCOM that he is satisfied that they are designed to secure, as nearly as may be and taking one year with another, that the aggregate fees received, or reasonably expected to be received, equal the costs incurred, or reasonably expected to be incurred, by OFCOM in discharging their duties under paragraphs (1), (2) and (3).

(5) The functions of OFCOM under paragraphs (1), (2) and (3), other than the function of determining the fees to be required for the purposes of paragraph (3), may be discharged on their behalf by some other person in pursuance of arrangements made by OFCOM with that other person.

26 Register to be kept for the purposes of regulation 21

(1) For the purposes of regulation 21 OFCOM shall maintain and keep up-to-date, in printed or electronic form, a register of the numbers allocated to individual subscribers, in respect of particular lines, who have notified them that they do not for the time being wish to receive unsolicited calls for direct marketing purposes on the lines in question.

(2) OFCOM shall remove a number from the register maintained under paragraph (1) where they have reason to believe that it has ceased to be allocated to the subscriber by whom they were notified pursuant to paragraph (1).

(3) On the request of—

(a)   a person wishing to make, or instigate the making of, such calls as are mentioned in paragraph (1), or

(b)   a subscriber wishing to permit the use of his line for the making of such calls,

for information derived from the register kept under paragraph (1), OFCOM shall, unless it is not reasonably practicable so to do, on the payment to them of such fee as is, subject to paragraph (4), required by them, make the information requested available to that person or that subscriber.

(4) For the purposes of paragraph (3) OFCOM may require different fees—

(a)   for making available information derived from the register in different forms or manners, or

(b)   for making available information derived from the whole or from different parts of the register,

but the fees required by them shall be ones in relation to which the Secretary of State has notified OFCOM that he is satisfied that they are designed to secure, as nearly as may be and taking one year with another, that the aggregate fees received, or reasonably expected to be received, equal the costs incurred, or reasonably expected to be incurred, by OFCOM in discharging their duties under paragraphs (1), (2) and (3).

(5) The functions of OFCOM under paragraphs (1), (2) and (3), other than the function of determining the fees to be required for the purposes of paragraph (3), may be discharged on their behalf by some other person in pursuance of arrangements made by OFCOM with that other person.

27   Modification of contracts

To the extent that any term in a contract between a subscriber to and the provider of a public electronic communications service or such a provider and the provider of an electronic communications network would be inconsistent with a requirement of these Regulations, that term shall be void.

28   National security

(1) Nothing in these Regulations shall require a communications provider to do, or refrain from doing, anything (including the processing of data) if exemption from the requirement in question is required for the purpose of safeguarding national security.

(2) Subject to paragraph (4), a certificate signed by a Minister of the Crown certifying that exemption from any requirement of these Regulations is or at any time was required for the purpose of safeguarding national security shall be conclusive evidence of that fact.

(3) A certificate under paragraph (2) may identify the circumstances in which it applies by means of a general description and may be expressed to have prospective effect.

(4) Any person directly affected by the issuing of a certificate under paragraph (2) may appeal to the Tribunal against the issuing of the certificate.

(5) If, on an appeal under paragraph (4), the Tribunal finds that, applying the principles applied by a court on an application for judicial review, the Minister did not have reasonable grounds for issuing the certificate, the Tribunal may allow the appeal and quash the certificate.

(6) Where, in any proceedings under or by virtue of these Regulations, it is claimed by a communications provider that a certificate under paragraph (2) which identifies the circumstances in which it applies by means of a general description applies in the circumstances in question, any other party to the proceedings may appeal to the Tribunal on the ground that the certificate does not apply in those circumstances and, subject to any determination under paragraph (7), the certificate shall be conclusively presumed so to apply.

(7) On any appeal under paragraph (6), the Tribunal may determine that the certificate does not so apply.

(8) In this regulation—

(a)   "the Tribunal" means the Information Tribunal referred to in section 6 of the Data Protection Act 1998;

(b)   Subsections (8), (9), (10) and (12) of section 28 of and Schedule 6 to that Act apply for the purposes of this regulation as they apply for the purposes of section 28;

(c)   section 58 of that Act shall apply for the purposes of this regulation as if the reference in that section to the functions of the Tribunal under that Act included a reference to the functions of the Tribunal under paragraphs (4) to (7) of this regulation; and

(d)   subsections (1), (2) and (5)(f) of section 67 of that Act shall apply in respect of the making of rules relating to the functions of the Tribunal under this regulation.

29   Legal requirements, law enforcement etc

(1) Nothing in these Regulations shall require a communications provider to do, or refrain from doing, anything (including the processing of data)—

(a)   if compliance with the requirement in question—

   (i)   would be inconsistent with any requirement imposed by or under an enactment or by a court order; or

   (ii)   would be likely to prejudice the prevention or detection of crime or the apprehension or prosecution of offenders; or

(b)   if exemption from the requirement in question—

   (i)   is required for the purposes of, or in connection with, any legal proceedings (including prospective legal proceedings);

   (ii)   is necessary for the purposes of obtaining legal advice; or

   (iii) is otherwise necessary for the purposes of establishing, exercising or defending legal rights.

30   Proceedings for compensation for failure to comply with requirements of the Regulations

(1) A person who suffers damage by reason of any contravention of any of the requirements of these Regulations by any other person shall be entitled to bring proceedings for compensation from that other person for that damage.

(2) In proceedings brought against a person by virtue of this regulation it shall be a defence to prove that he had taken such care as in all the circumstances was reasonably required to comply with the relevant requirement.

(3) The provisions of this regulation are without prejudice to those of regulation 31.

31   Enforcement—extension of Part V of the Data Protection Act 1998

(1) The provisions of Part V of the Data Protection Act 1998 and of Schedules 6 and 9 to that Act are extended for the purposes of these Regulations and, for those purposes, shall have effect subject to the modifications set out in Schedule 1.

(2) In regulations 32 and 33, "enforcement functions" means the functions of the Information Commissioner under the provisions referred to in paragraph (1) as extended by that paragraph.

(3) The provisions of this regulation are without prejudice to those of regulation 30.

32   Request that the Commissioner exercise his enforcement functions

Where it is alleged that there has been a contravention of any of the requirements of these Regulations either OFCOM or a person aggrieved by the alleged contravention may request the Commissioner to exercise his enforcement functions in respect of that contravention, but those functions shall be exercisable by the Commissioner whether or not he has been so requested.

33   Technical advice to the Commissioner

OFCOM shall comply with any reasonable request made by the Commissioner, in connection with his enforcement functions, for advice on technical and similar matters relating to electronic communications.

34   Amendment to the Telecommunications (Lawful Business Practice) (Interception of Communications) Regulations 2000

In regulation 3 of the Telecommunications (Lawful Business Practice) (Interception of Communications) Regulations 2000, for paragraph (3), there shall be substituted—

"(3) Conduct falling within paragraph (1)(a)(i) above is authorised only to the extent that Article 5 of Directive 2002/58/EC of the European Parliament and of the Council of 12 July 2002 concerning the processing of personal data and the protection of privacy in the electronic communications sector so permits.".

35   Amendment to the Electronic Communications (Universal Service) Order 2003

(1) In paragraphs 2(2) and 3(2) of the Schedule to the Electronic Communications (Universal Service) Order 2003, for the words "Telecommunications (Data Protection and Privacy) Regulations 1999" there shall be substituted "Privacy and Electronic Communications (EC Directive) Regulations 2003".

(2) Paragraph (1) shall have effect notwithstanding the provisions of section 65 of the Communications Act 2003 (which provides for the modification of the Universal Service Order made under that section).

36   Transitional provisions

The provisions in Schedule 2 shall have effect.

Stephen Timms,
Minister of State for Energy, E-Commerce and Postal Services,
Department of Trade and Industry
18th September 2003

SCHEDULE I
Modifications for the Purposes of these Regulations to Part V of the Data Protection Act 1998 and Schedules 6 and 9 to that Act as Extended by Regulation 31

Regulation 31

1   In section 40—

(a)   in subsection (1), for the words "data controller" there shall be substituted the word "person", for the words "data protection principles" there shall be substituted the words "requirements of the Privacy and Electronic Communications (EC Directive) Regulations 2003 (in this Part referred to as "the relevant requirements")" and for the words "principle or principles" there shall be substituted the words "requirement or requirements";

(b)   in subsection (2), the words "or distress" shall be omitted;

(c)   subsections (3), (4), (5), (9) and (10) shall be omitted; and

(d)   in subsection (6)(a), for the words "data protection principle or principles" there shall be substituted the words "relevant requirement or requirements."

2   In section 41(1) and (2), for the words "data protection principle or principles", in both places where they occur, there shall be substituted the words "relevant requirement or requirements".

3   Section 42 shall be omitted.

4   In section 43—

(a)   for subsections (1) and (2) there shall be substituted the following provisions—

"(1) If the Commissioner reasonably requires any information for the purpose of determining whether a person has complied or is complying with the relevant requirements, he may serve that person with a notice (in this Act referred to as "an information notice") requiring him, within such time as is specified in the notice, to furnish the Commissioner, in such form as may be so specified, with such information relating to compliance with the relevant requirements as is so specified.

(2) An information notice must contain a statement that the Commissioner regards the specified information as relevant for the purpose of determining whether the person has complied or is complying with the relevant requirements and his reason for regarding it as relevant for that purpose."

(b)   in subsection (6)(a), after the word "under" there shall be inserted the words "the Privacy and Electronic Communications (EC Directive) Regulations 2003 or";

(c)   in subsection (6)(b), after the words "arising out of" there shall be inserted the words "the said Regulations or"; and

(d)   subsection (10) shall be omitted.

5   Sections 44, 45 and 46 shall be omitted.

6   In section 47—

(a)   in subsection (1), for the words "an information notice or special information notice" there shall be substituted the words "or an information notice"; and

(b)   in subsection (2) the words "or a special information notice" shall be omitted.

7   In section 48—

(a)   in subsections (1) and (3), for the words "an information notice or a special information notice", in both places where they occur, there shall be substituted the words "or an information notice";

(b)   in subsection (3) for the words "43(5) or 44(6)" there shall be substituted the words "or 43(5)"; and

(c)   subsection (4) shall be omitted.

8   In section 49 subsection (5) shall be omitted.

9   In paragraph 4(1) of Schedule (6), for the words " (2) or (4)" there shall be substituted the words "or (2)".

10   In paragraph 1 of Schedule 9—

(a)   for subparagraph (1)(a) there shall be substituted the following provision—

"(a)   that a person has contravened or is contravening any of the requirements of the Privacy and Electronic Communications (EC Directive) Regulations 2003 (in this Schedule referred to as "the 2003 Regulations") or";

and

(b)   subparagraph (2) shall be omitted.

11   In paragraph 9 of Schedule 9—

(a)   in subparagraph (1)(a) after the words "rights under" there shall be inserted the words "the 2003 Regulations or"; and

(b)   in subparagraph (1)(b) after the words "arising out of" there shall be inserted the words "the 2003 Regulations or".

SCHEDULE 2
Transitional Provisions

Regulation 36

Interpretation

1   In this Schedule "the 1999 Regulations" means the Telecommunications (Data Protection and Privacy) Regulations 1999 and "caller" has the same meaning as in regulation 21 of the 1999 Regulations.

Directories

2   (1)   Regulation 18 of these Regulations shall not apply in relation to editions of directories first published before 11th December 2003.

(2)   Where the personal data of a subscriber have been included in a directory in accordance with Part IV of the 1999 Regulations, the personal data of that subscriber may remain included in that directory provided that the subscriber—

(a)   has been provided with information in accordance with regulation 18 of these Regulations; and

(b)   has not requested that his data be withdrawn from that directory.

(3)   Where a request has been made under subparagraph (2) for data to be withdrawn from a directory, that request shall be treated as having no application in relation to an edition of a directory that was produced before the producer of the directory received the request.

(4)   For the purposes of subparagraph (3), an edition of a directory, which is revised after it was first produced, shall be treated as a new edition.

Notifications

3   (1)   A notification of consent given to a caller by a subscriber for the purposes of regulation 22(2) of the 1999 Regulations is to have effect on and after 11th December 2003 as a notification given by that subscriber for the purposes of regulation 19(2) of these Regulations.

(2)   A notification given to a caller by a corporate subscriber for the purposes of regulation 23(2)(a) of the 1999 Regulations is to have effect on and after 11th December 2003 as a notification given by that subscriber for the purposes of regulation 20(1)(b) of these Regulations.

(3)   A notification of consent given to a caller by an individual subscriber for the purposes of regulation 24(2) of the 1999 Regulations is to have effect on and after 11th December 2003 as a notification given by that subscriber for the purposes of regulation 20(2) of these Regulations.

(4)   A notification given to a caller by an individual subscriber for the purposes of regulation 25(2)(a) of the 1999 Regulations is to have effect on and after the 11th December 2003 as a notification given by that subscriber for the purposes of regulation 21(1) of these Regulations.

Registers Kept Under Regulations 25 and 26

4 (1) A notification given by a subscriber pursuant to regulation 23(4)(a) of the 1999 Regulations to the Director General of Telecommunications (or to such other person as is discharging his functions under regulation 23(4) of the 1999 Regulations on his behalf by virtue of an arrangement made under regulation 23(6) of those Regulations) is to have effect on or after 11th December 2003 as a notification given pursuant to regulation 25(1) of these Regulations.

(2) A notification given by a subscriber who is an individual pursuant to regulation 25(4)(a) of the 1999 Regulations to the Director General of Telecommunications (or to such other person as is discharging his functions under regulation 25(4) of the 1999 Regulations on his behalf by virtue of an arrangement made under regulation 25(6) of those Regulations) is to have effect on or after 11th December 2003 as a notification given pursuant to regulation 26(1) of these Regulations.

References in these Regulations to OFCOM

5 In relation to times before an order made under section 411 of the Communications Act 2003 brings any of the provisions of Part 2 of Chapter 1 of that Act into force for the purpose of conferring on OFCOM the functions contained in those provisions, references to OFCOM in these Regulations are to be treated as references to the Director General of Telecommunications.

(This note is not part of the Regulations)

These Regulations implement Articles 2, 4, 5(3), 6 to 13, 15 and 16 of Directive 2002/58/EC of the European Parliament and of the Council of 12 July 2002 concerning the processing of personal data and the protection of privacy in the electronic communications sector (Directive on privacy and electronic communications) ("the Directive").

The Directive repeals and replaces Directive 97/66/EC of the European Parliament and of the Council of 15 December 1997 concerning the processing of personal data and the protection of privacy in the telecommunications sector which was implemented in the UK by the Telecommunications (Data Protection and Privacy) Regulations 1999. Those Regulations are revoked by regulation 3 of these Regulations.

Regulation 2 sets out the definitions which apply for the purposes of the Regulations.

Regulation 4 provides that nothing in these Regulations relieves a person of any of his obligations under the Data Protection Act 1998.

Regulation 5 imposes a duty on a provider of a public electronic communications service to take measures, if necessary in conjunction with the provider of the electronic communications network by means of which the service is provided, to safeguard the security of the service, and requires the provider of the electronic communications network to comply with the service provider's reasonable requests made for the purposes of taking the measures ("public electronic communications service" has the meaning given by section 151 of the Communications Act 2003 and "electronic communications network" has the meaning given by section 32 of that Act). Regulation 5 further requires the service provider, where there remains a significant risk to the security of the service, to provide subscribers to that service with certain information ("subscriber" is defined as "a person who is a party to a contract with a provider of public electronic communications services for the supply of such services").

Regulation 6 provides that an electronic communications network may not be used to store or gain access to information in the terminal equipment of a subscriber or user ("user" is defined as "any individual using a public electronic communications service") unless the subscriber or user is provided with certain information and is given the opportunity to refuse the storage of or access to the information in his terminal equipment.

Regulations 7 and 8 set out certain restrictions on the processing of traffic data relating to a subscriber or user by a public communications provider. "Traffic data" is defined as "any data processed for the purpose of the conveyance of a communication on an electronic communications network or for the billing in respect of that communication". "Public communications provider" is defined as "a provider of a public electronic communications network or a public electronic communications service".

Regulation 9 requires providers of public electronic communications services to provide subscribers with non-itemised bills on request and requires OFCOM to have regard to certain matters when exercising their functions under Chapter 1 of Part 2 of the Communications Act 2003.

Regulation 10 requires a provider of a public electronic communications service to provide users of the service with a means of preventing the presentation of calling line identification on a call-by-call basis, and to provide subscribers to the service with a means of preventing the presentation of such identification on a per-line basis. This regulation is subject to regulations 15 and 16. Regulation 11 requires the provider of a public electronic communications service to provide subscribers to that service with certain facilities where facilities enabling the presentation of connected line identification or calling line identification are available.

Regulation 12 requires a public electronic communications service provider to provide certain information to the public for the purposes of regulations 10 and 11, and regulation 13 requires communications providers (the term "communications provider" has the meaning given by section 405 of the Communications Act 2003) to co-operate with reasonable requests made by providers of public electronic communications services for the purposes of those regulations.

Regulation 14 imposes certain restrictions on the processing of location data, which is defined as "any data processed in an electronic communications network indicating the geographical position of the terminal equipment of a user of a public electronic communications service, including data relating to the latitude, longitude or altitude of the terminal equipment; the direction of travel of the user; or the time the location information was recorded."

Regulation 15 makes provision in relation to the tracing of malicious or nuisance calls and regulation 16 makes provision in relation to emergency calls, which are defined in regulation 16(1) as calls to the national emergency number 999 or the European emergency call number 112.

Regulation 17 requires the provider of an electronic communications service to a subscriber to stop, on request, the automatic forwarding of calls to that subscriber's line and also requires other communications providers to comply with reasonable requests made by the subscriber's provider to assist in the prevention of that forwarding.

Regulation 18 applies to directories of subscribers, and sets out requirements that must be satisfied where data relating to subscribers is included in such directories. It also gives subscribers the right to verify, correct or withdraw their data in directories.

Regulation 19 provides that a person may not transmit communications comprising recorded matter for direct marketing purposes by an automated calling system unless the line called is that of a subscriber who has notified the caller that he consents to such communications being made.

Regulations 20, 21 and 22 set out the circumstances in which persons may transmit, or instigate the transmission of, unsolicited communications for the purposes of direct marketing by means of facsimile machine, make unsolicited calls for those purposes, or transmit unsolicited communications by means of electronic mail for those purposes. Regulation 22 (electronic mail) applies only to transmissions to individual subscribers (the term "individual" means "a living individual" and includes "an unincorporated body of such individuals").

Regulation 23 prohibits the sending of communications by means of electronic mail for the purposes of direct marketing where the identity of the person on whose behalf the communication is made has been disguised or concealed or an address to which requests for such communications to cease may be sent has not been provided.

Regulation 24 sets out certain information that must be provided for the purposes of regulations 19, 20 and 21.

Regulation 25 imposes a duty on OFCOM, for the purposes of regulation 20, to maintain and keep up-to-date a register of numbers allocated to subscribers who do not wish to receive unsolicited communications by means of facsimile machine for the purposes of direct marketing. Regulation 26 imposes a similar obligation for the purposes of regulation 21 in respect of individual subscribers who do not wish to receive calls for the purposes of direct marketing.

Regulation 27 provides that terms in certain contracts which are inconsistent with these Regulations shall be void.

Regulation 28 exempts communications providers from the requirements of these Regulations where exemption is required for the purpose of safeguarding national security and further provides that a certificate signed by a Minister of the Crown to the effect that exemption from a requirement is necessary for the purpose of safeguarding national security shall be conclusive evidence of that fact. It also provides for certain questions relating to such certificates to be determined by the Information Tribunal referred to in section 6 of the Data Protection Act 1998.

Regulation 29 provides that a communications provider shall not be required by these Regulations to do, or refrain from doing, anything if complying with the requirement in question would be inconsistent with a requirement imposed by or under an enactment or by a court order, or if exemption from the requirement is necessary in connection with legal proceedings, for the purposes of obtaining legal advice or is otherwise necessary to establish, exercise or defend legal rights.

Regulation 30 allows a claim for damages to be brought in respect of contraventions of the Regulations.

Regulations 31 and 32 make provision in connection with the enforcement of the Regulations by the Information Commissioner (who is the Commissioner appointed under section 6 of the Data Protection Act 1998).

Regulation 33 imposes a duty on OFCOM to comply with any reasonable request made by the Commissioner for advice on technical matters relating to electronic communications.

Regulation 34 amends the Telecommunications (Lawful Business Practice) (Interception of Communications) Regulations 2000 and regulation 35 amends the Electronic Communications (Universal Service) Order 2003.

Regulation 36 provides for the transitional provisions in Schedule 2 to have effect.

A transposition note setting out how the main elements of the Directive are transposed into law and a regulatory impact assessment have been placed in the libraries of both Houses of Parliament. Copies are also available from the Department of Trade and Industry, Bay 202, 151 Buckingham Palace Road, London SW1W 9SS and can also be found on www.dti.gov.uk.

Appendix 8 – Guidance to the Privacy and Electronic Communications (EC Directive) Regulations 2003

This guidance is copyright of the Information Commissioner and subject to change. Part 2 of the guidance related more to telecoms and traffic data matters and should also be considered. All guidance is at www.informationcommissioner.gov.uk

Part 1: Marketing by Electronic Means

Introduction – General Questions

Do these Regulations apply to all marketing?

They apply to the sending of direct marketing messages by electronic means such as by telephone, fax, email, text message and picture (including video) message and by use of an automated calling system. The Regulations are designed to be more "technology neutral" than the Telecommunications (Data Protection and Privacy) Regulations 1999 (the "1999 Regulations") and thus to cover any new developments there may be in electronic communications.

What is the definition of direct marketing?

Section 11 of the Data Protection Act 1998 ("DPA") refers to direct marketing as "the communication (by whatever means) of any advertising or marketing material which is directed to particular individuals".

The Commissioner regards the term "direct marketing" as covering a wide range of activities which will apply not just to the offer for sale of goods or services, but also to the promotion of an organisation's aims and ideals. This would include a charity or a political party making an appeal for funds or support and, for example, an organisation whose campaign is designed to encourage individuals to write to their MP on a particular matter or to attend a public meeting or rally.

Which law should marketers comply with – these Regulations or the Data Protection Act?

They may need to comply with both.

When sending direct marketing by electronic means they must comply with the Regulations. If they are processing personal data (i.e., if they know the name of the person who will receive their message) they must also comply with DPA. In fact, Regulation 4 reminds marketers that they must remember their obligations under DPA (if applicable) as well as their obligations under these Regulations. For more information about DPA obligations, refer to our leaflet "Be Open" which is available from our_office or by clicking on http://www.dataprotection.gov.uk/dpr/dpdoc1.nsf and accessing our "Information Padlock/Signpost" page. (See also http://www.dataprotection.gov.uk/dpr/dpdoc.nsf, Data Protection Act 1998: Legal Guidance, paragraph 4.3).

The important point to note is that marketers do not need to know individuals' names in order to conduct a direct marketing exercise. For example, they may only have a list of telephone numbers to call with marketing messages. If marketers only hold telephone numbers and don't know the name of the person who can be reached on that telephone number, DPA does not apply. However, they must comply with these Regulations when they make those marketing calls. Once they know the name of the person who can be reached on that telephone number, they must also comply with their obligations under DPA.

How do the defined terms apply to marketing?

The Regulations refer to "person", "caller", "subscriber", "individual subscriber", "corporate subscriber" among other defined terms. We may be issuing more formal legal guidance at a later date covering all the defined terms in the Regulations but briefly:

When the Regs say ...

"person" – this means a legal person, e.g. a business, a charity, or a natural person, i.e. a living individual.

"caller" – this means the instigator of a call. This is usually a legal person. The call would not be made or the fax/email/text/picture message would not be sent unless this caller paid for it to be made or sent.

"subscriber" – this means the person that pays the bill for the use of the line (that is, the person legally responsible for the charges incurred).

"individual subscriber" – this means a residential subscriber, a sole trader or a non-limitedliability partnership in England, Wales and N. Ireland.

"corporate subscriber" – this includes corporate bodies such as a limited company in the UK, a limited liability partnership in England, Wales and N. Ireland or any partnership in Scotland. It also includes schools, government departments and agencies, hospitals and other public bodies e.g. the Information Commissioner's office.

What is the difference between a "solicited marketing message" and an "unsolicited marketing message that you consent to receiving"?

Put simply, a "solicited message" is one that you have actively invited. An "unsolicited marketing message that you consent to receiving" is one that you have not specifically invited but you have positively indicated that you do not mind receiving it. This is not the same as failing to object to receiving a message when you are given the opportunity to object.

By analogy, it is the difference between asking someone to buy you a drink and that person asking you if they may buy you a drink to which you answer "Yes". The outcome may be the same in both scenarios-you receive a drink. However, in the first scenario you have invited the drink whereas, in the second scenario, you haven't objected to someone buying you a drink but you didn't invite them to make the offer. To extend the analogy, when a person does not say "No" to a drink that is offered, it is not the same as saying "Yes". They may simply be ignoring the offer which they are entitled to do if it doesn't interest them.

Thus, if you call a travel agency and ask them to look into the cost of flights to Prague at New Year, you are soliciting a call back from that travel agency with a range of quotes for that trip. The travel agency could make further marketing calls to you about other flights to other destinations at a later date which **they** think might interest you. These would be unsolicited calls. For good practice, the travel agency should ask you first whether you agree to receive such calls from them. However, they should not, in any event, make such calls to you if you are a TPS registered subscriber unless you have told them that you do not mind receiving such calls.

Does consent mean ticking a box?

It is true that you need to have a positive indication of consent under these Regulations but it is not true that this must be obtained by means of ticking a box.

Recital 17 of the Directive on which these Regulations are based (2002/58/EC) gives the ticking of a box on an internet site as an example of an "appropriate method" for giving consent but it is only an example. It is not the only method by which consent can be obtained.

Directive 95/46/EC (the main Data Protection Directive on which the UK Data Protection Act is based) defines "the data subject's consent" as

> "any freely given specific and informed indication of his wishes by which the data subject signifies his agreement to personal data relating to him being processed"

In our view, therefore, there must be some form of communication whereby the individual knowingly indicates consent. This may involve clicking an icon, sending an email or subscribing to a service. The crucial consideration is that the individual must fully understand that by the action in question they will be signifying consent.

I'm confused about the terms "opt-in" and "opt-out". What do they mean?

We are concerned that the terms "opt-in" and "opt-out" can be misunderstood. They are commonly taken to refer to the use of tick-boxes. In this context, "opt-in" refers to a box that you tick to indicate agreement and "opt-out" refers to a box that you tick to indicate objection. Marketers have traditionally favoured the latter, i.e., where the default (an unticked "opt-out" box) indicates a failure to register an objection. The fact that someone has had an opportunity to object which they have not taken only means that they have not objected. It does not mean that they have consented.

By itself, the failure to register an objection will be unlikely to constitute valid consent. However, in context, a failure to indicate objection may be part of the mechanism whereby a person indicates consent. For example, if you receive a clear and prominent message along the following lines, the fact that a suitably prominent opt-out box has not been ticked may help establish that consent has been given: e.g. "By submitting this registration form, you will be indicating your consent to receiving email marketing messages from us unless you have indicated an objection to receiving such messages by ticking the above box".

> In summary, the precise mechanisms by which valid informed consent is obtained may vary. The crucial consideration is that individuals must fully appreciate that they are consenting and must fully appreciate what they are consenting to.

Does the phrase "for the time being" mean consent only lasts a finite period of time?

Many of the Regulations refer to consent being given "for the time being". We do not interpret the phrase "for the time being" as meaning that consent must inevitably lapse after a certain period. Consent, once given, will not inevitably last indefinitely. However, it will remain valid until there is good reason to consider it is no longer valid, for example, where it has been specifically withdrawn or it is otherwise clear that the recipient no longer wishes to receive such messages. The initial consent will remain valid where there are good grounds for believing that the recipient remains happy to receive the marketing communications in question, for example, where the recipient has responded positively (i.e., other than to object) to previous, reasonably recent marketing emails.

The phrase "for the time being" is also used in the Regulations in respect of notifications of objection. For example, Regulation 21(1)(a) (see Telephone marketing) provides that unsolicited direct marketing calls should not be made where the subscriber has notified that such calls should not be made "for the time being". We do not believe that this means the objection will lapse automatically. The objection will remain valid until there is good reason to ignore it, for example, where the individual has changed their mind and indicated that they now consent to receiving such calls.

How can I stop unsolicited electronic marketing messages?

> We recognise that many people are concerned about confirming their email address or mobile phone number where they make any response to such messages (even where that response is exercising their legal right to opt-out). Most spam email originates from outside the UK and should never be replied to unless you are familiar with the company and trust that company. For more information about this please read our Subscribers' FAQ's in the section on Electronic Mail.

If you receive a marketing message that you don't want from an identifiable UK source, the first thing to do is contact the company concerned and tell them to stop sending you further messages. You should be able to identify them because they are legally obliged to provide you with their contact details and not conceal their identity. Most responsible marketers will comply with an opt-out request. In most circumstances they are legally obliged to comply with an opt out request. The only circumstance where they are not legally obliged to comply with an opt-out request is when they are marketing corporate subscribers by electronic mail without processing personal data (see Electronic Mail for more information). Ensure you provide them with details of the number or email address that they contacted you on. This enables them to add those details to their suppression list which will ensure that they keep a record of your objection.

There are two statutory "do not call" lists. One is for telephone numbers (Telephone Preference Service). The other is for fax numbers (Fax Preference Service).

For more information about the Telephone Preference Service contact: online http://www.tpsonline.org.uk/, by telephone 0845 070 0707, by fax 0845 070 0706, in writing: The Telephone Preference Service DMA House 70 Margaret Street London W1M 8SS For more information about the Fax Preference Service contact: online http://www.fpsonline.org.uk by telephone 0845 070 0702 by fax 0845 070 0705 in writing: The Fax Preference Service DMA House 70 Margaret Street London W1M 8SS

There are a number of industry initiatives to facilitate opt-outs from other media such as the Mailing Preference Service and the Email Preference Service. Although these lists do not have a statutory basis, the Information Commissioner welcomes their widespread use by responsible marketers. For more information contact Direct Marketing Association DMA House 70 Margaret Street London W1M 8SS online http://www.dma.org.uk by telephone: 020 7291 3300.

How do I make a complaint about an unsolicited electronic marketing message?

For more information about making a complaint to the Information Commissioner, please refer to each set of Subscribers' FAQs in this guidance.

Complaints about automated calls

Complaints about telesales calls

Complaints about marketing faxes

Complaints about electronic mail

AUTOMATED CALLING SYSTEMS (Regulations 19 & 24)

How do the Regulations apply to automated calling systems?

The Regulations restate the requirement of the 1999 Regulations in respect of marketing by automated calling systems.

However, this Regulation clarifies the definition of "automated calling system". It refers to a system which is "capable of automatically initiating a sequence of calls to more than one destination in accordance with instructions stored in that system" and which transmits "sounds which are not live speech for reception by persons at some or all of the destinations so called" (Regulation 19(4) refers).

It is important to note that this does not cover marketing by text/picture/video message, by fax or by email, nor does it cover the technology used by some call centres to dial target numbers automatically in order to facilitate live telephone conversations, so called "power dialling". Text/picture/video messages, faxes, live telephone calls and emails are covered elsewhere in the Regulations and elsewhere in this guidance.

This is what the law requires:

1.   Marketing material cannot be transmitted by such a system without the **prior consent** of any subscriber. This is where the subscriber has told the caller that he/she she consents, for the time being, to such communications being sent on that line, by or at the instigation of the caller (Regulation 19(1) and (2) refer)

2.   A subscriber must not permit their line to be used to contravene Regulations 19. (Regulation 19(3) refers)

3.   All marketing messages sent by this method of communication must include the identity of the caller and an address or freephone number at which the caller can be contacted. (Regulation 24(1)(a) refers)

The mischief that Regulation 19 seeks to address is where a subscriber receives a marketing call which is a recorded message and where there is no opportunity to speak to a "live" person. In our view, even if an opportunity is provided at some point in the message, e.g. "to speak to a live operator, press 1", such a call would still be covered by the prior consent rule because not all telephones are "touch tone" phones. Such calls are particularly intrusive and can be unsettling for the recipient. We will therefore be taking a firm line on this point.

SUBSCRIBERS' FAQs

I keep getting calls where, when I pick up the phone, there is only silence. I put down the phone then it happens again. This is extremely distressing. The caller withholds their number and my service provider won't tell me who the caller is because they think it would breach the Data Protection Act. Does this Regulation or any other of the Regulations apply? What can I do?

We understand how distressing so-called "silent calls" can be. The natural assumption is that the call is made with malicious intent. Service providers have specific procedures for dealing with malicious calls. However, it is likely that, in this case, your service provider is not pursuing the matter as a malicious call because they have identified that the caller is a business using technology which dials target numbers automatically to facilitate a "live" conversation, so-called "power diallers". Sometimes, when power diallers are used, there can be a delay in the process of connecting the call centre worker to the target number which results in a disturbing silence. Although such systems can give the organisation certain efficiency savings, it can also result in silent calls that are subsequently terminated at times when the number of answered calls exceeds the number of available operators. Even though they are not a "malicious" calls, they are certainly a nuisance. As disturbing as silent calls can be, no marketing material is being transmitted and therefore the marketing rules in these Regulations do not apply.

There are three further points worth making. Firstly, Regulation 15 makes it clear that there is nothing in the Regulations to prevent service providers from telling a person "with a legitimate interest" the identity of whoever is making calls that are malicious or cause a nuisance. In our view, the recipient of repeated nuisance calls such as this clearly has a legitimate interest in knowing who made them.

Secondly, the Data Protection Act only applies to individuals and not to businesses. There is nothing in the Data Protection Act which prevents the service provider from disclosing a business name to you although we note that many service providers do not, as a policy decision, provide this information. They have concerns about individuals taking the law into their own hands and have therefore have decided, as a matter of policy, only to disclose caller information to the police.

If the call is made with malicious intent by an individual, the Data Protection Act permits disclosures which are necessary for the prevention or detection of crime. If you believe you are receiving calls made with malicious intent, speak to your service provider who will, if necessary, involve the appropriate law enforcement authorities.

Finally, persistent misuse of communications networks is subject to regulation by Oftel (who will be absorbed by OFCOM at the end of 2003) under the Communications Act 2003. This Act gives that regulator powers to take action against network use which causes avoidable nuisance, annoyance or anxiety. For more information contact Oftel at:

OFTEL
50 Ludgate Hill
London
EC4M 7JJ
Tel: 020 7634 8700
Fax: 020 7634 8845
or visit their website: http://www.oftel.gov.uk/publications/consumer/2003/misusestat0803.htm.

How do I stop unsolicited automated calls?

Contact the marketer and tell them to stop. They are legally obliged to provide you with their contact details in their marketing message. They are also legally obliged to stop calling you when you ask them to. Ensure you provide them with details of the number that they contacted you on. This enables them to add those details to their suppression list which will ensure that they keep a record of your objection. Keep a record of your request.

How do I make a complaint about unsolicited automated calls?

Contact our Information Line (01625) 545745 and ask for an Unsolicited Calls complaints form.

Am I entitled to compensation?

If you can demonstrate to a Court that the caller has breached these Regulations and that by doing so, you have been caused quantifiable damage, you may be entitled to compensation under Regulation 30 of these Regulations. Please note that if a caller can demonstrate to a Court that they did what could reasonably be required of them to comply with the Regulations, this would be a defence against any compensation claim.

We have produced two leaflets "Claiming Compensation" (Leaflet 7) and "Taking a Case to Court" (Leaflet 8) for those wishing to take action for compensation under Section 13 of DPA. Much of the information also applies to those who wish to seek compensation under Regulation 30 of these Regulations. These leaflets are available from our office.

MARKETERS' FAQs

A subscriber is not registered with TPS and has not contacted us to tell us that they object to us marketing them by telephone, can we call them with a pre-recorded marketing message?

No. You would need their prior consent to use this particular medium for marketing.

This Regulation does not spell out our obligation to respect an opt-out request from a subscriber? Does this mean we don't have to comply with such requests?

In our view, if you can only send marketing by automated calling systems to any subscriber where that subscriber has given their consent to such a call, implicit in this is the option for consent to be withdrawn at a later stage. We would cite the inclusion of the phrase "for_the_time_being " (Regulation 19(2)) in support of our view. We are likely to take enforcement action against those companies within UK jurisdiction who persistently fail to comply with opt-out requests from subscribers.

TELEPHONE MARKETING (Regulations 21 and 24)

How do the Regulations apply to telephone marketing?

The Regulations restate the 1999 Regulations with respect to marketing by telephone with one significant change. With effect from May 2004, corporate subscribers will be allowed to register their numbers on the Telephone Preference Service (TPS). At present, only residential subscribers, sole traders and unincorporated partnerships can register their numbers on TPS. Registration is free of charge.

This is what the law requires:

1.   If a subscriber has told you to stop making telesales calls to their number, you must comply with that request. (Regulation 21(1)(a) refers)

2.   You cannot make or instigate the making of unsolicited telesales calls to any number listed on the TPS register. (Regulation 21(1)(b) refers)

3.   TPS registration takes 28 days to come into force. Calls can be made to a number during the registration period unless an opt-out request has also been made to the caller (see 1. above). (Regulation 21(3) refers)

4.   You can make or instigate the making of unsolicited telesales calls to a TPS registered subscriber where that subscriber has notified you that, for the time being, they do not object to receiving such calls on that TPS registered number. (Regulation 21(4) refers)

5.   A subscriber can withdraw that over-riding consent at any time, in which case, further telesales calls must not be made to that number. (Regulation 21(5) refers)

6.   You must identify yourself when making a telesales call. If asked, you must provide a valid business address or freephone telephone number at which you can be contacted. When using a subcontractor, the subcontractor's call centre staff must identify the instigator of the call (i.e. the organisation on whose behalf they are making the call). (Regulation 24(1)(b) refers)

7.   Subscribers must not let their lines be used to contravene Regulation 21. (Regulation 21(2) refers).

What is the TPS?

The Telephone Preference Service list is a statutory list of telephone numbers where the subscriber to that number has registered a general objection to receiving unsolicited marketing faxes on that number.

Does TPS registration apply to mobile numbers?

Any mobile number can be registered on TPS to block unwanted "live" calls. Those who wish to market by text/picture/video message do not need to screen against TPS but they need to obtain prior consent before sending such messages. The rules on marketing by text/picture/video message are covered in the Electronic Mail section of this guidance.

Subscribers' FAQs

I registered my number on TPS before these Regulations came into force, do I have to register again?

No, your registration prior to 11 December 2003 is still valid

I'm ex-directory. Do I need to register on TPS if I want to stop unsolicited telesales calls?

Yes. Going ex-directory will not prevent unsolicited direct marketing calls. Many marketers use technology to generate telephone numbers at random, perhaps for a target postcode area. As a consequence, ex-directory numbers may be generated. Once a list of numbers is generated, marketers must ensure that this list is screened against TPS.

I asked a marketer not to call me before these Regulations came into force, do I need to write to them again?

No, your opt-out request made prior to 11 December 2003 is still valid.

Do I have to make my opt-out request in writing?

The Regulations do not state that you have to make an opt-out request in writing. However, if you were making a complaint to the Commissioner or seeking to enforce your rights yourself through the Courts, you would need to be able to demonstrate that you had made that request. A diary record of who you spoke to and when you spoke to them may not be sufficient where the caller contradicts your version of events, particularly where we were seeking to rely on your evidence in enforcement action or you were seeking to rely on it in a compensation action. The most practical way to overcome this potential problem is to make all opt-out requests in writing, preferably obtaining proof of posting when you do so.

I asked a company for a quote and now they won't stop calling me. Should I register on TPS to stop them calling me?

TPS registration may not prevent calls from any organisation whose calls you have previously invited and which has assumed that you are happy to receive calls from them. You should write directly to the company and ask them to stop calling you. You should remember to tell them which number(s) they should no longer call. They must comply with this request.

How do the Regulations apply to corporate registration on TPS?

The Regulations will be amended in May 2004 to give effect to corporate registration on TPS. Until we see the final details of the amendment we will not be able to provide guidance on this point. However, we will be providing further guidance on the amended Regulations once they have been laid before Parliament but before they come into force.

How do I stop unsolicited telesales calls?

Ask the marketer for their contact details. They are legally obliged to provide you with their contact details, if you ask them. This should be either an address or a freephone number. Next, contact them at that address or on that freephone number and tell them to stop. They are also legally obliged to stop making further calls to you if you ask them to. Ensure you provide them with details of the number that they contacted you on. This enables them to add those details to their suppression list which will ensure that they keep a record of your objection. Keep a record of your request.

If you have not done so already, you should also register your number on TPS.

How do I make a complaint about unsolicited telesales calls?

If you are TPS registered, you should, in the first instance, contact the TPS. The TPS will check that your number is registered accurately and then contact the marketer to advise them of your complaint. Most responsible marketers will take remedial action when the TPS contacts them about a complaint. The TPS also sends us a detailed statistical record of the complaints they have received. We use this record to assist us in identifying which companies are persistently failing to comply with their obligations.

If you want to make a complaint directly to the Information Commissioner, contact our Information Line (01625) 545745 and ask for an Unsolicited Calls complaints form.

Am I entitled to compensation?

If you can demonstrate to a Court that the caller has breached these Regulations and that by doing so, you have been caused quantifiable damage, you may be entitled to compensation under Regulation 30 of these Regulations. Please note that if a caller can demonstrate to a Court that they did what could reasonably be required of them to comply with the Regulations, this would be a defence against any compensation claim.

We have produced two leaflets "Claiming Compensation" (Leaflet 7) and "Taking a Case to Court" (Leaflet 8) for those wishing to take action for compensation under Section 13 of DPA. Much of the information also applies to those who wish to seek compensation under Regulation 30 of these Regulations. These leaflets are available from our office.

Marketers' FAQs

We pay a subcontractor to make the calls for us. Isn't it their responsibility to make sure we don't break the rules?

No, under the Regulations it's your responsibility as the instigator of the call. They may have a contractual obligation to make sure **you** don't break the rules but if they let you down, you are responsible under the Regulations as the person who instigated the call. If we were to take enforcement action, we would usually take it against **you** and not your subcontractor. You should check you have appropriate contracts in place to guard against such failures. If your subcontractor's failures cause you to break the rules, seek independent legal advice about an action for breach of contract and find another subcontractor who will ensure you don't break the rules.

It would be possible for the Commissioner to take action against subcontractors who allow their lines to be used in contravention of the Regulations (Regulation 21(2) refers) but this is more likely to apply where the subcontractor and their clients work in concert to disregard the Regulations. It is unlikely that this would apply, for example, to telemarketing activities conducted by individuals working at home on commission on behalf of a company using telephone lists provided by that company. This is because that individual could not be expected to know the full extent of the legal obligations by which that company is bound under these Regulations.

Do the rules mean that our call centre staff have to give out their names?

No. The rules mean that they have to give out the name of the company whose products or services they are promoting. If asked, they must also provide a valid address or freephone number at which that company can be contacted with an opt-out request.

If the subcontractor is making the calls on our behalf, do they have to provide their identity or ours?

They must provide your identity because you have instigated the call i.e., the call would not be made unless you paid for it to be made. If asked, your sub-contractor or his call centre staff must provide a valid address or freephone number at which you can be contacted with an opt-out request.

We delete numbers from our database whenever we get an opt-out request. Are we doing enough?

No. You must **suppress** details upon receipt of an opt-out request not delete them. If you delete them, you have no record to show that you should not call that number. You or your subcontractor might collect it again from a list broker. The only way you can legally call that number again is if the subscriber tells you directly that they have changed their mind and are now happy to hear from you again.

If you use subcontractors, you must make sure that they don't call numbers on your suppression list as well as ensuring that they don't call numbers registered on TPS.

Several members of a household use the same telephone number and may make different choices about who they want to hear from. How does the law apply?

If the subscriber to that phone line (i.e. the person who pays the bill) has registered the number on TPS, this indicates a general objection to receiving any unsolicited marketing calls on that number. This objection applies to the whole household but does not apply to calls which are "solicited".

Individual members of the household may invite, that is, **solicit**, marketing calls from different companies but those calls can only be made to the individual who has issued the invitation, not to other members of the household. This invitation can be revoked at any time.

Individual members of the household may also have existing relationships with a number of companies which pre-date TPS registration. Unsolicited marketing calls from those companies may be a feature of that relationship. If those individual members of the household wish to prevent marketing calls from any of those companies, they must each contact the company concerned directly to advise them that they no longer wish to receive marketing calls from them.

We have bought/rented a list of numbers where the subscribers have consented to receiving unsolicited marketing calls from third parties, some of the numbers are TPS registered, can we call them?

As outlined above, TPS registration indicates a general objection to receiving unsolicited marketing calls. The TPS list is a statutory list. Subscribers can give consent to receiving unsolicited marketing calls which over-rides TPS registration but this is only valid where that over-riding consent is given to the specific caller in question.

If you obtain a list of numbers where you are assured that the subscribers consent to receiving unsolicited marketing calls, you should ensure that the list is screened against TPS and your own suppression list before making any telesales calls. Such lists have no statutory basis and do not over-ride registration on TPS.

FAX MARKETING (Regulations 20 and 24)

How do the Regulations apply to fax marketing?

The Regulations duplicate the 1999 Regulations with respect to marketing by fax.

However, as a reminder this is what the law requires:

1. You cannot send or instigate the sending of an unsolicited marketing fax to the line of an individual_subscriber without that individual subscriber's prior consent. (Regulation 20(1)(a) refers)

2. You cannot send or instigate the sending of an unsolicited marketing fax to the line of a corporate_subscriber where that subscriber has asked you not to fax on that line. (Regulation 20(1)(b) refers)

3. You cannot send or instigate the sending of an unsolicited marketing fax to any number listed on the FPS register. (Regulation 20(1)(c) refers)

4. FPS registration takes 28 days to come into force. Faxes can be sent to a subscriber's number during the registration period unless an opt-out request has also been made to the caller (see 2 above). (Regulation 20(4) refers). If the subscriber is an individual subscriber, you cannot do so unless you have their prior consent (see 1 above).

5. You can send unsolicited marketing faxes to an FPS registered subscriber where the subscriber has notified you that, for the time being, they do not object to receiving such calls. (Regulation 20(5) refers)

6. A subscriber can withdraw that over-riding consent at any time, in which case, further marketing faxes must not be sent to that number. (Regulation 20(6) refers)

7. You must provide your identity (i.e., the name of the business being promoted) and a valid business address or freephone telephone number at which you can be contacted on each fax you send. (Regulation 24(1)(a) refers)

8. A subscriber must not allow their line to be used to contravene Regulation 20. (Regulation 20(3) refers).

What is the FPS?

The Fax Preference Service list is a statutory list of telephone numbers where the subscriber to that number has registered a general objection to receiving unsolicited marketing faxes on that number.

Subscribers' FAQs

Can individual subscribers register their number(s) on FPS?

Yes, they can. We recommend that they do so for extra protection, particularly if they are sole traders or unincorporated partnerships whose contact details may be available in business directories.

I registered my number on FPS before these Regulations came into force, do I have to register again?

No, your registration prior to 11 December 2003 is still valid.

I asked a marketer not to call me before these Regulations came into force, do I need to write to them again?

No, your request made prior to 11 December 2003 is still valid.

I'm ex-directory. Do I need to register on FPS if I want to stop unsolicited marketing faxes?

Yes. Going ex-directory will not prevent unsolicited marketing faxes. Many marketers use technology to generate fax numbers at random, perhaps for a target postcode area. As a consequence, ex-directory numbers may be generated. Once a list of numbers is generated, the marketer must use his best endeavours to ensure that numbers belonging to individual subscribers are removed. The list must also be screened against FPS.

I'm registered with FPS, I've written to the caller, I've complained to ICO and I am STILL getting unsolicited faxes? Can nothing be done to stop them?

Unsolicited marketing faxes are the subject of the most complaints we have received to date. We share your frustration. We have taken enforcement action against those companies who were the subject of the most complaints and continue to monitor the level of complaints we receive about other companies.

However, in the course of recent enforcement action we have identified some technical reasons which may explain why you might still be receiving marketing faxes despite registering your number on FPS.

Some telephony packages, especially those used by small businesses, are more sophisticated than we had appreciated. You may have an extra number or a bundle of numbers attached to your main number(s) that you were not previously aware of. These extra numbers are in place to facilitate other features of your telephony package e.g. "call sign" feature, ADSL. A call made to one of these extra numbers may be automatically diverted to a line that you use. If a fax machine is plugged into a line you use and the diverted call is an attempt to send a fax, you will receive a fax. If this applies to you, you should register all your numbers on FPS, even if you don't have a fax machine attached to them. A fax received on an FPS registered line via a divert from a non-FPS registered number is not a breach of the Regulations unless the subscriber to that non-FPS registered number is an individual subscriber.

You should be able to identify these extra numbers on your telephone bill or by checking with your service provider.

I am FPS registered and I have received an unsolicited fax asking me if I want to stop receiving further unsolicited faxes? If I don't want to receive further faxes I have to either fax back on a premium rate line or call a national rate number. Is this legal?

If you are FPS registered and/or an individual subscriber, it is likely that this fax has been sent to you in breach of the 1999 Regulations. If sent after 11 December 2003, it is likely that it also breaches these Regulations.

Although the premium rate line may be the most prominent contact detail, the sender is legally obliged to provide a valid address or freephone number. This is usually found in the small print at the bottom of the fax. Contact the caller and ask them not to fax you again. They are legally obliged to comply with this request. Ensure you tell them what your number is so they can add it to their suppression list which will ensure that they keep a record of your objection. Keep a record of your request and then write to the FPS to report what has happened. If they persist, you should contact the Information Commissioner (see Complaints about marketing faxes below).

You may also want to contact ICSTIS on 0800 500 212 (9:00am–4:00pm, Monday to Friday) or visit their website http://www.icstis.org.uk/. ICSTIS regulate the use of premium rate lines and have a strict Code of Practice which states what companies can and cannot do with premium rate lines. They also have the power to suspend premium rate lines and, if appropriate, impose large fines for a breach of their Code of Practice.

How do I stop unsolicited faxes?

There should be an address or freephone number on the fax (it may be in very small print so check carefully). Contact the marketer at that address or on that freephone number and tell them to stop. They are also legally obliged to stop making further calls to you if you ask them to. Ensure you provide them with details of the number that they contacted you on. This enables them to add those details to their suppression list which will ensure that they keep a record of your objection. Keep a record of your request.

If you have not done so already, you should also register your number on FPS.

How do I make a complaint about unsolicited faxes?

If you are FPS registered, you should, in the first instance, contact the FPS. The FPS will check your fax number is registered accurately and then contact the marketer to advise them of your complaint. Most responsible marketers will take remedial action when the FPS contacts them about a complaint. The FPS also sends us a detailed statistical record of the complaints they have received. We use this record to assist us in identifying which companies are persistently failing to comply with their obligations.

If you want to make a complaint directly to the Information Commissioner, contact our Information Line (01625) 545745 and ask for an Unsolicited Faxes complaints form.

Am I entitled to compensation?

If you can demonstrate to a Court that the caller has breached these Regulations and that by doing so, you have been caused quantifiable damage, you may be entitled to compensation under Regulation 30 of these Regulations. Please note that if a caller can demonstrate to a Court that they did what could reasonably be required of them to comply with the Regulations, this would be a defence against any compensation claim.

We have produced two leaflets "Claiming Compensation" (Leaflet 7) and "Taking a Case to Court" (Leaflet 8) for those wishing to take action for compensation under Section 13 of DPA. Much of the information also applies to those who wish to seek compensation under Regulation 30 of these Regulations. These leaflets are available from our office.

I keep getting calls where, when I pick up the phone, there is only a fax signal. I put down the phone then it happens again. This is extremely irritating. The caller withholds their number and my service provider won't tell me who the caller is because they think it would breach the Data Protection Act. Does this Regulation or any other of the Regulations apply? What can I do?

As with "silent calls", no marketing material is being transmitted and therefore such attempts to send faxes are not caught by the marketing rules of these Regulations. If it is possible to attach a fax machine to your line, you should be able to find out whether it is someone trying to send a marketing fax or not. You are also advised to register that number on the FPS. You don't need to have a fax machine to register your number on FPS.

There are three further points worth making. Firstly, Regulation 15 makes it clear that there is nothing in the Regulations to prevent service providers from telling a person "with a legitimate interest" the identity of whoever is making calls that are malicious or cause a nuisance. In our view, the recipient of repeated nuisance calls such as this clearly has a legitimate interest in knowing who made them.

Secondly, the Data Protection Act only applies to individuals and not to businesses. There is nothing in the Data Protection Act which prevents the service provider from disclosing a business name to you although we note that many service providers do not, as a policy decision, provide this information. They have concerns about individuals taking the law into their own hands and have therefore have decided, as a matter of policy, only to disclose caller information to the police.

If the call is made with malicious intent by an individual, the Data Protection Act permits disclosures which are necessary for the prevention or detection of crime. If you believe you are receiving calls made with malicious intent, speak to your service provider who will, if necessary, involve the appropriate law enforcement authorities.

Finally, persistent misuse of communications networks is subject to regulation by Oftel (who will be absorbed by OFCOM at the end of 2003) under the Communications Act 2003. This Act gives that regulator powers to take action against network use which causes avoidable nuisance, annoyance or anxiety. For more information contact Oftel at:

OFTEL
50 Ludgate Hill
London
EC4M 7JJ
Tel: 020 7634 8700
Fax: 020 7634 8845
or visit their website: http://www.oftel.gov.uk/publications/consumer/2003/misusestat0803.htm.

Marketers' FAQs

We delete numbers from our database whenever we get an opt-out request. Are we doing enough?

No. You must **suppress** details upon receipt of an opt-out request not delete them. If you delete them, you have no record to show that you should not fax that number. You or your subcontractor might collect it again from a list broker. The only way you can legally fax that number again is if the subscriber tells you directly that they have changed their mind and are now happy to hear from you again.

If you use subcontractors, you must make sure they screen against your suppression list as well as ensuring they don't fax numbers registered on FPS.

We pay a subcontractor to send faxes for us. Isn't it their responsibility to make sure we don't break the rules?

No, under the Regulations it's your responsibility. They may have a contractual obligation to make sure you don't break the rules but if they let you down, you are responsible under the Regulations as the person who instigated the sending of a fax. If we were to take enforcement action, we would usually take it against **you** and not your subcontractor. You should check you have appropriate contracts in place to guard against such failures. If your subcontractor's failures cause you to break the rules, seek independent legal advice about an action for breach of contract and find another subcontractor who will ensure you don't break the rules.

It would be possible for the Commissioner to take action against subcontractors who allow their lines to be used in contravention of the Regulations (Regulation 20(3) refers) but this is more likely to apply where the subcontractor and their clients work in concert to disregard the Regulations. It is unlikely that this would apply, for example, to fax marketing activities conducted by individuals working at home on commission on behalf of a company using contact lists provided by that company. This is because that individual could not be expected to know the full extent of the legal obligations by which that company is bound under these Regulations.

If the subcontractor is sending faxes on our behalf, do they have to provide their identity or ours?

They must provide your identity **and** a valid address or freephone number at which you can be contacted with an opt-out request.

We have bought/rented a list of fax numbers where the subscribers have consented to receiving unsolicited marketing faxes from third parties, some of the numbers are FPS registered, can we fax them?

As outlined above, FPS registration indicates a general objection to receiving unsolicited marketing calls. The FPS list is a statutory list. Subscribers can give consent to receiving unsolicited marketing faxes which over-rides FPS registration but this is only valid where that over-riding consent is given to the specific caller in question.

If you obtain a list of numbers where you are assured that the subscribers consent to receiving unsolicited marketing faxes, you should ensure that the list is screened against the FPS list and your own suppression list before sending any marketing faxes. Such lists have no statutory basis and do not override registration on FPS.

ELECTRONIC MAIL (Regulations 22 and 23)

How do the Regulations apply to marketing by electronic mail?

The Regulations define electronic mail as "any text, voice, sound, or image message sent over a public electronic communications network which can be stored in the network or in the recipient's terminal equipment until it is collected by the recipient and includes messages sent using a short message service" (Regulation 2 "Interpretation" refers).

In other words, both e-mail and text/picture/video marketing messages are considered to be "electronic mail".

We consider that this rule also applies to voicemail/answerphone messages left by marketers making marketing calls that would otherwise be "live". Therefore, there are stricter obligations placed upon those marketers who make live calls but who wish to leave messages on a person's voicemail or answerphone.

For the avoidance of doubt, faxes are not considered to be "electronic mail". Fax marketing is covered elsewhere in the Regulations. Also, so-called "silent_calls " or calls where a fax or other electronic signal is transmitted are not covered by these Regulations. This is because no marketing material is transmitted during such calls.

This is what the law requires:

1. You cannot transmit, nor instigate the transmission of, unsolicited marketing material by electronic mail to an **individual subscriber** unless the recipient of the electronic mail has previously notified you, the sender, that he consents, for the time being, to receiving such communications. There is an exception to this rule which has been widely referred to as the "soft opt in" (Regulation 22(2) refers).

2. A subscriber shall not permit their line to be used to contravene Regulation 22(2). (Regulation 22(4) refers)

3. You cannot transmit, nor instigate the transmission of any marketing by electronic mail (whether solicited or unsolicited) to **any subscriber** (whether corporate or individual) where

    a. the identity of the sender has been disguised or concealed; or

    b. a valid address to which the recipient can send an opt-out request has not been provided. (Regulation 23 refers)

What is the difference between a "solicited marketing message" and an "unsolicited marketing message that you consent to receiving"?

Put simply, a "solicited message" is one that you have actively invited. We accept that this invitation can be given via a third party (see below Third Party Electronic Mailing Lists). An "unsolicited marketing message that you have opted into receiving" is one that you have not invited but you have indicated that you do not, for the time being, object to receiving it. If challenged, marketers would need to demonstrate that you have positively opted into receiving further information from them.

What would constitute a "valid address" for the purpose of Regulation 23?

In an on-line environment, this could be a valid email address. We do not consider that the provision of a premium rate, national rate or freephone number would satisfy this obligation.

Is there any difference between an individual subscriber and the recipient of marketing material by electronic mail (Regulation 22(2))?

Yes, there is a difference.

The Directive which these Regulations give effect to says that unsolicited marketing should not be sent by electronic mail to an individual subscriber unless the subscriber has given consent. However, this Regulation refers to the consent of the recipient. We consider that the practical interpretation of the meaning of "the recipient" is the intended recipient. Where a household member has an individual email address then the consent of that individual is required unless the soft opt-in criteria are satisfied. Where a household has a household email address (e.g. familyname@domainname.com) then the consent of someone who there is no reason to believe does not speak on behalf of the family is sufficient unless the soft opt-in criteria are satisfied.

What is "soft opt-in" (Regulation 22(3))?

This is what the law goes on to state:

You may send or instigate the sending of electronic mail for marketing purposes to an individual subscriber where

1.   you have obtained the contact details of the recipient in the course of a sale or negotiations for the sale of a product or service to that recipient;

2.   the direct marketing material you are sending is in respect of your similar products and services only; and

3.   the recipient has been given a simple means of refusing (free of charge except for the cost of transmission) the use of his contact details for marketing purposes at the time those details were initially collected and, where he did not refuse the use of those details, at the time of each subsequent communication.

In other words, if you satisfy these criteria, you do not need prior consent to send marketing by electronic mail to individual subscribers. If you cannot satisfy these criteria you cannot send marketing by electronic mail to individual subscribers without their prior consent.

How does the Information Commissioner interpret "in the course of a sale or negotiations for the sale of a product or service"?

A sale does not have to be completed for this criterion to apply. It may be difficult to establish where negotiations may begin. However, where a person has actively expressed an interest in purchasing a company's products and services and not opted out of further marketing of that product or service or similar products and services at the time their details were collected, the company can continue to market them by electronic mail unless and until that person opts out of receiving such messages at a later date.

For the avoidance of doubt, the Commissioner does not consider that "negotiations for the sale of a product or service" includes the use of cookie technology to identify a person's area of interest when they are browsing your website. Unless that person has expressly communicated their interest to you by, for example, asking for a quote, no "negotiations" can be said to have taken place for the purpose of these Regulations.

As another example, if you send an email to a national retailer asking them if they are going to open a branch in your town, you would expect a response of "yes" with details or "no" perhaps with details of their other stores in your area. This query does not, however, constitute part of a negotiation for the sale of a product or service. It does not constitute an invitation to the retailer to send you further information about their products or services. Nor does it indicate consent to receive further promotional emails from that retailer. The retailer could send you emails promoting their products and services if you a) expressly invited them to, b) consented to their suggestion that they send you pro-motional emails or c) did not object to the receipt of emails in the course of a sale or negotiations for a sale.

How does the ICO interpret "similar products and services"?

We are taking a purposive approach here. In our view, the intention of this section is to ensure that an individual does not receive promotional material about products and services that they would not rea-sonably expect to receive. For example, someone who has shopped on-line at a supermarket's website (and has not objected to receiving further email marketing from that supermarket) would expect at some point in the future to receive further emails promoting the diverse range of goods available at that supermarket.

Ultimately, if an individual feels that the company has gone beyond the boundaries of their reasonable expectation that individual can opt-out, something which most responsible marketers will be keen to avoid. For the time being, therefore, we will be focussing particular attention on failures to comply with opt-out requests. We will continue to monitor the extent to which marketers take the reasonable expectations of individual subscribers into consideration.

Marketers' FAQs

This Regulation does not spell out our obligation to respect an opt-out request from indi-vidual subscribers? Does this mean we don't have to comply with such requests?

In our view, if you can only send marketing by electronic mail to individual subscribers where they have provided prior consent, implicit in this is the option to withdraw that consent at a later stage. We would cite the inclusion of the phrase "for the time being" in support of our view. We will take enforcement action against those companies within UK jurisdiction who persistently fail to comply with opt-out requests from individual subscribers.

Text/picture/video messaging

Surely SMS marketing can't be subject to the same rules as conventional email – after all, the standard mobile phone screen can only hold 160 characters!

The practical limitations of standard mobile screens do not mean that marketers can ignore the rules. Information about the marketing you intend to do can be given before you send a marketing message or even before you collect the mobile number in question. For example, in an advert, or on a website where the recipient signs up for the service.

Assuming the recipient has clearly consented to the receipt of messages, each message will have to identify the sender and provide a valid suppression address. This may take as few as 18 characters (e.g. PJLtdPOBox97SK95AF). If, however, the sender is relying on the relaxation of the prior consent rule (i.e., soft opt-in), there is an additional obligation to provide a simple means of refusing further mar-keting with every message. This may well take 40 characters or more (e.g.PJLtdPOBox97SK95AF.2STOPMSGSTXT'STOP'TO (then add 5 digit short code)).

Do we have to screen against TPS if we are sending unsolicited marketing by text/pic-ture/video messages?

TPS registration indicates a general objection to receiving live marketing calls. Text/picture/video messages are defined as "electronic mail" under the Regulations and, as such, they should not be sent without the prior consent of the individual subscribers unless the "soft opt-in" criteria are satisfied. You are, therefore, not obliged to screen against TPS before so doing because you should already have established prior consent or satisfied the "soft opt-in" criteria.

However, you must ensure that you identify yourself in any text/picture/text messages that you send and provide a valid address to which opt-out requests can be sent. If you are sending the message on a soft opt-in basis, you are obliged to provide simple means of refusing further messages which is free of charge except for the cost of transmitting the refusal (see below Mailing Lists Compiled before

11 December 2003). For the avoidance of doubt, if you only supply a premium rate or national rate number in these circumstances you would not satisfy this obligation.

We did a marketing exercise by sending unsolicited text/picture/video messages before these Regulations came into force and only received a few opt-outs. Does this mean that we have consent to contact those other numbers because the subscribers didn't opt-out first time round?

No, it does not mean you have consent to send further messages in this way. Provided you obtained the details in accordance with existing privacy law and used them recently, you can use them again. However, you must provide an opportunity for an opt-out with each subsequent message that is free of charge to exercise, except for the cost of transmission. (See below Mailing Lists Compiled before 11 December 2003). For the avoidance of doubt, the use of premium or national rate lines for opt-out requests will not satisfy this requirement.

We will collect email address/mobile phone numbers as part of a competition, could this be considered as being "in the course of negotiations for the sale of a product and service"?

A great deal will depend on the context and on what you tell the person when you collect their details. Arguably, where a competition is part of an inducement to raise interest in a product or service, this constitutes part of the negotiations for a sale. However, where you are unclear about what you will do with a person's email address or mobile phone number when you collect those details or where this information is not readily accessible, you are less likely to be able to rely on the "soft opt-in". If you have collected a person's name with their email address and/or mobile phone number and you have not been clear about what you are going to do with that information, you may also be in breach of the First Data Principle. (See our leaflet "Be Open" which is available from our office or by clicking on http://www.dataprotection.gov.uk/dpr/dpdoc1.nsf and accessing our "Information Padlock/Signpost" page).

Mailing Lists Compiled before 11 December 2003

Can we still use our own electronic mail mailing list that we compiled before 11 December 2003?

We recognise that this new legislation imposes upon marketers a higher standard for data collection than they were obliged to follow before 11 December 2003. For the time being, we take that view that where your own mailing lists were compiled in accordance with privacy legislation in force before 11 December 2003 and have been used recently, you can continue to use them unless the intended recipient has already opted out. You are reminded that it is our view that privacy legislation in force before 11 December 2003 did not permit the sending of unsolicited text/picture/video messages without prior consent.

When using our existing lists after 11 December 2003, do we need to provide an opt-out opportunity or do we just have to provide a valid address for opt outs?

If your existing lists were compiled on a clear prior consent basis, you only need to provide a valid address with every message. In either case, you must always ensure that you do not conceal your identity.

However, if your existing lists were compiled in accordance with privacy legislation in force before 11 December but were not compiled on a clear prior consent basis, you must provide an opt-out opportunity with every message. This accords with the requirements of the "soft opt-in" criteria.

As best practice, companies may wish to provide an opportunity to opt-out in every message, even if they are not obliged to. This may alleviate any practical difficulties that may arise in using lists compiled both before and after 11 December 2003 for the same mailing exercise.

While we are prepared to take a pragmatic view on pre-existing lists for the time being, we will expect marketers to ensure that any opt-out requests received either before or after 11 December 2003 are acted upon promptly. Responding promptly to an opt-out request is not a new requirement and organisations should already have efficient systems in place to deal with such requests.

For the avoidance of doubt, contact details should be "suppressed" rather than deleted when an opt-out request is received. This should ensure that a person's opt-out request is recorded, retained and respected until such time as that person provides consent which over-rides their previous opt-out request. It is our view that over-riding consent would only be valid where it is provided to the sender directly from the person concerned.

Third Party Electronic Mailing Lists

Must any consent or invitation to market by electronic mail always be provided directly to the sender? If so, does this mean that we can never use bought-in/ rented lists after 11 December 2003?

Notwithstanding our view about over-riding consent (see previous point), there is nothing in the Regulations which expressly rules out the provision of consent via a third party. However, if you are buying or renting a list from a broker, you will need to seek assurances about the basis upon which the information was collected.

We are prepared to exercise some latitude in the use of mailing lists that were compiled before 11 December 2003 in accordance with existing privacy legislation. However, it is difficult to see how third party lists can be compiled and used legitimately after 11 December 2003 on any other basis than one where the individual subscriber expressly invites, i.e., solicits marketing by electronic mail. This is because unsolicited marketing can only be sent to an individual subscriber where he has "previously notified the sender that he consents for the time being to such communications being sent by, or at the instigation of, the sender." (Regulation 22(2) refers)

The following is a list of scenarios that may apply to your list. It is by no means exhaustive.

1. List of individual subscribers who have INVITED contact from third parties on a particular subject

    You can send marketing material by electronic mail to contacts on this list provided that

    a)   this person has not already sent an opt-out request to you

    b)   you do not conceal your identity when you contact them and

    c)   you ensure that you have provided a valid contact address for subsequent opt-out requests.

    Given individuals' increased caution over disclosure of their contact details to third parties for marketing purposes, you should seek assurances on the veracity of such a list, i.e. are these genuine invitations for contact from anyone on a particular subject as opposed to 2. or 3. below.

2. List of individual subscribers who have INVITED contact from third parties on unspecified subjects

    You can send marketing material by electronic mail to contacts on this list provided that

    a) this person has not already sent an opt-out request to you

    b) you do not conceal your identity when you contact them and

    c) you ensure that you have provided a valid contact address for subsequent opt-out requests.

    Given individuals' increased caution over disclosure of their contact details to third parties for marketing purposes, you should seek assurances on the veracity of such a list i.e. are these genuine **invitations** for contact from **anyone** on **any** subject as opposed to 3. below.

3. List of individual subscribers who have CONSENTED TO receiving unsolicited marketing material by electronic mail from third parties on a particular subject (i.e., list compiled on an opt-in basis)

    You can send marketing material by electronic mail to contacts on this list provided that

    a) this person has not already sent an opt-out request to you

    b) you do not conceal your identity and

    c) you ensure that you have provided a valid contact address for subsequent opt-out requests.

    Given individuals' increased caution over disclosure of their contact details to third parties for marketing purposes, you should seek assurances on the veracity of such a list.

Where this consent was given after 11 December 2003, it is more likely that this person has genuinely consented to receiving unsolicited marketing messages from third parties about a particular subject (i.e. products and services similar to those in which they have already expressed an interest). It may, however, be difficult to demonstrate that the intended recipients have "notified the sender" and a great deal will depend on the wording of any statement made when the information was collected.

Where this consent was given before 11 December 2003, you may wish to check with the broker how recently it was compiled and whether it has already been used by their other clients. A list compiled in 2003 should have been compiled in the knowledge of the general requirements of these Regulations. Although we would be prepared to take a pragmatic view on the use of lists compiled in accordance with privacy legislation before 11 December 2003, you may wish to consider whether using a list compiled before 1 January 2003 is going to yield a sufficiently positive response because it may well be out of date.

To summarise, if there is no express invitation to receive marketing messages, you will need to consider whether any list you use constitutes a list of notifications of consent to you, the sender. Another point to consider is that the older the list that you buy or rent, the less likely it is that those contacts on the list are going to respond positively to marketing messages. It may even damage the reputation of your business to send poorly targeted unwanted marketing messages. You have a general obligation to ensure that the recipient is provided with a valid address for opt-out requests in every message. Should you receive such an opt-out request, you must ensure that you suppress that individual's details immediately. We will pay particular attention to those companies that fail to respect opt-out requests.

Can we advertise the products and services of third parties via electronic mail?

If you are offering a "host mailing" service, you are not disclosing your mailing list to a third party but you are willing, for a fee, to promote their goods and services alongside yours. It is unlikely you could send such messages on a "soft opt-in" basis because they are not your "similar products and services". You could, however, send such material on a clear "opt-in" basis provided you identify that you and not the third party are the sender.

Can we pass our list of email addresses/mobile numbers on to a third party for them to use for marketing purposes?

If the email addresses/mobile numbers in question are those of individual subscribers, the third party will not be able to use them to send unsolicited marketing material unless the subscriber has consented to receiving it from that third party (i.e. "the sender"). You must make it clear who you are proposing to pass the details on to and what sort of products and services they will be offering.

For example, a positive response to a phrase such as "We would like to pass your details on to specially selected third parties so that they can send you more information about holidays in America. Do you agree to this?" is likely to be sufficient to allow third parties to use those contact details for promoting holidays in America by electronic mail.

A phrase such as "We will pass your details on to third parties unless you write to us and tell us that you don't agree" will not be sufficient. You should not use contact lists which have been obtained in these circumstances. The decision about what happens to an individual's electronic contact details

731

must rest with the individual. No disclosure can be made to third parties for their marketing purposes unless that individual actively consents to such a disclosure taking place.

Group Companies/Trading Names

How do the rules on marketing by electronic mail rule apply to marketing by different companies within a group of companies?

If you disclosed individual subscribers' contact information within your Group in compliance with existing data protection rules prior to 11 December 2003 and those other Group companies have already used that information and not received an opt-out request, that contact information can still be used by those other Group companies as long as further opt-out opportunities are provided with every subsequent message (see Mailing Lists Compiled before 11 December 2003 for more information about whether a valid address or an opt-out opportunity is required for subsequent communications).

Moving forward, you will, as a minimum requirement, have to ask individuals whether they consent to receiving unsolicited marketing by electronic mail from other group companies when you collect their contact details. In an on-line environment, you could provide a link listing those group companies. You may even wish to consider providing separate opt-in opportunities for each company on that list in order to give the individual greater choice and to target your Group's marketing more efficiently.

Another option you may wish to consider is providing an opportunity for the individual to invite (i.e. **solicit**) contact from other companies within the Group.

Our company has a number of different trading names, surely an opt-in for one of the trading names is an opt-in for all the trading names because there is only one legal entity?

If you trade under several different names, particularly where those names are strong brands, you cannot assume that a customer who agrees to receive mailing from one trading entity is agreeing to receive marketing from your other trading entities. They may not even be aware of any connection between different trading names. You would need to ensure that the individual is made aware that they will receive unsolicited marketing from all of your trading names when they opt-in to receiving marketing from you. Similarly, when an individual opts-out of receiving unsolicited marketing from one of your trading names, this opt-out applies to all of your trading names unless they make it clear otherwise.

If you are collecting information on a "soft opt-in" basis, you may have considerable difficulty in satisfying the "similar products and services" criteria, if you want to send further unsolicited marketing relating to your full range of trading names. You could avoid this difficulty by providing an opportunity for the individual to invite contact from the wide range of trading names within the company.

Loyalty Schemes

We operate a loyalty scheme for our own products and services. How do the Regulations apply here?

If someone participates in a loyalty scheme, the minimum that they can expect to receive from you is an update about how many points/vouchers they have earned. In our view, under the "soft opt-in" rule, you can send them further information about other incentives that are available under the scheme unless and until they opt-out of receiving such further information. Once they have opted-out of receiving further information about other offers that are available under the scheme, you should not send such further information unless and until they opt back into receiving it again.

We operate a loyalty scheme in partnership with other companies. A great deal of information is transferred across the scheme and the partners do not necessarily offer similar products and services, how do the Regulations apply here?

Dealing first of all with the information you have already collected, we will assume that you have collected that contact information in accordance with your obligations under the Data Protection Act.

Each partner can continue to use contact information which was collected before 11 December 2003 for marketing by electronic mail provided the information has been recently used by that partner and provided no opt-outs have been received (see Mailing Lists Compiled before 11 December 2003 for more information about whether a valid address or an opt-out opportunity is also required for subsequent communications).

Moving forward, you may need to revisit the data protection and privacy wording of your application form where you are collecting information in order to conduct marketing exercises by electronic means. You must ensure that individuals are fully aware of the nature of the promotions you propose to send. The minimum that an individual can expect to receive from you is an update about how many points/vouchers they have earned. In our view, under the "soft opt-in" rule, you can send them further information about other incentives offered by all the participating companies in the scheme unless and until they opt-out of receiving such further information. Where there are a number of partners in a loyalty scheme, you may find it easier to provide an opportunity for the individual to invite (i.e. **solicit**) further marketing contact from each partner where those partners propose to contact the individual independently of this scheme.

Business to Business

How do the Regulations apply to business to business marketing by electronic mail?

Your obligations are as follows:

1. You must not conceal your identity when you send, or instigate the sending of a marketing message by electronic mail to anyone (including corporate subscribers)and

2. You must provide a valid address to which the recipient (including corporate subscribers) can send an opt-out request (Regulation 23 refers)

Only individual subscribers have an enforceable right of opt-out under these Regulations. This is where that individual withdraws the consent that they previously gave to receiving marketing by electronic mail (that consent only being valid "for the time being" (Regulation 22(2) refers)). This right is not extended to corporate subscribers.

Although recipients who are corporate subscribers do not have an enforceable opt-out right under the Regulations, where the sending of marketing material to the employee of a company includes the processing of personal data (i.e. the marketer knows the name of the person they are contacting), that individual has a fundamental and enforceable right under DPA Section 11 to request that a company cease sending them marketing material (See http://www.dataprotection.gov.uk/dpr/dpdoc.nsf, Data Protection Act 1998: Legal Guidance, paragraph 4.3).

In our view, it makes no business sense to continue to send marketing material to a business contact who no longer wishes to hear from you. Arguably, by failing to respect a business to business opt-out request you may give the impression that you are unconcerned about your commercial reputation. You should note that persistent failure to comply with a Section 11 request, whether or not it relates to a business to business communication, may result in our taking enforcement action against you.

How do these Regulations apply to unsolicited marketing material sent by electronic mail to individual employees of a corporate subscriber where that material promotes goods and services which are clearly intended for their personal/domestic use?

The Commissioner has no authority to take enforcement action based on the content of emails sent to corporate subscribers even though that content may be entirely inappropriate for business to business communications.

In the "Spam" report of an Inquiry by the All-Party Parliamentary Internet Group (APPIG) there was a recommendation that the Information Commissioner set out clear guidance as to how business-to-business communications are to be distinguished from messages intended for individual subscribers. This recommendation was prompted by the observation of one of the witnesses to the inquiry that an invitation to buy Viagra sent to the sales address of a shipping company could only be construed as being sent to an individual since it would not be of any business relevance. The problem is that the "opt-in" and "soft opt-in" rules do not extend to the sending of marketing emails to corporate subscribers. In the example quoted, the subscriber will be the shipping company because that is the person which is party to a contract with a provider of public electronic communications systems. This means, therefore, that even an email addressed to an individual within the company will not be covered by the Regulations although it may be subject to DPA and a Section 11 notice could be issued. In other words, the fact that an email sent to a corporate subscriber's address is obviously aimed at an individual (because it promotes a product that is for personal/domestic use) is not, for the purposes of the Regulations, relevant. Email communications sent to a corporate subscriber are simply not covered by the Regulations except in so far as there is a requirement to identify the sender and to provide contact details.

How do the Regulations apply to the sending of text/picture/video messaging to mobile phones which are supplied to individual employees by corporate subscribers.

The law applies in exactly the same way as it does to the sending of emails to corporate subscribers.

Electronic Mail Marketing To Partnerships

How do the Regulations apply to the sending of marketing messages by electronic mail to partnerships?

A non-limited liability partnership in England, Wales or N. Ireland is an individual subscriber under these Regulations. This means that such a partnership (which may consist of several individuals and which may have a large number of employees) is afforded the same protection under these Regulations as a residential subscriber or a sole trader. This protection is not available to limited liability partnerships, to Scottish partnerships or to corporate subscribers which include small and medium sized limited companies.

Strictly speaking, marketers must get prior consent to send emails to any email address used by an unincorporated partnership unless the "soft_opt_in" criteria apply. This may be the generic contact email address of the partnership e.g. mail@partnershipname.com or it may be the separate email addresses used by individuals (partners, associates, other employees) working at that partnership. This issue was the matter of some debate during the Department of Trade and Industry's consultation exercise prior to the implementation of these Regulations. (http://www.dti.gov.uk/industries/ecommunications/directive_on_privacy_electronic_communications_200258ec.html)

What does this mean in practice?

Although, strictly speaking, the partnership could be viewed as the commercial equivalent of a large household (see above comments on the issue of "recipient"), we recognise that there may be circumstances when the wishes of the subscriber, i.e., the unincorporated partnership (which is legally responsible for charges incurred on its lines) might over-ride the wishes of the employee. For example, an employer may insist that an employee keeps in regular contact with conference organisers. The employer's wishes in respect of unsolicited emails from conference organisers would over-ride the wishes of the employee.

However, if one individual working at the partnership consents to receiving unsolicited marketing material from the organiser, this does not mean that every individual working at the partnership has consented to receiving such material from the organiser.

Marketers must also remember that where they know the name of the person they are seeking to contact, that person's contact details must be processed in accordance with the Eight Data Protection Principles of DPA. For example, where DPA applies, all individuals have a fundamental opt-out right under Section 11.

Who is able to give consent on behalf of individuals working at a partnership?

If you are targeting an individual working at a partnership, you must ensure you obtain the consent of the individual (or a person who can be reasonably assumed to be entitled to give consent on that individual's behalf e.g. a secretary or assistant) before sending unsolicited electronic mail to that individual unless the "soft opt-in" criteria apply.

Partnerships may wish to ensure that their key frontline staff, e.g switchboard operators, receptionists, administrators, secretaries are advised of any office policy regarding the disclosure of employee contact details.

Individuals employed by partnerships must remember that in respect of their work email address and mobile phone, it is ultimately their employer's consent choices which take precedence over their individual choices.

Who is able to give consent on behalf of the partnership?

Marketers must ensure that they have obtained consent from a person working for that partnership who, it is reasonable to assume has the authority to give such consent. Partnerships may wish to ensure that their key frontline staff, e.g., switchboard operators, receptionists, administrators, secretaries, are advised of any office policy regarding the disclosure of office contact details.

Electronic Mail Marketing To Sole Traders

How do the Regulations apply to sending of marketing messages by electronic mail to sole traders?

Sole traders are also individual subscribers under the Regulations.

That said, we have recognised in earlier enforcement that marketers may have difficulty in distinguishing sole traders from small limited companies, particularly where a sole trader's contact details are available in business directories. However, marketers should use their best efforts to ensure that they do not send marketing messages by electronic mail to sole traders in contravention of the Regulations. For example, it is possible to check free of charge on Companies House website www.companieshouse.gov.uk whether or not a trading entity is a limited company.

Pan European Marketing

We plan to conduct a pan-European marketing campaign. Which jurisdiction'srules do we need to comply with?

It is our understanding that you must comply with the laws of the jurisdiction in which you are based. However, you should bear in mind that when implementing the EU Directive, each member state was given the option to decide whether the rights given to individual subscribers should extend to corporate subscribers. Some jurisdictions have chosen to do so to a greater extent than the UK has done. You may create a negative impression about your business if you don't respect the laws of the country to which you are sending your messages. We cannot offer guidance on how to comply with the legislation of other jurisdictions and you should seek your own legal advice if you wish to conduct pan-European marketing campaigns.

Marketing by more than one medium

We collect individuals' addresses, telephone numbers, mobile numbers and email addresses for marketing purposes on a paper form. We have limited room on the form and we have to provide other information in order to comply with other legislation. What is the minimum amount of information we have to provide in order to comply with data protection rules?

You do not need to provide reams of legalese in order to comply with your data protection obligations. If you are collecting information in order to market a person by a variety of media, the simplest method is to adopt the highest standard and apply it even where you do not need to.

Under DPA, the bare minimum that you are obliged to tell people is who you are and what you plan to do with their information, including any unexpected uses such as processing for marketing purposes and/or disclosures to third parties. Because you plan to market by electronic means, you also need to provide consent options. The very highest standard would be to provide the individual with the opportunity to solicit information from you e.g:

Please contact me by post, by telephone, by text/picture/video message, by email with further information about your products and services (tick as applicable).

However, if you use this wording, you cannot send marketing material to them by post, telephone, text message or email unless the individual ticks the box to invite further contact from you.

Charities/Political Parties/Not-for Profit Organisations

We are a charity/political party/not-for profit organisation, can we take advantage of "soft opt-in"?

No, not unless you are promoting commercial goods and services, for example, those offered by your trading arm. We recognise that this puts such organisations at a disadvantage and raised this point in our response to the consultation exercise conducted by the Department of Trade and Industry in advance of these Regulations (see http://www.dataprotection.gov.uk/dpr/dpdoc.nsf and click on "Codes of Practice Our Responses and Other Papers"). However, the EU Directive from which these Regulations are derived specify that the rules on marketing by electronic means apply to commercial relationships.

You may wish to revisit the wording of your data protection and privacy statements so that a person would actively "invite" promotional information from you via electronic mail. As outlined above there is a difference between a person actively soliciting promotional material by electronic mail and that same person consenting to the receipt of any promotional material you choose to send them by electronic mail (i.e. unsolicited marketing material). Alternatively, you could ask them whether they consent to the receipt of unsolicited marketing material.

You remain obliged to identify yourself and to provide a valid address for opt-outs in each electronic mailing.

Subscribers' FAQs

I have made all my consent choices using one email account/mobile number. How do the Regulations apply when I change my email address/mobile number?

The Regulation refers to you as the "recipient of the electronic mail". A company cannot be expected to know that you wish to transfer your consent options to a different email address or a different mobile phone number unless you tell them.

I use a number of different email addresses simultaneously, do my consent choices for one account automatically transfer to the others?

No. A company cannot be expected to know that you can receive marketing messages on a number of different email addresses. If you want to ensure that a company who has been marketing you via email never contacts you again at any of your existing email addresses, you must ensure that you provide that company with a list of all your email addresses. Alternatively, you should ensure that you opt out of receiving further marketing messages at each different email address. For the future, you will need to remember that your consent choices for one account do not automatically transfer to others.

I sometimes access my personal email account at work/at the library/at an internet café/at a hotel. Do my rights only apply when I access the account at home?

Not necessarily. A responsible marketer should be able to identify which domain names are generally used by individual subscribers rather than corporate subscribers. However, there may be difficulties in relying on your evidence in enforcement or compensation proceedings where you only access your personal email account via a line paid for by a corporate subscriber even if that subscriber charges you for the privilege.

We are a partnership and, therefore, an individual subscriber under the Regulations. How do the rules apply to our employees?

See Partnerships above in the Marketers' FAQs.

I am a sole trader and, therefore, an individual subscriber under the Regulations. How do the rules apply to me?

See Sole Traders above in the Marketers' FAQs.

How do I stop getting marketing messages sent by unsolicited electronic mail?

Pay close attention to the options that companies give you when they collect your information on-line. Companies have a general obligation under data protection law to be transparent about what they plan to do with your information. (See our leaflet "Be Open" which is available from our office or by clicking on http://www.dataprotection.gov.uk/dpr/dpdoc1.nsf and accessing our "Information Padlock/Signpost" page). These new Regulations now place additional obligations upon companies who collect your details for marketing by electronic mail. These obligations will give you more options. Even where you have opted in to receiving marketing by electronic mail, you should be given a valid address for opt-out requests.

If you have already been contacted by a company you do not wish to hear from, contact the identify themselves in their messages and to provide a valid address for opt-out requests. Ensure you provide them with details of the number or email address that they contacted you on. This enables them to add those details to their suppression list which will ensure that they keep a record of your objection.

We recognise that many people are reluctant to send opt-out requests to unsolicited marketing emails that come from senders that are outside UK jurisdiction. Many people are also concerned about some unscrupulous marketers fail to comply with their obligation to provide a valid address for opt-out requests that is free of charge. If this applies to you, we recommend that you do the following:

"Spam" Emails

Most spam email originates from outside the UK and should never be replied to unless you are familiar with the company and trust that company. We will be producing separate information about technical measures you can take to block spam. This information will be accessible from our website.

Text/picture/video messages with a premium rate line opt-out

1.   If you are certain that you have never given the company your prior consent, copy the text out, complete our complaints form and send the details to us.

2.   If you think you may have given your consent at some stage, look for a postal address in the message. This may be no more than a name and a PO Box number. Write to the company and tell them to stop sending messages to your number. You do not need to give them your name or address but you should state clearly that:

   a)   you are the subscriber to that number

   b)   you do not want to receive further messages from them on that number

   c)   keep a copy of your letter and proof of posting

3.   Contact ICSTIS. This message may breach their Code of Practice on the use of premium rate lines. Tel: 0800 500 212 (9:00am-4:00pm, Monday to Friday) Website: http://www.icstis.org.uk/.

There are no statutory lists similar to TPS and FPS for those who do not wish to receive unsolicited electronic mail. There are non-statutory direct marketing industry initiatives in this area and you may wish to contact the Direct Marketing Association for more information Direct Marketing Association

DMA House 70 Margaret Street London W1M 8SS online http://www.dma.org.uk by telephone: 020 7291 3300

How do I make a complaint about marketing by unsolicited electronic mail?

Before 11 December 2003

If you can be identified from your email address e.g. firstname.lastname@domainname.com and you can demonstrate that you have already asked the marketer to stop contacting you on that email address, this may be a breach of Section 11 DPA. Please complete our Request for Assessment form.

From 11 December 2003

If you wish to make a complaint to the Information Commissioner from 11 December 2003, download and complete our Unsolicited Electronic Mail Complaints form (not available until 11 December 2003) and submit it either by post or email.

PLEASE NOTE:

IT IS UNLIKELY THAT WE WILL BE ABLE TO CONSIDER YOUR COMPLAINT UNLESS YOU HAVE COMPLETED AND SUBMITTED THE APPROPRIATE FORM. THIS FORM IS DESIGNED TO ENSURE THAT YOU GIVE US THE SPECIFIC INFORMATION WE NEED IN ORDER TO CONSIDER YOUR COMPLAINT.

Am I entitled to compensation?

If you can demonstrate to a Court that the caller has breached these Regulations and that by doing so, you have been caused quantifiable damage, you may be entitled to compensation under Regulation 30 of these Regulations. Please note that if a caller can demonstrate to a Court that they did what could reasonably be required of them to comply with the Regulations, this would be a defence against any compensation claim.

We have produced two leaflets "Taking a Case to Court" and "Am I entitled to compensation" for those wishing to take action for compensation under Section 13 of DPA. Much of the information applies to those who wish to seek compensation under Regulation 30 of these Regulations.

CONTACTING THE INFORMATION COMMISSIONER

Information Commissioner's OfficeWycliffe House
Water Lane
Wilmslow
Cheshire: SK9 5AF
Publication Request: 01625 545700Information Line: 01625 545745
Fax: 01625 524510
Email: data@dataprotection.gov.uk
Website: www.informationcommissioner.gov.uk

© Information Commissioner 2003

Index